Generative Adversarial Networks in Practice

This book is an all-inclusive resource that provides a solid foundation on Generative Adversarial Networks (GAN) methodologies, their application to real-world projects, and their underlying mathematical and theoretical concepts.

Key Features:

- **G**uides you through the complex world of GANs, demystifying their intricacies
- **A**ccompanies your learning journey with real-world examples and practical applications
- **N**avigates the theory behind GANs, presenting it in an accessible and comprehensive way
- **S**implifies the implementation of GANs using popular deep learning platforms
- **I**ntroduces various GAN architectures, giving readers a broad view of their applications
- **N**urture your knowledge of AI with our comprehensive yet accessible content
- **P**ractice your skills with numerous case studies and coding examples
- **R**eviews advanced GANs, such as DCGAN, cGAN, and CycleGAN, with clear explanations and practical examples
- **A**dapts to both beginners and experienced practitioners, with content organized to cater to varying levels of familiarity with GANs
- **C**onnects the dots between GAN theory and practice, providing a well-rounded understanding of the subject
- **T**akes you through GAN applications across different data types, highlighting their versatility
- **I**nspires the reader to explore beyond this book, fostering an environment conducive to independent learning and research
- **C**loses the gap between complex GAN methodologies and their practical implementation, allowing readers to directly apply their knowledge
- **E**mpowers you with the skills and knowledge needed to confidently use GANs in your projects

Prepare to deep dive into the captivating realm of GANs and experience the power of AI like never before with Generative Adversarial Networks (GANs) in Practice. This book brings together the theory and practical aspects of GANs in a cohesive and accessible manner, making it an essential resource for both beginners and experienced practitioners.

Dr. Mehdi Ghayoumi is an Assistant Professor at the State University of New York (SUNY) at Canton. With a strong focus on cutting-edge technologies, he has dedicated his expertise to areas including Machine Learning, Machine Vision, Robotics, Human-Robot Interaction (HRI), and privacy. Dr. Ghayoumi's research revolves around constructing sophisticated systems tailored to address the complexities and challenges within these fields, driving innovation and advancing the forefront of knowledge in his respective areas of expertise.

Generative Adversarial Networks in Practice

Mehdi Ghayoumi
State University of New York

CRC Press
Taylor & Francis Group
Boca Raton London New York

CRC Press is an imprint of the
Taylor & Francis Group, an **informa** business

A CHAPMAN & HALL BOOK

First edition published 2024
by CRC Press
2385 NW Executive Center Drive, Suite 320, Boca Raton FL 33431

and by CRC Press
4 Park Square, Milton Park, Abingdon, Oxon, OX14 4RN

CRC Press is an imprint of Taylor & Francis Group, LLC

ISBN: 9781032248448 (hbk)
ISBN: 9781032250588 (pbk)
ISBN: 9781003281344 (ebk)

DOI: 10.1201/9781003281344

Typeset in Palatino
by KnowledgeWorks Global Ltd.

Contents

Preface

This book serves as a comprehensive guide to Generative Adversarial Networks (GANs) and their application in real-world projects. It is my sincere hope that this resource brings clarity and illumination to your understanding of GANs, bolstering your knowledge and practical application skills.

Contained within these pages, you'll find an in-depth exploration of GAN methodologies, including a breakdown of the most popular algorithms and the theory that underpins them. Each chapter unfolds with a careful balance of theory and practice, augmented by relevant case studies and coding examples to aid your comprehension. We delve into the crux of the matter, from understanding the mathematics behind GANs, their practical implementation, to their implications across various applications.

This book is structured into 15 concise chapters, each tackling a specific facet of GANs. We begin by grounding our exploration in necessary terms and definitions before venturing into data preprocessing and model evaluation techniques – the backbone of any successful deep learning project.

From here, we journey through the principles of TensorFlow and Keras, offering a high-level overview of these powerful deep learning platforms. This sets the stage for the ensuing chapters on Artificial Neural Networks (ANNs) and Deep Neural Networks (DNNs), where we unravel the core principles of these foundational architectures with real-world applications and hands-on examples.

At the heart of this book lies the detailed discourse on Generative Adversarial Networks (GANs). Here we dissect various architectures, highlighting their unique characteristics, potential, and challenges. Among these are the Deep Convolutional GAN (DCGAN), Conditional GAN (cGAN), Cycle GAN, Semi-Supervised GAN (SGAN), Least Squares GAN (LSGAN), and Wasserstein GAN (WGAN).

Finally, we hone our focus on GANs' applications in images, videos, voice, music, and song generation. Each chapter provides practical insights into the implementation steps, demonstrating GANs' versatility across these domains.

While writing this book, I was mindful of a wide range of readers – from students to professionals venturing into the world of deep learning. As such, this book is suitable for both beginners and advanced learners looking to strengthen their understanding and application of GANs. It's my hope that the clarity of explanations, practical code examples, and case studies will aid you in bringing your projects to fruition.

Thank you for embarking on this journey of discovery with me, and I look forward to the insights and innovations that will undoubtedly stem from your newfound knowledge.

Happy reading!

Mehdi Ghayoumi
Beverly Hills, Calif.
August 2023

Acknowledgments

In the process of creating this book, I have been profoundly influenced by the remarkable people who have shaped my life. I owe a great deal to many, but none more so than my beloved parents.

Firstly, I dedicate this book to my dear mother, Khadijeh Ghayoumi. Your steadfast belief in my abilities, infinite love, and unwavering support have been my pillars of strength throughout this journey. This book is a small testament to the monumental impact you have had on my life. Your priceless lessons continue to guide me, and your inspiring resilience serves as a constant reminder to persevere, even in the face of the greatest challenges.

In loving memory of my father, Aliasghar Ghayoumi, I dedicate this book as well. Though you may not be with us physically, your spirit continues to light my path. Your memory serves as a constant reminder of the integrity, perseverance, and wisdom that you exemplified.

In their unique ways, both of you have instilled in me the values I hold dear: the pursuit of knowledge, the importance of tenacity, and the virtue of humility. This book is the product of my academic journey, a journey enriched by the deep love and invaluable lessons you both have imparted. I hope it brings you pride.

To my extended family, I extend my deepest gratitude. Your belief in my abilities and your continuous encouragement have been instrumental in this achievement.

I express my sincerest thanks to my colleagues, mentors, and collaborators. Your shared wisdom, expertise, and guidance have steered me through the complex labyrinth of academia. The intellectual camaraderie we have shared has been pivotal in bringing this research to fruition.

Thank you from the bottom of my heart.

About the Author

Dr. Mehdi Ghayoumi currently holds a distinguished position as an Assistant Professor at the renowned Center of Criminal Justice, Intelligence, and Cybersecurity at the State University of New York (SUNY) at Canton. His past positions bear testament to his academic excellence and leadership. He has previously served as a Research Assistant Professor at SUNY Binghamton, where he took on the dynamic role of spearheading initiatives at the Media Core Lab. Moreover, his academic journey includes a noteworthy stint as a lecturer at Kent State University, where his exceptional teaching abilities were recognized with a prestigious Teaching Award for two consecutive years, 2016 and 2017.

Over the years, Dr. Ghayoumi has not only been instrumental in teaching but has also taken the lead in developing comprehensive courses in domains as diverse and interconnected as machine learning, data science, robotics, and programming. His research interests provide a broad glimpse into his scientific pursuits. From Machine Learning to Machine Vision, and from Robotics to Human-Robot Interaction (HRI) and privacy, Dr. Ghayoumi's research spans a broad spectrum. His research, focusing on creating viable systems for realistic environment settings, demonstrates his commitment to practical applications. His current projects cut across multiple fields, including Human-Robot Interaction, manufacturing, biometrics, and healthcare.

In addition to his research and teaching commitments, Dr. Ghayoumi is actively involved in the broader academic community. He is a member of the technical program committee for numerous conferences and workshops and serves on the editorial board of an array of respected journals in the realms of machine learning, mathematics, and robotics. These include but are not limited to ICML, ICPR, HRI, FG, WACV, IROS, CIBCB, and JAI.

Dr. Ghayoumi's substantial contributions to his field are not confined to his active participation in these committees. His research has found a receptive audience at several leading conferences and in prestigious journals in related fields. Noteworthy among these are Human-Computer Interaction (HRI), Robotics Science and Systems (RSS), and the International Conference on Machine Learning and Applications (ICMLA).

1

Introduction

This chapter introduces the topics that will be covered in this book and defines some terms that will be used while reading it.

- What is Learning?
- What is Machine Learning?
- What is Deep Learning?
- Generative Adversarial Networks (GANs)
- About this Book!
- Terminology
- Issues and Challenges in Machine Learning
- Issues and Challenges in Deep Learning
- Issues and Challenges in GANs
- Tips in Machine Learning Implementation
- Tips in Deep Learning Implementation
- Tips in GAN Implementation

1.1 Preface

This chapter reviews concepts such as learning, machine learning, and deep learning to help readers understand the connections between these concepts and how they relate to GANs. It provides a brief overview of each chapter in this book as well as some essential terminology for readers who are new to machine learning.

1.2 What Is Learning?

Many definitions of learning exist, but one that many people agree on is "learning is the acquisition of knowledge or skills through study or experience". Humans must enhance their social and personal situations to improve their lives, and they constantly face decision-making situations to achieve this. Acquiring new skills and information can help people make better decisions and contribute to success in their lives. Numerous research studies have been conducted to better understand the human learning process. One of the most crucial aspects of this research and analysis is determining how to simulate and improve the accuracy and effectiveness of machine learning (see Figure 1.1).

DOI: 10.1201/9781003281344-1

FIGURE 1.1
Individuals can enhance their lives through learning, and machines are capable of emulating this human learning process.

1.3 What Is Machine Learning?

In recent decades, machines have played a significant role in making human life more comfortable (see Figure 1.2). Making machines smarter to better assist humans is a challenge that many enjoy solving, and researchers are working toward this goal, continuously seeking ways to enhance machine intelligence. Numerous algorithms and techniques have been discovered and developed in this field, some traditional, such as Support Vector Machine (SVM)

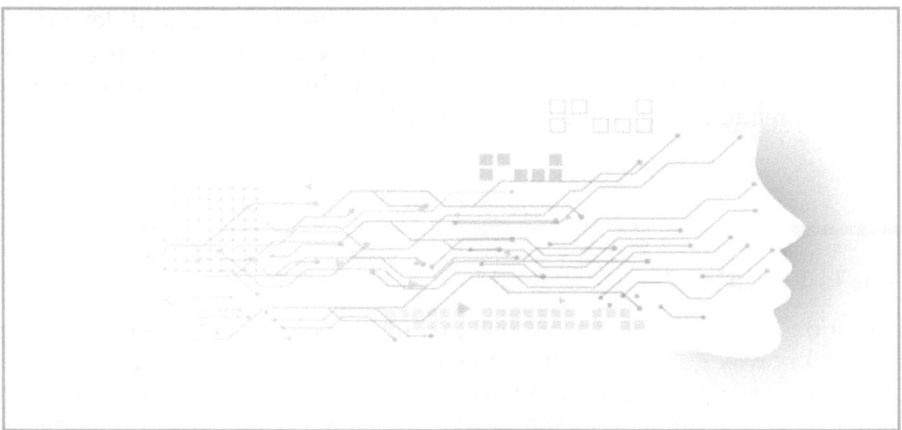

FIGURE 1.2
Machine learning is currently one of the most advanced and popular subjects, with numerous applications across various fields.

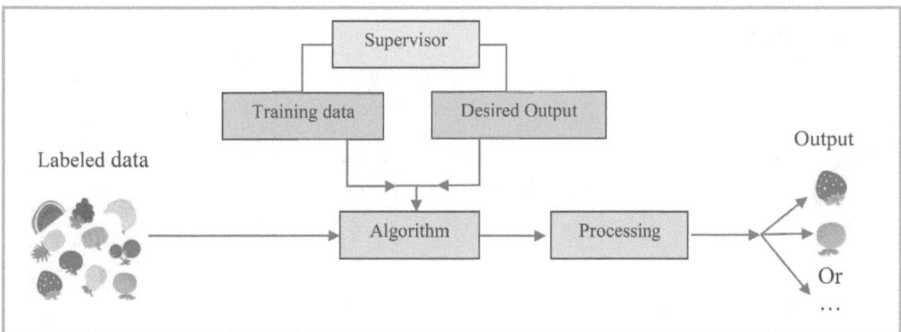

FIGURE 1.3
Supervised learning is one of the most prevalent methods of learning.

or Decision Tree (DT), and some novel, such as deep learning. These methods and studies form part of machine learning, an area of computer science that has recently piqued both academic and industry interests (see Figure 1.3).

1.3.1 Supervised Learning

Individuals utilize supervised learning in many applications, which, as the name suggests, involves teaching or training the machine using data that is already labeled. For instance, input data (a collection of fruits) and output data (classified fruits), as illustrated in Figure 1.3, are examples of supervised learning. Supervised learning employs algorithms to feed data into the model, which then processes the data before categorizing or classifying them. Regression and classification are the two main types of supervised learning. In the industry, both traditional and modern classifiers, such as Naive Bayes, decision trees, support vector machines, and deep learning, are widely used. Classification is the process of dividing objects, things, concepts, or entities into various classes or categories, and this process is linked to measuring similarities. The entities are defined by several characteristics, and comparing their similarities generates values that assist in classification. Recognition (speech, handwriting, face, etc.), identification (biometrics, etc.), and document categorization are some examples of classification applications.

1.3.2 Unsupervised Learning

Unsupervised learning involves training a machine to learn from unlabeled data. Without any preexisting data labeling, the machine's task is to categorize all data based on similarities, dissimilarities, and patterns. Consequently, the machine is left to discover the hidden structure of the unlabeled data independently, and the trained model produces results based on different categories or clusters. Unsupervised learning methods interpret, and extract features based on similarity and dissimilarity, grouping objects into distinct clusters. One of the most well-known types of unsupervised learning is clustering. Imagine an image containing some fruit, but we don't know what the labels are, and there is no teacher or supervisor present, nor is there any training data. Figure 1.4 depicts this situation, which includes unlabeled data, an algorithm, processing, and an output section. The unlabeled data will be utilized in some unsupervised learning algorithms to create a trained model, which will then be used for classification.

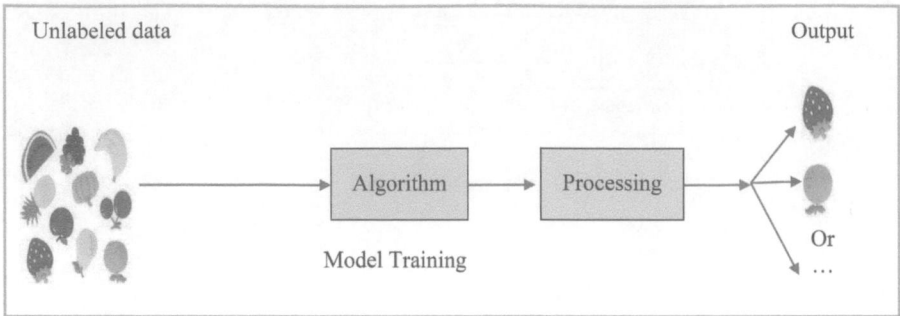

FIGURE 1.4
Unsupervised learning is also one of the most popular methods of learning.

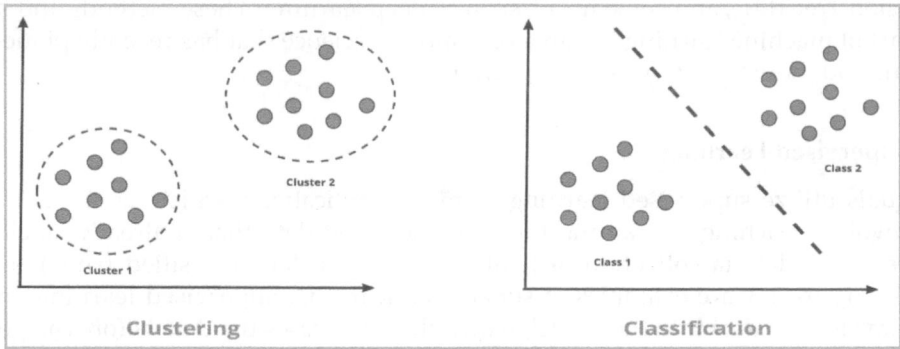

FIGURE 1.5
Clustering vs. classification.

1.3.2.1 Clustering

Clustering is an unsupervised learning technique that calculates the distances (or dissimilarities) between entity features to form clusters. K-means and Hierarchical clustering are two well-known clustering algorithms. They are used in a variety of applications, such as recommender systems, image segmentation, and anomaly detection. Figure 1.5 illustrates the differences between clustering and classification of the same data. In clustering, data is grouped into distinct groups or clusters based on similarities, whereas in classification, lines or hyperplanes are used to separate or classify the classes. The process of finding the line or hyperplane is conducted with labeled data while discovering similarities is achieved with methods like K-means, which aims to partition **n** samples into **k** clusters.

1.3.3 Semi-supervised Learning

Another type of learning algorithm is the semi-supervised learning algorithm, which trains to learn using a combination of labeled and unlabeled data. This combination typically comprises a small amount of labeled data and a large quantity of unlabeled data. The approach assumes that similar labeled data (a small portion of the data) will be grouped, and the remaining unlabeled data (a large part of the data) will be labeled based on the initially labeled data.

FIGURE 1.6
Unsupervised vs. semi-supervised vs. supervised.

1.3.4 Supervised vs. Semi-supervised vs. Unsupervised

Let's illustrate the comparison of these three different learning algorithms with an example. In this scenario, the learning algorithm is the teacher, the data represents the environments of home and school, and the model is the student. In supervised learning, a student is guided by a teacher both at home and at school. In unsupervised learning, the student must decipher the concept on their own. Finally, in semi-supervised learning, a teacher introduces a few concepts in class before assigning homework questions based on those concepts. Figure 1.6 depicts these approaches and how the students, serving as models, will be trained.

1.3.5 Reinforcement Learning

Another type of learning system is reinforcement learning, which focuses on making optimal decisions. Consider Figure 1.7, observing how the process begins gently with a specific focus on its goal but gradually improves with training until it achieves success. Positive or negative feedback can be used to refine the solution. Generally, it consists of five major components: state (s), reward (r), action (a), agent, and environment. The agent receives the state (s_t) and reward (r_t) and takes an action (a_t), which results in changes in the environment, yielding a new state (s_{t+1}) and reward (r_{t+1}).

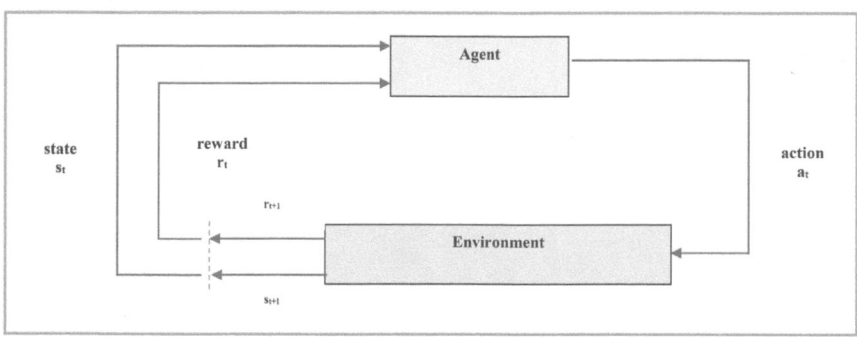

FIGURE 1.7
Reinforcement learning architecture.

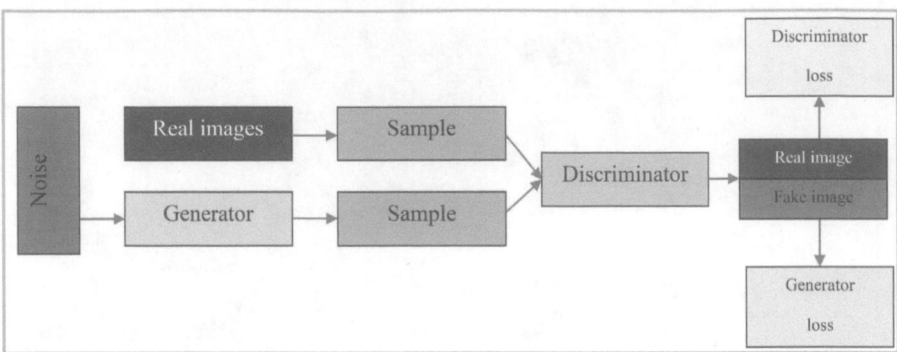

FIGURE 1.8
GAN learning architecture in general.

1.3.6 Generating Learning

Another type of machine learning method involves generating new data by simulating existing data (the new features required for the new data). This is one of the most exciting and recent topics in machine learning, and it's the main focus of this book, which we examine in depth. The general architecture of this learning method is depicted in Figure 1.8. It is divided into five major sections: the generator, the discriminator, the inputs (for the generator, which are noise, and for the discriminator, which are real data), the outputs (for the generator, which are the generated sample data, and for the discriminator, which are real or fake sample data), and the loss (for both the generator and the discriminator).

1.3.7 Regression

Regression is the use of statistical methods to determine the relationship between the features of a set of entities. It helps us make predictions by establishing the relationship between dependent and independent variables. Different types of regression analysis, such as linear, logistic, and polynomial regression, are employed to solve different problems with varying data. These methods are used for both prediction, as in the case of linear regression, and classification, as with logistic regression. Figure 1.9 illustrates various prediction lines (both linear and nonlinear) for different data distributions.

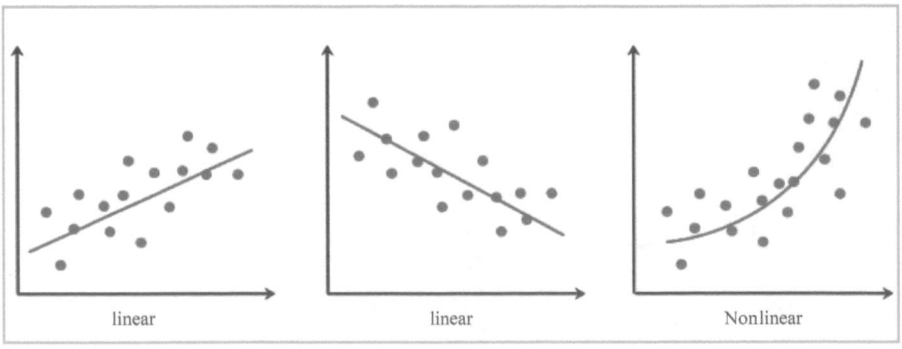

FIGURE 1.9
The linear and nonlinear data prediction lines.

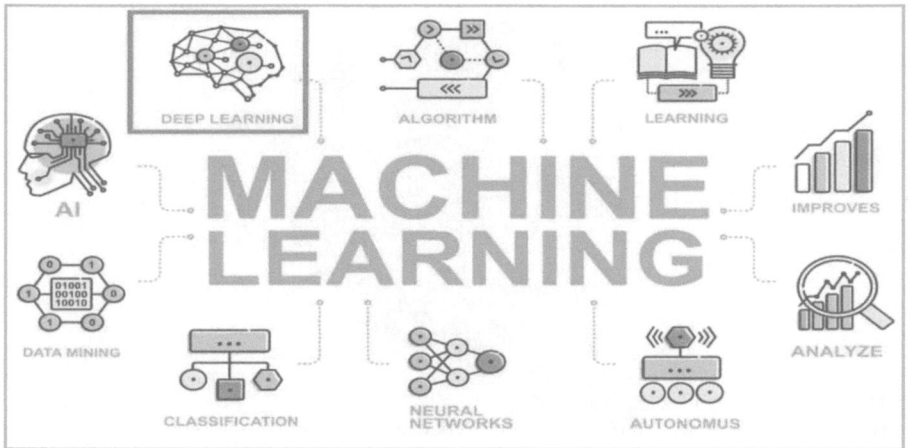

FIGURE 1.10
Deep learning is a subfield of machine learning.

1.4 What Is Deep Learning?

One of the research methods used in artificial intelligence to create systems that can learn involves mimicking human behavior, such as human learning. To achieve this, scientists and engineers began investigating how machines can learn to improve their capabilities. As a result, Artificial Neural Networks (ANNs) are among the most well-known examples of these efforts. For instance, the perceptron simulates the formation and processes of the human neural network and serves as the foundation for advanced ANNs methods, such as deep learning. ANNs' general architecture is divided into three sections: input, output, and hidden layers. Its learning process is split into two stages: creating a model by transforming data into a linear or nonlinear model, and then improving it. However, several architectural parameters, such as the number of neurons in each layer, weights, bias, and activation function, affect the outputs. Deep learning, as an advanced ANNs method, has produced fascinating results in a wide range of applications, particularly those involving image and audio data. Deep learning encompasses several algorithms and approaches that are used in various applications, and GANs are among the recent deep learning methods that have garnered significant attention. Figure 1.10 illustrates various subfields within machine learning.

1.5 Generative Adversarial Networks (GANs)

GANs are one of the most exciting and recently developed deep learning methods, showing several promising results in generating new data from existing data. They have a wide range of applications, which we will discuss in this book, along with information about their architectures and methods, as well as step-by-step instructions for implementing them. Figure 1.11 depicts GANs and some approaches as a subset of deep learning.

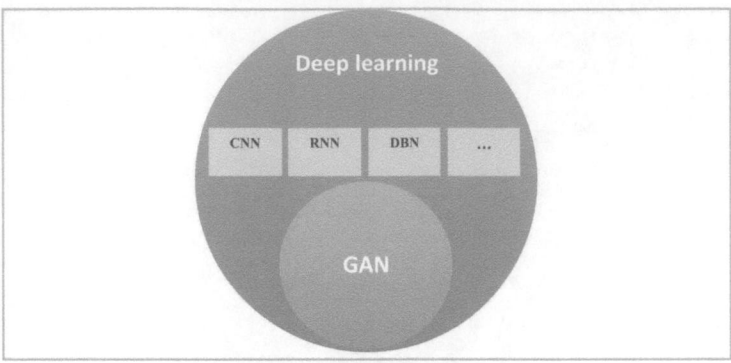

FIGURE 1.11
A Generative Adversarial Network (GAN) is a subfield of deep learning.

1.6 About This Book!

This book delves into GAN algorithms and provides code examples for the most commonly used methods. Its goal is to teach you GAN methodologies and present several case studies to aid you in learning and understanding how to complete your project using GANs. This 15-chapter book focuses on applying the latest and most popular GAN algorithms to real-world projects, along with their associated mathematics and theories. This book reviews the concept, mathematics, and theory behind each approach before providing some examples of its application and, finally, some coding examples to understand the practical implementation.

1.6.1 Introduction

This chapter provides a summary of the other chapters in this book and gives a brief description of the content within each. It also includes a section on necessary terms and definitions, added to facilitate the reader's understanding of this book.

1.6.2 Data Preprocessing

Data preprocessing is a critical component of deep learning approaches, such as GANs. This chapter explores some of the most common data preprocessing techniques. It includes code examples to facilitate your understanding of these methods.

1.6.3 Model Evaluation

Model evaluation is a key component in the design of machine learning architectures. This section explains how to evaluate a model and adjust its hyperparameters for improved performance.

1.6.4 TensorFlow and Keras Fundamentals

TensorFlow is a renowned deep learning platform developed by Google. This book provides a high-level overview of the platform, demonstrating how to define tensors and simplify implementations. It also includes an introduction to Keras, supplemented with practical examples.

1.6.5 Artificial Neural Networks (ANNs)

To learn deep learning more effectively, you should first understand the fundamentals of ANNs. This chapter goes over the fundamentals of ANN architectures and presents well-known ANNs with examples using TensorFlow and Keras.

1.6.6 Deep Neural Networks (DNNs)

This chapter introduces the fundamentals of deep learning, providing examples of the most well-known and popular architectures as well as their applications. It equips you with crucial knowledge required to understand the core principles of deep learning.

1.6.7 Generative Adversarial Networks (GANs)

This chapter introduces the key concepts, definitions, and architectures of GANs. It presents the general characteristics of GAN architecture, along with the advantages and disadvantages of well-known approaches, supplemented by an example to illustrate the implementation steps.

1.6.8 Deep Convolutional Generative Adversarial Network (DCGAN)

The Convolutional Neural Network (CNN) is incorporated into the structure of GAN, forming one of the most popular GAN architectures, the DCGAN. This section elaborates on the DCGAN structure, providing examples of its functioning and potential applications.

1.6.9 Conditional Generative Adversarial Network (cGAN)

cGAN is a type of GAN algorithm that utilizes labels during the training process. It's a widely recognized GAN model. This chapter explains its structure and provides examples to facilitate your understanding of its functioning.

1.6.10 Cycle Generative Adversarial Network (CycleGAN)

CycleGAN is one of the architectures of the GAN model and is used for a variety of applications, such as image-to-image translation. This chapter explores this architecture and provides examples to help you understand its concepts and implementation.

1.6.11 Semi-supervised Generative Adversarial Network (SGAN)

This section discusses the SGAN approach and provides examples to enhance your learning. An SGAN employs a generator and both supervised and unsupervised discriminators working in parallel.

1.6.12 Least Squares Generative Adversarial Network (LSGAN)

This section will go over the LSGAN method, providing some coding examples for better understanding. For the discriminator, the LSGAN employs the least squares loss function.

1.6.13 Wasserstein Generative Adversarial Network (WGAN)

This section explores the WGAN approach, providing examples to facilitate comprehension and learning. In its formulation, the WGAN model employs a unique type of distance measure.

1.6.14 Generative Adversarial Networks (GANs) for Images and Video

This chapter outlines the steps for implementing a GAN and provides a practical example. Image generation is one of the most common applications of GANs. Their use in image and video processing includes tasks such as image synthesis and generation, image translation, image restoration, and generating images from text.

1.6.15 Generative Adversarial Networks (GANs) for Voice, Music, and Song

Speech synthesis is another application of GANs. This chapter introduces key concepts related to using GANs for audio data. It is followed by examples of its applications, such as speech, music, and song generation, to help you familiarize yourself with the practical use of these concepts.

1.7 Terminology

We will review some terminology used throughout the chapters, which you should familiarize yourself with before beginning to read this book.

1.7.1 Inputs

Learning algorithms, such as ANNs, use data to train models. This input data is often represented as a vector of data samples, denoted by x. A collection of x vectors forms an input matrix, X. Each sample vector x contains $1...m$ features, which are the data values of the vector. Let's say we have $N = 1000$ apples, and each apple is represented by a data vector $X = [x_1 = \text{price}, x_2 = \text{color}, x_3 = \text{shape}]$. The value of m denotes the number of features in the data sample vector, which in this case is 3. Therefore, we have $N = 1000$ samples, each of which is a vector with dimensions of $m = 3 \times 1$. The dimension of the feature vector is 1000×3, indicating that we have 1000 samples, each with 3 features.

Figure 1.12 illustrates how a local patch of an image with a size of 3×3 ($X = [x_0, x_1, x_2, x_3, x_4, x_5, x_6, x_7, x_8]$) is converted into a feature vector with dimensions of 9×1. These vectors serve as inputs for machine learning approaches during training. If the image size is 28×28, the feature vector dimensions are 784×1. If we have 60,000 data samples, like in the MNIST dataset, the size of all feature vectors in MNIST is $60,000 \times 784 \times 1$. If we select 40,000 samples for training, the input matrix size for the learning model is $40,000 \times 784 \times 1$, which is the size of X. Understanding these concepts is crucial for the implementation steps when working with real-world data.

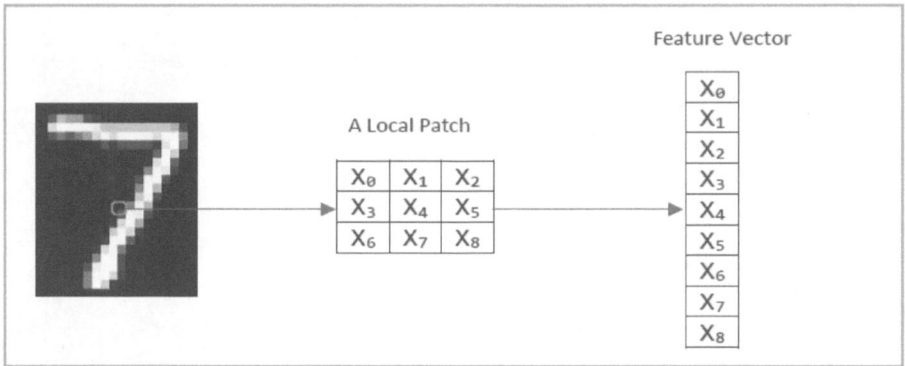

FIGURE 1.12
A feature vector is generated from image data.

1.7.2 Weights

The weights, denoted as w_{ij}, are the values that the learning algorithms update to train the model. Each weight represents the connection between two nodes (node **i** and node **j**). A collection of these weights forms a matrix, which we denote by **W**. Typically, the values of **W** are initialized randomly within the range [0, 1].

1.7.3 Outputs (Targets)

In the final step, the learning algorithms generate a set of output data. These values are typically represented as a vector of output values, **Y**, with individual elements denoted by y_j (j = 1…k). For instance, if the outputs are 0 (apple) and 1 (non-apple), the dimension of **Y** is **k** = 2, indicating a binary classification problem. Depending on the algorithm and the problem, the output can vary, including numerical values, strings, etc. These values, which have the same dimension as the output (**k**), are needed by supervised learning algorithms. They provide us with the correct values (targets) that the model should output.

1.7.4 Activation Function

ANNs can simulate both linear and nonlinear behavioral models. To model nonlinear behaviors, which are common in most real-world problems, they utilize activation functions. The most commonly used activation functions include the sigmoid (Sig), hyperbolic tangent (Tanh), rectified linear unit (ReLU), leaky ReLU, and SoftMax functions. The question arises, which one is the best to use? To identify the most suitable one, methods such as cross-validation are employed, alongside insights from recent research.

1.7.4.1 Sigmoid (sig)

Every event has a probability ranging between 0 and 1, and the sigmoid function, which also outputs values in this range, may be the best fit for such problems. Additionally, the sigmoid function is differentiable, meaning the slope of its curve can be calculated at any point. Figure 1.13 depicts its shape: if **z** represents the x-axis, then $\emptyset(\mathbf{z})$ corresponds to the y-axis:

$$\emptyset(z) = \frac{1}{1+e^{-1}}$$

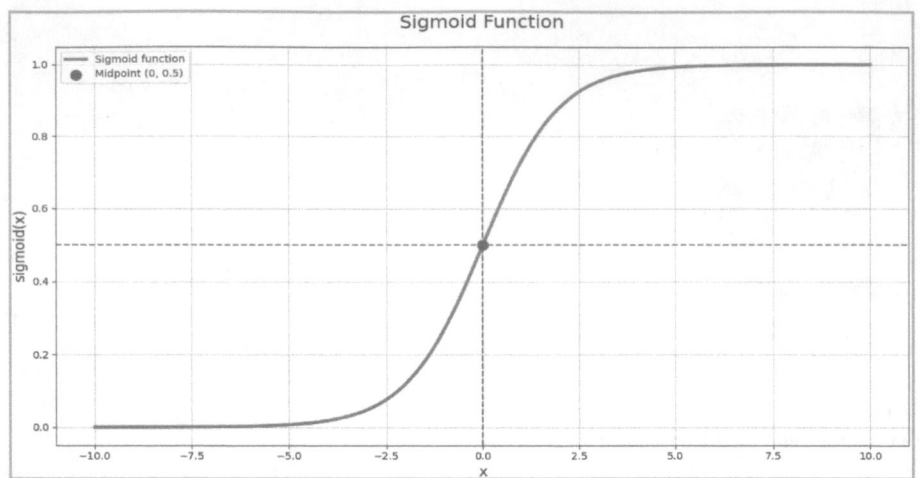

FIGURE 1.13
Sigmoid (sig) function.

1.7.4.2 Tanh or Hyperbolic Tangent (tan)

The hyperbolic tangent (Tanh) activation function has a value range of [–1 to 1]. It maps negative inputs to negative values, so inputs close to zero yield outputs close to zero. It's differentiable and is primarily used for classification problems. Figure 1.14 illustrates its shape: if **z** is the *x*-axis, then $\varnothing(\mathbf{z})$ corresponds to the *y*-axis:

$$\varnothing(z) = \tanh(z) = \frac{\sinh(z)}{1 + e^{-1}\cosh(z)} = \frac{e^z - e^{-z}}{e^z + e^{-z}}$$

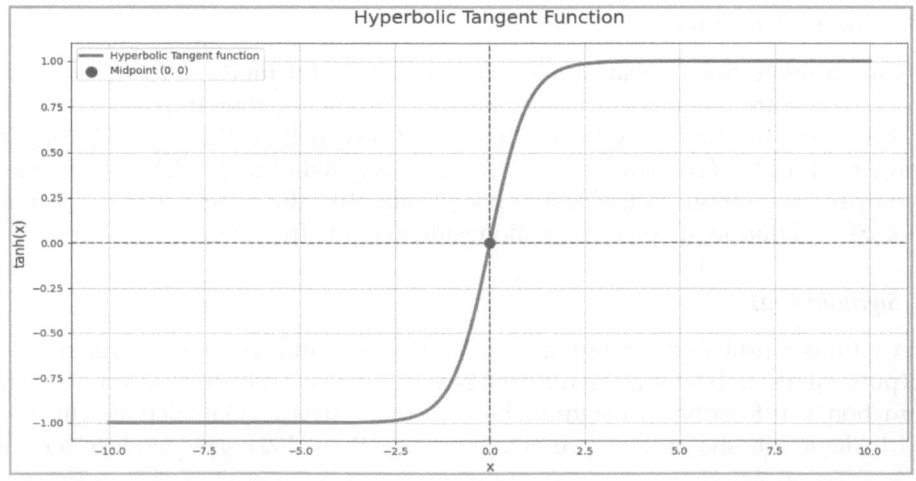

FIGURE 1.14
Hyperbolic tangent (tan) function.

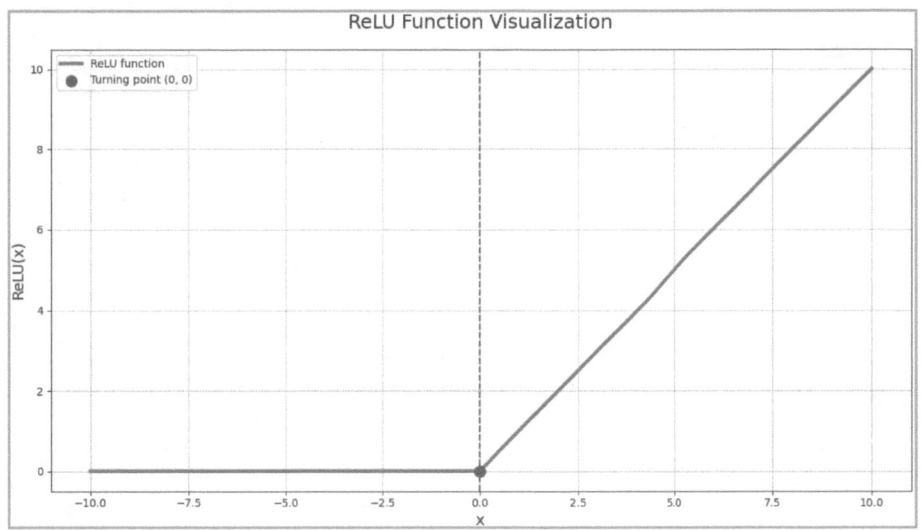

FIGURE 1.15
Rectified linear unit (ReLU) function.

1.7.4.3 Rectified Linear Unit (ReLU)

ReLU activation function has a value range of [0, infinity]. Its output is zero when **z** is less than zero and equal to **z** when **z** is greater than or equal to zero (max (0, **z**)). This means that all negative input values are mapped to zero by ReLU. While this may cause the network to fail to map negative values properly, it does help alleviate the vanishing gradient problem and reduce computation costs. Hence, it's widely used in deep learning algorithms. Figure 1.15 shows the shape of the ReLU function. As can be seen, values less than zero are mapped to zero, while values greater than zero follow a linear function. If **z** is on the *x*-axis, the function R(**z**) is expressed as: R(**z**) = max(0,**z**).

1.7.4.4 leaky ReLU

The Leaky version of the ReLU function maps negative values to other negative values and positive values to themselves. It has an infinite range, from negative infinity to positive infinity. If we consider "**z**" as the *x*-axis, then the function for negative data is given by f(**z**) = **a** × **z**, and for positive data, it's f(**z**) = **z**. Figure 1.16 illustrates its shape.

1.7.4.5 SoftMax

SoftMax is typically used for the final or output layer. It produces multiple outputs and can handle multi-class problems. SoftMax normalizes the output for each class to a value between 0 and 1, which is the probability value divided by the sum. If "**y**" represents the input vector, then the formula for SoftMax is as follows:

$$S(y_i) = \frac{e^{y_i}}{\sum_{i=1}^{n} e^{y_i}}$$

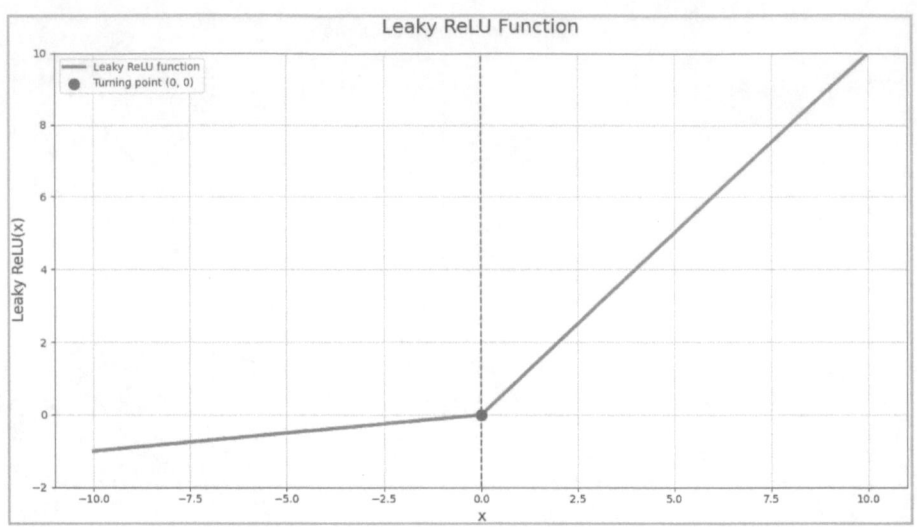

FIGURE 1.16
Leaky rectified linear unit (LReLU).

The SoftMax function, denoted as "**S**", takes "**y**", an input vector with "**n**" classes (such as y_i), which can have a value ranging between negative infinity and positive infinity for "**n**" classes. The standard exponential function is denoted by "**e**". Figure 1.17 illustrates the operation of the SoftMax function. Here, we perform some calculations to find the SoftMax values of the input data. The input data vector is [1,2,3,4], and we also consider an example of a normalized patch from a cat image. We find the exponential ('exp ()') of each value, sum them, and finally, calculate the "s_i" values.

Exp() for each value as follows:

exp(1) = **2.718**,
exp(2) = **7.389**,
exp(3) = **20.085**,
exp(4) = **54.598**.

And their summation:

$$exp(1) + exp(2) + exp(3) + exp(4) = 2.718 + 7.389 + 20.085 + 54.598 = \mathbf{84.790}$$

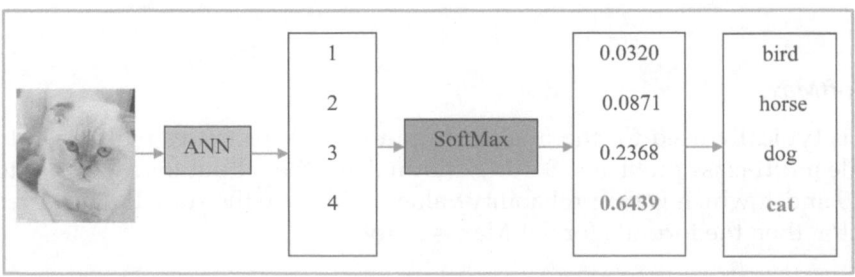

FIGURE 1.17
The SoftMax process.

And their softmax values:

$$s_1 = 2.718/84.790 = \mathbf{0.0320}$$
$$s_2 = 7.389/84.790 = \mathbf{0.0871}$$
$$s_3 = 20.085/84.790 = \mathbf{0.2368}$$
$$s_4 = 54.598/84.790 = \mathbf{0.6439}$$
$$s_1 + s_2 + s_3 + s_4 = 1$$

Its code is like this in Python:

```
from scipy.special import softmax
# define data values
data = [1, 2, 3, 4]
# calculate softmax value
result = softmax(data)
# print the probabilities
print(result)
# print the sum of the probabilities
print(sum(result))
```

And the output is:

```
[0.0320586 0.08714432 0.23688282 0.64391426]
s₁ + s₂ + s₃ + s₄ = 1.0
```

1.7.5 Vanishing Gradient

The vanishing gradient problem is a significant challenge in deep learning. The gradient, which is crucial for optimization, can become very small and approach zero when the network's weights are updated during training. This happens especially when the weights are negative. As weights approach zero, their gradient also tends toward zero. The problem is that when the gradient is close to zero, the network cannot be updated effectively, and it gets stuck, unable to further adjust its weights. This is known as the "vanishing gradient" problem, as the gradient essentially disappears and is no longer useful for training the model. Several solutions exist to mitigate this problem, including the use of Rectified Linear Units (ReLU). We will go over it in more detail in each approach.

1.7.6 Channel

In deep learning, inputs can possess multiple channels. For instance, if you're working with images using the RGB color representation standard, these images comprise three channels: red, green, and blue. Features are extracted from each of these channels.

1.7.7 Embedding

An embedding represents input data as vectors, such as images, text, etc. For instance, we can embed image data into matrices. In sentiment analysis, the embedding process converts text, including individual words, into vectors.

1.7.8 Fine-tuning

This refers to a technique where the parameters of a network are initially set up for one task and then updated for a new task. For example, in a natural language processing (NLP) system, there may be pre-trained word embeddings like word vectors. These parameters can be modified to suit a specific application, such as content analysis or sentiment analysis.

1.7.9 Data Augmentation

These methods employ a range of techniques to generate new data from existing ones, depending on the type of data. For instance, flipping and rotation are two techniques used to generate new image data from an original image.

1.7.10 Generalization

The performance of a neural network is primarily determined by its potential for generalization, which improves as the model is exposed to new data. A DNN, as a type of ANN, excels in promoting this generalization and enhancing the flexibility of the deep learning model. Regularization is one of the methods used to boost this generalization.

1.7.11 Regularization

Regularization is a technique used to enhance model generalization by making slight modifications to the learning process. Some common regularization methods include L_1, L_2, and dropout.

1.7.12 L_1 and L_2

These are among the most common regularization techniques. In these methods, we introduce a regularization term and modify the cost function accordingly.

$$\text{Cost function} = \text{loss} + \text{regularization term}$$

Increasing these values decreases the weight value, which helps simplify and generalize the model. L_1 and L_2 are the two primary terms. L_2 is:

$$\text{Cost function} = \text{loss} + \frac{\text{lambda}}{2m} \times \sum \|w\|^2$$

Lambda is a hyperparameter. L_2 is also known as weight decay, as it diminishes the weights to values close to zero but not exactly zero. Additionally, L_1 is:

$$\text{Cost function} = \text{loss} + \frac{\text{lambda}}{2m} \times \sum \|w\|$$

We usually prefer L_2 over L_1, unless we intend to make the model sparser, because, in L_1 regularization, the weights may be reduced to zero.

1.7.13 Dropout

Dropout operates by masking (or removing) some of the network nodes during the training phase. We will explain this in more detail later.

1.7.14 End-to-end Learning

Deep learning facilitates end-to-end learning, solving problems more efficiently. Traditional AI methods or ANNs, for instance, require steps, such as cropping, translation, detection, and recognition. However, deep learning bypasses these steps, as the layers in the network automatically extract the features from the data.

1.7.15 Error

Error is the difference between the output value and the target value. It is denoted by "**E**", and the objective of learning is to minimize this error within given constraints. There are several methods and criteria for calculating and defining errors.

1.7.16 Training, Testing, and Validation Sets

Data in a database is divided into three major categories: (1) training data, which is used to train the model; (2) validation data, which is used to verify the model; and (3) testing data, which is used to test the trained model. We will discuss these three types in greater detail later.

1.7.17 Overfitting

When training the model, we should always keep generalization in mind. It's possible that if we train the model excessively, it will not generalize well and will fail to fit new data correctly. This concept is also applicable in regression when the model is unable to replicate the behavior of the data. Generally, such a model performs well on training data but poorly on unseen data, as shown in Figure 1.18 (c).

1.7.18 Underfitting

Underfitting occurs when a learning model is unable to capture the underlying patterns and relationships between the values in a dataset and the target variable. Such a model performs poorly on the training data and does not generalize well to new data, as shown in Figure 1.18 (a).

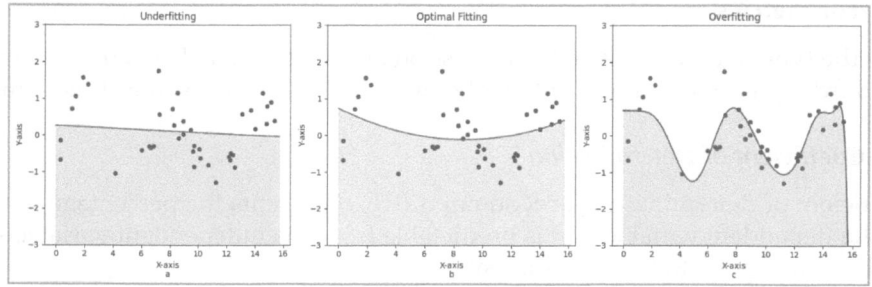

FIGURE 1.18
(a) Underfitting: model too simplistic. (b) Optimal Fit: model captures underlying trend. (c) Overfitting: model overly complex, capturing noise.

TABLE 1.1

Confusion Matrix for Two Classes

		Predicted Values	
		C_1	C_2
Targets	C_1	4	1
	C_2	2	7

1.7.19 Confusion Matrix

There are several methods for determining the accuracy of an algorithm. For classification problems, we can use a confusion matrix. To create a confusion matrix, we construct a square matrix with the classes represented in both rows and columns. The predicted values are listed across the top of the table, while the actual target values are listed down the side. The cell at row "i" and column "j" tells us how many times the model predicted class "j" when the actual target was class "i". For instance, with two classes, we would have a 2×2 table, as illustrated in Table 1.1.

The value of $t_{(1,1)} = 4$ means that four times the output was correctly predicted as class C_1 when the actual target was C_1. The value $t_{(2,1)} = 2$ indicates that two times the output was incorrectly predicted as class C_1 when the actual target was C_2. Similarly, $t_{(1,2)} = 1$ means that once, the output was incorrectly predicted as class C_2 when the actual target was C_1. Lastly, $t_{(2,2)} = 7$ means that seven times the output was correctly predicted as class C_2 when the actual target was C_2. If you're seeking a single accuracy score, you can sum the values on the main diagonal and divide them by the sum of all the matrix values. For instance, in this case, the accuracy value is:

values on diagonal $= 4 + 7 = 11$

whole values $= 4 + 1 + 2 + 7 = 14$

then we have:

$11/14 = .785$

You can multiply this number by 100 and find a percentage:

$.785 \times 100 = \mathbf{78.5\%}$

1.7.20 Error Metrics

Based on the type of problem, whether regression or classification, there are various metrics and standards to assess accuracy. In the following, we will review some of these metrics.

1.7.20.1 Coefficient of Determination

The coefficient of determination, or R-squared (R^2), represents the percentage of the variance in the dependent variable that is predictable from the independent variable(s). It can be calculated using the following formula:

$$R^2 = \frac{\Sigma\left(\hat{y_i} - y^-\right)^2}{\Sigma\left(y_i - y^-\right)^2}$$

1.7.20.2 Mean Squared Error (MSE)

MSE is the average of the squared differences between the observed and predicted values. It can be calculated using the following formula:

$$MSE = \frac{1}{n} \sum \left(y_i - \hat{y_i} \right)^2$$

1.7.20.3 Root Mean Squared Error (RMSE)

RMSE is calculated by taking the square root of the average of the squared differences between the observed and predicted values.

$$RMSE = \sqrt{MSE} = \sqrt{\frac{1}{n} \sum \left(y_i - \hat{y_i} \right)^2}$$

1.7.20.4 Mean Absolute Error (MAE)

MAE is calculated by taking the average of the absolute values of the differences between the observed and predicted values.

$$MAE = \frac{1}{n} \sum \left| y_i - \hat{y_i} \right|$$

1.7.20.5 True Positive (TP)

TP occurs when an observation is correctly identified. For example, in a classification task distinguishing apples from non-apples, an object is a true positive if it is an apple and is correctly classified as an apple.

1.7.20.6 False Positive (FP)

FP occurs when an observation is incorrectly classified. For example, in a classification task distinguishing apples from non-apples, an object is an FP if it is not an apple but is wrongly classified as an apple.

1.7.20.7 True Negative (TN)

TN occurs when an observation is correctly classified as a negative instance. For example, in a classification task distinguishing apples from non-apples, an object is a TN if it is not an apple and is correctly classified as not being an apple.

1.7.20.8 False Negative (FN)

FN occurs when an observation is incorrectly classified as a negative instance. For example, in a classification task distinguishing apples from non-apples, an object is an FN if it is an apple but is incorrectly classified as not being an apple.

TABLE 1.2

Accuracy Metrics Parameters

		Actual	
		Positive	Negative
Predicted	Positive	TP	FP
	Negative	FN	TN

Table 1.2 displays these values. Based on the four values we discussed, the following are the most commonly used definitions of accuracy.

1.7.20.9 Accuracy (ACC)

Its value is equal to the following:

$$ACC = \frac{TP + TN}{TP + FP + TN + FN}$$

Accuracy is a suitable metric, but only if the datasets are balanced, meaning the counts of false negatives and false positives are relatively equal. Figure 1.19 depicts accuracy, highlighting how measurements align with the known or true value.

1.7.20.10 Precision or Positive Predictive Value (PPV)

Its value is equal to the following formula:

$$PPV = \frac{TP}{TP + FP} = 1 - FDR$$

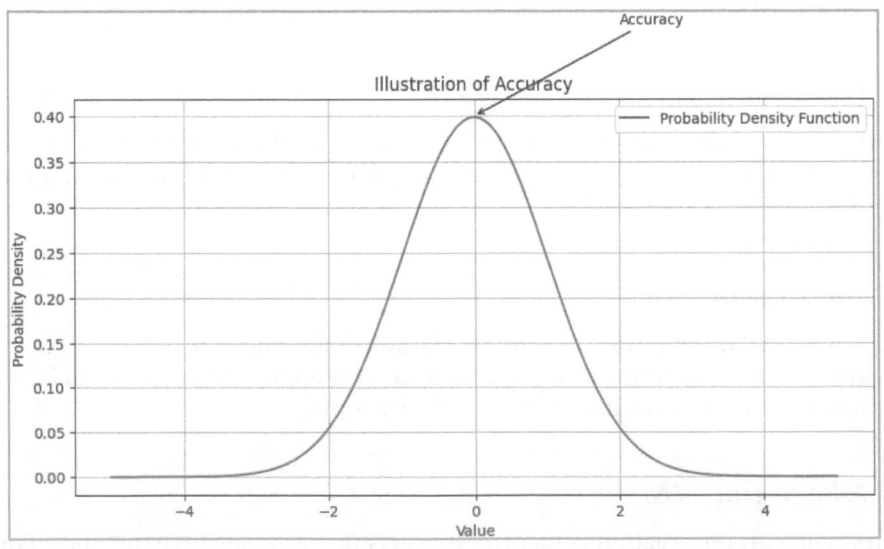

FIGURE 1.19
Accuracy value.

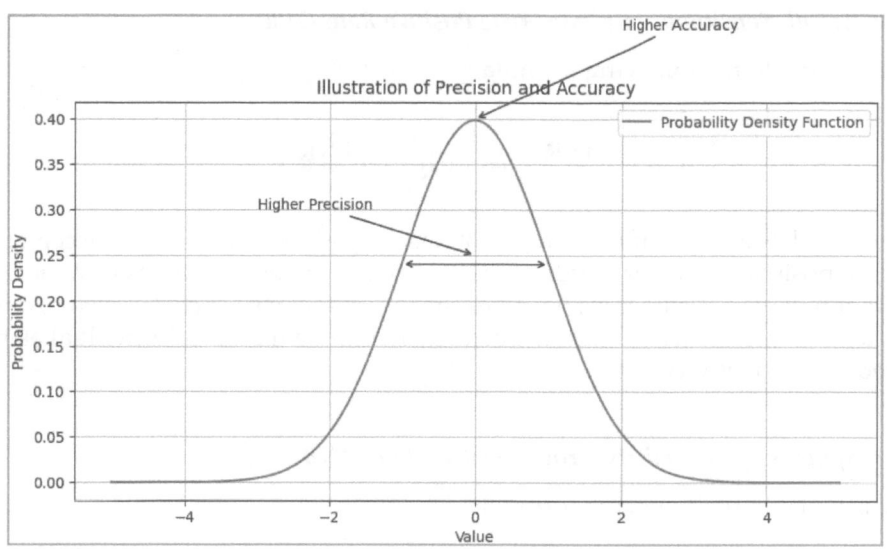

FIGURE 1.20
Precision and Accuracy.

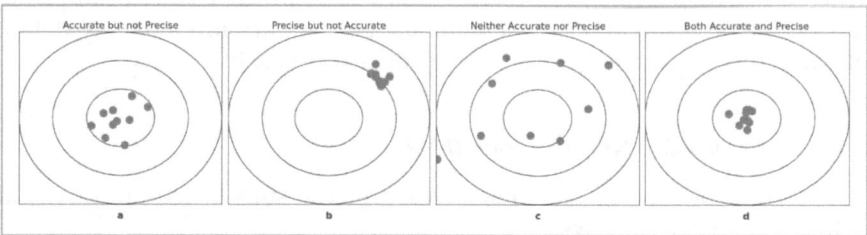

FIGURE 1.21
Four scenarios visualized: (1) Accurate, not precise; (2) Precise, not accurate; (3) Neither accurate nor precise; (4) Both accurate and precise

Choose precision as a metric if you want to be more confident about your true positives (e.g., in the case of spam emails). Figure 1.20 showcases precision, emphasizing the consistency in results from repeated measurements under stable conditions.

Figure 1.21 demonstrates how accuracy can be low regardless of whether the precision value is high or low.

1.7.20.11 Negative Predictive Values (NPV)

NPV is a statistical measure used in diagnostic testing to evaluate the performance of a test. It is particularly useful in medical diagnostics and screening where there's a need to determine if a person has a specific condition or not based on test results. Its value can be calculated as follows:

$$\mathbf{NPV} = \frac{\text{TN}}{\text{TN} + \text{FN}} = 1 - \text{FOR}$$

1.7.20.12 Recall, Sensitivity, Hit Rate, True Positive Rate (TPR)

Its value is equal to the following formula:

$$\mathbf{TPR} = \frac{TP}{TP + FN} = 1 - FNR$$

Choose recall as a metric if the concept of false negatives is far more unacceptable than that of false positives. In other words, if the occurrence of false negatives is intolerable and you'd rather have some extra false positives than miss some true positives. For example, in medical testing, the ability of a test to correctly identify a diseased individual as positive is referred to as sensitivity.

1.7.20.13 Specificity, Selectivity, True Negative Rate (TNR)

Its value is equal to the following formula:

$$\mathbf{TNR} = \frac{TN}{FP + TN} = 1 - FPR$$

To capture all true negatives, you don't want any false positives. For example, if you are administering a drug test and all those who test positive are immediately detained, you would not want anyone who is drug-free to be detained falsely.

1.7.20.14 Miss Rate or False Negative Rate (FNR)

It represents the proportion of false negatives over the sum of true positives and false negatives. Its formula is as follows:

$$\mathbf{FNR} = \frac{FN}{TP + FN} = 1 - TPR$$

1.7.20.15 Fall-out or False Positive Rate (FPR)

It represents the proportion of false positives over the sum of false positives and true negatives. Its formula is as follows:

$$\mathbf{FPR} = \frac{FP}{FP + TN} = 1 - TNR$$

1.7.20.16 False Discovery Rate (FDR)

It represents the proportion of false positives over the sum of false positives and true positives. Its formula is as follows:

$$\mathbf{FDR} = \frac{FP}{FP + TP} = 1 - PPV$$

1.7.20.17 *False Omission Rate (FOR)*

It represents the proportion of false positives over the sum of false positives and true negatives. Its formula is as follows:

$$\mathbf{FOR} = \frac{FP}{FP + TN} = 1 - TNR$$

1.7.20.18 *Positive Likelihood Ratio (LR+)*

It is the ratio of True Positive Rate (TPR) to False Positive Rate (FPR). Its formula is as follows:

$$\mathbf{LR+} = \frac{TPR}{FPR}$$

1.7.20.19 *Negative Likelihood Ratio (LR-)*

It is the ratio of False Negative Rate (FNR) to True Negative Rate (TNR). Its formula is as follows:

$$\mathbf{LR-} = \frac{FNR}{TNR}$$

1.7.20.20 *F_1-score (aka F-Score/F-Measure)*

Its value is equal to the following:

$$\mathbf{F_1 - score} = 2 \times \frac{(Recall \times Precision)}{(Recall + Precision)} = \frac{2 \times TP}{2 \times TP + FP + FN}$$

F_1 score comes to your rescue if the costs of false positives and false negatives are different. F_1 is the best choice if your class distribution is skewed.

1.7.21 Balanced and Unbalanced Datasets

A dataset is considered balanced if it contains an equal number of positive and negative examples. We often assume that a dataset is balanced, but this is not typically the case with real-world datasets (unbalanced datasets). To evaluate accuracy in a balanced dataset, we can calculate and apply the following value:

$$\mathbf{Accuracy} = \frac{(Sensitivity + Specificity)}{2}$$

Another metric derived from these four values is the Matthews Correlation Coefficient (MCC), which is calculated as follows:

$$\mathbf{MCC} = \frac{((TP \times TN) - (FP \times FN))}{(\sqrt{(TP + FP)} \times (TP + FN) \times (TN + FP) \times (TN + FN))}$$

1.7.22 Standardization

Features are transformed to a range centered at 0, with 1 representing the standard deviation.

$$x_{standardized} = \frac{x_{original} - \mu_x}{\sigma_x}$$

μ_x is the mean and σ_x is the standard deviation of the feature, and when there are outliers, standardization works best.

1.7.23 Normalization

It scales a feature to a specific range. For example, one well-known normalization method scales data to the range [0,1].

$$x_{normalized} = \frac{x_{original} - min_x}{max_x - min_x}$$

When all features must be on the same scale, normalization comes in handy.

1.7.24 One-hot Encoding

Suppose the dataset has categorical features (e.g., color) with three main color channels (R = Red, G = Green, and B = Blue). Then, the string values can be encoded into numbers for use in a machine-learning algorithm. For instance, red can be assigned 0, green 1, and blue 2. These values are distinct; in the data, if there are k features (here $k = 3$), there are k distinct numbers, with each feature assigned a unique value.

In Table 1.3, the input is {Green, Red, Blue, Red} with dimensions 4×1, and the output is {(0,1,0), (1,0,0), (0,0,1), (1,0,0)} with dimensions 4×3. Please keep in mind that this method increases the dimensionality of the dataset. In the preceding example, the input dimension is 4×1, while the output dimension is 4×3. When dealing with real-world data, the input dimension may be large, resulting in a large output dimension and extensive computations.

1.7.25 Generator

It generates synthetic data from random noise and progressively refines it based on feedback from the discriminator.

1.7.26 Discriminator

It is a classifier that distinguishes between real and fake data. The real data is sourced directly from the input, whereas the fake data is artificially generated.

TABLE 1.3

Encoding RGB Values

Color Values	Red	Green	Blue
Green	0	1	0
Red	1	0	0
Blue	0	0	1
Red	1	0	0

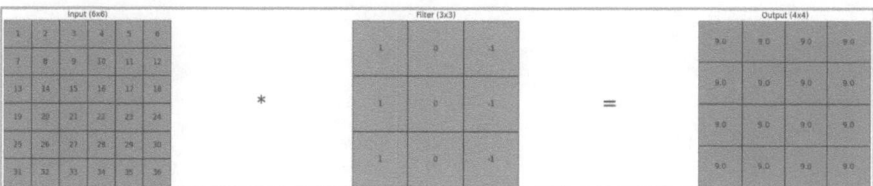

FIGURE 1.22
The convolution processes.

1.7.27 Convolutional Layers

Convolutions are instrumental in quickly extracting relevant information from data. They require an input (like a 2D image), a filter or kernel, and yield an output known as the convolved feature. Figure 1.22 illustrates how a convolved feature of 4×4 dimensions is created by applying a 3×3 dimension filter to a 6×6 dimension image. A neural network can comprise multiple convolutional layers, along with additional pooling layers, to decrease the overall size of the convolved features. Convolutional layers are utilized in both the discriminator and the final layers of generative models.

1.7.28 Deconvolution

The objective of the deconvolution computational technique is to obtain a more precise estimate of image intensity. This is achieved by applying a mathematical equation that performs the inverse of the imaging process. The term "deconvolution" originally comes from signal processing and refers to the process of reversing the effects of convolution to retrieve the original signal. In the context of neural networks, "deconvolution" has sometimes been used to describe layers that perform an operation that is the inverse of a convolution in terms of reversing the forward and backward passes, but it is a bit of a misnomer because it does not perform a mathematical deconvolution. It would be more accurately described as fractionally-strided or transposed convolution. Figure 1.23 provides a visual comparison between the convolution and deconvolution processes, elucidating their respective operations in signal or image processing.

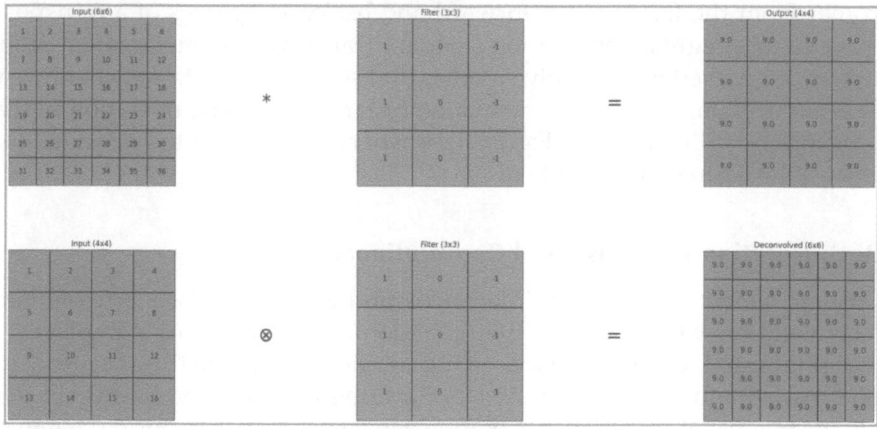

FIGURE 1.23
The convolution vs. deconvolution process.

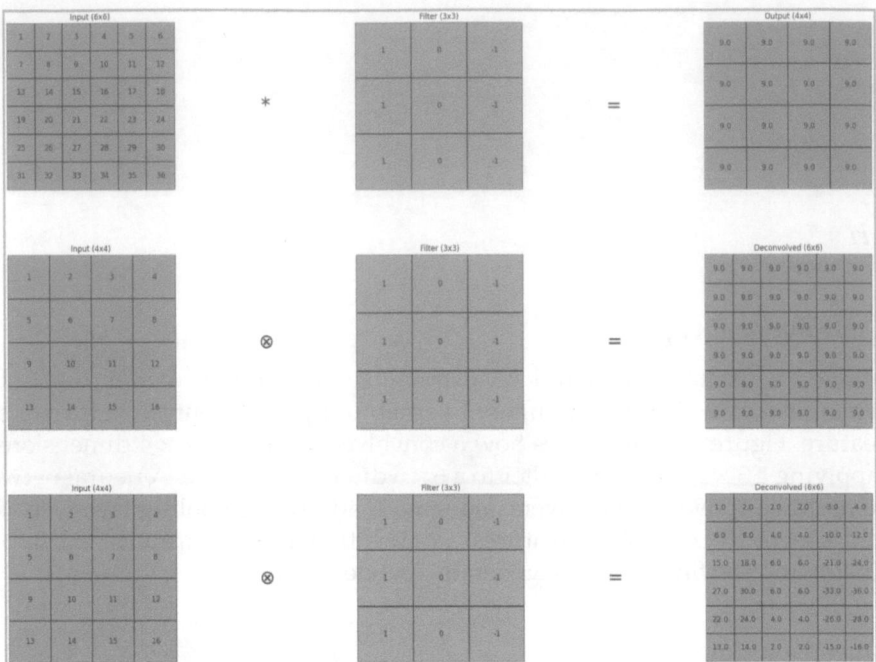

FIGURE 1.24
The convolution vs. deconvolution vs. transposed convolution process.

1.7.29 Transposed Convolutional Layers

Transposed convolutions utilize filters to process the input in the same way as regular convolutions. However, their objective is the inverse of a standard convolution. In contrast to traditional convolutions, which downsample the data, transposed convolutions are used to upsample the input, producing a larger feature map. Transposed convolution, also sometimes referred to as "fractionally-strided convolution", "backward convolution", or incorrectly as "deconvolution", is an operation that increases the spatial resolution of the input, effectively performing the opposite of a normal convolution. The name "transposed" comes from the fact that the forward and backward passes of a transposed convolution layer and a regular convolution layer are transposes of one another. Transposed convolution is often used in generative models and segmentation tasks where we want to upsample a feature map to a higher resolution or larger size. The operation of the transposed convolution is illustrated in Figure 1.24, where a 4×4 input is upscaled to a 6×6 output using a 3×3 filter and a stride of 1.

1.7.30 Deconvolution vs. Transposed Convolutional

The key difference between a "true" deconvolution and transposed convolution is that a true deconvolution would reverse the operation of a convolution completely, getting back the original input, while a transposed convolution doesn't do this – instead, it merely swaps the forward and backward passes, performing an operation that is similar to but not exactly the inverse of a regular convolution. However, it's worth noting that in practice, these terms can sometimes be used interchangeably, and you may find "deconvolution" being used to describe a transposed convolution operation. This is technically incorrect but is common in the literature. As always, the key is to understand the context in which these terms are being used.

1.7.31 Loss Functions

A loss function, also known as a cost function, quantifies the disparity between our model's predictions and the desired targets. It is calculated by determining the loss values, which are the differences between the predicted and desired (target) outputs. Loss functions can be categorized into three major types: regression loss functions, classification loss functions, and embedding loss functions.

1.7.31.1 Regressive Loss Functions

Mean Square Error (MSE) and Absolute Error (AE) are two common methods used in regression loss functions.

- **Mean Square Error (MSE):** This is one of the most commonly used loss functions for regression problems. It calculates the average of the squared difference between the predicted and actual values. The MSE provides a good measure of the model's performance, as larger errors are penalized more due to the squaring.
- **Absolute Error (AE):** Also known as Mean Absolute Error (MAE), this loss function computes the average of the absolute differences between the predicted and actual values. Unlike MSE, it doesn't penalize larger errors as heavily, which can make it more robust to outliers.

These loss functions are used to guide the optimization algorithm (like gradient descent) to adjust the parameters of the model in order to minimize the loss and improve the model's predictive performance.

1.7.31.2 Classification Loss Functions

There are some approaches in this field, such as Binary Cross-Entropy (BCE), Negative Log-Likelihood (NLL), and Soft Margin Classifier (SMC). BCE, also known as log loss, is a loss function used in binary classification tasks in machine learning. This function calculates the cross-entropy loss between true labels and predictions and is especially suitable for models that output probabilities, such as logistic regression or models with a sigmoid activation in the final layer. NLL is a common loss function used in various machine learning algorithms, particularly in tasks like classification and density estimation. It is based on principles of probability and statistics. An SMC is a variation of the Support Vector Machine (SVM) algorithm. SVMs are a popular class of methods used in supervised learning for classification and regression.

1.7.31.3 Embedding Loss Functions

There are several embedding loss functions, such as Cosine Error (CE). "Cosine Error" is typically referred to as "Cosine Similarity Loss" or "Cosine Distance" in the context of machine learning, and it is often used in tasks that involve learning embeddings. The Cosine Similarity measures the cosine of the angle between two vectors. The resulting similarity ranges from –1, meaning exactly opposite, to 1, meaning exactly the same, with 0 indicating orthogonality (decorrelation) and in-between values indicating intermediate similarity or dissimilarity.

1.7.31.4 Cross-entropy Loss

Cross-entropy loss, also known as log loss, is a commonly used loss function in machine learning and deep learning for classification problems. It measures the dissimilarity between the predicted probability distribution and the true distribution. It represents a probability value that indicates the difference between the expected and actual costs; this is illustrated in Figure 1.25.

1.7.31.5 MSE (L₂) Loss

L_2 is calculated by:

$$\text{MSE} = \frac{\sum_{i=1}^{n}(y_i - y_i^p)^2}{n}$$

Figure 1.26 illustrates the L_2 graph for an MSE function, where the MSE loss reaches its minimum value when the prediction equals 100.

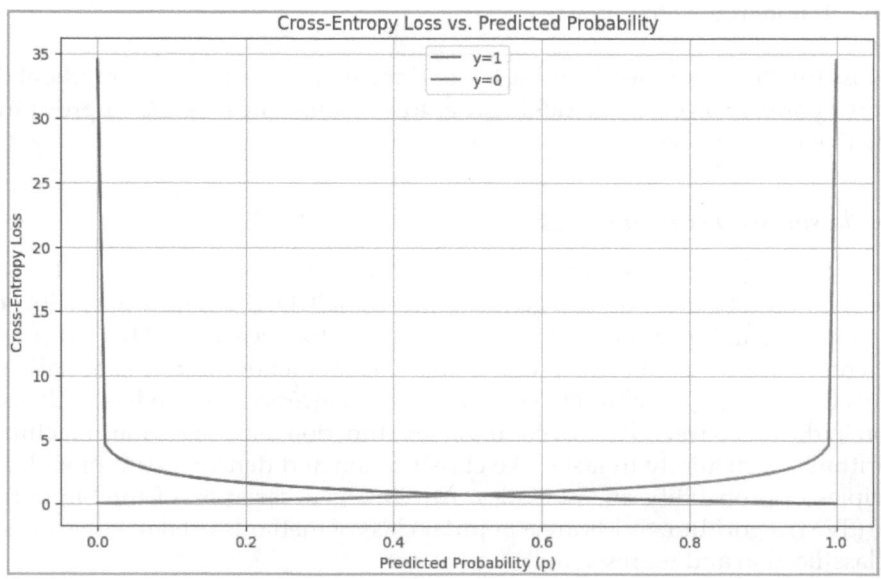

FIGURE 1.25
Cross-entropy loss graph.

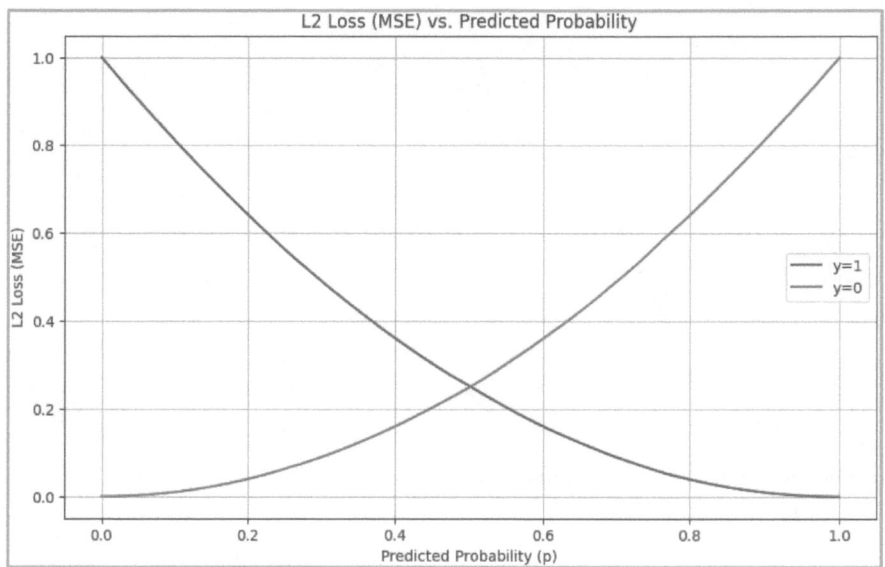

FIGURE 1.26
MSE (L_2) loss graph.

1.7.32 Optimization Functions

Gradient Descent (GD), Stochastic Gradient Descent (SGD), Adagrad, and Adam are the four most popular optimization algorithms. In general, SGD is much faster than the others. There is a trade-off between speed and higher-quality results (accuracy). As the amount of data increases, the model becomes more complex, and selecting an optimization function becomes challenging. Before we proceed to discuss some well-known optimization methods, we need to understand two concepts: learning rate and convexity.

1.7.32.1 Learning Rate

In the context of machine learning and optimization, the learning rate is a hyperparameter that determines the step size at each iteration while moving toward a minimum of loss function. Essentially, it controls how much we are adjusting the weights of our network with respect to the loss gradient. Optimization algorithms use two types of learning rates to update the network's weights and biases: constant and adaptive learning rate. The value is usually small, typically between 0.0 and 1.0. Choosing an appropriate learning rate can be challenging. If it's too high, the algorithm might overshoot the minimum and diverge. If it's too low, the algorithm will converge slowly. The optimal learning rate might also change during training, decreasing as we approach the minimum. Techniques like learning rate schedules or adaptive learning rates can help handle these challenges. Figure 1.27 illustrates some of these scenarios.

1.7.32.2 Convex

Convexity refers to a characteristic of a function. A curve is convex if any line drawn between two points on the graph lies either entirely above or entirely below the graph. Figure 1.28 shows a convex curve (bottom) and a non-convex curve (top).

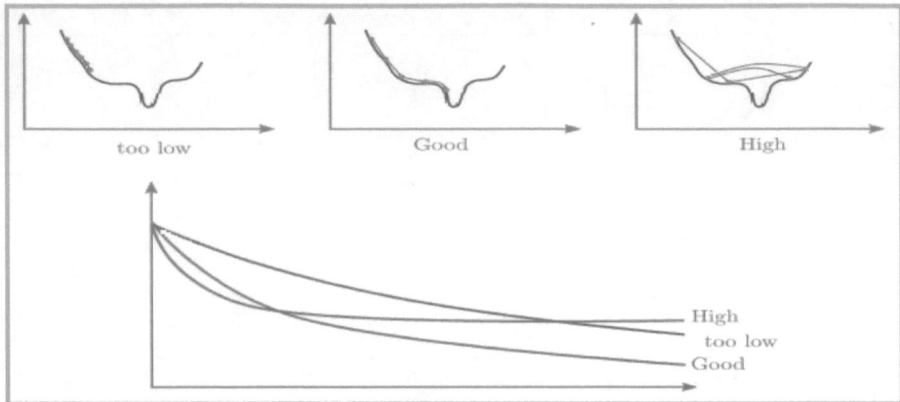

FIGURE 1.27
How different learning rate values affect training convergence.

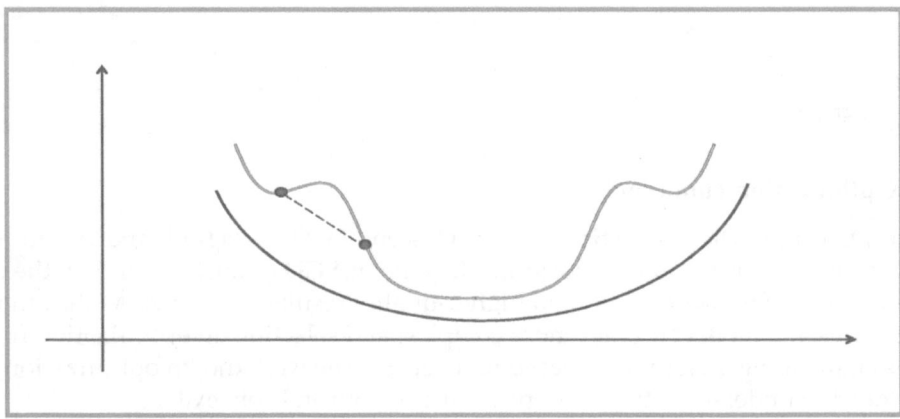

FIGURE 1.28
The top curve is non-convex, and the bottom one is convex.

1.7.32.3 *Gradient Descent*

GD is a popular optimization method that returns the optimal value along the direction of the gradient descent. This method is the most general and popular solution when the objective function is convex. One of its challenges is that it doesn't update the process at every step. When the gradient of all data is computed, the computational cost of GD significantly increases, especially with large datasets. It also takes longer to converge when the data contains more noise or is biased.

1.7.32.4 *Stochastic Gradient Descent*

GD computes the gradient to find local minima, whereas SGD updates the parameters for each training example. SGD changes the parameters randomly, and its computational cost is efficient, not always dependent on the entire dataset. Its challenge lies in determining the appropriate learning rate. Simply selecting the same learning rate for all parameters may not be the best solution, and it could potentially lead to convergence at a saddle point.

1.7.32.5 Adagrad

Adagrad adjusts the learning rate for each parameter at each step based on the previous gradients. This means that manually tuning the learning rate is unnecessary. The learning rate in this method is adaptively adjusted according to the squares of all previous gradient values, making it faster with a larger learning rate. This method works well for problems with sparse gradients. However, over time, it's possible that all gradient values will increase, causing the learning rate to approach zero and resulting in incorrect parameter updates. Please note that this method does not work well for non-convex problems.

1.7.32.6 Adam

ADAM, which stands for Adaptive Moment Estimation, combines the concepts of momentum and adaptability. It is suitable for non-convex problems that involve large amounts of data and a large dimensional feature space. Since most deep learning methods require extensive datasets, Adam may be a suitable candidate for these applications.

Figure 1.29 shows the differences between the four convergence methods, including GD, SGD, Adagrad, and Adam.

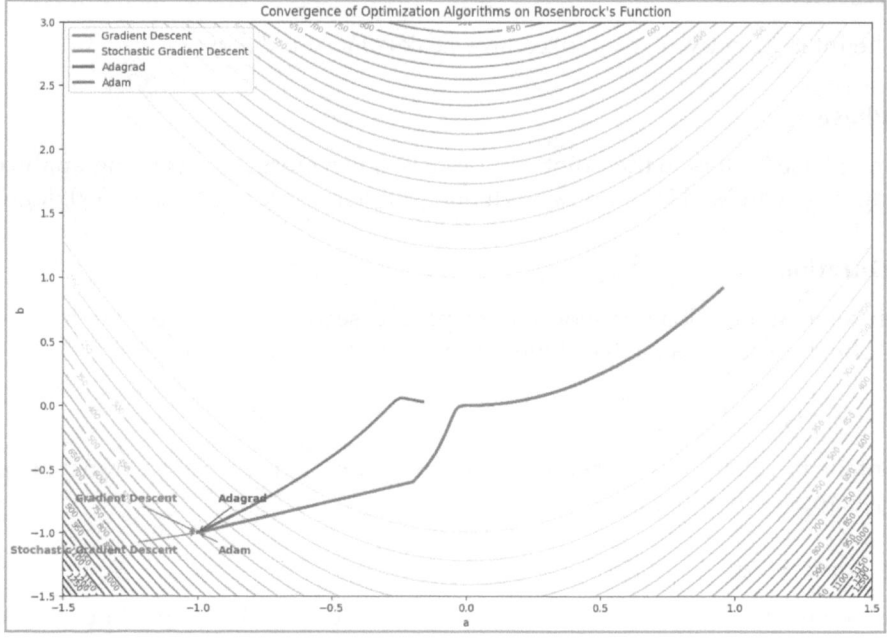

FIGURE 1.29
Four optimization function convergence graphs.

1.7.33 Frequency

The frequency of a sound wave refers to the number of cycles it completes per unit of time, typically per second.

1.7.34 Amplitude

Volume, also known as amplitude, refers to the loudness or quietness of a sound. It is measured in a unit called "decibel", abbreviated as "dB".

1.7.35 Timbre

Timbre is what allows us to distinguish between two different instruments playing the same note at the same volume. It's often referred to as the "color" or "tone quality" of the sound and is determined by the unique characteristics of the sound's production and resonance.

1.7.36 Pitch

In addition to the fundamental frequency, there are other subtle frequencies at play. Some have a lower pitch than the fundamental frequency, which is why they're called subtones, while others have a higher pitch, which is why they're called overtones.

1.7.37 Wavelength

This is the interval between two successive peaks of a sound wave.

1.7.38 Phase

The term "phase" refers to the point in a cycle of a waveform that is being analyzed. The phase angle is expressed in degrees, with one complete cycle equating to 360 degrees.

1.7.39 Duration

Duration refers to how long or short a note, phrase, section, or composition lasts. In other words, "The duration of a pitch or tone is the amount of time it is sounded".

1.7.40 Intensity

Sound intensity refers to the amount of power that sound waves can transport perpendicularly across a given area.

1.7.41 Sample Rate

The sample rate refers to the number of times a sound wave is sampled per unit of time. A lower sampling rate results in less information and a lower computational cost, while a higher sampling rate captures more details but incurs a higher computational cost.

1.7.42 Score (in Sound)

A score is a notated representation of music that can be read and interpreted by people or computer programs to create music. This representation is composed of discrete symbols that effectively express the musical composition. Music notation allows both human musicians and computer programs to understand and recreate the intended sounds.

1.7.43 Performance (in Sound)

Notated music serves as a guideline for performers, allowing them to interpret and perform a piece of music according to their preferences for tempo, rhythm, and other musical elements. It provides a framework within which musicians can express their creativity and individuality.

1.7.44 Zero-sum Game

In a situation where one person's gain equals another's loss, the net gain or loss is zero. This is often referred to as a zero-sum game.

1.8 Issues and Challenges in Machine Learning

There are several issues in machine learning, some of which include:

1.8.1 Bias and Fairness

Machine learning models can exhibit bias if the training data is not representative of the population. This can lead to unfair outcomes and discrimination. Ensuring fairness and reducing bias are significant areas of research in machine learning.

1.8.2 Overfitting

When a model is excessively complex and fits the training data too closely, it performs poorly on new, previously unseen data. Overfitting can be mitigated using regularization techniques.

1.8.3 Data Quality and Quantity

Machine learning models require substantial amounts of high-quality data to learn and generalize effectively. Poor quality or inadequate data can result in subpar model performance.

1.8.4 Interpretability

Many machine learning models are considered "black boxes" because understanding how they make predictions can be challenging. This can make it difficult to trust and use these models in certain domains.

1.8.5 Scalability

Some machine learning algorithms are not scalable and may perform poorly with large datasets or in distributed computing environments.

1.8.6 Privacy and Security

Machine learning models can potentially reveal sensitive information about individuals or organizations. Ensuring the privacy and security of the data and models is an important consideration in machine learning applications.

1.8.7 Hyperparameter Tuning

Choosing the optimal hyperparameters for a machine learning model can be challenging and time-consuming. Automated hyperparameter tuning techniques are being developed to address this issue.

1.8.8 Transfer Learning

Training machine learning models can be time-consuming and computationally expensive. Transfer learning techniques allow pre-trained models to be fine-tuned on new tasks, reducing the amount of training data and computation required.

1.8.9 Adversarial Attacks

Adversarial attacks involve intentionally perturbing input data to fool machine learning models into making incorrect predictions. Developing robust models that can withstand such attacks is an active area of research.

1.8.10 Ethics and Accountability

As machine learning models are increasingly used to make decisions that impact individuals and society, ensuring the ethical use and accountability of these models is becoming increasingly important.

1.9 Issues and Challenges in Deep Learning

There are several issues in deep learning that can affect the performance and reliability of the models. Here are some common issues:

1.9.1 Overfitting

Overfitting occurs when a model becomes overly complex and begins to learn from the noise in the training data. This can result in poor performance when dealing with new data.

1.9.2 Underfitting

Overly simple models fail to capture the underlying patterns in the data. This can also result in poor performance when dealing with new data.

1.9.3 Vanishing and Exploding Gradients

DNNs can suffer from vanishing and exploding gradients, occurring when the gradients become very small or large during training. This can make it challenging to train deep models.

1.9.4 Computational Complexity

Deep learning models can be very computationally expensive to train, especially when dealing with large datasets.

1.9.5 Data Quality

The quality of data used to train deep learning models can significantly impact their performance. Poor quality data can lead to poor performance, even with the most advanced algorithms.

1.9.6 Interpretability

Deep learning models can be extremely complex and difficult to interpret, which makes it difficult to understand why a model makes a particular prediction.

1.9.7 Generalization

Deep learning models can struggle to generalize to new data that is significantly different from the training data.

1.9.8 Ethical Considerations

Deep learning models can be used to make decisions that significantly impact people's lives, such as in healthcare, finance, and criminal justice. This raises important ethical considerations around fairness, transparency, and accountability.

1.10 Issues and Challenges in GANs

GANs have gained popularity in recent years for their ability to generate high-quality samples that closely resemble real data. When working with GANs, however, several issues must still be addressed. Some of these issues include:

1.10.1 Mode Collapse

This occurs when the generator produces a limited number of samples, causing the discriminator to become too good at distinguishing between real and fake data. This results in the generator focusing on generating only a few types of samples and ignoring the rest.

1.10.2 Training Instability

Because of their unstable nature, GANs can be difficult to train. The generator and discriminator are trained concurrently, and if either becomes overly powerful, it can result in "gradient vanishing" or "gradient exploding", in which the gradients become too small or too large, respectively.

1.10.3 Overfitting

GANs can also suffer from overfitting, where the generator produces samples that are too similar to the training data, resulting in poor generalization to new data.

1.10.4 Evaluation

Unlike other generative models, objectively evaluating the quality of GAN-generated samples can be challenging. While metrics, such as the Inception Score and Fréchet Inception Distance, have been proposed, they are not perfect and can be misleading in some cases.

1.10.5 Limited Data

GANs require large amounts of data to train effectively. In some cases, obtaining a large dataset can be challenging, which can limit the effectiveness of GANs.

1.10.6 Hyperparameters

GANs have several hyperparameters that need to be tuned carefully to achieve optimal results. This can be a time-consuming process and requires significant expertise.

1.11 Tips in Machine Learning Implementation

Implementing machine learning models can be a challenging task, and several tips can help improve the success and efficiency of the process. Here are some tips for machine learning implementation.

1.11.1 Understand the Problem

Before beginning the implementation process, understand the details of the problem you are attempting to solve. Understand the data, the domain, and the business context to create a well-defined problem statement.

1.11.2 Choose the Right Algorithm

The choice of algorithm can significantly impact the model's performance. Choose an algorithm that is appropriate for the problem at hand and the data available.

1.11.3 Data Preprocessing

Ensure the data is clean, well-structured, and contains all the relevant features required for the model.

1.11.4 Feature Selection

The process of selecting the most relevant features from data is known as feature selection. It contributes to decreasing the dimensionality of the dataset and improving the model's performance.

1.11.5 Hyperparameter Tuning

Hyperparameters are parameters determined prior to training and not learned by the model. Tuning the hyperparameters can help to optimize the model's performance.

1.11.6 Cross-validation

It ensures that the model does not overfit the data and gives a more accurate estimate of its performance.

1.11.7 Regularization

Regularization is a technique for preventing model overfitting. It aids in the reduction of variance and the improvement of the model's generalization performance.

1.11.8 Monitoring and Logging

Monitoring and logging the model's performance and behavior can help to identify potential issues and improve the model's performance over time.

1.11.9 Interpretability

Interpretability is the ability to understand and explain the model's behavior. It is essential to ensure that the model's decisions are transparent and can be easily understood by stakeholders.

1.11.10 Reproducibility

Reproducibility is the ability to replicate the results of the model. It is important to ensure that the implementation process is well-documented and that others can reproduce the results.

1.12 Tips in Deep Learning Implementation

Here are some tips for deep learning implementation.

1.12.1 Start with a Small Dataset

When implementing a deep learning model, it's best to start with a small dataset to test the architecture and hyperparameters. This allows you to quickly iterate and improve before scaling to larger datasets.

1.12.2 Use Pre-trained Models

Pre-trained models can save you a lot of time and computational resources. They enable you to train a model on a large dataset before fine-tuning it for your specific task.

1.12.3 Use Transfer Learning

Transfer learning is the process of adapting a previously trained model to a new task. Because the pre-trained model has already learned many useful features that can be applied to your new task, you can save a lot of time and resources.

1.12.4 Regularize Your Model

Regularization techniques, such as L_1 and L_2 regularization, dropout, and batch normalization, can help prevent overfitting and improve generalization performance.

1.12.5 Use Early Stopping

Early stopping is a technique where you stop training your model when the validation loss starts to increase. This can help prevent overfitting and improve generalization performance.

1.12.6 Use a Graphics Processing Unit (GPU)

Training deep learning models can be computationally intensive, and using a GPU can significantly speed up the training process.

1.12.7 Visualize Your Results

Visualizing your results can help you understand what your model is learning and where it may be making mistakes. This can help you make improvements to your model.

1.12.8 Document Your Experiments

Documenting your experiments is important for reproducibility and for keeping track of what works and what doesn't. This can save you time in the long run and help you make informed decisions about future experiments.

1.12.9 Use Good Coding Practices

Good coding practices, such as modularization, version control, and code reviews, can make your code more maintainable and reduce errors.

1.12.10 Stay Up to Date

Because deep learning is a rapidly evolving field, staying current on the latest techniques and research is essential. When implementing deep learning models, attending conferences, reading research papers, and participating in online communities can help you stay informed and make better decisions.

1.13 Tips in GAN Implementation

When implementing a GAN, here are some tips that can help improve the training process and the quality of generated samples.

1.13.1 Use a Smaller Learning Rate

GANs are notoriously difficult to train, and using a smaller learning rate can help prevent the generator from overpowering the discriminator too quickly.

1.13.2 Normalize Input Data

Normalizing input data to the range [–1, 1] can aid in preventing mode collapse, which occurs when the generator learns to produce only a limited set of samples.

1.13.3 Use Batch Normalization

Batch normalization can help stabilize the training process and improve the quality of generated samples.

1.13.4 Add Noise to Input Data

Adding noise to input data can help prevent overfitting and improve the diversity of generated samples.

1.13.5 Use Different Activation Functions

Experimenting with different activation functions in the generator and discriminator can help find the ones that work best for the specific problem.

1.13.6 Use Different Loss Functions

Conducting experiments with various loss functions can assist in identifying the ones that are most effective for a specific problem, thereby preventing mode collapse.

1.13.7 Monitor the Training Process

Monitoring the training process, for example, by plotting the discriminator and generator losses, can aid in identifying when the training process is not progressing as expected, allowing for appropriate adjustments to the hyperparameters.

1.13.8 Use Early Stopping

Employing early stopping can aid in preventing overfitting and enhancing the model's ability to generalize.

1.13.9 Generate Samples Periodically

Periodically generating samples during training can assist in tracking the model's progress and identifying when the quality of the generated samples ceases to improve.

1.13.10 Evaluate the Model Using Multiple Metrics

Evaluating the model using multiple metrics, such as Fréchet Inception Distance (FID) and Inception Score, can provide a comprehensive understanding of the model's performance.

Remember, hands-on experience is key when working with machine learning models. Therefore, consistently practicing implementation and troubleshooting is crucial for mastering these concepts.

1.14 Lessons Learned

- Learn the definition and concept of learning.
- Learn the definition and concept of machine learning and its relation to learning.
- Learn the different types of machine learning algorithms.
- Learn the general concept of ANNs, Deep learning, and GAN and their relations.
- Learn some terminology that is needed to read this book.
- Learn the issues and challenges in machine learning, deep learning, and GAN.
- Learn the implementation tips for machine learning, deep learning, and GAN.

1.15 Problems

1.15.1 What is machine learning, how many approaches are there, and what are their benefits and drawbacks?

1.15.2 What exactly is deep learning? Describe some of its applications.

1.15.3 What are GANs, and what is the relationship between GANs, Deep Learning, Machine Learning, and Artificial Intelligence?

1.15.4 What is the difference between supervised and unsupervised learning?

1.15.5 What is overfitting, and how can it be avoided?

1.15.6 What is regularization, and why is it used?

1.15.7 What is cross-validation, and how is it used in machine learning?

1.15.8 What is clustering, and what are some popular clustering algorithms?

1.15.9 What are the differences between logistic regression and linear regression?

1.15.10 What is the difference between a generative and a discriminative model?

1.15.11 What is reinforcement learning, and what are some popular applications of it?

1.15.12 What are the differences between parametric and non-parametric models?

1.15.13 What is the difference between a classification and a regression problem?

1.15.14 What are the differences between L_1 and L_2 regularization?

1.15.15 What is the difference between a batch gradient descent and a stochastic gradient descent?

1.15.16 What are the differences between K-nearest neighbors and K-means clustering?

1.15.17 What are some common evaluation metrics used in machine learning?

1.15.18 What is the difference between precision and recall?

1.15.19 How does the bias-variance tradeoff affect machine learning models?

1.15.20 What are the differences between deep learning and traditional machine learning?

1.15.21 What is a neural network, and how does it work?

1.15.22 What is backpropagation, and why is it important?

1.15.23 What are some popular neural network architectures?

1.15.24 What is transfer learning, and how is it used in deep learning?

1.15.25 What are some common challenges in training deep neural networks?

1.15.26 What are some popular deep learning frameworks?

1.15.27 What are the differences between a convolutional neural network and a recurrent neural network?

1.15.28 What are some popular applications of natural language processing using machine learning?

1.15.29 What is the difference between a single-layer perceptron and a multi-layer perceptron?

1.15.30 How does the bias term in a machine learning model affect the predictions?

1.15.31 What are some common techniques used for data preprocessing in machine learning?

1.15.32 What are some popular ensemble learning methods?

1.15.33 What are some techniques used for dealing with imbalanced datasets?

1.15.34 What is the difference between a hyperparameter and a parameter in a machine-learning model?

1.15.35 What are some common data-cleaning techniques used in machine learning?

1.15.36 What is the difference between a perceptron and a neural network?

1.15.37 What is the meaning of the term "deep" in deep learning?

1.15.38 What is the difference between supervised, unsupervised, and reinforcement learning?

1.15.39 What is the purpose of an activation function in a neural network?

1.15.40 What is a loss function, and how is it used in training a neural network?

1.15.41 What is meant by the term "batch size" in deep learning?

1.15.42 What is regularization, and how is it used in training a neural network?

1.15.43 What is the difference between overfitting and underfitting in machine learning?

1.15.44 What is the purpose of a dropout layer in a neural network?

1.15.45 What is a generative model, and how is it used in deep learning?

1.15.46 What is transfer learning, and how is it used in deep learning?

1.15.47 What is the difference between a model and an algorithm in machine learning?

1.15.48 What is the purpose of a validation set in machine learning?

1.15.49 What is backpropagation, and how is it used in training a neural network?

1.15.50 What is the difference between gradient descent and stochastic gradient descent?

1.15.51   What is a hyperparameter, and how is it different from a model parameter?

1.15.52   What is the purpose of a convolutional layer in a convolutional neural network?

1.15.53   What is the purpose of a pooling layer in a convolutional neural network?

1.15.54   What is a recurrent neural network (RNN), and how is it used in deep learning?

1.15.55   What is a long short-term memory (LSTM) network, and how is it used in deep learning?

1.15.56   What is the difference between a one-hot encoding and a label encoding?

1.15.57   What is the difference between a regression problem and a classification problem in machine learning?

1.15.58   What is the purpose of a confusion matrix in evaluating the performance of a classification model?

1.15.59   What is the purpose of principal component analysis (PCA) in machine learning?

2

Data Preprocessing

This chapter discusses data processing approaches and includes the following:

- Data Preprocessing
- Data Cleaning
- Data Transformation
- Balancing Data
- Data Augmentation
- Data Reduction
- Dataset Partitioning
- Data Preparation Steps
- Data Preprocessing Examples
- Data Preprocessing Issues
- Data Preprocessing Implementation Tips

2.1 Preface

Data preparation is a crucial step in creating a machine learning model. It involves a series of operations performed on raw data to transform it into a format that can be readily processed by machines, thereby enhancing the reliability of the output and results. Raw data in any format, including video, audio, and text, is typically unsuitable for direct machine processing due to the presence of noise, errors, or missing information. Furthermore, the data may contain sensitive information or be insufficient for the machine learning model's requirements. Data preprocessing steps rectify these issues, structuring and cleaning the data, which improves the processes of machine learning modeling, data science, and data mining. Here are some common tasks involved in data preprocessing:

1. **Data cleaning:** This involves removing irrelevant, duplicate, or inaccurate data points from the dataset.
2. **Data transformation:** This involves converting the raw data into a more useful format. For example, categorical data might be transformed into numerical data, or text might be converted into a format that machine learning algorithms can process.
3. **Data normalization:** This involves scaling the data so that it falls within a specific range. Normalization ensures that different features have equal weight in the analysis.

DOI: 10.1201/9781003281344-2

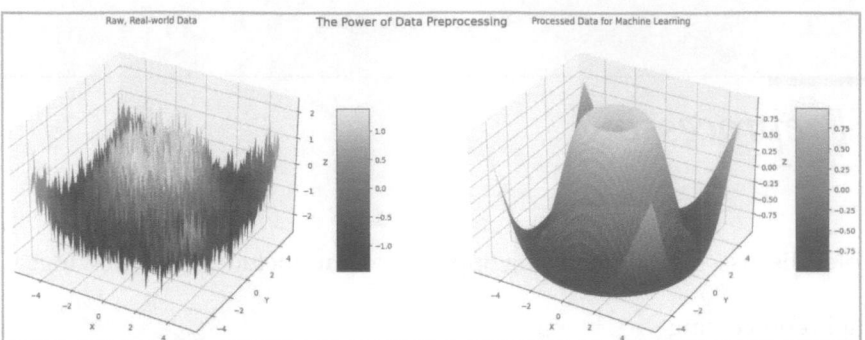

FIGURE 2.1
The data preprocessing prepares raw data (real-world data) for use in machine learning systems.

4. **Data reduction:** This involves reducing the size of the dataset while preserving its essential information. Techniques, such as principal component analysis (PCA) or feature selection, are often used.

5. **Data augmentation:** This involves creating new data points by applying various transformations to the existing data. Data augmentation is often used to increase the size of the dataset and improve the performance of machine learning models.

In summary, data preprocessing is a vital step in machine learning that can significantly impact the performance of the models. By properly cleaning, transforming, and preparing the data, we can ensure that our machine learning models yield accurate, efficient, and effective results. We review these approaches in this chapter in more detail. Figure 2.1 illustrates the process of data preprocessing, transforming raw real-world data to be suitable for machine learning systems.

2.2 Data Preprocessing

Unclean data often contain extraneous information, which can lead to inaccurate training and evaluation. Even the most advanced and powerful machine learning techniques cannot yield accurate results when the input data is of poor quality. The data carries all the vital features and information, and optimal results in machine learning model training are achieved through proper data preprocessing, which is the first step in machine learning modeling. Similarly, well-prepared data yields the best outcomes when evaluating machine learning models, the second step in machine learning modeling. Therefore, to achieve the best results in machine learning modeling, proper data preprocessing is essential, and that is the primary focus of this chapter. No matter which machine learning techniques we employ, "garbage in" inevitably results in "garbage out" or inaccurate outcomes (Figure 2.2).

Figure 2.3 illustrates some of the most commonly used data preprocessing techniques, including data reduction, transformation, cleaning, augmentation, balancing, and partitioning, along with some of their subsets.

The data can reveal various types of errors that manifest as inaccurate characteristics in raw data. For example, an image of an apple would be considered an error in a dataset consisting of orange images. Other errors include values that are outside their expected range, such as negative ages or heights, incorrect word usage, and irrelevant symbols in a specific language. As shown in Table 2.1, data preparation typically includes a quality check of the data.

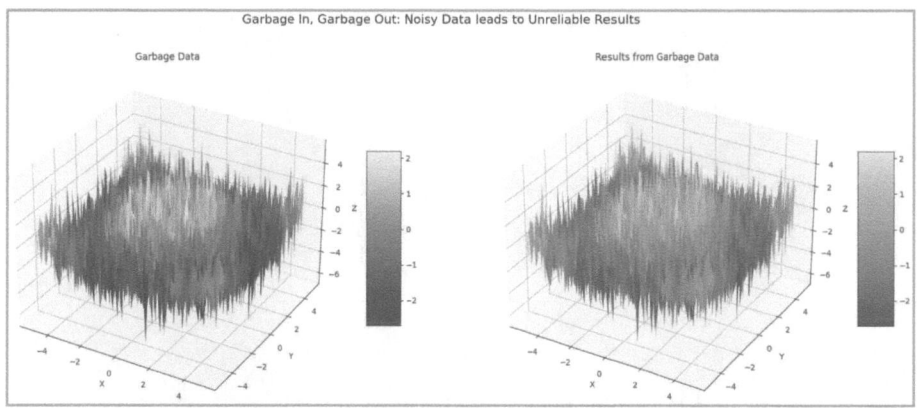

FIGURE 2.2
Garbage data produce garbage results.

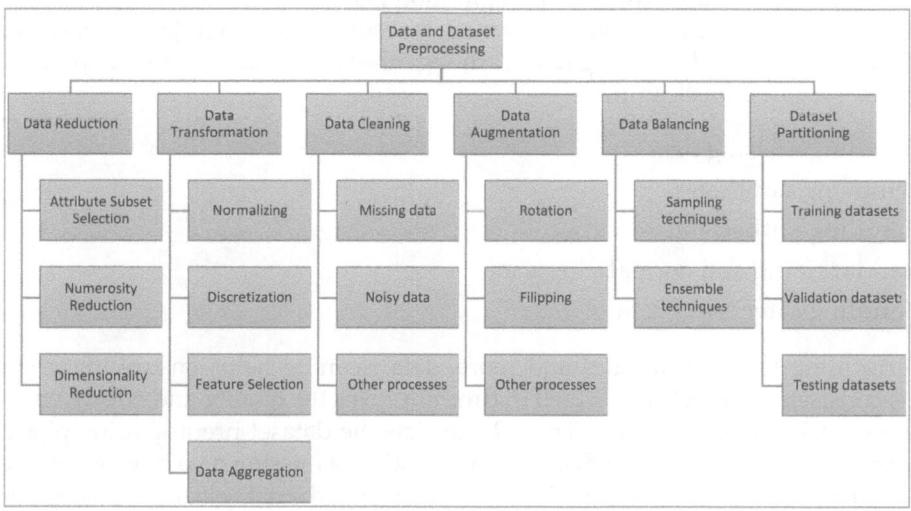

FIGURE 2.3
Data and dataset preprocessing approaches.

TABLE 2.1

Parameters for Data Quality Evaluation

Parameters	Definition
Accuracy	It determines how much of the data is accurate. For example, positive or negative, cat or dog.
Completeness	It verifies the existence of data.
Consistency	It verifies the data's location. For example, data in the same location may have the same or different values.
Timeliness	It determines whether or not the data is up-to-date.
Believability	It determines whether or not the data is reliable.
Interpretability	It ensures that the data is relevant and that the machine can interpret and understand it.

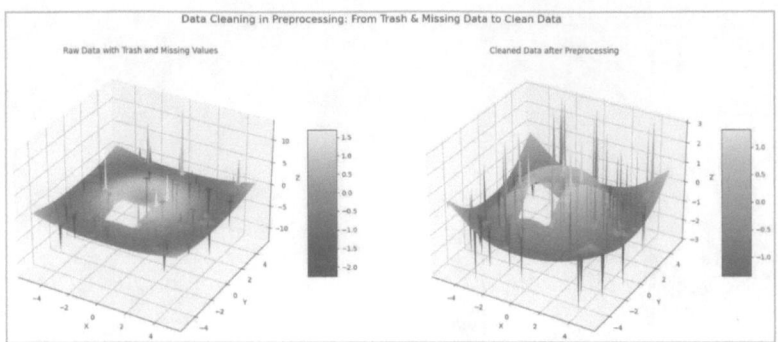

FIGURE 2.4
In the dataset preprocessing, data cleaning removes trash data or adds missing data.

2.3 Data Cleaning

Data cleaning, a subfield within "data preparation", is a collection of procedures designed to improve data quality by removing incorrect, inaccurate, or incomplete data, substituting certain missing data, and reducing noise, among other operations. Here are some common techniques used in data cleaning:

1. Handling missing data
2. Removing duplicates
3. Handling outliers
4. Standardizing and normalizing data
5. Handling categorical data

By performing these techniques and more, data cleaning helps ensure that the data is accurate, consistent, and reliable, which in turn improves the quality and effectiveness of the subsequent analysis or modeling. Figure 2.4 depicts the dataset preprocessing phase, highlighting the removal of unwanted data and the addition of missing data during data cleaning.

Data can be added to fill in missing information during the data cleaning process, or incorrect data can be removed. Adding or removing data is a significant part of the data cleaning process. Figure 2.5 demonstrates that data cleaning involves handling missing or noisy data, along with other data preprocessing, to make it pure and ready for model training.

FIGURE 2.5
In the dataset preprocessing, the data cleaning removes trash data or adds missing data.

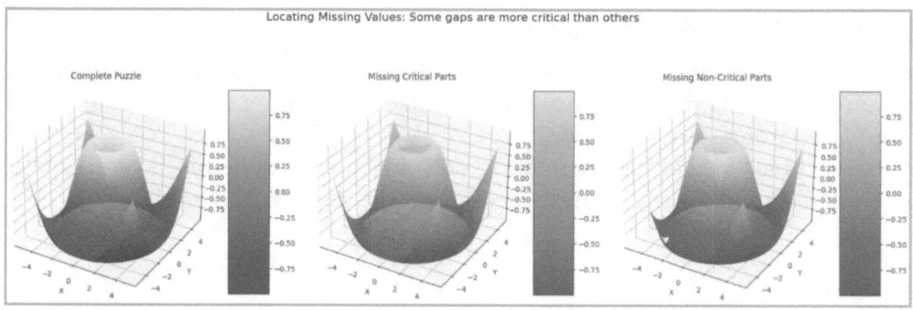

FIGURE 2.6
The data distribution type is an easy approach for locating the missing value.

2.3.1 Missing Data

One of the issues we encounter is that some values in the raw data are missing. To make use of this information, we must fill in the blanks with some values, and there are a few different strategies to replace this missing data. One such technique is to discover the distribution function and then input the appropriate data based on it. If the data follows a typical distribution pattern, the mean value of the dataset is a good place to start. If the data does not have a normal distribution, we can use the median value to fill in the missing data. Furthermore, probability can be useful to us, and we can replace these values in the dataset with the value that is most likely to occur by using techniques, such as regression or decision trees. Different distributions affect the data that we intend to select. For example, one of the most popular is the normal distribution, which can be used in the case of missing data. Here are the steps for replacing missing data:

1. Identify missing values,
2. Eliminate data with missing values (or Estimate missing values), and
3. Fill in the missing values.

Missing values are sometimes critical for our model training. For example, missing some critical parts in a puzzle makes the entire image incomplete, while other parts are not as important (Figure 2.6). Missing data refers to situations where some data points or values are absent or not recorded in a dataset. This can occur due to various reasons, such as measurement errors, equipment failures, or data entry errors. Missing data can cause problems in data analysis and modeling as it can lead to biased or inaccurate results. There are different methods for dealing with missing data, including:

2.3.1.1 Deleting the Missing Data

One approach is to simply remove any observations or variables that contain missing values. However, this can lead to a loss of information and may not be feasible if the missing data is substantial.

2.3.1.2 Imputing the Missing Data

Imputation is a technique where the missing data is replaced with estimated or imputed values. This can be done using various methods, such as mean imputation, median imputation, regression imputation, and multiple imputation.

2.3.1.3 Using Machine Learning Algorithms

Machine learning algorithms, such as decision trees, random forests, and gradient boosting, can handle missing data. These algorithms use a split point that separates the missing values into a separate branch or node.

Overall, the choice of method for dealing with missing data depends on the nature and extent of the missing data, the analysis goals, and the data characteristics.

2.3.2 Noisy Data

The term "noisy data" refers to data that contains errors as well as unexpected points or features. Fixing noisy data is one of the data-cleaning processes. There are various types of noise in data, and in general, two main types are class noise and attribute noise. Class noise can be caused by a variety of factors, including subjectivity during the labeling process, data entry errors, or insufficient information used to label each example. Another type is attribute noise, which refers to corruption in one or more attribute values. Noisy data refers to the presence of errors or inconsistencies in the data that can negatively impact the accuracy of a model. These errors can occur due to various reasons, such as measurement errors, data entry errors, or even random fluctuations in the data. Some common techniques for handling noisy data include:

2.3.2.1 Removing Outliers

Outliers are extreme values in the data that may not follow the same pattern as the rest of the data. Removing them can help reduce the impact of noisy data.

2.3.2.2 Smoothing

Smoothing techniques, such as moving averages or Gaussian smoothing, can be used to reduce the impact of noisy data by removing random fluctuations in the data.

2.3.2.3 Interpolation

To fill in missing or noisy data points, interpolation techniques, such as linear or spline interpolation, can be used.

2.3.2.4 Feature Scaling

Scaling the features can help reduce the impact of noisy data by reducing the range of values and making the data more consistent.

Some methods for removing noise from data include Binning, Regression, and Clustering. Figure 2.7 showcases the presence of noise in raw data, emphasizing the need for data cleaning before utilization.

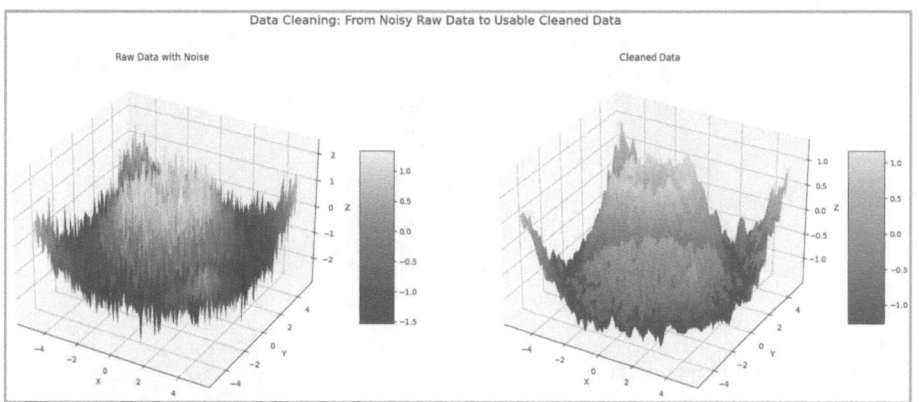

FIGURE 2.7
Noise is in the raw data, and the data should be cleaned before use.

2.3.2.4.1 Binning

Binning is a data smoothing strategy used to minimize the effects of minor observation errors. This strategy involves sorting data into bins or containers, and it's typically used for dealing with continuous numerical variables. Binning helps improve the accuracy of machine learning models by making them less sensitive to minor differences and errors. Binning can be performed through various methods, including:

1. **Mean/Median/Minimum/Maximum binning:** For each bin, these methods calculate the mean, median, minimum, or maximum values, respectively, and then substitute these calculated values for the original data points within each bin. The aim here is to replace the entire data within a particular bin with its central tendency, which could be mean or median, or with its extremes, which could be minimum or maximum.

2. **Boundary binning:** In this method, the data points are replaced by the closest boundary values. This method is particularly useful when dealing with outliers. For instance, consider a dataset with values ranging from 1 to 60. We can create six bins, such as [1–10], [11–20], [21–30], [31–40], [41–50], [51–60]. If there are five data points in the range of 1–10 and 11 data points in the range of 11–20, the data points in these bins can be replaced with the mean, median, minimum, or maximum of each bin, or the closest boundary value, depending on the method used. Using such binning techniques, we can handle noisy data by reducing the effect of individual data points, thereby improving the accuracy of our machine learning models.

Figure 2.8, as an example, would show the distribution of data across these bins. Figure 2.9 illustrates four categories, each with three bins. These bins demonstrate the distribution of data within each category.

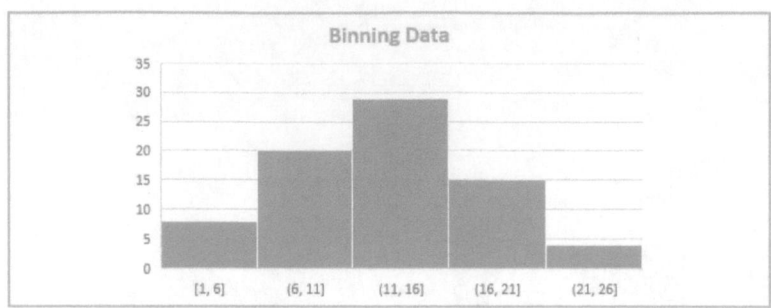

FIGURE 2.8
Binning data based on a different range.

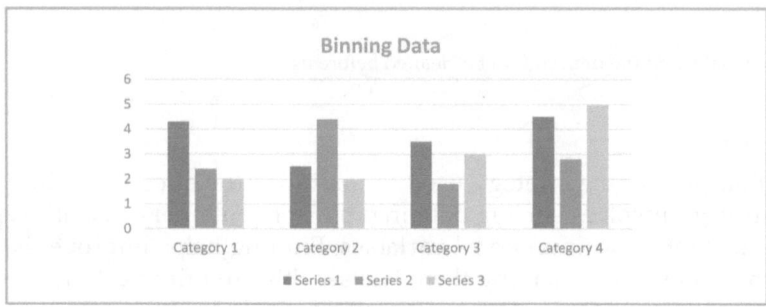

FIGURE 2.9
Binning data based on different categories.

2.3.2.4.2 Regression

One of the primary objectives of regression analysis is to eliminate irrelevant or unnecessary variables, thereby smoothing out the data values. This method can help you identify the most valuable data for analysis and remove the unnecessary data (noise). Several techniques can be employed to achieve this, one of which is known as the Random Sample Consensus (RANSAC). Some data points are classified as "outliers", which are data values that significantly deviate from others. Several techniques exist for identifying these outliers and subsequently removing them as noisy data. Consider Figure 2.10, which depicts three different types of outliers.

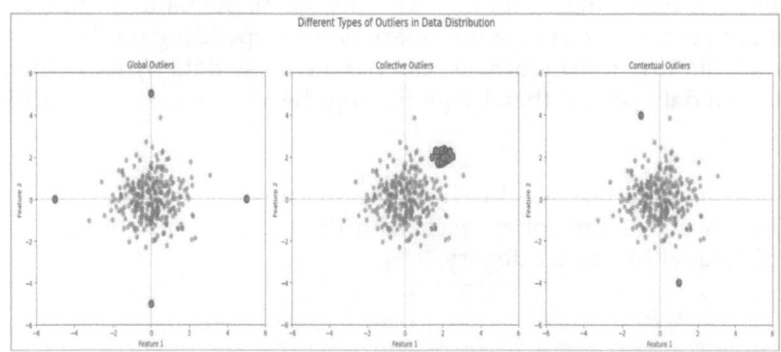

FIGURE 2.10
Noise in the raw data should be cleaned before use (Outliers may be present in the raw data).

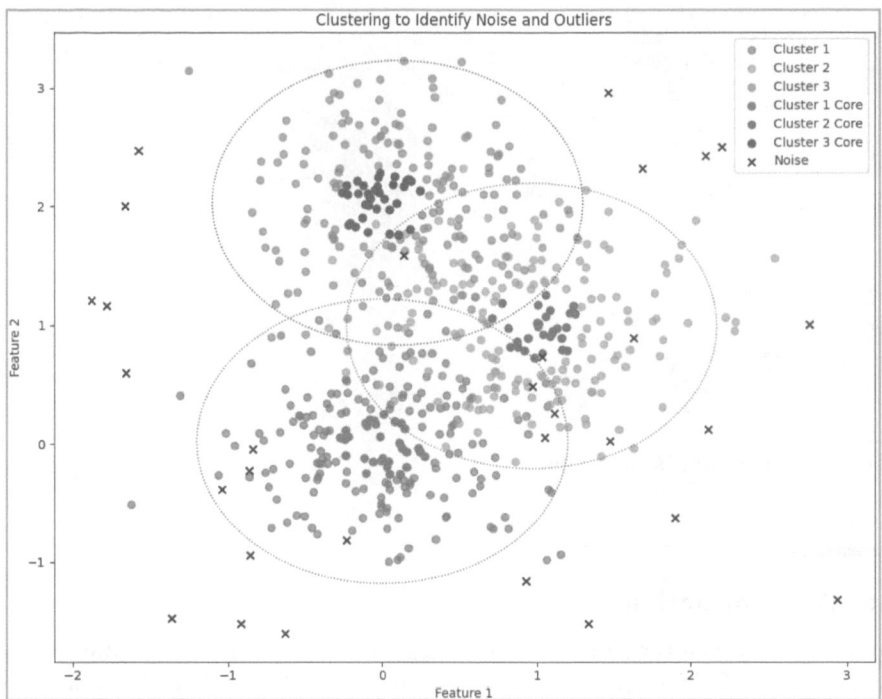

FIGURE 2.11
Clustering can be used to identify noise and outliers.

2.3.2.4.3 Clustering

Clustering, a technique typically employed in unsupervised learning, can be a useful tool when we lack sufficient information about the data and the relationships among the data. We can use clustering techniques to identify appropriate clusters and group certain data points while treating the remaining data as noise. This enables us to identify unrelated data or data with little or no correlation to others, which can then be removed. Figure 2.11 illustrates the general concepts and method of clustering and how it can assist in noise removal.

2.3.3 Other Processes

We have discussed the two most common issues with raw data: missing data and noisy data, along with their typical solutions. Apart from these two problems, there are numerous other measures that can be taken to clean the data and prepare it for processing. For instance, having redundant or duplicate data can increase the computational cost without noticeably affecting the results, and there are several techniques available for removing such data. The solutions we adopt depend on the nature of the data, the values it represents, the problem that requires data deployment, and our ultimate objectives. For instance, if our data consists of images, these images will be quite large. When we convert each image into a feature vector, these vectors will contain a lot of redundancies. Such redundancies can be removed using methods like Principal Component Analysis (PCA) or Linear Discriminant Analysis (LDA).

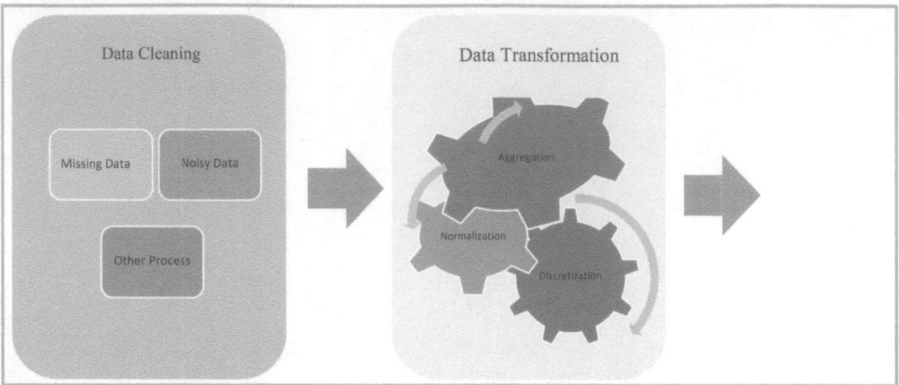

FIGURE 2.12
Data transformation is a part of data cleaning.

2.4 Data Transformation

Data transformation is a type of data preprocessing task that involves changing the data format or structure. This process is crucial for enhancing the quality of cleaned data, making it more suitable for data science and machine learning applications. Data transformation is the process of converting data from one form or format to another to facilitate improved analysis or modeling. Transformations can be undertaken for various purposes, such as normalization, scaling, encoding, and feature extraction. Normalization is a form of data transformation where data is scaled to have a zero mean and unit variance. This approach is beneficial when dealing with data that have varying scales and ranges, especially when using an algorithm that is sensitive to these scales. Another type of data transformation is scaling. This involves reducing or expanding the data to fit within a specific range, such as [0, 1] or [–1, 1]. Scaling is useful when the data has a specific range, and the algorithm requires the data to be within that range. Encoding is a transformation method that converts categorical data into numerical data. This is helpful when the algorithm cannot directly process categorical data. Feature extraction is another form of data transformation. It involves extracting relevant features from the data. This approach is beneficial when the dataset has a large number of features, and not all of them are pertinent to the analysis or modeling. Figure 2.12 demonstrates the role of data transformation as an integral component of the data cleaning process. There are several data transformation methods, and the most popular ones are:

1. Aggregation
2. Normalization
3. Discretization

2.4.1 Aggregation

Aggregation in data preprocessing refers to the process of combining multiple data instances or variables into a single unit. This is often achieved by summarizing or computing statistical representations of the data. For instance, if you have a dataset of sales

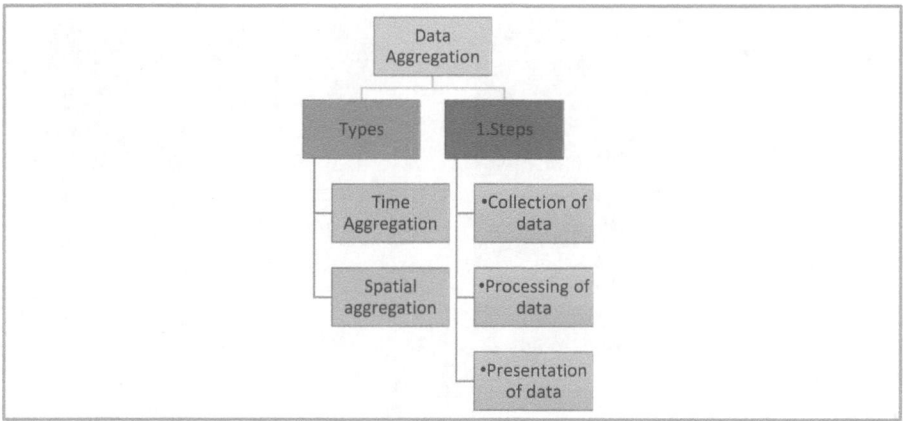

FIGURE 2.13
Aggregation types and steps.

records comprising individual transactions, you can aggregate the data by summing up the sales revenue or calculating the average sales per transaction for a specific time period. Aggregation is advantageous in simplifying the dataset and deriving insights from the data. Aggregation can be performed using various functions, such as sum, mean, median, mode, count, min, max, variance, and standard deviation. These functions can be applied to different subsets of the data based on grouping criteria, such as time period, location, category, or any other relevant factor. The aggregated data can then be used for further analysis, visualization, or modeling to gain insights into trends, patterns, and relationships within the data. Figure 2.13 shows the types and steps of data aggregation approaches.

The increasing prevalence of data science and machine learning applications working with data from multiple sources underscores the importance of data aggregation as a stage in the data preparation process. This process combines data from various sources into a unified format. Some challenges associated with aggregation deployment include integrating information, identifying entities, and combining data from multiple sources. Several strategies can be employed to mitigate these issues' impact on the overall outcomes and performance.

2.4.2 Normalizing

Normalization is indeed a crucial operation performed on data. It is a process that involves transforming and scaling data to fit within a specific range, thereby facilitating data management. This can be achieved through various methods, such as general or batch normalization. Normalization helps reduce computational costs, enhances the reliability of results, and can even expedite convergence. By scaling the data, normalization ensures that all features have the same scale so that no particular feature dominates the others, which can lead to skewed or biased results in data analysis or machine learning models. In the context of machine learning, normalization often leads to better performance and faster training. For instance, many gradient-based optimization algorithms, which are used to train machine learning models, converge faster when the features are on a similar scale. Figure 2.14, for instance, may illustrate how normalization can bring all values within a dataset to converge faster. This common scale allows for a more accurate comparison of

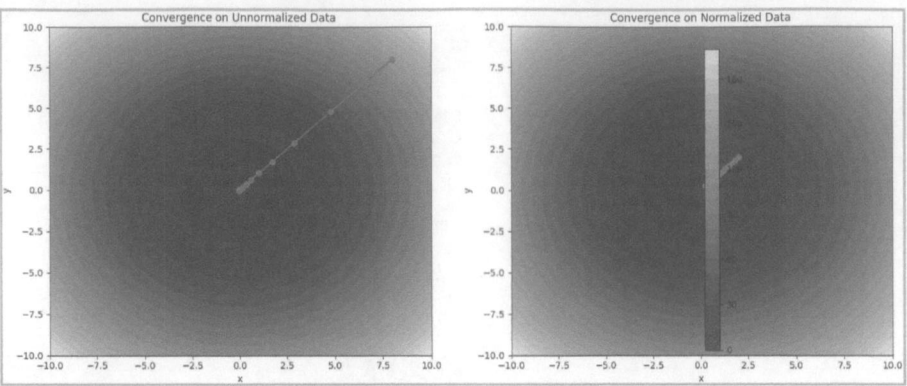

FIGURE 2.14
Normalizing data is a type of transformation.

values and can lead to improved model performance. To summarize, normalization is a vital preprocessing step that can enhance the efficiency and effectiveness of data analysis and machine learning models.

2.4.3 Discretization

The process of discretization subdivides continuous data, models, and functions into smaller chunks. This preprocessing step validates the information in the data prior to its processing. For instance, if our data pertains to time, which is a continuous variable, we could discretize it into distinct intervals to expedite the process (e.g., into intervals of every five minutes, ten minutes, and so forth). This is similar to the binning process we discussed earlier, and it can be performed after the data has been cleaned. Discretization is a technique in data preprocessing that involves dividing a continuous variable into discrete intervals or bins. This is useful when we have a large number of observations and a continuous variable, and we want to group the observations into categories based on the values of that variable. Discretization can be carried out in several ways, including equal width, equal frequency, and k-means clustering. In the equal width method, we divide the range of values into a fixed number of bins of equal width. In the equal frequency method, we divide the range of values into a fixed number of bins with approximately the same number of observations in each bin. In the k-means clustering method, we use a clustering algorithm to group the observations into k clusters based on the variable values. Discretization can prove useful in several applications, including machine learning, where we might want to use the discrete variable as a feature in a model. However, it's important to remember that discretization can lead to information loss, as the exact values of the variable are no longer used. Therefore, carefully considering the appropriate number of bins and the method of discretization for each application is crucial. To illustrate this process, we can create some containers for each interval using various techniques, such as histograms (this procedure is shown in Figure 2.15).

There are two types of data discretization: supervised and unsupervised discretization. Supervised discretization utilizes class data, while unsupervised discretization differs based on how the operation is carried out. It uses a top-down splitting strategy and a bottom-up merging strategy. Some software, such as MATLAB® and Python, have data discretization modules that facilitate data cleaning before usage.

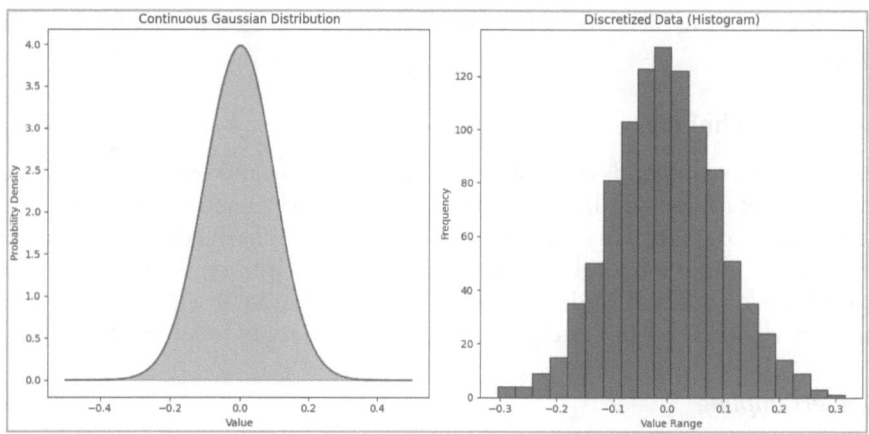

FIGURE 2.15
Discretization process as a transformation.

2.5 Balancing Data

One of the challenges with a dataset is achieving balance. A balanced dataset contains an equal number of input samples for all output classes. Several approaches exist to address this issue, but they are generally categorized into sampling or ensemble methods. To achieve class balance in a dataset, the data values of majority classes can be reduced, or those of minority classes can be increased. Before balancing, and prior to utilizing balancing data techniques, some preparations should be undertaken, such as splitting data into training and testing datasets. This allows for the testing of your model on an unbiased dataset, which will yield a more accurate evaluation of the model's performance. Balancing data involves ensuring that the number of instances in each class of a dataset is approximately equal or within an acceptable range. This is particularly crucial in machine learning tasks where class imbalance can affect the model's performance. There are several approaches for data balancing, and the choice of technique depends on the size and distribution of the dataset, the complexity of the problem, and the performance metric of interest. Figure 2.16 highlights the technique of data balancing as an alternative approach within data preprocessing.

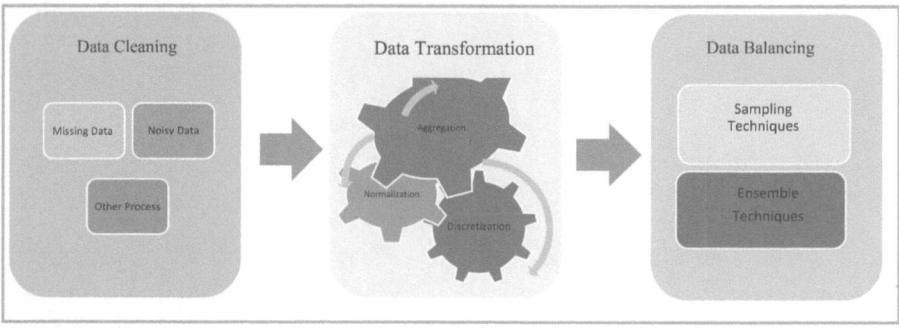

FIGURE 2.16
Another method of data preprocessing is data balancing.

Here we are looking at two main approaches for data balancing: sampling and ensembling.

2.5.1 Sampling Techniques

There are two primary methods of sampling: undersampling and oversampling. Several different techniques of undersampling and oversampling can be used to achieve balance in the data included in the dataset. This is important as it ensures that the classes in the dataset are well-balanced, given that the total number of data samples influences both the training and the results. However, because undersampling has the potential to alter the overall distribution of the data, it should not be used as the initial method for balancing data in your design.

2.5.1.1 Undersampling

This involves reducing the number of instances in the majority class to match the number in the minority class. This can be done randomly or using specific sampling techniques, such as Tomek links or Edited Nearest Neighbors (ENN).

2.5.1.2 Oversampling

This involves increasing the number of instances in the minority class to match the number in the majority class. Techniques, such as Synthetic Minority Over-sampling Technique (SMOTE), Adaptive Synthetic Sampling (ADASYN), or Random Oversampling, can be used. Figure 2.17 illustrates two data balancing techniques across four subfigures: (a) shows the original dataset where class B is larger than class A, (b) displays the result after applying undersampling to balance the classes, resulting in an equal number of instances

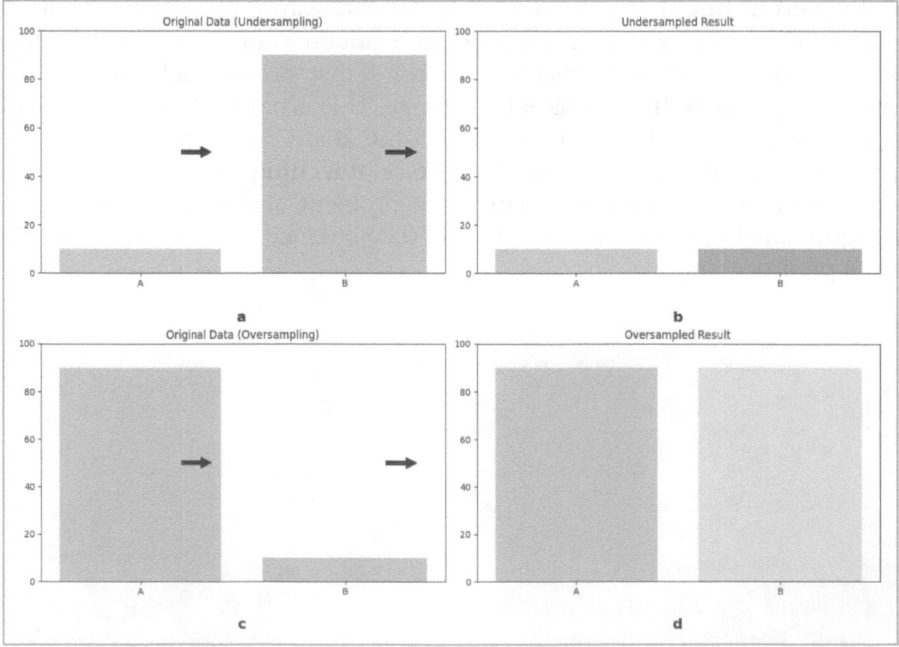

FIGURE 2.17
Data Balancing Techniques. (a) Original dataset with class B larger than class A. (b) Dataset after undersampling to balance class sizes. (c) Original dataset with class A larger than class B. (d) Dataset after oversampling to equalize class sizes.

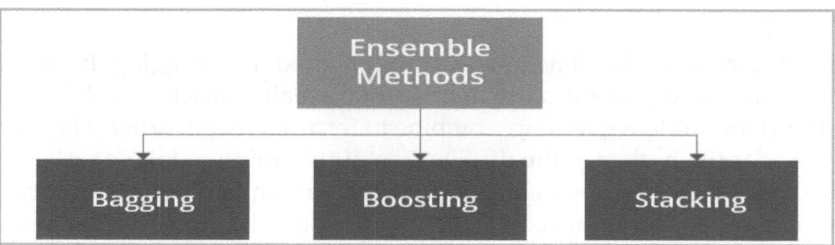

FIGURE 2.18
There are several approaches as ensemble methods.

as the smaller class A, (c) presents the original dataset with class A larger than class B, and (d) demonstrates the effect of oversampling on class B to match the size of the larger class A, achieving balanced classes.

2.5.2 Ensemble Techniques

Ensemble methods involve combining several classifiers to find the best one for the new data. Some of the approaches to ensemble the data include bagging, boosting, and Stacking. Each approach has advantages and disadvantages that determine whether it is suitable for specific tasks or datasets. In conclusion, ensemble methods can improve the performance of classifiers by combining the strengths of multiple models, but choosing the appropriate method depends on the specific task and dataset at hand. Figure 2.18 illustrates various techniques categorized under ensemble methods.

2.5.2.1 Bagging

Bagging, which stands for Bootstrap Aggregating, is a powerful ensemble machine learning method. It was designed to improve the stability and accuracy of machine learning algorithms used in statistical classification and regression. The main benefit of bagging is that it can reduce the variance of a prediction by introducing randomization into the model building process and making an ensemble (i.e., combination) of models. It can help prevent overfitting by averaging multiple models' predictions, leading to a smoother estimate that's less likely to be influenced by noise in the data. A well-known algorithm that uses bagging is the Random Forest algorithm, which creates an ensemble of decision trees using bootstrapped samples of the dataset. Here's a brief explanation of bagging.

1. **Bootstrap sampling:** The main principle behind bagging is to create several subsets of the original data through a process called bootstrapping. Bootstrapping is a method of resampling where we create subsets of observations from the original dataset with replacement. The size of the subsets is the same as the size of the original set.
2. **Model building:** Bagging then fits a separate decision tree (or any other base model) on these subsets. Because the sampling is done with replacement, each model is built independently of the others.
3. **Aggregation:** Once each model has made its prediction, bagging makes a final prediction by averaging the predictions (in the case of regression) or using a majority vote (in the case of classification) of all the models. This process of averaging or voting is a form of aggregation, hence the term "aggregating" in the name.

2.5.2.2 Boosting

Boosting is another ensemble machine learning method, like bagging. It operates on the principle of learners' collaboration, where several weak learners (models that do only slightly better than random guessing) combine to form a strong learner. The idea of boosting is thus to adaptively change the distribution of the training data sample set based on the performance of the previous classifiers so the subsequent classifiers focus more on the difficult instances. One important thing to note is that boosting can lead to overfitting if the number of weak learners (iterations) is too high. However, certain boosting algorithms, such as AdaBoost and Gradient Boosting, have shown excellent performance with appropriate settings. In essence, boosting algorithms aim to reduce bias and variance in supervised learning to enhance the prediction power of the model. They are highly effective and are often used in machine learning competitions and practical problem-solving. Here's a brief explanation of boosting:

2.5.2.2.1 Sequential Learning

Unlike bagging, where models are built independently, boosting involves building models sequentially. In each iteration, a new weak model is trained with respect to the total error made by the existing ensemble of weak models.

2.5.2.2.2 Weight Adjustment

After each iteration, the algorithm assigns higher weights to the instances that were incorrectly predicted by the previous model and lower weights to the instances that were predicted correctly. This procedure forces the next model to pay more attention to the instances that the previous models misclassified, aiming to correct the mistakes of the previous models.

2.5.2.2.3 Final Prediction

Predictions are made by a weighted vote (in the case of classification) or a weighted sum (in the case of regression). The weights for each model depend on their overall accuracy so that more accurate models have more influence on the final prediction.

2.5.2.3 Stacking

Stacking, also known as a stacked generalization, is another ensemble machine learning method where the key idea is to combine the predictions of several base models and use another machine learning model to compute the final prediction. The main advantage of stacking is that it can represent a wider hypothesis space by combining different models, which can lead to improved prediction performance. The idea behind stacking is to try to use the strengths of different models to improve predictions, and the meta-model can learn which base model predictions are more reliable. However, stacking may be computationally intensive and more complex to set up than simpler methods, such as bagging or boosting, since it requires training multiple layers of models. It can also be more prone to overfitting if not designed and trained carefully. Here's a brief explanation of stacking:

2.5.2.3.1 Base Model Training

In the first step, several base models are trained independently on the complete training set. These models can be of all the same type or of different types. The variety among models can be in terms of the algorithm used or the configuration settings for the algorithms.

2.5.2.3.2 Meta-Model Training

The base models' predictions are used as inputs to train a higher-level learner, called the meta-model or meta-learner. The meta-model takes the predictions from all the base models and then makes the final prediction. The meta-model can be trained using the predictions of the base learners as features and the original labels as the target variable.

2.5.2.3.3 Final Prediction

When predicting with a stacking ensemble, each model in the first layer makes a prediction for each instance in the test set. Then these predictions are used as input for the meta-model to make the final prediction.

2.5.3 Combination of Undersampling and Oversampling

This involves using a combination of both techniques to achieve a balanced dataset.

2.5.4 Class Weighting

This involves assigning different weights to different classes during model training to give more importance to the minority class.

2.5.5 Generating Synthetic Data

This involves generating new instances for the minority class using techniques, such as Generative Adversarial Networks (GANs) or Variational Autoencoders (VAEs).

2.6 Data Augmentation

Data augmentation is a process used in machine learning and deep learning that generates and forms new data, aiding the model in its training. This method can be particularly useful if data is lost and needs to be replaced. By applying transformations to all instances in the dataset, data augmentation can increase the size of the dataset. This technique, often used offline, is particularly beneficial for smaller datasets. Data augmentation artificially expands a dataset by creating additional training examples from existing ones. It does this by applying various transformations, such as rotation, flipping, cropping, scaling, or adding noise, to the existing data, thereby creating new samples. These new samples are similar to the original ones but exhibit variations. Data augmentation is especially useful when the available dataset is small, and there's a risk of overfitting or poor generalization performance. By increasing the number of training examples, the model can learn more robust features and patterns, thus improving its ability to generalize to new, unseen data. Several libraries and tools are available for implementing data augmentation in machine learning, including the ImageDataGenerator class in Keras, the imgaug library, and the Albumentations library. These tools allow users to apply various data augmentation techniques and customize the parameters, such as the magnitude or probability of the transformation. GAN models are used for generating new synthetic data. This approach can produce novel data, improve model accuracy, reduce data collection costs, and mitigate issues related to data privacy. Various transformations can be applied to augment image data, providing us with additional useful information. Let us check some examples.

2.6.1 Padding

Adding extra pixels around the image, which can be useful when parts of relevant objects might be located at the image borders.

2.6.2 Random Rotating

Rotating the image by a certain angle.

2.6.3 Rescaling

Changing the size of the image.

2.6.4 Vertical and Horizontal Flipping

Mirroring the image vertically or horizontally.

2.6.5 Translation

Shifting the image in the X or Y direction.

2.6.6 Cropping

Cutting out a part of the image.

2.6.7 Zooming

Enlarging a section of the image.

2.6.8 Darkening and Brightening/Color Modification

Adjusting the brightness or color of the image.

2.6.9 Grayscaling

Converting the image to grayscale, which removes color information.

2.6.10 Changing Contrast

Adjusting the contrast of the image.

2.6.11 Adding Noise

Adding random pixel values to the image.

FIGURE 2.19
Data augmentation is widely used in deep learning, particularly in GANs.

2.6.12 Random Erasing

Randomly selecting a rectangle region in the image and setting the pixel values within that region to zero. These processes are depicted in Figure 2.19. By augmenting the data in these ways, we can create a more robust dataset for training our machine learning or deep learning models.

2.7 Data Reduction

Working with large volumes of data often presents numerous challenges, even after preliminary data preprocessing, such as conversion and cleaning. In particular, high-dimensional data can be difficult to manage and interpret. Dimension reduction techniques can be very helpful in these situations, as they can reduce the dimensionality of the data while retaining most of the important information. For instance, consider an image with dimensions of 40×40 pixels. This image has a dimensionality of 1600, which is rather large even for such a small image. Dimension reduction techniques, like PCA and LDA, can reduce this dimensionality while maintaining the critical structure and variance in the data. These methods are commonly used with image and audio data. PCA works by identifying the directions (principal components) in which the data varies the most and projecting the data onto these directions. The first principal component captures the most variance, the second principal component (orthogonal to the first) captures the second most variance, and so on. This process effectively reduces the dimensionality of the data while preserving as much variance as possible.

LDA, on the other hand, is a supervised method that aims to identify the directions that maximize the separation between different classes in the data. It is particularly useful when the goal is to perform classification or when class labels are important. However, it's crucial to be aware of the potential risks associated with data compression. While dimension reduction techniques can greatly simplify data analysis and processing, they can also result in the loss of certain data if not done carefully. Therefore, the choice of technique and the number of dimensions to retain should be considered carefully based on the specific requirements of the task at hand. Figure 2.20 demonstrates these two methods and how they project data onto key directions, such as LD_1 and LD_2 in LDA, and PC_1 and PC_2 in PCA.

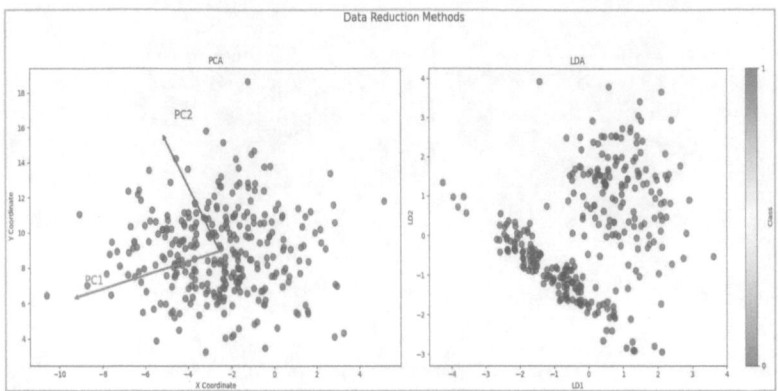

FIGURE 2.20
Data reduction methods make the computation cost less. Left: PCA reduces dimensionality retaining variance.
Right: LDA maximizes class separability in lower-dimensional space.

2.8 Dataset Partitioning

Let's start by discussing the categories of data needed for projects. Typically, the original
data is divided into three subsets: (1) training data, (2) validation data, and (3) test data.
The ratio of these subsets, for example, 70% for training, 15% for validation, and 15% for
testing, is a crucial aspect to consider. If the model, when tested with the test data, achieves
the required level of accuracy, then it is deemed ready for use with new real-world data.
However, these proportions are not set in stone. Depending on the specific project, they
can be adjusted. By comparing the results, you can find the proportions that yield the best
performance for your specific task. Once the training phase is completed and the initial
model is built using the training data, the validation data can be used to evaluate its performance. This assessment helps in determining whether the trained model is suitable for
your objective. If the model doesn't perform well on the validation set, adjustments can be
made to the model parameters, and it can be retrained. The performance of the model can
be affected by several factors, including the characteristics of the data, the nature of the
data, the parameters of the network, and the hyperparameters. Therefore, the process of
training, validating, and testing a model is usually iterative, involving multiple rounds of
training and adjustment until the model's performance is satisfactory. Figure 2.21 demonstrates the division of the original data into three distinct segments.

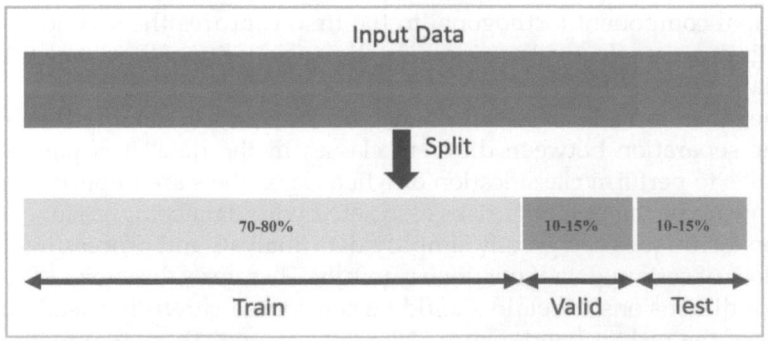

FIGURE 2.21
Split the original data into three parts.

2.9 Data Preparation Steps

In practice, data preparation can indeed be divided into four main steps.

2.9.1 Importing Libraries

This involves loading the necessary libraries for your project. There are many libraries available, and the ones you use will depend on the type of project you are working on and the platforms you are using. Some commonly used libraries in data science include NumPy, Pandas, Matplotlib, and Scikit-learn.

2.9.2 Reading Data

After setting up your environment with the necessary libraries, the next step is to read the data into your project. Data can be read from various sources, such as local files (e.g., CSV, Excel), databases, or online sources. The specific method of reading data will depend on the format and location of your data.

2.9.3 Data Cleaning

Once you've loaded the data into your project, the next step is to clean it. This involves handling missing values, dealing with outliers, correcting inconsistent or incorrect data, and transforming data types if necessary. The goal is to ensure that your data is accurate, complete, and in a suitable format for your subsequent analysis or modeling.

2.9.4 Data Splitting

The last step before feeding data into your model is to split the data. However, as mentioned earlier, some data cleaning and preprocessing should not be done on the entire dataset. If you plan to do such preprocessing, it is better to split the data first. Typically, the data is divided into three subsets: training, validation, and testing. The training set is used to train the model, the validation set is used to tune the model and select the best parameters, and the test set is used to evaluate the final performance of the model.

After these steps, you'll have a set of data ready to be used to train your model. It's important to remember that the process can be iterative, and you may need to go back and adjust your data preparation steps based on the results you get from your model.

2.10 Data Preprocessing Examples

Here, we present some data preparation examples that will serve as good practice for you to undertake yourself.

TABLE 2.2

Incorrect Data

Name	Age	Company
Karen Lynch	59	CVS Health
Elon Musk	51	Apple
Jeff Bezos	59	Amazon
Tim Cook	62	Tesla

TABLE 2.3

Remove Incorrect Data

Name	Age	Company
Karen Lynch	59	CVS Health
Jeff Bezos	59	Amazon

TABLE 2.4

Data Transformation

Name	Age	Company
Karen Lynch	59	CVS Health
Elon Musk	51	Tesla
Jeff Bezos	59	Amazon
Tim Cook	62	Apple

2.10.1 Data-based Example

In this example, there are some inaccuracies in rows 2 and 4 regarding company names. Specifically, "Elon Musk" is incorrectly listed for Apple, and "Tim Cook" is incorrectly associated with Tesla. Table 2.2 displays the instances of incorrect data.

In the first step, we can remove these two-row data as the data cleaning. Table 2.3 lists the instances where incorrect data has been removed.

Or we can do a data transformation to fix the error. Table 2.4 presents the details related to data transformation.

2.10.2 Project-based Example

In this example, we'll cover all four main steps of data preprocessing in a project context.

2.10.2.1 Import Libraries and the Dataset

The first step involves loading the required libraries. For this project, we primarily use Pandas, Numpy, Matplotlib, and Seaborn. Additionally, we utilize various techniques and algorithms from the Scikit-learn library for data preprocessing.

```
#This line imports the pandas library, which is used for data
manipulation and analysis. It is particularly useful for working with
numerical tables or data frames.
import pandas as pd

#This line imports the numpy library, which is used for numerical
operations and supports arrays and matrices. It also contains
mathematical functions to operate on these arrays.
import numpy as np
```

```
#This line imports the time module, which provides various time-related
functions. It's often used for benchmarking how long code takes to run.
import time
```

```
This line imports the pyplot module from matplotlib, which is used for
creating static, animated, and interactive visualizations in Python.
from matplotlib import pyplot as plt
```

```
#This line imports the K-Nearest Neighbors (KNN) classifier from the
sklearn library. KNN is a simple, easy-to-implement supervised machine
learning algorithm that can be used to solve both classification and
regression problems.
from sklearn.neighbors import KneighborsClassifier
```

```
#This line imports the train_test_split function from sklearn, which is
used to split your dataset into training and testing sets.
from sklearn.model_selection import train_test_split
```

```
This line imports the normalize function from sklearn, which is used to
scale input vectors individually to unit norm (a length of 1).
from sklearn.preprocessing import normalize
```

```
#This line imports several functions from sklearn's metrics module, which
are used to evaluate the performance of a machine learning model.
from sklearn.metrics import (confusion_matrix, accuracy_score,
precision_score,
                        recall_score, f1_score, matthews_corrcoef,
classification_report, roc_curve)
```

```
#This line imports the joblib module, which is used for saving and
loading scikit-learn models.
import joblib
```

```
#This line imports the StandardScaler class from sklearn, which is used
to standardize features by removing the mean and scaling to unit
variance.
from sklearn.preprocessing import StandardScaler
```

```
#This line imports the PCA class from sklearn, which is a dimensionality
reduction technique used to reduce the dimensionality of large datasets,
by transforming a large set of variables into a smaller one that still
contains most of the information in the large set.
from sklearn.decomposition import PCA
```

```
#This line sets the style of the plots to 'ggplot', which is a popular
plot style that emulates the aesthetics of ggplot (a plotting package
for R).
plt.style.use('ggplot')
```

	Time	V1	V2	V3	V4	V5	V6	V7	V8	V9	...	V21	V22	V23	V24
0	0.0	-1.359807	-0.072781	2.536347	1.378155	-0.338321	0.462388	0.239599	0.098698	0.363787	...	-0.018307	0.277838	-0.110474	0.066928	0.12
1	0.0	1.191857	0.266151	0.166480	0.448154	0.060018	-0.082361	-0.078803	0.085102	-0.255425	...	-0.225775	-0.638672	0.101288	-0.339846	0.16
2	1.0	-1.358354	-1.340163	1.773209	0.379780	-0.503198	1.800499	0.791461	0.247676	-1.514654	...	0.247998	0.771679	0.909412	-0.689281	-0.32
3	1.0	-0.966272	-0.185226	1.792993	-0.863291	-0.010309	1.247203	0.237609	0.377436	-1.387024	...	-0.108300	0.005274	-0.190321	-1.175575	0.64
4	2.0	-1.158233	0.877737	1.548718	0.403034	-0.407193	0.095921	0.592941	-0.270533	0.817739	...	-0.009431	0.798278	-0.137458	0.141267	-0.20

FIGURE 2.22
Dataset data values.

2.10.2.2 Read Data

In the second step, the data should be read to be processed by the algorithm. It is also good practice to check the data values and perform some presentation and visualization to see how they are distributed. Make sure there are no unnecessary spaces in your file path. Figure 2.22 displays the values within the dataset.

```
# Using the pandas library, you read the data from the CSV file.
# The pd.read_csv function is used to read a CSV file and convert it into
a pandas DataFrame.
df = pd.read_csv('/content/creditcard.csv')

# df.head() function is used to get the first 5 rows of the DataFrame df.
# This is useful to quickly test if your object has the right type of
data in it.
df.head()
```

2.10.2.3 Data Cleaning

In this section, we'll do some data cleaning, including checking for missing values and categorical data.

2.10.2.3.1 Checking for Missing Values

As a result, the dataset is labeled as 0s and 1s. This section of the code is designed to give you an understanding of the distribution of fraudulent and non-fraudulent transactions in your data. This is important as it can influence how you handle data preprocessing and model training. For example, if your data is heavily imbalanced (i.e., there are far more non-fraudulent transactions than fraudulent ones), you might decide to use techniques like oversampling the minority class, undersampling the majority class, or using a combination of both.

```
# df.isnull().any().sum() checks if there are any null values in the
DataFrame.
# If the sum is greater than 0, it means there are null values present in
the DataFrame.
df.isnull().any().sum()
```

```
# Here, 'Class' is a column in your DataFrame which signifies whether a
transaction is fraud or not.
# '0' represents a non-fraudulent transaction, and '1' represents a
fraudulent transaction.
# So, 'fraud' is a subset of your DataFrame where all transactions are
fraudulent.
fraud = df[df['Class'] == 1]

# Similarly, 'nonFraud' is a subset of your DataFrame where all
transactions are non-fraudulent.
nonFraud = df[df['Class'] == 0]

# 'All' is a variable that contains the total number of transactions in
the DataFrame.
All = df.shape[0]
# 'x' is a variable that contains the proportion of fraudulent
transactions in your DataFrame.
x - len(fraud)/All

# 'y' is a variable that contains the proportion of non-fraudulent
transactions in your DataFrame.
y = len(nonFraud)/All

# The next two lines print the percentage of fraudulent and non-fraudulent
transactions.
print('frauds :',x*100,'%')
print('non frauds :',y*100,'%')
```

Output:
```
frauds: 0.1727485630620034 %
non frauds: 99.82725143693798 %
```

Let's plot the Transaction class against the Frequency. This section of the code is creating a bar plot to visualize the distribution of fraudulent and non-fraudulent transactions in your dataset. This can help you understand the balance of the classes in your data. Figure 2.23 represents the relationship between Transaction Class and its corresponding Frequency.

```
# labels is a list of two strings: 'non frauds' and 'fraud'. These labels
will be used in the bar plot.
labels = ['non frauds', 'fraud']

# classes is a Series object that contains the counts of unique values in
the 'Class' column of your DataFrame.The values are sorted in descending
order so that the first element is the most frequently-occurring element.
classes = pd.value_counts(df['Class'], sort = True)

# The classes.plot() function is used to generate a bar plot of the
'classes' Series.
# The 'kind' parameter is set to 'bar' to generate a bar plot.
# The 'rot' parameter is set to 0 to keep the x-axis labels horizontal.
classes.plot(kind = 'bar', rot=0)
```

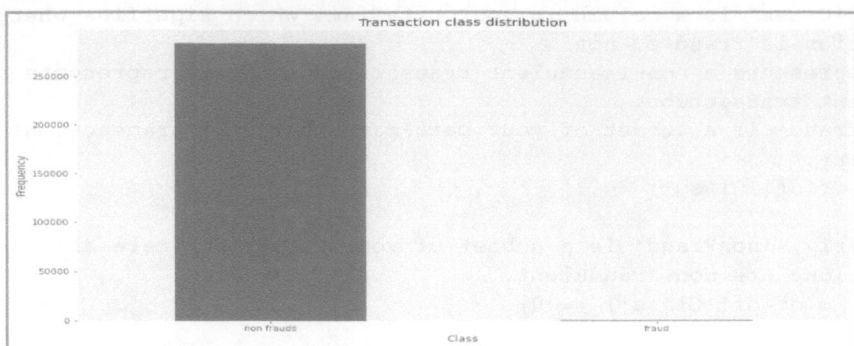

FIGURE 2.23
Transaction class vs. frequency.

```
# plt.title() is used to set a title for the bar plot.
plt.title("Transaction class distribution")

# plt.xticks() is used to set the x-axis tick values, which are the
positions along the x-axis where the tick marks appear, and labels.
plt.xticks(range(2), labels)

# plt.xlabel() is used to set the label for the x-axis.
plt.xlabel("Class")

# plt.ylabel() is used to set the label for the y-axis.
plt.ylabel("Frequency")
```

2.10.2.3.2 *Checking for Categorical Data*

The target variable is the only categorical variable in this dataset. Since the other attributes already have a numerical representation, there's no need to convert them into categorical data. Let's create a feature distribution chart. We used the seaborn distplot() function to better understand the distribution of features across the dataset. Besides the target variable, the dataset contains 30 additional characteristics. This section of the code generates a distribution plot for the "Amount" column in our dataset. This plot can offer insights into the transaction amounts' distribution in our data, which can be especially useful for identifying patterns or anomalies. Figure 2.24 illustrates the

FIGURE 2.24
Distribution of amount values.

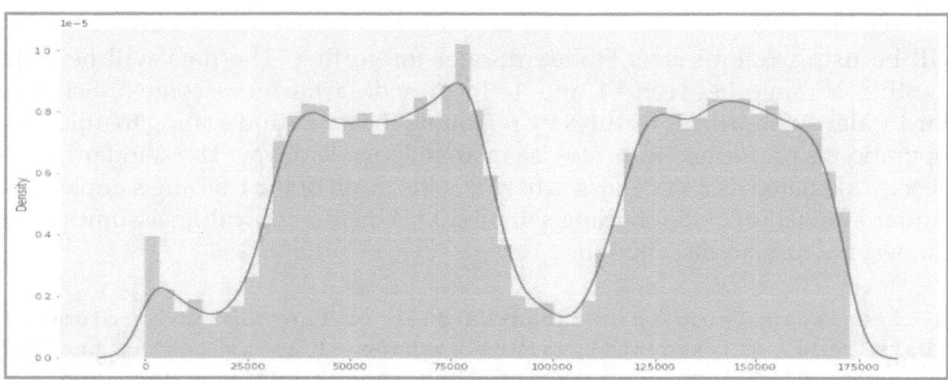

FIGURE 2.25
Distribution of amount.

distribution of various amount values and Figure 2.25 visualizes the distribution of the amount values.

```
# 'amount' is a list that contains one numpy array, which consists of the
values of the 'Amount' column in your DataFrame.
amount = [df['Amount'].values]

# sns.distplot() function is used to plot a univariate distribution of
observations.
# In this case, it's plotting the distribution of the 'amount' list.
sns.distplot(amount)

#This line is extracting the 'Time' column from your DataFrame df
and converting it into a NumPy array. The. values attribute of a
DataFrame returns the numpy representation of the DataFrame—only the
values in the DataFrame will be returned, the axes labels will be
removed.
time = df['Time'].values

#This line is creating a distribution plot of the 'Time' variable using
seaborn's distplot function. distplot is a function in seaborn which is
used to flexibly plot a univariate distribution of observations. This
means that you can visualize the distribution of a single variable (in
this case, 'Time'). The distplot function will draw a histogram and fit a
kernel density estimate (KDE), giving you a good idea of the distribution
of your data
sns.displot(time, kde=True)
```

2.10.2.4 Transformation the Data

As previously stated, data transformation is one method of data cleaning. In this section, we'll explore data transformation techniques. Data transformation is an important part of data preprocessing. It can include a variety of activities depending on your specific needs.

2.10.2.4.1 Normalizing

We will be using Scikit-learn's StandardScaler for scaling. The data will be reshaped to fit within a range between –1 and 1. To provide a bit more context, Scikit-learn's StandardScaler standardizes features by removing the mean and scaling to unit variance. This operation is performed feature-wise in an independent way. The standard score of a sample **x** is calculated as z = (x – u)/s, where **u** is the mean of the training samples, and **s** is the standard deviation of the training samples. This method of scaling assumes that your data follows a Gaussian distribution.

```
#This line is applying the StandardScaler to the 'Amount' column of
your DataFrame. df['Amount'].values.reshape(-1,1) is taking the values
of the 'Amount' column, converting them into a numpy array, and
reshaping that array into a 2D array because StandardScaler expects a
2D array. The -1 in reshape allows numpy to calculate the unknown
dimension for you. StandardScaler().fit_transform() calculates the
mean and standard deviation on the given data (the 'Amount' column),
then standardizes it using those values (i.e., it subtracts the mean
and divides by the standard deviation). The result of the
standardization is then stored in a new column in your DataFrame
called 'Vamount'.
df['Vamount'] = StandardScaler().fit_transform(df['Amount'].values.
reshape(-1,1))


#This line is doing the exact same thing as the previous line, but for
the 'Time' column instead of the 'Amount' column.
df['Vtime'] = StandardScaler().fit_transform(df['Time'].values.
reshape(-1,1))


#After creating the standardized columns, you no longer need the original
'Time' and 'Amount' columns, so this line drops them from the DataFrame.
The axis = 1 parameter tells pandas to look for these labels in the
DataFrame's columns, not its index.
df = df.drop(['Time','Amount'], axis = 1)


#Finally, this line prints out the first 5 rows of the DataFrame so you can
check your work. The head() function in pandas returns the first n rows for
the object based on position. By default, it returns the first 5 rows.
df.head()
```

Now all the features are standardized into the unit scale (mean = 0 and variance = 1). Your DataFrame should now have two new columns "Vamount" and "Vtime", that contain the standardized values of the "Amount" and "Time" columns, respectively, and the original "Time" and "Amount" columns should be gone. Figure 2.26 depicts the dataset after undergoing standardization.

V22	V23	V24	V25	V26	V27	V28	Class	Vamount	Vtime
0.277838	-0.110474	0.066928	0.128539	-0.189115	0.133558	-0.021053	0	0.244964	-1.996583
-0.638672	0.101288	-0.339846	0.167170	0.125895	-0.008983	0.014724	0	-0.342475	-1.996583
0.771679	0.909412	-0.689281	-0.327642	-0.139097	-0.055353	-0.059752	0	1.160686	-1.996562
0.005274	-0.190321	-1.175575	0.647376	-0.221929	0.062723	0.061458	0	0.140534	-1.996562
0.798278	-0.137458	0.141267	-0.206010	0.502292	0.219422	0.215153	0	-0.073403	-1.996541

FIGURE 2.26
Standardized dataset.

2.10.2.5 Data Reduction

As previously stated, the data reduction approach allows us to eliminate noise or unrelated data from the dataset. Some methods include PCA and LDA. In this section, we will practice some code to understand how to implement data reduction. Remember, the choice between PCA and LDA will depend largely on whether you're working with labeled data or not, and whether class separation is a concern.

2.10.2.5.1 PCA

The purpose of PCA is to reduce the size of the feature. This code is performing PCA on your data and reducing it to two principal components, then creating a new DataFrame that includes these components along with the original "Class" column. Figure 2.27 showcases the process of dimensional reduction applied to the dataset.

```
#This line is creating a new DataFrame X that includes all the columns
from df except 'Class'. The drop function removes the specified labels
from the rows or columns. Here, axis=1 indicates that labels should be
dropped from the columns.
X = df.drop(['Class'], axis = 1)
```

	principal component 1	principal component 2	Class
0	1.571633	-0.675537	0
1	-1.086136	-0.282819	0
2	2.053450	1.077546	0
3	1.150128	-0.427471	0
4	1.143864	-1.342195	0

FIGURE 2.27
Dimensional reduction.

```
#This line is creating a Series y that includes only the 'Class' column
from df.
y = df['Class']
```

```
#This line is initializing a PCA object with two components. This means
that the PCA will reduce your data down to two dimensions. But please
note, there seems to be a typo. The variable PCA should be in lowercase
as pca because Python is case sensitive. The corrected line should be pca
= PCA(n_components=2).
from sklearn.decomposition import PCA
PCA = PCA(n_components=2)
```

```
#This line is applying the PCA to the data in X and storing the result in
principal components. The fit_transform function first fits the model to
the data and then transforms the data to its first n principal components.
principal components = pca.fit_transform(X.values)
```

```
#This line is creating a new DataFrame from principalComponents and
naming the columns 'principal component 1' and 'principal component 2'.
principalDf = pd.DataFrame(data = principalComponents, columns =
['principal component 1', 'principal component 2'])
```

```
#This line is concatenating the principalDf DataFrame and the y Series
along axis=1, which means it's adding 'Class' as a new column to
principalDf and storing the result in finalDf.
finalDf = pd.concat([principalDf, y], axis = 1)
```

```
#Finally, this line is printing out the first five rows of finalDf so you
can check your work. The head() function in pandas returns the first n rows
for the object based on position. By default, it returns the first 5 rows.
finalDf.head()
```

The result of the following code should be a scatter plot where points of class 0 are shown in red and points of class 1 are shown in green. The x-axis represents the first principal component, and the y-axis represents the second principal component. This visualization helps you understand the distribution of classes in the context of the two principal components. Figure 2.28 presents a scatter plot resulting from the PCA (Principal Component Analysis) transformation.

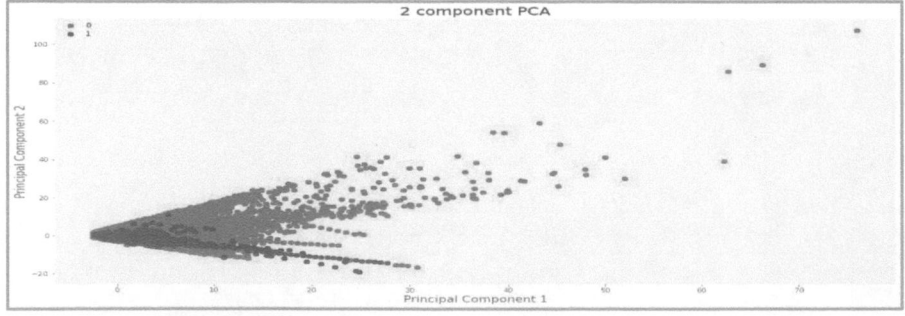

FIGURE 2.28
Scatter plot of PCA transformation.

```
#This line is creating a new matplotlib figure with a size of 8x8 inches.
fig = plt.figure(figsize = (8,8))

#This line is adding a new subplot to your figure. The arguments (1,1,1)
mean that there's just one plot in your figure.
ax = fig.add_subplot(1,1,1)

#This line is setting the label for the x-axis to 'Principal Component 1'
and the fontsize to 15.
ax.set_xlabel('Principal Component 1', fontsize = 15)

#This line is setting the label for the y-axis to 'Principal Component 2'
and the fontsize to 15.
ax.set_ylabel('Principal Component 2', fontsize = 15)

#This line is setting the title of the plot to '2 component PCA' and the
fontsize to 20.
ax.set_title('2 component PCA', fontsize = 20)

#This line is creating a list of the target values you're interested in.
In this case, it's 0 and 1.
targets = [0, 1]

#This line is creating a list of the colors that will be used for each
target. Red ('r') will be used for 0, and green ('g') will be used
for 1.
colors = ['r', 'g']
#This line is starting a loop that will iterate over your targets and
colors simultaneously.
for target, color in zip(targets,colors):

#Within the loop, this line is creating a Boolean Series that's True for
all rows in finalDf where 'Class' is equal to the current target
    indicesToKeep = finalDf['Class'] == target

#This line is adding a scatter plot to your subplot for all rows where
'Class' is equal to the current target. The x-values are the values in
the 'principal component 1' column, the y-values are the values in the
'principal component 2' column, the color is the current color, and the
size of the markers is 50.
    ax.scatter(finalDf.loc[indicesToKeep, 'principal component 1'],
finalDf.loc[indicesToKeep, 'principal component 2'],  c = color,
s = 50)

#This line is adding a legend to your plot. The labels for the legend are
your targets.
ax.legend(targets)

#Finally, this line is adding a grid to your plot.
ax.grid()
```

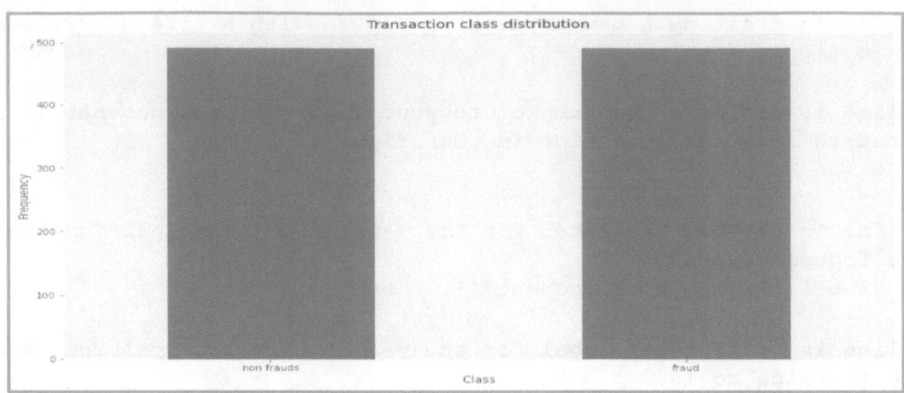

FIGURE 2.29
Distribution of classes.

This block of code is shuffling the rows in the DataFrame, creating a new DataFrame new_df that contains all non-fraudulent and fraudulent transactions, shuffling new_df, and then creating a bar plot of the transaction class distribution. The resulting plot shows the distribution of the "Class" variable in your shuffled DataFrame, giving you an idea of the balance (or imbalance) between non-fraudulent and fraudulent transactions. Figure 2.29 illustrates the distribution of different classes within the dataset.

```
#This line shuffles the entire DataFrame df. The sample function with the
frac=1 parameter returns a random sample of items from an axis of the
DataFrame, and when frac=1, it shuffles all items.
df = df.sample(frac=1)

#This line subsets df to only the rows where 'Class' is 1 (indicating a
fraudulent transaction) and stores this in frauds.
frauds = df[df['Class'] == 1]
#This line subsets df to only the rows where 'Class' is 0 (indicating a
non-fraudulent transaction) and stores this in non_frauds.
non_frauds = df[df['Class'] == 0][:]

#This line concatenates non_frauds and frauds to form a new DataFrame
new_df.
new_df = pd.concat([non_frauds, frauds])

#This line shuffles the rows of new_df. The random_state=42 parameter
ensures that the shuffle is reproducible, meaning that if you run the
code multiple times, you'll get the same shuffle every time.
new_df = new_df.sample(frac=1, random_state=42)

This line creates a list labels for labeling the x-axis of the bar plot.
labels = ['non frauds','fraud']

#This line counts the number of each unique value in the 'Class' column
of new_df and stores the result in classes.
classes = pd.value_counts(new_df['Class'], sort = True)
```

```
#This line creates a bar plot of classes. The rot=0 parameter makes the
x-axis labels horizontal.
classes.plot(kind = 'bar', rot=0)

#This line sets the title of the plot.
plt.title("Transaction class distribution")

#This line sets the labels for the x-axis ticks. The ticks are at
positions [0, 1], and the corresponding labels are 'non frauds' and
'fraud'.
plt.xticks(range(2), labels)

#These lines label the x-axis and y-axis of the plot, respectively.
plt.xlabel("Class")
plt.ylabel("Frequency")
```

2.11 Data Preprocessing Issues

Data preprocessing techniques indeed come with a variety of challenges that need to be addressed during their application. Here are some common issues.

2.11.1 Data Quality

Data preprocessing can reveal data quality problems, such as missing values, inconsistent data, and noisy data. These problems must be identified and addressed before proceeding with data analysis. Using robust data validation methods and data cleaning techniques can help address these issues.

2.11.2 Bias and Fairness

Data preprocessing can inadvertently introduce bias into the data, which can impact the accuracy and fairness of subsequent analyses or predictions. It's essential to consider these issues and ensure that the data is representative and unbiased. Techniques like stratified sampling and careful feature selection can help reduce bias.

2.11.3 Data Privacy

Data preprocessing may involve dealing with sensitive information, raising privacy concerns. It's essential to take measures to protect data privacy, such as anonymizing or de-identifying the data, and to ensure compliance with regulations like the GDPR.

2.11.4 Scalability

Data preprocessing can be computationally intensive, especially for large datasets. It's vital to consider scalability and ensure that the preprocessing steps are efficient and can handle the data's size. Using distributed computing frameworks like Apache Spark or Dask can help with scalability issues.

2.11.5 Interpretability

Data preprocessing can sometimes make it more challenging to interpret the results of subsequent analyses. It's crucial to thoroughly document the preprocessing steps and ensure that the results remain interpretable. Techniques like dimensionality reduction and feature importance analysis can help with interpretability.

Overall, while data preprocessing techniques aim to improve the quality and utility of data for analysis, it's crucial to be aware of these potential challenges and adopt strategies to address them.

2.12 Data Preprocessing Implementation Tips

Here are some tips for using data preprocessing approaches.

2.12.1 Understand Your Data

Before applying any preprocessing techniques, get to know your data. Understand the types of features, their distributions, the presence of missing or noisy data, and the nature of your target variable.

2.12.2 Choose Appropriate Techniques

Different datasets and problems require different preprocessing techniques. Choose the ones that best suit your data and the problem you're trying to solve.

2.12.3 Document Changes

Keep a record of any changes made during data preprocessing, including missing data imputation, feature scaling, and data transformation. This helps maintain transparency and reproducibility in your analysis.

2.12.4 Avoid Overfitting

While techniques like oversampling and undersampling can help balance class distributions, be wary of overfitting your model to the training data. Use cross-validation or similar techniques to ensure your model generalizes well.

2.12.5 Use Established Libraries

Libraries like scikit-learn, TensorFlow, and Pandas provide robust and tested implementations of common preprocessing techniques. Using these can save time and help avoid errors.

2.12.6 Continuously Monitor Data Quality

Data preprocessing isn't a one-time process. Keep monitoring data quality and adjust preprocessing techniques as needed to maintain the performance of your model.

2.12.7 Start with Simple Techniques

Start with straightforward preprocessing techniques, such as handling missing values, scaling data, or encoding categorical variables. These can often provide substantial improvements without adding significant complexity.

2.12.8 Test Multiple Techniques

It's often beneficial to test various preprocessing techniques to see their impact on model performance. This way, you can identify the most effective techniques for your specific problem.

2.12.9 Document Your Steps

Keep a thorough record of your preprocessing steps, including the rationale for each step, the code used, and any parameters or settings used. This will ensure the reproducibility of your analysis and allow others to understand and validate your work.

Remember, hands-on experience is key when working with data preprocessing or any other machine learning models. Therefore, consistently practicing implementation and troubleshooting is crucial for mastering these concepts.

2.13 Lessons Learned

- Learn Data Preprocessing Concepts, Steps, and Approaches
- Learn Data Cleaning
- Learn Data Transformation
- Learn Data Balancing
- Learn Data Augmentation
- Learn Data Reduction
- Learn Dataset Partitioning
- Learn Data Preparation Steps
- Learn Data Preprocessing with some examples
- Learn Data Preprocessing Issues
- Learn Data Preprocessing Implementation Tips

2.14 Problems

2.14.1 Name three major types of data cleaning approaches and describe the general steps involved.

2.14.2 What exactly is data transformation? Name three of its primary approaches.

2.14.3   What is data balancing, and how do sampling and undersampling work?

2.14.4   What exactly is data augmentation, and why is it crucial?

2.14.5   What is data reduction, and how does it differ from PCA and LDA?

2.14.6   In general, how many partitions are there in data splitting?

2.14.7   What are the main steps involved in data preparation?

2.14.8   Define a sample data set of students' grades with the following fields: first name, last name, ID, and grade. Provide some sample data and perform data cleaning and transformation.

2.14.9   Select an Excel file and perform data preprocessing steps, such as cleaning, transformation, and reduction.

2.14.10 Try to identify the Principal Components (PCs) and Linear Discriminants (LDs) using PCA and LDA on your data. Check the outputs and determine how these methods can reduce your computation cost.

2.14.11 What is data preprocessing, and why is it significant in machine learning?

2.14.12 What are some common techniques used for the imputation of missing data?

2.14.13 How can we handle noisy data in a dataset?

2.14.14 What is feature scaling, and why is it necessary in certain machine learning algorithms?

2.14.15 How can we manage imbalanced datasets in machine learning?

2.14.16 What is the difference between data augmentation and data generation in the context of machine learning?

2.14.17 What is dimensionality reduction, and why is it employed in machine learning?

2.14.18 What are some common techniques used for the detection and removal of outliers?

2.15 Programming Questions

- **Easy**

    2.15.1   Write a Python program to remove missing values from a dataset using the Pandas library.

    2.15.2   Implement a program to normalize the values of a dataset using Min-Max scaling.

    2.15.3   Write a Python function to perform one-hot encoding on categorical variables in a dataset.

    2.15.4   Build a program to split a dataset into training and testing sets using the scikit-learn library.

    2.15.5   Implement a Python script to remove outliers from a dataset using the z-score method.

    2.15.6   Write a program to apply Principal Component Analysis (PCA) on a dataset using the scikit-learn library.

2.15.7 Implement a program to perform feature scaling using standardization.

2.15.8 Build a script to apply data discretization using the k-means algorithm.

2.15.9 Write a Python function to perform text preprocessing on a text dataset.

2.15.10 Build a program to perform data augmentation on image data using the Keras library.

2.15.11 Write a Python function to remove duplicates from a list of strings.

2.15.12 Write a Python script to convert a CSV file to a JSON file.

2.15.13 Write a Python program to count the number of occurrences of each word in a text file.

2.15.14 Write a Python function to tokenize a sentence into words.

2.15.15 Write a Python program to remove stop words from a text file.

2.15.16 Write a Python script to merge multiple CSV files into a single CSV file.

2.15.17 Write a Python function to perform stemming on a list of words.

2.15.18 Write a Python program to convert text to lowercase and remove punctuation marks.

2.15.19 Write a Python script to split a large text file into smaller files based on the number of lines.

2.15.20 Write a Python program to replace missing values in a dataset with the mean or median of the feature.

2.15.21 Write a Python function to remove duplicate rows from a CSV file.

2.15.22 Write a Python script to replace all occurrences of a specific value in a CSV file with a new value.

2.15.23 Write a Python program to merge two CSV files based on a common column.

- **Medium**

  2.15.24 Write a Python function to convert all categorical variables in a dataset to one-hot encoded variables.

  2.15.25 Write a Python program to perform feature scaling on a dataset.

  2.15.26 Write a Python function to impute missing values in a dataset using mean imputation.

  2.15.27 Write a Python program to perform principal component analysis (PCA) on a dataset.

  2.15.28 Write a Python function to detect and remove outliers from a dataset.

- **Hard**

  2.15.29 Write a Python function to preprocess text data for natural language processing (NLP).

3

Model Evaluation

This chapter discusses Model Evaluation and Hyperparameters Setting and includes the following:

- Hyperparameter Setting
- Optimize the Model
- Bias/Variance
- Identifying Weaknesses in a Model
- Model Evaluation
- Model Evaluation Issues
- Model Evaluation Implementation Tips

3.1 Preface

Model evaluation and hyperparameter tuning are among the most crucial tasks in machine learning, encompassing deep learning and Generative Adversarial Networks (GANs). GAN models can be assessed using a multitude of methods, both quantitative and qualitative. If the model has certain limitations, such as knowledge of the target domain or a substantial amount of data computed in a reasonable timeframe, we can save it using training epochs. Evaluating the model with validation error to determine the best model for testing with test data is also crucial. Selecting the right features, parameters, and hyperparameters is equally vital for finding the best model. In deep learning, model evaluation is an indispensable step in the development and deployment of any machine learning algorithm. It involves assessing a trained model's performance using various metrics to determine its effectiveness on unseen data. One of the most common evaluation metrics in deep learning is accuracy, which measures the percentage of correct predictions made by the model. However, accuracy alone may not be sufficient to evaluate a model's performance, especially when dealing with imbalanced datasets where classes are not evenly represented. In such cases, other metrics, such as precision, recall, and F1-score, are commonly used. Precision represents the proportion of true positives (correctly identified instances) out of all positive instances predicted, whereas recall signifies the proportion of true positives out of all actual positive instances. The F1-score is the harmonic mean of precision and recall, providing a balanced evaluation metric that considers both measures. Cross-validation is another crucial aspect of model evaluation. It involves dividing the data into training and testing sets to avoid overfitting. K-fold cross-validation splits the data into "k" equal parts, each part serving once as the test set while the remaining parts form the training set. This ensures the model's performance is assessed on unseen data, thereby reducing the risk of overfitting. Alongside

DOI: 10.1201/9781003281344-3

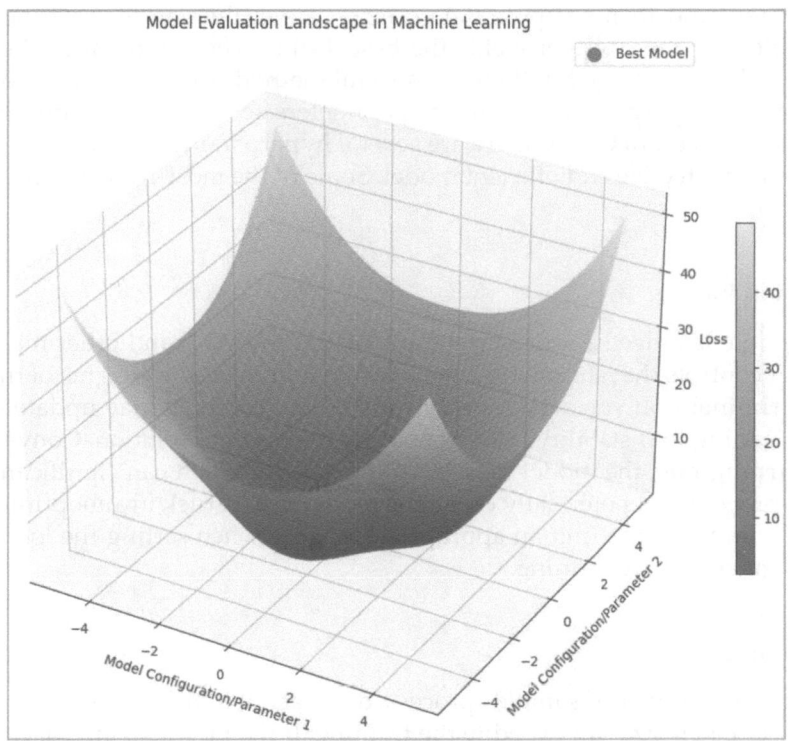

FIGURE 3.1
In machine learning, model evaluation is critical.

cross-validation, other techniques like early stopping and regularization can improve model performance and prevent overfitting. Regularization involves adding a penalty term to the loss function to minimize model complexity and prevent overfitting, while early stopping ends the training process when the validation loss no longer improves. In summary, model evaluation is a vital step in the development and deployment of deep learning models. It requires careful consideration of evaluation metrics, cross-validation techniques, and other methods to ensure the model performs well on unseen data and proves robust in different scenarios.

In this chapter, we will review the most validated model evaluation approaches and learn how to set hyperparameters to optimize the model. Figure 3.1 highlights the importance of model evaluation in the realm of machine learning.

3.2 Hyperparameter Setting

Parameters are generally divided into two types: training parameters, which are learned from the training data, and hyperparameters, which are optimized separately from the training parameters. Various methods can be employed to enhance a model's performance, such as adjusting individual hyperparameters or finding the optimal combination of values. Grid search is one method to achieve this. In grid search, we define a set of hyperparameters and then compute the performance evaluation for each possible combination to identify the one that yields the best results. The computational cost for this evaluation can be quite high, but there are several methods to mitigate this cost, like randomized search. Hyperparameters are the parameters set before the training process of the model commences. In GANs, there are several hyperparameters that need to be established to train an effective and efficient model. Some of the most critical hyperparameters in GANs include:

3.2.1 Learning Rate

The learning rate is indeed a crucial hyperparameter in GANs and other machine learning models. It controls the rate at which the optimizer updates the weights of the generator and the discriminator. If you set a high learning rate, the model may update the weights too quickly, leading to instability or overshooting the optimal solution. Conversely, if you set a low learning rate, the model may learn too slowly, which can significantly prolong the training process and potentially cause the model to get stuck in suboptimal solutions. Therefore, it's important to find an appropriate balance when setting the learning rate to ensure efficient and stable training.

3.2.2 Batch Size

This refers to the number of samples processed in each iteration of the training process. Setting a larger batch size can expedite the training, but it may also increase the memory requirements and potentially lead to overfitting.

3.2.3 Number of Epochs

During training, this refers to the number of times the entire training dataset is passed through the model. Setting a larger number of epochs can lead to a more accurate model, but it can also increase the risk of overfitting.

3.2.3.1 Risk of Overfitting

More complex models with a larger number of parameters (such as deeper networks) are more prone to overfitting, especially when training data is limited. Overfitting occurs when a model learns the training data too well, including the noise or random fluctuations in the training data, leading to poor generalization to unseen data (i.e., the test data).

3.2.3.2 Increased Computational Demand

Deeper networks require more computational resources for training. They take longer to train and require more memory to store the model parameters.

3.2.3.3 Vanishing/Exploding Gradients

Very deep networks can suffer from vanishing or exploding gradients, which makes them harder to train effectively. Although there are techniques to mitigate these issues, they remain a challenge in designing and training deep networks. So, while adding more layers might improve the performance of your GANs up to a point, it's essential to carefully consider these trade-offs. Further, it's always a good idea to validate the model's performance using a hold-out validation set or cross-validation to ensure that it generalizes well to unseen data, and does not merely memorize the training data.

3.2.4 Number of Neurons

This pertains to the number of layers in the generator and discriminator networks. Increasing the number of layers can lead to a more complex model. However, it can also heighten the risk of overfitting and potentially decelerate the training process. In deep learning models like GANs, adding more layers often helps the model to learn more complex, higher-level features. But it also comes with challenges:

3.2.4.1 Overfitting

More complex models (those with more layers/parameters) may overfit to the training data, especially when there's not enough data. Overfitting refers to the model learning the noise and outliers in the training data, reducing its ability to generalize to unseen data.

3.2.4.2 Training Time

Deeper models generally take longer to train due to the increased number of parameters.

3.2.4.3 Vanishing/Exploding Gradients

This problem becomes more prominent as the model gets deeper. It can hinder the learning process and requires specific techniques to mitigate.

3.2.5 Activation Functions

Choosing the appropriate activation functions can significantly impact the model's performance. Activation functions play a crucial role in neural networks, including GANs. By introducing nonlinearity, they allow the model to learn and represent more complex patterns in the data, which linear models might not capture effectively. Common choices include Rectified Linear Unit (ReLU), sigmoid, and tanh, each having different properties that may make them more suitable for certain tasks or types of data. It's important to experiment with different activation functions to see which works best for your specific use case.

Setting hyperparameters in GANs often involves a trial-and-error process, and methods like grid or random searches are commonly used to identify the optimal hyperparameters for a specific problem. The model's performance can be evaluated using metrics, such as accuracy, precision, recall, F1 score, and AUC-ROC. Hyperparameters can significantly impact the performance of a GAN, and choosing the right ones often requires trial and error, as there's no one-size-fits-all solution. Techniques, such as grid search or random search, can help find a good set of hyperparameters. The performance metrics (accuracy, precision, recall, F1 score, and AUC-ROC) are important for evaluating how well the GAN performs, and each offers a different perspective on the model's effectiveness. Figure 3.2

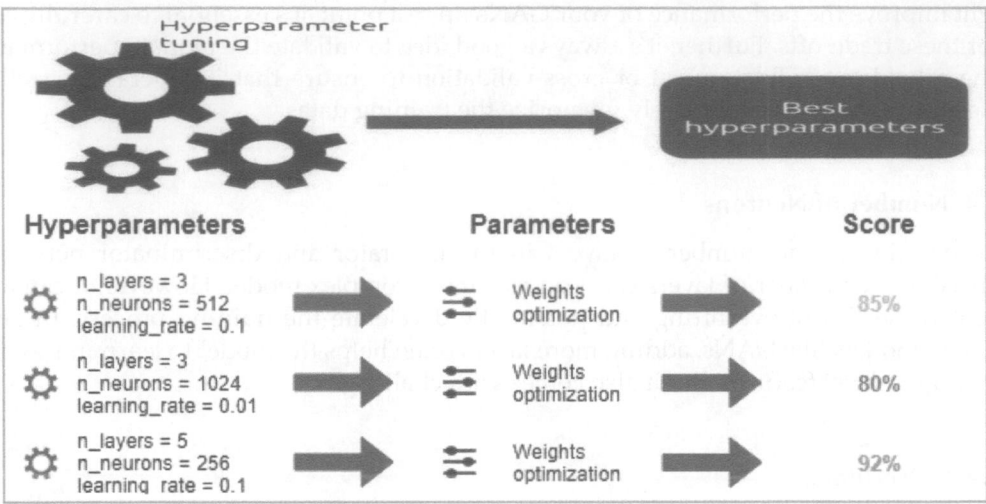

FIGURE 3.2
It is critical to identify the best hyperparameters for the machine learning model.

emphasizes the significance of identifying optimal hyperparameters for a machine learning model.

3.3 Optimize the Model

The initial step in model evaluation involves calculating its accuracy or identifying its errors. If the error is substantial and the accuracy is low, it indicates that the model is not performing optimally and isn't accurately representing the intended target. In the context of GANs, a superior model is one that generates high-quality synthetic samples that are visually similar to the real training data samples. This implies that the generated samples should mirror the same statistical properties as the real samples, including the distribution of colors, textures, shapes, and patterns. The quality of the generated samples can be evaluated using various metrics, such as the Inception Score (IS), Fréchet Inception Distance, or through visual inspection by human evaluators. Moreover, an effective GAN model should also converge to a stable state during training without experiencing mode collapse or oscillation. This implies that the discriminator should be proficient at distinguishing between real and fake samples with high accuracy, while the generator should be capable of producing diverse and realistic samples that deceive the discriminator. Hyperparameter tuning and careful selection of loss functions are crucial factors in achieving an effective GAN model. Several methods and measures can be used to ascertain accuracy or identify errors. Validation errors and test errors are two types of errors that can occur during model validation. By focusing on the validation error, you can determine the model's effectiveness. Evaluating the model using validation error is essential to identify the optimal model for testing with actual data. If the validation error is significant, or the model doesn't meet your requirements, the model is deemed insufficient. Evaluating GANs indeed relies on a balance of quantitative metrics and qualitative assessment. The stability of the training

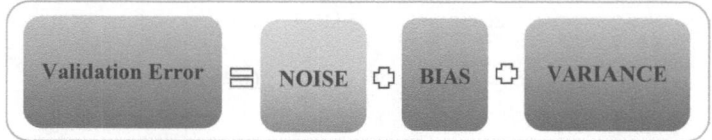

FIGURE 3.3
Error definition consists of three major components.

process, the visual quality of generated samples, and the diversity of those samples are all crucial aspects to consider. To ascertain this value, you first need to decompose the validation error as follows:

Figure 3.3 illustrates the validation error segments, and calculating these segments is the first step in analyzing and evaluating the model. Using the formula, the variance, bias, and noise can be calculated as follows:

$$\text{Noise} = \mathbb{E}\left[\left(\bar{y}(\mathbf{x}) - y(\mathbf{x})\right)^2\right]$$

$$\text{Bias} = \mathbb{E}\left[\left(\bar{h}(\mathbf{x}) - \bar{y}(\mathbf{x})\right)^2\right]$$

$$\text{Variance} = \mathbb{E}\left[\left(h_D(\mathbf{x}) - \bar{h}(\mathbf{x})\right)^2\right]$$

Now let us put these values into one formula:

$$\underset{\text{Validation Error} =}{\mathbb{E}\left[\left(h_D(\mathbf{x}) - y\right)^2\right]} = \underset{\text{Noise} \quad +}{\mathbb{E}\left[\left(\bar{y}(\mathbf{x}) - y(\mathbf{x})\right)^2\right]} + \underset{\text{Bias} \quad +}{\mathbb{E}\left[\left(\bar{h}(\mathbf{x}) - \bar{y}(\mathbf{x})\right)^2\right]} + \underset{\text{Variance}}{\mathbb{E}\left[\left(h_D(\mathbf{x}) - \bar{h}(\mathbf{x})\right)^2\right]}$$

Let's take a closer look at these parameters and see how they can affect our model.

3.3.1 What Is the Noise?

Handling noise in data is an essential part of any data analysis process. Noise can introduce inaccuracies and inconsistencies that can adversely impact the performance of machine learning models. Various techniques are available for noise detection and removal, including statistical methods, machine learning-based methods, and data preprocessing techniques. The choice of method often depends on the nature of the noise and the specific characteristics of the data. A variety of factors, including data corruption and the presence of data that customers cannot interpret or evaluate, can lead to these errors. The influence of such information on the training process might result in an inaccurate trained model and unreliable results. Challenges then arise, such as determining the cause of this problem and identifying suitable solutions to address it. This becomes particularly critical when the noise level is extremely high or reaches an unacceptable value. At this stage, we'll begin by calculating the total amount of noise. When estimating the volume of the noise, consider the following factors:

$$\text{Noise} = \mathbb{E}\left[\left(\bar{y}(\mathbf{x}) - y(\mathbf{x})\right)^2\right] = 1/n\left(\Sigma_{(i=0:n)}\left(\bar{y}(x_i) - y(x_i)\right)^2\right)$$

where:

$$\bar{y}(\mathbf{x}) = 1 * p(y = 1 \mid \mathbf{x}) + 2 * p(y = 2 \mid \mathbf{x})$$

Let's assume we have a database represented by $\mathbf{D} = [(\mathbf{x}_1, \mathbf{y}_1), \ldots, (\mathbf{x}_n, \mathbf{y}_n)]$, along with the distribution $\mathbf{P(X, Y)}$. Here, the labels are denoted by $\mathbf{y}_i$, while the sample data points are represented by $\mathbf{x}_1$ through $\mathbf{x}_n$. Each pair $(\mathbf{x}_i, \mathbf{y}_i)$ for $\mathbf{i} = 1 \ldots n$ forms a feature vector for each sample, where the coordinates $\mathbf{x}_1 \ldots \mathbf{x}_n$ symbolize the sample data. The actual label is represented by the variable $\mathbf{y}$, and $\mathbf{x} = \mathbf{x}_1, \ldots, \mathbf{x}_n$ represents all the sample values obtained. Sometimes, noise is present in the data. In such cases, you might need to preprocess the data before using it for training, which could include noise removal. If the noise level remains substantial even after completing all the preprocessing steps, further investigation into other potential causes is necessary to reduce or eliminate the noise. The two primary contributors to the volume of the noise are:

1. Incorrect labeling
2. Incorrect feature extraction

For these two problems, there are two corresponding solutions:

1. Relabeling the data
2. Changing the features and repeating the feature extraction process

It's important to remember that these definitions for individual data samples are not about the nature of the data. Noise can corrupt any type of data. For instance, Figure 3.4 might show noise in image data that has completely corrupted the image.

3.3.1.1 Labeling

When there is a lot of background noise, incorrect labeling is more likely. In such a scenario, it's advised to revisit the data and relabel everything. Let's elaborate with an example. Suppose you label a certain data point as "orange" when it should be "apple".

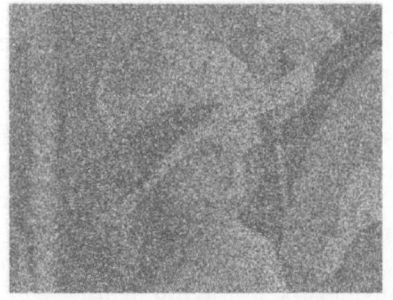

FIGURE 3.4
The noise in data can change the results.

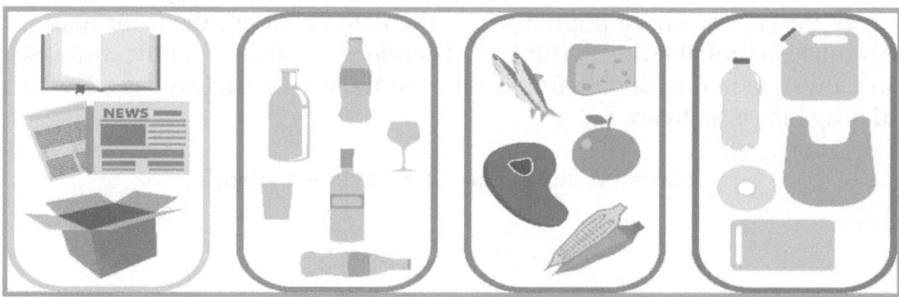

FIGURE 3.5
Incorrect labeling data can make the noise value high.

This mislabeling introduces problems in the training process, much like noisy data, leading to a flawed model. To address this issue, follow these steps:

1. Review the labels.
2. Identify the data points that have been incorrectly labeled.
3. Repeat the data labeling process.
4. Recalculate the noise to assess if the noise level has changed.

If you find that the noise level has decreased after these steps, mislabeling is likely the primary source of the noise. If not, other causes need to be investigated to eliminate the noise. Mislabeling is the most probable cause if you observe a decrease in noise after the above steps. Figure 3.5 illustrates how poor labeling can lead to noisy data and high error values. For instance, in Figure 3.5, the data points are classified based on their material, shape, group, or usage. Generally, we could group all food items into one category, but this classification would be incorrect if we aim to distinguish between vegetables, fruits, and meats.

3.3.1.2 Incorrect Features

Choosing the right features is crucial for model accuracy, as they directly and indirectly influence the training and classification outcomes. Selecting inappropriate features can inflate the error. Therefore, if the noise level remains high even after relabeling, consider the following steps:

1. Examine the existing features.
2. Reanalyze the problem.
3. Assess if the current features adequately represent your sample definition.
4. Identify potential new features.
5. Update the feature vectors.
6. Train the model using the new features.
7. Recalculate the noise to assess how these changes affect the noise level.

3.3.2 What Is the Bias?

Bias is another component of error values. Our dataset will always contain some form of bias. When we discuss data bias, we're referring to the inability of data samples to accurately represent the entire population. If the data is biased, the information used to train the model isn't reliable due to this bias. Therefore, we must compute the bias, analyze it, and find a way to make the data impartial or, at the very least, less biased. One method for calculating bias is as follows:

$$\text{Bias} = |\text{predicted classifier} - \text{average labels}|$$

$$\text{Bias} = \mathbb{E}\left[\left(\bar{h}(\mathbf{x}) - \bar{y}(\mathbf{x})\right)2\right]$$

where:

$$\bar{h}(\mathbf{x}) \approx 1/m\left(\Sigma_{i=1:m}\, h_{Di}(\mathbf{x})\right)$$

$$\bar{y}(\mathbf{x}) = 1 * p(y = 1 \,|\, \mathbf{x}) + 2 * p(y = 2 \,|\, \mathbf{x})$$

In this case, "m" denotes the number of classifiers, "$\mathbf{D_i}$" represents the dataset, and "$\mathbf{h_{Di}}$" signifies the trained classifier of "$\mathbf{D_i}$". Here, $\bar{y}(\mathbf{x})$ is the expected label, $y(\mathbf{x})$ is the actual label, and $\mathbf{x}$ is the set $\{\mathbf{x_1}, \ldots, \mathbf{x_n}\}$. There are several reasons for high bias in the model, and the following are two major sources of bias:

- Choosing an incorrect classifier, and
- Using inappropriate features (we discussed this and how to solve it in the previous section).

The same discussion and examples apply in cases where incorrect features are chosen, illustrating how it can lead to inaccurate modeling.

3.3.2.1 Incorrect Classifier

If the bias is high, it may suggest that the chosen classifier is inappropriate, and thus the classifier might fail to learn the pattern in the data. Take, for instance, a scenario where linear classifiers are used on nonlinear data. Figure 3.6 illustrates how the appropriate classifier can reduce bias.

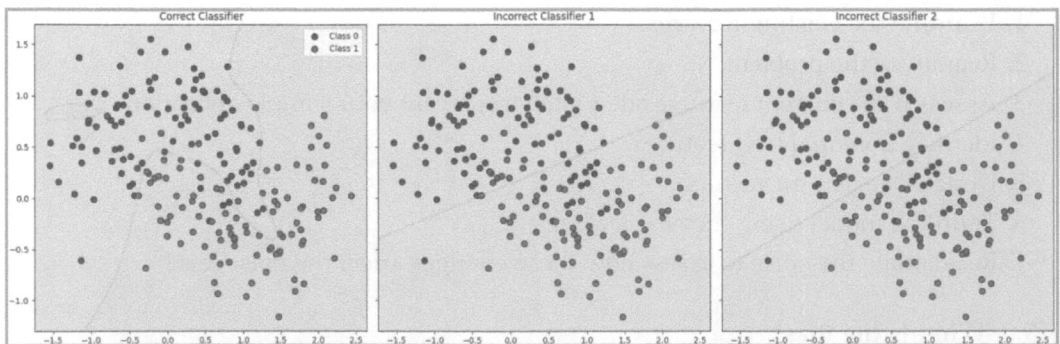

FIGURE 3.6
The correct classifier can make the bias less.

3.3.3 What Is the Variance?

Variance (σ^2) is another component of the error. Variance measures the spread of the data points from the mean value of the dataset. Generally, variance is calculated by subtracting the mean from each data point, squaring the results, summing them up, and then dividing by the number of data points. In this context, we calculate variance as a part of the error, and if it is high, it suggests a significant portion of the error is due to variance. In such cases, we try to find ways to reduce it. There are some methods for reducing variance, such as bagging or selecting a good dataset. Here, $\bar{y}(x)$ represents the expected label, $y(x)$ represents the actual label, $\mathbf{x} = \{x_1, \ldots, x_n\}$ represents the feature vectors, $\mathbf{m}$ represents the number of classifiers, $\mathbf{D_i}$ represents a dataset, and $\mathbf{h_{Di}}$ represents the classifier trained on $\mathbf{D_i}$. Let's look at the formula in more detail:

$$\textbf{Variance} = \mathbb{E}\left[\left(h(\mathbf{x}) - \bar{h}(\mathbf{x})\right)^2\right]$$

$$\mathbb{E}_D\left[\left(h_D(\mathbf{x}) - \bar{h}(\mathbf{x})\right)^2\right] \approx 1/m\left(\sum_{j=1:m}\left(h_{Dj}(\mathbf{xi}) - \bar{h}(\mathbf{xi})\right)^2\right)$$

where:

$$\bar{h}(\mathbf{x}) \approx 1/m\left(\sum_{i=1:m} h_{Di}(\mathbf{x})\right)$$

$$\bar{y}(\mathbf{x}) = 1 * p(y=1 \mid \mathbf{x}) + 2 * p(y=2 \mid \mathbf{x})$$

Figure 3.7 illustrates how high and low variance affect final results and whether they are far from or close to the best model.

3.3.3.1 New Dataset

Variance can be influenced by different datasets or data preprocessing techniques, such as data augmentation. You could modify your dataset or look for a different one, or you could apply additional preprocessing to your data, such as data augmentation and other techniques to generate new data and alter the data's variance. Following this, calculate the variance, explore how the new data impacts the variance, and contemplate how this change can enhance the trained model, thereby guiding your decisions.

3.4 Bias/Variance

Let's now consider the relationship between bias and variance, and how their values can be close to the target. There are four major states in the tradeoff between bias and variance (L: Low, H: High, B: Bias, V: Variance).

1. LB/LV
2. HB/LV
3. LB/HV
4. HB/HV

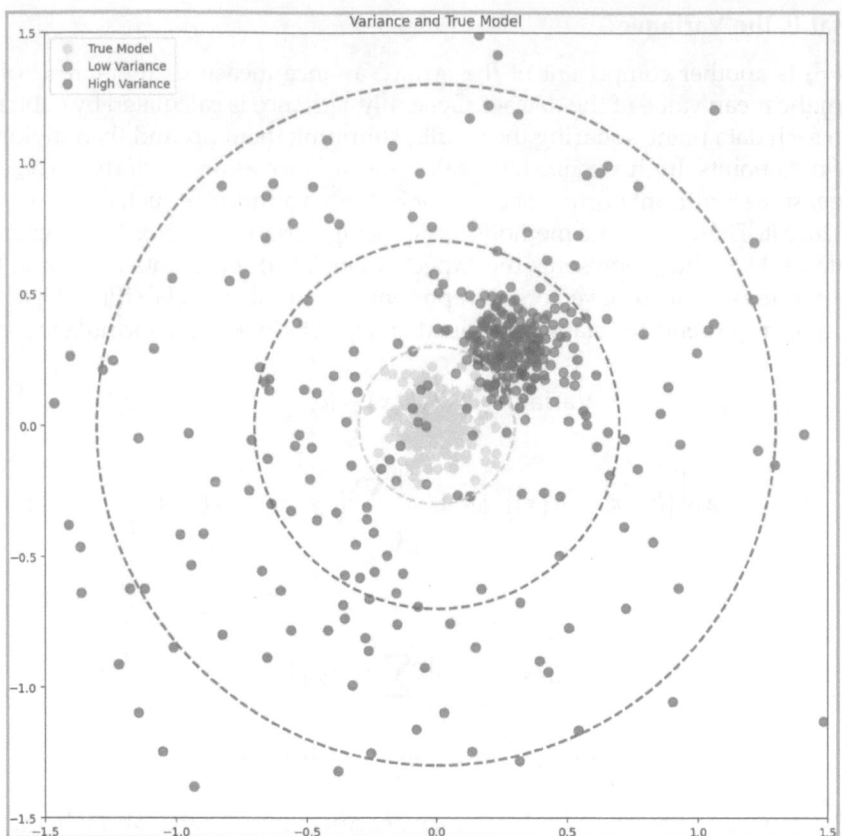

FIGURE 3.7
Variance value changes the accuracy.

Figure 3.8 represents each of these four states. It shows that the optimal state is Low Bias and Low Variance (LB/LV), and the values are very close to the target. Even in the formula for validation error, low bias and variance decrease validation error, leading to more accurate results. Another challenge is determining the optimal bias and variance values. Figure 3.9 illustrates the tradeoff between bias and variance, as well as their relationship to model complexity. This is analogous to minimizing the total value, which equals the sum of bias and variance. The dotted vertical line signifies the optimal point for model complexity. There are two states:

a. When the variance is high, and
b. When the bias is high.

So, in the first step, check the values of these two parameters and then proceed with steps to identify and resolve the problems. A point of contention is the data's high variance and bias. The problems causing the model to be inaccurate are underfitting and overfitting. When the model has low variance and high bias, it underfits the target; however, a model with high variance results in overfitting. To avoid these two issues, we can recognize the conditions causing the model's variance or bias to be high and then attempt to mitigate these high values. These two scenarios are discussed in the following section.

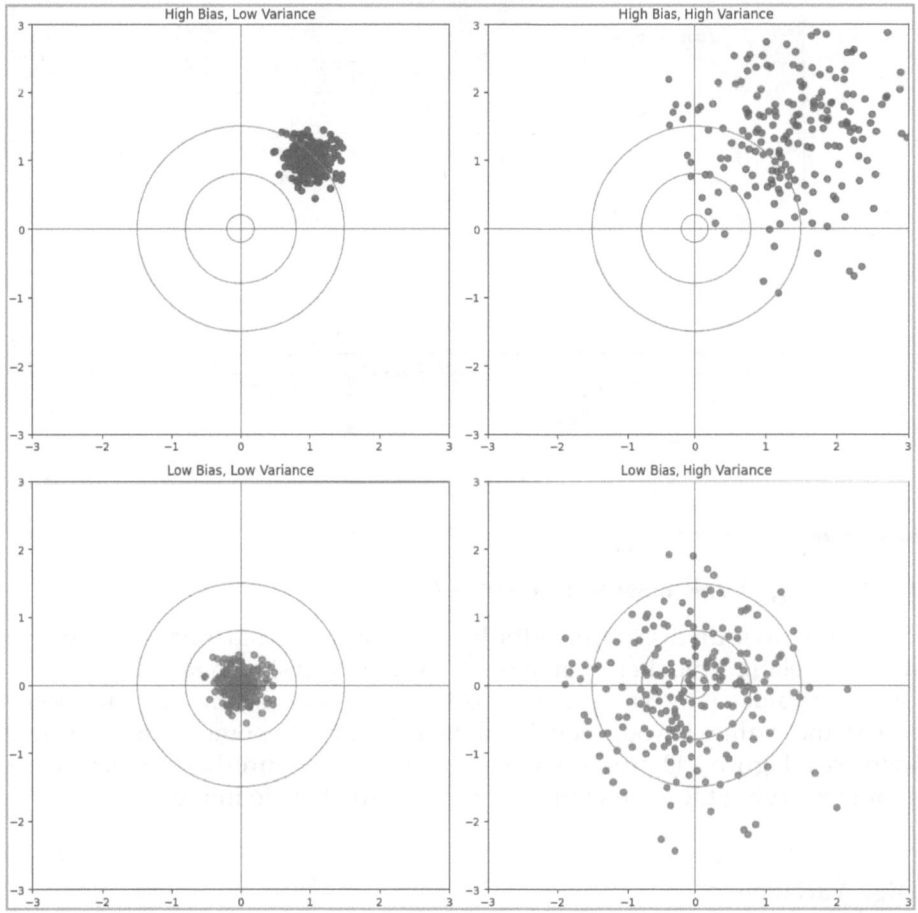

FIGURE 3.8
Bias/variance changes.

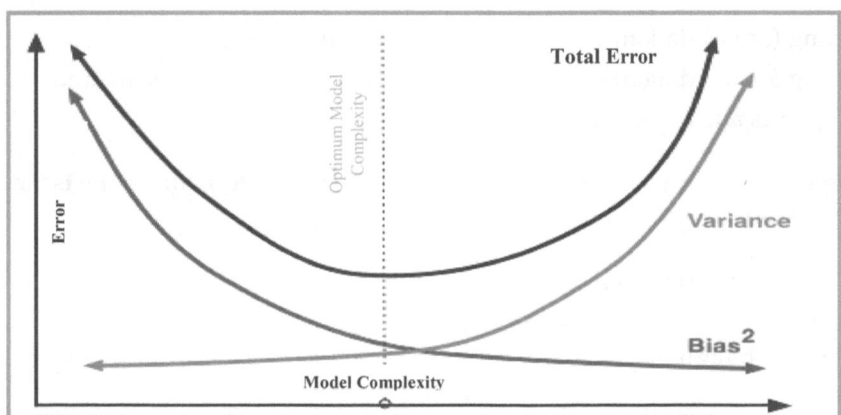

FIGURE 3.9
Bias/variance tradeoff.

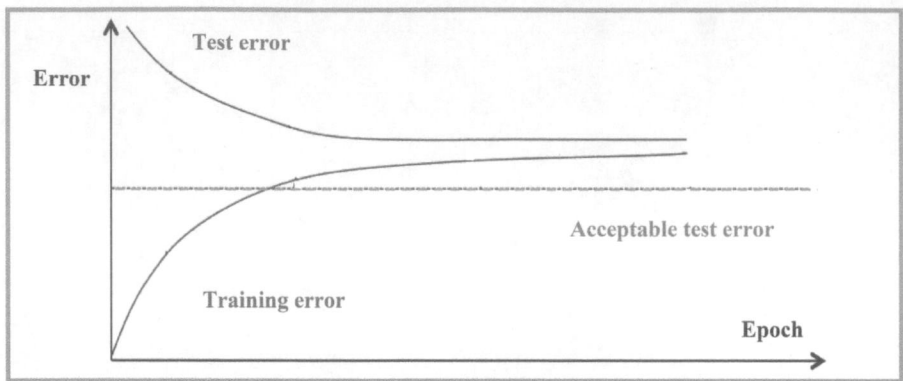

FIGURE 3.10
Testing and training errors.

3.5 Identifying Weaknesses in a Model

Based on the previous discussion, once the bias and variance values have been determined, along with the relationships between these two values, you should take appropriate action based on these values if the variance or bias is high. Consequently, you can ascertain the bias and variance values in your model and then identify the point at which the total error value increases. Figure 3.10 presents some graphs and the threshold, which serve as the criteria for identifying the issue with a poor model and how to improve it.

3.5.1 High Variance

When data points are spread out from the mean value, they exhibit high variance. Overfitting can occur when the variance is high; hence, to prevent this problem, we must determine whether the variance is indeed high. You can identify high variance by observing the following (as depicted in Figure 3.10):

1. Training (or validation) error is lower than the test error,
2. Training (or validation) error is lower than an acceptable test error, and
3. Test error is above the acceptable error.

After identifying high variance, it's crucial to know how to address the issue. Here are some potential solutions:

1. Add more training data,
2. Reduce the model complexity, or
3. Implement bagging.

As previously stated, these are the most commonly used solutions for dealing with high variance. Nonetheless, there is ongoing research in this field to devise more effective strategies.

3.5.2 High Bias

High bias occurs when predictions or classifications are consistently incorrect. This often happens when the data is heavily skewed, leading to flawed conclusions and assumptions. High bias can lead to underfitting. Figure 3.10 indicates that high bias is present when:

1. Training error is higher than the acceptable error.

You can address this issue by:

1. Increasing the number of features or modifying them,
2. Using a more complex model, for example, one with greater depth, and
3. Applying boosting techniques.

3.6 Model Evaluation

Evaluating GANs can be challenging due to the absence of a clear, universally-accepted metric for assessing their performance. However, several techniques have been developed to evaluate GANs, including the IS, the Frechet Inception Distance (FID), Visual inspection, Human evaluation, and the Precision and Recall for Distributions. Each of these methods provides a different perspective on the GAN's performance, helping to ensure a comprehensive evaluation. The following are some commonly used evaluation metrics for GANs.

3.6.1 Inception Score (IS)

The IS is a widely-used metric for evaluating the quality of images generated by GANs. It measures the quality of the generated images based on how well they represent different classes. The score is calculated by computing the softmax probabilities of the generated images using the pre-trained Inception-v3 network. A higher score indicates that the generated images are diverse and have good class representation.

3.6.2 Frechet Inception Distance (FID)

The FID is another commonly-used metric for evaluating GANs. It measures the distance between the distributions of the real and generated images in the feature space, using the pre-trained Inception-v3 network. A lower FID score indicates that the generated images closely resemble the real images in terms of feature representation.

3.6.3 Precision and Recall

Precision and recall are commonly-used evaluation metrics in classification tasks. In the context of GANs, precision refers to the percentage of generated images that the discriminator classifies as real, while recall refers to the percentage of real images that the discriminator correctly identifies as real. Higher precision and recall values indicate that the generated images are of higher quality and more closely resemble the real images.

3.6.4 Visual Inspection

Visual inspection is a subjective evaluation metric in which human evaluators examine the generated images and compare them with real images. This is often used in conjunction with objective evaluation metrics to achieve a more comprehensive assessment of the GAN. In conclusion, it's important to employ a combination of objective and subjective evaluation metrics for a thorough evaluation of the GAN. This can help identify areas of improvement and refine the training process to yield higher quality images.

3.6.5 Human Evaluation

In certain cases, the ultimate evaluation of GANs is performed by humans, who assess the realism of the generated images in comparison to actual ones. Although this approach may be subjective and time-consuming, it offers invaluable insights into the quality of the images produced by the GAN.

3.6.6 The Hold-out Method

This strategy is considered one of the more traditional approaches to model evaluation in the field of machine learning. We divide the initial dataset into training data to instruct the model and test data to evaluate the performance of the trained model. We decide on the models to use by modifying various parameters to improve their performance. The final parameters chosen are referred to as hyperparameters. It is crucial not to reuse the test data because doing so contributes to the problem of overfitting. To prevent this, divide the data into three subsets: the training dataset, the validation dataset, and the test dataset. Using this strategy, you can validate the model multiple times to identify the best hyperparameters before assessing it with the test dataset at the end. One disadvantage of this method is that it splits the original dataset into three parts. To address this issue, techniques like K-fold cross-validation could be employed.

3.6.7 K-fold Cross-validation

K-fold cross-validation is a method used in machine learning for model evaluation. In this technique, the original dataset is divided into **k** equally-sized subsamples, or "folds". The model is trained **k** times, with each fold serving as the testing set once, while the remaining folds serve as training data. The results from these **k** folds are then averaged to obtain a final performance metric for the model. K-fold cross-validation is employed to mitigate the problem of overfitting, where the model performs well on the training data but poorly on the test data. By training and evaluating the model on multiple different subsets of the data, K-fold cross-validation provides a more accurate estimate of how the model will perform on unseen data. The value of **k** is typically set to 5 or 10, but can be adjusted based on the size of the dataset and the computational resources available. This technique is commonly used in deep learning and other machine learning applications to evaluate model performance and to tune hyperparameters. The process works by randomly splitting the training dataset into **K** folds. One fold is reserved for evaluation, while the others are used for training. This procedure is repeated for each of the **K** folds, resulting in **K** models and **K** evaluations upon completion. After determining the optimal values for its hyperparameters, the model can be evaluated by applying it to the test data. This is a "once-only" approach: each sample goes through the training and validation processes

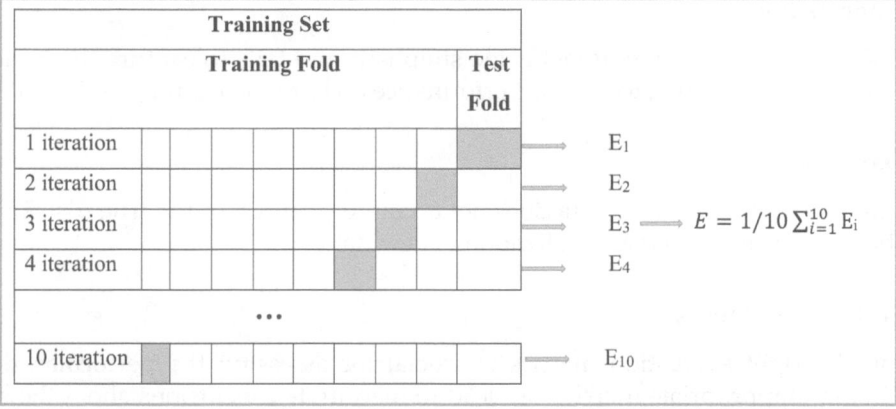

FIGURE 3.11
K-fold example.

just once. There are numerous possibilities for the value of **K**, but ten is often considered optimal as it provides a good balance between bias and variance. Increasing the value of **K** improves generalization but also increases the time required for the method to complete, and the training fold becomes more similar. For large datasets, a lower value for **K**, such as 5, can be used to minimize runtime. Figure 3.11 showcases an example of K-fold cross-validation. The two most common choices are:

1. **K** = 10, which is widely used in data science as it typically yields satisfactory results with low computational cost.
2. **K** = the number of observations in the training data, which trains models on all subsets of all but one observation, validating the remaining observation for each model. This is known as leave-one-out cross-validation (LOOCV), a form of K-fold cross-validation where K equals the number of observations in the training data.

3.7 Model Evaluation Issues

Model evaluation is an important step in the development of machine learning models because it allows us to assess the model's performance and make necessary improvements. Some common issues that can arise during model evaluation include overfitting, where the model performs well on the training data but poorly on unseen data; underfitting, where the model does not capture the underlying patterns in the training data; and bias-variance tradeoff, where a balance has to be struck between the model's complexity and its ability to generalize to new data. Let us look at some of these issues and when they occur.

3.7.1 Overfitting

Overfitting occurs when the model becomes overly complex and starts to fit the noise in the training data, resulting in poor generalization to unseen data.

3.7.2 Underfitting

Underfitting occurs when the model is too simplistic and fails to capture the underlying patterns in the data, leading to subpar performance on both the training and test datasets.

3.7.3 Data Bias

This occurs when the training data does not accurately represent the true distribution of the problem, leading to poor generalization to new data.

3.7.4 Evaluation Metrics

Choosing the right evaluation metrics is crucial for assessing the performance of the model. Using inappropriate metrics can lead to inaccurate conclusions about the model's performance.

3.7.5 Imbalanced Data

This occurs when the classes in the data are not evenly represented, leading to the model's poor performance on the minority class.

3.7.6 Data Leakage

This occurs when information from the test data leaks into the training data, resulting in overly optimistic performance estimates.

3.7.7 Hyperparameter Tuning

Selecting the appropriate hyperparameters for the model is crucial for obtaining optimal performance. However, improper hyperparameter tuning can result in poor performance on new data.

3.8 Model Evaluation Implementation Tips

Here are some implementation tips for model evaluation.

3.8.1 Define Evaluation Metrics

Before training the model, it's important to define evaluation metrics based on the task at hand. For example, if the task is classification, common metrics are accuracy, precision, recall, and the F_1 score. For regression tasks, mean squared error (MSE), root mean squared error (RMSE), and mean absolute error (MAE) are commonly used. Define the metrics beforehand and use them to evaluate the model during training and testing.

3.8.2 Split Data into Train, Validation, and Test Sets

Split the data into three sets – training, validation, and testing sets. The training set is used to train the model, the validation set is used to evaluate the model and adjust hyperparameters during training, and the testing set is used to evaluate the final model's performance after training.

3.8.3 Use Cross-validation

Use K-fold cross-validation to evaluate the model's performance on different subsets of the data. This method ensures that the model does not overfit the training data and provides a more accurate estimate of the model's performance.

3.8.4 Visualize Performance

Visualize the performance of the model during training using graphs and plots. This helps to identify if the model is overfitting, underfitting, or if the training has converged.

3.8.5 Regularization

Use regularization techniques, such as L_1, L_2, or dropout, to prevent overfitting of the model to the training data.

3.8.6 Early Stopping

To avoid overfitting, stop the training process when the model's performance on the validation set starts to deteriorate.

3.8.7 Ensemble Models

Ensemble multiple models to improve performance. This can be done by averaging the predictions of several models or combining them using a weighted average.

3.8.8 Fine-tune Hyperparameters

Experiment with various hyperparameters, such as learning rate, batch size, and epoch count, to find the best combination that optimizes model performance.

Remember, hands-on experience is key when working with model evaluation or any other machine learning models. Therefore, consistently practicing implementation and troubleshooting is crucial for mastering these concepts.

3.9 Lessons Learned

- Learn How to Set Hyperparameters
- Learn How to Optimize the Mode
- Learn Bias/Variance and its Relationship and Effects on Model
- Learn How to Identify Model Weaknesses
- Learn How to Do Model Evaluation
- Learn the Model Evaluation Issues
- Learn the Model Evaluation Implementation Tips

3.10 Problems

3.10.1 Why are hyperparameters important, and how can we achieve the best results?

3.10.2 What is the correct model, what is error, and how can we calculate it?

3.10.3 What exactly is noise, and how can it be calculated?

3.10.4 What is bias, and how is it calculated?

3.10.5 What is variance, and how is it calculated?

3.10.6 What is the relationship between bias and variance, and what condition produces the best results?

3.10.7 What are a model's flaws, and how can you identify them?

3.10.8 What are the three main approaches to model evaluation? Briefly explain each of them.

3.10.9 What is the purpose of model evaluation?

3.10.10 What are some commonly used evaluation metrics for classification models?

3.10.11 How do you interpret a confusion matrix?

3.10.12 How do you calculate precision, recall, and the F1 score?

3.10.13 What is overfitting, and how do you prevent it during model evaluation?

3.10.14 What is cross-validation, and why is it important for model evaluation?

3.10.15 What is the purpose of a ROC curve, and how do you interpret it?

3.10.16 What is the difference between precision and recall?

3.10.17 How do you choose which evaluation metric to use for your model?

3.10.18 What is the difference between validation and test sets in model evaluation?

3.10.19 What is overfitting, and how can it be detected?

3.10.20 What are some common evaluation metrics for binary classification problems?

3.10.21 What are precision and recall, and how are they used in model evaluation?

3.10.22 What is the F1 score, and how is it calculated?

3.10.23 What is cross-validation, and how is it used to evaluate model performance?

3.10.24 How do you evaluate the performance of a regression model?

3.10.25 What are some common evaluation metrics for multi-class classification problems?

3.10.26 What is the confusion matrix, and how is it used to evaluate model performance?

3.10.27 What is the ROC curve, and how is it used to evaluate model performance in binary classification problems?

3.11 Programming Questions

- **Easy**

  3.11.1 How can you evaluate the accuracy of a classification model in scikit-learn?

  3.11.2 What is the distinction between accuracy and precision in model evaluation?

3.11.3 How can you compute the confusion matrix of a classification model in TensorFlow?

3.11.4 Write a Python function to calculate and print the accuracy of a binary classification model.

3.11.5 Implement a function to calculate the precision and recall of a multiclass classification model.

3.11.6 Write a function to calculate the F1 score of a regression model.

3.11.7 Implement a function to calculate the mean squared error (MSE) of a regression model.

3.11.8 Write a Python function to calculate and print the confusion matrix of a classification model.

- **Medium**

  3.11.9 How can you perform K-fold cross-validation in TensorFlow for model evaluation?

  3.11.10 What is AUC-ROC, and how can you use it to evaluate a binary classification model in Keras?

  3.11.11 Implement a function to calculate and print the ROC curve of a binary classification model.

  3.11.12 Write a Python function to calculate and print the precision-recall curve of a binary classification model.

  3.11.13 Implement a function to calculate the Area Under the Curve (AUC) of a ROC curve.

  3.11.14 Write a Python function to perform cross-validation on a classification model using K-fold cross-validation.

  3.11.15 Implement a function to calculate the R-squared score of a regression model.

- **Hard**

  3.11.16 How can you use Bayesian optimization to tune hyperparameters for a machine learning model in scikit-learn?

  3.11.17 In TensorFlow, how can you evaluate the performance of a deep learning model using precision-recall curves?

  3.11.18 How can you perform leave-one-out cross-validation in Keras for model evaluation?

  3.11.19 Write a Python function to perform nested cross-validation on a classification model.

  3.11.20 Implement a function to calculate the Brier score of a binary classification model.

  3.11.21 Write a function to calculate and plot the learning curve of a classification or regression model.

  3.11.22 Implement a function to calculate the average precision (AP) of a binary classification model.

  3.11.23 Write a Python function to perform hyperparameter tuning on a classification or regression model using grid search.

4

TensorFlow and Keras Fundamentals

This chapter covers TensorFlow and Keras Fundamentals approaches, as well as the following:

- How Does TensorFlow Work?
- Tensors
- TensorFlow
- Indexing and Slicing
- Building an NN Using TensorFlow
- Building a CNN Using TensorFlow
- Keras
- TensorFlow Issues
- TensorFlow Implementation Tips
- Keras Issues
- Keras Implementation Tips

4.1 Preface

TensorFlow, a comprehensive open-source machine learning platform, was developed internally by the Google Brain team and later released under the Apache license in 2015. Over time, TensorFlow has expanded to include many application programming interfaces (APIs) and modules, specifically designed for tasks, such as data transformation, feature engineering, model building, serving, and more. Keras, on the other hand, is a high-level, open-source deep learning API developed by François Chollet, an AI researcher. It aims to simplify the syntax and coding style for those who wish to build deep learning models, without the need to delve into the complexities of low-level computations. Keras is compatible with several machine learning libraries, including TensorFlow, Theano, and Microsoft Cognitive Toolkit (CNTK). With the introduction of TensorFlow 2.0 in 2019, Keras was officially incorporated as TensorFlow's primary API, now referred to as tf.keras, for all future releases. Consequently, TensorFlow has closely integrated tf.keras with several other critical modules. This chapter provides an overview of these two essential platforms, TensorFlow and Keras, equipping readers with the necessary knowledge to follow the coding examples in this book. Figure 4.1 compares the functionalities and features of TensorFlow and Keras.

DOI: 10.1201/9781003281344-4

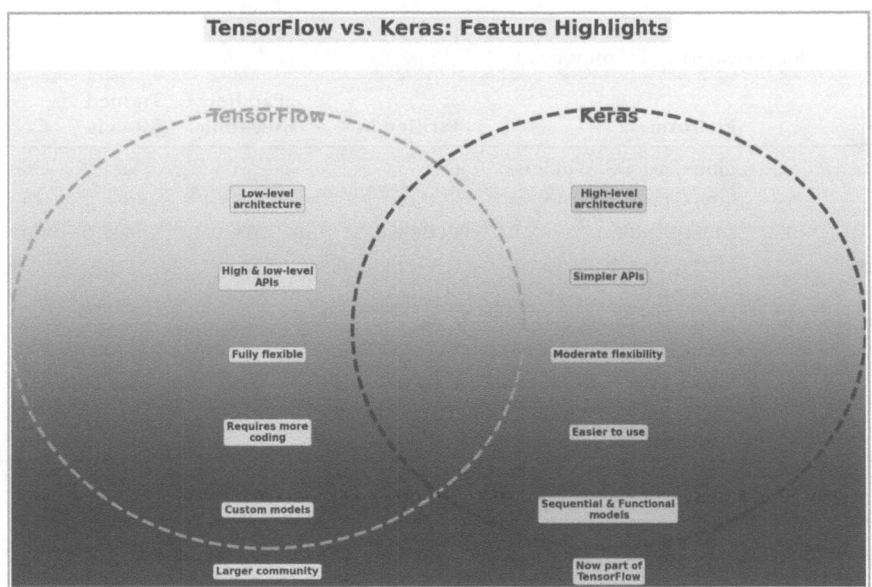

FIGURE 4.1
TensorFlow vs. Keras.

4.2 How Does TensorFlow Work?

TensorFlow is a robust framework widely utilized for numerical computation, particularly in the development and implementation of machine learning algorithms and deep neural networks. It's favored by academics, programmers, and data scientists alike for its versatility and power. As a machine learning library, TensorFlow is platform-agnostic and can operate on a multitude of operating systems, including Windows, MacOS, and Linux. Moreover, it can be run on various platforms, ranging from desktop computers and mobile devices (iOS or Android) to cloud services like Amazon Web Services (AWS) and Google Cloud. Comparisons between TensorFlow and other frameworks are outlined in Table 4.1, showcasing both its similarities and distinctions. TensorFlow is currently available in two versions: TensorFlow 1 and TensorFlow 2. It visualizes computations as a dataflow graph, where data within each graph are defined by a sequence of operations, depicted as nodes and edges. These operations could range from simple arithmetic functions, like addition, to more complex machine learning processes.

TensorFlow is rooted in the concept of graph computation. It operates with both the central processing unit (CPU) and the graphics processing unit (GPU) of various devices. This flexibility allows TensorFlow to leverage the computational power of different hardware architectures. TensorFlow provides a wide range of libraries that integrate with various APIs, making them freely accessible to all developers. This accessibility contributes to TensorFlow's popularity on platforms like GitHub. Owing to its capabilities and versatility, TensorFlow has emerged as one of the most intriguing platforms for developing deep learning algorithms. It enables developers to build complex models and perform advanced

TABLE 4.1

Most Popular Deep Learning Frameworks

Library	Platform	Written in	Parallel Execution	Trained Models	CNN	RNN
Torch	Linux, macOS, Windows	Lua	Yes	Yes	Yes	Yes
Kears	Linux, macOS, Windows	Python	Yes	Yes	Yes	Yes
Theano	Cross-platform	Python	Yes	Yes	Yes	Yes
TensorFlow	Linux, macOS, Windows, Android	C++, Python, CUDA	Yes	Yes	Yes	Yes
Microsoft Cognitive Toolkit	Linux, Windows, and macOS with Docker	C++	Yes	Yes	Yes	Yes
Caffe	Linux, macOS, Windows	C++	Yes	Yes	Yes	Yes
MXNet	Linux, macOS, Windows, Android, ios, JavaScript	C++	Yes	Yes	Yes	Yes

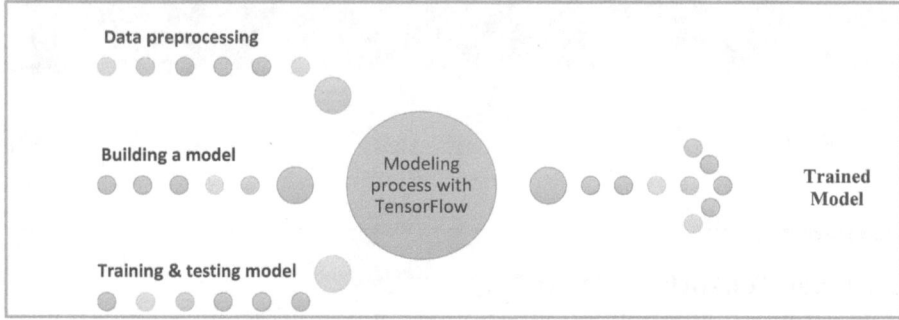

FIGURE 4.2
Model building steps using TensorFlow.

computations with ease. The modeling process in TensorFlow typically involves three basic steps: defining a computational graph, training the model using data, and using the trained model to make predictions or perform other tasks. These steps ensure a systematic approach to model development and deployment. Figure 4.2, as mentioned, showcases the three basic steps involved in the modeling process with TensorFlow, providing a visual representation of the workflow.

4.3 Tensors

A tensor, which serves as the foundation of TensorFlow, is a vector or an n-dimensional matrix used to represent data. Tensors, or multidimensional data, proceed to the subsequent node after undergoing a series of operations. The leaf in each graph houses the actual tensor. There are two types of tensors:

1. Constant
2. Variable

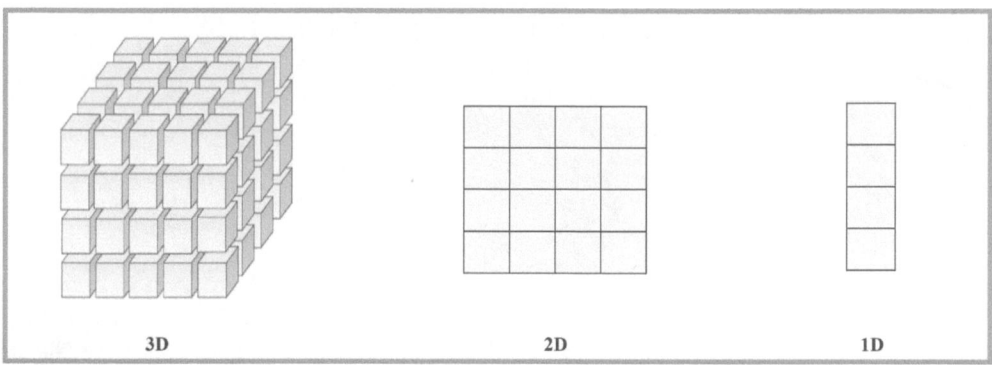

FIGURE 4.3
Three examples for three tensors dimensions.

A tensor possesses several characteristics, including:

- **Dimension:** This signifies the structure of a tensor. Figure 4.3 presents three instances of dimensions.
- **Rank:** This is the number of directions in the tensor. It is zero for a scalar number (based on the dimensions). For instance, in Figure 4.3, the rank for 1^D is 1; for 2^D, the rank is 2; for 3^D, the rank is 3; and so forth.
- **Shape:** This is the number of values in each dimension. For example, the shapes of the tensors in Figure 4.3 are: 3^D: (4,5,4), 2^D: (4,4), 1^D: 4
- **Size:** This is the total number of items in the tensor, and it equals the product of the shape vector. For instance, in Figure 4.3: 3^D: $4 \times 5 \times 4 = 80$, 2^D: $4 \times 4 = 16$, and 1^D: 4

Moreover, a tensor has three principal properties:

1. A unique label (name)
2. Dimension (shape)
3. Data type (dtype)

In TensorFlow, we can create three types of tensors:

1. "**tf.Variable**": This defines the variable.
2. "**tf.constant**": This determines the constant.
3. "**tf.SparseTensor**": This defines the sparse tensor.

TensorFlow comprises nodes and edges, where the edges transfer scalar values from the nodes at the current level to the nodes at the next level. Consider the following example:

$$K = \frac{(3 \times x + y)}{y + 7}$$

Figure 4.4 illustrates the computational graph for **K = m/n**.

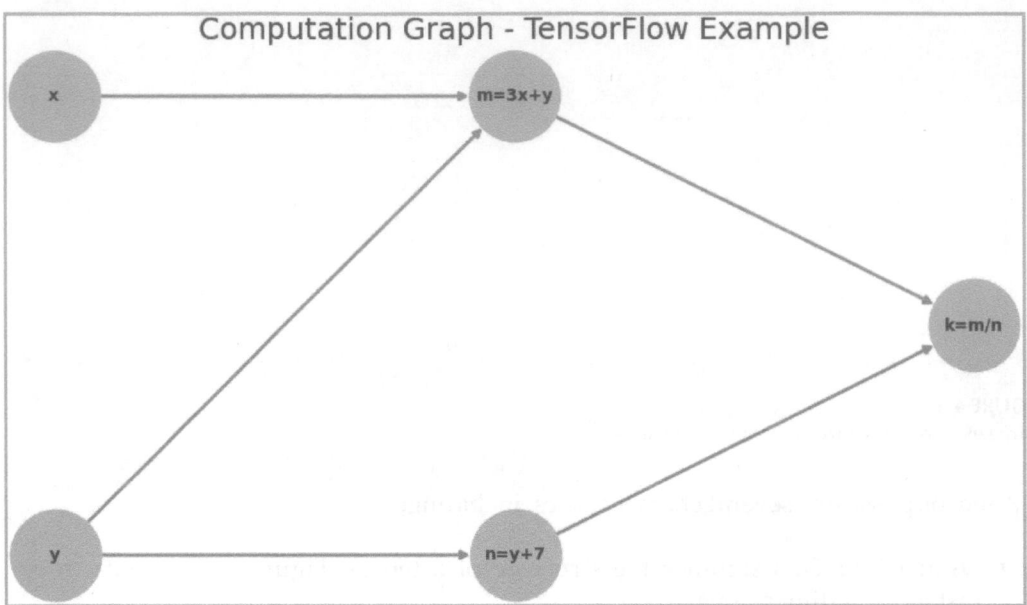

FIGURE 4.4
An example of a computation graph.

In the given example, the value "x" at the lowest leaf level is multiplied by 3, and the value "y" is multiplied by 1. The results are added together in a new node that represents the level above, and the values currently stored in the node are assigned to "m". Moreover, the value of "n" will be determined by adding 7 to another node's y-value and assigning that value. A new operation will be used to move the values of the newly created nodes to the nodes on the next level. The first step in TensorFlow is defining a tensor. Now, let's understand this with some practical examples.

1. Consider the creation of a 0^D tensor (scalar). In the following Python code, we first import the TensorFlow library and then create a constant tensor named "r0_tensor" using the "tf.constant()" function with a value of 7. The "tf.constant()" function creates an immutable tensor that cannot be changed once it's defined. Finally, the code prints the tensor "r0_tensor".

   Example:
   ```
   import tensorflow as tf
   # Define a 0D tensor (scalar)
   r0_tensor = tf.constant(7)
   # Print the tensor
   print(r0_tensor)
   ```

   Output:
   "Const:0" is the name of the tensor. In TensorFlow, every tensor and operation gets assigned a name automatically. Here, "Const" signifies that this tensor was created as a constant, and "0" is the unique identifier for this tensor. "shape=()" suggests that the tensor is a scalar, as the shape is an empty tuple, meaning it has

no dimensions. "dtype=int32" indicates that the data type of the values in the tensor is a 32-bit integer.

```
Tensor("Const:0", shape=(), dtype=int32)
```

2. Let's create a float 1^D tensor. This code imports the TensorFlow library and creates a constant tensor, r_1_tensor, using the tf.constant() function with values [1.0, 2.0, 3.0]. The tf.constant() function creates an immutable tensor that cannot be changed once it's defined. Finally, the code prints the tensor r_1_tensor.

Example:
```
import tensorflow as tf
r1_tensor = tf.constant([1.0, 2.0, 3.0])
print(r1_tensor)
```

Output:
This output displays the information about the tensor, including the shape (3,), which indicates a 1-dimensional tensor with three elements, the data type float32, and the values [1., 2., 3.] in a NumPy array.

```
<tf.Tensor: shape=(3,), dtype=float32, numpy=array([1., 2., 3.],
dtype=float32)>
```

3. Let's create a 2^D tensor. This code imports the TensorFlow library and creates a constant tensor, rank_2_tensor, using the tf.constant() function. The tensor has a shape of (3, 2), indicating three rows and two columns, and the data type is set to float16. The tf.float16 data type represents half-precision floating-point numbers. Finally, the code prints the tensor rank_2_tensor.

Example:
```
import tensorflow as tf
rank_2_tensor = tf.constant([[1, 2], [3, 4], [5, 6]], dtype=tf.float16)
print(rank_2_tensor)
```

Output:
This output displays the information about the tensor, including the tensor's values, the shape (3, 2), indicating three rows and two columns, and the data type float16.

```
tf.Tensor([[1. 2.] [3. 4.] [5. 6.]], shape=(3, 2), dtype=float16)
```

4. Let's create a 3^D tensor. This code imports the TensorFlow library and creates a constant tensor, r3_tensor, using the tf.constant() function. The tensor has a shape of (3, 2, 5), indicating three matrices, each with two rows and five columns. The data type is inferred as int32 based on the provided values. Finally, the code prints the tensor r3_tensor.

Example:
```
import tensorflow as tf
r3_tensor = tf.constant([[[1, 2, 3, 4, 5], [6, 7, 8, 9, 10]],
[[11, 12, 13, 14, 15], [16, 17, 18, 19, 20]], [[21, 22, 23, 24, 25],
[26, 27, 28, 29, 30]]])
print(r3_tensor)
```

Output:
This output displays the information about the tensor, including the tensor's values, the shape (3, 2, 5), indicating three matrices, each with two rows and five columns, and the data type int32.

```
tf.Tensor([[[ 1  2  3  4  5]  [ 6  7  8  9 10]] [[11 12 13 14 15]
[16 17 18 19 20]] [[21 22 23 24 25]  [26 27 28 29 30]]], shape=(3,
2, 5), dtype=int32)
```

5. Let's find the shape, size, and dimension of the matrix using TensorFlow. This code imports the TensorFlow library and creates a tensor, r3D_tensor, using the tf.zeros() function with a shape of (4, 5, 4), indicating a 3^D tensor with four matrices, each with five rows and four columns. The elements of the tensor are initialized to zero. The code then prints various properties and information about the tensor. The dtype property indicates the data type of the elements in the tensor, which in this case is inferred as the default float32. The ndim property shows the number of dimensions of the tensor, which is three. The shape property provides the shape of the tensor as a tuple, (4, 5, 4), indicating four matrices, each with five rows and four columns. The elements along specific axes can be accessed using indexing, and the code demonstrates accessing the elements along the first axis (axis 0) and the last axis (axis −1). Finally, the tf.size() function is used to calculate the total number of elements in the tensor, which is 80, and this value is printed.

Example:
```
import tensorflow as tf
r3D_tensor = tf.zeros([4, 5, 4])
print("Type of every element:", r3D_tensor.dtype)
print("Number of dimensions:", r3D_tensor.ndim)
print("Shape of tensor:", r3D_tensor.shape)
print("Elements along axis 0 of tensor:", r3D_tensor.shape[0])
print("Elements along the last axis of tensor:", r3D_tensor.
shape[-1])
print("Total number of elements (4*5*4):", tf.size(r3D_tensor).
numpy())
```

Output:
This output provides information about the tensor's data type, number of dimensions, shape, specific elements along axes, and the total number of elements in the tensor.

```
Type of every element: <dtype: 'float32'>
Number of dimensions: 3
Shape of tensor: (4, 5, 4)
Elements along axis 0 of tensor: 4
Elements along the last axis of tensor: 4
Total number of elements (4*5*4): 80
```

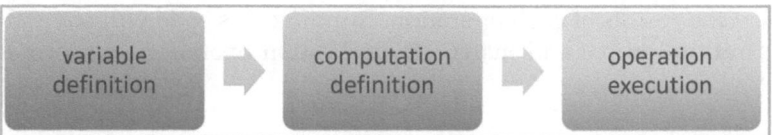

FIGURE 4.5
Steps in using TensorFlow.

4.4 TensorFlow

There are three main steps when you are using TensorFlow. Figure 4.5 shows these three steps.

Let's learn them better with some examples.

4.4.1 Define the Variable

This code imports the TensorFlow library and creates two tensors, X_1 and X_2, using the tf.constant() function. The first tensor, X_1, contains the values [1, 3, 5], while the second tensor, X_2, contains the values [2, 4, 6]. Both tensors are created as constant tensors, meaning their values cannot be changed once initialized. These tensors can be used for various operations in TensorFlow, such as mathematical computations, neural network training, or other data processing tasks.

Example:
```
import tensorflow as tf
X1 = tf.constant([1, 3, 5])
X2 = tf.constant([2, 4, 6])
```

4.4.2 Define the Computation

In this code, the tf.multiply() function is used to perform element-wise multiplication between X_1 and X_2. The resulting tensor, "multiply", will have the same shape as the input tensors and will contain the element-wise product of the corresponding elements in X_1 and X_2.

Example:
```
import tensorflow as tf
X1 = tf.constant([1, 3, 5])
X2 = tf.constant([2, 4, 6])
multiply = tf.multiply(X1, X2)
```

4.4.3 Operation Execution and Print Results

In this code, the tf.add() function is used to perform element-wise addition between tensors "a" and "b", resulting in the "addition" tensor. The tf.multiply() function performs element-wise multiplication between tensors "a" and "b", resulting in the "multiplication" tensor. Finally, the tf.matmul() function performs matrix multiplication between tensors "a" and "b", resulting in the "matrix_multiplication" tensor. The print() statements are used to display the results of each operation. Running this code will show the outputs of the addition, multiplication, and matrix multiplication operations performed on tensors "a" and "b".

Example:
```
import tensorflow as tf
a = tf.constant([[2, 5], [1, 4]])
b = tf.constant([[1, 1], [1, 1]])
addition = tf.add(a, b)
multiplication = tf.multiply(a, b)
matrix_multiplication = tf.matmul(a, b)
print(addition, "\n")
print(multiplication, "\n")
print(matrix_multiplication, "\n")
```

Output:
```
tf.Tensor([[3 6] [2 5]], shape=(2, 2), dtype=int32)
tf.Tensor([[2 5] [1 4]], shape=(2, 2), dtype=int32)
tf.Tensor([[7 7] [5 5]], shape=(2, 2), dtype=int32)
```

Example:
In the next code, the tf.matmul() function is used to perform matrix multiplication between tensors "a" and "x". The result is added to the variable "b" using the + operator. The print() statement then displays the value of the resulting tensor "y" using the numpy() method. Running this code will output the numerical values of the tensor "y", which is the result of the matrix multiplication and addition operations.

```
import tensorflow as tf
a = tf.constant([[12, 10], [2., 10.]])
x = tf.constant([[1., 0.], [0., 1.]])
b = tf.Variable(2.)
y = tf.matmul(a, x) + b
print(y.numpy())
```

Output:
```
[[14. 12.]  [4. 12.]]
```

4.5 Indexing and Slicing

4.5.1 Indexing

Indexing is supported in TensorFlow like [i][j] and comma and ":". For example, a 2^D image with size 28 × 28 is like this:[28,28] as follows. In this code, the "tf.random.normal()" function is used to create a random tensor "x" with a shape of (28, 28). The values in the tensor are drawn from a normal distribution. Please note that this code snippet only creates the random tensor "x".

```
import tensorflow as tf
x = tf.random.normal([28, 28])
```

Here, "[28, 28]" is the shape of the tensor, indicating a 2^D tensor (or a matrix) with 28 rows and 28 columns. This could represent a grayscale image with a resolution of 28×28 pixels, where each element in the tensor corresponds to the pixel intensity at a specific location in the image. After the tensor "x" is created, you can index into it using either bracket notation like "x[i][j]" or comma notation like "x[i, j]". The colon ":" can be used to represent a slice of the tensor along a specific dimension. For instance, "x[i,:] " would give you the "i"-th row of the tensor, and "x[:, j]" would give you the "j"-th column.

4.5.2 Slicing

This is the format for slicing **start: end: step**, that starts and ends are the start and end position, and the step is the sampling step size.

4.6 Building an NN Using TensorFlow

Here is an example of the Fashion-MNIST dataset by Zalando (see Figure 4.6). It contains 70,000 images in 10 different categories, each image being a 28×28 pixel representation of a clothing item. The steps to create a neural network structure are as follows:

4.6.1 Import the Data

In the first step, we import the necessary libraries and the dataset from scikit-learn. The "__future__" import statement is used to enable certain features that are not default in older versions of Python. The numpy and TensorFlow libraries are then imported, and the Keras module from the TensorFlow package is imported as well. Finally, the MinMaxScaler class from the sklearn.preprocessing module is imported.

```
from __future__ import absolute_import, division, print_function,
unicode_literals
import numpy as np
import tensorflow as tf
from tensorflow import keras
from sklearn.preprocessing import MinMaxScaler
```

4.6.2 Loading and Normalizing the Data

Now, load the dataset and normalize the data for better training. The normalization of data facilitates more efficient computation and reduces computational costs. It can also increase the accuracy of the results. In this code, the train_labels and test_labels arrays are

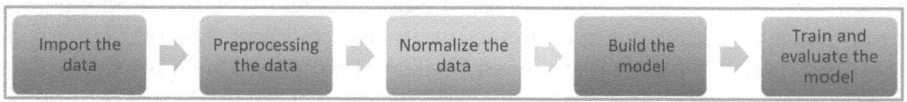

FIGURE 4.6
Steps in building a NN model using TensorFlow.

cast to int using the astype method. The batch_size is set to the length of the train_images array. Then, a MinMaxScaler object, named scaler, is created to scale the image data. The fit_transform method of the scaler is applied to both train_images and test_images arrays to scale the pixel values between 0 and 1. The print statements display the shapes of the datasets and the number of labels.

```
from sklearn.preprocessing import MinMaxScaler
import numpy as np
from tensorflow import keras
(train_images, train_labels), (test_images, test_labels) = keras.
datasets.fashion_mnist.load_data()

# Reshape the data to 2D (from 3D) to use MinMaxScaler
train_images = train_images.reshape(-1, 1)
test_images = test_images.reshape(-1, 1)
train_labels = train_labels.astype(int)
test_labels = test_labels.astype(int)
scaler = MinMaxScaler()
train_images = scaler.fit_transform(train_images.astype(np.float64))

# Use transform, not fit_transform
test_images = scaler.transform(test_images.astype(np.float64))

# Reshape the data back to 3D after scaling
train_images = train_images.reshape(-1, 28, 28)
test_images = test_images.reshape(-1, 28, 28)
print('Training Images Dataset Shape: {}'.format(train_images.shape))
print('No. of Training Images Dataset Labels: {}'.
format(len(train_labels)))
print('Test Images Dataset Shape: {}'.format(test_images.shape))
print('No. of Test Images Dataset Labels: {}'.format(len(test_labels)))
```

Output:
```
Training Images Dataset Shape: (60000, 28, 28)
No. of Training Images Dataset Labels: 60000
Test Images Dataset Shape: (10000, 28, 28)
No. of Test Images Dataset Labels: 10000
```

4.6.3 Build the Model

The model can be defined by specifying its parameters and hyperparameters. Examples of these include the activation function, data shape, and the number of layers. In this case, the data shape is set to 28 × 28, and the hidden and output activation functions are ReLU and softmax, respectively. This code defines the input_data_shape variable as the shape of the input data. The hidden_activation_function variable is set to "relu", specifying the activation function for the hidden layer. The output_activation_function variable is set to "softmax", indicating the activation function for the output layer. The nn_model is created as a sequential model, and layers are added using the add method. The first layer is a flatten layer that converts the 2^D input shape into a 1^D array. The second layer is a dense layer with 32 units, using the specified hidden_activation_function. The third layer is another dense layer with 10 units, representing the number of classes in the output, and uses the specified output_activation_function. Finally, the summary method is called on the nn_model to display the model's details, including the layer names, output shapes, and the number of parameters.

```
input_data_shape = (28, 28)
hidden_activation_function = 'relu'
output_activation_function = 'softmax'
nn_model = ks.models.Sequential()
nn_model.add(ks.layers.Flatten(input_shape=input_data_shape,
name='Input_layer'))
nn_model.add(ks.layers.Dense(32, activation=hidden_activation_function,
name='Hidden_layer'))
nn_model.add(ks.layers.Dense(10, activation=output_activation_function,
name='Output_layer'))
nn_model.summary()
```

This code defines a simple neural network with one hidden layer of 32 units using a ReLU activation function, and an output layer of 10 units using a softmax activation function. The model summary will provide details about each layer, including the number of parameters.

Output:
```
Layer (type)                    Output Shape              Param #
=================================================================
Input_layer (Flatten)           (None, 784)               0
Hidden_layer (Dense)            (None, 64)                50240
Output_layer (Dense)            (None, 10)                650
=================================================================
Total params: 50,890
Trainable params: 50,890
Non-trainable params: 0
```

4.6.4 Train and Evaluate the Model

In the next step, you'll need to train and evaluate the model. Here, the optimizer used is ADAM, although other optimizers can also be used.

4.6.4.1 Training

First, define the model and train it using the training data. In this code, the optimizer variable is set to "adam", a popular optimization algorithm. The loss_function variable is set to "sparse_categorical_crossentropy", which is suitable for multi-class classification problems with integer labels. The metrics variable is a list containing "accuracy" as the only evaluation metric. The compile method is then called on the nn_model to configure the model with the specified optimizer, loss function, and metrics. Finally, the fit method is used to train the model with the training images (train_images) and corresponding labels (train_labels). The epochs parameter is set to 40, indicating that the entire training dataset should be iterated through 40 times during training.

```
# Define the optimizer to be used during training.
optimizer = 'adam'
```

```
# Define the loss function suitable for a multi-class classification
loss_function = 'sparse_categorical_crossentropy'  problem.

# Define the metric(s) to be used for model evaluation.
metrics = ['accuracy']

# Configure the model for training.
nn_model.compile(optimizer=optimizer, loss=loss_function,
metrics=metrics)

# Train the model using the training images and labels over 40 epochs.
nn_model.fit(train_images, train_labels, epochs=40)
```

In this code, the model is trained using the ADAM optimizer, the sparse categorical cross-entropy loss function, and accuracy as the evaluation metric. The training is performed over 40 epochs, which means the entire dataset will be passed forward and backward through the neural network 40 times.

Output:
```
....
1875/1875 [==============================] - 2s 967us/step - loss: 0.1831 -
accuracy: 0.9317
Epoch 19/20
1875/1875 [==============================] - 2s 1ms/step - loss: 0.1779 -
accuracy: 0.9339
Epoch 20/20
1875/1875 [==============================] - 2s 978us/step - loss: 0.1765 -
accuracy: 0.9345
...
```

4.6.4.2 Evaluation

Evaluate the model using a subset of the original data as evaluation data. This provides us with an estimate of the model's performance before testing it with real-world problems. In this code, the "evaluate" method is called on the "nn_model" to assess the model's performance on the training data. The "train_images" and "train_labels" are passed as input to calculate the loss and accuracy. The returned values "train_loss" and "train_accuracy" represent the loss and accuracy of the model on the training data, respectively. The print statement displays the training data accuracy using the formatted string "Training Data Accuracy: {}". The "round" function is used to round the float value of "train_accuracy" to two decimal places.

```
# Evaluate the model's performance on the training data.
train_loss, train_accuracy = nn_model.evaluate(train_images,
train_labels)
# Print the training data accuracy, rounded to two decimal places.
print('Training Data Accuracy: {}'.format(round(float(train_accuracy), 2)))
```

4.6.4.3 Testing

Next, test the model using the testing data. In this code, the "evaluate" method is called on the "nn_model" to assess the model's performance on the test data. The "test_images" and

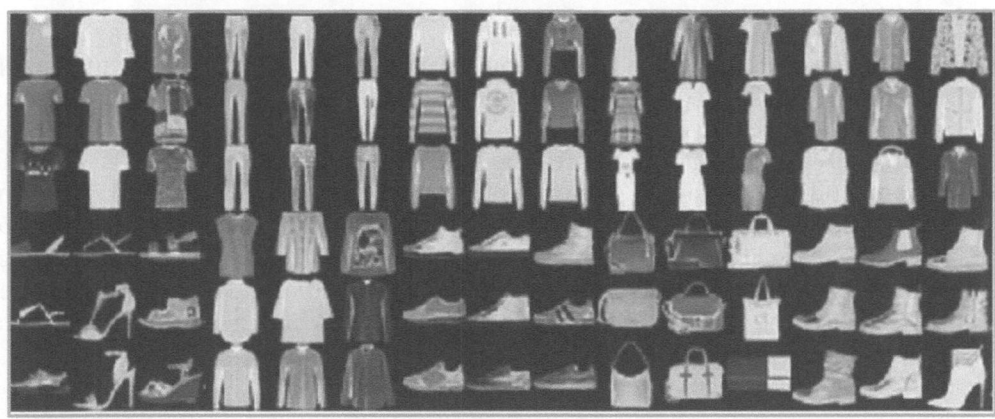

FIGURE 4.7
Fashion-MNIST data.

"test_labels" are passed as input to calculate the loss and accuracy. The returned values "test_loss" and "test_accuracy" represent the loss and accuracy of the model on the test data, respectively. The print statement displays the test data accuracy using the formatted string "Test Data Accuracy: {}". The "round" function is used to round the float value of "test_accuracy" to two decimal places.

```
# Evaluate the model's performance on the test data.
test_loss, test_accuracy = nn_model.evaluate(test_images, test_labels)

# Print the test data accuracy, rounded to two decimal places.
print('Test Data Accuracy: {}'.format(round(float(test_accuracy), 2)))
```

The Fashion-MNIST dataset values are displayed in Figure 4.7. The output here is 88 percent, which may vary depending on the specific approaches employed.

4.7 Building a CNN Using TensorFlow

Here are the steps for creating a Convolutional Neural Networks (CNN) using TensorFlow. Upload the data in the first step. We are using the dataset in the previous example (Fashion-MNIST). Figure 4.8 depicts the sequential steps involved in implementing a Convolutional Neural Network (CNN) using TensorFlow.

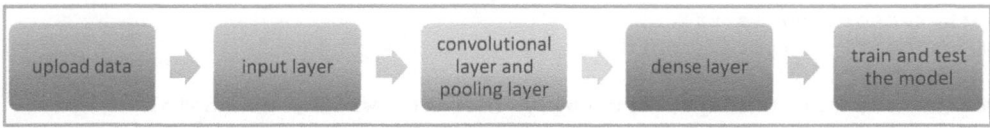

FIGURE 4.8
Steps in CNN using TensorFlow.

4.7.1 Input Layer

You should define the parameters of the input layer, such as the activation function and data shape, before you start coding. In this code, "input_data_shape" represents the shape of the input data, which is set to (28,28) for an image with dimensions of 28 × 28 pixels. "hidden_activation_function" represents the activation function to be used in the hidden layers, and in this case, it's set to "relu", which stands for Rectified Linear Unit. "output_activation_function" represents the activation function to be used in the output layer, and in this case, it's set to "softmax", which is commonly used for multi-class classification problems. The "dnn_model" is created as a sequential model using "ks.models. Sequential()". However, since no layers have been added to the model yet, the "summary()" function will display an empty model summary.

```
# Set the input data shape for an image of 28x28 pixels.
input_data_shape = (28, 28)

# Set the activation function for the hidden layers to ReLU.
hidden_activation_function = 'relu'

# Set the activation function for the output layer to softmax.
output_activation_function = 'softmax'

# Create a new sequential model.
dnn_model = ks.models.Sequential()

# Display the summary of the model, which will be empty since no layers
have been added yet.
dnn_model.summary()
```

This code defines the shape of the input data and the activation functions for the hidden and output layers. It then creates a new sequential model. However, since no layers have been added yet, the summary of the model will be empty.

4.7.2 Convolutional and Pooling Layers and Dense Layer

In this example, two sets of convolutional and pooling layers are used, followed by a dense layer and the output layer. The number of filters, kernel size, and other parameters might need to be adjusted based on your specific task and the complexity of the input data. The number of neurons in the output layer (in this case, 10) should match the number of classes in your classification problem. Here's the corresponding code with line-by-line explanations:

```
import tensorflow as tf
from tensorflow.keras import layers

# Define the input shape, typically (height, width, channels)
input_shape = (28, 28, 1)
```

```python
# Create a Sequential model
model = tf.keras.models.Sequential()

# Add the first convolutional layer
model.add(layers.Conv2D(32, (3, 3), activation='relu', input_shape=input_
shape, name='Conv_layer_1'))

# Add a max pooling layer
model.add(layers.MaxPooling2D((2, 2), name='MaxPool_layer_1'))

# Add the second convolutional layer
model.add(layers.Conv2D(64, (3, 3), activation='relu',
name='Conv_layer_2'))

# Add a max pooling layer
model.add(layers.MaxPooling2D((2, 2), name='MaxPool_layer_2'))

# Flatten the tensor output by the convolutional layers
model.add(layers.Flatten(name='Flatten_layer'))

# Add a dense layer
model.add(layers.Dense(64, activation='relu', name='Dense_layer'))

# Add the output layer
model.add(layers.Dense(10, activation='softmax', name='Output_layer'))

# Print the model summary
model.summary()

Model: "sequential"
```

Layer (type)	Output Shape	Param #
Conv_layer_1 (Conv2D)	(None, 26, 26, 32)	320
MaxPool_layer_1 (MaxPooling2	(None, 13, 13, 32)	0
Conv_layer_2 (Conv2D)	(None, 11, 11, 64)	18496
MaxPool_layer_2 (MaxPooling2	(None, 5, 5, 64)	0
Flatten_layer (Flatten)	(None, 1600)	0
Dense_layer (Dense)	(None, 64)	102464
Output_layer (Dense)	(None, 10)	650

```
Total params: 121,930
Trainable params: 121,930
Non-trainable params: 0
```

4.7.3 Train the Model

The model is now compiled and ready to be trained. The process of training the model involves providing it with the training data and allowing it to adjust its internal parameters to better predict the classes of the training data.

```
# Defining training parameters
batch_size = 128
epochs = 10

# Compile the model
model.compile(optimizer='adam', loss='sparse_categorical_crossentropy',
metrics=['accuracy'])

# Train the model
history = model.fit(train_data, train_labels, batch_size=batch_size,
epochs=epochs, validation_split=0.2)
```

In the code above:

- "batch_size" is the number of training examples utilized in one iteration.
- "epochs" refers to the number of times the learning algorithm will work through the entire training dataset.
- "optimizer='adam'" means that we're using the Adam optimization algorithm.
- "loss='sparse_categorical_crossentropy'" sets the loss function. For multiclass classification problems like this, "sparse_categorical_crossentropy" is commonly used.
- "metrics=['accuracy']" means we're evaluating the model performance based on accuracy.
- "model.fit()" is the function that trains the model. The training data and labels are the inputs ("train_data", "train_labels"). The "validation_split=0.2" means that 20% of the training data is used as validation data.

4.7.4 Test the Model

After the model is trained, we evaluate it using the testing dataset.

```
# Evaluate the model
test_loss, test_acc = model.evaluate(test_data, test_labels, verbose=2)

# Print the test accuracy
print('\nTest accuracy:', test_acc)
```

In the testing code:

- "model.evaluate()" is the function used to evaluate the model. The testing data and labels are the inputs ("test_data", "test_labels").
- The accuracy of the model based on the testing data is printed. The higher the accuracy, the better the model is at making predictions for unseen data.

4.8 Keras

Keras is a Python library that provides a convenient and user-friendly platform for developing deep learning models. It works on top of machine learning frameworks, such as TensorFlow. Examples of models that can be created with ease using Keras include CNN and Recurrent Neural Networks (RNN). While TensorFlow offers both low-level and high-level APIs, Keras only provides high-level APIs, making it more straightforward to use for common tasks. Notably, Keras also aids in reducing computation costs. This guide will outline some fundamental concepts and usage of Keras, supplemented with examples. For more comprehensive information and tutorials, you may wish to visit the official Keras website (https://keras.io/). To use Keras effectively, the following prerequisites are needed:

1. Python 3.5 or higher
2. SciPy, complemented with NumPy
3. TensorFlow
4. A compatible operating system: Windows, Linux, or Mac are all suitable

4.8.1 Setup and Install

To set up and install Keras, you can follow these steps:

1. Ensure that you have Python installed on your system. Keras is compatible with Python 3.6 or higher.
2. Install Keras using pip, which is a package installer for Python. You can do this by opening your command prompt or terminal and running the command "pip install keras". This command will download and install the latest version of Keras along with its dependencies, such as TensorFlow or Theano.
3. If you prefer a specific backend, you can specify it during the installation. Keras defaults to TensorFlow as the backend if none is specified.
4. Once the installation is complete, verify the installation by importing Keras in a Python script or interactive shell. You can import the Keras module and look for any error messages. If no errors occur, then Keras has been successfully installed.
5. Depending on your requirements, you may also need to install specific libraries or frameworks, such as TensorFlow or PyTorch. Keras can use these as backends for more advanced operations.

Overall, setting up and installing Keras is a straightforward process, enabling you to leverage the powerful deep learning capabilities it offers for your projects.

4.8.1.1 Create a Virtual Environment

Creating a virtual environment helps you manage different installed packages for various projects separately. For instance, you can set one up with Python 3. This command will generate a new virtual environment called "kerasenv" in the current directory, utilizing

Python 3. Please ensure that Python 3 is installed on your system before running this command.

```
python3 -m venv kerasenv
```

- **"python3"**: This is the command to start the Python 3 interpreter. It will execute the following command.
- **"-m"**: This option allows the subsequent module, venv, to be executed as a script. It effectively treats the specified module as a standalone program.
- **"venv"**: This is the module that Python provides for creating virtual environments. It is included in the standard library in Python 3.3 and later.
- **"kerasenv"**: This is the name of the virtual environment that you're creating. It will be a directory in your current location that contains the Python executable files and a copy of the pip library, which you can use to install other packages within this virtual environment.

4.8.1.2 Activate the Environment

After creating the virtual environment, you should activate it if you like to use it.

4.8.1.2.1 *Linux/Mac*

To activate the virtual environment on Linux/Mac, use the following commands:

```
cd kerasenv
source bin/activate
```

These commands will activate the virtual environment. You should then see "(kerasenv)" in your terminal prompt. This indicates that the virtual environment is active.

- **cd kerasenv:** This command changes your current directory to the "kerasenv" directory, which is the virtual environment you created.
- **Source bin/activate:** The source command reads and executes commands from the file specified as its argument in the current shell environment. Here, it activates the Python virtual environment.

```
source kerasenv/bin/activate
```

4.8.1.2.2 *Windows*

To activate the virtual environment on Windows, use the following command. Make sure to replace "kerasenv" with the actual name of your virtual environment if it's different. After running this command, the virtual environment will be activated, and you should see the environment name in the command prompt.

```
.\kerasenv\Scripts\activate
```

This command navigates to the Scripts folder inside your virtual environment (here, "kerasenv") and runs the activate script, which activates the virtual environment. You'll know it's activated because the name of the virtual environment (in this case, "kerasenv") will appear at the start of the command prompt line.

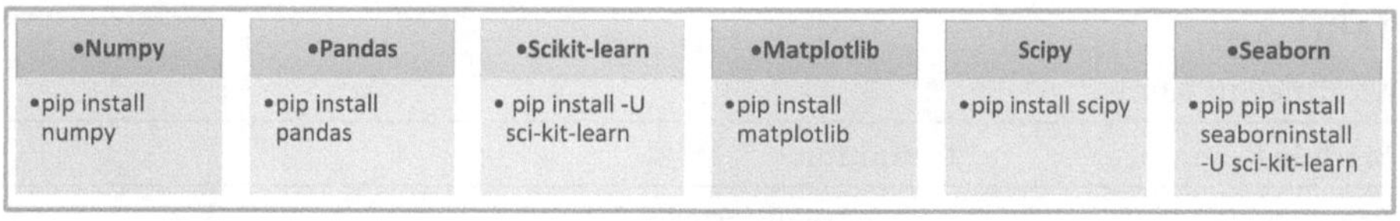

FIGURE 4.9
Python libraries installation.

4.8.1.3 Python Libraries

In your project, you may need to install certain Python dependencies using pip or pip3. Let's discuss some of these requirements with examples, focusing on installing Keras and its related libraries. Please note that you may encounter errors related to the platform version or the libraries you are using, so check their compatibility before use. For those unfamiliar with these settings, applications like Anaconda or Google Colab can be beneficial as they provide some ready-to-use libraries and resources. Figure 4.9 illustrates the process of installing various Python libraries.

Now, let's install Keras. This command will download and install the latest version of Keras and its dependencies. Ensure you have an active Internet connection and the latest version of pip installed on your system.

```
pip install keras
```

Next, install TensorFlow. This command will download and install the latest version of TensorFlow and its dependencies. Ensure you have an active Internet connection and the latest version of pip installed on your system.

```
pip install tensorflow
```

After completing all parts of your project, you can exit the environment. These commands will deactivate the current virtual environment and return you to your system's default environment. To deactivate a virtual environment, you can use the following command:

For Windows:

```
deactivate
```

For Linux/macOS:

```
source deactivate
```

Please check your Python version and its requirements for using pip or pip3. Creating, activating, and deactivating the virtual environment helps organize your code and modules for different projects.

4.8.2 Available Modules

These are the key modules available in Keras that you should familiarize yourself with and learn to utilize when planning to create a model using Keras. Table 4.2 provides an overview of the various modules available in Keras.

TABLE 4.2

Modules in Keras

Module Name	Definition
Regularizes	A list of regularizes
Constraints	A list of constraints
Activations	A list of activator functions
Losses	A list of the loss functions
Metrics	A list of metrics functions
Optimizers	A list of optimizer functions
Callback	A list of the callback functions
Text processing	Functions to convert text into NumPy array
Image processing	Functions to convert images into NumPy
Sequence processing	Functions to generate time-based data from the given input data
Backend	Function of the backend library like TensorFlow
Utilities	Many utility functions are useful in deep learning

4.8.3 Import Libraries and Modules

Here are some of the most commonly used libraries and modules when working with Keras, along with the commands for importing them. Please try executing these commands and steps on your computer. These libraries are essential for most projects involving Keras. Table 4.3 outlines the various libraries and their associated modules for importing.

4.8.4 Train and Predict the Model

After importing the necessary libraries, the next steps are to train and test the model. Keras provides several modules for these tasks.

4.8.4.1 Compile

This method configures the learning process. The compile function in Keras is used to prepare the model for training. It requires specifying the optimizer, loss function, and metrics to use during training.

Example:
In this example, the model is compiled with the SGD optimizer, mean squared error loss function, and categorical accuracy as the evaluation metric.

```
model.compile(optimizer='sgd', loss='mean_squared_error',
metrics=['categorical_accuracy'])
```

TABLE 4.3

Libraries and Modules Importing

Libraries and Modules	Code Example
NumPy	import numpy as np
Keras model module	from keras.models import Sequential
Keras core layers	from keras.layers import Dense, Dropout, Activation, Flatten
Keras CNN Layers	from Keras.layers import Convoluton2D, MaxPooling2D
Utilities	from keras.utils import np_utils

4.8.4.2 *Fit*

This method trains the model using training data. In the fit function of Keras, you need to specify the number of epochs and batch size.

Example:
In this example, the model will be trained for 10 epochs, and each batch will contain 32 samples.

```
model.fit(X, y, epochs=10, batch_size=32)
```

Where:

- **X, y:** Input data and corresponding labels.
- **Epochs:** The number of times the model should be evaluated during training.
- **batch_size:** The number of training instances in one forward/backward pass (updating weights once).

4.8.4.3 *Evaluate*

This method evaluates the model using evaluation or test data. The evaluate function in Keras is used to determine the performance of a trained model on a test dataset.

Example:
This example calculates the loss and any specified metrics on the x_test and y_test data, without displaying verbose output. The results can be accessed using the score variable.

```
score = model.evaluate(x_test, y_test, verbose=0)
```

4.8.4.4 *Predict*

This method generates predictions for new input data using a trained model. The predict function in Keras is used for this purpose.

Example:
This example generates predictions for the input data x using the trained model. You can access the predictions using the predictions variable.

```
predictions = model.predict(x, batch_size=None, verbose=0, steps=None,
callbacks=None, max_queue_size=10, workers=1, use_multiprocessing=False)
```

4.8.5 Implement an Example Using Keras

The Keras API consists of three main components:

1. **Model:** There are two main types of models – "Sequential" for simple architectures, and "Functional" for more complex ones.

2. **Layer:** Keras provides various types of layers, such as convolutional, pooling, and recurrent layers.
3. **Module:** Keras also includes modules, such as activation functions (e.g., softmax, ReLU), loss functions (e.g., MSE), optimizers (e.g., Adam, SGD), and regularizers (e.g., L_1, L_2).

Let's illustrate the usage of these components with an example on the MNIST dataset.

4.8.5.1 Import the Necessary Modules

The code imports the necessary modules from Keras and NumPy. "Sequential", "Dense", "Dropout", "Flatten", "Conv2D", "MaxPooling2D" are different types of layers and models provided by Keras. "backend" is used for checking the image data format.

```
import keras
from keras.datasets import mnist
from keras.models import Sequential
from keras.layers import Dense, Dropout, Flatten
from keras.layers import Conv2D, MaxPooling2D
from keras import backend as K
import numpy as np
```

4.8.5.2 Load the Data

This line of code loads the MNIST dataset. "(x_train, y_train)" are the training images and labels, and "(x_test, y_test)" are the testing images and labels.

```
(x_train, y_train), (x_test, y_test) = mnist.load_data()
```

4.8.5.3 Preprocess the Data

This block of code reshapes the input images to ensure they have the right dimensions for training the CNN. It also normalizes the image data to the range [0, 1] and converts the labels to categorical (one-hot encoding) format.

```
img_rows, img_cols = 28, 28
if K.image_data_format() == 'channels_first':
    x_train = x_train.reshape(x_train.shape[0], 1, img_rows, img_cols)
    x_test = x_test.reshape(x_test.shape[0], 1, img_rows, img_cols)
    input_shape = (1, img_rows, img_cols)
else:
    x_train = x_train.reshape(x_train.shape[0], img_rows, img_cols, 1)
    x_test = x_test.reshape(x_test.shape[0], img_rows, img_cols, 1)
    input_shape = (img_rows, img_cols, 1)
x_train = x_train.astype('float32')
x_test = x_test.astype('float32')
x_train /= 255
x_test /= 255
y_train = keras.utils.to_categorical(y_train, 10)
y_test = keras.utils.to_categorical(y_test, 10)
```

4.8.5.4 Create the Model

Here, a Sequential model is defined, and several layers are added to it. "Conv2D" layers for convolution, "MaxPooling2D". For pooling, "Dropout" for regularization, "Flatten" to flatten the output before passing it to "Dense" layers, and "Dense" layers for classification. The last layer uses a "softmax" activation function for multi-class classification.

```
model = Sequential()
model.add(Conv2D(32, kernel_size=(3, 3), activation='relu',
input_shape=input_shape))
model.add(Conv2D(64, (3, 3), activation='relu'))
model.add(MaxPooling2D(pool_size=(2, 2)))
model.add(Dropout(0.25))
model.add(Flatten())
model.add(Dense(128, activation='relu'))
model.add(Dropout(0.5))
model.add(Dense(10, activation='softmax'))
```

4.8.5.5 Compile the Model

This line compiles the model by specifying the loss function, optimizer, and metrics to track during training.

```
model.compile(loss=keras.losses.categorical_crossentropy,
optimizer=keras.optimizers.Adadelta(), metrics=['accuracy'])
```

4.8.5.6 Train the Model

Here, the model is trained for 12 epochs using the training data with a batch size of 128. The "validation_data" parameter is set to the test data to evaluate the model after every epoch.

```
model.fit(x_train, y_train, batch_size=128, epochs=12, verbose=1,
validation_data=(x_test, y_test))
```

4.8.5.7 Evaluate the Model

The model's performance is evaluated on the test data, and the loss and accuracy are printed.

```
score = model.evaluate(x_test, y_test, verbose=0)
print('Test loss:', score[0])
print('Test accuracy:', score[1])
```

4.8.5.8 Test the Model

Finally, the model's predictions for the test data are compared to the true labels. The "argmax" function is used to convert the predicted probabilities back to class labels.

```
pred = model.predict(x_test)
pred = np.argmax(pred, axis=1)[:5]
```

```
label = np.argmax(y_test, axis=1)[:5]
print("Predicted labels:", pred)
print("True labels:", label)
```

4.9 TensorFlow Issues

Below are some common issues encountered while working with TensorFlow, along with potential solutions:

4.9.1 Installation Errors

You may experience errors during TensorFlow's installation due to Python compatibility issues, operating system conflicts, or library clashes. To address this, consider installing TensorFlow in a virtual environment or updating Python to a compatible version.

4.9.2 GPU Compatibility Issues

If you're utilizing TensorFlow with a GPU, compatibility issues may arise with your GPU drivers. Updating your drivers or downgrading TensorFlow to a version compatible with your GPU might help.

4.9.3 Out-of-memory Error

Training large models with high-resolution images or videos can sometimes lead to out-of-memory errors in TensorFlow. You can resolve this by reducing the batch size or using smaller images.

4.9.4 Slow Training Time

Training deep neural networks can be time-consuming, particularly with large datasets. Using pre-trained models or techniques like transfer learning may expedite the training process.

4.9.5 Overfitting

Overfitting occurs when a model learns the training data too well, leading to suboptimal performance on unseen data. Regularization or dropout techniques can be employed to prevent overfitting.

4.9.6 Underfitting

Underfitting happens when a model is overly simplistic, failing to capture the data's intricacies. To mitigate underfitting, consider increasing the model's capacity, using more training data, or modifying the architecture.

4.9.7 NaN or Infinity Values

Occasionally, TensorFlow may generate NaN or infinity values during training, which can cause the model to fail. Reducing the learning rate, adding more training data, or using a different optimizer might help in this case.

4.9.8 Dataset Loading Errors

Errors may occur while loading datasets in TensorFlow due to incorrect file formats, wrong file paths, or corrupted files. Checking the file formats, paths, and data integrity can help solve this issue.

4.9.9 Debugging Issues

Debugging TensorFlow models can be challenging, especially when dealing with intricate architectures. Tools like TensorBoard or simple print statements can assist in debugging your model.

4.9.10 Performance Optimization

TensorFlow offers various tools to optimize the performance of deep learning models, such as the tf.data API, parallelization techniques, and the XLA compiler. These tools can help reduce your model's training and inference time.

4.10 TensorFlow Implementation Tips

Here are some tips for implementing TensorFlow.

1. Utilize TensorFlow's built-in functions whenever possible. This can expedite computations and enhance performance.
2. During graph definition, use TensorFlow's name_scope and variable_scope for better organization and readability of the code.
3. Always use the "with tf.Session()" block for executing the graph and evaluating tensors.
4. When handling large datasets, consider employing TensorFlow's Dataset API. It provides efficient data loading and preprocessing.
5. Simplify the model-building process and enable distributed training with TensorFlow's Estimator API.
6. If you have access to GPUs, take advantage of TensorFlow's GPU support to speed up training and inference.
7. Use TensorBoard for visualizing the training progress and monitoring the model's performance.
8. If you're working with deep learning models, use TensorFlow's high-level APIs like Keras or tf.layers to simplify the model-building process.
9. For debugging, make use of TensorFlow's eager execution mode. It allows for easy inspection of the values of intermediate tensors and line-by-line debugging.
10. Stay updated with the latest TensorFlow releases to take advantage of new features and improvements.

4.11 Keras Issues

Here are some common issues and their solutions related to Keras.

4.11.1 Keras Installation Errors

Occasionally, Keras installation may fail due to version conflicts or dependencies. In such cases, upgrading or reinstalling Keras using pip or conda package managers is recommended.

4.11.2 Overfitting

Overfitting is a common issue in deep learning models. Keras offers a number of solutions to prevent this, including dropout, regularization, and early stopping. These techniques can help improve the model's generalization.

4.11.3 Unbalanced Datasets

Dealing with unbalanced datasets can cause the model to become biased toward the majority class. Keras provides several techniques to handle class imbalance, such as class weighting and oversampling/undersampling.

4.11.4 Gradient Vanishing/Exploding

When the gradients become too small or too large, it can lead to poor performance of the model. This can be addressed by using appropriate weight initialization techniques, gradient clipping, and batch normalization.

4.11.5 Memory Issues

When working with large datasets or complex models, memory usage can become a bottleneck. To address this, one can use techniques, such as data generators, batch processing, and memory-efficient data structures.

4.11.6 Slow Training

Training deep learning models can be computationally expensive and time-consuming. To speed up the training process, techniques, such as distributed training, GPU acceleration, and model pruning, can be used.

4.11.7 Hyperparameter Tuning

Choosing the right set of hyperparameters can significantly impact the performance of the model. Keras provides several tools for hyperparameter tuning, such as Keras Tuner and GridSearchCV.

4.11.8 Debugging

Debugging deep learning models can be challenging due to their complexity. Keras provides several tools for debugging, such as TensorBoard and the Keras Debugger, which can help in visualizing and diagnosing issues with the model.

4.11.9 Compatibility Issues

Keras is a high-level deep learning library that supports multiple backends, including TensorFlow, Theano, and CNTK. However, some functionalities may not be compatible across different backends. Therefore, ensuring compatibility before using any advanced features of Keras is recommended.

4.12 Keras Implementation Tips

Here are some tips for implementing Keras.

4.12.1 Use Keras Functional API for Complex Models

If you need to build a complex model with multiple inputs, outputs, or shared layers, use the Keras functional API instead of the sequential model API. It allows you to define a directed acyclic graph of layers, making it more flexible and powerful.

4.12.2 Normalize Input Data

Normalizing the input data can stabilize the training process and improve the speed of convergence. You can use the MinMaxScaler or StandardScaler from the scikit-learn library, or write your own normalization function.

4.12.3 Use Early Stopping

Early stopping is a technique that prevents overfitting by monitoring the validation loss and halting the training when the loss ceases to improve. You can implement this technique using the EarlyStopping callback from Keras.

4.12.4 Use Regularization

Another method to prevent overfitting is to add a penalty term to the loss function. You can use the L_1 or L_2 regularization provided by Keras, or write your own regularization function.

4.12.5 Use Data Augmentation

Data augmentation is a technique that increases the size of the training dataset by randomizing the input data. This can help prevent overfitting and improve the model's generalization. You can implement data augmentation using the ImageDataGenerator class from Keras.

4.12.6 Monitor the Training Process

To monitor the training process and plot the training and validation loss and accuracy curves, use Keras's History callback. This can help you understand the model's behavior and identify potential issues.

4.12.7 Use Transfer Learning

Transfer learning is a method for reusing previously trained models and adapting them to a new task. Keras provides a large number of pre-trained models from which you can build your own models. By freezing some layers and training others, you can fine-tune the pre-trained models.

4.12.8 Use GPU Acceleration

If you have access to a GPU, you can use it to accelerate the training process. Keras supports many popular deep learning frameworks, such as TensorFlow and PyTorch, which provide GPU acceleration. You can also use cloud-based GPU services, like Google Colab or AWS, to train your models.

4.12.9 Tune Hyperparameters

Hyperparameters are the parameters that define the model's architecture and training process, such as the learning rate, batch size, or number of epochs. Tuning these hyperparameters can significantly affect the model's performance. To find the best hyperparameters for your model, consider using techniques like grid search or random search.

Remember, hands-on experience is key when working with TensorFlow and Keras or any other machine learning models. Therefore, consistently practicing implementation and troubleshooting is crucial for mastering these concepts.

4.13 Lessons Learned

- Learn How TensorFlow Works
- Learn What Tensors Are
- Learn What TensorFlow Is
- Learn Indexing and Slicing in TensorFlow
- Learn Building an NN Using TensorFlow
- Learn Building a CNN Using TensorFlow
- Learn How Keras Works
- Learn TensorFlow Issues
- Learn Implementation Tips Using TensorFlow
- Learn Keras Issues
- Learn Implementation Tips Using Keras

4.14 Problems

4.14.1 What is TensorFlow, and what are its main features?

4.14.2 How does one install TensorFlow?

4.14.3 What are the different types of tensors in TensorFlow?

4.14.4 What does a TensorFlow session entail, and how is one created?

4.14.5 How does one define a TensorFlow computation graph?

4.14.6 What are placeholders and variables in TensorFlow, and how do they differ?

4.14.7 How does one train a model in TensorFlow?

4.14.8 What is the difference between a tensor and a variable in TensorFlow?

4.14.9 What distinguishes a placeholder from a variable in TensorFlow?

4.14.10 What are the various activation functions in TensorFlow?

4.14.11 What is backpropagation in TensorFlow, and how does it function?

4.14.12 How does one save and load a TensorFlow model?

4.14.13 What optimization algorithms are available in TensorFlow?

4.14.14 What purpose does the TensorFlow Serving API serve?

4.14.15 What is TensorFlow Lite, and how does it differ from TensorFlow?

4.14.16 What is Keras, and how does it differentiate from TensorFlow?

4.14.17 What types of Keras models are available for building deep learning models?

4.14.18 What role do callbacks play in Keras?

4.14.19 How can overfitting in Keras models be addressed?

4.14.20 How can Keras models be saved and loaded?

4.14.21 What are the different types of layers available in Keras?

4.14.22 What is the difference between the Sequential and Functional APIs in Keras?

4.14.23 How is transfer learning implemented using Keras?

4.14.24 What is data augmentation in Keras, and how is it implemented?

4.14.25 How can Keras be utilized for image classification tasks?

4.15 Programming Questions

- **Easy**

    4.15.1 Implement a linear regression model using TensorFlow.

    4.15.2 Develop a program to create a 2D convolutional layer in TensorFlow.

    4.15.3 Build a simple feedforward neural network in TensorFlow.

    4.15.4 Design a program to calculate the accuracy of a trained model using TensorFlow.

    4.15.5 Compose a TensorFlow program to visualize the training progress of a model.

    4.15.6 Construct a basic neural network with Keras to classify images from the MNIST dataset.

    4.15.7 Train a Keras model to predict the output of a logical OR gate.

    4.15.8 Develop a Keras model to classify images from the CIFAR-10 dataset.

4.15.9   Train a Keras model to predict house prices based on their features.

4.15.10   Create a Keras model that predicts a person's gender based on their height and weight.

- **Medium**

  4.15.11   Design a program to implement a recurrent neural network using TensorFlow.

  4.15.12   Develop a program for image classification using a pre-trained model in TensorFlow.

  4.15.13   Compose a TensorFlow program to implement a generative adversarial network (GAN) for image generation.

  4.15.14   Construct a program to train a convolutional neural network (CNN) for image recognition using TensorFlow.

  4.15.15   Develop a program to implement a long short-term memory (LSTM) network in TensorFlow.

  4.15.16   Build a Keras model for sentiment analysis on movie reviews.

  4.15.17   Train a Keras model to generate new text in the style of a given author.

  4.15.18   Design a Keras model to recognize emotions in speech.

  4.15.19   Train a Keras model for image segmentation on medical images.

  4.15.20   Develop a Keras model to predict company stock prices based on historical data.

- **Hard**

  4.15.21   Implement a deep neural network with multiple hidden layers using TensorFlow.

  4.15.22   Design a program for transfer learning using a pre-trained model in TensorFlow.

  4.15.23   Compose a TensorFlow program to implement a variational autoencoder (VAE) for image generation.

  4.15.24   Develop a multi-GPU training program for a deep learning model using TensorFlow.

  4.15.25   Construct a program for object detection using a deep learning model trained with TensorFlow.

  4.15.26   Build a Keras model for object detection in real-time video streams.

  4.15.27   Train a Keras model to generate realistic 3D models of objects from 2D images.

  4.15.28   Develop a Keras model to generate new music based on a given style or genre.

  4.15.29   Design a Keras model for automatic machine translation between two languages.

  4.15.30   Train a Keras model for real-time facial recognition and identification.

5

Artificial Neural Networks
Fundamentals and Architectures

This chapter covers the following topics in Artificial Neural Network Fundamentals and Architectures:

- Artificial Neural Networks (ANNs)
- Linear and Nonlinear Functions
- ANNs Architectures
- Artificial Neural Networks Issues
- Artificial Neural Networks Implementation Tips

5.1 Preface

Artificial Neural Networks (ANNs) are computational models inspired by the human brain. These networks form the foundation of Deep Learning algorithms and are crucial to a plethora of Artificial Intelligence (AI) applications. ANNs consist of layers of nodes or artificial neurons, each of which mimics a biological neuron. These nodes receive inputs, process them, and pass the resultant outputs to the subsequent layer. The structure of an ANN comprises an input layer, one or more hidden layers, and an output layer. Within this structure, every node in a layer is linked to all nodes in the following layer. Each of these connections carries a specific weight. As an input traverses a node, the node multiplies the input by the corresponding weight and employs an activation function. If the output from this function exceeds a predetermined threshold, the node "fires", sending the result to the next layer. ANNs learn by processing training data, during which they adjust the weights of their connections to minimize the difference between their outputs and the target values. This learning procedure involves optimization strategies, such as gradient descent and backpropagation. Once trained, ANNs can handle new data, carrying out tasks, such as classification, recognition, prediction, and decision-making. Figure 5.1 juxtaposes the intricacies of a biological neural network with that of an artificial neural network. On one side, the visualization captures the complex organization of neurons, synapses, and dendrites that make up the human brain's network. In contrast, the other side showcases the structured layers, nodes, and connections found in artificial neural networks as commonly used in machine learning. This side-by-side comparison offers a compelling insight into how nature's design has inspired and paralleled advancements in computational modeling and artificial intelligence.

Feedforward Neural Networks (FFNNs) and Recurrent Neural Networks (RNNs) represent two key categories of ANNs. In FFNNs, signals move in a single direction – from input to output, without looping back. Conversely, RNNs boast connections that

DOI: 10.1201/9781003281344-5

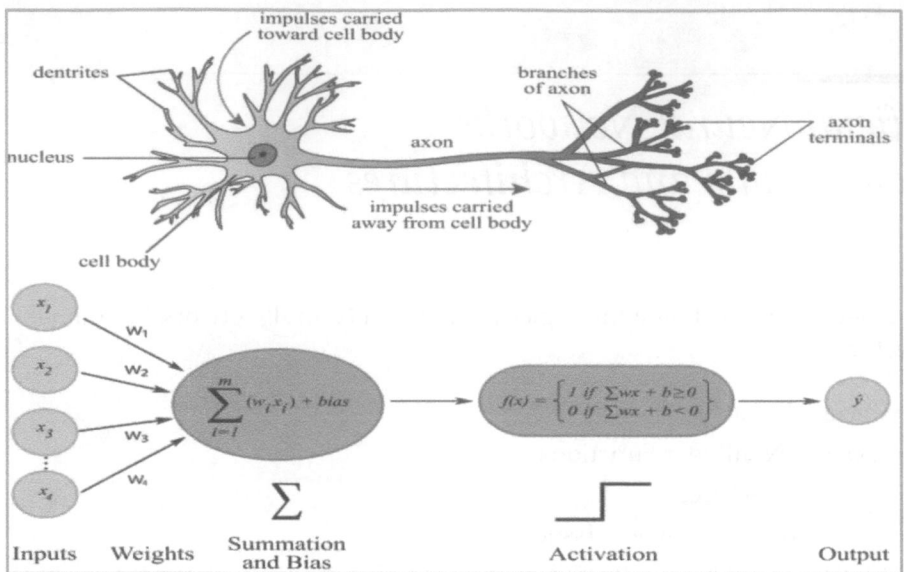

FIGURE 5.1
Artificial neural networks are an imitation of biological neural networks.

form directed cycles, allowing for the creation of internal memory. This unique feature enables them to exhibit dynamic temporal behavior, making them proficient at processing sequences of inputs. Despite their widespread application and numerous successes, ANNs do have inherent limitations. A common issue is overfitting, a phenomenon where the model becomes too attuned to the training data, subsequently performing inadequately on new, unseen data. Nevertheless, ANNs continue to be a dynamic area of research and development. Consistent efforts are underway to enhance their performance, robustness, and interpretability, as well as to broaden their applicability to a wider array of tasks. Given the rapid advancement in computational power, ANNs hold enormous potential for furthering the progression of AI.

5.2 Artificial Neural Networks (ANNs)

The concept of ANNs has a rich history dating back to 1943, when Warren McCulloch and Walter Pitts introduced a computational model to emulate the functioning of neurons in the brain. Their insightful contributions marked the early steps toward the development of artificial neurons, paving the way for contemporary artificial intelligence and neural network models. The displayed portraits offer a tribute to these visionaries, acknowledging their lasting impact on the intersection of biology and computation. This pivotal introduction marked the birth of ANNs. A significant advancement came in 1957 when Frank Rosenblatt invented the perceptron, a pattern recognition algorithm based on a two-layer computer learning network. This innovation was implemented on an IBM 704 at Cornell University, representing one of the earliest applications of ANNs in computing. Interest in ANNs experienced a resurgence in the 1980s, driven by the development of new architectural frameworks and learning algorithms. However, during the same period, alternative machine learning techniques like Support Vector Machines (SVMs) emerged and, in certain cases, outperformed ANNs. Despite these challenges, the field of ANNs underwent a renaissance with the advent of deep learning in the late 2000s. Deep learning, a subset of ANNs characterized by multiple hidden layers, allows models to learn complex patterns in large datasets. The increasing availability of computational resources and vast volumes of data have catapulted deep learning to prominence in numerous fields, including image and speech recognition and natural language processing. Deep learning has brought about significant advancements and holds immense potential to revolutionize technology and the way we live. This chapter will delve into the principles and architectures of ANNs, explore some renowned ANN architectures, and examine their wide range of applications.

5.2.1 Biological Neuron

Neurons, the fundamental units of the brain and the nervous system in both animals and humans, are truly fascinating. Each neuron is composed of a central body known as the soma, which is surrounded by a multitude of extensions identified as dendrites and axons. Intriguingly, dendrites receive signals from other neurons in the form of electrical impulses. These impulses then journey toward the soma, where the signals undergo integration. When the total sum of these signals exceeds a certain threshold, the neuron undergoes a process known as "firing" or activation. This prompts the transmission of an impulse down the axon, connecting with other neurons. The intricate interplay of electrical impulses and the complex interaction of neurons serve as the foundation for all brain activities, ranging from basic physiological functions to complex cognitive tasks. Nevertheless, the precise mechanisms behind neuron communication and information processing within these elaborate networks remain the subjects of intense research. The quest of scientists to deepen our understanding of these biological networks continues, from the exploration of individual neuron communication to understanding the role of extensive neural networks in various physiological and cognitive processes. This ongoing research offers revealing insights into the complexity of the nervous system, enriching our knowledge of biology and catalyzing advancements in fields like AI. Figure 5.2 provides

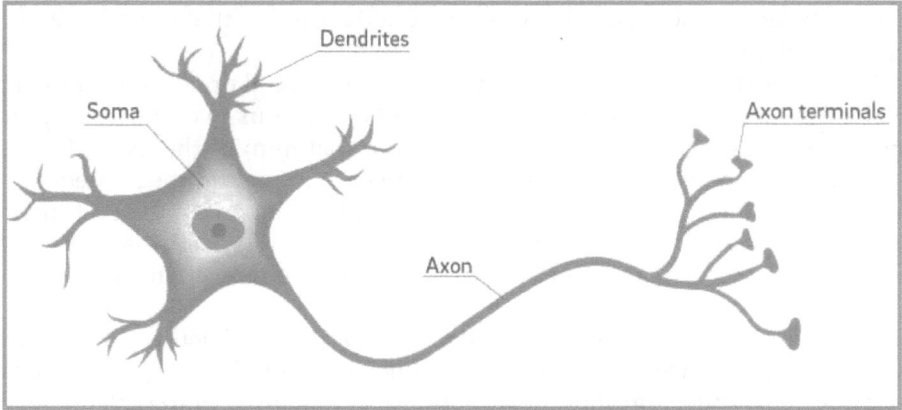

FIGURE 5.2
Biological neural cell.

TABLE 5.1

The Similarity between Biological and Artificial Neurons

Biological Neuron	Artificial Neuron
Dendrites	Input connections
Soma	Activation function
Axons	Output connections
Neuron size and shapes, and features	Weights and bias

a detailed illustration of a biological neuron, highlighting its main components. These components include the cell body (soma), dendrites, which receives signals from other neurons, and the axon, which transmits signals to other neurons. At the end of the axon, axon terminals or synaptic terminals connect to the dendrites or soma of other neurons through synapses. This visual representation underscores the complexity of individual neural cells, which collectively form the intricate neural network in living organisms, and serves as the inspiration behind artificial neural networks.

5.2.2 Artificial Neuron

Artificial neurons are ingeniously designed to simulate the structure and function of their biological counterparts. Table 5.1 serves as a useful reference for comparing the elements of biological neurons with those of ANNs. In biological neurons, dendrites and axons are crucial conduits for signal transmission. ANNs emulate this functionality via their input and output layers, which are tasked with receiving and transmitting data, respectively. The role of the soma in a biological neuron, which integrates incoming signals, is mirrored in ANNs by activation functions. These functions manage the output of artificial neurons based on their inputs. The structure of biological neurons, encompassing aspects, such as their shape, size, and arrangement, greatly influences their signal transmission abilities and their role within the neural network. Analogous factors in ANNs are the weights assigned to the inputs of artificial neurons. These weights dictate each neuron's importance in the network and are integral to the processing of information. By integrating these components, all inspired by the traits of biological neurons, ANNs are structured to imitate the behavior of biological neural networks. This allows them to undertake complex computations on input data, a trait that is at the heart of their effectiveness and versatility.

Figure 5.3 presents the architecture of an artificial neural cell or neuron. Drawing parallels to its biological counterpart, it showcases inputs analogous to dendrites, a processing unit similar to the cell body (soma), and an output that mimics the axon. The neuron's behavior is determined by the weights assigned to each input and the subsequent aggregation of weighted inputs followed by a transformation using an activation function. The design serves as a foundational building block for more complex artificial neural network structures, underscoring its inspiration from biological neural mechanisms.

1. **Inputs:** These are analogous to the dendrites in a biological neuron and are where the data samples and weights enter the artificial neuron. Each input is associated with a weight, which signifies the importance of that input in the calculation.
2. **Impulse signals:** Similar to the electrical impulses in biological neurons, impulse signals in ANNs are the weighted sum of the inputs.

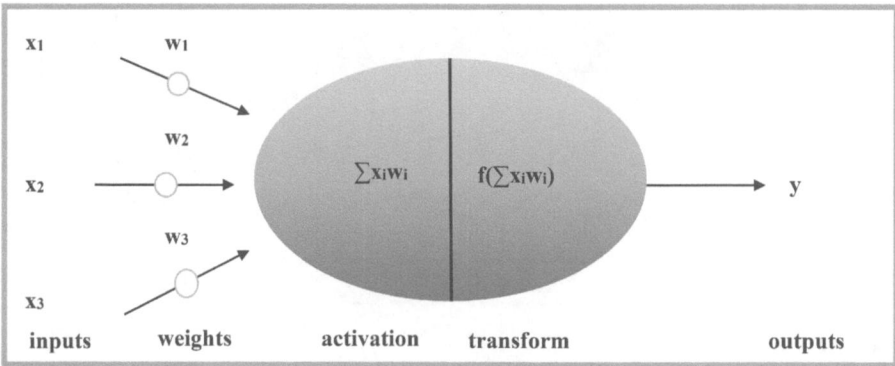

FIGURE 5.3
Artificial neuron element.

3. **Neuron structure:** This refers to the entire structure of the artificial neuron, including the inputs, weights, bias (an extra input to shift the activation function), and the activation function.

4. **Activation function:** This is analogous to the soma in a biological neuron. The activation function takes the impulse signal and transforms it, typically in a non-linear way, to produce the output. Some common activation functions include sigmoid, Rectified Linear Unit (ReLU), and tanh (Hyperbolic Tangent).

5. **Output:** The output of an artificial neuron is the result of the activation function, similar to the axon in a biological neuron. This output can then be passed on as input to the neurons in the next layer.

5.3 Linear and Nonlinear Functions

In a neural network, several input variables, such as sample inputs (**x**), weights (**w**), and bias (**b**), contribute to the network's formula. By adjusting these parameters, we can identify different decision boundaries to partition the data. If the data cannot be separated linearly, we can use kernel functions to transform the data into a new space. This transformation allows the data to become linearly separable in the transformed space, facilitating effective data partitioning.

5.3.1 Linear Function

In ANNs, a linear function is a mathematical operation applied to the inputs of a layer, resulting in an output that is a linear combination of the inputs. Typically, a nonlinear activation function follows the linear function to introduce nonlinearity to the model. In ANNs, a linear function can be represented by performing a matrix multiplication of the input vector and the weight matrix, followed by the addition of a bias vector. The output of the linear function is then passed through a nonlinear activation function, such as the sigmoid or ReLU function. Linear functions are utilized in the input and output layers of ANNs, as well as in some hidden layers. In the input layer, a linear function is employed to

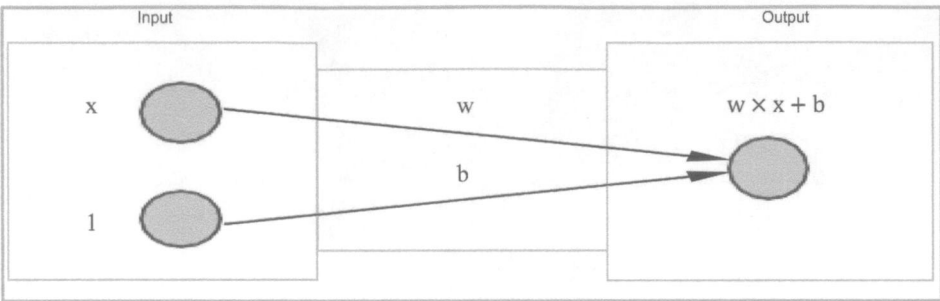

FIGURE 5.4
Vertices are neurons (data samples), and edges are weights and biases.

convert the input data into a format suitable for network processing. In the output layer, a linear function is used to generate the final network output. In certain hidden layers, linear functions are employed to combine the outputs of preceding layers and create new sets of features. While linear functions are simple and efficient, they have limitations in modeling complex relationships between variables. They can only capture linear relationships and are unable to model nonlinear relationships. Therefore, it is common to use nonlinear activation functions in conjunction with linear functions in ANNs to capture complex patterns in the data. Here, we present the basic version of a neural network for modeling linear functions:

$$f(x) = w \times x + b$$

where "**x**" represents the input samples, "**w**" denotes the weights, and "**b**" signifies the bias. Figure 5.4 illustrates a connection network that establishes connections between these components. The vertices and edges in this graph symbolize the neuron cells within the network. The learning method aims to identify the optimal values for the parameters (**w, b**) to achieve the best possible model approximation that fits the data (**x**) to the desired goal function **f(x)**. By iteratively adjusting the weights and biases, the neural network aims to minimize the difference between the predicted output of the model and the actual output, improving its ability to accurately approximate the desired function **f(x)**.

The *x*-axis in the given context represents the matrix of input vectors, where each vector in the matrix contains the feature values of the data items. For example, consider apples, where their characteristics may include color, flavor, and price, resulting in three values. If there are seven distinct apples, the size of the input matrix would be 7 × 3, which amounts to 21. In this matrix, each row represents an apple, and each column represents one of the specified characteristics. The value of "**w**" is typically chosen randomly, and the objective of network training is to find the optimal value of "**w**" that yields the best results in regression or classification problems. When using the linear activation function, backpropagation does not work effectively because the derivative remains constant. Consequently, it cannot assist in determining the best weights or updating existing ones when backpropagating to the inputs. Therefore, with this approach, it is not possible to accurately replicate the nonlinear behavior of a problem. Figure 5.5 depicts a linear function represented by the blue line, while its derivative is indicated by the red

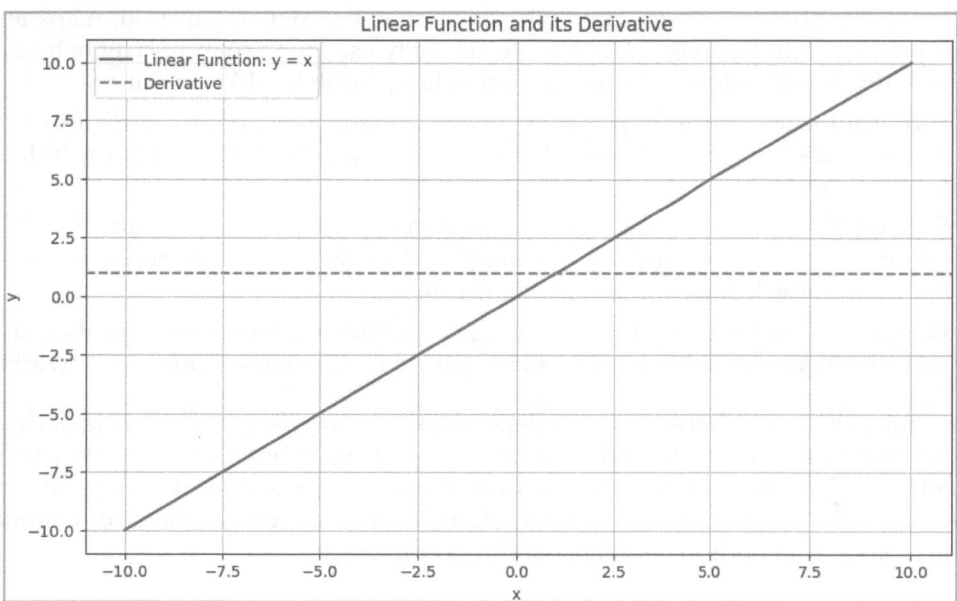

FIGURE 5.5
Linear function and its derivative.

dotted line). Figure 5.5 illustrates the nature and behavior of a Linear Function and its derivative:

- The primary graph plots a straight line, representing the linear function $y = x$. As one moves horizontally along the x-axis, the value of y increases at a consistent rate, showcasing the function's linearity.
- Superimposed on the same graph is a horizontal line, which depicts the derivative of the linear function. This constant line underscores the fact that the rate of change or slope of a linear function is constant throughout.

In essence, Figure 5.5 conveys that while a linear function changes linearly with the input, its derivative remains constant, reflecting a consistent rate of change.

5.3.2 Nonlinear Functions

Nonlinearity in real-world actions can indeed present challenges. To effectively simulate such scenarios, it is crucial to incorporate nonlinear functions, particularly activation functions (AF), in the modeling process. ANNs utilize nonlinear functions to capture the complex relationships between input features and output targets. These functions enable ANNs to learn from data and make predictions based on nonlinear patterns. Some commonly used nonlinear functions in ANNs are:

- **Rectified Linear Unit (ReLU):** ReLU is a piecewise linear function that outputs 0 for negative inputs and the input value itself for positive inputs. ReLU has gained popularity due to its computational efficiency and its ability to mitigate the vanishing gradient problem.

- **Sigmoid:** The sigmoid function, also known as the logistic function, maps any input to a value between 0 and 1. It is commonly used in the output layer of binary classification problems, where it can provide a probability-like output.
- **Hyperbolic tangent (tanh):** Similar to the sigmoid function, the tanh function maps inputs to values between −1 and 1. It is frequently employed in the hidden layers of ANNs.
- **Softmax:** The softmax function is utilized in the output layer of multiclass classification problems. It produces a probability distribution over the possible classes, aiding in the selection of the most likely class.
- **Gaussian:** The Gaussian function assigns weights to inputs based on their distance from a specified point. It is often utilized in radial basis function networks.

The choice of the nonlinear function depends on the specific problem being addressed and the architecture of the neural network. By selecting an appropriate nonlinear function, an ANN model can effectively capture underlying patterns in the data and make accurate predictions. In this example, the sigmoid function, one of the most commonly used activation functions in neural networks, is employed:

$$f(x) = sig(w \times x + b)$$

Figure 5.6 illustrates how to simulate nonlinearity with the sigmoid function, which produces a continuous gradient as well as an accurate forecast. It visually presents the use of the sigmoid function for modeling nonlinearity within a neural computation framework. Displayed are input variables x and a bias unit (1), connected to weights (w) and a bias term (b). These components come together in the formula sig(wx + b) to calculate the output. The graph emphasizes how the weighted input, combined with the bias, undergoes a transformation via the sigmoid function to produce an output between 0 and 1, effectively capturing nonlinearity.

The nonlinear activation function addresses two problems discussed in the previous section: its utilization in backpropagation, and its influence on the training process when incorporating more neurons and layers, particularly in deep neural networks. However, there are certain drawbacks associated with specific activation functions. Firstly, the computational cost of certain functions can be high. Secondly, the gradients tend to remain

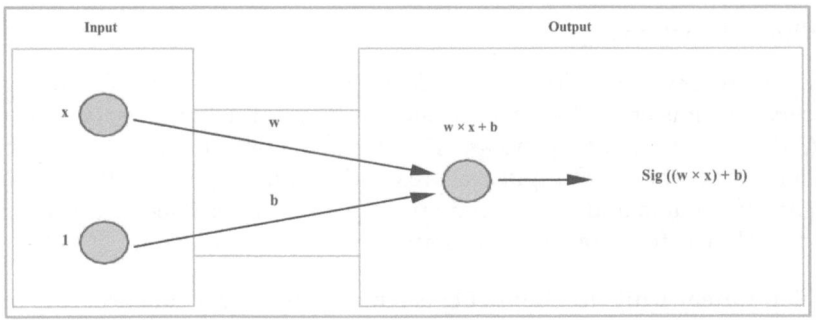

FIGURE 5.6
Using sigmoid for nonlinearity modeling.

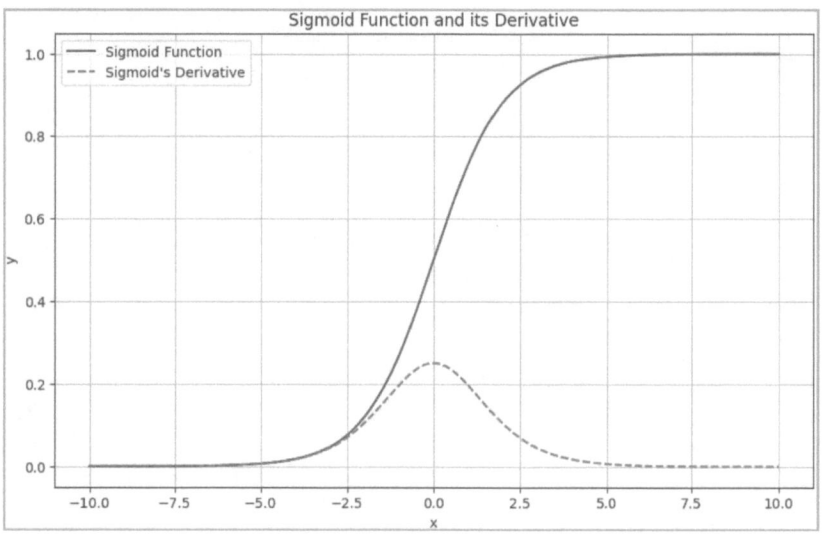

FIGURE 5.7
Derivatives for sigmoid.

unchanged when applied to very large input values, leading to the vanishing gradient problem. To overcome these challenges, the ReLU function can be employed as it introduces nonlinearity and offers computational efficiency. However, a limitation of ReLU is its inability to handle negative values, which can hinder its performance. leaky ReLU is a variation that addresses this problem by allowing a small nonzero gradient for negative input values. It is possible that leaky ReLU can resolve some issues associated with ReLU, enhancing the performance and capabilities of the network. Figures 5.7 and 5.8 illustrate the derivative values for the sigmoid and ReLU functions, respectively. These derivative values play a significant role in the backpropagation algorithm, as they determine the gradients used to update the network's weights during training. Understanding the derivative values provides insights into the behavior and characteristics of these activation functions.

Figure 5.7 delves into the **Sigmoid Function** and its derivative, which are pivotal components in neural network activations:

- The primary curve visualizes the sigmoid function, characterized by its distinct "S" shape. This function maps any input value to a range between 0 and 1, making it a popular choice for producing probabilities and binary classifications.

- Superimposed on the same graph is another curve, representing the derivative of the sigmoid function. This curve captures how the rate of change in the sigmoid function varies across different input values. Notably, the derivative is highest at the midpoint (where the sigmoid curve is steepest) and approaches zero as the input values move toward the extremes, indicating regions of the sigmoid function where changes are minimal.

In summary, it illuminates the behavior of the sigmoid function and how its rate of change evolves across its domain, offering insights into why it can lead to vanishing gradient issues in deep networks.

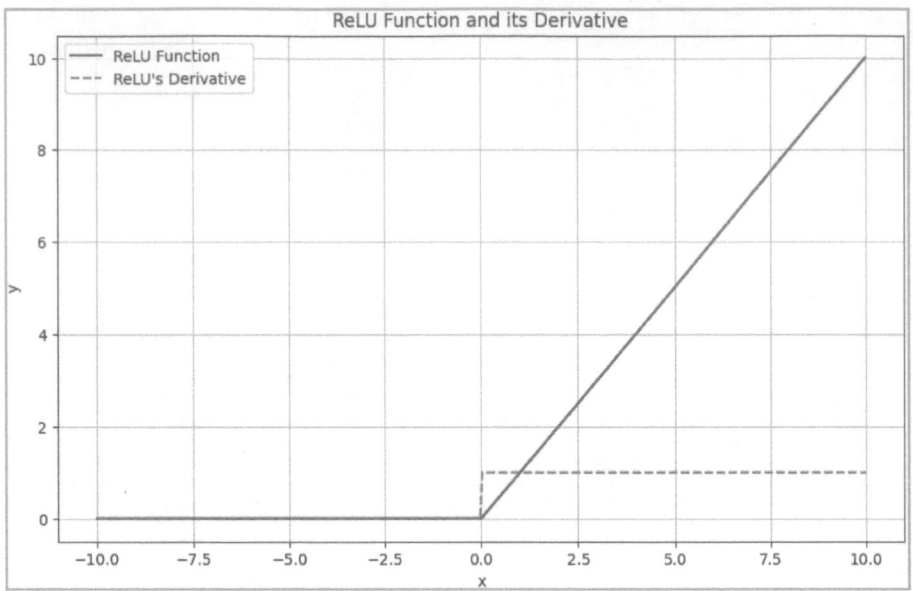

FIGURE 5.8
Derivatives for ReLU.

Figure 5.8 offers a detailed visualization of the **Rectified Linear Unit (ReLU)** function and its derivative, which are instrumental in deep learning activations:

- The primary curve displays the ReLU function, which is simple yet powerful: it outputs the input directly if it's positive; otherwise, it outputs zero. This nonlinearity helps deep networks learn complex representations without the computational complexities of other functions.

- The graph also incorporates a representation of the derivative of the ReLU. The derivative is 1 for positive input values and 0 for negative values, indicating that for positive inputs, the function has a constant rate of change, while for negative inputs, it doesn't change at all.

In essence, it encapsulates how ReLU operates, allowing activations to pass through largely unchanged if positive, but nullifying negative activations, and its derivative underscores the regions of change and nonchange in the function.

5.4 ANNs Architectures

ANNs come in various architectures that determine the network's structure and how information flows within it. Here, we will explore some common ANN architectures: FFNNs, RNNs, Convolutional Neural Networks (CNNs), Modular Neural Networks, and Autoencoders. These are just a few examples of ANN architectures. Many variations and hybrid architectures combine different components to address specific tasks and challenges. The choice of architecture depends on the data's nature, the problem's complexity, and the desired output.

5.4.1 Feedforward Neural Networks (FFNNs)

FFNNs exhibit a streamlined flow of information from the input layer to the output layer without any feedback connections. This means data is input into the network, undergoes a series of nonlinear transformations in the hidden layers, and ultimately yields an output at the final layer. Unlike RNNs, FFNNs lack any loops that feed information back into preceding layers. A typical FFNN architecture comprises three primary sections: an input layer, one or more hidden layers, and an output layer. The input layer is equipped with neurons that receive the initial data, while the output layer comprises neurons responsible for generating the final predictions. Sandwiched between these two layers are the hidden layers, which carry out nonlinear transformations on the input data. Each neuron within the network processes a weighted sum of inputs from the prior layer, a value that is then transmuted by a nonlinear activation function. This function introduces nonlinearity into the network, empowering it to model complex, nonlinear relationships between the input and output data. FFNNs have proven their value across a spectrum of domains, including image and speech recognition, natural language processing, and financial forecasting. They have also been utilized to boost the performance of other deep learning models, such as CNNs for image processing and RNNs for sequential data handling. Figure 5.9 offers a clear visual breakdown of the architecture of a Feedforward Neural Network (FFNN). The diagram prominently showcases distinct layers, starting with the "input layer", where raw data enters the network. This is followed by an intermediate "hidden layer" which captures complex patterns and relationships from the input data. The diagram culminates with the "output layer", delivering the final predictions or classifications. The pathways between these layers, representing weighted connections, underline the flow of information from input to output, highlighting the layered and hierarchical structure inherent to FFNNs.

An FFNN is a type of artificial neural network in which the connections between its nodes do not form a cycle. The data is only transmitted in one direction, from the input to the hidden layer, and then to the output layer. FFNNs process information in only one direction, making them the type of neural network with the fewest steps. The FFNN is a straightforward network with input, hidden, and output layers. The combinations of neurons from the first layer are transferred to the next layer. Then, these combinations go through the activation function, and the outputs, along with their combinations, become

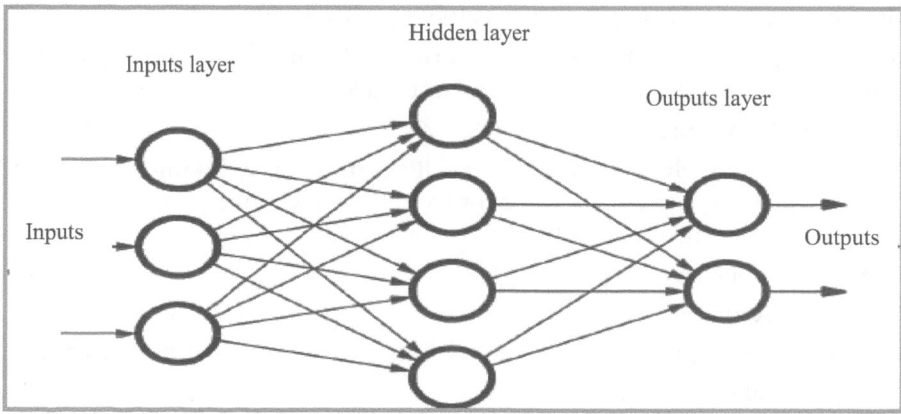

FIGURE 5.9
FFNN general architecture.

the inputs of the next layer. This process continues until the final layer produces the final outputs. For example, if the network has one input, one hidden, and one output layer, as shown in Figure 5.9, and X is the sample input vector, $X = (x_1, x_2)$, and $W_h = (w_{h11}, w_{h12}, w_{h21}, w_{h22})$ are the hidden layer weights, and b_h is the bias, $W_o = (w_{o11}, w_{o12}, w_{o13}, w_{o21}, w_{o22}, w_{o23}, w_{o31}, w_{o32}, w_{o33})$ are the output layer weights, b_o is the bias, and "a" is the activation function, then:

$$Output = a(a(X \times W_h + b_h) \times W_o + b_o)$$

The FFNN general algorithm is as follows:

```
Forward (x):
y₀ = x
# Step 3
for i = 1: L do:
      # Step 1
      cᵢ = wᵢᵀyᵢ₋₁ + bᵢ
      # Step 2
      yᵢ = a(cᵢ)
end
return (yᵢ)
```

These are the three main steps for an FFNN:

Step 1: Calculate the weighted input for the hidden layer by multiplying the input (**X**) by the hidden weight (W_h).

Step 2: Apply the activation function to the calculated result and pass this output to the next layer.

Step 3: Repeat steps 1 and 2 for all layers.

The algorithm computes a combination of data (**X**), weights (**W**), and bias (**b**), then applies the activation function through all layers to generate the final output. Single-layer and multi-layer perceptron are two well-known types of feedforward networks. Here's a breakdown of algorithm:

1. **Initialization**: y_0 is set to x, where x is the input to the network.
2. **Loop through Layers**: The loop is set to run for L times, representing the number of layers in the network (excluding the input layer).
   2.1. **Compute Weighted Sum:**
       - c_i is the weighted sum for layer i. It's computed by taking the dot product of the weight matrix w_i for layer i and the activations y_{i-1} from the previous layer, and then adding the bias b_i for layer i.
       - Symbolically, $c_i = w_i^T y_{i-1} + b_i$.
   2.2. **Apply Activation Function**:
       - y_i is the output of layer i after applying the activation function a to c_i.
       - Symbolically, $y_i = a(c_i)$
3. **Output**: Finally, the function returns y_i, which represents the output of the last layer.

The code provides a general sequence for forward propagation. However, a few things to note:

- The specific type of activation function *a* isn't specified here.
- Weight matrices and biases are referenced but not defined in the given snippet. They are typically initialized beforehand and adjusted during training.
- This is a high-level representation. In a practical implementation, there would likely be more details and optimizations.

5.4.1.1 FFNN with Pseudocode

Here's a pseudocode representation of an FFNN. It's important to note that this pseudocode is based on a basic structure of an FFNN with sigmoid activation and weight updates using gradient descent. Depending on the specific implementation or requirements, modifications or additional functions may be necessary.

```
# X: Input data
# y: Target labels
# layers: List of layer sizes, including input and output layers
# learning_rate: Learning rate for updating weights
# epochs: Number of training epochs
# Initialize weights and biases randomly
This block of code initializes the weights and biases of the neural
network randomly. The layers parameter is a list that represents the
sizes of each layer, including the input and output layers. The
initialize_weights function will create weight matrices and bias
vectors for each layer.
initialize_weights(layers)

# Training loop
This block of code represents the training loop, where the network goes
through multiple epochs. In each epoch, it performs a forward pass to
compute the output of the network given the input data X. Then, it
performs backpropagation to calculate the gradients and update the
weights and biases. The learning_rate determines the step size of the
weight updates.
for epoch in range(epochs):
    # Forward pass
    output = forward_pass(X)

    # Backpropagation
    backward_pass(output, y)

    # Update weights and biases
    update_weights(learning_rate)

# Forward pass function
This function performs the forward pass through the neural network. It
takes the input X and propagates it through each layer. The output of
```

each layer is computed by applying the activation function to the
weighted sum of the inputs plus the bias term.

```
function forward_pass(X):
    output = X
    for layer in layers:
        output = activate(layer * output + bias)
    return output
```

Backpropagation function

This function performs the backpropagation algorithm to calculate the
gradients of the weights and biases. It starts by computing the error
between the network output and the target labels y. Then, it iterates
through the layers in reverse order and calculates the deltas, which
represent the contribution of each layer to the overall error. The
deltas are computed by multiplying the error by the derivative of the
activation function, and then backpropagating the error to the previous
layers

```
function backward_pass(output, y):
    error = output - y
    for layer in reversed(layers):
        delta = error * derivative(activate(layer * output + bias))
        update_delta(delta)
        error = delta * transpose(layer)
```

Update weights and biases function

This function updates the weights and biases of each layer based on the
calculated deltas. It applies the gradient descent algorithm by
subtracting the learning rate multiplied by the deltas from the weights
and biases.

```
function update_weights(learning_rate):
    for layer in layers:
        layer.weights = layer.weights - learning_rate * layer.delta
        layer.bias = layer.bias - learning_rate * layer.delta
```

#These helper functions play a crucial role in initializing the network,
computing activations, derivatives, and updating deltas, which are
essential components of the feedforward neural network algorithm.This
function initializes the weights and biases of each layer in the network.
It iterates over the layers list, starting from the second layer (index
1) since the first layer is the input layer. For each layer, it retrieves
the sizes of the previous layer and the current layer. Then, it generates
random weight matrices and bias vectors for each layer. The dimensions of
the weight matrix depend on the size of the previous layer and the
current layer.

```
function initialize_weights(layers):
    for i in range(1, len(layers)):
        layer_size_prev = layers[i-1]
        layer_size_curr = layers[i]
        layer.weights = random_matrix(layer_size_prev, layer_size_curr)
        layer.bias = random_vector(layer_size_curr)
```

#This function computes the activation of a given input x using the
sigmoid activation function. The sigmoid function squeezes the input

```
value between 0 and 1, providing non-linear behavior in the network. It
is defined as 1 / (1 + exp(-x))
function activate(x):
    return 1 / (1 + exp(-x))  # Sigmoid activation function
```

```
#This function calculates the derivative of the sigmoid activation
function. It takes the output x of the activation function and returns the
derivative value. The derivative of the sigmoid function is computed as the
product of the sigmoid function itself (activate(x)) and 1 - activate(x)
function derivative(x):
        return activate(x) * (1 - activate(x))  # Derivative of sigmoid
function
#This function updates the delta attribute of a layer with the given
value. The delta represents the contribution of a layer to the overall
error during the backpropagation process. It is used to calculate the
weight gradients and propagate the error back through the network.
function update_delta(delta):
        layer.delta = delta
```

5.4.1.2 FFNN with TensorFlow

We implement the FFNN using TensorFlow in eight steps, from importing libraries to testing the model.

5.4.1.2.1 Import Libraries

TensorFlow, NumPy, and Keras are the primary libraries required for this implementation. Importing these libraries grants access to their functionality and tools, enabling you to work with neural networks and execute a range of deep learning tasks using TensorFlow and Keras.

```
# import the required libraries
import tensorflow as tf
import numpy as np
from tensorflow import keras
```

Here's the breakdown of each code line:

```
#This line imports the TensorFlow library, which is a popular deep
learning library for building and training neural networks.
import tensorflow as tf
```

```
#This line imports the NumPy library, which is a fundamental library for
scientific computing in Python. NumPy provides powerful tools for working
with multi-dimensional arrays and mathematical functions.
import numpy as np
```

```
#This line imports the Keras module from TensorFlow. Keras is a user-
friendly deep learning library that provides a high-level API for
defining and training neural networks. It is integrated into TensorFlow
and offers a simplified interface for building and training models
efficiently.
from tensorflow import keras
```

5.4.1.2.2 Load Data

This implementation utilizes the MNIST dataset, which we've imported from Keras data-sets and divided into training and testing sets. By executing this code, you'll load the MNIST dataset and have it split into these sets, thus preparing it for the training and evaluation of your neural network models.

```
# load the minst dataset from keras
from keras.datasets import mnist
(x_train, y_train), (x_test, y_test) = mnist.load_data()
```

Here's the breakdown of each line:

```
#This line imports the MNIST dataset module from Keras. The MNIST dataset
is a widely used benchmark dataset in machine learning, consisting of
60,000 training images and 10,000 test images of handwritten digits.
from keras.datasets import mnist
```

```
#This line loads the MNIST dataset and assigns it to the variables
`x_train`, `y_train`, `x_test`, and `y_test`. The `load_data()`
function retrieves the dataset and returns four NumPy arrays:
```

- `x_train`: Training images. It is a 3D array of shape `(num_samples, 28, 28)`, where `num_samples` is the number of training samples, and each image is a 28x28 grayscale image represented as an array.
- `y_train`: Training labels. It is a 1D array of shape `(num_samples,)`, containing the corresponding labels (integers) for each training image.
- `x_test`: Test images. It is a 3D array of shape `(num_samples, 28, 28)`, where `num_samples` is the number of test samples, and each image is a 28x28 grayscale image represented as an array.
- `y_test`: Test labels. It is a 1D array of shape `(num_samples,)`, containing the corresponding labels (integers) for each test image.

```
(x_train, y_train), (x_test, y_test) = mnist.load_data()
```

5.4.1.2.3 One Hot and Normalization Data

The TensorFlow one-hot module can be utilized for one-hot encoding operations, and nor-malizing the data can be achieved by dividing it by 255. By executing this code, the labels will be one-hot encoded, and the pixel values of the images will be normalized to fall within the range of 0 to 1. This process prepares the data for training a neural network model using the MNIST dataset.

```
y_train = tf.one_hot(y_train, 10)
y_test = tf.one_hot(y_test, 10)
x_train = x_train / 255.0
x_test = x_test / 255.0
```

Here's the breakdown of each line:

```
#These lines use the `tf.one_hot` function from TensorFlow to perform
one-hot encoding on the labels (`y_train` and `y_test`). One-hot encoding
```

converts categorical labels into a binary vector representation, where each label is represented as a vector with a single element set to 1 and the rest set to 0. In this case, the labels are converted into one-hot encoded vectors of size 10 (since there are 10 possible classes in the MNIST dataset).

```
y_train = tf.one_hot(y_train, 10)
y_test = tf.one_hot(y_test, 10)
```

```
#These lines normalize the pixel values of the training and test data
(`x_train` and `x_test`) by dividing them by 255.0. Normalizing the pixel
values to the range of 0 to 1 is a common preprocessing step in machine
learning tasks. In the MNIST dataset, the pixel values range from 0 to
255, where 0 represents black and 255 represents white. By dividing by
255.0, the pixel values are scaled down to the range of 0 to 1, which can
help improve the convergence and performance of the neural network.
x_train = x_train / 255.0
x_test = x_test / 255.0
```

5.4.1.2.4 *Making Model*

A model is created using the Sequential module from Keras, and layers are defined by specifying inputs and activation functions. By defining this model architecture, you will have established a sequential neural network with multiple layers, aptly designed for processing the MNIST dataset.

```
model = keras.Sequential([
    keras.layers.Flatten(input_shape=(28, 28)),
    keras.layers.Dense(256, activation='relu'),
    keras.layers.Dense(32, activation='relu'),
    keras.layers.Dense(10, activation='softmax')
])
```

Here's the breakdown of each line:

```
#This code defines a sequential model using the Keras Sequential class.
The sequential model allows you to stack multiple layers on top of each
other, forming a linear stack of layers.
model = keras.Sequential([])
```

```
#This line adds a Flatten layer to the model. The Flatten layer
transforms the input into a 1D array by reshaping the input tensor of
shape `(batch_size, 28, 28)` into `(batch_size, 28*28)`. It prepares the
image data for the fully connected layers.
keras.layers.Flatten(input_shape=(28, 28))
```

```
#This line adds a Dense layer with 256 units to the model. The Dense layer
is a fully connected layer where each neuron is connected to every neuron
in the previous layer. The activation function used in this layer is ReLU
(Rectified Linear Unit), which introduces non-linearity to the network.
keras.layers.Dense(256, activation='relu')
```

```
#This line adds another Dense layer with 32 units to the model.
Similarly, it is a fully connected layer with ReLU activation.
keras.layers.Dense(32, activation='relu')
```

```
#This line adds the output Dense layer with 10 units (one for each class
in the MNIST dataset). The activation function used is softmax, which
produces a probability distribution over the classes, indicating the
likelihood of each class for a given input.
keras.layers.Dense(10, activation='softmax')
```

5.4.1.2.5 Model Summary

A model summary is a good practice for providing a high-level overview of the network architecture.

```
# Check the model summary for more information about the architecture and
its parameters.
model.summary()
Model: "sequential"
```

Layer (type)	Output Shape	Param #
flatten_2 (Flatten)	(None, 784)	0
dense_6 (Dense)	(None, 256)	200960
dense_7 (Dense)	(None, 32)	8224
dense_8 (Dense)	(None, 10)	330

```
Total params: 209,514
Trainable params: 209,514
Non-trainable params: 0
```

5.4.1.2.6 Compile the Model

In Keras, you can prepare the model for training by specifying parameters like the metric value and optimizer type. By compiling the model with the specified loss function, metrics, and optimizer, you effectively set up the model for training and evaluation using the MNIST dataset.

```
# compile the model using the compile of the model module
model.compile(loss='categorical_crossentropy', metrics=['accuracy'],
optimizer='adam')
```

Here's the breakdown of each line:

```
This line compiles the model and configures the learning process. The
`compile` function takes several arguments:
```

- `loss='categorical_crossentropy'`: This argument specifies the loss
  function to be used during training. Since the labels are one-hot
  encoded, `categorical_crossentropy` is a suitable loss function for
  multi-class classification problems.
- `metrics=['accuracy']`: This argument specifies the evaluation
  metric(s) to be used during training and testing. In this case, the
  model will be evaluated based on accuracy, which calculates the
  percentage of correctly classified samples.
- `optimizer='adam'`: This argument specifies the optimizer
  algorithm to be used during training. In this case, the Adam

> **optimizer is used. Adam is an adaptive learning rate optimization algorithm that adjusts the learning rate during training to improve convergence.**

```
model.compile(loss='categorical_crossentropy', metrics=['accuracy'],
optimizer='adam')
```

5.4.1.2.7 Train the Model

During the training step, parameters, such as batch size and epochs, are set, and then the "fit" method from a Keras model is used to train the model. By executing this code, the model will be trained on the MNIST dataset. The TensorBoard callback will log the training progress, including loss and accuracy metrics. The "history" variable will store the training history, including metrics at each epoch.

```
n_val = 5000
n_train = 60000
n_test = 10000
batch_size=100
epochs=100
steps_per_epoch = int((n_train-n_val)/batch_size)
n_val = 5000
validation_split = n_val/n_train
validation_steps = int(n_val / batch_size)
test_steps = int(n_test/batch_size)
history = model.fit(x_train, y_train, epochs=epochs, steps_per_
epoch=steps_per_epoch, validation_split= validation_split, validation_
steps=validation_steps, callbacks=[tensorboard_callback])
```

Here's the explanation for each code line:

```
#This line sets the variable `n_val` to the value 5000. `n_val`
represents the number of validation samples.
n_val = 5000
```

```
#This line sets the variable `n_train` to the value 60000. `n_train`
represents the number of training samples.
n_train = 60000
```

```
#This line sets the variable `n_test` to the value 10000. `n_test`
represents the number of test samples.
n_test = 10000
```

```
#This line sets the variable `batch_size` to the value 100. `batch_size`
determines the number of samples per gradient update during training.
batch_size=100
```

```
#This line sets the variable `epochs` to the value 100. `epochs`
represents the number of training epochs.
epochs=100
```

```
#This line calculates the variable `steps_per_epoch` by subtracting the
number of validation samples (`n_val`) from the number of training
```

samples (`n_train`), and then dividing it by the `batch_size`. It represents the number of steps required to cover the training data once based on the batch size and the difference between the number of training samples and the number of validation samples.

```
steps_per_epoch = int((n_train-n_val)/batch_size)
```

```
#This line calculates the variable `validation_split` by dividing the number of validation samples (`n_val`) by the number of training samples (`n_train`). It represents the fraction of the training data to be used for validation during training.
validation_split = n_val/n_train
```

```
#This line calculates the variable `validation_steps` by dividing the number of validation samples (`n_val`) by the `batch_size`. It represents the number of steps required to cover the validation data once based on the batch size.
validation_steps = int(n_val / batch_size)
```

```
#This line calculates the variable `test_steps` by dividing the number of test samples (`n_test`) by the `batch_size`. It represents the number of steps required to cover the test data once based on the batch size.
test_steps = int(n_test/batch_size)
```

```
#This line trains the model using the `fit` function. It takes the training data (`x_train` and `y_train`) as input along with other arguments:
```

- `epochs`: The number of training epochs.
- `steps_per_epoch`: The number of steps to iterate over the training data in each epoch.
- `validation_split`: The fraction of the training data to be used for validation during training.
- `validation_steps`: The number of steps to iterate over the validation data in each epoch.
- `callbacks`: Additional callbacks to be applied during training. Here, `tensorboard_callback` is used as a callback for logging the training progress.

```
history = model.fit(x_train, y_train, epochs=epochs, steps_per_
epoch=steps_per_epoch, validation_split= validation_split, validation_
steps=validation_steps, callbacks=[tensorboard_callback])
```

5.4.1.2.8 *Test the Model*

Finally, before deploying the trained model on real-world data, it can be tested using the test dataset. By executing this code, you will obtain both the test loss and accuracy metrics of the model, as trained on the MNIST test dataset.

```
score = model.evaluate(x_test,  y_test, steps=test_steps, verbose=0)
print('Test loss:', score[0])
print('Test accuracy:', score[1])
```

Here's the breakdown of each line:

```
This line evaluates the model on the test data (`x_test` and `y_test`).
The `evaluate` function calculates the loss value and any specified
metrics of the model on the provided test data. The `steps` argument
specifies the number of steps to iterate over the test data, based on the
`test_steps` value calculated earlier. The `verbose=0` argument indicates
that no progress bar or logging should be displayed during evaluation.
The evaluation result is stored in the `score` variable.
score = model.evaluate(x_test, y_test, steps=test_steps, verbose=0)


These lines print the evaluation results. `score[0]` corresponds to the
test loss value, and `score[1]` corresponds to the test accuracy. By
printing these values, you can assess the performance of the trained
model on the unseen test data.
print('Test loss:', score[0])
print('Test accuracy:', score[1])
```

5.4.2 Backpropagation

Backpropagation is a supervised learning algorithm used to train ANNs. The core objective of the algorithm is to fine-tune the weights of the network's connections, enabling it to more accurately approximate a given function. In order to achieve this, the backpropagation algorithm calculates the gradient of the loss function with respect to each weight in the network. The gradient provides direction on how the weight should be adjusted to minimize the loss function. Starting from the output layer and moving toward the input layer, the gradient is then propagated backward through the network. At each layer, the gradient is multiplied by the local derivative of the activation function in relation to the net input. This product is used to compute the gradients of the weights and biases at that layer. Following this, the weights and biases are updated using a learning rate and the recently computed gradients. The backpropagation algorithm relies on a set of training sample data to adjust the network's weights and improve its overall performance. With each pass of the algorithm, the network becomes progressively better at approximating the desired function.

5.4.2.1 Forward Propagation

Forward propagation, also known as feedforward propagation, is the procedure in which input data is passed through a neural network to produce an output or prediction. This process is characterized by the unidirectional flow of information from the input layer toward the output layer, with no feedback loops or recurrences. At the start of forward propagation, each neuron in the input layer takes in an input value. This value is multiplied by a weight and then processed through an activation function to produce an output. The output from one layer serves as the input for the subsequent layer, continuing until the final output layer is reached. Activation functions introduce nonlinearity into the network, enabling it to model complex input-output relationships. Several activation functions, such as the sigmoid function, ReLU function, and hyperbolic tangent function, are widely used in practice. Upon reaching the output layer, the generated output values can be compared with the desired output values to compute the error. This error is then utilized during the backpropagation phase, where the weights of the network are adjusted to minimize the error and improve the accuracy of the network's predictions. Figure 5.10 presents the inner workings of the backpropagation algorithm in a neural network's architecture. From the

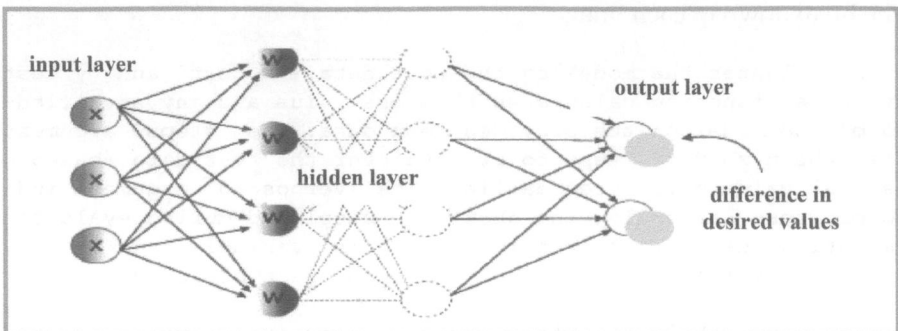

FIGURE 5.10
Backpropagation architecture.

input layer through several hidden layers to the output layer, the diagram visually captures the flow of data and subsequent calculations of errors. Once the network produces its predictions in the output layer, the differences between these predictions and the true values are measured. This prediction error is then propagated backward through the network. This backpropagation helps in adjusting the weights of the connections, optimizing the network for more accurate future predictions. The interconnected nodes and directed arrows emphasize the iterative and layered nature of this learning process, underlining the importance of each step in refining the model's performance.

5.4.3 Single-layer Perceptron

Frank Rosenblatt introduced the single-layer perceptron, a rudimentary type of FFNN, in 1964. This network architecture consists of just one layer of input nodes directly connected to a layer of output nodes, with no intervening hidden layers. The primary application of a single-layer perceptron lies in binary classification problems, where the goal is to separate input data into two distinct classes based on a linear decision boundary. In the training phase, the perceptron learning algorithm is employed to adjust the network's weights and biases. This adjustment is based on the errors that the network produces on the training data. As a result, the perceptron gets better at correctly classifying the input data into the respective classes. Figure 5.11 visually captures the essence of a single-layer perceptron.

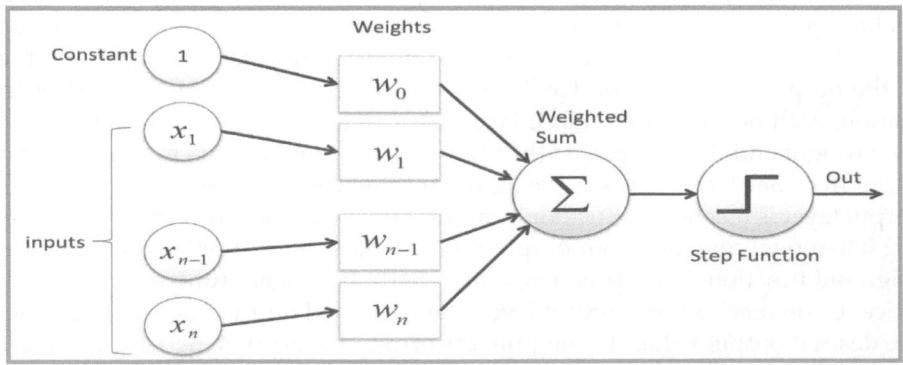

FIGURE 5.11
Single-layer perceptron.

At the forefront, it showcases an array of input nodes that receive various data points. Among these input nodes, a distinct node, labeled "constant = 1", represents the bias unit which aids in shifting the decision boundary. Each input node is associated with a specific weight, signifying its importance in the decision-making process. All these weighted inputs converge to be summed up, forming a weighted sum. This sum is then passed through a step function, which essentially decides the final output of the perceptron based on whether the sum is above or below a certain threshold. The resulting output node captures this decision, providing a clear visual journey from data intake to decision output in the simplistic yet foundational architecture of a single-layer perceptron.

5.4.4 Multi-layer Perceptron (MLP)

MLP is a powerful neural network architecture predominantly used for tackling classification problems involving nonlinear functions. It is structured with three key components: the input layer, one or more hidden layers, and the output layer. The input layer takes data from the dataset, while the output layer generates the final output. The hidden layers, positioned between the input and output layers, are where most data transformations occur. In an MLP, each node processes incoming signals by applying a nonlinear activation function to the weighted sum of the inputs. This activation function introduces nonlinearity into the network, which is critical for learning complex data patterns. MLPs commonly employ activation functions, such as sigmoid, tanh, or ReLU. Learning in an MLP involves adjusting the weights of the connections between nodes to better map the input data to the correct outputs. This process leverages the backpropagation algorithm, which calculates the error between the network's predicted output and the actual output, then propagates this error backward through the network to adjust the weights iteratively, thus minimizing the error. Due to its versatility and capacity to learn intricate patterns in data, MLPs find applications in diverse domains, such as image recognition, natural language processing, and financial analysis. Figure 5.12 provides a visual breakdown of a Multi-Layer Perceptron (MLP) architecture. Starting from the left, we have the input layer consisting of three nodes labeled as input 1, input 2, and input 3. These nodes are responsible for receiving individual data points or features. From the input layer, connections branch out to a hidden layer containing four nodes. This hidden layer serves

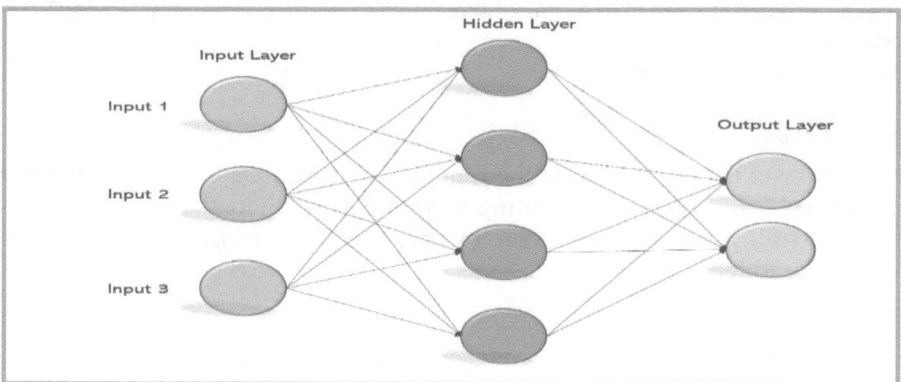

FIGURE 5.12
Multi-layer perceptron.

as a computational space where the network can internally process and transform the inputs, making it possible to capture complex patterns and relationships in the data. The figure culminates on the right with an output layer, comprising two nodes, representing the final decision or prediction made by the MLP. It's worth noting, as suggested, that additional hidden layers can be introduced between the depicted input and output layers to further enhance the network's learning capacity and tackle even more intricate data complexities.

5.4.4.1 MLP with TensorFlow

Here we implement the MLP using TensorFlow.

5.4.4.1.1 Import Libraries

The main libraries required for this implementation are TensorFlow, NumPy, and Keras. By importing these libraries, you gain access to the functionality and tools they offer, enabling you to work with neural networks and carry out various deep learning tasks using TensorFlow and Keras.

```
import tensorflow as tf
import numpy as np
from tensorflow import keras
```

Here's the breakdown of each code line:

```
#This line imports the TensorFlow library, which is a popular deep
learning library for building and training neural networks.
import tensorflow as tf

#This line imports the NumPy library, which is a fundamental library for
scientific computing in Python. NumPy provides powerful tools for working
with multi-dimensional arrays and mathematical functions.
import numpy as np

#This line imports the Keras module from TensorFlow. Keras is a user-
friendly deep learning library that provides a high-level API for
defining and training neural networks. It is integrated into TensorFlow
and offers a simplified interface for building and training models
efficiently.
from tensorflow import keras
```

5.4.4.1.2 Load Data

The MNIST dataset is imported from the Keras dataset, and the data samples are divided into training and testing sets. By executing this code, you can load the MNIST dataset and partition it into training and test sets, thereby preparing it for training and evaluating your neural network models.

```
from keras.datasets import mnist
(x_train, y_train), (x_test, y_test) = mnist.load_data()
```

Here's the breakdown of each line:

```
#This line imports the MNIST dataset module from Keras. The MNIST
dataset is a widely used benchmark dataset in machine learning,
consisting of 60,000 training images and 10,000 test images of
handwritten digits.
from keras.datasets import mnist
```

```
#This line loads the MNIST dataset and assigns it to the variables `x_
train`, `y_train`, `x_test`, and `y_test`. The `load_data()` function
retrieves the dataset and returns four NumPy arrays:
```

- `x_train`: Training images. It is a 3D array of shape `(num_samples, 28, 28)`, where `num_samples` is the number of training samples, and each image is a 28x28 grayscale image represented as an array.
- `y_train`: Training labels. It is a 1D array of shape `(num_samples,)`, containing the corresponding labels (integers) for each training image.
- `x_test`: Test images. It is a 3D array of shape `(num_samples, 28, 28)`, where `num_samples` is the number of test samples, and each image is a 28x28 grayscale image represented as an array.
- `y_test`: Test labels. It is a 1D array of shape `(num_samples,)`, containing the corresponding labels (integers) for each test image.

```
(x_train, y_train), (x_test, y_test) = mnist.load_data()
```

5.4.4.1.3 One Hot and Normalization Data

The TensorFlow one-hot module can be used for one-hot encoding operations, and normalization can be achieved by dividing the data by 255. By executing this code, the labels will be one-hot encoded, and the pixel values of the images will be normalized to a range between 0 and 1. This prepares the data for training a neural network model on the MNIST dataset.

```
y_train = tf.one_hot(y_train, 10)
y_test = tf.one_hot(y_test, 10)
x_train = x_train / 255.0
x_test = x_test / 255.0
```

Here's the breakdown of each code line:

```
#This line uses the `tf.one_hot` function from TensorFlow to perform
one-hot encoding on the training labels (`y_train`). Each label in
`y_train` is converted into a binary vector representation with a single
element set to 1 and the rest set to 0. The resulting one-hot encoded
labels have a size of 10, corresponding to the number of classes in the
MNIST dataset.
y_train = tf.one_hot(y_train, 10)
```

```
#This line uses the `tf.one_hot` function again, but this time it
performs one-hot encoding on the test labels (`y_test`). Similar to the
previous line, each label in `y_test` is converted into a one-hot encoded
binary vector representation with a size of 10.
y_test = tf.one_hot(y_test, 10)
```

```
#This line normalizes the pixel values of the training images (`x_train`)
by dividing each pixel value by 255.0. By dividing by 255.0, the pixel
values are scaled down to the range of 0 to 1, which is a common
preprocessing step in machine learning tasks. This normalization step
ensures that the pixel values are in a consistent and appropriate range
for training the neural network model.
x_train = x_train / 255.0
```

```
#This line performs the same normalization process as the previous line,
but it applies it to the test images (`x_test`). The pixel values of the
test images are divided by 255.0 to normalize them between 0 and 1,
similar to the training images.
x_test = x_test / 255.0
```

5.4.4.1.4 Making Model

A model is provided by using the Sequential module in Keras and defining the layers by specifying the inputs and activation functions. By defining this model architecture, you have created a Sequential neural network with multiple layers suitable for processing the MNIST dataset.

```
model = keras.Sequential([
    keras.layers.Flatten(input_shape=(28, 28)),
    keras.layers.Dense(128, activation='relu'),
    keras.layers.Dropout(.2, input_shape=(2,)),
    keras.layers.Dense(32, activation='relu'),
    keras.layers.Dropout(.2, input_shape=(2,)),
    keras.layers.Dense(10, activation='softmax')])
```

Here's the breakdown of each code line:

```
#This line adds a Flatten layer to the model. The Flatten layer
transforms the input into a 1D array by reshaping the input tensor of
shape `(batch_size, 28, 28)` into `(batch_size, 28*28)`. It prepares the
image data for the fully connected layers.
keras.layers.Flatten(input_shape=(28, 28))
```

```
#This line adds a Dense layer with 128 units to the model. The Dense
layer is a fully connected layer where each neuron is connected to every
neuron in the previous layer. The activation function used in this layer
is ReLU (Rectified Linear Unit), which introduces non-linearity to the
network.
keras.layers.Dense(128, activation='relu')
```

```
#This line adds a Dropout layer with a dropout rate of 0.2. Dropout is
a regularization technique that randomly sets a fraction of input
units to 0 during training, which helps prevent overfitting. The
`input_shape` parameter is not necessary in this case and can be
omitted.
keras.layers.Dropout(.2, input_shape=(2,))
```

```
#This line adds another Dense layer with 32 units to the model.
Similarly, it is a fully connected layer with ReLU activation.
keras.layers.Dense(32, activation='relu')
```

```
#This line adds another Dropout layer with a dropout rate of 0.2.
keras.layers.Dropout(.2, input_shape=(2,))

#This line adds the output Dense layer with 10 units (one for each class
in the MNIST dataset). The activation function used is softmax, which
produces a probability distribution over the classes, indicating the
likelihood of each class for a given input.
keras.layers.Dense(10, activation='softmax')
```

5.4.4.1.5 Model Summary

For providing a high-level overview of the network architecture, a model summary is a good practice.

```
# Check the model summary for more information about the architecture and
its parameters.
model.summary()
Model: "sequential"
```

Layer (type)	Output Shape	Param #
flatten_4 (Flatten)	(None, 784)	0
dense_12 (Dense)	(None, 128)	100480
dropout_5 (Dropout)	(None, 128)	0
dense_13 (Dense)	(None, 32)	4128
dropout_6 (Dropout)	(None, 32)	0
dense_14 (Dense)	(None, 10)	330

```
Total params: 104,938
Trainable params: 104,938
Non-trainable params: 0
```

5.4.4.1.6 Compile the Model

The model in Keras can be run by defining its parameters, such as the metric value and optimizer type. By compiling the model with the specified loss function, metrics, and optimizer, the model is now ready to be trained and evaluated on the MNIST dataset.

```
model.compile(loss='categorical_crossentropy', metrics=['accuracy'],
optimizer='adam')
```

Here's the breakdown of each line:

```
#This line compiles the model and configures the learning process. The
`compile` function takes several arguments:
```

- `loss='categorical_crossentropy'`: This argument specifies the loss function to be used during training. Since the labels are one-hot encoded, `categorical_crossentropy` is a suitable loss function for multi-class classification problems.

- `` `metrics=['accuracy']` ``: This argument specifies the evaluation metric(s) to be used during training and testing. In this case, the model will be evaluated based on accuracy, which calculates the percentage of correctly classified samples.
- `` `optimizer='adam'` ``: This argument specifies the optimizer algorithm to be used during training. In this case, the Adam optimizer is used. Adam is an adaptive learning rate optimization algorithm that adjusts the learning rate during training to improve convergence.

```
model.compile(loss='categorical_crossentropy', metrics=['accuracy'],
optimizer='adam')
```

5.4.4.1.7 Train the Model

In the training step, parameters, such as batch size and epochs, are set. Then, the fit module from a model in Keras is used to train the model. By executing this code, the model will be trained on the MNIST dataset. The training progress, including loss and accuracy metrics, will be logged using the TensorBoard callback. The training history, which includes the metrics at each epoch, will be stored in the "history" variable.

```
n_val = 5000
n_train = 60000
n_test = 10000
batch_size=100
epochs=100
steps_per_epoch = int((n_train-n_val)/batch_size)
n_val = 5000
validation_split = n_val/n_train
validation_steps = int(n_val / batch_size)
test_steps = int(n_test/batch_size)
history = model.fit(x_train, y_train, epochs=epochs, steps_per_
epoch=steps_per_epoch, validation_split= validation_split, validation_
steps=validation_steps, callbacks=[tensorboard_callback])
```

Here's the breakdown of each code line:

```
#This line sets the variable `n_val` to the value 5000. `n_val`
represents the number of validation samples.
n_val = 5000

#This line sets the variable `n_train` to the value 60000. `n_train`
represents the number of training samples.
n_train = 60000

#This line sets the variable `n_test` to the value 10000. `n_test`
represents the number of test samples.
n_test = 10000

#This line sets the variable `batch_size` to the value 100. `batch_size`
determines the number of samples per gradient update during training.
batch_size=100

#This line sets the variable `epochs` to the value 100. `epochs`
represents the number of training epochs.
epochs=100
```

```
#This line calculates the variable `steps_per_epoch` by subtracting the
number of validation samples (`n_val`) from the number of training
samples (`n_train`), and then dividing it by the `batch_size`. It
represents the number of steps required to cover the training data once
based on the batch size and the difference between the number of training
samples and the number of validation samples.
steps_per_epoch = int((n_train-n_val)/batch_size)
```

```
#This line sets the variable `n_val` to the value 5000. This line is
repeated, but it doesn't have any effect on the subsequent calculations
since `n_val` has already been set earlier.
n_val = 5000
```

```
#This line calculates the variable `validation_split` by dividing the
number of validation samples (`n_val`) by the number of training samples
(`n_train`). It represents the fraction of the training data to be used
for validation during training.
validation_split = n_val/n_train
```

```
#This line calculates the variable `validation_steps` by dividing the
number of validation samples (`n_val`) by the `batch_size`. It represents
the number of steps required to cover the validation data once based on
the batch size.
validation_steps = int(n_val / batch_size)
```

```
#This line calculates the variable `test_steps` by dividing the number of
test samples (`n_test`) by the `batch_size`. It represents the number of
steps required to cover the test data once based on the batch size.
test_steps = int(n_test/batch_size)
```

```
#This line trains the model using the `fit` function. It takes the
training data (`x_train` and `y_train`) as input along with other
arguments:
```

- `epochs`: The number of training epochs.
- `steps_per_epoch`: The number of steps to iterate over the training data in each epoch.
- `validation_split`: The fraction of the training data to be used for validation during training.
- `validation_steps`: The number of steps to iterate over the validation data in each epoch.
- `callbacks`: Additional callbacks to be applied during training. Here, `tensorboard_callback` is used as a callback for logging the training progress.

```
history = model.fit(x_train, y_train, epochs=epochs, steps_per_
epoch=steps_per_epoch, validation_split= validation_split, validation_
steps=validation_steps, callbacks=[tensorboard_callback])
```

5.4.4.1.8 *Test the Model*

Finally, before applying the trained model to real-world data, it can be tested with test data. By executing this code, you will obtain the test loss and test accuracy of the model, trained on the MNIST dataset, when evaluated against the test dataset.

```
score = model.evaluate(x_test,  y_test, steps=test_steps, verbose=0)
print('Test loss:', score[0])
print('Test accuracy:', score[1])
```

Here's the breakdown of each line:

```
#This line evaluates the model on the test data (`x_test` and `y_test`).
The `evaluate` function calculates the loss value and any specified
metrics of the model on the provided test data. The `steps` argument
specifies the number of steps to iterate over the test data, based on the
`test_steps` value calculated earlier. The `verbose=0` argument indicates
that no progress bar or logging should be displayed during evaluation.
The evaluation result is stored in the `score` variable.
score = model.evaluate(x_test,  y_test, steps=test_steps, verbose=0)
```

```
#These lines print the evaluation results. `score[0]` corresponds to the
test loss value, and `score[1]` corresponds to the test accuracy. By
printing these values, you can assess the performance of the trained
model on the unseen test data.
print('Test loss:', score[0])
print('Test accuracy:', score[1])
```

5.5 Artificial Neural Networks Issues

ANNs are powerful machine learning models widely used in various applications, such as image recognition, speech recognition, natural language processing, and more. However, like any technology, ANNs have their limitations and challenges. These issues highlight the importance of careful design, optimization, and testing when developing ANNs for practical applications. Here are some issues commonly associated with ANNs.

5.5.1 Overfitting

ANNs are prone to overfitting, where the model learns the training data too well, thus hampering its ability to generalize to new data.

5.5.2 Underfitting

On the other hand, ANNs can also underfit, where the model is too simple to capture the complexity of the data, leading to poor performance.

5.5.3 Gradient Vanishing/Exploding

The vanishing or exploding gradient problem can occur during the training of deep neural networks, making it difficult to optimize the model.

5.5.4 Training Time

Training ANNs can be time-consuming, especially for deep neural networks with a large number of parameters.

5.5.5 Data Requirements

ANNs require large amounts of data for effective training, which may not be available for some applications.

5.5.6 Hardware Requirements

Training and running ANNs can be computationally intensive, requiring specialized hardware, such as GPUs or TPUs.

5.5.7 Interpretability

ANNs can be challenging to interpret, making it difficult to understand how the model is making predictions.

5.5.8 Robustness

ANNs can be sensitive to adversarial attacks, where minor changes to the input can cause the model to misclassify the data.

5.5.9 Bias

ANNs can suffer from bias, where the model's predictions are influenced by the biases present in the training data.

5.5.10 Transferability

ANNs may not transfer well to new domains or tasks, requiring retraining on new data.

5.5.11 Architecture Selection

Choosing the right architecture for ANNs can be challenging, as there are many different architectures to choose from, each with their strengths and weaknesses.

5.5.12 Hyperparameter Tuning

ANNs have many hyperparameters that need to be tuned to achieve optimal performance, which can be time-consuming.

5.5.13 Scalability

ANNs can be challenging to scale for large datasets and distributed computing environments.

5.5.14 Continual Learning

ANNs may not be well-suited for continual learning tasks, where the model needs to adapt to new data over time.

5.5.15 Cost

ANNs can be expensive to develop and deploy, requiring significant resources and expertise.

5.6 Artificial Neural Networks Implementation Tips

Here are some implementation tips for ANNs.

5.6.1 Normalize Input Data

Normalizing input data can improve the performance of neural networks by ensuring that the input data has a similar range.

5.6.2 Use Appropriate Activation Functions

Choosing the right activation functions for the hidden and output layers can enhance the performance of the neural network.

5.6.3 Implement Early Stopping

Early stopping can help prevent overfitting by halting the training process before the neural network starts to memorize the training data.

5.6.4 Use Regularization

Regularization techniques like L_1, L_2, and dropout can prevent overfitting by adding penalties to the weights and biases of the neural network.

5.6.5 Use Batch Normalization

Batch normalization can improve the performance of neural networks by normalizing the output of the hidden layers.

5.6.6 Implement Learning Rate Decay

Implementing learning rate decay can enhance the performance of the neural network by gradually reducing the learning rate over time.

5.6.7 Use a Suitable Loss Function

Choosing the right loss function can help in optimizing the neural network for a specific task.

5.6.8 Avoid Using Too Many Layers

Using too many layers in a neural network can lead to overfitting and can slow the training process.

5.6.9 Use an Appropriate Optimizer

Choosing the right optimizer can enhance the performance of the neural network by optimizing the weights and biases.

5.6.10 Use Dropout

Dropout, a regularization technique, can help prevent overfitting by randomly dropping out neurons during training.

5.6.11 Use Data Augmentation

Data augmentation can improve the performance of the neural network by creating additional training data from existing data.

5.6.12 Use Cross-validation

Cross-validation can aid in evaluating the performance of the neural network and preventing overfitting.

5.6.13 Choose Appropriate Network Architecture

Selecting the right network architecture is crucial for improving the performance of the neural network.

5.6.14 Use Transfer Learning

Transfer learning can enhance the performance of the neural network by leveraging pre-trained models for specific tasks.

Remember, hands-on experience is key when working with ANN or any other machine learning models. Therefore, consistently practicing implementation and troubleshooting is crucial for mastering these concepts.

5.7 Lessons Learned

- Learn Artificial Neural Networks (ANNs) Architecture and Types
- Learn Linear and Nonlinear Functions in ANNs
- Learn ANNs Architectures
- Learn Implementing the FFNN
- Multi-Layer Perceptron (MLP)
- Learn Implementing the MLP
- Learn the Issue of ANNs
- Learn the Implementation Tips of ANNs

5.8 Problems

5.8.1   What exactly are ANNs?

5.8.2   Explain how ANNs are similar to the biological neuron system in the human body.

5.8.3   What is the difference between a feedforward neural network and a recurrent neural network?

5.8.4   What is backpropagation, and how does it function in training an artificial neural network?

5.8.5   How can overfitting be prevented during the training of an artificial neural network?

5.8.6   What is the role of activation functions in a neural network, and which are some commonly used activation functions?

5.8.7   How can dropout be utilized to prevent overfitting in a neural network?

5.8.8   What is a convolutional neural network, and how does it differ from a traditional feedforward neural network?

5.8.9   What is a recurrent neural network, and how is it useful in applications like natural language processing?

5.8.10 How can hyperparameters, such as learning rate, number of hidden layers, and batch size, be optimized during neural network training?

5.8.11 What is transfer learning, and how can it be utilized in training a neural network for a specific task?

5.8.12 What are the differences between supervised, unsupervised, and semi-supervised learning in the context of neural networks?

5.8.13 What is the difference between a regression and a classification task in neural networks?

5.8.14 How can regularization be used to prevent overfitting in a neural network?

5.8.15 What is the vanishing gradient problem, and how can it be addressed in deep neural networks?

5.8.16 How can early stopping be utilized to prevent overfitting in a neural network?

5.8.17 What is the role of normalization techniques, such as batch normalization, in the training of neural networks?

5.8.18 How can the performance of a trained neural network be evaluated and compared with other models?

5.8.19 How can imbalanced data be managed in the context of training a neural network for a classification task?

5.8.20 What are some common pitfalls to avoid when training a neural network?

5.8.21 How can neural networks be employed for unsupervised learning tasks such as clustering and dimensionality reduction?

5.8.22 How can transfer learning be utilized in neural network applications like image recognition and natural language processing?

5.9 Programming Questions

- **Easy**
    - **5.9.1** Implement a single-layer perceptron in Python.
    - **5.9.2** Build a feedforward neural network with one hidden layer using Keras.
    - **5.9.3** Train a neural network to classify the MNIST dataset in Python.

- **Medium**
    - **5.9.4** Implement a multi-layer perceptron in Python.
    - **5.9.5** Build a convolutional neural network using TensorFlow.
    - **5.9.6** Train a recurrent neural network for sequence prediction in TensorFlow.

- **Hard**
    - **5.9.7** Implement a neural network from scratch using only NumPy.
    - **5.9.8** Build a generative adversarial network for image generation using Tensorflow.
    - **5.9.9** Train a deep reinforcement learning agent to play a game using TensorFlow.

6

Deep Neural Networks (DNNs) Fundamentals and Architectures

The following topics are covered in this chapter about Fundamentals and Architectures of Deep Neural Networks:

- Deep Neural Networks (DNNs)
- Deep Learning Applications
- Deep Learning Algorithms and Architectures
- Deep Learning Issues
- Deep Learning Implementation Tips

6.1 Preface

Deep learning is a subfield of machine learning that utilizes artificial neural networks (ANNs) to model and solve complex problems. An ANN with multiple hidden layers between its input and output layers is referred to as a deep neural network (DNN). The primary purpose of a neural network in real-world problem-solving, such as classification, is to accept a series of data inputs, process them using increasingly complex algorithms, and generate results. In deep learning, a deep network comprises both an input and an output layer, operating on a stream of sequential data. Most of the hidden layers in deep learning models are nonlinear. Deep learning models often exhibit superior performance compared to standard machine learning networks in terms of output accuracy. Deep learning algorithms are designed to automatically learn representations of data through multiple layers of interconnected nodes. This enables them to perform tasks like image recognition, natural language processing, and speech recognition with previously unattainable accuracy. The success of deep learning can be attributed to the availability of large datasets and the development of powerful computing technologies, such as graphics processing units (GPUs), capable of handling the massive amounts of data and calculations required for training these models. Several popular deep learning architectures exist, including Convolutional Neural Networks (CNNs) for image recognition, Recurrent Neural Networks (RNNs) for sequential data processing, and Generative Adversarial Networks (GANs) for generating new data. The applications of deep learning are vast and varied, spanning from self-driving cars and virtual assistants to medical image analysis and even art generation. As the field continues to advance, it is expected to have a significant impact on various industries and aspects of our daily lives. This chapter provides an overview of deep learning architectures, features, concepts, and applications. Figure 6.1 delineates the fundamental workflow differences between traditional machine learning and deep learning when it comes to image classification.

DOI: 10.1201/9781003281344-6

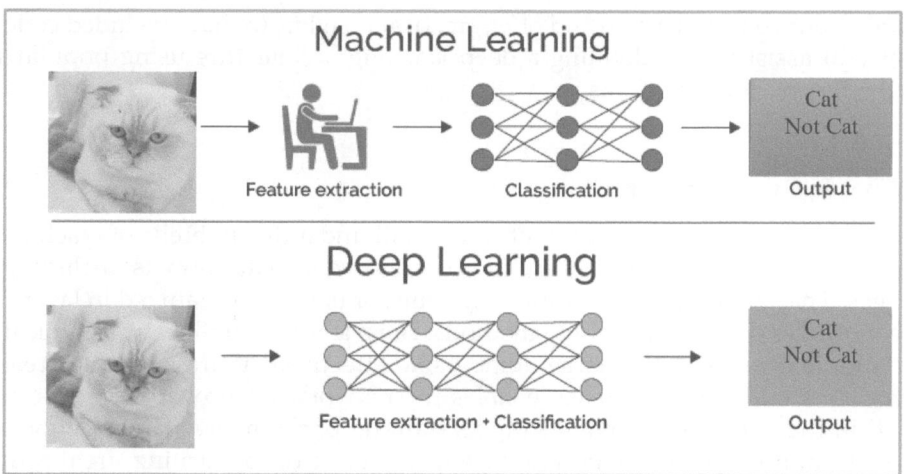

FIGURE 6.1
Machine Learning vs. Deep Learning in simple view.

For the machine learning side, the process is divided into distinct stages:

1. Starting with the "input" stage, we begin with an image.
2. This transitions into the "feature extraction" phase, where handcrafted methods or algorithms are used to identify and extract meaningful attributes from the image.
3. The extracted features then proceed to the "classification" step, which uses algorithms to determine the category of the image.
4. Finally, we arrive at the "output", where the system predicts whether the image represents a "cat" or "not a cat".

In contrast, the deep learning approach streamlines the process:

1. With the same image "input" as the starting point.
2. The data feeds directly into the "deep learning" phase. Within this step, both "feature extraction" and "classification" happen concurrently, utilizing layers of interconnected nodes or neurons.
3. This leads to the final "output", delivering a prediction of "cat" or "not a cat".

This side-by-side depiction underscores the power and efficiency of deep learning in directly learning from raw data without the necessity of manual feature engineering, unlike its machine learning counterpart.

6.2 Deep Neural Networks (DNNs)

When working with deep learning algorithms, it is crucial to familiarize yourself with a variety of key concepts. This chapter aims to delve into various deep learning models, ideas, and definitions, providing a comprehensive understanding of this intricate field.

To enhance your comprehension and offer practical insights, we have included code examples that will assist you in defining a deep learning architecture using popular frameworks like TensorFlow and Keras.

6.2.1 What Is Deep Learning?

Deep learning algorithms, as a subset of ANNs, fall under the umbrella of machine learning. These algorithms have the ability to process diverse data formats, including audio and images. They achieve this by employing units, or neurons, organized in layers, where each layer utilizes distinct processing methods. Deep learning architectures typically consist of multiple layers, often in large numbers, to effectively address complex real-world problems. This multilayer approach enables the network to uncover more intricate features within the data, thereby enhancing its training performance. The selection of various crucial parameters and hyperparameters within a deep learning architecture can impact learning characteristics, such as speed and accuracy. Figure 6.2 visually illustrates the relationship between machine learning and deep learning, demonstrating how deep learning is a subset of neural networks. This subset encompasses advanced architectures like GANs and others.

6.2.2 Deep Learning Needs

To train deep learning algorithms effectively, a substantial amount of data is necessary, which in turn contributes to the considerable computational cost associated with deep learning. Overcoming the challenges posed by large datasets and high computation costs is essential for enabling more efficient application of deep learning algorithms. Ongoing research is focused on improving the efficiency and performance of these algorithms, as well as developing methods for generating new data from existing datasets.

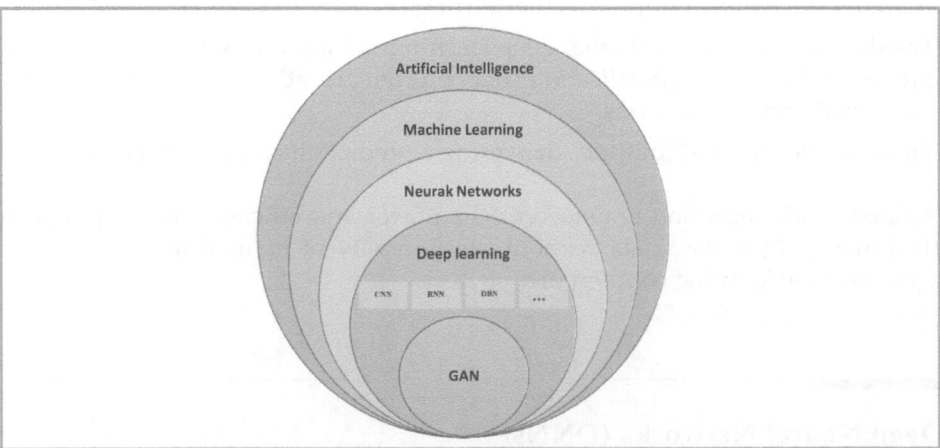

FIGURE 6.2
GAN is a subset of artificial intelligence.

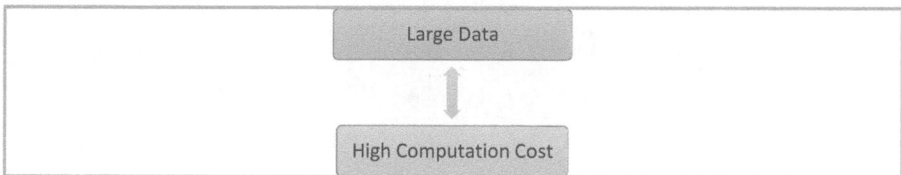

FIGURE 6.3
There is a challenge between the value of large amounts of data and the high computational costs.

Figure 6.3 underscores two pivotal considerations central to deep learning implementations:

1. **Large data requirement:** The graphic emphasizes that deep learning models thrive on vast amounts of data. These models, due to their complexity and high number of parameters, necessitate substantial data volumes to train effectively and avoid overfitting. The illustration might depict increasing data volumes or show a comparison between traditional learning with smaller datasets and deep learning with larger ones.

2. **High computational Cost:** Parallel to the data depiction, the figure also brings attention to the substantial computational resources deep learning models demand. Training deep neural networks requires advanced hardware, often in the form of GPUs or TPUs, to handle the extensive matrix operations and computations. The visualization might represent a computer or server infrastructure, signifying the heavy computational machinery that supports these models.

Together, these two points serve as a reminder that while deep learning techniques are powerful, they come with prerequisites that one needs to be prepared for when venturing into this domain. Researchers are actively seeking solutions to address this challenge within the field of deep learning approaches.

6.2.3 How to Deploy Deep Learning More Efficiently?

When striving to optimize the use of deep learning, it is important to keep in mind several key foundational factors. Selecting and implementing deep learning architectures accurately and effectively are crucial steps. However, once the initial model has been trained, further optimization becomes possible. Figure 6.4 visually underscores essential considerations for deploying deep learning techniques. At its foundation, the emphasis is on having a relevant and properly curated dataset, ensuring the model generalizes effectively to real-world scenarios. Preprocessing data, including tasks such as normalization, missing value handling, and feature engineering, stands out as a paramount step, echoing the principle of "garbage in, garbage out". Further annotations in the diagram likely delve into the importance of selecting the appropriate model architecture, properly evaluating model performance, assessing computational requirements, and ethically managing data. Altogether, this diagram serves as a comprehensive checklist for practitioners navigating the deep learning landscape.

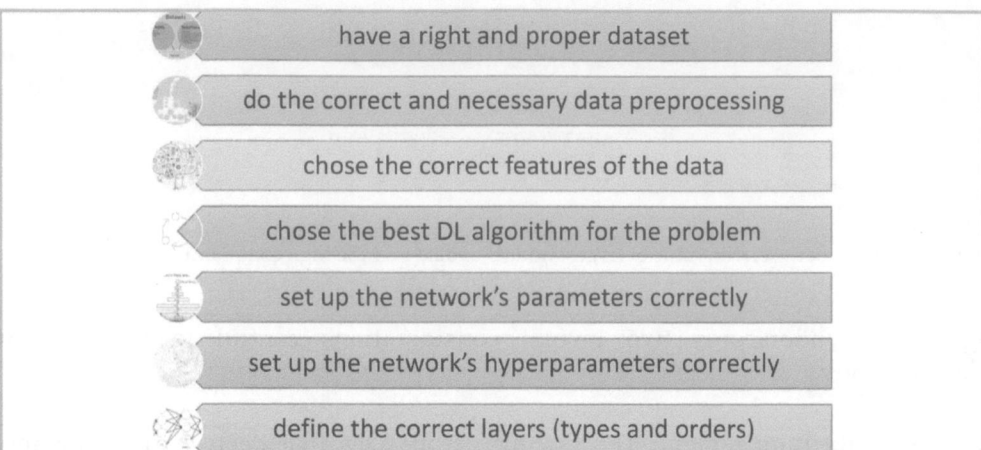

FIGURE 6.4
Key points to consider when deploying deep learning approaches.

6.3 Deep Learning Applications

Deep learning is a powerful tool for modeling complex real-world problems, extending beyond image and audio data to various types of signal data. Its applications span a wide range of fields, exhibiting remarkable performance in numerous scenarios. Depending on the data and problem at hand, deep learning can effectively tackle specific challenges. Examples of deep learning applications are abundant. Real-time human behavior analysis, language translation, and natural disaster prediction are just a few instances where deep learning has shown its potential. The development of self-driving cars has captured significant attention, with major companies like Google, Apple, Tesla, and Uber heavily investing in this technology. Deep learning is also employed in the banking industry to prevent and detect fraudulent financial transactions, resulting in substantial savings for banks and insurance companies. Virtual assistants, such as Alexa, Siri, and Google Assistant, have become integral parts of our daily lives. They possess the ability to comprehend human language and provide intelligent, self-directed responses, offering services, such as email management and organization. A notable recent advancement in this field is ChatGPT, an AI chatbot system developed by OpenAI to showcase and evaluate the capabilities of robust AI systems. Users can ask a variety of questions, and ChatGPT typically responds with helpful information. However, the use of AI applications also brings forth certain challenges, including ethical considerations in AI and data science. These challenges explore the responsible and ethical use of AI, considering its potential impact on human life.

6.3.1 Computer Vision

Deep learning has been used for image classification, object detection, face recognition, and image segmentation. Some applications include self-driving cars, medical image analysis, and security surveillance.

6.3.2 Natural Language Processing

Deep learning has been utilized for various applications, including speech recognition, language translation, sentiment analysis, and chatbots. It has been applied in areas, such as virtual assistants, customer service, and content creation.

6.3.3 Robotics

Deep learning has been employed in diverse applications, such as robot control, object recognition, and task planning. Areas of use include industrial automation, warehouse logistics, and healthcare robotics.

6.3.4 Finance

Deep learning has been applied to various applications, including fraud detection, stock price prediction, and credit risk assessment. Specific uses include fraud detection in credit card transactions, algorithmic trading, and loan underwriting.

6.3.5 Biology and Healthcare

Deep learning has been extensively employed in medical image analysis, drug discovery, and genomics research. It has proven valuable in applications, such as disease diagnosis, drug development, and personalized medicine.

6.3.6 Gaming

Deep learning has found applications in game AI, player behavior prediction, and content generation. Tasks include developing game bots, enabling adaptive difficulty in games, and facilitating procedural content generation.

6.3.7 Agriculture

Deep learning has been employed in various agricultural applications, including crop yield prediction, soil analysis, and pest detection. It has been instrumental in the field of precision agriculture, aiding in tasks, such as crop disease diagnosis and enabling robotic farming systems.

These are just a few examples of the numerous applications of deep learning, and new applications are constantly being explored and developed. Figure 6.5 illustrates several applications that leverage deep learning algorithms.

self-driving cars	natural language processing	content analysis	visual recognition	fashion	chatbots
virtual agents	text generation	handwritten generation	machine translation	advertising	fraud detection

FIGURE 6.5
Deep learning has numerous applications.

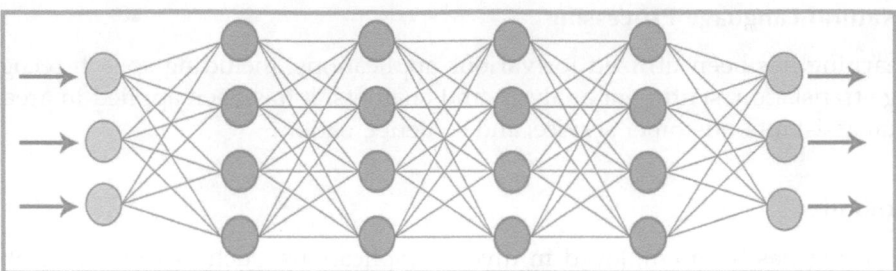

FIGURE 6.6
DNN with four hidden layers.

6.4 Deep Learning Algorithms and Architectures

DNNs are characterized by their multiple hidden layers. When we refer to "deep" in neural networks, we're implying that these models are highly complex.

Figure 6.6 showcases the architecture of a Deep Neural Network (DNN) consisting of four hidden layers. Each of these hidden layers is equipped with four nodes, suggesting a consistent structure across the network's depth. The input layer introduces the data with three nodes, and the output layer, also with three nodes, presents the network's predictions or classifications. The consistent node distribution across the layers signifies a balanced design, possibly aimed at handling a specific type of data or problem. This depiction offers a clear visualization of the depth and symmetry present in some DNN designs. In this architecture, there's a specific layer designated for input, another for output, and four additional layers that are hidden.

6.4.1 Recurrent Neural Networks (RNNs)

An RNN is a type of neural network often used for time series prediction problems. Unlike regular neural networks, RNNs can handle problems involving sequential data with order, storing past data to use for future predictions. RNNs process each element in a sequence, retaining characteristics of the previous element before advancing to the next. Each neuron cell, also known as a node, is not only linked to another node but also to itself, which facilitates the memory of sequential data. RNNs are trained using the stochastic gradient descent method and process data through both feed-forward and backpropagation methods. These techniques offer feedback of the processed data output values to the hidden and input layers, respectively. This process is illustrated in Figure 6.7, which shows the design of an RNN and the connections between the output and hidden layers. RNNs come in two basic types: bidirectional RNNs and deep RNNs. Importantly, all layers within an RNN share the same parameter settings, leveraging the same values across the network. RNNs have a broad range of applications. They can predict an event's outcome by analyzing previous data, such as stock market data. One common application is sentiment analysis, which identifies whether a sentence or phrase carries a positive or negative sentiment. With the rapid advancements in deep learning structures and computational capacity, RNNs are quickly becoming one of the most captivating types of DNNs.

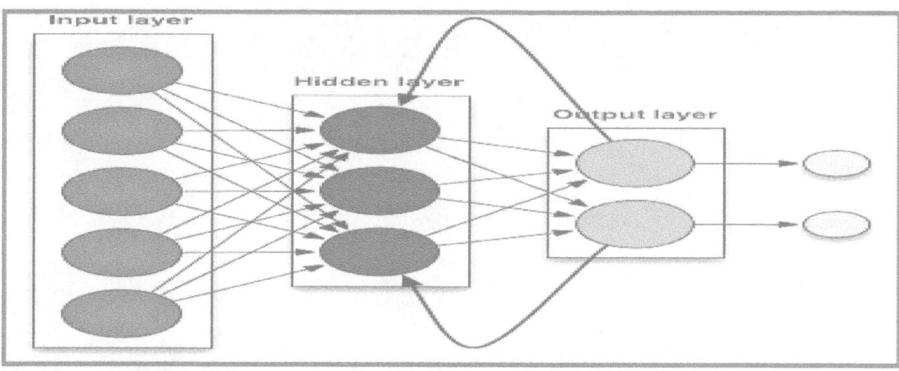

FIGURE 6.7
RNN uses the features of previous layers.

6.4.2 Long Short-term Memory (LSTM)

RNNs often struggle with processing long-term data, but LSTM networks provide a solution to this problem. An LSTM is a type of RNN that incorporates memory blocks within the neurons for layer connections and utilizes backpropagation for training. LSTM networks diverge from traditional RNNs in three significant ways: the control of input data, the retention of sample data, and the management of outputs. This specialization has allowed LSTMs to be successfully deployed in various fields, including language translation, emotion analysis, financial market prediction, and photo captioning. RNNs commonly encounter the "vanishing gradient" problem during training, where changes to weights become so small that they impede effective learning. Combined with their limitations in handling short-term memory, RNNs often find it challenging to process lengthy sequences or series of data. LSTMs, however, help to address these challenges by enabling RNNs to distinguish between short-term memory (represented by input data in sequence) and long-term memory (the selection and operation on data drawn from short-term memory). This differentiation plays a crucial role in mitigating the vanishing gradient problem. Figure 6.8 provides an illustration of the overall architecture of LSTMs, highlighting their major components.

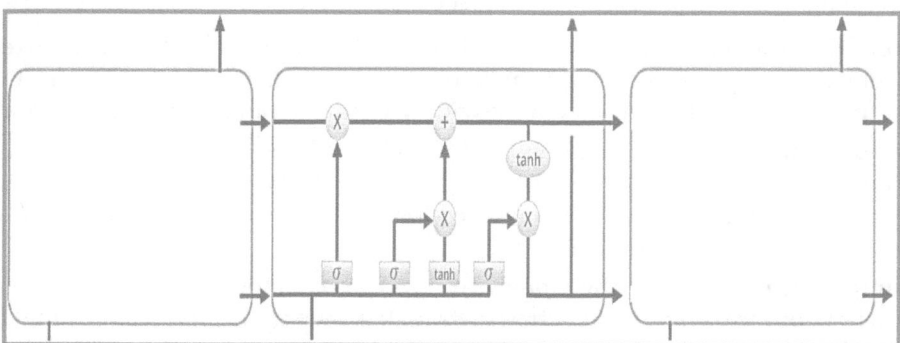

FIGURE 6.8
LSTMs are RNNs with memory that use backpropagation.

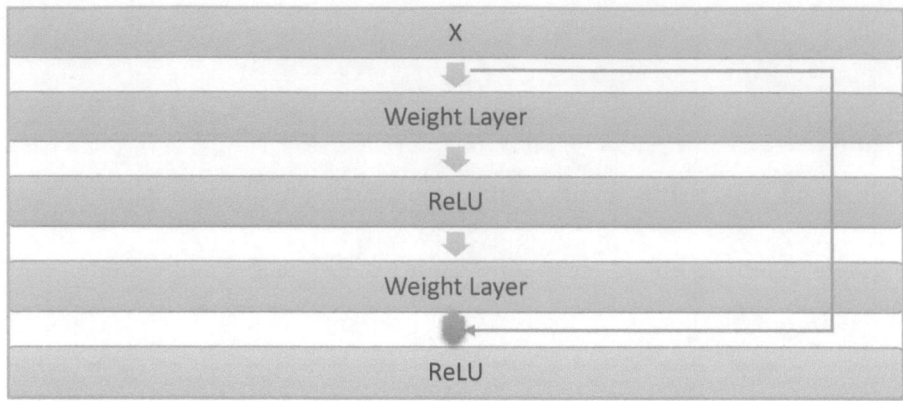

FIGURE 6.9
ResNets architecture.

6.4.3 Residual Neural Networks (ResNets)

ResNet is used when other methods, such as CNNs, struggle with complex problems. It incorporates several residual modules, often referred to as layers, each capable of performing various operations on the input data. ResNet is recognized for its precision and efficiency, requiring fewer weights compared to RNNs. Figure 6.9 depicts the ResNet architecture, where the input (represented as X) passes through successive layers before reaching the ReLU layer.

6.4.3.1 Designing an RNN

TensorFlow and Keras are utilized in building an RNN model for classifying the MNIST database. The LSTM model is specifically employed, and the implementation involves five main stages, which are described below.

1. **Importing the required libraries:** The necessary libraries, including TensorFlow and Keras, are imported to provide the foundational framework for building the RNN model.

2. **Loading the MNIST dataset:** The MNIST dataset, consisting of handwritten digit images, is loaded for training and testing the RNN model. This dataset is commonly used for image classification tasks.

3. **Preparing the data:** The loaded MNIST dataset is preprocessed to normalize the pixel values, typically ranging from 0 to 255, to a normalized scale between 0 and 1. This ensures that the input data is within a suitable range for the RNN model.

4. **Building the LSTM model:** The LSTM model architecture is constructed using TensorFlow and Keras. This involves defining the LSTM layer, specifying the input shape, and adding any additional layers or modifications based on the requirements of the classification task.

5. **Compiling and training the model:** The model is compiled by specifying the loss function, optimizer, and evaluation metrics. It is then trained on the training dataset using the fit() function, with the specified number of epochs and batch size. The model learns from the training data to classify the images correctly.

These five stages outline the implementation process of building an RNN model using TensorFlow and Keras for MNIST database classification.

6.4.3.1.1 *Import Libraries*

The first step is to import libraries, such as NumPy, TensorFlow, and Keras. By importing these libraries and modules, you gain access to a wide range of powerful tools and functions that facilitate efficient numerical computations, provide support for machine learning algorithms, and offer an intuitive interface for building and training deep learning models.

```
import numpy as np
import tensorflow as tf
from tensorflow import keras
from tensorflow.keras import layers
```

Here's the explanation of each code line:

```
#This line imports the NumPy library and assigns it the alias `np`. NumPy
is a widely used library in Python for numerical computations,
particularly when working with arrays and matrices. It provides efficient
implementations of mathematical operations and functions.
import numpy as np
```

```
#This line imports the TensorFlow library, which is a popular open-source
framework for machine learning. TensorFlow offers a comprehensive set of
tools and functionalities for building and training various types of
machine learning models, including deep learning models.
import tensorflow as tf
```

```
#This line imports the Keras API from TensorFlow. Keras is a high-level
deep learning API that simplifies the process of building neural
networks. It provides a user-friendly interface and supports multiple
backend frameworks, including TensorFlow, making it easier to design,
train, and evaluate deep learning models.
from tensorflow import keras
```

```
#This line imports the `layers` module from the Keras API within
TensorFlow. Keras layers serve as the building blocks for constructing
neural networks. Different types of layers, such as dense (fully
connected), convolutional, recurrent, and more, can be imported from this
module to create complex network architectures for deep learning tasks.
from tensorflow.keras import layers
```

6.4.3.1.2 *Load and Normalize the Dataset*

Using MNIST as a database, you can load the dataset, divide the data into training and testing categories, and normalize it (assuming the maximum value for pixel data is 255). By executing these lines of code, you load the MNIST dataset, split it into training and testing sets, normalize the pixel values, and extract a sample image along with its corresponding label for further use in your code.

```
mnist = keras.datasets.mnist
(x_train, y_train), (x_test, y_test) = mnist.load_data()
x_train, x_test = x_train / 255.0, x_test / 255.0
sample, sample_label = x_train[3], y_train[3]
```

Here's an explanation of each code line:

```
#This line assigns the `mnist` variable to the `mnist` dataset in the
Keras library. The MNIST dataset is a widely used dataset in machine
learning, consisting of handwritten digits from 0 to 9.
mnist = keras.datasets.mnist
```

```
#This line loads the MNIST dataset and assigns the training and testing
data to the variables `x_train`, `y_train`, `x_test`, and `y_test`. The
training data `(x_train, y_train)` consists of input images and their
corresponding labels, while the testing data `(x_test, y_test)` contains
images and labels for evaluating the trained model.
(x_train, y_train), (x_test, y_test) = mnist.load_data()
```

```
#This line normalizes the pixel values of the input images. By dividing
each pixel value by 255.0, the pixel values are scaled to a range between
0 and 1. This normalization step is often performed to ensure that the
input data falls within a consistent and manageable range for model
training.
x_train, x_test = x_train / 255.0, x_test / 255.0
```

```
#This line assigns the fourth image (`x_train[3]`) from the training
data to the variable `sample` and its corresponding label (`y_train[3]`)
to the variable `sample_label`. This allows you to extract a sample
image and its label from the dataset for further analysis or
visualization.
sample, sample_label = x_train[3], y_train[3]
```

6.4.3.1.3 Build the Model

Each MNIST image data has a size of 28 × 28, and any batch in the dataset is represented as a tensor with a shape of (batch_size, 28, 28). The corresponding labels for the images range from 0 to 9, representing handwritten digits (a total of 10 labels). By utilizing the "build_model" function, you can create a sequential model with LSTM or RNN layers. Additionally, you have the option to enable or disable the use of the cuDNN kernel, which can provide faster performance on compatible GPUs.

```
batch_size = 64
input_dim = 28
units = 64
output_size = 10
def build_model(allow_cudnn_kernel=True):
    if allow_cudnn_kernel:
        lstm_layer = keras.layers.LSTM(units, input_shape=(None,
input_dim))
    else:
        lstm_layer = keras.layers.RNN(keras.layers.LSTMCell(units), input_
shape=(None, input_dim) )
    model = keras.models.Sequential([ lstm_layer, keras.layers.
BatchNormalization(), keras.layers.Dense(output_size),])
    return model
```

Here's an explanation of each code line:

```
#These lines define the values for batch size, input dimension, number of
units in the LSTM layer, and the output size. These values can be
adjusted based on the requirements of the model.
batch_size = 64
input_dim = 28
units = 64
output_size = 10
```

```
#This function, `build_model`, takes an optional argument `allow_cudnn_
kernel` which defaults to `True`. It creates a sequential model using
Keras. If `allow_cudnn_kernel` is `True`, it creates an LSTM layer
(`keras.layers.LSTM`) with the specified number of units and input shape.
The input shape is set to `(None, input_dim)`, indicating that the model
can handle input sequences of variable lengths. If `allow_cudnn_kernel`
is `False`, it creates an RNN layer (`keras.layers.RNN`) with an LSTM
cell (`keras.layers.LSTMCell`) and the same number of units and input
shape. Next, the model is defined as a sequential model, with the LSTM
layer as the first layer, followed by a batch normalization layer (`keras.
layers.BatchNormalization`) to normalize the activations, and finally a
dense layer (`keras.layers.Dense`) with the output size specified.
def build_model(allow_cudnn_kernel=True):
    if allow_cudnn_kernel:
        lstm_layer = keras.layers.LSTM(units, input_shape=(None, input_dim))
    else:
        lstm_layer = keras.layers.RNN(keras.layers.LSTMCell(units), input_
shape=(None, input_dim) )
    model = keras.models.Sequential([ lstm_layer, keras.layers.
BatchNormalization(), keras.layers.Dense(output_size),])
```

```
This line returns the constructed model.
return model
```

6.4.3.1.4 Train the Model

To accomplish this, you can compile the model with the desired parameters, such as the loss function, optimizer, and metrics like accuracy. Next, you can train the model using the test data values. By executing this code, the model will be compiled with the specified loss function, optimizer, and metrics. It will then be trained on the training data for the specified number of epochs, with performance evaluation performed on the validation data.

```
model = build_model(allow_cudnn_kernel=True)
model.compile(loss=keras.losses.SparseCategoricalCrossentropy(from_logits
=True),optimizer="adam",metrics=["accuracy"],)
model.fit(x_train, y_train, validation_data=(x_test, y_test), batch_
size=batch_size, epochs=100)
```

The code utilizes the compiled model and the fit module in Keras to train the model. Here's an explanation of each code line:

```
#This line calls the `build_model` function to create the model. The
`allow_cudnn_kernel` argument is set to `True`, which means the cuDNN
kernel can be used for faster performance if available.
model = build_model(allow_cudnn_kernel=True)
```

```
#This line compiles the model. The `compile` method is used to configure
the model for training. It takes several arguments:
```

- `loss`: The loss function to optimize during training. Here,
  `SparseCategoricalCrossentropy` is used, which is suitable for
  multi-class classification problems.
- `optimizer`: The optimizer algorithm to use. In this case, "adam" is
  used, which is a popular optimizer known for its effectiveness in
  training deep neural networks.
- `metrics`: The evaluation metrics to monitor during training. Here,
  "accuracy" is used to track the model's classification accuracy.

```
model.compile(loss=keras.losses.SparseCategoricalCrossentropy(from_
logits=True), optimizer="adam", metrics=["accuracy"])
```

```
#This line trains the model using the `fit` method. The `fit` method
trains the model on the provided training data and labels. It takes
several arguments:
```

- `x_train`: The input training data.
- `y_train`: The corresponding training labels.
- `validation_data`: Optional validation data to evaluate the model's
  performance on during training. Here, it uses the testing data `(x_
  test, y_test)` as the validation data.
- `batch_size`: The number of samples per gradient update. It is set
  to the previously defined `batch_size` value.
- `epochs`: The number of epochs or iterations to train the model.
  Here, it is set to 100.

```
model.fit(x_train, y_train, validation_data=(x_test, y_test), batch_
size=batch_size, epochs=100)
```

6.4.3.1.5 *Evaluate the Model*

To check and evaluate the model with some sample data, you can obtain the model's
predictions for the sample image, print them to the console, and display the sample
image using matplotlib.pyplot. By executing this code, the model's predictions for the
sample image are obtained, printed to the console, and the sample image is displayed
using "matplotlib.pyplot".

```
import matplotlib.pyplot as plt
with tf.device("CPU:0"):
    cpu_model = build_model(allow_cudnn_kernel=True)
    cpu_model.set_weights(model.get_weights())
    result = tf.argmax(cpu_model.predict_on_batch(tf.expand_dims(sample,
0)), axis=1)
    print("Predicted result is: %s, target result is: %s" % (result.
numpy(), sample_labe)
    plt.imshow(sample, cmap=plt.get_cmap("gray"))
```

   Here's the breakdown of each line:

```
#This line imports the `matplotlib.pyplot` module, which provides
functions for visualizing data and creating plots.
import matplotlib.pyplot as plt
```

```
#This line uses a context manager to specify that the following code
should be executed on the CPU. It ensures that the code runs on the CPU
instead of any available GPU devices.
with tf.device("CPU:0"):

#This line creates a new model on the CPU using the `build_model`
function, with `allow_cudnn_kernel` set to `True`. It assigns the created
model to the `cpu_model` variable.
cpu_model = build_model(allow_cudnn_kernel=True)

#This line sets the weights of the `cpu_model` to the weights of the
previously trained model. It ensures that the CPU model has the same
weights as the trained model.
cpu_model.set_weights(model.get_weights())

#This line performs a prediction on the `cpu_model` using the `predict_
on_batch` method. It takes the `sample` image, expands its dimensions to
match the model's input shape, and predicts the output. `tf.argmax` is
then used to find the index of the predicted class with the highest
probability along `axis=1`.
result = tf.argmax(cpu_model.predict_on_batch(tf.expand_dims(sample, 0)),
axis=1)

#This line prints the predicted result and the target result (sample
label) to the console. It uses string formatting to include the values of
`result.numpy()` (the predicted result) and `sample_label` (the target
result).
print("Predicted result is: %s, target result is: %s" % (result.numpy(),
sample_label))

#This line displays the `sample` image using `plt.imshow` from
`matplotlib.pyplot`. It visualizes the image using the "gray" colormap,
which shows the image in grayscale.
plt.imshow(sample, cmap=plt.get_cmap("gray"))
```

6.4.4 Convolutional Neural Networks (CNNs)

CNNs are a renowned type of deep learning algorithm that excels in visual classification tasks. A CNN is composed of four key components:

1. Convolution filters,
2. Pooling or subsampling,
3. Activation (transition) function, and
4. Fully-connected layer.

The primary innovation of CNNs lies in their use of convolution filters. These filters allow each neuron to connect to the filter outputs, effectively creating a receptive field.

6.4.4.1 CNN Layers

The layers in a CNN play a crucial role in processing and extracting features from the input data. These layers are designed to learn and recognize patterns in the data, making them especially suited for tasks, such as image classification, object detection, and image segmentation. There are several types of layers commonly used in CNN architectures.

6.4.4.1.1 *Convolution Layers*

The primary component of a CNN is its convolution layers. These layers work by applying a convolution function to a data matrix, such as an image, which results in a convolved or filtered output. The "stride" refers to the step by which the convolution function moves across the data. For instance, a "stride of 2" means the convolution window shifts two elements to the right or down, typically moving from left to right and top to bottom. CNN filters are crafted using kernels that match the size of the convolution windows. The pixel values within these windows are multiplied by the corresponding values in the kernel. In designing a CNN, it is critical to understand and select the right number of filters, kernel size, and stride value.

For instance, if the kernel filter has a size of 4 × 4, resulting in 16 elements, each neuron in the receptive field connects with 16 weights and one bias. CNNs can have multiple convolution layers, and the outputs of these layers are known as feature maps. Figure 6.10 provides an illustration of a 3 × 3 filter moving across an original image. The pixel values within the area covered by the filter are multiplied by the corresponding kernel values. In this example, the first computation results in a convolution output of –2. It is worth noting that the outputs of the filters for each layer can be observed and analyzed.

Figure 6.10 provides a clear depiction of the **Convolution** operation, a foundational component in convolutional neural networks:

- The **Input Data** matrix represents a slice of an image or a feature map.
- The **Filter or Kernel** is a smaller matrix, which slides or "convolves" around the input data to produce the **Convolved Output**. This output, often referred to as a feature map, highlights specific features from the input data depending on the filter values.
- In the **Convolved Output** section, each value is obtained by performing an element-wise multiplication between the filter and a sub-matrix of the input, and then summing up the results.

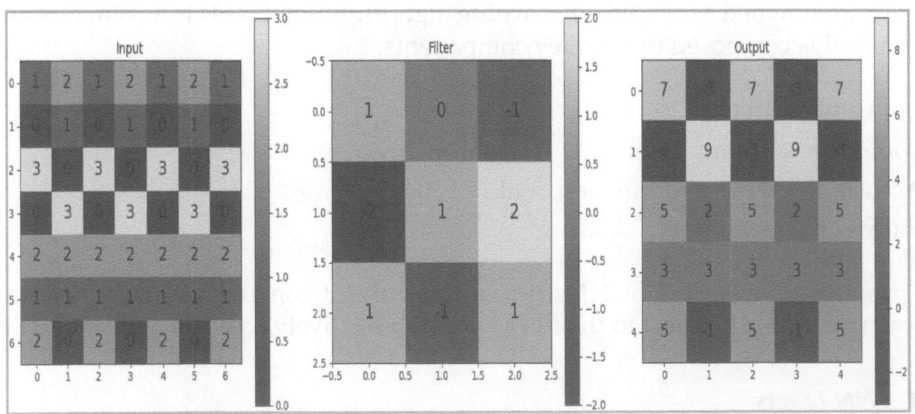

FIGURE 6.10
Convolving by a 3 × 3 filter.

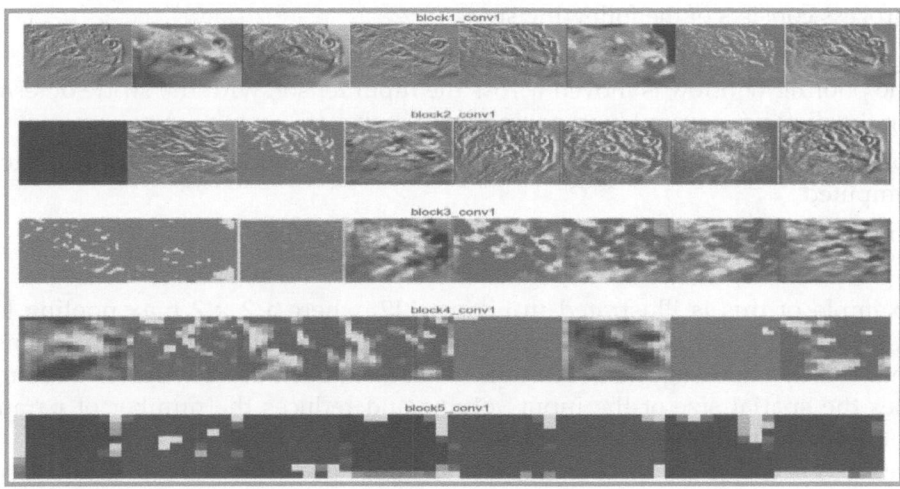

FIGURE 6.11
The outputs of filters are in a different layer.

In essence, it elucidates how a convolution filter processes input data to emphasize certain features, thereby allowing neural networks to learn and identify patterns within the data.

Figure 6.11 showcases the final output from processing the original image. As discussed earlier, the initial layers of the CNN identify low-level features, while the subsequent layers capture high-level ones. Refer to Figure 6.11 to witness how the features evolve as represented by the CNN outputs in blocks 1 and 5. In this specific instance, a lightweight CNN is employed to analyze multilevel feature maps of cat images. A visual examination of pixel patterns in the feature maps extracted from each block is carried out. Each block holds unique information that is vital to the classification process within the CNN. The output shapes of the feature maps from block 15 follow this sequence: 56×56 with 92 channels, 28×28 with 192 channels, 14×14 with 384 channels, and 7×7 with 512 channels. For analysis, eight feature maps per block are displayed, with each block respectively containing 92, 192, 384, and 512 channels. Upon analyzing these feature maps, it becomes clear that block 5 contains the majority of image information. However, the resulting maps are less visually interpretable to humans despite their informational richness.

6.4.4.2 Pooling Layers

The role of pooling layers in CNNs is indispensable. Their purpose is to reduce the spatial dimensions (width and height) of the input volume before it's passed to the next convolutional layer, without affecting the depth of the volume. This reduction is achieved by performing a transformation on the input volume – selecting the maximum value (max pooling), computing the average value (average pooling), or adding up all the values (sum pooling) within a defined window. The result is a decrease in computational complexity for the subsequent layers. This design aims to diminish the size of the volume while controlling overfitting and retaining the most crucial information. Pooling layers are usually inserted after convolutional layers in CNNs. The pooling operation is applied independently to each input feature map, processing a patch of the input tensor at a time. The size of this patch is determined by the pooling window.

The process consists of the following steps:

1. The pooling window is moved across the input tensor, with the stride determining the distance covered by the window in each step.
2. For every position of the window, the pooling operation (max, average, etc.) is computed.
3. The outcome is a new tensor with reduced dimensions.

An example of this is illustrated in Figure 6.12, where a 2×2 max pooling layer is applied to a 4×4 input tensor. The pooling layer reduces the spatial dimensions from 4×4 to 2×2 by choosing the maximum value from each 2×2 window. This method decreases the spatial size of the input volume and reduces the number of parameters, which helps in controlling overfitting.

Figure 6.12 visualizes the mechanism of **Max Pooling**, a dimensionality reduction technique often employed in convolutional neural networks:

- The **Input Data** segment showcases a higher resolution data matrix, often representing the output activations from a convolutional layer.
- In the **After Max Pooling** section, one can observe a down-sampled representation. This reduced matrix is obtained by selecting the maximum value from non-overlapping sub-regions in the input. The connecting lines in the visualization demonstrate which specific values from the input matrix have been carried over to the pooled output.

In summary, it elucidates how Max Pooling operates by taking the maximum values from localized regions of the input to produce a condensed, yet representative output, effectively reducing computational demands while retaining important features.

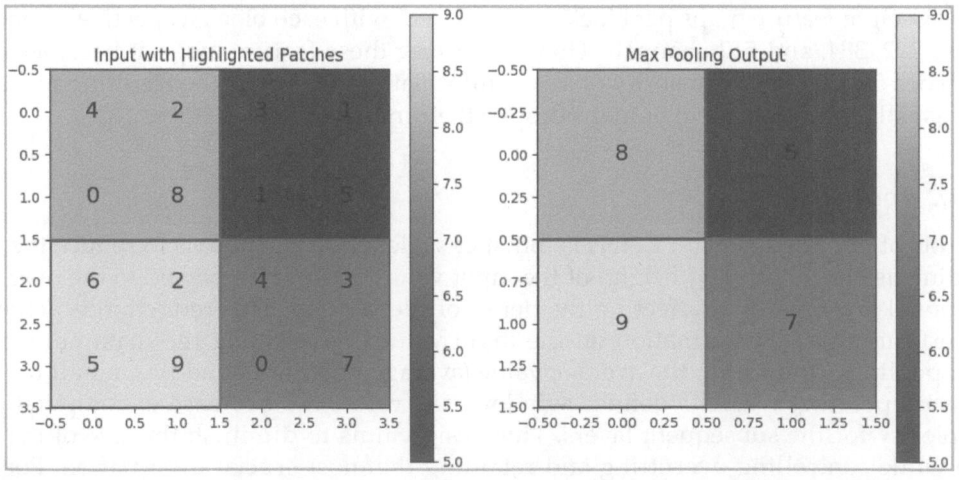

FIGURE 6.12
Max pooling.

6.4.4.3 *Dropout*

Dropout is a regularization technique employed in neural networks to curb overfitting. During training, a certain number of layer outputs are randomly ignored or "dropped out". This action effectively makes the layer appear and function as if it has a different number of nodes and connectivity to the preceding layer. As a result, each update to a layer during training occurs with a different "view" of the configured layer. As a consequence, the network becomes less sensitive to the specific weights of neurons. This leads to a network that is capable of better generalization and is less likely to overfit the training data. While dropout is often used in fully connected layers, it can also be applied to convolutional layers. In the Keras framework, dropout can be implemented by adding dropout layers into our model.

Figure 6.13 illustrates the concept of **Dropout**, a regularization technique used in deep neural networks:

- The **Input Data** section presents a typical data layer or neuron activations from a specific layer of a neural network.
- The **After Dropout** section visually represents the effect of dropout. Some cells (or neurons) are dimmed or "dropped out", meaning during this specific forward and backward pass, they're inactive and don't contribute to the network's learning. This is done to prevent the model from becoming overly reliant on any specific neuron and to promote generalization.

In essence, it highlights how Dropout works by randomly deactivating certain neurons during training, ensuring the network remains robust and avoids overfitting to the training data.

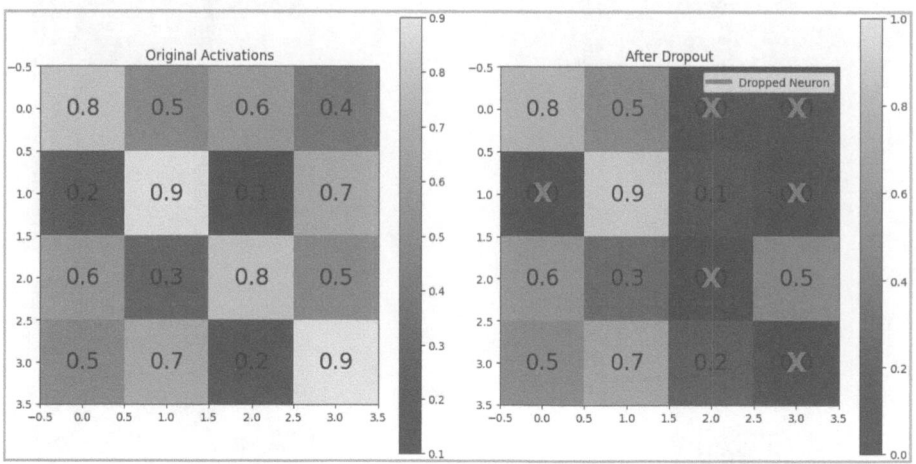

FIGURE 6.13
Demonstrates the effect of dropout on neural network activations. Left: Original activations before applying dropout. Right: Activations post-dropout, showcasing thinned network with reduced overfitting potential.

6.4.4.4 Batch Normalization

Batch Normalization and Group Normalization are techniques used to normalize the activations of a layer in a neural network. They aim to make the distribution of the inputs to a layer more consistent, leading to faster learning and higher overall accuracy.

Figure 6.14 provides a detailed visual comparison between the effects of Batch Normalization and Group Normalization on two sample images.

- **Original Input Data:** The top row showcases the original values of the two images. Each heatmap in this row represents an image's channels and their respective data points. The color intensity of each cell corresponds to the magnitude of the data point value.
- **Batch Normalized Data:** The middle row displays the images after undergoing Batch Normalization. This technique normalizes the data across the entire batch, adjusting the values so that they have a mean of zero and a standard deviation of

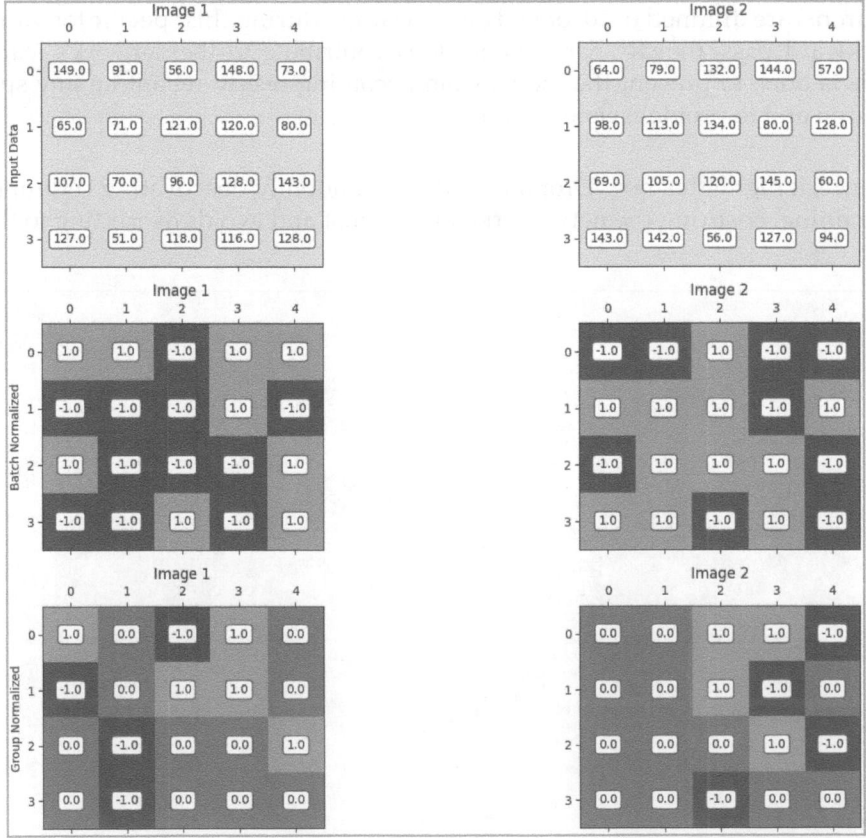

FIGURE 6.14
Visual comparison of Batch Normalization and Group Normalization on two sample images. Top Row: Original Input Data with each heatmap representing an image's channels. Middle Row: Batch Normalized Data showing a shift and scaling in values. Bottom Row: Group Normalized Data with channels normalized within groups, evident in similar color intensities across certain channels/groups.

one. By comparing the original input data to the batch normalized data, one can observe a shift and scaling in the values, which is evident from the changes in color intensity in the heatmaps.

- **Group Normalized Data:** The bottom row represents the images after Group Normalization. Unlike Batch Normalization, Group Normalization divides the channels into groups and normalizes within these groups. This is evident in the heatmaps where certain channels (or groups of channels) have similar color intensities, indicating they've been normalized together.

Both of these methods have proven effective in different settings. Batch Normalization tends to be more commonly used due to its long-standing history and proven success in various tasks. Group Normalization, on the other hand, may be more suitable for tasks where smaller batch sizes are necessary or where applying batch normalization is challenging, such as in certain recurrent networks.

Figure 6.14 offers a visual comparison of data normalization techniques crucial for deep neural network training: **Batch Normalization (BN)** and **Group Normalization (GN)**:

- The **Input Data** segment displays two multi-channel "images" or data sets.
- In the **Batch Normalized** section, BN standardizes the readings across the entire batch, resulting in brighter cells for values above average and darker ones below.
- The **Group Normalized** section depicts GN's approach, which normalizes within individual data samples but across designated groups of channels. Here, channels are collectively adjusted to ensure a balanced distribution within each group.

In a nutshell, it demonstrates how BN operates across an entire data batch, while GN focuses on channel groupings within single data samples, both aiming to provide consistent data for optimized neural network performance.

6.4.4.5 Fully Connected Layer

Fully connected layers, also known as dense layers, are often used at the end of deep learning models. These layers are called "fully connected" because every node in the current layer is connected to every node in the subsequent layer. The neurons in a fully connected layer have full connections to all activations in the previous layer. In the context of a CNN, after several convolutional and pooling layers, the high-level reasoning in the neural network happens via fully connected layers. The output from the convolutional layers represents high-level features in the data. While the convolutional layers are learning local features in the earlier stages of the network, the fully connected layer learns from the global information, combining these features to form a complete "picture". A typical structure of a CNN might look like this:

1. **Convolutional layer:** responsible for the convolutional operation.
2. **Pooling layer:** responsible for the pooling operation.
3. **Fully connected layer:** responsible for output generation.

In Figure 6.15, the last fully connected layer is also the classification layer, which uses an activation function like the SoftMax function. The SoftMax function converts the network's raw output scores into probabilities, which are easier to interpret. The node in

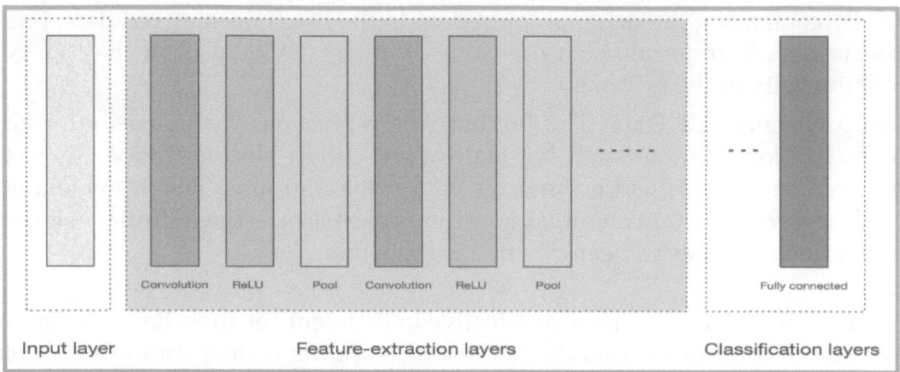

FIGURE 6.15
Fully-connected layer.

the final layer with the highest probability is the model's output, or prediction. The fully connected layers serve as a bridge between the feature extraction and classification. The learned image features from the convolutional layers are flattened into a single vector of values and used as input to the fully connected layer. The fully connected layer then uses these features to classify the input image into various classes based on the training dataset.

6.4.4.6 Design a CNN

Here, we are implementing the LeNet5 architecture. It utilizes a sequence of convolutional and pooling layers and consists of two fully connected layers and one classifier layer. The implementation procedures of a single CNN architecture are nearly identical across various architectures.

6.4.4.6.1 Import Libraries

In the first step, it is important to determine and import the necessary libraries for the implementation. These libraries provide valuable functionality, enhance code robustness and accuracy, and help reduce computational costs. By importing these libraries and modules, you gain access to a wide range of functions, classes, and tools that facilitate working with TensorFlow, NumPy, and the MNIST dataset efficiently in your code.

```
import tensorflow as tf
import numpy as np
from tensorflow.examples.tutorials.mnist import input_data
```

Here's an explanation of each code line:

```
#This line imports the TensorFlow library, which is an open-source
machine learning framework developed by Google. TensorFlow provides tools
and APIs for building and training various machine learning models.
import tensorflow as tf

#This line imports the NumPy library and assigns it the alias `np`. NumPy
is a popular library for numerical computations in Python, particularly
when working with arrays and matrices. It provides efficient
implementations of mathematical operations and functions.
import numpy as np
```

```
#This line imports the `input_data` module from the TensorFlow's MNIST
tutorial examples. The `input_data` module provides functions for
downloading and loading the MNIST dataset, which is a widely used dataset
for training and testing machine learning models on handwritten digit
recognition tasks.
from tensorflow.examples.tutorials.mnist import input_data
```

6.4.4.6.2 *Setup Training and Testing Sets*

To set up the number of samples for the training and testing steps, the image size, and the number of classes, you can define placeholders. These placeholders act as symbolic placeholders within the TensorFlow computational graph. They will be later filled with actual input data and labels when the graph is executed. By using placeholders, you enable the flexible feeding of data during the training or inference process.

```
batch_size = 128
test_size = 256
img_size = 28
num_classes = 10
X = tf.placeholder("float", [None, img_size, img_size, 1])
Y = tf.placeholder("float", [None, num_classes])
```

Here's the breakdown of each code line:

```
#These lines define the values for `batch_size`, `test_size`, `img_size`,
and `num_classes`. These parameters are used to specify the batch size
for training, the size of the test set, the image size, and the number of
classes in the classification task, respectively.
batch_size = 128
test_size = 256
img_size = 28
num_classes = 10
```

```
#This line creates a placeholder `X` using `tf.placeholder`.
Placeholders are symbolic tensors that will be used to pass input data
into the TensorFlow computational graph. Here, `X` is a placeholder for
the input data. The `tf.float32` indicates the data type of the
placeholder, and `[None, img_size, img_size, 1]` specifies the shape of
the placeholder. The `None` dimension allows for a variable batch size,
while `img_size` represents the height and width of the input image,
and `1` represents the number of color channels (assuming grayscale
images).
X = tf.placeholder(tf.float32, [None, img_size, img_size, 1])
```

```
#This line creates a placeholder `Y` using `tf.placeholder`. Similarly to
`X`, `Y` is a placeholder, but it is used for the labels or target
values. It is defined with the data type `tf.float32` and a shape of
`[None, num_classes]`. The `None` dimension allows for a variable batch
size, while `num_classes` represents the number of classes in the
classification task. Each label will be represented as a one-hot encoded
vector.
Y = tf.placeholder(tf.float32, [None, num_classes])
```

6.4.4.6.3 Load Data and Initialize the Weights and Outputs

By executing these code lines, you collect the data and create training and testing categories. The MNIST dataset is loaded, and the training and testing data are extracted and reshaped. Additionally, the weights for the neural network layers are initialized.

```
mnist = mnist_data.read_data_sets("data/")
Xtr, Ytr, Xte, Yte = mnist.train.images, mnist.train.labels,mnist.test.
images, mnist.test.labels
Xtr = Xtr.reshape(-1, img_size, img_size, 1)
Xte = Xte.reshape(-1, img_size, img_size, 1)
def init_weights(shape):
    return tf.Variable(tf.random_normal(shape, stddev=0.01))
w₁ = init_weights([3, 3, 1, 32])
w₂ = init_weights([3, 3, 32, 64])
w₃ = init_weights([3, 3, 64, 128])
w₄ = init_weights([128 * 4 * 4, 625])
w_o = init_weights([625, num_classes])
```

Here's an explanation of each code line in:

#This line reads the MNIST dataset using the `read_data_sets` function
from the `mnist_data` module. The dataset is downloaded and stored in
the specified directory "data/". The `mnist` variable holds the
dataset.
mnist = mnist_data.read_data_sets("data/")
#This line extracts the training and testing data from the `mnist`
dataset. `Xtr` contains the training images, `Ytr` contains the
corresponding training labels, `Xte` contains the testing images, and
`Yte` contains the corresponding testing labels.
Xtr, Ytr, Xte, Yte = mnist.train.images, mnist.train.labels, mnist.test.
images, mnist.test.labels

#These lines reshape the training and testing images. The `reshape`
function is used to modify the shape of the arrays. `-1` in the reshaping
indicates that the size in that dimension should be automatically
determined based on the other dimensions. The images are reshaped to have
dimensions `(img_size, img_size, 1)`, where `img_size` represents the
height and width of the image, and `1` represents the number of color
channels (assuming grayscale images).
Xtr = Xtr.reshape(-1, img_size, img_size, 1)
Xte = Xte.reshape(-1, img_size, img_size, 1)

#This code defines a function called `init_weights` that initializes the
weights of the neural network. It takes a `shape` argument as input and
returns a TensorFlow variable with random values. The `tf.random_normal`
function is used to generate random values from a normal distribution
with a standard deviation of 0.01.
def init_weights(shape):
    return tf.Variable(tf.random_normal(shape, stddev=0.01))

#These lines initialize the weights for each layer of the neural network.
The `init_weights` function is called to generate random weights for each

layer. The shapes of the weight matrices are specified, representing the dimensions of the filters or connections between layers.

```
w1 = init_weights([3, 3, 1, 32])
w2 = init_weights([3, 3, 32, 64])
w3 = init_weights([3, 3, 64, 128])
w4 = init_weights([128 * 4 * 4, 625])
```

#This line initializes the weights for the output layer of the neural network. The shape of the weight matrix is `[625, num_classes]`, where `625` represents the number of units in the previous layer, and `num_classes` represents the number of classes in the classification task.

```
w_o = init_weights([625, num_classes])
```

6.4.4.6.4 Define the Model

By executing these code lines, the model is defined with various layers including convolution layers, pooling layers, dropout layers, and ReLU layers. These lines specifically define the operations for the fully connected layers. The reshaped FC_layer is multiplied by the weight matrix w_4. When executing these code lines, the model function is defined with the provided input tensor X and weight matrices (w_1, w_2, w_3, w_4, w_o). It also takes in dropout placeholders (p_keep_conv and p_keep_hidden). The function applies convolutional layers, activation functions, pooling, and dropout to construct the neural network model. Finally, the logits for each class are computed and returned as the output of the function.

```
p_keep_conv = tf.placeholder("float")
p_keep_hidden = tf.placeholder("float")
def model(X, w, w₂, w₃, w₄, w_o, p_keep_conv, p_keep_hidden):
    conv1 = tf.nn.conv2d(X, w,strides=[1, 1, 1, 1], padding='SAME')
    conv1 = tf.nn.relu(conv1)
    conv1 = tf.nn.max_pool(conv1, ksize=[1, 2, 2, 1], strides=[1, 2, 2, 1],
padding='SAME')
    conv1 = tf.nn.dropout(conv1, p_keep_conv)
    conv2 = tf.nn.conv2d(conv1, w₂,strides=[1, 1, 1, 1],padding='SAME')
    conv2 = tf.nn.relu(conv2)
    conv2 = tf.nn.max_pool(conv2, ksize=[1, 2, 2, 1],strides=[1, 2, 2, 1],
padding='SAME')
    conv2 = tf.nn.dropout(conv2, p_keep_conv)
    conv3 = tf.nn.conv2d(conv2, w₃,strides=[1, 1, 1, 1],padding='SAME')
    conv3_a = tf.nn.relu(conv3)
    FC_layer = tf.nn.max_pool(conv3, ksize=[1, 2, 2, 1],strides=[1, 2, 2, 1],
padding='SAME')
    FC_layer = tf.reshape(FC_layer, [-1,w₄.get_shape().as_list()[0]])
    FC_layer = tf.nn.dropout(FC_layer, p_keep_conv)
    output_layer = tf.nn.relu(tf.matmul(FC_layer, w₄))
    output_layer = tf.nn.dropout(output_layer, p_keep_hidden)
    result = tf.matmul(output_layer, w_o)
  return result
```

Here's the breakdown of each code line:

#These lines create placeholders `p_keep_conv` and `p_keep_hidden` for the dropout probabilities. These placeholders will be used to control the dropout rates during training and inference.

```
p_keep_conv = tf.placeholder("float")
p_keep_hidden = tf.placeholder("float")
```

#This line defines a function called `model` that takes input `X` and various weight matrices (`w`, `w2`, `w3`, `w4`, `w_o`) as well as dropout placeholders (`p_keep_conv` and `p_keep_hidden`).

```
def model(X, w, w2, w3, w4, w_o, p_keep_conv, p_keep_hidden):
```

#These lines define the operations for the first convolutional layer (`conv1`). It performs convolution (`tf.nn.conv2d`), applies the ReLU activation function (`tf.nn.relu`), performs max pooling (`tf.nn.max_pool`), and applies dropout (`tf.nn.dropout`) using the `p_keep_conv` placeholder.

```
conv1 = tf.nn.conv2d(X, w, strides=[1, 1, 1, 1], padding='SAME')
conv1 = tf.nn.relu(conv1)
conv1 = tf.nn.max_pool(conv1, ksize=[1, 2, 2, 1], strides=[1, 2, 2, 1],
padding='SAME')
conv1 = tf.nn.dropout(conv1, p_keep_conv)
```

#These lines define the operations for the second convolutional layer (`conv2`). Similar to the first layer, it performs convolution, ReLU activation, max pooling, and dropout.

```
conv2 = tf.nn.conv2d(conv1, w2, strides=[1, 1, 1, 1], padding='SAME')
conv2 = tf.nn.relu(conv2)
conv2 = tf.nn.max_pool(conv2, ksize=[1, 2, 2, 1], strides=[1, 2, 2, 1],
padding='SAME')
conv2 = tf.nn.dropout(conv2, p_keep_conv)
```

#These lines define the operations for the third convolutional layer (`conv3`) and an activation (`conv3_a`) using ReLU. The result is then max pooled to obtain the fully connected (`FC_layer`) output.

```
conv3 = tf.nn.conv2d(conv2, w3, strides=[1, 1, 1, 1], padding='SAME')
conv3_a = tf.nn.relu(conv3)
FC_layer = tf.nn.max_pool(conv3, ksize=[1, 2, 2, 1], strides=[1, 2, 2,
1], padding='SAME')
```

#These lines reshape the `FC_layer` to a 2D tensor and apply dropout using the `p_keep_conv` placeholder.

```
FC_layer = tf.reshape(FC_layer, [-1, w4.get_shape().as_list()[0]])
FC_layer = tf.nn.dropout(FC_layer, p_keep_conv)
output_layer = tf.nn.relu(tf.matmul(FC_layer, w4))
output_layer = tf.nn.dropout(output_layer, p_keep_hidden)
```

#This line performs matrix multiplication between the `output_layer` tensor and the weight matrix `w_o` using `tf.matmul`. It produces the final output tensor, `result`, which represents the logits for each class.

```
result = tf.matmul(output_layer, w_o)
```

#This line returns the `result` tensor as the output of the `model` function. The `result` tensor contains the logits that represent the predicted values for each class.

```
return result
```

6.4.4.6.5 Train and Evaluate the Model

Finally, you can utilize the TensorFlow training and evaluation module to train the designed model with your data and evaluate the trained model. By executing these code lines, the model is trained using the training data and evaluated using the testing data for a specified number of epochs. The training process employs mini-batch optimization, and the accuracy of the model is monitored throughout the training.

```
py_x = model(X, w, w₂, w₃, w₄, w_o, p_keep_conv, p_keep_hidden)
Y_ = tf.nn.softmax_cross_entropy_with_logits(py_x, Y)
cost = tf.reduce_mean(Y_)
optimizer = tf.train.RMSPropOptimizer(0.001, 0.9).minimize(cost)
predict_op = tf.argmax(py_x, 1)
with tf.Session() as sess:
    tf.initialize_all_variables().run()
    for I in range(100):
        training_batch =  zip(range(0, len(Xtr), batch_size),
range(batch_size, len(Xtr)+1, batch_size))
        for start, end in training_batch:
            sess.run(optimizer, feed_dict={X: Xtr [start:end],Y: Ytr
[start:end],p_keep_conv: 0.8, p_keep_hidden: 0.5})
        test_indices = np.arange(len(Xte))
        np.random.shuffle(test_indices)
        test_indices = test_indices[0:test_size]
        print(I, np.mean(np.argmax(Yte[test_indices], axis=1) ==sess.
run(predict_op, feed_dict={X: Xte[test_indices], Y: Yte [test_indices],
p_keep_conv: 1.0, p_keep_hidden: 1.0})))
```

Here's the breakdown of each code line:

```
#This line calls the `model` function with the provided parameters and
assigns the result to the variable `py_x`. It represents the predicted
output of the model.
py_x = model(X, w, w2, w3, w4, w_o, p_keep_conv, p_keep_hidden)

#This line calculates the cross-entropy loss between the predicted output
`py_x` and the true labels `Y`. It uses the `softmax_cross_entropy_with_
logits` function from TensorFlow's neural network module. The result is
assigned to the variable `Y_`.
Y_ = tf.nn.softmax_cross_entropy_with_logits(py_x, Y)

#These lines define the cost function (`cost`) as the mean of the cross-
entropy loss `Y_` using `tf.reduce_mean`. The optimizer (`optimizer`) is
created using the RMSProp optimization algorithm with a learning rate of
0.001 and a decay factor of 0.9. The `minimize` method is then called on
the optimizer to minimize the cost.
cost = tf.reduce_mean(Y_)
optimizer = tf.train.RMSPropOptimizer(0.001, 0.9).minimize(cost)

#This line determines the predicted class labels by finding the index
with the highest probability in the `py_x` tensor using `tf.argmax`. The
`1` argument specifies the axis along which to perform the operation. The
result is assigned to the variable `predict_op`.
predict_op = tf.argmax(py_x, 1)

#These lines define a TensorFlow session and perform the training and
evaluation loop. The session is created using the `with tf.Session()
```

as sess˘ context manager, which automatically handles session cleanup. Within the session, the variables are initialized using ˘tf.initialize_ all_variables().run()˘. Then, for each epoch (100 in this case), the training data is divided into mini-batches using the ˘zip˘ function. The optimizer is run for each mini-batch, updating the model's parameters. After each epoch, a subset of the testing data is randomly selected and used to evaluate the model's accuracy. The accuracy is computed by comparing the predicted labels (˘sess.run(predict_op)˘) with the true labels (˘Yte[test_indices]˘). The average accuracy is then printed for each epoch.

```
with tf.Session() as sess:
    tf.initialize_all_variables().run()
    for I in range(100):
        training_batch = zip(range(0, len(Xtr), batch_size), range(batch_
size, len(Xtr)+1, batch_size))
        for start, end in training_batch:
            sess.run(optimizer, feed_dict={X: Xtr[start:end], Y:
Ytr[start:end], p_keep_conv: 0.8, p_keep_hidden: 0.5})
        test_indices = np.arange(len(Xte))
        np.random.shuffle(test_indices)
        test_indices = test_indices[0:test_size]
        print(I, np.mean(np.argmax(Yte[test_indices], axis=1) == sess.
run(predict_op, feed_dict={X: Xte[test_indices], Y: Yte[test_indices],
p_keep_conv: 1.0, p_keep_hidden: 1.0})))
```

6.4.5 Generative Adversarial Networks (GANs)

GANs constitute a thrilling and swiftly advancing domain within deep learning. GANs comprise two principal components: the Generator and the Discriminator. The Generator is tasked with creating new data instances. Starting with some form of noise as input, it transforms this noise into data instances that closely resemble the training data. The Generator's objective is to deceive the Discriminator into believing that the data it generated is genuine. On the contrary, the Discriminator is a classifier that distinguishes between instances from the actual training data and instances fabricated by the Generator. Over time, the Discriminator becomes more proficient at differentiating real from fake data. The two networks engage in a continuous game of cat and mouse, with the Generator striving to produce increasingly convincing data, while the Discriminator improves its ability to distinguish this data from the real thing. This adversarial process results in the Generator creating high-quality data instances that closely mimic real instances from the training data. Loss functions have a vital role in training both the Generator and the Discriminator. For the Generator, the loss function is formulated to incentivize it to generate data that the Discriminator classifies as real. In the case of the Discriminator, the loss function encourages it to correctly classify real data as real and generated data as fake. Figure 6.16 likely portrays this setup, illustrating the Generator network receiving a noise vector as input and producing a data instance. This generated data, along with real data from the training dataset, is then supplied to the Discriminator, which tries to differentiate between the two. In Chapter 7, we will delve further into GANs, exploring their structure in greater detail, understanding the complexities of their training process, and examining various applications where GANs have proven to be highly effective.

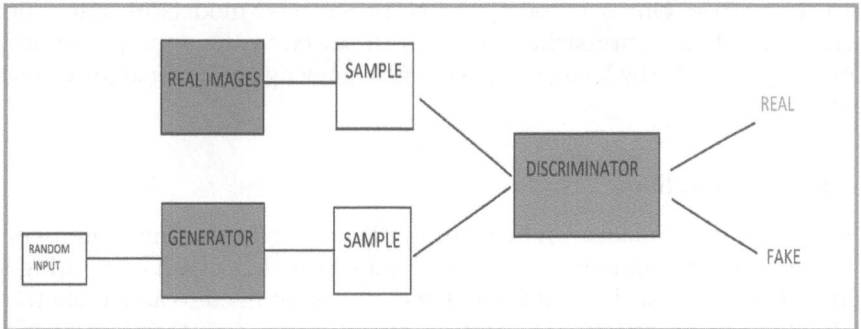

FIGURE 6.16
GAN networks architecture.

6.5 Deep Learning Issues

Deep learning is a complex field with many challenges that researchers and practitioners face. Here are some common issues and solutions in deep learning.

6.5.1 Vanishing Gradients

When training DNNs, the gradients can become very small, resulting in slow convergence or no convergence at all. These issues can be addressed by implementing better weight initialization techniques, exploring different activation functions, or applying regularization techniques.

6.5.2 Overfitting

Overfitting occurs when a model becomes overly specialized to the training data and performs poorly on new, unseen data. To mitigate overfitting, various strategies can be employed. Regularization techniques, such as dropout or weight decay, can be applied to prevent the model from overemphasizing certain features or parameters. Additionally, increasing the amount of training data can help the model generalize better and reduce overfitting.

6.5.3 Data Preprocessing

Deep learning models are highly sensitive to the quality and quantity of training data. To enhance model performance, it is essential to employ proper data preprocessing techniques. These techniques may include data normalization, which scales the data to a standard range, ensuring consistent inputs across features. Additionally, data augmentation techniques, such as image rotation, flipping, or adding noise, can be used to artificially expand the training dataset, improving the model's ability to generalize and handle variations in the data.

6.5.4 Model Architecture

Choosing the right model architecture for the problem at hand is crucial for good performance. However, there are many choices to make, and it can be difficult to know which architecture to choose. One solution is to use pre-trained models or automated model search techniques. These approaches can help in selecting the appropriate architecture and improve performance by leveraging existing knowledge or using algorithms to search for the best architecture.

6.5.5 Hardware Limitations

Training deep learning models can be computationally intensive, making it challenging to train large models on standard hardware. To address this, cloud computing solutions or specialized hardware, such as GPUs or TPUs, can be utilized to accelerate the training process. These high-performance computing resources provide the necessary computational power to train complex models efficiently and reduce the training time significantly.

6.5.6 Interpretability

Deep learning models are sometimes labeled as "black boxes" because understanding their internal workings and decision-making processes can be challenging. This lack of interpretability can be problematic in scenarios where the model's predictions have substantial implications. To address this concern, explainable AI techniques, such as Local Interpretable Model-agnostic Explanations (LIME) or Shapley Additive Explanations (SHAP), can be employed. These methods aim to provide insights into the factors influencing the model's predictions and offer explanations for individual decisions. By incorporating explainability techniques, stakeholders can gain a better understanding of how the model reaches its conclusions, increasing transparency and trust in the system.

6.5.7 Generalization

Deep learning models occasionally exhibit a phenomenon called overfitting, where they perform exceptionally well on the training data but struggle to generalize to new, unseen data. To mitigate this issue, several techniques can be employed. Cross-validation is a common approach that involves dividing the available data into multiple subsets. The model is trained on a portion of the data and evaluated on the remaining subset. This process is repeated multiple times, with different subsets used for training and evaluation. By averaging the performance across these iterations, a more reliable estimate of the model's generalization ability can be obtained. Another technique is early stopping, which involves monitoring the model's performance on a validation set during training. If the model's performance on the validation set starts to deteriorate after an initial improvement, training is halted early to prevent overfitting. This ensures that the model is not overly tailored to the training data and can generalize better to new data. By incorporating cross-validation and early stopping, deep learning models can strike a balance between capturing the patterns in the training data and avoiding overfitting, resulting in improved performance on unseen data.

6.5.8 Labeling Data

Deep learning models typically require a large amount of labeled data for training. However, labeling data can be a time-consuming and expensive process. One potential solution to this challenge is to leverage semi-supervised learning techniques, which can achieve satisfactory results with fewer labeled examples.

6.5.9 Adversarial Attacks

Adversarial attacks occur when an attacker intentionally manipulates input data in order to deceive a deep learning model. These attacks can be mitigated by employing adversarial training techniques or by utilizing models that are inherently less vulnerable to such attacks.

6.5.10 Ethical Considerations

Deep learning models can have profound societal effects, and it is crucial to contemplate the ethical ramifications during their design and implementation. This entails addressing concerns, such as fairness, bias, and privacy. Potential solutions involve incorporating diverse training data to mitigate bias and evaluating models to ensure fairness and mitigate any discriminatory outcomes. Additionally, stringent privacy safeguards should be implemented to protect sensitive user information.

6.6 Deep Learning Implementation Tips

Here are some implementation tips for deep learning.

6.6.1 Choose the Right Framework

There are several deep learning frameworks available, including TensorFlow, Keras, PyTorch, and Caffe. The choice of framework depends on the specific requirements of your project. TensorFlow is a widely used and versatile framework with excellent support for large-scale deep learning applications. Keras, which is now part of TensorFlow, provides a high-level API that simplifies the development process. PyTorch is known for its dynamic computational graph and is popular for research purposes. Caffe is a framework known for its efficiency in computer vision tasks. Consider the features, documentation, community support, and compatibility with your existing infrastructure when selecting the framework that best suits your project.

6.6.2 Use GPU

Training deep learning models can be computationally expensive, so utilizing a GPU can significantly accelerate the process. GPUs are designed to handle parallel computations, which aligns well with the matrix operations commonly performed in deep learning algorithms. By offloading computations to the GPU, deep learning models can benefit from faster training times, enabling quicker experimentation and iteration. It is important to note that not all deep learning frameworks have native GPU support, so ensure compatibility between the chosen framework and the GPU you intend to use. Additionally, cloud-based GPU solutions are available, allowing access to powerful GPU resources without the need for dedicated hardware.

6.6.3 Preprocess the Data

Preprocessing the data is a crucial step in deep learning to enhance model accuracy and speed. There are several preprocessing techniques that can be applied to the data before feeding it into the model. Normalization is a common preprocessing technique that scales the data to a standard range, typically between 0 and 1 or –1 and 1. This helps in preventing features with larger values from dominating the learning process. Resizing is often necessary when dealing with images or data of different sizes. Resizing the data to a consistent size ensures that the model receives inputs of the same dimensions, allowing it to learn effectively. Data augmentation is another powerful technique where the training data is artificially expanded by applying transformations, such as rotation, translation, flipping, or adding noise. This increases the diversity and variability of the training data, leading to a more robust and generalizable model. Other preprocessing techniques may include feature scaling, one-hot encoding for categorical variables, handling missing data, and handling imbalanced classes. It is important to carefully select and apply the appropriate preprocessing techniques based on the characteristics of the data and the requirements of the model. Proper preprocessing can improve the model's ability to learn meaningful patterns from the data and ultimately enhance its performance.

6.6.4 Start with a Simple Model

Deep learning models can indeed be complex and challenging to tune. Starting with a simple model and gradually increasing its complexity is a recommended approach to avoid overwhelming complexity and facilitate better understanding and optimization of the model. Beginning with a simple model allows you to establish a baseline performance and gain insights into the data and problem at hand. It helps in understanding the relationship between model architecture, parameters, and the task's requirements. This step allows you to identify potential bottlenecks, limitations, or areas for improvement. Once you have a solid foundation with a simple model, you can gradually introduce complexity by adding additional layers, increasing the number of units or neurons, or incorporating more advanced techniques, such as regularization, dropout, or attention mechanisms. This incremental approach allows you to observe the impact of each modification and evaluate if the increase in complexity leads to improved performance. By iteratively building on simpler models, you can effectively identify the optimal model architecture and hyperparameters for your specific task. It also helps in avoiding overfitting, as excessive complexity without sufficient data or regularization can lead to poor generalization. Remember, deep learning models often require experimentation and fine-tuning, and starting with a simple model serves as a solid foundation for iterative improvements. It allows you to strike a balance between model complexity and performance, leading to better results and a more efficient training process.

6.6.5 Regularization

Overfitting is a common challenge in deep learning, and it can significantly impact the performance and generalization ability of a model. Regularization techniques play a crucial role in mitigating overfitting and improving the model's ability to generalize well to unseen data. L_1 and L_2 regularization are two commonly used regularization techniques in deep learning. They both introduce a regularization term to the loss function during training, which helps control the complexity of the model and prevent overfitting. L_1 regularization, also known as Lasso regularization, adds the absolute values of the model's weights multiplied by a regularization parameter to the loss function. This encourages the model to reduce the impact of less important features by driving their corresponding weights toward zero. As a result, L_1 regularization can help with feature selection and create sparse models. L_2 regularization, also known as Ridge regularization, adds the squared values of the model's weights multiplied by a regularization parameter to the loss function. This encourages the model to distribute the weights more evenly across different features, reducing their overall impact. L_2 regularization promotes smoother weight values and can help prevent excessive reliance on a few dominant features. By incorporating L_1 or L_2 regularization, or a combination of both, the model's weights are effectively constrained, preventing them from becoming too large and causing overfitting. The regularization term adds a penalty for complex models, striking a balance between fitting the training data well and avoiding overfitting. It's important to note that the choice between L_1 and L_2 regularization (or their combination) depends on the specific problem and the characteristics of the data. Experimentation and tuning of the regularization parameter are typically required to find the optimal balance. Regularization techniques like L_1 and L_2 regularization are valuable tools in the deep learning practitioner's toolkit to combat overfitting and enhance the generalization performance of models.

6.6.6 Use Transfer Learning

Transfer learning is a powerful technique in deep learning that involves leveraging knowledge from pre-trained models and applying it to new, related tasks. By using a pre-trained model as a starting point, rather than training a model from scratch, transfer learning can save significant time and computational resources. In transfer learning, a pre-trained model is typically trained on a large-scale dataset, such as ImageNet, which contains a vast amount of labeled images. This pre-training allows the model to learn generic features and patterns that are useful for a wide range of visual recognition tasks. The learned representations capture valuable information about low-level features, object shapes, and higher-level concepts. To apply transfer learning, the pre-trained model is used as a feature extractor, where the input data is passed through the pre-trained layers to obtain a fixed set of features. These features are then fed into a new classifier or additional layers that are specifically designed for the target task. The classifier or additional layers are typically trained using a smaller task-specific dataset, which requires less data and computational resources. By using a pre-trained model as a starting point, transfer learning offers several benefits. First, it allows the model to leverage the knowledge learned from a large-scale dataset, which enhances its ability to capture relevant patterns in the new task. Second, transfer learning can overcome the limitation of insufficient training data for the target task by using the pre-trained model's knowledge. Finally, it accelerates the training process since only the task-specific layers need to be trained, reducing the overall training time and resource requirements. It's important to choose a pre-trained model that is relevant to the target task and domain. For example, if the task involves image classification, pre-trained models like VGG, ResNet, or Inception can be used as a starting point. Fine-tuning of the pre-trained model may be necessary, where the weights of the pre-trained layers are updated during training to adapt to the target task. Transfer learning has become a common practice in deep learning, enabling the application of deep models to various tasks with limited data and resources. It is a valuable technique that allows practitioners to build powerful models efficiently and effectively.

6.6.7 Monitor the Training Process

Monitoring the training process is indeed essential for understanding the behavior and performance of a deep learning model. It allows us to identify potential issues, track progress, and make informed decisions to improve the model's performance. There are several aspects to consider when monitoring the training process. First, tracking metrics, such as accuracy and loss, provides insights into how well the model is learning and generalizing. These metrics can be calculated on both the training and validation datasets and plotted over time to observe trends and potential overfitting. Visualizing the training process is also beneficial. TensorBoard, a visualization tool provided by TensorFlow, is widely used for this purpose. It allows for real-time monitoring of various aspects of the training, such as loss curves, accuracy curves, and histograms of weights and biases. TensorBoard provides a visual representation of the model's performance, making it easier to identify patterns and anomalies. Additionally, it can be helpful to visualize example predictions or misclassifications during the training process. This provides a qualitative assessment of the model's behavior and helps in identifying areas that require improvement. Another aspect of monitoring is observing the convergence of the model. This involves checking if the loss is decreasing and stabilizing over time. If the loss is not converging, it may indicate issues, such as a suboptimal learning rate, incorrect model architecture, or insufficient training data. Regular checkpoints should also be saved during training to ensure that the model's progress is not lost in case of any interruptions. These checkpoints allow for model evaluation and further training from a specific point. By actively monitoring the training process, practitioners can gain valuable insights into their model's behavior and performance. This information helps in making informed decisions to address issues, fine-tune hyperparameters, and ultimately improve the model's accuracy and generalization capabilities.

6.6.8 Hyperparameter Tuning

Deep learning models typically involve a large number of hyperparameters that control various aspects of the model's architecture, optimization process, and regularization. Tuning these hyperparameters is crucial for achieving optimal performance. Grid search and random search are popular techniques used to explore and find the best hyperparameter settings. Grid search involves defining a grid of possible hyperparameter values and exhaustively evaluating the model's performance for all possible combinations of these values. It systematically searches through the entire parameter space, evaluating the model's performance using a predefined evaluation metric. This approach provides a comprehensive view of the model's performance across different hyperparameter configurations but can be computationally expensive when the search space is large. Random search, on the other hand, randomly samples hyperparameters from a defined distribution and evaluates the model's performance using these randomly selected settings. This approach offers the advantage of being more computationally efficient compared to grid search, as it does not exhaustively search the entire parameter space. Instead, it explores different hyperparameter combinations based on random sampling. Random search can be particularly effective when the impact of individual hyperparameters on the model's performance is not well understood. Both grid search and random search help in identifying hyperparameter configurations that yield the best performance for a given task. By systematically exploring different settings, these techniques assist in finding the optimal balance between model complexity, regularization, and optimization parameters. It is important to perform cross-validation during the hyperparameter search to ensure the selected configuration is robust and generalizes well to unseen data. It's worth noting that advanced optimization techniques, such as Bayesian optimization and evolutionary algorithms, can also be employed to automate the hyperparameter search process and further improve efficiency. In summary, grid search and random search are valuable techniques for hyperparameter tuning in deep learning. They allow practitioners to explore different hyperparameter configurations and identify the optimal settings for achieving the best model performance.

6.6.9 Save the Model

Saving the trained deep learning model is a crucial step to preserve its learned parameters and architecture for future use. TensorFlow provides the SavedModel format, which is a standard way to save and load models in a language-neutral format. Saving a model in the SavedModel format involves capturing both the model's architecture and its learned parameters. The architecture includes information about the layers, connections, and operations of the model, while the learned parameters consist of the trained weights and biases. To save a model in the SavedModel format, you can use TensorFlow's tf.saved_model.save function. This function takes the model object and the desired save location as input. It will create a directory containing the saved model artifacts.

6.6.10 Use a Reproducible Environment

To ensure reproducibility in deep learning projects, creating a consistent and reproducible environment is essential. Two commonly used tools for achieving this are Docker and Anaconda.

Docker is a platform that allows you to create lightweight, portable containers that encapsulate the necessary dependencies and environment for running your code. With Docker, you can package your deep learning project along with all its dependencies, including specific versions of libraries and packages, into a container. This container can then be shared and run on different machines, ensuring that the code will produce consistent results regardless of the underlying system. Anaconda, on the other hand, is a distribution of Python and a package manager that simplifies the management of packages and environments. With Anaconda, you can create isolated Python environments that contain specific versions of libraries and dependencies required for your deep learning project. By defining and managing these environments using Anaconda, you can ensure that the code will run consistently across different machines. To use Docker or Anaconda for reproducibility in your deep learning project, follow these general steps.

1. **Docker:**
   - Define a Dockerfile that specifies the necessary environment, including the base image, dependencies, and installation steps.
   - Build a Docker image from the Dockerfile using the "docker build" command.
   - Run the Docker container from the built image using the "docker run" command, providing the necessary inputs and executing the code inside the container.
2. **Anaconda:**
   - Create a new Anaconda environment using the "conda create" command, specifying the required packages and their versions.
   - Activate the created environment using the "conda activate" command.
   - Install additional packages and dependencies using the "conda install" or "pip install" commands.
   - Run your deep learning code within the activated Anaconda environment.

Both Docker and Anaconda provide ways to document and share the environment configuration, allowing others to replicate the same environment and reproduce your results. By using Docker or Anaconda to create reproducible environments, you can ensure that your deep learning code will run consistently across different machines and produce reliable and reproducible results.

Remember, hands-on experience is key when working with deep learning or any other machine learning models. Therefore, consistently practicing implementation and troubleshooting is crucial for mastering these concepts.

6.7 Lessons Learned

- Learn the concept of deep learning
- Learn the architecture of deep learning
- Learn the most popular deep learning approaches architectures
- Learn the most popular deep learning applications
- Learn the Issues of deep learning
- Learn the implementation Tips for deep learning

6.8 Problems

6.8.1   What is deep learning, and how is it different from traditional machine learning?

6.8.2   What is a neural network, and how does it work in deep learning?

6.8.3   What are the different types of neural networks used in deep learning?

6.8.4   How do you choose the right activation function for a neural network?

6.8.5   What is backpropagation, and how is it used in deep learning?

6.8.6   How do you prevent overfitting in a deep learning model?

6.8.7   What is transfer learning, and how is it used in deep learning?

6.8.8   What are some common optimization algorithms used in deep learning?

6.8.9   What is the vanishing gradient problem, and how can it be mitigated?

6.8.10 How do you choose the right hyperparameters for a deep learning model?

6.8.11 What is the difference between supervised, unsupervised, and semi-supervised learning in deep learning?

6.8.12 What is reinforcement learning, and how is it used in deep learning?

6.8.13 What is adversarial training, and how is it used in deep learning?

6.8.14 How do you measure the performance of a deep learning model?

6.8.15 What is the role of regularization in deep learning?

6.8.16 What is a convolutional neural network, and how is it used in deep learning?

6.8.17 What is a recurrent neural network, and how is it used in deep learning?

6.8.18 What is a generative adversarial network, and how is it used in deep learning?

6.8.19 What is deep reinforcement learning, and how is it different from traditional reinforcement learning?

6.8.20 How do you scale a deep learning model to handle large datasets?

6.9 Programming Questions

- **Easy**

  6.9.1 Implement a simple neural network to classify images of digits from the MNIST dataset.

  6.9.2 Write a Python script to load and preprocess image data for use in a deep learning model.

  6.9.3 Train a simple convolutional neural network (CNN) to classify images of cats and dogs.

  6.9.4 Implement a feedforward neural network to predict housing prices based on input features, such as location, number of rooms, and square footage.

- **Medium**

  6.9.5 Train a CNN on the CIFAR-10 dataset and evaluate its performance on the test set.

  6.9.6 Implement a recurrent neural network (RNN) for sentiment analysis on movie reviews.

  6.9.7 Build a deep learning model to generate captions for images using the COCO dataset.

  6.9.8 Implement a variational autoencoder (VAE) to generate new images of faces from the CelebA dataset.

- **Hard**

  6.9.9 Implement a deep reinforcement learning algorithm for playing a game like Atari Breakout or Pac-Man.

  6.9.10 Train a deep learning model to predict the 3D structure of a protein from its amino acid sequence.

  6.9.11 Build a neural network to generate music using MIDI files and evaluate its performance using human evaluation metrics.

  6.9.12 Develop a deep learning model to detect and classify objects in satellite imagery for use in disaster response or urban planning.

7

Generative Adversarial Networks (GANs) Fundamentals and Architectures

The following topics are covered in this chapter about Fundamentals and Architectures of Generative Adversarial Networks (GANs):

- Introducing Adversarial Learning
- GAN Architecture
- Loss Functions
- GAN Training
- GAN Applications
- Most popular GANs
- Develop GAN Models
- Issues in GAN
- Training Approaches and Implementation Tips for GAN

7.1 Preface

Generative Adversarial Networks (GANs) are deep learning-based models that have been used to address various problems. First described in a 2014 article by Ian Goodfellow and colleagues, GANs have found applications in image-to-image translation, achieving photorealism, and generating photorealistic images. Current research focuses on common issues that make GANs susceptible to a wide range of failure scenarios. They function through a two-part competitive strategy involving generators and discriminators, with the aim of maximizing performance and enhancing both components. The generator network is responsible for creating new data similar to the training data, while the discriminator network tries to differentiate between real and generated data. Both networks are trained concurrently in a two-player minimax game until the generator produces data indistinguishable from the real data. GANs have diverse applications in fields, such as computer vision, natural language processing, and audio processing. In computer vision, they have been used for image synthesis, image super-resolution, image-to-image translation, and style transfer. In natural language processing, applications include text generation, text-to-image synthesis, and sentiment analysis. GANs have also been employed in audio processing for music generation, speech synthesis, and audio-to-image synthesis. One of the main advantages of GANs is their ability to generate new data, similar to the training data, without explicitly modeling the data distribution. This makes them ideal for data augmentation and synthesis tasks, where additional data is required for training machine learning models. GANs can also

DOI: 10.1201/9781003281344-7

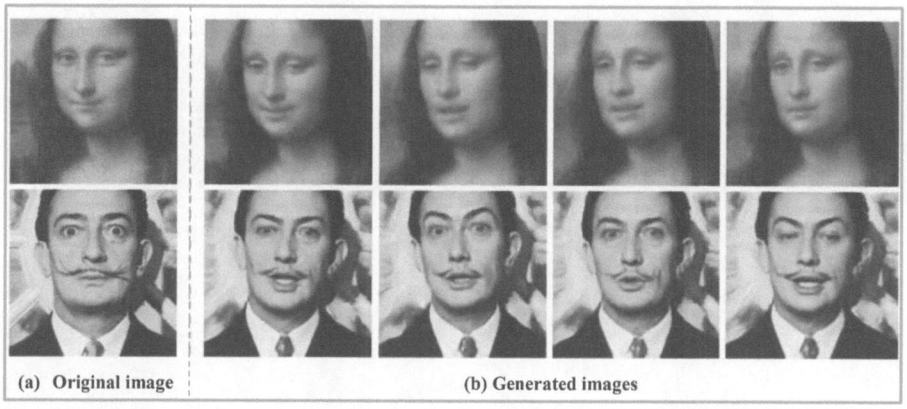

FIGURE 7.1
Examples of talking head image synthesis using face landmark tracks. (a) The left images are original. (b) The right ones are the generated images using GAN.

be used for unsupervised learning with unlabeled training data. However, GANs are not without their issues. They can suffer from instability during training, mode collapse, and lack of diversity in the generated data. Several techniques have been proposed to address these issues, such as using alternative loss functions, regularizing the generator, and incorporating feedback from the discriminator into the generator. Overall, GANs are a powerful tool for data generation and have the potential to revolutionize various fields, including art, design, and entertainment. Figure 7.1 presents a compelling visual comparison between original and synthesized images of talking head shots using face landmark tracks. On the left side (a), we see the original images that serve as a reference point. In contrast, the right side (b) displays the generated images that have been crafted using Generative Adversarial Networks (GANs). The juxtaposition provides a clear insight into the capabilities of GANs in creating realistic representations based on facial landmarks, highlighting the advancements in image synthesis techniques. This chapter will further review the general architecture of GANs, their applications, and the most well-known and popular methods.

7.2 Introducing Adversarial Learning

This section delves into the characteristics of adversarial neural networks, focusing on their general architectures, methods, and applications.

7.2.1 What Is Adversarial Learning?

Generative models utilize unsupervised machine learning to automatically discover and learn patterns in input data, which enables them to generate new examples that resemble those from the original dataset. The architecture of GANs is divided into two sub-models: the generator model, which strives to create new examples, and the discriminator model, which aims to classify examples as either real or fake. These two models are trained concurrently in an adversarial, zero-sum game until the discriminator model is fooled approximately half of the time. This indicates that the generator model is producing convincing

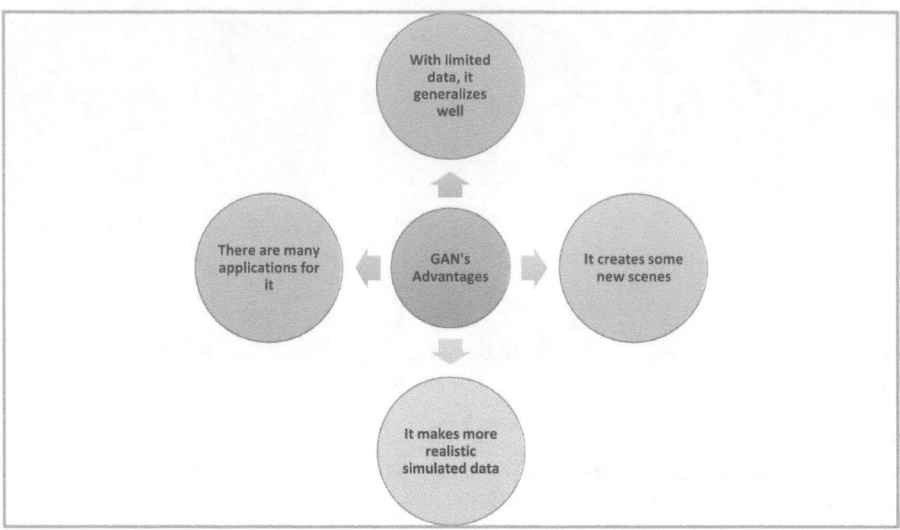

FIGURE 7.2
Advantages of GANs.

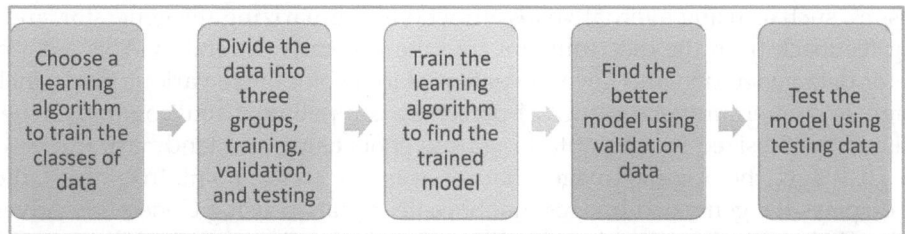

FIGURE 7.3
Steps to finding a model using deep learning approaches.

instances. GANs have found use in a variety of problem areas, including image-to-image translation tasks, such as converting summer photos into winter ones or daytime photos into nighttime ones. They can also generate photorealistic images of objects, scenes, and people that are indistinguishable to the human eye. GANs offer numerous advantages, some of the most significant of which are shown in Figure 7.2.

Discriminative or generative methods are typically used for discrimination (classification) and generation (simulation) of new scenes or data. There are various methods and approaches for training a GAN model, and the training process generally involves several steps common to many deep learning methods, as illustrated in Figure 7.3.

7.3 GAN Architecture

A GAN consists of two components: the Generator and the Discriminator. The Generator is designed to generate data consistent with acceptability criteria, while the Discriminator is trained to distinguish between fake data generated by the Generator and real data. If the

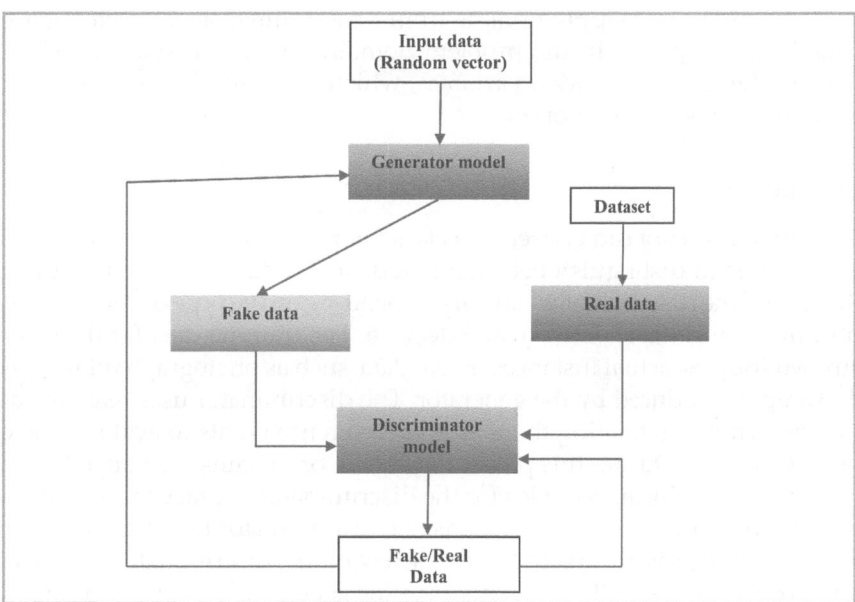

FIGURE 7.4
General GAN architecture.

Generator produces improbable results, the Discriminator penalizes it. Both the generation and discrimination processes employ neural networks, with the Generator's output directly connected to the Discriminator's input. The Discriminator's classification sends a signal to the Generator, prompting it to update its weights through backpropagation.

Let's review the general process of GANs. Initially, random input vectors, such as those generated by a Gaussian distribution, are fed into the Generator to create a generator model. This model then generates new examples, resulting in two sets: real examples from the original database and generated examples from the generator model. The Discriminator uses both these sets to classify them as real or fake. After this classification, the generator model is updated based on the Discriminator's output. If the Discriminator fails to distinguish between real and fake data, the update of the generator model and Discriminator model parameters can be skipped. Figure 7.4 illustrates the general architecture of GANs, where the inputs are random vectors (e.g., noise) following a defined distribution, and the output is classified as either real or fake data.

7.3.1 Generator

Training the generator requires closer integration between the generator and the discriminator compared to training the discriminator. During neural network training, weights are adjusted to minimize output error or loss. In the GAN framework, the generator loss penalizes the generator for producing fake samples as evaluated by the discriminator network. The generator model takes a random vector of a predetermined length as input and generates a sample from the desired domain. To initiate the generative process, a vector is randomly selected from a Gaussian distribution and used as input. Experiments have shown that the specific distribution of the noise isn't crucial, allowing for simpler choices, such as a uniform distribution. After training, the GAN model forms a compressed representation of the data distribution by mapping points from a multidimensional vector space (known as the latent space) to points in the problem domain. The latent space consists of latent variables, also referred to as hidden variables, which are essential to the domain but not immediately observable to an observer.

7.3.2 Discriminator

In a GAN, the discriminator can be seen as a classifier rather than a traditional discriminator. Its main objective is to distinguish between real data and data generated by the generator. The architecture of the discriminator can vary depending on the type of data it's categorizing, and it can utilize any suitable network architecture. The training data for the discriminator comes from two sources: actual instances of real data, such as photographs of real people, and generated examples produced by the generator. The discriminator uses real data as positive examples during training, treating them as good reference points to evaluate the quality of the generated fake data. During this phase, the generator remains unchanged, retaining the same weights while producing samples for the discriminator to practice on. The discriminator is connected to two distinct loss functions: the discriminator loss and the generator loss. During its training, the discriminator focuses solely on the discriminator loss, disregarding the generator loss. Conversely, the generator uses the generator loss for its training. If the discriminator misclassifies a real instance as fake or a fake instance as real, it experiences a loss due to its mistake. The discriminator network updates its weights through backpropagation based on the discriminator loss. In other words, the discriminator learns from its errors and adjusts its parameters accordingly. In practice, an instance from the input domain is fed into the discriminator model, which then makes a classification decision by assigning it a true or false class label, indicating whether it belongs to the real or fake data category.

7.4 Loss Functions

The loss methods discussed here focus on deriving generator and discriminator losses from a single measure of distance between probability distributions. Two common approaches are:

1. The minimax loss function, which was used in the original research paper that introduced GANs.
2. The Wasserstein loss function, initially outlined in a 2017 study.

These approaches represent different ways to measure the discrepancy between the generated and real data distributions. Their effectiveness and applicability depend on the specific problem and dataset at hand. Ongoing research aims to explore and refine these loss functions and potentially introduce new ones to improve the training stability and performance of GANs.

7.4.1 Minimax Loss

In the first research article introducing GANs, the generator's goal was described as minimizing the value of the loss function, while the discriminator's goal was to maximize it.

7.4.2 Wasserstein Loss

This loss function is based on the "Wasserstein GAN" or "WGAN", which is a variant of the GAN system. In WGAN, the discriminator doesn't classify instances but instead returns a numerical value for each instance. Because it doesn't differentiate between true and false content, the WGAN discriminator is more accurately referred to as a "critic" rather than a "discriminator".

7.5 GAN Training

To learn how to distinguish between real and fake data, the training of the discriminator must initially focus on identifying the mistakes made by the generator. This poses a unique challenge, particularly for a well-trained generator compared to one that produces random output without any training. During the training process of a GAN, the discriminator remains unmodified while the generator is being trained, aiming to reach a specific target. The discriminator's prediction method can be likened to coin flipping, and ideally, with a well-trained generator, the discriminator's accuracy should be around 50%. However, as the training progresses, the discriminator's feedback becomes less significant, which presents a challenge for the overall convergence of the GAN. The training of a GAN typically involves three steps, as shown in Figure 7.5. The initial input to the generator is random data, which is not part of the training process. As previously mentioned, the loss function is used for training, and the initial training is performed on the discriminator, which then updates the generator based on its outputs. This process is repeated iteratively until the discriminator reaches a point where it cannot distinguish between real and fake data. At this stage, the generator is considered to be evaluated and tested. By going through these training steps and iterations, a GAN aims to achieve a state where the generated data becomes highly convincing and indistinguishable from real data.

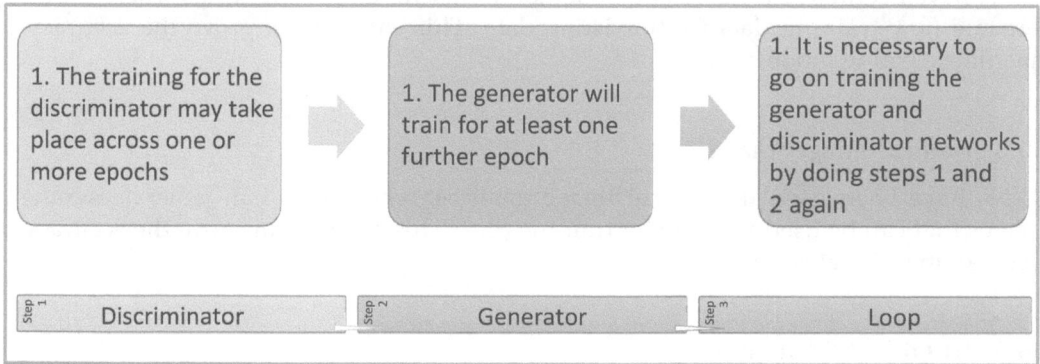

FIGURE 7.5
GAN training procedures.

7.6 GAN Applications

GANs have numerous applications, the most exciting of which is the use of GANs for tasks requiring the creation or concepts of new examples. The ability to create unique and creative paintings, drawings, and other forms of visual expression. Converting images from one format to another can transform photos into different states, such as day to night, summer to winter, and so on. GANs have created photographs that are so realistic that humans are unable to tell that they illustrate objects, settings, or people that do not exist in the real world. GANs have shown great potential in various applications, such as image and video synthesis, text-to-image synthesis, style transfer, and data augmentation.

7.6.1 Image and Video Synthesis

GANs have been widely used in image and video synthesis, where they generate realistic images or videos that look like real-world data. For example, GANs have been used to create realistic face images, which can be used in applications like virtual reality and computer vision.

7.6.2 Text-to-Image Synthesis

GANs have also been used to generate images from text descriptions. Given a textual description, a GAN can generate an image that corresponds to that description. This application has many potential uses, including in the fields of design and art.

7.6.3 Style Transfer

GANs have also been used for style transfer, where the style of one image is transferred to another image. This application can be used for artistic purposes as well as in the fields of fashion and design.

7.6.4 Data Augmentation

GANs have been used for data augmentation in machine learning tasks, where they can generate new training data from existing data. This can help improve the accuracy of machine learning models.

7.6.5 Medical Image Analysis

GANs have been used in medical image analysis, where they can generate synthetic images that can be used to augment training data. This can help improve the accuracy of medical image analysis algorithms.

7.6.6 3D Object Generation

GANs have been used to generate 3D objects, which can be used in virtual reality and other applications.

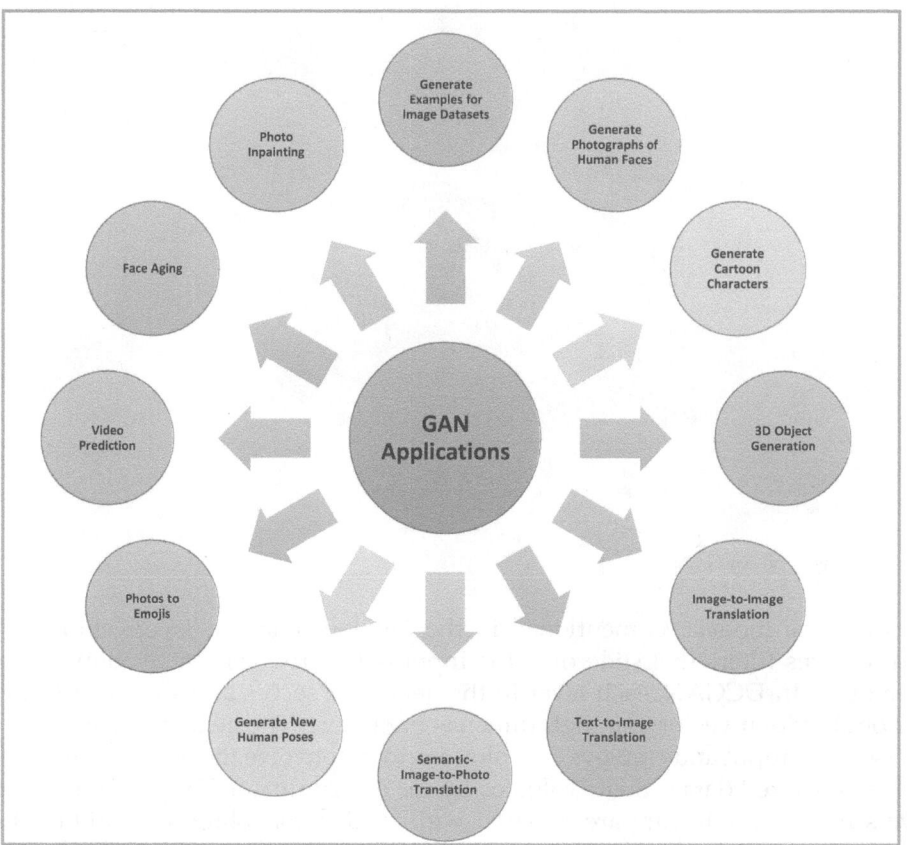

FIGURE 7.6
GAN has a wide range of applications.

7.6.7 Speech Synthesis

GANs have also been used for speech synthesis, where they can generate speech that sounds like a human voice. This application has many potential uses, including in the field of voice assistants and chatbots.

These are just a few examples of the many potential applications of GANs, and their usage is still being explored in various fields. Figure 7.6 illustrates a few of these applications, and we also discuss some of these in each chapter from 8 to 15.

7.7 Most Popular GANs

There are several types of GAN, but the most popular ones are as follows in Figure 7.7.

7.7.1 Deep Convolutional GANs (DCGANs)

The core of the Deep Convolutional Generative Adversarial Network (DCGAN) architecture is based on a standard Convolutional Neural Network (CNN) architecture for

FIGURE 7.7
There are various types of GAN.

a discriminative model. As mentioned in the previous chapter, a convolutional neural network utilizes filters that slide over the input data, producing activations using a set of parameters. In DCGAN, each layer in the generator serves as a mapping from a low-dimensional hidden vector to a high-dimensional image. The generator begins with random noise as an input and employs convolutions to deconvolve the noise and generate fake data. This generated data is then evaluated by the discriminator. To accomplish this, pooling layers in the architecture are replaced with strided convolutions. Additionally, both the generator and discriminator employ normalization techniques and use convolutional layers instead of fully connected layers, which allow for a deeper architecture. Chapter 8 delves into the features of DCGAN in more detail, providing a comprehensive exploration of its architecture and characteristics.

7.7.2 Conditional GANs (cGANs)

Conditional GAN (cGAN) is a variant of GAN where the generator model generates images conditionally, based on additional information. This additional information serves as a constraint on the data to be fed into the discriminator as real data. When working with a conditional GAN, it is crucial to condition both the generator and discriminator so that they are aware of the specific type of data they are dealing with. It is important to note that cGANs can be conditioned on a wide range of inputs. For example, in the context of image-to-image translation, other images can be used as additional information for conditioning the GAN. In Chapter 9, a deeper exploration of cGAN is provided, offering more comprehensive insights into its workings, applications, and characteristics.

7.7.3 Cycle Generative Adversarial Networks (CycleGAN)

CycleGAN is a type of GAN used for mapping the distribution of one image domain to another or transferring the characteristics of one image to another. In CycleGAN, the problem is approached as an image reconstruction task. It starts with an input image, denoted as **x**, which is processed by the generator **G** to generate a reconstructed image. Then, using the generator **F**, the process is reversed to reconstruct the original image from the generated image. One notable advantage of CycleGAN is its ability to perform image translation even when the input and output images are not directly paired, meaning there is no explicit correspondence between them. This flexibility allows for more versatile and diverse image transformations. Chapter 10 provides a more comprehensive discussion of CycleGAN, offering detailed insights into its methodology, applications, and further exploration of the algorithm.

7.7.4 Semi-supervised Generative Adversarial Network (SGAN)

Semi-supervised learning represents a promising and highly valuable domain for the practical implementation of GANs. The objective of semi-supervised learning is to learn from a limited number of labeled data points and successfully classify unlabeled data by leveraging the latent structures present in the data. It is essential for the labeled and unlabeled data to be derived from the same underlying distribution to ensure the effectiveness of semi-supervised learning. The utilization of GANs in semi-supervised learning is explored in detail in Chapter 11, providing a comprehensive examination of this approach. This chapter delves into the intricacies of employing GANs for semi-supervised learning, shedding light on the underlying principles, applications, and potential benefits of this methodology.

7.7.5 Least Squares Generative Adversarial Network (LSGAN)

Unsupervised learning using GANs has shown remarkable effectiveness. In traditional GANs, the discriminator is typically treated as a classifier, and the sigmoid cross entropy loss function is used to model its behavior. However, research has revealed that using this loss function exclusively throughout the learning process can lead to vanishing gradients, which hamper effective training. To address this challenge, the use of least squares GANs (LSGANs) has emerged as a beneficial alternative to standard GANs. LSGANs offer two notable advantages. Firstly, the generated images produced by LSGANs tend to be of higher quality compared to those generated by standard GANs. Secondly, LSGANs demonstrate more stable performance throughout the learning process, resulting in improved stability and convergence. Chapter 12 delves into a detailed discussion of LSGANs, providing a comprehensive exploration of their characteristics, mechanisms, and benefits.

7.7.6 Wasserstein Generative Adversarial Networks (WGAN)

This specific GAN tackles several critical aspects, including enhancing learning stability, mitigating issues, such as mode collapse, and providing meaningful learning curves for effective debugging and hyperparameter optimization. It showcases successful solutions to the associated optimization problem and presents a substantial body of theoretical work that underscores the significant relationships between different distribution distances. Chapter 13 delves into a comprehensive examination of this GAN, offering detailed insights into its architecture, optimization techniques, and theoretical foundations.

7.7.7 Auxiliary Classifier Generative Adversarial Networks (AC-GAN)

In recent years, the use of image-based methodologies and treating executables as images have gained popularity in the field of malware research. In this context, some

researchers have employed AC-GAN to generate synthetic malware samples and evaluate the performance of various classification strategies on these generated samples.
While achieving good results in distinguishing between real and fake samples, the
resulting multiclass classification problem proves to be challenging, according to their
findings. Although the AC-GAN-generated images often exhibit a high degree of similarity to actual malware images, the researchers concluded that the AC-GAN-generated
samples do not reach the level of "deep fake" malware images in terms of deep learning.
For further details, I recommend reading their paper, which provides a more comprehensive exploration of these AC-GANs and their applications in the context of malware
research.

7.7.8 Stacked Generative Adversarial Networks (StackGAN)

The described GAN is composed of a hierarchical stack of GANs, each of which is trained
to generate lower-level representations based on higher-level representations. At each
level of the feature hierarchy, a representation discriminator is implemented to encourage
the alignment of the generator's representation manifold with that of the bottom-up discriminative network. This approach allows the generative model to leverage powerful and
biased representations to guide its generation process. In addition to the representation
discriminator, the GAN incorporates a conditional loss that promotes the utilization of
dependent information from the layer above. It also introduces an entropy loss that maximizes a variational lower bound on the conditional entropy of the generator output. These
losses act as incentives for the generator to make effective use of conditional information.
The training process involves training each stack of GANs separately before training the
entire model from start to finish. Unlike the original GAN, which represents all variations
with a single noise vector, this hierarchical GAN divides variations into multiple levels,
gradually resolving uncertainties in the top-down generation process. For further insights
and a more detailed understanding of this GAN, I recommend referring to the original
research paper, which offers a comprehensive exploration of its architecture, training
methodology, and experimental results.

7.7.9 Progressive, Growing Generative Adversarial Networks (PGAN)

The utilization of GANs in generating metasurfaces from a training set of high-performance
device layouts holds the potential to significantly reduce the computational requirements
for metasurface design. This could lead to substantial cost savings. However, traditional
GAN designs may struggle to capture the intricate properties of complex metasurfaces
accurately. Consequently, additional computationally expensive design modifications are
necessary for the produced devices to function properly. The research demonstrates that
by progressively expanding both the network architecture and the training set, GANs
can effectively learn spatially fine features from high-resolution training data. This
approach proves more effective in creating high-quality devices compared to traditional
gradient-based topology optimization methods. As a result, further design refinements
are no longer necessary to achieve optimal device performance. For a more comprehensive understanding of these GANs and their application in generating metasurfaces, I
recommend referring to the original research paper. It provides detailed insights into the
GAN architecture, training techniques, and experimental results, shedding light on the
benefits and advancements achieved in the field of metasurface design.

7.7.10 Big Generative Adversarial Networks (BigGAN)

BigGAN is a specialized GAN designed to handle the generation of high-resolution and high-fidelity images. It incorporates several improvements and modifications compared to the baseline GAN architecture. The following changes were made to enhance the performance of BigGAN:

- Self-Attention GAN (SAGAN) was utilized as a baseline, along with spectral normalization for both the generator (**G**) and discriminator (**D**), and the Two Time-Scale Update Rule (TTUR) was implemented for training stability.
- A GAN objective with Hinge Loss was employed, which has been shown to improve the quality of generated images.
- Class-conditional batch normalization was utilized, where classified information is provided to the generator (**G**). However, instead of using a Multi-Layer Perceptron (MLP), a linear projection was used.
- Class information was provided to the discriminator (**D**) through a projection discriminator.
- An evaluation method called Exponentially Weighted Moving Average (EWMA) of G's weights was introduced, similar to the approach used in Progressive GANs (ProGANs).

In addition to these modifications, BigGAN introduces several innovations that contribute to its performance:

- The batch size was increased, which has a significant impact on the inception score, a metric used to evaluate the quality of generated images.
- The inception score was further enhanced by increasing the width of each layer in the network.
- More skip connections were added from the latent variable to subsequent layers, which help improve performance.
- A novel iteration of orthogonal regularization was introduced, a technique used to encourage orthogonal weight matrices.

For a more in-depth understanding of BigGAN and its architecture, I recommend reading the original research paper.

7.7.11 Style-based Generative Adversarial Networks (StyleGAN)

StyleGAN is a GAN that generates fake images in a multi-stage process, starting from a low resolution and gradually progressing to a high resolution of 1024 × 1024 pixels in each iteration. This staged generation allows for independent control over the visual characteristics expressed at each level. By adjusting the input at each level independently, StyleGAN enables control over various visual traits, ranging from broad features like pose and face shape to more specific attributes like hair color. Importantly, these adjustments have no impact on other levels, ensuring the targeted control of specific characteristics.

This approach not only provides a deeper understanding of the generated output but also yields impressive results, particularly in generating high-resolution images that appear more realistic and genuine compared to previous methods. To gain a more comprehensive understanding of StyleGAN and its architecture, I recommend referring to the original research paper.

7.8 Develop GAN Models

There are several major steps to developing a GAN model. We will first review these steps before deploying TensorFlow and Keras to implement some examples.

7.8.1 Analyze the Problem

Correctly analyzing your problem and identifying all of its needs, inputs, outputs, and features is critical.

7.8.2 Select GAN Architecture

We have looked at some of the most common GAN architectures. It is crucial to determine which GAN architecture is suitable for our data and problem. This can be determined based on previous GAN applications, related architectures, features of each GAN architecture, including advantages and disadvantages, and your goals for using GAN for your problem.

7.8.3 Train the Discriminator on Real Dataset

In this step, GAN's discriminator is trained on the dataset using real data. This step contains only real data; there is no fake data. The discriminator is a tool for distinguishing between real and fake data that is noisy or generated by a generator, and it should only be trained on real data.

7.8.4 Train Generator

In this step, some random noise (or something similar) will be fed to the generator for training. This type of data is used to train the initial generator.

7.8.5 Fake Data on the Discriminator

In this step, the generated fake data will be fed to the trained discriminator to determine whether it is real or fake.

7.8.6 Train Generator

The discriminator's feedback will be passed to the generator in this step to improve the generated data.

7.9 Issues in GAN

GANs have been shown to be a powerful tool for generating realistic and diverse data, including images, voice, and music. However, there are several issues and challenges associated with GANs. We'll go over some of them here before getting into more detail in the following chapters.

7.9.1 Mode Collapse

In some cases, GANs can suffer from mode collapse, which occurs when the generator produces a limited variety of samples, ignoring some modes in the real data distribution.

7.9.2 Training Instability

The training process of GANs can be unstable and difficult to converge, especially when the discriminator is too strong or too weak compared to the generator.

7.9.3 Evaluation of Generated Data

There is no clear and definitive way to evaluate the quality and diversity of the generated data, and different metrics may give different results.

7.9.4 Dataset Bias

GANs are sensitive to the distribution of the training data, and if the dataset is biased or unrepresentative of the real data distribution, the generated data may also be biased or unrealistic.

7.9.5 Computational Resources

Training GANs requires significant computational resources, including powerful GPUs and large amounts of memory, which can be costly and time-consuming.

7.9.6 Lack of Interpretability

GANs are often referred to as black box models, as it is difficult to understand how the generator produces the generated samples and what features it learns from the input data.

7.9.7 Data Privacy and Security

GANs can potentially be used for malicious purposes, such as generating fake data for fraud or impersonation, raising concerns about data privacy and security.

7.9.8 Transferability

GANs trained on one dataset may not generalize well to other datasets or domains, and fine-tuning or retraining may be required to adapt the model to new data.

7.10 Training Approaches and Implementation Tips for GAN

There are some training skills that can assist you in your implementation. We will go over some of them here and go over in more details each in other GAN approaches in the following chapters.

7.10.1 Feature Matching

Some of the GAN's instabilities are caused by the generators' targets failing to converge to the discriminator's target. The proposed solution to this problem is to install a supervisor signal that instructs the generator to act as an intermediate layer. The intermediate layer of this technique has some expected value of the features, and when training the discriminator, we look for those features to distinguish between genuine and false data provided by the generator.

7.10.2 Normalizing the Inputs, Mini-batch, and Batch Norm

There are several normalizing methods. It is preferable to use a mini-batch of samples rather than a single input for the discriminator to look at because this avoids some collapses in the training steps. If you don't want to use the batch norm, you can normalize the data by subtracting the mean value and dividing it by the standard deviation value. Finally, if the batch norm is not used, you can have different mini-batches, each containing either real or generated image data.

7.10.3 Use Batch Normalization

Batch normalization can help in stabilizing the training process by reducing internal covariate shift.

7.10.4 Use Different Learning Rates for the Generator and Discriminator

In most cases, the generator needs to learn slower than the discriminator. Therefore, it is recommended to use a smaller learning rate for the generator.

7.10.5 Use Different Loss Functions for the Generator and Discriminator

The generator is trained to minimize the difference between the generated and real data, while the discriminator is trained to distinguish between the generated and real data. Therefore, it is important to use different loss functions for each of them.

7.10.6 Use a Variety of Evaluation Metrics

While the most common evaluation metric for GANs is the Inception score, it is important to use a variety of evaluation metrics to get a comprehensive understanding of model's performance.

7.10.7 Monitor the Gradients

Monitoring the gradients during training can help in diagnosing issues, such as vanishing or exploding gradients.

7.10.8 Use Regularization Techniques

Regularization techniques, such as weight decay, dropout, and data augmentation, can help in preventing overfitting.

7.10.9 Use Appropriate Activation Functions

The choice of activation function can have a significant impact on the performance of the model. It is recommended to use ReLU or leaky ReLU for the generator and discriminator.

7.10.10 Use Appropriate Initialization Techniques

The choice of initialization technique can also have a significant impact on the performance of the model. It is recommended to use techniques, such as Xavier initialization or He initialization.

7.10.11 Use Early Stopping

Early stopping can help in preventing overfitting and improving the generalization ability of the model.

7.10.12 Use Transfer Learning

Transfer learning can help in improving the performance of the model by leveraging the pre-trained weights of another model. For example, the pre-trained weights of a convolutional neural network can be used as the initial weights for the discriminator.

7.10.13 Use Progressive Training

Progressive training involves gradually increasing the complexity of the model during training. This can help in preventing mode collapse and improving the stability of the training process.

7.10.14 Use Wasserstein Distance

Wasserstein distance is a more stable alternative to the traditional GAN loss function. It can help in improving the stability of the training process and preventing mode collapse.

7.10.15 Use Label Smoothing

Label smoothing involves replacing the binary labels (0 or 1) with smoothed labels (e.g., 0.1 or 0.9). This can help in preventing the discriminator from becoming too confident in its predictions and improving the stability of the training process.

7.10.16 Use Noise Injections

Noise injections involve adding random noise to the input of the discriminator or generator. This can help in preventing the discriminator from overfitting to the training data and improving the generalization ability of the model.

7.10.17 Use Mini-batch Discrimination

Mini-batch discrimination involves computing statistics over a mini-batch of samples and using them to augment the input of the discriminator. This can help in preventing mode collapse and improving the diversity of the generated samples.

Remember, hands-on experience is key when working with GANs or any other machine learning models. Therefore, consistently practicing implementation and troubleshooting is crucial for mastering these concepts.

7.11 Lessons Learned

- Learn the Adversarial learning concept
- Learn the GAN general architecture and concept
- Learn Loss Functions
- Learn Training in GAN
- Learn the GAN applications
- Learn the most popular GAN approaches
- Learn the steps for GAN approach development
- Learn the GAN issues
- Learn the Implementation tips for GAN

7.12 Problems

7.12.1   What is the difference between a generator and a discriminator in GANs?

7.12.2   How does the training process of GANs work?

7.12.3   What is the objective function of GANs?

7.12.4   What are some common loss functions used in GANs?

7.12.5   What is the role of the noise vector in GANs?

7.12.6   How can we evaluate the performance of GANs?

7.12.7   What is mode collapse in GANs?

7.12.8   How can we prevent mode collapse in GANs?

7.12.9   What is the difference between vanilla GANs and DCGANs?

7.12.10   What are some practical applications of GANs?

7.12.11   How can we generate high-resolution images using GANs?

7.12.12   What is the difference between conditional GANs and unconditional GANs?

7.12.13   How can we use GANs for data augmentation?

7.12.14   What is the role of batch normalization in GANs?

7.12.15 How can we generate new examples from a trained GAN model?

7.12.16 What are some challenges in training GANs?

7.12.17 What is the difference between a generator and an encoder in GANs?

7.12.18 How can we use GANs for image-to-image translation?

7.12.19 What is the difference between adversarial training and traditional supervised training?

7.12.20 How can we use GANs for unsupervised learning?

7.13 Programming Questions

- **Easy**

  7.13.1 Implement a Normal GAN to generate images of a specific category, such as cats or dogs.

  7.13.2 Train a Normal GAN on a small dataset of handwritten digits and generate new samples of digits.

  7.13.3 Modify the Normal GAN code to use different activation functions in the generator and discriminator.

- **Medium**

  7.13.4 Implement a Normal GAN that generates 3D objects, such as chairs or cars.

  7.13.5 Train a Normal GAN on a large dataset of images and evaluate the quality of the generated images using various metrics, such as inception score or FID.

  7.13.6 Implement a Normal GAN that generates images conditioned on a specific input, such as a sentence describing the image.

- **Hard**

  7.13.7 Implement a Normal GAN that generates high-resolution images, such as 4K or 8K resolution.

  7.13.8 Train a Normal GAN that generates video sequences instead of static images.

  7.13.9 Implement a Normal GAN that can generate images with multiple objects and complex backgrounds, and evaluate its performance against other state-of-the-art GAN models.

8

Deep Convolutional Generative Adversarial Networks (DCGANs)

This chapter covers the following topics in Deep Convolutional Generative Adversarial Networks (DCGANs):

- DCGAN Architecture
- DCGAN Applications
- DCGAN for CelebA
- DCGAN for MNIST
- DCGAN Issues
- DCGAN Implementation Tips

8.1 Preface

Radford et al. (2015) introduced Deep Convolutional Generative Adversarial Networks (DCGANs), which have proven to be an effective approach for image synthesis. They also provided guidelines for implementing DCGANs, which include the following steps:

1. Replace pooling layers with stride convolutions in the discriminator and fractional-stride convolutions in the generator.
2. Apply batch normalization in both the generator and discriminator.
3. Remove fully connected hidden layers from the network architecture.
4. Use ReLU activation for all generator layers, except for the output layer, where Tanh activation should be used.
5. Utilize leaky ReLU activation for all layers in the discriminator.

By adhering to these guidelines, improved results can be achieved when implementing DCGANs. Additionally, other techniques found beneficial in DCGAN implementations include:

1. Downsampling and upsampling using stride convolutions.
2. Using leaky ReLU activation.
3. Applying batch normalization.
4. Utilizing Gaussian weight initialization.
5. Implementing the Adam optimizer.

DOI: 10.1201/9781003281344-8

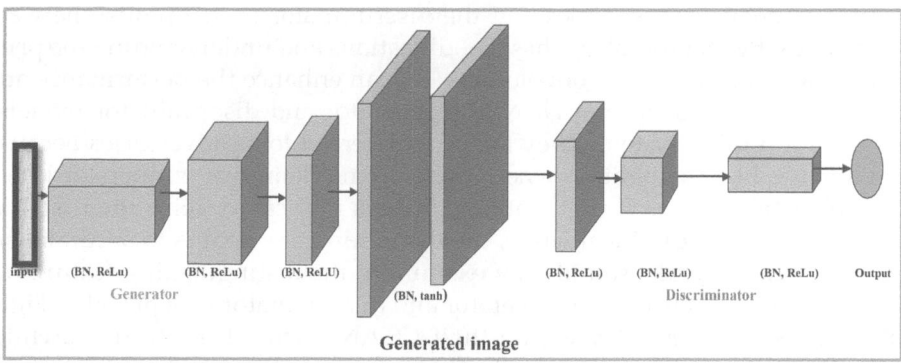

FIGURE 8.1
DCGAN general architecture.

DCGANs are powerful generative models that leverage deep convolutional neural networks to learn and generate new data. They have successfully generated high-quality images and found applications across various domains. DCGANs excel in creating large, detailed images by capturing fine-grained features through their convolutional layers. However, they are not without challenges. Issues, such as mode collapse and training instability, can arise during training. Techniques, such as mini-batch discrimination, spectral normalization, and alternative loss functions, have been proposed to address these issues. In industries such as entertainment, fashion, and healthcare, DCGANs have the potential to be revolutionary. They offer a powerful means to generate high-quality images. Figure 8.1 showcases the architecture of a Deep Convolutional Generative Adversarial Network (DCGAN). The diagram is bifurcated into two main sections: the generator and the discriminator. The generator is responsible for creating synthetic data, while the discriminator evaluates the authenticity of the generated samples against real data. The structure is designed to illustrate the intricate interplay between these two components, highlighting the iterative nature of their relationship as they vie to outperform each other. The representation serves as a visual guide to understanding the mechanics and intricacies of the DCGAN model. The use of convolutional and transposed convolutional layers is crucial, as discussed in Chapter 1. This chapter aims to review the DCGAN approach and provide coding examples to facilitate the understanding and implementation of DCGANs.

8.2 DCGAN Architecture

To optimize the DCGAN, several adjustments were made to the discriminator, generator, and the convergence of the GAN architecture. In this modified setup, pooling layers are not utilized at all. Neurons are not required to connect and combine their outputs to form pooling, and any convolutional classification strategy can be used for the discriminator if necessary. Batch normalization, also developed by the creators of DCGAN, helps stabilize the training process by normalizing the inputs at each layer. This normalization helps mitigate issues such as internal covariate shift and ensures a more stable gradient flow during training. Having covered the fundamentals of convolutions and transposed convolutions, let's delve into how these operations are implemented within the context of a GAN. These operations play a vital role in transforming and manipulating data, allowing the generator to create new samples and the discriminator to distinguish between real and fake samples. By incorporating these modifications and understanding the principles of convolutions and transposed convolutions, we can enhance the performance and convergence of the GAN model. In a GAN, the generator and discriminator models operate together as a unified system. They are often referred to as adversaries because they engage in a game-like competition where there are no definitive winners or losers. The generator's objective is to produce synthetic images that can deceive the discriminator into believing they are real. Meanwhile, the discriminator's goal is to accurately distinguish between real and fake samples by examining the distinguishing features of each image. The interaction between the generator and discriminator is depicted in Figure 8.2, which showcases their interplay within the DCGAN architecture. In this architecture, convolutional and transposed convolutional layers are utilized instead of dense layers. Several design considerations come into play, such as incorporating batch normalization, selecting appropriate activation functions for different layers, carefully choosing the optimizer, and designing upscaling and downscaling layers in a specific way. The discriminator model essentially functions as a convolutional classification model, as its primary task is to classify the input images as real or fake based on their distinguishing features. This involves using convolutional layers to extract relevant features and making predictions based on these features.

Overall, the GAN framework brings together the generator and discriminator models, allowing them to learn from each other and iteratively improve their performance. Through their competition and cooperation, GANs have proven to be highly effective in generating realistic and high-quality synthetic samples.

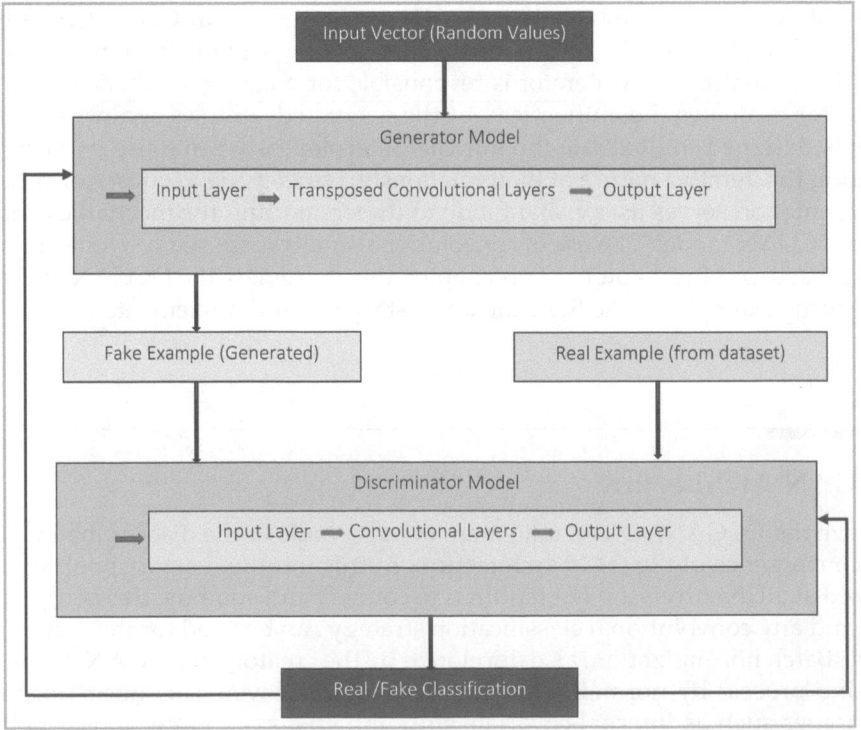

FIGURE 8.2
DCGAN architecture.

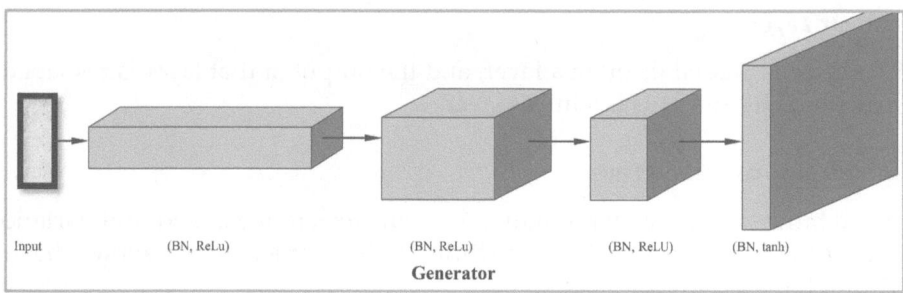

FIGURE 8.3
Generator architecture.

8.2.1 Generator

The initialization step and the requirements for constructing the DCGAN model differ significantly. The generator starts by generating initial images from random noise and iteratively refines them until the desired images are obtained. Figure 8.3 illustrates the general architecture of the generator, highlighting its key components. It presents a detailed visualization of the generator's architecture within the Deep Convolutional Generative Adversarial Network (DCGAN). The diagram emphasizes its core components, starting from the initial noise input layer, progressing through various convolutional and upsampling layers, and culminating in the final generated image output. Each layer's structure and interconnections are meticulously displayed, providing a comprehensive view of how the generator synthesizes new data from random noise. This visualization aids in grasping the intricacies and importance of the generator within the broader DCGAN framework. It is evident from the figure that batch normalization is applied to all layers, and ReLU activation is used for all layers except the final layer, which employs the Tanh activation function.

Let's go over how to create a generator class. Figure 8.4 shows the three main steps for implementing the generator.

The generator's main components are several layers and activation functions. Now, let's take a closer look at the generator's architecture.

FIGURE 8.4
Generator implementation steps.

8.2.1.1 Linear Layer

The noise vector is passed through a layer, and the output of that layer is reshaped into a four-dimensional tensor. This is a linear layer.

8.2.1.2 Batch Normalization Layer

This layer stabilizes learning by normalizing inputs to zero mean and unit variance. This prevents training issues such as the vanishing gradient problem and allows the gradient to flow through the network.

8.2.1.3 2D Convolutional Layer

The generator sends the matrix through a convolutional layer with the same padding as the generator upsample. This allows the generator to learn from the upsampled data.

8.2.1.4 ReLU Layer

The DCGAN paper recommends using ReLU for the generator rather than leaky ReLU because it allows the model to train quickly and fill the distribution's color space compared to leaky ReLU.

8.2.1.5 Tanh Activation

The DCGAN paper recommends using the tanh activation function for the generator, most likely due to tanh's properties, which allow the model to converge more quickly.

8.2.2 Discriminator

For the discriminator, we observe a similar distinction in terms of step initialization and model construction as we do with the generator. Let's review the steps involved in creating a discriminator class. The discriminator utilizes batch normalization in all layers, applies the Tanh activation function in the first layer, and employs the leaky ReLU activation function in the remaining layers. Figure 8.5 provides a general overview of the discriminator architecture. It offers an encompassing look at the discriminator's architecture within the Deep Convolutional Generative Adversarial Network (DCGAN). The visual representation meticulously outlines the structure, starting with the input image and traversing through a series of convolutional layers, downsampling stages, and finally converging to a single output

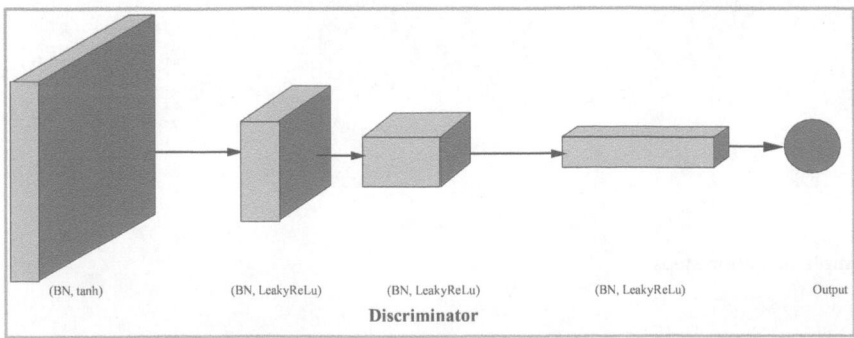

FIGURE 8.5
Discriminator architecture.

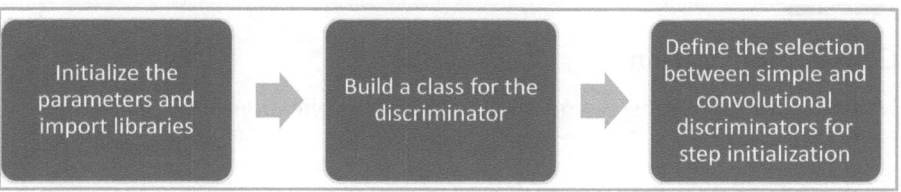

FIGURE 8.6
Discriminator implementation steps.

node determining the authenticity of the given image. The diagram underscores the integral role of the discriminator in evaluating and distinguishing between genuine and generated images, offering viewers a clear insight into its operation within the DCGAN system.

Figure 8.6 illustrates the three main steps in implementing a discriminator in DCGAN.

The discriminator has several components, including an activation function and a dropout layer. We will discuss these in more detail.

8.2.2.1 Concat Layer

This layer combines fake and real images into a single batch for feeding the discriminator. However, this step can be performed separately to obtain the generator loss.

8.2.2.2 Convolutional Layer

This layer uses stride convolution to downsample the image and learn filters simultaneously.

8.2.2.3 leaky ReLU

According to research papers, leaky ReLU is better for discriminators than the max-out function used in the original GAN work because it simplifies training.

8.2.2.4 Dropout

Dropout is a training-only task that helps prevent overfitting. The model tends to memorize actual image data, and training can fail at this point because the generator can no longer fool the discriminator.

8.2.2.5 Batch Normalization

The use of batch normalization is discussed in the paper. It is used at the end of each discriminator block except for the first one. According to the paper, applying batch normalization across all blocks can cause sample oscillation, leading to model instability.

8.2.2.6 Fully Connected Layer

This layer is called a fully connected layer because it applies a reshaped vector from the 2D batch normalization and linear layers.

8.2.2.7 Sigmoid Activation

Because the discriminator deals with binary classifications, a sigmoid activation function makes the most sense for its output.

Some additional tips and tricks come from practicing with different types of data using DCGAN.

8.3 DCGAN Applications

DCGANs have shown impressive results in various applications.

8.3.1 Image Generation

DCGANs have been widely used for generating high-quality images of different categories, such as faces, animals, and landscapes. This has potential applications in fields, such as graphic design, gaming, and art.

8.3.2 Data Augmentation

DCGANs can be used to generate new training data, augmenting the size of the original dataset. This can help improve the performance of machine learning models, especially in scenarios where there is limited available data.

8.3.3 Style Transfer

DCGANs can be used to transfer the style of one image to another, creating a new image that combines the content of one image with the style of another. This has applications in fields, such as art and design.

8.3.4 Super-resolution

DCGANs can be used to enhance the resolution of low-resolution images, resulting in high-quality images with more detail. This has applications in fields, such as medical imaging and surveillance.

8.3.5 Anomaly Detection

DCGANs can be trained to detect anomalies in images, such as defects in manufacturing processes or abnormalities in medical images. This can help improve the accuracy and efficiency of quality control processes.

Overall, DCGANs have shown great potential in various applications that require the generation or manipulation of images, and they continue to be an active area of research.

8.4 DCGAN for CelebA

Using the CelebA dataset and implementing DCGAN on it is considered a good practice. This process can be carried out in six steps, starting with some initial settings. The necessary datasets, libraries, and packages for implementing DCGAN on CelebA are described below.

8.4.1 Import the Libraries

We will need libraries, such as TensorFlow, Keras, NumPy, and Matplotlib. Some libraries, such as ZipFile, also assist in unzipping the loaded files. These import statements are used to bring in the necessary libraries and modules that will be used in the code.

```
import tensorflow as tf
from tensorflow import keras
from tensorflow.keras import layers
import numpy as np
import matplotlib.pyplot as plt
import os
import gdown
from zipfile import ZipFile
```

Here's an explanation of each line of the code:

```
#This line imports the TensorFlow library, which is a popular open-source
library for machine learning and deep learning.
import tensorflow as tf

#This line imports the `keras` module from TensorFlow. Keras is a high-
level API for building and training neural networks.
from tensorflow import keras

#This line imports the `layers` module from TensorFlow's Keras API. The
`layers` module provides various types of layers that can be used to
build neural networks.
from tensorflow.keras import layers

#This line imports the NumPy library, which is a fundamental package for
scientific computing in Python. It provides support for multi-dimensional
arrays and mathematical functions.
import numpy as np

#This line imports the `pyplot` module from the Matplotlib library.
Matplotlib is a plotting library in Python, and `pyplot` provides a
MATLAB-like interface for creating plots and visualizations.
import matplotlib.pyplot as plt

#This line imports the `os` module, which provides a way to interact with
the operating system. It allows you to perform various operations related
to file and directory manipulation.
import os

#This line imports the `gdown` module, which is a Python library for
downloading files from Google Drive. It provides a convenient way to
download files using their Google Drive URL.
import gdown

#This line imports the `ZipFile` class from the `zipfile` module. The
`ZipFile` class provides tools for creating, reading, writing, and
extracting ZIP files.
from zipfile import ZipFile
```

8.4.2 Prepare Data

We'll resize the face images from the CelebA dataset to 64×64 pixels. Other preprocessing steps can be performed based on your expectations. The data can be loaded from a local machine or an online source. The code downloads a ZIP file from a specified URL, creates a directory to store the downloaded file and extracted contents, and extracts the ZIP file into the created directory.

```
os.makedirs("celeba_gan")
url = "https:// "
output = "celeba_gan/data.zip"
gdown.download(url, output, quiet=True)
with ZipFile("celeba_gan/data.zip", "r") as zipobj:
    zipobj.extractall("celeba_gan")
```

This code snippet performs the following tasks.

```
#This line creates a new directory named "celeba_gan" using the `os.
makedirs()` function. This directory will be used to store the downloaded
and extracted files.
os.makedirs("celeba_gan")

#These lines assign values to the variables `url` and `output`. The `url`
variable represents the URL from which the file will be downloaded, and the
`output` variable specifies the path and filename of the downloaded file.
url = "https:// "
output = "celeba_gan/data.zip"

#This line uses the `gdown.download()` function to download the file
specified by the `url` to the location specified by `output`. The
`quiet=True` argument suppresses the download progress output.
gdown.download(url, output, quiet=True)

#This block of code opens the downloaded ZIP file (`data.zip`) using the
`ZipFile` class from the `zipfile` module. The `"r"` argument indicates
that the file should be opened in read mode. The `zipobj.extractall()`
method is then called to extract all the contents of the ZIP file to the
"celeba_gan" directory.
with ZipFile("celeba_gan/data.zip", "r") as zipobj:
    zipobj.extractall("celeba_gan")

#This line creates an image dataset using the `image_dataset_from_
directory()` function from the `keras.preprocessing` module. It reads
images from the "celeba_gan" directory and creates a dataset. The
`label_mode=None` argument indicates that the dataset does not have any
labels. The `image_size=(64, 64)` argument specifies that the images
should be resized to a size of 64x64 pixels. The `batch_size=32`
argument determines the number of images in each batch of the dataset.
dataset = keras.preprocessing.image_dataset_from_directory("celeba_gan",
label_mode=None, image_size=(64, 64), batch_size=32)

#This line applies a mapping function to the dataset using the `map()`
method. The lambda function `lambda x: x / 255.0` is used to normalize
the pixel values of the images. It divides each pixel value by 255.0,
```

which scales the pixel values to the range of [0, 1]. This normalization step is commonly performed to ensure that the pixel values are in a suitable range for training machine learning models.
```
dataset = dataset.map(lambda x: x / 255.0)
```

It is a good practice to display the data before using it in order to check the values and distribution, and to see if any preprocessing is required. This can be done by displaying the first image in the dataset using Matplotlib or other visualization tools. Prior to displaying the image, it is common to convert the pixel values to the appropriate range and data type for image visualization. By inspecting the displayed image, you can visually assess the data and determine if any further preprocessing steps are necessary:

```
for x in dataset:
    plt.axis("off")
    plt.imshow((x.numpy() * 255).astype("int32")[0])
    break
```

Here's a breakdown of each line:

```
#This line initiates a loop that iterates over the `dataset`, where `x`
represents each batch of images.
for x in dataset:
```

```
#This line turns off the axis labels and ticks in the matplotlib plot. By
setting it to "off", it hides the axes' values and removes the axis
lines.
plt.axis("off")
```

```
#This line displays the first image from the current batch. `x.numpy()`
converts the tensor `x` to a NumPy array, allowing us to perform element-
wise operations. `(x.numpy() * 255)` scales the pixel values back to the
original range (0-255). `astype("int32")` casts the values to integers,
as matplotlib expects integer values for displaying images. `[0]` selects
the first image from the batch.
plt.imshow((x.numpy() * 255).astype("int32")[0])
```

```
#This line exits the loop after displaying the first image. It is used to
display only one image and prevent the loop from iterating over the
entire dataset.
Break
```

Figure 8.7 showcases two sample images from the CelebA dataset, a popular and extensive collection of celebrity images used in machine learning research. These images give viewers an idea of the dataset's quality, diversity, and resolution, underscoring its suitability for training sophisticated image-generating models like GANs. The displayed celebrities highlight the range of facial features, expressions, and attributes present in the dataset, making it a valuable resource for deep learning experiments.

FIGURE 8.7
CelebA dataset data sample.

8.4.3 Discriminator

The code defines a discriminator model for a GAN setup. The model is designed to map a 64×64 image to a binary classification score, indicating whether the input image is real or fake. The layers and their parameters can be reviewed and modified to observe the impact on the output results. It is possible to add more layers by iterating and experimenting with different configurations.

```
discriminator = keras.Sequential(
    [
        keras.Input(shape=(64, 64, 3)),
        layers.Conv2D(64, kernel_size=4, strides=2, padding="same"),
        layers.LeakyReLU(alpha=0.2),
        layers.Conv2D(128, kernel_size=4, strides=2, padding="same"),
        layers.LeakyReLU(alpha=0.2),
        layers.Conv2D(128, kernel_size=4, strides=2, padding="same"),
        layers.LeakyReLU(alpha=0.2),
        layers.Flatten(),
        layers.Dropout(0.2),
        layers.Dense(1, activation="sigmoid"),
    ],
    name="discriminator",
)
discriminator.summary()
Model: "discriminator"
```

Layer (type)	Output Shape	Param #
conv2d (Conv2D)	(None, 32, 32, 64)	3136
leaky_re_lu (LeakyReLU)	(None, 32, 32, 64)	0
conv2d_1 (Conv2D)	(None, 16, 16, 128)	131200
leaky_re_lu_1 (LeakyReLU)	(None, 16, 16, 128)	0
conv2d_2 (Conv2D)	(None, 8, 8, 128)	262272
leaky_re_lu_2 (LeakyReLU)	(None, 8, 8, 128)	0
flatten (Flatten)	(None, 8192)	0
dropout (Dropout)	(None, 8192)	0
dense (Dense)	(None, 1)	8193

```
Total params: 404,801
Trainable params: 404,801
Non-trainable params: 0
```

Here's an explanation of each line:

```
#This line creates a Sequential model object named "discriminator" using
`keras.Sequential()`. The model will consist of a sequence of layers
defined within the brackets. The layers within the brackets define the
architecture of the discriminator model:
discriminator = keras.Sequential([...], name="discriminator")
```

```
#This line defines the input shape of the model. It specifies that the
input should have a shape of (64, 64, 3), representing an RGB image with
dimensions 64x64 pixels.
keras.Input(shape=(64, 64, 3))
```

```
#This line adds a Conv2D layer with 64 filters, a kernel size of 4x4, a
stride of 2, and "same" padding. This layer performs convolutional
operations on the input image.
layers.Conv2D(64, kernel_size=4, strides=2, padding="same")
```

```
#This line adds a LeakyReLU activation layer. LeakyReLU introduces a
small slope (alpha=0.2) for negative input values, which helps to
alleviate the vanishing gradient problem.
layers.LeakyReLU(alpha=0.2)
```

```
#This line adds a Flatten layer. It flattens the output from the previous
layer into a 1-dimensional tensor, which can be connected to a fully
connected layer.
layers.Flatten()
```

```
#This line adds a Dropout layer with a dropout rate of 0.2. Dropout
randomly sets a fraction of input units to 0 during training, which helps
prevent overfitting.
layers.Dropout(0.2)
```

```
#This line adds a Dense layer with 1 unit and a sigmoid activation
function. The output of this layer represents the discriminator's
prediction on whether the input is real or fake.
layers.Dense(1, activation="sigmoid")
```

```
#This line prints a summary of the model's architecture, displaying
the layer names, output shapes, and the total number of trainable
parameters.
discriminator.summary()
```

8.4.4 Generator

The code defines a generator model for a GAN setup. The generator is designed to generate images based on a latent space vector as input. It is a mirror image of the discriminator, where Conv2D layers are replaced with Conv2DTranspose layers. The generator architecture includes dense, reshape, transpose convolutional, and activation layers. These layers work together to transform the input latent vector into a realistic image output.

By modifying the layers and their parameters, you can observe how these changes affect the generated image results.

```
latent_dim = 128
generator = keras.Sequential(
    [
        keras.Input(shape=(latent_dim,)),
        layers.Dense(8 * 8 * 128),
        layers.Reshape((8, 8, 128)),
        layers.Conv2DTranspose(128, kernel_size=4, strides=2,
padding="same"),
        layers.LeakyReLU(alpha=0.2),
        layers.Conv2DTranspose(256, kernel_size=4, strides=2,
padding="same"),
        layers.LeakyReLU(alpha=0.2),
        layers.Conv2DTranspose(512, kernel_size=4, strides=2,
padding="same"),
        layers.LeakyReLU(alpha=0.2),
        layers.Conv2D(3, kernel_size=5, padding="same",
activation="sigmoid"),
    ],
    name="generator",)
generator.summary()
```

```
Model: "generator"

Layer (type)                            Output Shape             Param #
=========================================================================
dense_1 (Dense)                         (None, 8192)             1056768
reshape (Reshape)                       (None, 8, 8, 128)        0
conv2d_transpose (Conv2DTranspose)      (None, 16, 16, 128)      262272
leaky_re_lu_3 (LeakyReLU)               (None, 16, 16, 128)      0
conv2d_transpose_1 (Conv2Dtranspose)    (None, 32, 32, 256)      524544
leaky_re_lu_4 (LeakyReLU)               (None, 32, 32, 256)      0
conv2d_transpose_2 (Conv2DTranspose)    (None, 64, 64, 512)      2097664
leaky_re_lu_5 (LeakyReLU)               (None, 64, 64, 512)      0
conv2d_3 (Conv2D)                       (None, 64, 64, 3)        38403
=========================================================================
Total params: 3,979,651
Trainable params: 3,979,651
Non-trainable params: 0
```

Here's an explanation of each line:

```
#This line sets the dimensionality of the latent space, which is the
input to the generator model. In this case, the latent space has a
dimensionality of 128.
latent_dim = 128
```

```
#This line creates a Sequential model object named "generator" using
`keras.Sequential()`. The model will consist of a sequence of layers
defined within the brackets. The layers within the brackets define the
architecture of the generator model:
generator = keras.Sequential([...], name="generator")
```

```
#This line defines the input shape of the model. It specifies that the
input should have a shape of (latent_dim,), where latent_dim is the
dimensionality of the latent space.
keras.Input(shape=(latent_dim,))
```

```
#This line adds a Dense layer with 8x8x128 units. This layer serves as
the initial decoder, expanding the latent space to a higher-dimensional
representation.
layers.Dense(8 * 8 * 128)
```

```
#This line adds a Reshape layer to reshape the output of the previous
layer into a 4D tensor with dimensions (8, 8, 128). This prepares the
data for subsequent transpose convolutional layers.
layers.Reshape((8, 8, 128))
```

```
#This line adds a transpose convolutional layer (also known as
Deconvolution) with 128 filters, a kernel size of 4x4, a stride of 2, and
"same" padding. This layer upsamples the input.
layers.Conv2DTranspose(128, kernel_size=4, strides=2, padding="same")
```

```
#This line adds a LeakyReLU activation layer with a small negative slope
(alpha=0.2), introducing non-linearity to the model.
layers.LeakyReLU(alpha=0.2)
```

```
#This line adds another transpose convolutional layer with 256 filters, a
kernel size of 4x4, a stride of 2, and "same" padding.
layers.Conv2DTranspose(256, kernel_size=4, strides=2, padding="same")
```

```
#This line adds another LeakyReLU activation layer.
layers.LeakyReLU(alpha=0.2)
```

```
#This line adds another transpose convolutional layer with 512 filters, a
kernel size of 4x4, a stride of 2, and "same" padding.
layers.Conv2DTranspose(512, kernel_size=4, strides=2, padding="same")
```

```
#This line adds another LeakyReLU activation layer.
layers.LeakyReLU(alpha=0.2)
```

```
#This line adds a final Conv2D layer with 3 filters, a kernel size of
5x5, "same" padding, and a sigmoid activation function. This layer
produces the output of the generator, representing a generated image.
layers.Conv2D(3, kernel_size=5, padding="same", activation="sigmoid")
```

```
#This line prints a summary of the generator model's architecture,
displaying the layer names, output shapes, and the total number of
trainable parameters.
generator.summary()
```

8.4.5 Train

Define a training class that includes all modules, such as compiling and metrics, as well as training the discriminator and generator and updating the metric. The code defines a

GAN model by subclassing the Keras. Model class. Here's an explanation of each method and its functionality:

```
#The __init__ method initializes the GAN model. It takes the
discriminator, generator, and latent dimension as input arguments and
assigns them as attributes of the GAN object.
class GAN(keras.Model):
    def __init__(self, discriminator, generator, latent_dim):
        super(GAN, self).__init__()
        self.discriminator = discriminator
        self.generator = generator
        self.latent_dim = latent_dim
```

```
#The compile method sets up the optimizer, loss function, and
evaluation metrics for the GAN model. It takes discriminator
optimizer, generator optimizer, and loss function as input arguments.
Additionally, it initializes the loss metrics for the discriminator
and generator.
    def compile(self, d_optimizer, g_optimizer, loss_fn):
        super(GAN, self).compile()
        self.d_optimizer = d_optimizer
        self.g_optimizer = g_optimizer
        self.loss_fn = loss_fn
        self.d_loss_metric = keras.metrics.Mean(name="d_loss")
        self.g_loss_metric = keras.metrics.Mean(name="g_loss")
```

```
#The metrics property returns the list of metrics associated with the GAN
model. In this case, it returns the discriminator loss metric and
generator loss metric
    @property
    def metrics(self):
        return [self.d_loss_metric, self.g_loss_metric]
```

```
#The train_step method performs a single training step for the GAN model.
It takes real images as input
    def train_step(self, real_images):
        # Sample random points in the latent space
        batch_size = tf.shape(real_images)[0]
        random_latent_vectors = tf.random.normal(shape=(batch_size, self.
latent_dim))
        # Decode them to fake images
        generated_images = self.generator(random_latent_vectors)
        # Combine them with real images
        combined_images = tf.concat([generated_images, real_images],
axis=0)
        # Assemble labels discriminating real from fake images
        labels = tf.concat( [tf.ones((batch_size, 1)), tf.zeros((batch_
size, 1))], axis=0)
        # Add random noise to the labels - an important trick!
        labels += 0.05 * tf.random.uniform(tf.shape(labels))
        # Train the discriminator
        with tf.GradientTape() as tape:
            predictions = self.discriminator(combined_images)
            d_loss = self.loss_fn(labels, predictions)
```

```
        grads = tape.gradient(d_loss, self.discriminator.trainable_weights)
        self.d_optimizer.apply_gradients(
            zip(grads, self.discriminator.trainable_weights)
        )
        # Sample random points in the latent space
        random_latent_vectors = tf.random.normal(shape=(batch_size, self.
latent_dim))
        # Assemble labels that say "all real images"
        misleading_labels = tf.zeros((batch_size, 1))
        # Train the generator (note that we should *not* update the
weight of the discriminator)!
        with tf.GradientTape() as tape:
            predictions = self.discriminator(self.generator(random_
latent_vectors))
            g_loss = self.loss_fn(misleading_labels, predictions)
        grads = tape.gradient(g_loss, self.generator.trainable_weights)
        self.g_optimizer.apply_gradients(zip(grads, self.generator.
trainable_weights))
        # Update metrics
        self.d_loss_metric.update_state(d_loss)
        self.g_loss_metric.update_state(g_loss)
        return {
            "d_loss": self.d_loss_metric.result(),
            "g_loss": self.g_loss_metric.result(),
        }
```

8.4.6 Save Generated Images and Train the Model

Overall, this "GANMonitor" callback class generates a specified number of images at the end of each training epoch and saves them as PNG files, providing visual feedback on the progress of the GAN model.

```
class GANMonitor(keras.callbacks.Callback):
    def __init__(self, num_img=3, latent_dim=128):
        self.num_img = num_img
        self.latent_dim = latent_dim
    def on_epoch_end(self, epoch, logs=None):
        random_latent_vectors = tf.random.normal(shape=(self.num_img,
self.latent_dim))
        generated_images = self.model.generator(random_latent_vectors)
        generated_images *= 255
        generated_images.numpy()
        for i in range(self.num_img):
            img = keras.preprocessing.image.array_to_img(generated_
images[i])
            img.save("generated_img_%03d_%d.png" % (epoch, i))
```

Here's a breakdown of each line of the "GANMonitor" callback class code:

```
#This method defines the constructor for the `GANMonitor` class. It
initializes the `num_img` and `latent_dim` attributes with default values
or the provided values as arguments.
def __init__(self, num_img=3, latent_dim=128):
    self.num_img = num_img
    self.latent_dim = latent_dim
```

#This method is called at the end of each training epoch. It generates random latent vectors (`random_latent_vectors`) from a normal distribution, with a shape of `(num_img, latent_dim)`. These latent vectors are passed through the generator model (`self.model.generator`), resulting in generated images (`generated_images`). The pixel values of the generated images are scaled up by multiplying them with 255. Finally, the `numpy()` method is called to convert the generated images to NumPy arrays.

```
def on_epoch_end(self, epoch, logs=None):
    random_latent_vectors = tf.random.normal(shape=(self.num_img, self.
latent_dim))
    generated_images = self.model.generator(random_latent_vectors)
    generated_images *= 255
    generated_images.numpy()
```

#This block of code iterates over the generated images using a `for` loop. For each image, it converts the NumPy array representation to a PIL Image object (`img`) using `keras.preprocessing.image.array_to_img()`. Then, it saves the image to a file using the `save()` method, with a filename format that includes the epoch number and the index of the image.

```
for i in range(self.num_img):
    img = keras.preprocessing.image.array_to_img(generated_images[i])
    img.save("generated_img_%03d_%d.png" % (epoch, i))
```

Overall, this code trains the GAN model using the specified dataset and training configuration, while utilizing the "GANMonitor" callback to monitor the training progress visually.

```
epochs = 1
gan = GAN(discriminator=discriminator, generator=generator,
latent_dim=latent_dim)
gan.compile(
    d_optimizer=keras.optimizers.Adam(learning_rate=0.0001),
    g_optimizer=keras.optimizers.Adam(learning_rate=0.0001),
    loss_fn=keras.losses.BinaryCrossentropy(),
)
gan.fit(dataset, epochs=epochs, callbacks=[GANMonitor(num_img=10,
latent_dim=latent_dim)])
```

Here's an explanation of each line:

#This line assigns the value 1 to the variable `epochs`, specifying the number of training epochs.
```
epochs = 1
```
#This line creates an instance of the `GAN` model by passing the discriminator, generator, and latent dimension as arguments.
```
gan = GAN(discriminator=discriminator, generator=generator,
latent_dim=latent_dim)
```

#This line compiles the `gan` model. It specifies the discriminators' optimizer (`d_optimizer`), the generator's optimizer (`g_optimizer`), and the loss function (`loss_fn`) to be used during training. In this case, the Adam optimizer with a learning rate of 0.0001 is used for both the

discriminator and generator, and the BinaryCrossentropy loss function is used.

```
gan.compile(
    d_optimizer=keras.optimizers.Adam(learning_rate=0.0001),
    g_optimizer=keras.optimizers.Adam(learning_rate=0.0001),
    loss_fn=keras.losses.BinaryCrossentropy(),
)

#This line starts the training process for the `gan` model. It trains the
model on the provided `dataset` for the specified number of `epochs`.
Additionally, it uses the `GANMonitor` callback during training, which
generates and saves 10 images at the end of each epoch for visual
monitoring.
gan.fit(dataset, epochs=epochs, callbacks=[GANMonitor(num_img=10,
latent_dim=latent_dim)])
```

8.5 DCGAN for MNIST

This section goes over the steps for implementing handwritten generation with the MNIST dataset, TensorFlow, and Keras.

8.5.1 Import Libraries

In the first step, we should do several setups like importing the libraries and packages and installing the requirements. These import statements ensure that the necessary libraries and modules are available for performing tasks related to TensorFlow, image processing, plotting, and visualization in the subsequent code.

```
import tensorflow as tf
import imageio
import matplotlib.pyplot as plt
import numpy as np
import os
import PIL
from tensorflow.keras import layers
from IPython import display
```

Here's an explanation of each import statement:

```
#This line imports the TensorFlow library, which is an open-source
machine learning framework.
import tensorflow as tf
#This line imports the `imageio` library, which provides functions for
reading and writing various image formats.
import imageio

#This line imports the `pyplot` module from the Matplotlib library.
Matplotlib is a plotting library in Python, and `pyplot` provides a
MATLAB-like interface for creating plots and visualizations.
import matplotlib.pyplot as plt
```

```
#This line imports the NumPy library, which is a fundamental package for
scientific computing in Python. It provides support for multi-dimensional
arrays and mathematical functions.
import numpy as np

#This line imports the `os` module, which provides a way to interact with
the operating system. It allows you to perform various operations related
to file and directory manipulation.
import os

#This line imports the Python Imaging Library (PIL), which provides support
for opening, manipulating, and saving many different image file formats.
import PIL

#This line imports the `layers` module from TensorFlow's Keras API. The
`layers` module provides various types of layers that can be used to
build neural networks.
from tensorflow.keras import layers

#This line imports the `display` module from the IPython library, which
provides enhanced interactive capabilities for the Jupyter Notebook
environment.
from IPython import display
```

8.5.2 Load and Prepare the Dataset

Overall, this code loads the MNIST dataset, preprocesses the training images by reshaping and normalizing them, and creates a TensorFlow Dataset object for batching and shuffling the training data. This prepared dataset can be used for training a GAN model on the MNIST images.

```
(train_images, train_labels), (_, _) = tf.keras.datasets.mnist.
load_data()
train_images = train_images.reshape(train_images.shape[0], 28, 28,
1).astype('float32')
train_images = (train_images - 127.5) / 127.5
BUFFER_SIZE = 60000
BATCH_SIZE = 256
train_dataset = tf.data.Dataset.from_tensor_slices(train_images).
shuffle(BUFFER_SIZE).batch(BATCH_SIZE)
```

Here's an explanation of each line:

```
#This line loads the MNIST dataset using the `load_data()` function from
`tf.keras.datasets.mnist`. It returns the training images, training
labels, testing images, and testing labels. In this case, the testing
data is not used, so it is assigned to `_` to indicate that it is not
necessary to store.
(train_images, train_labels), (_, _) = tf.keras.datasets.mnist.load_data()

#This line reshapes the training images from a 3D shape `(num_samples,
28, 28)` to a 4D shape `(num_samples, 28, 28, 1)`. The additional
```

dimension of size 1 indicates that the images are grayscale. The images are also cast to the data type `'float32'`.

```
train_images = train_images.reshape(train_images.shape[0], 28, 28,
1).astype('float32')
```

#This line normalizes the pixel values of the training images to the range of `[-1, 1]`. It subtracts 127.5 from each pixel value and then divides by 127.5. This normalization brings the pixel values from the original range of `[0, 255]` to `[-1, 1]`.

```
train_images = (train_images - 127.5) / 127.5
```

#These lines create a TensorFlow Dataset object `train_dataset` from the training images. The `from_tensor_slices()` method converts the tensor of images into a dataset by slicing it along the first dimension. The dataset is then shuffled with a buffer size of 60000, which is the total number of training samples. Finally, the dataset is batched into batches of size 256 for more efficient training.

```
BUFFER_SIZE = 60000
BATCH_SIZE = 256
train_dataset = tf.data.Dataset.from_tensor_slices(train_images).
shuffle(BUFFER_SIZE).batch(BATCH_SIZE)
```

8.5.3 Generator

Overall, this code generates a sample image using the generator model and displays it using Matplotlib, providing a visual representation of the output of the generator.

```
def make_generator_model():
    model = tf.keras.Sequential()
    model.add(layers.Dense(7*7*256, use_bias=False, input_shape=(100,)))
    model.add(layers.BatchNormalization())
    model.add(layers.LeakyReLU())
    model.add(layers.Reshape((7, 7, 256)))
    assert model.output_shape == (None, 7, 7, 256)
    model.add(layers.Conv2DTranspose(128, (5, 5), strides=(1, 1),
padding='same', use_bias=False))
    assert model.output_shape == (None, 7, 7, 128)
    model.add(layers.BatchNormalization())
    model.add(layers.LeakyReLU())
    model.add(layers.Conv2DTranspose(64, (5, 5), strides=(2, 2),
padding='same', use_bias=False))
    assert model.output_shape == (None, 14, 14, 64)
    model.add(layers.BatchNormalization())
    model.add(layers.LeakyReLU())
    model.add(layers.Conv2DTranspose(1, (5, 5), strides=(2, 2),
padding='same', use_bias=False, activation='tanh'))
    assert model.output_shape == (None, 28, 28, 1)
    return model
generator = make_generator_model()
noise = tf.random.normal([1, 100])
generated_image = generator(noise, training=False)
plt.imshow(generated_image[0, :, :, 0], cmap='gray')
```

The code defines a generator model for a GAN and generates a sample image using the generator. Here's an explanation of each line:

```
#This line defines a function named `make_generator_model()` that creates
a sequential model object for the generator.
def make_generator_model():
    model = tf.keras.Sequential()
```

```
#This line adds a dense layer to the model with 7*7*256 units. The `use_
bias=False` argument indicates that no bias term is used, and `input_
shape=(100,)` specifies the shape of the input to the generator.
model.add(layers.Dense(7*7*256, use_bias=False, input_shape=(100,)))
```

```
#These lines add a batch normalization layer and a LeakyReLU activation
layer to the model. Batch normalization helps stabilize the learning
process, and LeakyReLU introduces non-linearity while mitigating the
vanishing gradient problem.
model.add(layers.BatchNormalization())
model.add(layers.LeakyReLU())
```

```
#This line adds a reshape layer to the model, transforming the output
into a 4D tensor with dimensions (7, 7, 256).
model.add(layers.Reshape((7, 7, 256)))
```

```
#This line asserts that the output shape of the model is as expected,
ensuring that the model has been defined correctly.
assert model.output_shape == (None, 7, 7, 256)
```

```
#This line adds a transposed convolutional layer (also known as
Deconvolution) to the model. It has 128 filters, a kernel size of (5, 5),
strides of (1, 1), and "same" padding.
model.add(layers.Conv2DTranspose(128, (5, 5), strides=(1, 1),
padding='same', use_bias=False))
```

```
This line asserts that the output shape of the model is as expected.
assert model.output_shape == (None, 7, 7, 128)
```

```
#These lines add another batch normalization layer and LeakyReLU
activation layer to the model.
model.add(layers.BatchNormalization())
model.add(layers.LeakyReLU())
```

```
#This line adds another transposed convolutional layer to the model with
64 filters, a kernel size of (5, 5), strides of (2, 2), and "same"
padding.
model.add(layers.Conv2DTranspose(64, (5, 5), strides=(2, 2),
padding='same', use_bias=False))
```

```
#This line asserts that the output shape of the model is as expected.
assert model.output_shape == (None, 14, 14, 64)
```

```
#These lines add batch normalization and LeakyReLU activation layers.
model.add(layers.BatchNormalization())
model.add(layers.LeakyReLU())
```

```
#This line adds the final transposed convolutional layer to the model. It
has 1 filter, a kernel size of (5, 5), strides of (2, 2), and "same"
padding. The activation function is set to 'tanh', which maps the output
values to the range [-1, 1].
model.add(layers.Conv2DTranspose(1, (5, 5), strides=(2, 2),
padding='same', use_bias=False, activation='tanh'))

#This line asserts that the output shape of the model is as expected.
assert model.output_shape == (None, 28, 28, 1)

#This line returns the completed generator model.
return model

#The code generates a sample image using the generator model and displays
it using matplotlib. Here's an explanation of each line:
generator = make_generator

#This line generates random noise using `tf.random.normal()`. The `noise`
tensor has a shape of `[1, 100]`, indicating a batch size of 1 and
100-dimensional noise vectors.
noise = tf.random.normal([1, 100])

#This line generates an image using the generator model by passing the
`noise` tensor as input. The `training=False` argument ensures that the
model is not in training mode, which is important for proper behavior of
certain layers like batch normalization.
generated_image = generator(noise, training=False)

#This line displays the generated image using `plt.imshow()`. It selects
the first (and only) image from the `generated_image` tensor using
indexing (`[0, :, :, 0]`). The `cmap='gray'` argument specifies that the
colormap should be grayscale. Finally, `plt.imshow()` shows the image in
the current plot.
plt.imshow(generated_image[0, :, :, 0], cmap='gray')
```

8.5.4 Discriminator

Overall, this code defines a discriminator model and evaluates its decision on a generated image, providing an indication of the discriminator's output on the generated image.

```
def make_discriminator_model():
    model = tf.keras.Sequential()
    model.add(layers.Conv2D(64, (5, 5), strides=(2, 2), padding='same',
input_shape=[28, 28, 1]))
    model.add(layers.LeakyReLU())
    model.add(layers.Dropout(0.3))
    model.add(layers.Conv2D(128, (5, 5), strides=(2, 2), padding='same'))
    model.add(layers.LeakyReLU())
    model.add(layers.Dropout(0.3))
    model.add(layers.Flatten())
    model.add(layers.Dense(1))
    return model
discriminator = make_discriminator_model()
decision = discriminator(generated_image)
print (decision)
```

Here's an explanation of each line:

```
#This line defines a function named `make_discriminator_model()` that
creates a sequential model object for the discriminator.
def make_discriminator_model():
    model = tf.keras.Sequential()
```

```
#This line adds a convolutional layer to the model with 64 filters, a
kernel size of (5, 5), strides of (2, 2), and "same" padding. The `input_
shape` argument specifies the shape of the input to the discriminator.
model.add(layers.Conv2D(64, (5, 5), strides=(2, 2), padding='same',input_
shape=[28, 28, 1]))
```

```
#These lines add a LeakyReLU activation layer and a dropout layer to the
model. The LeakyReLU introduces non-linearity, and the dropout layer
helps prevent overfitting by randomly setting a fraction of the input
units to 0 during training.
model.add(layers.LeakyReLU())
model.add(layers.Dropout(0.3))
```

```
#This line adds another convolutional layer to the model with 128 filters,
a kernel size of (5, 5), strides of (2, 2), and "same" padding.
model.add(layers.Conv2D(128, (5, 5), strides=(2, 2), padding='same'))
```

```
#These lines add another LeakyReLU activation layer and dropout layer.
model.add(layers.LeakyReLU())
model.add(layers.Dropout(0.3))
```

```
#This line adds a flatten layer to the model. It flattens the output from
the previous layer into a 1-dimensional tensor.
model.add(layers.Flatten())
```

```
#This line adds a dense layer to the model with 1 unit. This layer serves
as the output layer of the discriminator, producing a single scalar value
indicating the discriminator's decision on the input image.
model.add(layers.Dense(1))
```

```
#This line returns the completed discriminator model.
return model
```

```
#This line creates an instance of the discriminator model by calling the
`make_discriminator_model()` function.
discriminator = make_discriminator_model()
```

```
#This line passes the `generated_image` through the discriminator model,
generating a decision value indicating the discriminator's prediction on
the generated image.
decision = discriminator(generated_image)
```

```
#This line prints the decision value.
print(decision)
```

8.5.5 Discriminator Loss

Overall, this code defines a discriminator loss function that calculates the cross-entropy loss between the discriminator's predictions and the target labels (1 for real samples and 0 for fake samples). The function returns the total loss, which is the sum of the losses for real and fake samples.

```
def discriminator_loss(real_output, fake_output):
    real_loss = cross_entropy(tf.ones_like(real_output), real_output)
    fake_loss = cross_entropy(tf.zeros_like(fake_output), fake_output)
    total_loss = real_loss + fake_loss
    return total_loss
```

Here's an explanation of each line:

```
#This line defines a function named `discriminator_loss` that takes two
arguments: `real_output` and `fake_output`. These arguments represent the
discriminator's predictions on real and fake/generated samples,
respectively.
def discriminator_loss(real_output, fake_output):
```

```
#This line calculates the loss for the real samples. It uses the `cross_
entropy` function (presumably defined elsewhere) to compute the cross-
entropy loss between the discriminator's predictions (`real_output`) and
a tensor of ones (`tf.ones_like(real_output)`). The `tf.ones_like()`
function creates a tensor with the same shape as `real_output` but with
all elements set to 1.
real_loss = cross_entropy(tf.ones_like(real_output), real_output)
```

```
#This line calculates the loss for the fake/generated samples. It uses
the `cross_entropy` function to compute the cross-entropy loss between
the discriminator's predictions (`fake_output`) and a tensor of zeros
(`tf.zeros_like(fake_output)`). The `tf.zeros_like()` function creates
a tensor with the same shape as `fake_output` but with all elements set
to 0.
fake_loss = cross_entropy(tf.zeros_like(fake_output), fake_output)
```

```
#This line computes the total loss by summing the individual losses for
the real and fake samples.
total_loss = real_loss + fake_loss
```

```
#This line returns the computed total loss.
return total_loss
```

8.5.6 Generator Loss

Overall, this code defines a generator loss function that computes the cross-entropy loss between the discriminator's predictions on the generated samples and a tensor of ones. It also creates Adam optimizers with the same learning rate for both the generator and discriminator. These components are typically used in training a GAN model, where the generator aims to minimize its loss while the discriminator aims to maximize its loss.

```
def generator_loss(fake_output):
    return cross_entropy(tf.ones_like(fake_output), fake_output)
generator_optimizer = tf.keras.optimizers.Adam(1e-4)
discriminator_optimizer = tf.keras.optimizers.Adam(1e-4)
```

Here's an explanation of each line:

```
#This function, `generator_loss`, calculates the loss for the generator.
It takes the `fake_output` as an argument, which represents the
discriminator's predictions on the generated samples. The loss is
computed using the `cross_entropy` function (presumably defined
elsewhere) between the discriminator's predictions (`fake_output`) and a
tensor of ones (`tf.ones_like(fake_output)`). The `tf.ones_like()`
function creates a tensor with the same shape as `fake_output` but with
all elements set to 1. This loss measures how well the generator can
generate samples that are classified as real by the discriminator.
def generator_loss(fake_output):
    return cross_entropy(tf.ones_like(fake_output), fake_output)
```

```
#This line creates an Adam optimizer for the generator. The optimizer is
initialized with a learning rate of `1e-4` (0.0001), which determines the
step size taken during the optimization process to update the generator's
weights.
generator_optimizer = tf.keras.optimizers.Adam(1e-4)
```

```
#This line creates an Adam optimizer for the discriminator. It uses the
same learning rate of `1e-4` (0.0001) as the generator optimizer.
discriminator_optimizer = tf.keras.optimizers.Adam(1e-4)
```

8.5.7 Define the Training Loop

Overall, these lines ensure that the final set of generated images is displayed and saved after the training process is completed for the specified number of epochs.

```
EPOCHS = 50
noise_dim = 100
num_examples_to_generate = 16
seed = tf.random.normal([num_examples_to_generate, noise_dim])
@tf.function
def train_step(images):
    noise = tf.random.normal([BATCH_SIZE, noise_dim])
    with tf.GradientTape() as gen_tape, tf.GradientTape() as disc_tape:
        generated_images = generator(noise, training=True)
        real_output = discriminator(images, training=True)
        fake_output = discriminator(generated_images, training=True)
        gen_loss = generator_loss(fake_output)
        disc_loss = discriminator_loss(real_output, fake_output)
    gradients_of_generator = gen_tape.gradient(gen_loss, generator.
trainable_variables)
    gradients_of_discriminator = disc_tape.gradient(disc_loss,
discriminator.trainable_variables)
```

```
    generator_optimizer.apply_gradients(zip(gradients_of_generator,
generator.trainable_variables))
    discriminator_optimizer.apply_gradients(zip(gradients_of_
discriminator, discriminator.trainable_variables))
def train(dataset, epochs):
  for epoch in range(epochs):
    start = time.time()
    for image_batch in dataset:
      train_step(image_batch)
    display.clear_output(wait=True)
    generate_and_save_images(generator,epoch + 1,seed)
    if (epoch + 1) % 20 == 0:
      checkpoint.save(file_prefix = checkpoint_prefix)
    print ('Time for epoch {} is {} sec'.format(epoch + 1, time.
time()-start))
    display.clear_output(wait=True)
  generate_and_save_images(generator,epochs,seed)
```

Here's an explanation of each component:

```
#These lines set the number of training epochs (`EPOCHS`), the
dimensionality of the noise vector (`noise_dim`), the number of examples
to generate and save during training (`num_examples_to_generate`), and a
seed noise vector for generating consistent images during training
(`seed`).
EPOCHS = 50
noise_dim = 100
num_examples_to_generate = 16
seed = tf.random.normal([num_examples_to_generate, noise_dim])
```

```
#This line decorates the `train_step` function with `tf.function`,
allowing TensorFlow to compile the function for improved performance.
Inside the `train_step` function:
@tf.function
def train_step(images):
```

```
#This line generates a batch of noise vectors (`noise`) using the noise
dimension and the batch size.
noise = tf.random.normal([BATCH_SIZE, noise_dim])
```

```
#This line starts gradient tapes for both the generator and
discriminator, enabling automatic differentiation to calculate
gradients.
with tf.GradientTape() as gen_tape, tf.GradientTape() as disc_tape:
```

```
#These lines generate images from the generator using the noise vectors
(`generated_images`), and obtain the discriminator's predictions on both
real and generated images (`real_output` and `fake_output`,
respectively).
generated_images = generator(noise, training=True)
real_output = discriminator(images, training=True)
fake_output = discriminator(generated_images, training=True)
```

#These lines calculate the generator loss (`gen_loss`) and discriminator loss (`disc_loss`) using the generator and discriminator losses defined earlier.

```
gen_loss = generator_loss(fake_output)
disc_loss = discriminator_loss(real_output, fake_output)
```

#These lines compute the gradients of the generator and discriminator losses with respect to their trainable variables using the gradient tapes.

```
gradients_of_generator = gen_tape.gradient(gen_loss, generator.
trainable_variables)
gradients_of_discriminator = disc_tape.gradient(disc_loss, discriminator.
trainable_variables)
```

#These lines apply the computed gradients to update the generator and discriminator weights using their respective optimizers.

```
generator_optimizer.apply_gradients(zip(gradients_of_generator,
generator.trainable_variables))
discriminator_optimizer.apply_gradients(zip(gradients_of_discriminator,
discriminator.trainable_variables))
```

#This line defines the `train` function that takes a dataset and the number of epochs as arguments.
Inside the `train` function:

```
def train(dataset, epochs):
```

#This line starts the training loop over the specified number of epochs.

```
for epoch in range(epochs):
```

#This line records the current time at the start of each epoch.

```
start = time.time()
```

#This loop iterates over each batch in the dataset and calls the `train_step` function to perform one step of training using the batch.

```
for image_batch in dataset:
    train_step(image_batch)
```

#This line clears the output and calls a function `generate_and_save_images` to generate and save a set of example images using the generator at the current epoch.

```
display.clear_output(wait=True)
generate_and_save_images(generator,epoch + 1,seed)
```

#This conditional statement saves the model's checkpoints every 20 epochs.

```
if (epoch + 1) % 20 == 0:
    checkpoint.save(file_prefix = checkpoint_prefix)
```

#This line prints the time taken for each epoch.

```
print ('Time for epoch {} is {} sec'.format(epoch + 1, time.time()-start))
```

#This line clears the output to ensure that only the final set of generated images is displayed without any intermediate outputs from previous epochs.

```
display.clear_output(wait=True)
```

```
#This line calls the function `generate_and_save_images` to generate and
save a set of example images using the generator model. It takes three
arguments: the generator model (`generator`), the number of epochs
(`epochs`), and the seed noise vector (`seed`). This function is not
provided in the code snippet, but it is likely defined elsewhere and
performs the task of generating and saving the images.
generate_and_save_images(generator, epochs, seed)
```

8.5.8 Generate and Save Images

Overall, this function generates a set of images using the generator model and saves them as an image file with the corresponding epoch number in the filename. The images are displayed in a 4×4 grid plot.

```
def generate_and_save_images(model, epoch, test_input):
  predictions = model(test_input, training=False)
  fig = plt.figure(figsize=(4, 4))
  for i in range(predictions.shape[0]):
      plt.subplot(4, 4, i+1)
      plt.imshow(predictions[i, :, :, 0] * 127.5 + 127.5, cmap='gray')
      plt.axis('off')
  plt.savefig('image_at_epoch_{:04d}.png'.format(epoch))
  plt.show()
```

Here's an explanation of each line:

```
#This line defines a function named `generate_and_save_images` that takes
three arguments: the generator model (`model`), the current epoch number
(`epoch`), and the test input noise (`test_input`).
def generate_and_save_images(model, epoch, test_input):
```

```
#This line generates images using the generator model by passing the test
input noise (`test_input`) to the model. The `training=False` argument
ensures that the model runs in inference mode, which means that layers
like batch normalization will use the learned statistics and not update
their internal states.
predictions = model(test_input, training=False)
```

```
#This line creates a new figure with a size of 4x4 inches using `plt.
figure()` from Matplotlib.
fig = plt.figure(figsize=(4, 4))
```

```
#These lines create subplots within the figure and display the generated
images. The loop iterates over the number of predictions in `predictions`
(which corresponds to the number of images to be generated) and plots
each image in a subplot. The images are rescaled by multiplying by 127.5
and then adding 127.5 to bring them back to the range [0, 255]. The
`cmap='gray'` argument specifies that the colormap should be grayscale.
The `plt.axis('off')` command removes the axis ticks and labels from the
plot.
for i in range(predictions.shape[0]):
    plt.subplot(4, 4, i+1)
    plt.imshow(predictions[i, :, :, 0] * 127.5 + 127.5, cmap='gray')
    plt.axis('off')
```

```
#These lines save the figure as an image file with the format `image_at_
epoch_{epoch}.png`, where `{epoch}` is replaced with the current epoch
number. The `plt.savefig()` function saves the figure to disk, and `plt.
show()` displays the figure in the output.
plt.savefig('image_at_epoch_{:04d}.png'.format(epoch))
plt.show()
```

8.6 DCGAN Issues

Despite the success of DCGANs in generating realistic images, several issues can arise during training.

8.6.1 Mode Collapse

Mode collapse is a common issue in GANs, including DCGANs. When mode collapse occurs, the generator produces a limited diversity of samples, often just replicating a few modes of the real data distribution. As a result, the generator fails to capture the true underlying data distribution. Mode collapse typically happens when the generator starts to produce samples that can easily fool the discriminator. Once the generator finds these "tricks", it keeps generating the same or very similar samples, since these are already enough to fool the discriminator.

Solutions:

1. **Mini-batch discrimination:** This technique makes the discriminator consider sets of samples instead of individual samples. This helps prevent mode collapse by making the discriminator more sensitive to the diversity of generated samples.

2. **Unrolled GANs:** Unrolling the optimization of the discriminator allows the generator to have a more stable target to learn. It means running a few steps of the discriminator's optimization to compute the direction in which it will be updated, then using that direction to update the generator.

3. **Wasserstein GAN (WGAN) and WGAN with Gradient Penalty (WGAN-GP):** The Wasserstein distance metric used in these GAN variations helps to stabilize the training process and prevent mode collapse.

4. **Experience replay:** Keep some of the previous samples from the generator and mix them with the current batch of new samples for the discriminator to evaluate. This allows the discriminator to remember past generator distributions and encourages the generator to produce diverse samples.

5. **Using more diverse and larger datasets:** This gives the model a wider scope of learning, making it harder for the model to keep reusing the same "tricks".

6. **Regularization:** Regularizers can be added to the GAN loss function to encourage diversity.

Remember that addressing mode collapse often involves trade-offs and different solutions might work better depending on the specific dataset and task.

8.6.2 Instability during Training

Training DCGANs can indeed be unstable. This instability is often due to the adversarial nature of GANs: the generator and the discriminator are competing against each other, and the continual adjustments each one makes in response to the other's actions can lead to oscillations and divergence.

Solutions:

1. **Use of batch normalization:** Implementing batch normalization in both the generator and discriminator can help standardize the inputs to each layer and stabilize training.

2. **Suitable activation functions:** Using the right activation functions can also help stabilize training. For example, in DCGAN, it's suggested to use ReLU in the generator (except for the output layer where Tanh is used), and leaky ReLU in the discriminator.

3. **Wasserstein GAN (WGAN) or WGAN with Gradient Penalty (WGAN-GP):** These versions of GANs use a different loss function (the Wasserstein distance), which provides more stable training.

4. **Learning rate scheduling:** Gradually reducing the learning rate can help stabilize training.

5. **Two Time-Scale Update Rule (TTUR):** Using different learning rates for the generator and the discriminator can help stabilize training. Usually, the learning rate for the discriminator is higher than that for the generator.

6. **Spectral normalization:** This technique can be applied to normalize the weights in the discriminator, ensuring that it satisfies the Lipschitz continuity condition, which can improve training stability.

7. **Experience replay:** Storing past generated images and including them in the batches can help to stabilize training by presenting the discriminator with a more diverse range of samples.

8. **Avoid sparse gradients:** Architectures like max-pooling and ReLU activation result in sparse gradients, which can make GANs harder to train. Instead, try using architectures that produce more consistent gradients, such as strided convolutions for downsampling and leaky ReLU activation.

Remember that each of these solutions has its own trade-offs, and their effectiveness can depend on the specific application and dataset.

8.6.3 Difficulty in Generating High-resolution Images

Generating high-resolution images with DCGANs is indeed a challenging task. There are several reasons for this:

1. **Increased model complexity:** High-resolution images have more pixels and, therefore, require more computational resources for processing. This means more complex models and longer training times.

2. **Overfitting:** As the resolution increases, the model may start to memorize the training data instead of learning to generalize. This leads to overfitting, where the model performs well on the training data but poorly on unseen data.

3. **Mode collapse:** This is a common problem in GANs where the generator starts to produce the same or very similar outputs regardless of the input. This problem becomes more prominent when trying to generate high-resolution images.

Solutions:

1. **Progressive Growing of GANs (ProGANs):** ProGANs start by training on low-resolution images and gradually increase the resolution as training progresses. This approach has been used to generate realistic, high-resolution images.

2. **StyleGAN and StyleGAN2:** These are improved versions of GANs specifically designed for generating high-resolution images. They introduce new techniques, such as adaptive instance normalization (AdaIN) and noise injection.

3. **Using larger and deeper networks:** This can help the model learn more complex patterns, but it will also increase the computational requirements.

4. **Regularization techniques:** Regularization techniques, such as weight decay, dropout, or early stopping, can help to prevent overfitting.

5. **Data augmentation:** Data augmentation can help the model generalize better and prevent overfitting.

6. **Spectral normalization:** Spectral normalization can help in controlling the Lipschitz constant of the discriminator, which can stabilize the training process and reduce mode collapse.

7. **Conditional GANs (cGANs):** Providing additional information to the generator (e.g., class labels or some part of the image) can help in generating high-resolution images.

It is essential to remember that generating high-resolution images with GANs is still an active area of research, and there is no one-size-fits-all solution to these problems. Different approaches might work better depending on the specific application and dataset.

8.6.4 Sensitivity to Initialization

DCGANs, like other types of GANs, can be sensitive to the initialization of the model weights. The random initialization of the network parameters can have a significant impact on the training dynamics and the performance of the network. Poor initialization can lead to issues, such as vanishing/exploding gradients, getting stuck in poor local minima, or mode collapse.

Solutions:

1. **He or Xavier initialization:** Proper weight initialization can help to alleviate these issues. Techniques, such as He initialization or Xavier initialization, can help by initializing weights in such a way as to maintain the variance of the inputs and outputs across layers.

2. **Orthogonal initialization:** This is another weight initialization method that can improve the training stability of GANs. It initializes the weight matrix as a

random orthogonal matrix, which can prevent the vanishing and exploding gradients issue during the training process.

3. **Batch normalization:** The use of batch normalization can alleviate the sensitivity to initialization by standardizing the input to a layer. It can help in stabilizing the learning process and reduce the importance of initialization.

4. **Spectral normalization:** Spectral normalization controls the Lipschitz constant of the discriminator, which can help in stabilizing the GAN training. This can be beneficial in situations where initialization may cause unstable training dynamics.

5. **Gradient penalty:** Techniques, such as gradient penalty or spectral normalization, can reduce the sensitivity to initialization and improve the training stability of GANs.

6. **Use of learning rate schedulers:** Implementing a learning rate schedule, which starts with a larger learning rate and then decreases it over time, can also help to mitigate the sensitivity to initialization.

In summary, weight initialization is a crucial aspect of neural network training, and more so in GANs. It's always a good idea to experiment with different initialization strategies and stabilization techniques to find what works best for your specific use case.

8.6.5 Vanishing Gradients

In DCGANs, as in many deep learning models, the issue of vanishing gradients can be encountered. This problem is characterized by the gradients of the loss function becoming increasingly smaller as they backpropagate through the layers of the network. The earlier layers of the network receive very small gradient updates, slowing down the learning process or causing it to halt altogether.

Solutions:

1. **Use leaky ReLU activation:** In DCGAN, one of the changes from traditional GANs is the use of the leaky ReLU activation function instead of regular ReLU. This helps alleviate the vanishing gradient problem because, unlike the ReLU function, which clamps negative values to zero (thus causing the gradient to vanish during backpropagation), leaky ReLU allows small negative values when the input is less than zero. This results in a small, nonzero gradient that allows the continued training of the model.

2. **Batch normalization:** Batch normalization, another component of DCGAN, standardizes the inputs to a layer, which can help mitigate the vanishing gradient problem. It normalizes the output of a previous activation layer by subtracting the batch mean and dividing by the batch standard deviation, thereby ensuring the network always creates activations with the same distribution that we desire.

3. **Weight initialization:** Proper weight initialization can also be critical in dealing with vanishing gradients. The authors of the DCGAN paper suggest initializing the weights from a normal distribution with mean 0 and standard deviation 0.02.

4. **Use of alternative GANs:** Some variants of GANs, such as Wasserstein GANs (WGAN) or Least Squares GANs (LSGAN), modify the loss function to ensure more stable gradients.

5. **Avoid sigmoid activation in the last layer of the generator:** In DCGANs, it's recommended to use Tanh activation function in the last layer of the generator rather than the sigmoid. The range of Tanh (–1 to 1) helps with the vanishing gradient problem by spreading out the input values better than sigmoid.

6. **Skip connections/residual blocks:** In very deep networks, vanishing gradients can still be a problem despite these mitigations. In such cases, adding skip connections, as in ResNet, can help by creating an alternative pathway for the gradient to flow through.

Remember that these solutions can help but might not completely eliminate the vanishing gradient problem, which remains a complex challenge in training deep neural networks.

8.6.6 Overfitting

Overfitting in DCGANs can occur when the generator learns to recreate the training data too perfectly and fails to generalize to unseen examples. In other words, it's memorizing the training data instead of learning the underlying distribution, resulting in the generation of images that lack diversity and appear almost identical to the training examples.

Solutions:

1. **Data augmentation:** Increase the variety of your training data by applying transformations, such as rotation, scaling, and flipping. Although this technique is typically used in supervised learning, it can also be effective in the context of GANs by providing the model with a richer understanding of the data distribution.

2. **Regularization:** Regularization techniques like dropout and weight decay (L_2 regularization) can be applied during training to discourage overfitting.

3. **Noise injection:** Injecting noise into the inputs of the discriminator or the generator can help prevent overfitting. This noise makes it harder for the generator to simply memorize the training examples.

4. **Early stopping:** Monitor the model's performance on a validation set during training. If the model's performance on the validation set starts to degrade (indicating overfitting), stop the training process.

5. **Model architecture:** Opt for a simpler model architecture. Complex models with many parameters are more prone to overfitting. If overfitting is observed, reducing the model complexity could be beneficial.

6. **Use more training data:** If possible, increase the amount of training data. More data can help the model generalize better and reduce overfitting.

Remember, though, that GANs are inherently difficult to evaluate, and detecting overfitting may not be as straightforward as in traditional supervised learning models. The solutions proposed above might help in reducing overfitting but striking the right balance between underfitting and overfitting in GANs remains a challenging task.

8.6.7 Computational Complexity

Computational complexity is a significant issue in DCGANs, mainly due to the depth of the model and the extensive amount of computation needed during the training process.

This complexity can lead to slow training times and high computational resource requirements, especially when dealing with large datasets or high-resolution images.

Solutions:

1. **Hardware acceleration:** Use GPUs for training instead of CPUs. GPUs are designed to handle parallel operations, which are common in deep learning, and they can significantly speed up the training process.
2. **Batch normalization:** This can stabilize learning and accelerate convergence by reducing internal covariate shift. It standardizes the inputs to a layer, which can help manage the computational complexity.
3. **Distributed training:** By leveraging multiple GPUs or multiple machines, the computation can be distributed across devices, thus reducing training time.
4. **Gradient checkpointing:** This is a technique to reduce GPU memory usage during training. It trades off computation for memory by recomputing tensors during the backward pass.
5. **Efficient convolution techniques:** Depending on the specific architecture of your model and the shape of your data, certain types of convolution (e.g., dilated, separable, etc.) might be more efficient than others.
6. **Model pruning:** This technique reduces the size of the model by removing less important connections, thus reducing the computational complexity. Pruned models have fewer parameters and thus require less computational resources.
7. **Quantization:** It involves reducing the precision of the weights and biases of the model. Quantization not only reduces the model size but also speeds up the model inference.

It's worth mentioning that, often, these solutions involve a trade-off between computational efficiency and model performance. Therefore, it is essential to carefully consider these trade-offs when deciding which method to use.

8.6.8 Hyperparameter Tuning

Hyperparameter tuning is an inherent issue in DCGANs, as with any machine learning model. Hyperparameters in DCGANs include the learning rate, the number of layers in the discriminator and generator, the number of units in each layer, the type of optimizer, batch size, and the type and scale of initialization, among others. The quality of the generated samples and the stability of the training process greatly depend on the correct setting of these hyperparameters. However, finding the right values can be a time-consuming and computationally expensive process.

Solutions:

1. **Grid search:** One straightforward approach to hyperparameter tuning involves defining a set of possible values for each hyperparameter and then systematically trying out all combinations of these values. However, this can be quite time-consuming for models with many hyperparameters like DCGANs.

2. **Random search:** An alternative to grid search, this involves randomly sampling from a distribution of possible hyperparameter values. This method can be more efficient than a grid search, particularly when some hyperparameters are more important than others.

3. **Bayesian optimization:** This method builds a probabilistic model of the function mapping from hyperparameters to the objective evaluated on a validation set. By iteratively selecting hyperparameters that perform best on the probabilistic model, Bayesian optimization aims to find the optimal hyperparameters in as few steps as possible.

4. **Evolutionary algorithms and genetic programming:** These are population-based methods that iteratively update the hyperparameters over generations.

5. **Gradient-based optimization:** Some hyperparameters are amenable to gradient-based optimization. For example, if a differentiable function of the learning rate exists, it can be adjusted using gradient descent.

6. **Automated Machine Learning (AutoML) frameworks:** Tools like Google's AutoML, H2O's AutoML, and others provide automatic hyperparameter optimization and can save a lot of time and computational resources.

In all cases, remember to use separate training and validation sets to avoid overfitting during the hyperparameter tuning process. Always confirm the performance of the chosen hyperparameters on a test set to ensure their generalizability.

8.7 DCGAN Implementation Tips

DCGANs are a type of GANs that use CNNs as both the generator and the discriminator. Here are some implementation tips for DCGANs:

1. Employ convolutional layers in both the generator and discriminator instead of fully connected layers to leverage the spatial relationships among pixels in images.

2. Integrate batch normalization in both the generator and discriminator to stabilize learning and enhance the quality of the generated images.

3. Utilize the leaky ReLU activation function in the discriminator to mitigate the vanishing gradient problem.

4. Apply the ReLU activation function in the generator to ensure positive output.

5. Use the Adam optimizer with a learning rate of 0.0002 and a beta1 value of 0.5 for both the generator and discriminator.

6. Implement a loss function that balances the generator and discriminator losses, such as binary cross-entropy loss.

7. Train the discriminator for one or more epochs before initiating the training of the generator to ensure its proficiency in distinguishing between real and fake images.

8. Alternate training between the generator and discriminator, with one epoch of generator training for every n epochs of discriminator training.

9. Utilize data augmentation techniques like image flipping and rotation to enhance the training set size and minimize overfitting.

10. Adopt progressive training to incrementally increase the resolution of generated images, starting from a low resolution and gradually adding details as training progresses.

11. Ensure a sufficiently large batch size to maintain accurate gradient estimates.

12. Use early stopping to prevent overfitting.

13. Monitor the loss and quality of generated images during training to identify issues and adjust hyperparameters accordingly.

14. Leverage pre-trained models like VGG-16 or Inception to compute perceptual loss and improve the quality of generated images.

15. Employ various evaluation metrics, such as the inception score, Frechet Inception Distance (FID), and precision, and recall to assess the quality of generated images.

16. Regularize the model using techniques like weight decay or dropout to prevent overfitting.

17. Implement ensembling to improve the diversity of generated images.

18. Experiment with diverse architectures, hyperparameters, and loss functions to identify the optimal combination for your dataset and task.

19. Leverage transfer learning to utilize pre-trained models for tasks like style transfer or image-to-image translation.

20. Use techniques like progressive growing or style mixing to boost the diversity and quality of generated images.

Remember, the specific approaches and parameters you use may need to be adjusted depending on the specifics of your data and the task at hand. Also, hands-on experience is key when working with DCGANs or any other machine learning models. Therefore, consistently practicing implementation and troubleshooting is crucial for mastering these concepts.

8.8 Lessons Learned

- Learn the DCGAN architecture and concept
- Learn the DCGAN applications
- Learn the Implementation of DCGAN for CelebA
- Learn the Implementation of DCGAN for MNIST
- Learn the DCGAN issues
- Learn the DCGAN implementation Tips

8.9 Problems

8.9.1 What is a DCGAN?

8.9.2 How does a DCGAN differ from a traditional GAN?

8.9.3   What are some applications of DCGANs?

8.9.4   How do you prevent mode collapse in DCGANs?

8.9.5   What is the role of the generator in a DCGAN?

8.9.6   What is the role of the discriminator in a DCGAN?

8.9.7   How do you determine if a DCGAN is producing realistic images?

8.9.8   What is the loss function used in a DCGAN?

8.9.9   How can you improve the quality of images produced by a DCGAN?

8.9.10 Can DCGANs be used for other types of data besides images?

8.10 Programming Questions

- **Easy**

    8.10.1   Implement a DCGAN to generate images of a specific class, such as cats or dogs.

    8.10.2   Modify a pre-trained DCGAN to generate images with specific attributes, such as color or shape.

    8.10.3   Implement a DCGAN with a conditional input, such as adding a label to generate images of different classes.

    8.10.4   Train a DCGAN on a large dataset, such as ImageNet, to generate high-resolution images.

    8.10.5   Implement a DCGAN that can generate sequences of images, such as frames of a video.

    8.10.6   Modify a DCGAN to generate images that are both realistic and diverse, avoiding the problem of mode collapse.

    8.10.7   Implement a DCGAN that can generate images with different styles, such as painting styles or photography styles.

    8.10.8   How to load the dataset for DCGAN?

    8.10.9   What are the input and output shapes of the generator and discriminator networks?

    8.10.10 How to create a generator network using Keras layers?

    8.10.11 How to create a discriminator network using Keras layers?

    8.10.12 How to compile the discriminator network using binary cross-entropy loss and optimizer?

- **Medium**

    8.10.13 Train a DCGAN with limited resources, such as on a mobile device or a low-power computer.

    8.10.14 Implement a DCGAN with a loss function that encourages the generator to create images that are not only realistic but also informative or useful for downstream tasks.

8.10.15 Modify a DCGAN to handle missing or incomplete data, such as generating images of objects from partial or noisy input.

8.10.16 Implement a DCGAN that can generate images with multiple attributes, such as color and shape, and allow users to control these attributes.

8.10.17 Train a DCGAN to generate images with better interpretability, such as medical images that can be easily interpreted by doctors.

8.10.18 Implement a DCGAN that can generate images of 3D objects or scenes, such as buildings or landscapes.

8.10.19 Modify a DCGAN to generate images in a constrained domain, such as generating images of animals in a specific habitat or environment.

8.10.20 How to create a DCGAN model by combining the generator and discriminator networks?

8.10.21 How to train the DCGAN model using the dataset?

8.10.22 How to generate new images using the trained generator network?

8.10.23 How to visualize the generated images using Matplotlib?

8.10.24 How to implement gradient penalty regularization in the discriminator network?

- **Hard**

  8.10.25 Implement a DCGAN that can generate images in real-time, such as for use in video games or virtual reality.

  8.10.26 Train a DCGAN to generate images that are resistant to adversarial attacks, such as images that are robust to small perturbations or modifications.

  8.10.27 Implement a DCGAN that can generate images with controllable attributes, such as generating images of faces with specific expressions or poses.

  8.10.28 Modify a DCGAN to generate images with higher diversity, such as by adding noise or randomness to the generator input.

  8.10.29 Implement a DCGAN that can generate images with novel compositions or arrangements, such as images with unusual or creative compositions.

  8.10.30 Train a DCGAN to generate images that can be used for data augmentation, such as generating additional training data for a supervised learning task.

  8.10.31 How to implement conditional GAN using DCGAN architecture?

  8.10.32 How to use spectral normalization to stabilize the training of DCGAN?

  8.10.33 How to use a progressive growing strategy to train DCGAN for higher resolution images?

  8.10.34 How to implement WGAN-GP (Wasserstein GAN with gradient penalty) using DCGAN architecture?

  8.10.35 How to implement self-attention mechanism in the generator and discriminator networks of DCGAN?

9

Conditional Generative Adversarial Network (cGAN)

The following topics are covered in this chapter about Conditional Generative Adversarial Networks (cGANs):

- cGAN Architecture
- cGAN for Fashion Clothing Data
- CDCGAN
- Pix2Pix GAN for Image-to-Image Translation
- cGAN Applications
- Implementation Pix2Pix: image-to-image translation with a conditional GAN
- cGAN Issues
- cGAN Implementation Tips

9.1 Preface

Conditional Generative Adversarial Networks (cGANs) are a type of GAN that allows the generation of data that satisfies specific conditions. Unlike traditional GANs, which generate random data, cGANs use a conditional vector to control the output. This conditional vector is typically a class label or a set of attributes that define the desired output. cGANs consist of two neural networks: a generator and a discriminator. The generator takes a noise vector and a conditional vector as inputs and generates an output that attempts to match the conditional vector. The discriminator, on the other hand, takes the generated output and the corresponding conditional vector or real data and tries to distinguish between the two. cGANs have a wide range of applications, including image-to-image translation, text-to-image synthesis, and image editing. For instance, given an input image of a face with a specific attribute, such as glasses, a cGAN can generate an output image with the same face but without glasses. Another application is converting an image from one domain to another, such as changing a daytime image to a night-time image. One of the significant advantages of cGANs is their ability to generate data that meets specific conditions, making them useful for various tasks, such as data augmentation, image restoration, and style transfer. However, cGANs also face several challenges, including mode collapse and instability during training. Addressing these issues requires careful selection of the architecture and hyperparameters, as well as appropriate training strategies, such as minimizing the Jensen-Shannon divergence between the generated and real distributions. Overall, cGANs have shown promising results in various applications, and their ability to generate specific data makes them a valuable addition to the GAN family. This chapter provides a comprehensive review of this type of GAN.

DOI: 10.1201/9781003281344-9

9.2 cGAN Architecture

This section discusses the major components of the cGAN architecture, including the generator, discriminator, and general architecture. This discussion demonstrates the connection between the previous sections and compares it to a standard GAN.

9.2.1 cGAN Generator

The generator in cGAN uses labels or tags to provide additional information. The labels are represented as "**y**", and "**z**" is used as a random number to represent the initial noise data, which leads the generator to produce the output $x'|y$. The generator takes in the label and a vector of random numbers as input, and the output includes samples that are intended to be as convincing as possible in terms of how well they match their labels: $G(z, y) = x'|y$. Figure 9.1 presents the foundational architecture of the generator in a cGAN. This architecture, distinct from traditional GANs, incorporates conditional information, allowing for directed generation processes. The illustration likely emphasizes how the conditional data is introduced into the generator and how it interacts with the latent variables to produce outputs that align with specific conditions. Such a visualization underscores the unique capability of cGANs to generate targeted content based on specific criteria or labels. The output of the generator is not simply x', but fake samples that try to match the label **y** as closely as possible. These outputs, denoted as x', are then sent to the discriminator along with the label **y**.

9.2.2 cGAN Discriminator

The discriminator in cGAN takes in two types of inputs:

1. Real training dataset samples labeled with their respective labels: **(x, y)**, and
2. Fake samples generated by the generator along with the label: **(x'|y, y)**.

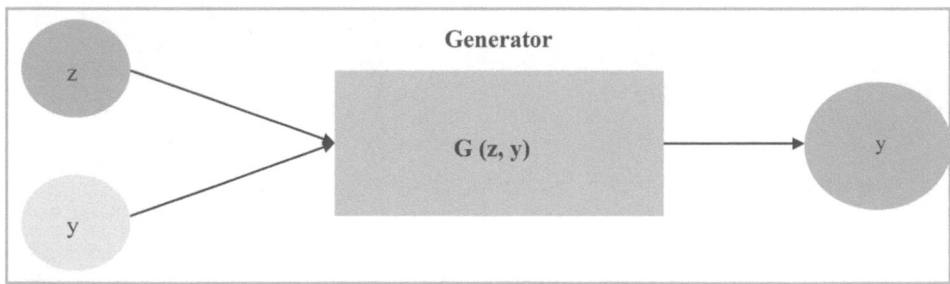

FIGURE 9.1
General cGAN Generator structure.

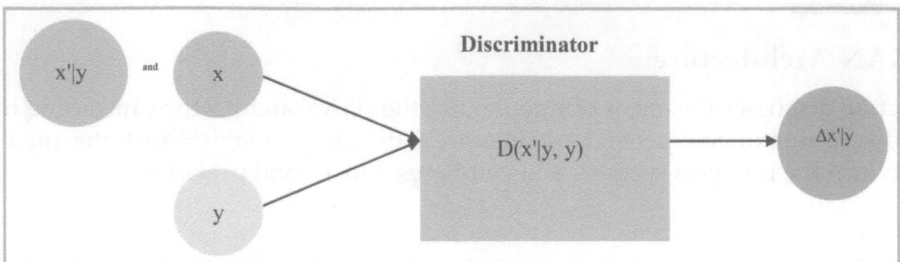

FIGURE 9.2
General cGAN discriminator structure.

The output from the discriminator is a single probability indicating whether the inputted example is a true example-label pair. The aim is to distinguish between fake example-label pairs generated by the generator and real example-label pairs from the training data set. Figure 9.2 showcases the typical architecture of the discriminator within a cGAN. This structure is designed to evaluate the authenticity of input samples while considering the conditional context. The depiction likely emphasizes how the conditional information is seamlessly integrated into the discriminator, influencing its decision-making process. By doing so, the cGAN discriminator can distinguish between genuine and generated samples more effectively in a conditional setting. This visualization helps elucidate the nuanced differences between traditional GAN discriminators and their conditional counterparts.

9.2.3 General Architecture

Figure 9.3 presents a comparative high-level architectural diagram of both traditional GAN and cGAN. At a glance, one can discern the differences and similarities between the two structures. In the cGAN side of the diagram, it's evident that the label **y** is fed into both the generator and the discriminator, emphasizing the conditional nature of its operation. By juxtaposing these models side by side, the visualization clearly illustrates

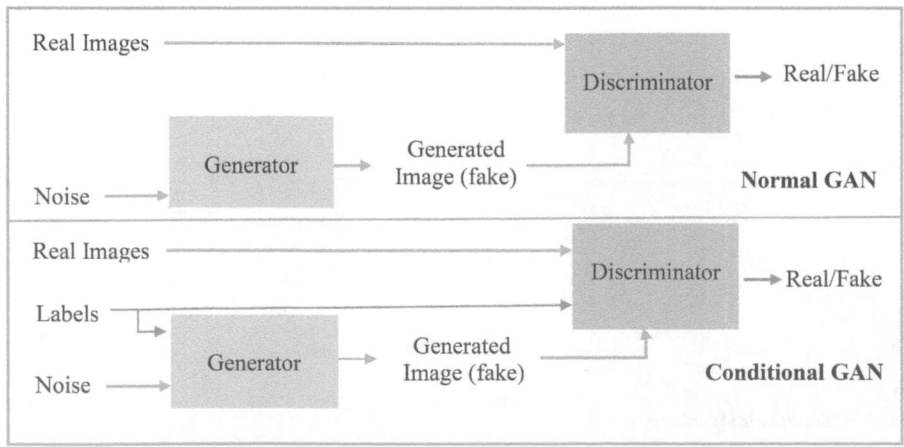

FIGURE 9.3
cGAN architecture.

how the incorporation of conditionality in cGANs offers an extended capability compared to the standard GAN, enabling more targeted and context-aware generation of samples. This side-by-side representation serves as an efficient tool for understanding the advancements and modifications brought by cGAN in the realm of generative models. The discriminator is trained to accept only true matching pairs, and as a result, it develops the ability to recognize mismatched pairs. The cGAN discriminator is fed both fake labeled samples **(x'|y, y)** generated by the generator and real labeled samples **(x, y)**, and it learns to determine whether a particular example-label pair is real or fake. To optimally train a conditional GAN, both the generator and discriminator must be trained simultaneously:

1. The generator is trained to generate data that will "fool" the discriminator into categorizing it as real.
2. The discriminator is trained to recognize the "real" category of labeled data provided by the generator.

The goal is to minimize the loss of the discriminator when it is fed batches of real and fake labeled data. If implemented correctly, these strategies will result in a generator that produces convincingly realistic data corresponding to the input labels, and a discriminator that has learned powerful feature representations for each label characteristic of the training data.

9.3 cGAN for Fashion Clothing Data

The Fashion-MNIST dataset comprises 6000 small, square, grayscale photographs of items of clothing from ten different categories, including shoes, t-shirts, dresses, and more. Each image in the dataset has a size of 28×28 pixels. In Keras, the function "fashion_mnist.load_data()" is available to access the Fashion-MNIST dataset. This function returns two sets of data: one for the standard training dataset, consisting of input and output components, and another for the standard test dataset, which also includes input and output components. To use this dataset with a cGAN, the following steps can be undertaken:

Step 1: Define a new input variable to hold the conditions.
Step 2: Incorporate this new input variable, denoted as "**y**", into the generator "**G**" and the discriminator "**D**" as additional information.
Step 3: Define a loss function that considers the conditions.
Step 4: During the training process, include the conditions "**y**" in both the generator "**G**" and the discriminator "**D**".
Step 5: Set the condition "**y**" to a specific value or label for generating desired outputs.

By following these steps, the cGAN can leverage the condition variable to generate specific outputs based on the provided conditions.

9.3.1 Data Loading

Load data from online or local paths. Here we loaded data from Keras and then two sets of pairs, including train and test data with labels. Overall, this code imports the Fashion MNIST dataset using Keras, assigns the training and test images as well as their corresponding labels to variables, and then prints the shapes of the training and test data.

```
from keras.datasets.fashion_mnist import load_data
(trainX, trainy), (testX, testy) = load_data()
print('Train', trainX.shape, trainy. shape)
print('Test', testX.shape, testy.shape)
```

Here's a breakdown of each line of code:

```
#This line imports the `load_data` function from the `fashion_mnist`
module within the `keras.datasets` package. The `fashion_mnist` dataset
is a collection of 60,000 28x28 grayscale images of 10 different clothing
categories for training, and 10,000 test images.
from keras.datasets.fashion_mnist import load_data
#This line calls the `load_data` function, which loads the Fashion MNIST
dataset and returns four variables: `trainX` (training images), `trainy`
(training labels), `testX` (test images), and `testy` (test labels). The
code uses tuple unpacking to assign these four variables in a single
line.
(trainX, trainy), (testX, testy) = load_data()

#This line prints the string `'Train'` followed by the shape of the
`trainX` array and the shape of the `trainy` array. The `trainX.shape`
returns the dimensions (number of samples and image size) of the
training images, while `trainy.shape` returns the shape of the training
labels.
print('Train', trainX.shape, trainy.shape)

#This line prints the string `'Test'` followed by the shape of the
`testX` array and the shape of the `testy` array. Similarly, `testX.
shape` returns the dimensions of the test images, and `testy.shape`
returns the shape of the test labels.
print('Test', testX.shape, testy.shape)
```

9.3.2 Show the Data Values

Checking the data values is a good habit for working with data and making models. Using matplotlib libraries and plot 100 images in a 10×10 output. Figure 9.4 showcases a selection of data samples from the Fashion MNIST dataset. This curated collection of grayscale images provides a visual snapshot into the various categories of fashion items present in the dataset, such as shirts, shoes, dresses, and more. Each image, standardized to a size of 28×28 pixels, offers a clear representation of a distinct fashion item, making it an essential resource for training and testing machine learning models. By presenting these images, Figure 9.4 provides viewers with a tangible sense of the dataset's content and diversity, laying a foundation for understanding subsequent modeling and results. Overall, this code loads the Fashion MNIST dataset, creates a grid of subplots, displays the first 100 training

FIGURE 9.4
The database data sample.

images within the subplots, and shows the plot. This allows you to visualize a subset of the training images from the dataset.

```
from keras.datasets.fashion_mnist import load_data
from matplotlib import pyplot
(trainX, trainy), (testX, testy) = load_data()
for i in range(100):
pyplot.subplot(10, 10, 1 + i)
pyplot.axis('off')
pyplot.imshow(trainX[i], cmap='gray_r')
pyplot.show()
```

Here's a breakdown of each line of code:

```
#This line imports the `load_data` function from the `fashion_mnist`
module within the `keras.datasets` package. This function is used to load
the Fashion MNIST dataset.
from keras.datasets.fashion_mnist import load_data
```

```
#This line imports the `pyplot` module from the `matplotlib` library, which
provides a collection of functions for creating visualizations and plots.
from matplotlib import pyplot
```

```
#This line calls the `load_data()` function, which loads the Fashion MNIST
dataset and returns four variables: `trainX` (training images), `trainy`
(training labels), `testX` (test images), and `testy` (test labels). The
code uses tuple unpacking to assign these four variables in a single line.
(trainX, trainy), (testX, testy) = load_data()
```

```
#This line starts a loop that iterates 100 times, with `i` taking values
from 0 to 99.
for i in range(100):
```

```
#This line creates a subplot within a grid of 10 rows and 10 columns. The
`1 + i` argument specifies the position of the subplot within the grid,
incrementing from 1 to 100.
pyplot.subplot(10, 10, 1 + i)
```

```
#This line turns off the axis labels and ticks for the current subplot,
resulting in a cleaner image display.
pyplot.axis('off')
```

```
#This line displays the `i`-th image from the `trainX` array using the
`imshow` function. The `cmap='gray_r'` argument specifies that the
image should be displayed in grayscale with reversed (black-to-white)
colormap.
pyplot.imshow(trainX[i], cmap='gray_r')
```

```
#This line displays all the subplots created within the loop, showing the
images one by one.
pyplot.show()
```

9.3.3 Generator

In this step, we implement the generator with a similar structure to a regular GAN but with the addition of labels for data samples. The general network architecture of the GAN is as follows:

- This network takes random vectors of size 100 and converts them into 4-by-4-by-1024 arrays using a fully connected layer and a reshape operation.
- The categorical labels are converted into embedding vectors and reshaped into a 4-by-4 array.
- The images produced by the two inputs are concatenated along the channel dimension, resulting in a 4-by-4-by-1025 array.
- A series of transposed convolution layers with batch normalization and ReLU layers are used to upscale the resulting arrays to 64-by-64-by-3 arrays.

The network properties are defined and specified as follows:

- An embedding dimension of 50 is used for categorical inputs.
- 5×5 filters, a stride of 2, and "same" cropping of the output are specified for the transposed layers.
- The final transposed convolution layer uses three 5×5 filters, corresponding to the three RGB channels of the generated images.
- A Tanh layer is added at the end of the network.

Figure 9.5 presents an intricate architectural depiction of the generator component within the cGAN tailored for the Fashion MNIST dataset. Through this diagram, one can discern the nuanced layers, interconnections, and components specifically designed to accommodate fashion item generation. As the generator receives both noise and label information, it crafts synthetic fashion images that adhere to the stipulated conditions. The visual representation elucidates the depth and complexity of this structure, highlighting the tailored adjustments made to cater to the unique challenges and intricacies of generating diverse fashion images based on specific categories within the dataset.

Let us start coding for this structure. Overall, the code defines a generator model that takes a latent space vector ("in_lat") and a label ("in_label") as input and generates a 28×28 grayscale image as output. The generator combines the label information with the latent

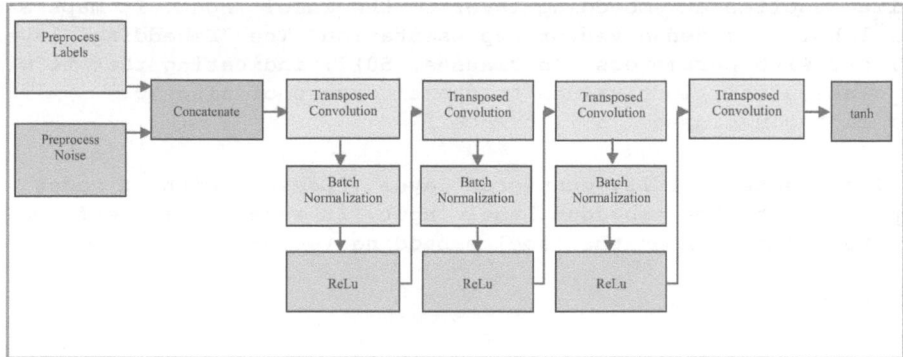

FIGURE 9.5
The generator architecture.

space vector and progressively upsamples the feature maps until the desired output size is reached.

```
def define_generator(latent_dim, n_classes=10):
in_label = Input(shape=(1,))
li = Embedding(n_classes, 50)(in_label)
n_nodes = 7 * 7
 li = Dense(n_nodes)(li)
li = Reshape((7, 7, 1))(li)
in_lat = Input(shape=(latent_dim,))
n_nodes = 128 * 7 * 7
 gen = Dense(n_nodes)(in_lat)
 gen = LeakyReLU(alpha=0.2)(gen)
 gen = Reshape((7, 7, 128))(gen)
 merge = Concatenate()([gen, li])
 gen = Conv2DTranspose(128, (4,4), strides=(2,2), padding='same')(merge)
 gen = LeakyReLU(alpha=0.2)(gen)
 gen = Conv2DTranspose(128, (4,4), strides=(2,2), padding='same')(gen)
 gen = LeakyReLU(alpha=0.2)(gen)
out_layer = Conv2D(1, (7,7), activation='tanh', padding='same')(gen)
model = Model([in_lat, in_label], out_layer)
 return model
```

Here's a breakdown of the code:

```
#This is a function definition for a generator model. It takes two
parameters: `latent_dim`, which represents the dimensionality of the
input noise vector, and `n_classes` (with a default value of 10), which
represents the number of classes or categories for conditional
generation.
def define_generator(latent_dim, n_classes=10):

#This line defines an input layer for the labels. It creates a Keras
`Input` tensor with a shape of `(1,)`, indicating that it expects a
single integer value representing the label.
in_label = Input(shape=(1,))
```

```
#This line applies an embedding layer to the label input. It maps each
integer label to a dense vector representation. The `Embedding` layer is
initialized with parameters `(n_classes, 50)`, indicating that it will
map `n_classes` distinct values to dense vectors of size 50.
li = Embedding(n_classes, 50)(in_label)
```

```
#This line creates a fully connected layer (`Dense`) with `n_nodes` units
and applies it to the embedded label input. It essentially performs a
linear transformation on the label embedding vectors.
n_nodes = 7 * 7
li = Dense(n_nodes)(li)
```

```
#This line reshapes the output of the previous layer to have a shape of
`(7, 7, 1)`. It adds an additional channel to the label representation,
making it compatible for merging with the image generator later.
li = Reshape((7, 7, 1))(li)
```

```
#This line defines an input layer for the latent space vector. It creates
a Keras `Input` tensor with a shape of `(latent_dim,)`, indicating that
it expects a vector of size `latent_dim` as input.
in_lat = Input(shape=(latent_dim,))
```

```
#These lines define the foundation of the generator model for generating
a 7x7 image. The latent space vector is passed through a fully connected
layer (`Dense`) with `n_nodes` units. Then, a LeakyReLU activation
function is applied to introduce non-linearity. The output is reshaped to
have a shape of `(7, 7, 128)`.
n_nodes = 128 * 7 * 7
gen = Dense(n_nodes)(in_lat)
gen = LeakyReLU(alpha=0.2)(gen)
gen = Reshape((7, 7, 128))(gen)
```

```
#This line concatenates the outputs from the image generator (`gen`) and
the label input (`li`). It merges the image generation pathway with the
conditional information represented by the label.
merge = Concatenate()([gen, li])
```

```
#These lines upsample the merged feature maps to a size of 14x14. A
`Conv2DTranspose` layer is used to perform the upsampling operation. The
resulting feature maps are then passed through a LeakyReLU activation
function.
gen = Conv2DTranspose(128, (4,4), strides=(2,2), padding='same')(merge)
gen = LeakyReLU(alpha=0.2)(gen)
```

```
#These lines further upsample the feature maps to a size of 28x28,
following a similar process as the previous upsampling step.
gen = Conv2DTranspose(128, (4,4), strides=(2,2), padding='same')(gen)
gen = LeakyReLU(alpha=0.2)(gen)
```

```
#This line applies a convolutional layer (`Conv2D`) to the output of the
previous upsampling step (`gen`). It uses a kernel size of `(7, 7)` and
produces a single-channel output. The activation function used is
```

`'tanh'`, which squashes the output values to the range of [-1, 1]. The padding is set to `'same'`, meaning the input and output have the same spatial dimensions.

```
out_layer = Conv2D(1, (7,7), activation='tanh', padding='same')(gen)
```

#This line creates a Keras `Model` object, specifying the inputs as a list `[in_lat, in_label]` and the output as `out_layer`. It constructs the generator model by connecting the inputs (`in_lat` and `in_label`) to the output (`out_layer`).

```
model = Model([in_lat, in_label], out_layer)
```

#This line returns the generator model as the output of the `define_generator` function.

```
return model
```

9.3.4 Discriminator

Create a network that utilizes convolution layers with batch normalization and leaky ReLU layers to produce a scalar prediction score from $64 \times 64 \times 1$ images and labels. Figure 9.6 offers a detailed architectural visualization of the discriminator component within the cGAN designed for the Fashion MNIST dataset. The diagram clearly delineates how the discriminator, unlike traditional GAN discriminators, incorporates label information alongside the image input, enhancing its ability to distinguish between real and generated fashion images based on specific conditions. The representation captures the layered composition, interconnections, and unique components that make up this enhanced discriminator. It serves as an illustrative guide to understanding how the discriminator has been specifically crafted to handle the nuances of the Fashion MNIST dataset, ensuring it can adeptly evaluate the authenticity of generated images while considering their categorical context. Set the dropout layer's dropout probability to 0.75. The convolution layers should be defined with 5×5 filters, and the number of filters should increase with each layer. Additionally, specify a stride of 2 and output padding on each edge. For the leaky ReLU layers, set the scale to 0.2. Finally, for the last layer, utilize a convolution layer with a single 4×4 filter.

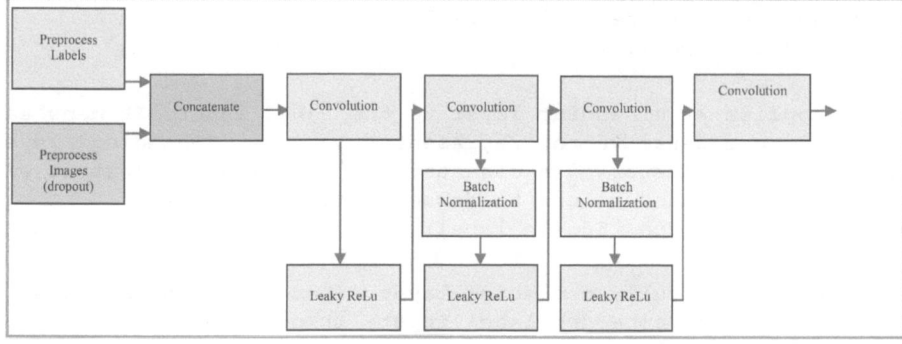

FIGURE 9.6
The discriminator architecture.

Let us start and do some coding.

```
def define_discriminator(in_shape=(28,28,1), n_classes=10):
in_label = Input(shape=(1,))
li = Embedding(n_classes, 50)(in_label)
n_nodes = in_shape[0] * in_shape[1]
li = Dense(n_nodes)(li)
li = Reshape((in_shape[0], in_shape[1], 1))(li)
in_image = Input(shape=in_shape)
merge = Concatenate()([in_image, li])
fe = Conv2D(128, (3,3), strides=(2,2), padding='same')(merge)
fe = LeakyReLU(alpha=0.2)(fe)
fe = Conv2D(128, (3,3), strides=(2,2), padding='same')(fe)
fe = LeakyReLU(alpha=0.2)(fe)
fe = Flatten()(fe)
fe = Dropout(0.4)(fe)
out_layer = Dense(1, activation='sigmoid')(fe)
model = Model([in_image, in_label], out_layer)
opt = Adam(lr=0.0002, beta_1=0.5)
model.compile(loss='binary_crossentropy', optimizer=opt,
metrics=['accuracy'])
return model
```

Overall, the code defines a discriminator model that takes an image input ("in_image") and a label input ("in_label") and predicts the probability of the input being real or fake. The discriminator uses convolutional layers to extract features from the input and a fully connected layer to make the final prediction. The model is compiled with an Adam optimizer and binary cross-entropy loss. Here's a breakdown of the code:

```
#This is a function definition for a discriminator model. It takes two
parameters: `in_shape`, which represents the shape of the input image,
and `n_classes` (with a default value of 10), which represents the number
of classes or categories for conditional discrimination.
def define_discriminator(in_shape=(28,28,1), n_classes=10):
```

```
#This line defines an input layer for the labels. It creates a Keras
`Input` tensor with a shape of `(1,)`, indicating that it expects a
single integer value representing the label.
in_label = Input(shape=(1,))
```

```
#This line applies an embedding layer to the label input. It maps each
integer label to a dense vector representation. The `Embedding` layer is
initialized with parameters `(n_classes, 50)`, indicating that it will
map `n_classes` distinct values to dense vectors of size 50.
li = Embedding(n_classes, 50)(in_label)
```

```
#This line creates a fully connected layer (`Dense`) with `n_nodes` units
and applies it to the embedded label input. It performs a linear
transformation on the label embedding vectors, scaling them up to the
dimensions of the input image.
n_nodes = in_shape[0] * in_shape[1]
li = Dense(n_nodes)(li)
```

```
#This line reshapes the output of the previous layer to have the same shape
as the input image `(in_shape)`. It adds an additional channel to the label
representation, allowing it to be concatenated with the image input later.
li = Reshape((in_shape[0], in_shape[1], 1))(li)
```

```
#This line defines an input layer for the image. It creates a Keras
`Input` tensor with the shape `in_shape`, which represents the shape of
the input image.
in_image = Input(shape=in_shape)
```

```
#This line concatenates the image input (`in_image`) and the label input
(`li`). It merges the image and label information by concatenating them
along the channel dimension.
merge = Concatenate()([in_image, li])
```

```
#These lines perform downsampling operations on the concatenated feature
maps. A `Conv2D` layer is used with a kernel size of `(3, 3)` and a
stride of `(2, 2)` to reduce the spatial dimensions. The downsampling is
followed by a LeakyReLU activation function.
fe = Conv2D(128, (3,3), strides=(2,2), padding='same')(merge)
fe = LeakyReLU(alpha=0.2)(fe)
```

```
#These lines further downsample the feature maps using another `Conv2D`
layer with the same parameters as before, followed by a LeakyReLU
activation.
fe = Conv2D(128, (3,3), strides=(2,2), padding='same')(fe)
fe = LeakyReLU(alpha=0.2)(fe)
```

```
#This line flattens the feature maps into a 1D vector. It transforms the
spatial information into a linear sequence of values.
fe = Flatten()(fe)
```

```
#This line applies dropout regularization to the flattened feature
vector. It randomly sets a fraction of the input units to 0 at each
update during training, which helps prevent overfitting.
fe = Dropout(0.4)(fe)
```

```
#This line applies a fully connected layer (`Dense`) to the output of the
previous layer. It produces a single output
out_layer = Dense(1, activation='sigmoid')(fe)
```

```
#This line creates a Keras `Model` object, specifying the inputs as a
list `[in_image, in_label]` and the output as `out_layer`. It constructs
the discriminator model by connecting the inputs (`in_image` and `in_
label`) to the output (`out_layer`).
model = Model([in_image, in_label], out_layer)
```

```
#This line creates an Adam optimizer with a learning rate of 0.0002 and a
decay rate (`beta_1`) of 0.5. The Adam optimizer is commonly used for
training deep learning models.
opt = Adam(lr=0.0002, beta_1=0.5)
```

```
#This line compiles the discriminator model. It specifies the loss
function as `'binary_crossentropy'`, which is appropriate for binary
```

classification tasks. The optimizer is set to `opt`, which was defined earlier. Additionally, the metric `'accuracy'` is specified to evaluate the performance of the model during training.

```
model.compile(loss='binary_crossentropy', optimizer=opt,
metrics=['accuracy'])
```

```
#This line returns the compiled discriminator model as the output of the
`define_discriminator` function.
return model
```

9.3.5 Load Real Sample Data

Processing data before using them with tasks like normalization (where the range is 0–255 for grayscale images) is crucial. In this case, the output consists of the input data, denoted as "x", and the corresponding labels, denoted as "y". Overall, this code loads the Fashion MNIST dataset, expands the dimensions of the training images, converts the data type to float32, and performs data normalization. The function then returns the normalized images and their corresponding labels.

```
def load_real_samples():
(trainX, trainy), (_, _) = load_data()
X = expand_dims(trainX, axis=-1)
X = X.astype('float32')
X = (X - 127.5) / 127.5
 return [X, trainy]
```

Here's a breakdown of the code:

```
#This is a function definition for loading the real samples from the dataset.
def load_real_samples():
```

```
#This line calls the `load_data()` function to load the Fashion MNIST
dataset. It returns two tuples, one for the training set and the other
for the test set. However, this code only assigns the training set tuples
to `(trainX, trainy)` while ignoring the test set tuples.
(trainX, trainy), (_, _) = load_data()
```

```
#This line expands the dimensions of the `trainX` array by adding an
extra dimension at the end. This is done using the `expand_dims` function
with `axis=-1`, which means the new dimension is added as the last axis.
This is commonly done to represent grayscale images as 3D arrays.
X = expand_dims(trainX, axis=-1)
```

```
#This line converts the data type of the `X` array from integers to
floats. It is done using the `astype` method, specifying `'float32'` as
the desired data type.
X = X.astype('float32')
```

```
#This line performs data normalization. The pixel values in `X` are scaled
from the original range of `[0, 255]` to the normalized range of `[-1, 1]`.
The operation subtracts 127.5 from each pixel and then divides the result by
127.5. This centers the pixel values around 0 and scales them accordingly.
X = (X - 127.5) / 127.5
```

```
#This line returns a list containing the normalized images `X` and the
corresponding labels `trainy` as the output of the `load_real_samples`
function.
return [X, trainy]
```

9.3.6 Select a Real Sample and Generate Data for the Generator and Labels

Split the data into images and labels, choose random data samples, select the image data and their labels, and finally generate labels for the selected real samples. Overall, this code takes a dataset consisting of images and labels, randomly selects "n_samples" instances, retrieves the images and labels corresponding to those instances, generates class labels indicating the samples are real, and returns the selected images, labels, and class labels as the output of the "generate_real_samples" function.

```
def generate_real_samples(dataset, n_samples):
images, labels = dataset
ix = randint(0, images.shape[0], n_samples)
X, labels = images[ix], labels[ix]
y = ones((n_samples, 1))
 return [X, labels], y
```

Here's a breakdown of the code:

```
#This is a function definition for generating real samples from a given
dataset.
def generate_real_samples(dataset, n_samples):
```

```
#This line unpacks the `dataset` into `images` and `labels`. The
`dataset` is expected to be a list containing the images and their
corresponding labels.
images, labels = dataset
```

```
#This line generates random indices (`ix`) for selecting `n_samples`
instances from the `images` array. The `randint` function is used with
the range of indices from 0 to the number of images in the dataset
(`images.shape[0]`).
ix = randint(0, images.shape[0], n_samples)
```

```
#This line selects the images and labels corresponding to the randomly
chosen indices `ix`. It retrieves the images from the `images` array and
their respective labels from the `labels` array.
X, labels = images[ix], labels[ix]
```

```
#This line generates class labels (`y`) for the real samples. It creates
an array of shape `(n_samples, 1)` filled with ones. This indicates that
the generated samples are real.
y = ones((n_samples, 1))
```

```
#This line returns a list containing the selected images (`X`), their
corresponding labels (`labels`), and the generated class labels (`y`). It
represents the real samples and their labels.
return [X, labels], y
```

Generate points in latent space as input for the generator. Overall, this code generates random points in the latent space by drawing from a standard normal distribution, reshapes them into a batch of inputs for the generator, generates random labels for the latent points, and returns the generated latent points and labels as the output of the "generate_latent_points" function.

```
def generate_latent_points(latent_dim, n_samples, n_classes=10):
x_input = randn(latent_dim * n_samples)
z_input = x_input.reshape(n_samples, latent_dim)
labels = randint(0, n_classes, n_samples)
 return [z_input, labels]
```

Here's a breakdown of the code:

```
#This is a function definition for generating latent points in the latent
space.
def generate_latent_points(latent_dim, n_samples, n_classes=10):
```

```
#This line generates random numbers from a standard normal distribution
using the `randn` function. The total number of random numbers generated
is `latent_dim * n_samples`, representing `latent_dim`-dimensional
vectors for `n_samples` points.
x_input = randn(latent_dim * n_samples)
```

```
#This line reshapes the generated random numbers (`x_input`) into a batch
of inputs for the network. It changes the shape from `(latent_dim *
n_samples,)` to `(n_samples, latent_dim)`, where each row represents a
latent point of dimension `latent_dim`.
z_input = x_input.reshape(n_samples, latent_dim)
```

```
#This line generates random integer labels for the latent points. The
labels are chosen from the range of integers `[0, n_classes)`, with a
total of `n_samples` labels generated.
labels = randint(0, n_classes, n_samples)
```

```
#This line returns a list containing the generated latent points (`z_
input`) and their corresponding labels (`labels`). It represents the
latent points and labels used as input for the generator model.
return [z_input, labels]
```

9.3.7 Generate Fake Sample

We can generate examples with class labels. Overall, this code generates latent points and labels using the "generate_latent_points" function, feeds them to the generator model to obtain fake images, creates class labels indicating that the samples are fake, and returns the generated fake images, input labels, and class labels as the output of the "generate_fake_samples" function.

```
def generate_fake_samples(generator, latent_dim, n_samples):
z_input, labels_input = generate_latent_points(latent_dim, n_samples)
images = generator.predict([z_input, labels_input])
y = zeros((n_samples, 1))
 return [images, labels_input], y
```

Here's a breakdown of the code:

```
#This is a function definition for generating fake samples using a
generator model.
def generate_fake_samples(generator, latent_dim, n_samples):

#This line calls the `generate_latent_points` function to generate latent
points (`z_input`) and their corresponding labels (`labels_input`). It
provides the `latent_dim` and `n_samples` parameters to the function.
z_input, labels_input = generate_latent_points(latent_dim, n_samples)

#This line uses the generator model to predict fake images given the
generated latent points (`z_input`) and labels (`labels_input`). It calls
the `predict` method of the `generator` model, passing the latent points
and labels as inputs.
images = generator.predict([z_input, labels_input])

#This line creates class labels (`y`) for the fake samples. It creates an
array of shape `(n_samples, 1)` filled with zeros. This indicates that
the generated samples are fake.
y = zeros((n_samples, 1))

#This line returns a list containing the generated fake images (`images`),
the corresponding labels used as input (`labels_input`), and the generated
class labels (`y`). It represents the fake samples and their labels.
return [images, labels_input], y
```

9.3.8 Training

Train the generator and discriminator using training data. Overall, this code trains a cGAN by alternating between training the discriminator and the generator models. It uses batches of real and fake samples to update the discriminator, and it uses the generator's output and latent points to update the generator via the discriminator's error. The training progress is printed, and the generator model is saved at the end of training.

```
def train(g_model, d_model, gan_model, dataset, latent_dim, n_epochs=100,
n_batch=128):
 bat_per_epo = int(dataset[0].shape[0] / n_batch)
 half_batch = int(n_batch / 2)
for i in range(n_epochs):
  for j in range(bat_per_epo):
    [X_real, labels_real], y_real = generate_real_samples(dataset,
half_batch)
    d_loss1, _ = d_model.train_on_batch([X_real, labels_real], y_real)
    [X_fake, labels], y_fake = generate_fake_samples(g_model, latent_dim,
half_batch)
    d_loss2, _ = d_model.train_on_batch([X_fake, labels], y_fake)
    [z_input, labels_input] = generate_latent_points(latent_dim, n_batch)
    y_gan = ones((n_batch, 1))
    g_loss = gan_model.train_on_batch([z_input, labels_input], y_gan)
    print('>%d, %d/%d, d1=%.3f, d2=%.3f g=%.3f'%
    (i+1, j+1, bat_per_epo, d_loss1, d_loss2, g_loss))
  g_model.save('cgan_generator.h5')
```

Here's a breakdown of the code:

```
#This is a function definition for training a conditional generative
adversarial network (cGAN).
def train(g_model, d_model, gan_model, dataset, latent_dim, n_epochs=100,
n_batch=128):
```

```
#These lines calculate the number of batches per epoch (`bat_per_epo`)
based on the size of the dataset and the batch size. The `half_batch`
variable is set to half of the batch size and will be used for training
the discriminator with half real and half fake samples.
bat_per_epo = int(dataset[0].shape[0] / n_batch)
half_batch = int(n_batch / 2)
```

```
#This line starts a loop over the number of epochs specified by `n_epochs`.
for i in range(n_epochs):
```

```
#This line starts a loop over the number of batches per epoch.
for j in range(bat_per_epo):
```

```
#These lines generate real samples (`X_real` and `labels_real`) using
the `generate_real_samples` function and their corresponding class
labels (`y_real`). Then, the discriminator model (`d_model`) is trained
on this batch of real samples using the `train_on_batch` method.
[X_real, labels_real], y_real = generate_real_samples(dataset, half_batch)
d_loss1, _ = d_model.train_on_batch([X_real, labels_real], y_real)
```

```
#These lines generate fake samples (`X_fake` and `labels`) using the
generator model (`g_model`) and their corresponding class labels
(`y_fake`). The discriminator model is then trained on this batch of fake
samples.
[X_fake, labels], y_fake = generate_fake_samples(g_model, latent_dim,
half_batch)
d_loss2, _ = d_model.train_on_batch([X_fake, labels], y_fake)
```

```
#These lines generate latent points (`z_input`) and labels (`labels_input`)
using the `generate_latent_points` function. The generator model (`g_model`)
is trained on this batch of latent points and labels, aiming to generate
fake samples that are classified as real. The class labels (`y_gan`) are
set to ones to indicate that the generated samples are real.
[z_input, labels_input] = generate_latent_points(latent_dim, n_batch)
y_gan = ones((n_batch, 1))
g_loss = gan_model.train_on_batch([z_input, labels_input], y_gan)
```

```
#This line prints the training progress, including the current epoch
number (`i+1`), the batch number within the epoch (`j+1`), the
discriminator loss for real samples (`d_loss1`), the discriminator loss
for fake samples (`d_loss2`), and the generator loss (`g_loss`).
print('>%d, %d/%d, d1=%.3f, d2=%.3f g=%.3f' % (i+1, j+1, bat_per_epo,
d_loss1, d_loss2, g_loss))
```

```
#This line saves the generator model (`g_model`) to a file named `'cgan_
generator.h5'`.
g_model.save('cgan_generator.h5')
```

9.4 CDCGAN

Several advanced variants of cGAN, including CDCGAN, incorporate conditional design from DCGAN. This allows us to generate specific data by providing additional information or conditions. By repeating the process, we can generate the desired data. CDCGAN combines the characteristics of conditional GAN and DCGAN, and it was developed by Google. Let's proceed with implementing this type of GAN.

9.4.1 Importing Libraries

Set up the libraries and requirements. Overall, these import statements provide the necessary tools and components for building and working with deep learning models using Keras and TensorFlow.It imports the necessary libraries and modules for working with Keras and TensorFlow.

```
import keras
import tensorflow as tf
import numpy as np
import matplotlib.pyplot as plt
import tensorflow.keras as tk
from keras.layers import Input, Dense, Conv2D, Conv2DTranspose, Reshape,
LeakyReLU, Embedding, Concatenate, Flatten, Dropout
from keras.models import Model
```

Here's a breakdown of the imports:

These lines import the `keras` and `tensorflow` libraries. `tensorflow` is imported as `tf` for convenience.
```
import keras
import tensorflow as tf
```

These lines import the `numpy` library for numerical operations and the `matplotlib.pyplot` module for plotting.
```
import numpy as np
import matplotlib.pyplot as plt
```

This line imports the `tensorflow.keras` module, which is the TensorFlow 2. x implementation of Keras. It is imported as `tk` for convenience.
```
import tensorflow.keras as tk
```

These lines import specific layers and classes from Keras. Each line imports a different layer or class that can be used to build neural network models.
```
from keras.layers import Input, Dense, Conv2D, Conv2DTranspose, Reshape,
LeakyReLU, Embedding, Concatenate, Flatten, Dropout
```

This line imports the `Model` class from Keras, which is used to define and work with models in Keras.
```
from keras.models import Model
```

9.4.2 Load Data

It loads the fashion MNIST dataset from the Keras dataset. Overall, this code loads the Fashion MNIST dataset, expands the dimensions of the images, performs data normalization, and returns the preprocessed training images and labels.This code defines a function "load_data()" that loads and preprocesses the Fashion MNIST dataset.

```
def load_data():
  (X_train, y_train), (_,_) = keras.datasets.fashion_mnist.load_data()
  X_train = np.expand_dims(X_train, -1)
  X_train = (X_train - 127.5)/127.5
  return [X_train, y_train]
```

   Here's a breakdown of the code:

```
#This is a function definition for loading and preprocessing the Fashion
MNIST dataset.
def load_data():
```

```
#This line loads the Fashion MNIST dataset using the `load_data()` function
from `keras.datasets.fashion_mnist`. It assigns the training images and
labels to `(X_train, y_train)` and ignores the test images and labels.
X_train, y_train), (_,_) = keras.datasets.fashion_mnist.load_data()
```

```
#This line expands the dimensions of the `X_train` array by adding an
extra dimension at the end. It uses `np.expand_dims` function with
`axis=-1`, which means the new dimension is added as the last axis. This
is commonly done to represent grayscale images as 3D arrays.
X_train = np.expand_dims(X_train, -1)
```

```
#This line performs data normalization on the `X_train` array. It subtracts
127.5 from each pixel value to center the values around 0, and then divides
the result by 127.5 to scale the values between -1 and 1. This normalization
is often applied to improve the training process of deep learning models.
X_train = (X_train - 127.5)/127.5
```

```
#This line returns a list containing the preprocessed training images
(`X_train`) and their corresponding labels (`y_train`) as the output of
the `load_data()` function.
return [X_train, y_train]
```

9.4.3 Discriminator

Discriminator structure definition using the proper layers. This code defines a discriminator model for a cGAN.

```
def discriminator(inp_shape = (28,28,1 ), n_classes = 10):
  in_label = Input(shape = (1,))
  li = Embedding(input_dim= n_classes, output_dim = 50)(in_label)
  n_nodes = inp_shape[0] * inp_shape[1]
  li = Dense(n_nodes)(li)
  li = Reshape(target_shape=(inp_shape[0], inp_shape[1],1))(li)
  in_image = Input(shape = inp_shape)
```

```
    merge = Concatenate()([in_image, li])
    ds = Conv2D(128, (4,4), strides = (2,2), padding = "same")(merge)
    ds = LeakyReLU(0.2)(ds)
    ds = Conv2D(128, (4,4), strides = (2,2), padding = "same")(ds)
    ds = LeakyReLU(0.2)(ds)
    ds = Flatten()(ds)
    ds = Dropout(0.4)(ds)
    out_layer = Dense(1, activation = "sigmoid")(ds)
    model = Model([in_image, in_label], out_layer)
    model.compile(optimizer = tf.optimizers.Adam(0.0002, beta_1 = 0.5),
loss = "binary_crossentropy", metrics = ['acc'])
    return model
```

Here's a breakdown of the code:

**#This is a function definition for the discriminator model. It takes two
parameters: `inp_shape`, which represents the shape of the input image,
and `n_classes` (with a default value of 10), which represents the number
of classes or categories for conditional discrimination.**
```
def discriminator(inp_shape=(28, 28, 1), n_classes=10):
```

**#These lines define the label input layer (`in_label`) and apply an
embedding layer (`Embedding`) to the label input. The `Embedding` layer
maps each integer label to a dense vector representation. The `input_dim`
parameter is set to `n_classes` to specify the number of distinct values
for the labels, and the `output_dim` parameter is set to 50 to specify
the size of the embedding vectors.**
```
in_label = Input(shape=(1,))
li = Embedding(input_dim=n_classes, output_dim=50)(in_label)
```

**#These lines create a fully connected layer (`Dense`) that maps the
embedded labels to a shape of `(inp_shape[0], inp_shape[1], 1)`. The
`target_shape` parameter of the `Reshape` layer reshapes the output of
the dense layer to match the shape of the input image.**
```
n_nodes = inp_shape[0] * inp_shape[1]
li = Dense(n_nodes)(li)
li = Reshape(target_shape=(inp_shape[0], inp_shape[1], 1))(li)
```

**#These lines define the image input layer (`in_image`) and concatenate it
with the reshaped label representation (`li`). The `Concatenate` layer
combines the image and label information by concatenating them along the
channel dimension.**
```
in_image = Input(shape=inp_shape)
merge = Concatenate()([in_image, li])
```

**#These lines apply two convolutional layers (`Conv2D`) to the concatenated
features. Each convolutional layer has 128 filters with a kernel size of
`(4, 4)` and a stride of `(2, 2)`. The padding is set to `"same"`, meaning
the input and output have the same spatial dimensions. The convolutional
layers are followed by the LeakyReLU activation function.**
```
ds = Conv2D(128, (4, 4), strides=(2, 2), padding="same")(merge)
ds = LeakyReLU(0.2)(ds)
ds = Conv2D(128, (4, 4), strides=(2, 2), padding="same")(ds)
ds = LeakyReLU(0.2)(ds)
```

```
#These lines flatten the feature maps, apply dropout regularization, and
produce the final output of the discriminator. The flattened features are
passed through a dropout layer to randomly set a fraction of the input
units to 0. Finally, a dense layer with a single unit and a sigmoid
activation function is used to generate the output, which represents the
probability of the input being real or fake.
ds = Flatten()(ds)
ds = Dropout(0.4)(ds)
out_layer = Dense(1, activation="sigmoid")(ds)
```

```
#These lines create the discriminator model by specifying the inputs as a
list `[in_image, in_label]` and the output as `out_layer`. The model is
compiled with the Adam optimizer, a learning rate of 0
model = Model([in_image, in_label], out_layer)
model.compile(optimizer=tf.optimizers.Adam(0.0002, beta_1=0.5),
loss="binary_crossentropy", metrics=['acc'])
```

```
#The `return model` statement simply returns the compiled discriminator
model as the output of the `discriminator` function. This allows the
caller of the function to obtain and use the discriminator model for
further processing or training.
return model
```

9.4.4 Generator

Generator structure definition using the proper layers. Overall, this code defines the generator architecture for a cGAN. It takes a latent vector and a label as inputs and generates an output image based on the provided label. The generator model is defined using the Keras functional API.

```
def generator(latent_dim = 100, n_classes = 10):
  in_label = Input(shape = (1,))
  gl = Embedding(input_dim = n_classes, output_dim = 50)(in_label)
  n_nodes = 7 * 7
  gl = Dense(n_nodes)(gl)
  gl = Reshape((7,7,1))(gl)
  in_lat = Input(shape = (latent_dim,))
  ls = Dense(7 * 7 * 128)(in_lat)
  ls = LeakyReLU(0.2)(ls)
  ls = Reshape((7,7,128))(ls)
  merge = Concatenate()([ls, gl])
  gen = Conv2DTranspose(128, 4, strides=(2,2), padding = "same")(merge)
  gen = LeakyReLU(0.2)(gen)
  gen = Conv2DTranspose(128, 4, strides=(2,2), padding = "same")(gen)
  gen = LeakyReLU(0.2)(gen)
  output_layer = Conv2D(1, 7, padding="same", activation = "tanh")(gen)
  model = Model([in_lat, in_label], output_layer)
  return model
```

Here's a breakdown of the code:

```
#This is a function definition for the generator model. It takes two
parameters: `latent_dim`, which represents the dimensionality of the
latent space, and `n_classes` (with a default value of 10), which
```

represents the number of classes or categories for conditional generation.

```
def generator(latent_dim=100, n_classes=10):
```

#These lines define the label input layer (`in_label`) and apply an embedding layer (`Embedding`) to the label input. The `Embedding` layer maps each integer label to a dense vector representation. The `input_dim` parameter is set to `n_classes` to specify the number of distinct values for the labels, and the `output_dim` parameter is set to 50 to specify the size of the embedding vectors.

```
in_label = Input(shape=(1,))
gl = Embedding(input_dim=n_classes, output_dim=50)(in_label)
```

#These lines create a fully connected layer (`Dense`) that maps the embedded labels to a shape of `(7, 7, 1)`. The `Reshape` layer reshapes the output of the dense layer to match the shape of the initial generator input.

```
n_nodes = 7 * 7
gl = Dense(n_nodes)(gl)
gl = Reshape((7, 7, 1))(gl)
```

#These lines define the latent input layer (`in_lat`) and apply a fully connected layer (`Dense`) to it. The output of the dense layer is then reshaped to a shape of `(7, 7, 128)`, matching the shape of the initial generator input.

```
in_lat = Input(shape=(latent_dim,))
ls = Dense(7 * 7 * 128)(in_lat)
ls = LeakyReLU(0.2)(ls)
ls = Reshape((7, 7, 128))(ls)
```

#These lines concatenate the latent and label representations (`ls` and `gl`) and then apply a series of transposed convolutional layers (`Conv2DTranspose`) to upsample the input. The output of each transposed convolutional layer is passed through a LeakyReLU activation function.

```
merge = Concatenate()([ls, gl])
gen = Conv2DTranspose(128, 4, strides=(2, 2), padding="same")(merge)
gen = LeakyReLU(0.2)(gen)
gen = Conv2DTranspose(128, 4, strides=(2, 2), padding="same")(gen)
gen = LeakyReLU(0.2)(gen)
```

#This line applies a convolutional layer (`Conv2D`) with a kernel size of 7 and `tanh` activation function to generate the final output image. The `Model` class is used to define the generator model, specifying the inputs as a list `[in_lat, in_label]` and the output as `output_layer`.

```
output_layer = Conv2D(1, 7, padding="same", activation="tanh")(gen)
model = Model([in_lat, in_label], output_layer)
```

#This line returns the generator model as the output of the `generator` function.

```
return model
```

9.4.5 Model

Define the GAN model and compile it. Overall, this code defines the GAN model by connecting the generator and discriminator models. It sets the discriminator as non-trainable, creates a new model that takes the generator's noise and label inputs and produces the GAN output, and compiles the model with the necessary optimizer and loss function.

```
def gan(g_model, d_model):
  d_model.trainable = False
  gen_noise, gen_label = g_model.input
  gen_output = g_model.output
  gan_output = d_model([gen_output, gen_label])
  model = Model([gen_noise, gen_label], gan_output)
  model.compile(optimizer = tf.optimizers.Adam(0.0002, beta_1 = 0.5),
loss = "binary_crossentropy")
  return model
```

Here's a breakdown of the code:

```
#This is a function definition for the GAN model. It takes two parameters:
`g_model`, which represents the generator model, and `d_model`, which
represents the discriminator model.
def gan(g_model, d_model):
```

```
#This line sets the `trainable` attribute of the discriminator model to
`False`. This is done to freeze the weights of the discriminator during
GAN training, so only the generator is updated.
d_model.trainable = False
```

```
#These lines retrieve the input layers and output layer of the generator
model. The `gen_noise` and `gen_label` represent the input layers of the
generator, and `gen_output` represents the output layer.
gen_noise, gen_label = g_model.input
gen_output = g_model.output
```

```
#This line connects the generator output (`gen_output`) and label input
(`gen_label`) as inputs to the discriminator model (`d_model`). The
resulting output is stored in `gan_output`, representing the output of
the GAN model.
gan_output = d_model([gen_output, gen_label])
```

```
#This line creates a new model using the Keras functional API, specifying
the inputs as `[gen_noise, gen_label]` and the output as `gan_output`.
This represents the GAN model, where the generator and discriminator are
connected.
model = Model([gen_noise, gen_label], gan_output)
```

```
#This line compiles the GAN model with the Adam optimizer, a learning
rate of 0.0002, and a beta value of 0.5. The loss function used is binary
cross-entropy, which is commonly used for GANs.
model.compile(optimizer=tf.optimizers.Adam(0.0002, beta_1=0.5),
loss="binary_crossentropy")
```

```
#This line returns the compiled GAN model as the output of the `gan`
function.
return model
```

9.4.6 Generate Data

Calling the defined modules for generating real and fake data samples. These functions are used to generate real and fake samples for training a GAN model. These functions can be used in a GAN training loop to generate real and fake samples for training the discriminator and generator models.

```
def generate_real_samples(dataset, n_samples):
  ind = np.random.randint(0, len(dataset[0]), n_samples)
  img, labels = dataset
  X, labels = img[ind], labels[ind]
  y = np.ones((n_samples, 1))
  return [X,labels], y
def generate_latent_space(n_size = 128, latent_dim = 100, n_classes =
10):
  points = np.random.randn(n_size * latent_dim)
  points = points.reshape((n_size, latent_dim))
  y = np.random.randint(0, n_classes, n_size )
  return points, y
def generate_fake_examples(g_model, n_size = 128):
  points, label_inp = generate_latent_space()
  images = g_model.predict([points, label_inp])
  y = np.zeros((n_size, 1))
  return [images, label_inp], y
```

Here's a breakdown of each function:

```
#This function generates real samples from a dataset. It takes two
parameters: `dataset`, which contains the images and labels, and `n_
samples`, which represents the number of samples to generate.
def generate_real_samples(dataset, n_samples):
```

```
#These lines randomly select `n_samples` indices from the dataset using
`np.random.randint`. Then, it retrieves the images and labels
corresponding to those indices. The function returns a list containing
the selected images (`X`), the corresponding labels (`labels`), and an
array `y` filled with ones, indicating that the samples are real.
ind = np.random.randint(0, len(dataset[0]), n_samples)
img, labels = dataset
X, labels = img[ind], labels[ind]
y = np.ones((n_samples, 1))
return [X, labels], y
```

```
#This function generates random points in the latent space. It takes
three parameters: `n_size`, which represents the number of points to
generate, `latent_dim`, which is the dimensionality of the latent space,
and `n_classes`, which represents the number of classes or categories.
def generate_latent_space(n_size=128, latent_dim=100, n_classes=10):
```

```
#These lines generate random numbers from a standard normal distribution
using `np.random.randn`. The total number of random numbers generated is
`n_size * latent_dim`, representing the points in the latent space. The
points are then reshaped into a 2D array with `n_size` rows and `latent_
dim` columns. Random labels (`y`) are also generated using `np.random.
randint` with values ranging from 0 to `n_classes`. The function returns
the generated points and labels.
points = np.random.randn(n_size * latent_dim)
points = points.reshape((n_size, latent_dim))
y = np.random.randint(0, n_classes, n_size)
return points, y


#This function generates fake examples using the generator model. It
takes two parameters: `g_model`, which represents the generator model,
and `n_size`, which is the number of fake examples to generate.
def generate_fake_examples(g_model, n_size=128):

#These lines generate latent points and labels using the `generate_latent_
space` function. The generator model is then used to predict fake images
given the generated points and labels. The function returns a list
containing the generated fake images (`images`), the corresponding labels
(`label_inp`), and an array `y` filled with zeros, indicating that the
samples are fake.
points, label_inp = generate_latent_space()
images = g_model.predict([points, label_inp])
y = np.zeros((n_size, 1))
return [images, label_inp], y
```

9.4.7 Training

Define the training module and calling generator module for generating data samples. This code defines a training function that trains a GAN model by calling the previously defined modules and initializing hyperparameters. Overall, this code defines a training function that iterates over epochs and batches to train the GAN model. It generates real and fake samples, trains the discriminator and generator models, and prints the loss values for monitoring the training progress.

```
def train(g_model, d_model, gan_model, dataset, n_size = 128, epochs =
70, latent_dim = 100):
  batch_per_epoch = int(dataset[0].shape[0]/n_size)
  half_batch = int(n_size/2)
  for i in range(epochs):
    for j in range(batch_per_epoch):
      [X_real, labels_real], y_real = generate_real_samples(dataset,
half_batch)
      d_loss1, _ = d_model.train_on_batch([X_real, labels_real], y_real)
      [x_fake, labels], y_fake = generate_fake_examples(g_model)
      d_loss2, _ = d_model.train_on_batch([x_fake, labels], y_fake)
      [z_input, labels_input] = generate_latent_space()
      y_gan = np.ones((n_size, 1))
      gan_loss = gan_model.train_on_batch([z_input, labels_input], y_gan)
      if((j+1)%50 == 0):
        print('>%d, %d/%d, d1=%.3f, d2=%.3f g=%.3f' % (i+1, j+1, batch_
per_epoch, d_loss1, d_loss2, gan_loss))
```

Here's a breakdown of the code:

```
#This is a function definition for training the GAN model. It takes
several parameters: `g_model`, which represents the generator model,
`d_model`, which represents the discriminator model, `gan_model`,
which represents the combined GAN model, `dataset`, which contains
the training dataset, `n_size`, which is the number of samples in
each batch, `epochs`, which is the number of training epochs, and
`latent_dim`, which represents the dimensionality of the latent
space.
def train(g_model, d_model, gan_model, dataset, n_size=128, epochs=70,
latent_dim=100):
```

```
#These lines calculate the number of batches per epoch (`batch_per_
epoch`) by dividing the total number of samples in the dataset by `n_
size`. The `half_batch` represents half the size of a batch and is used
for training the discriminator with real and fake samples.
batch_per_epoch = int(dataset[0].shape[0]/n_size)
half_batch = int(n_size/2)
```

```
#These lines define nested loops to iterate over the epochs and batches
for training the model.
for i in range(epochs):
  for j in range(batch_per_epoch):
```

```
#These lines generate real samples using the `generate_real_samples`
function and train the discriminator (`d_model`) on these real samples
using the `train_on_batch` method. The discriminator loss (`d_loss1`) is
computed and stored.
[X_real, labels_real], y_real = generate_real_samples(dataset,
half_batch)
d_loss1, _ = d_model.train_on_batch([X_real, labels_real], y_real)
```

```
#These lines generate fake samples using the generator (`g_model`)
and train the discriminator on these fake samples. The discriminator
loss (`d_loss2`) is computed and stored.
[x_fake, labels], y_fake = generate_fake_examples(g_model)
d_loss2, _ = d_model.train_on_batch([x_fake, labels], y_fake)
```

```
#These lines generate latent space points and labels using the `generate_
latent_space` function. Then, the GAN model (`gan_model`) is trained on
these points and labels. The GAN loss (`gan_loss`) is computed and
stored.
[z_input, labels_input] = generate_latent_space()
y_gan = np.ones((n_size, 1))
gan_loss = gan_model.train_on_batch([z_input, labels_input], y_gan)
```

```
#This block of code prints the discriminator loss (`d_loss1` and `d_
loss2`) and GAN loss (`gan_loss`) every 50 batches. It shows the progress
of the training process.
if((j+1)%50 == 0):
  print('>%d, %d/%d, d1=%.3f, d2=%.3f g=%.3f' % (i+1, j+1, batch_per_
epoch, d_loss1, d_loss2, gan_loss))
```

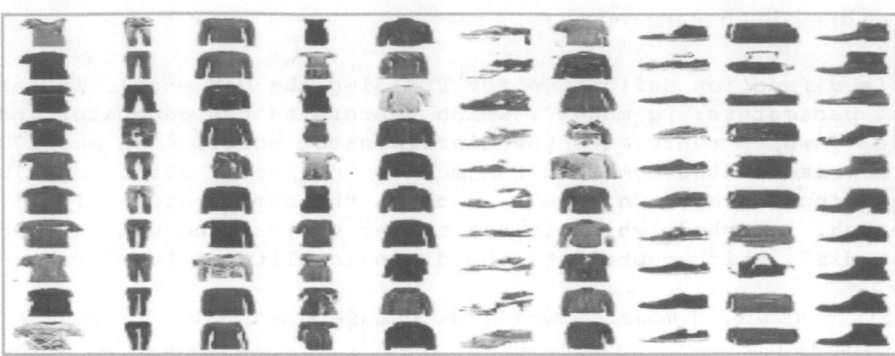

FIGURE 9.7
The output results of CDCGAN.

Figure 9.7 shows the output of the trained model. It showcases a selection of generated samples from the cGAN when trained on the Fashion MNIST dataset. These samples, which are conditioned on specific labels or categories, highlight the ability of cGAN to produce diverse fashion items corresponding to distinct categories within the dataset. The displayed outputs exemplify the efficacy of cGAN in adhering to the conditions set, generating realistic and varied fashion-related images that could range from footwear to tops, providing a visual testament to the capabilities of conditional generation in capturing intricate patterns and designs inherent to the Fashion MNIST data. You can change the hyperparameter values and compile them with more iterations to see different results.

9.5 Pix2Pix GAN for Image-to-Image Translation

It's a type of cGAN where a preceding image serves as a condition for image generation. The application of a GAN in this context pertains to the process of translating one image into another. Both the generator and discriminator models employ batch normalization and ReLU. This type of cGAN is often used in tasks like image-to-image translation. In this scenario, a GAN is used to translate or transform one image into another. This could involve colorizing black and white photos, transforming satellite images into map routes, and so on. The U-Net architecture is a popular choice for these tasks due to its effective design for semantic segmentation tasks, which can be thought of as a form of image-to-image translation. U-Net's architecture is a type of encoder-decoder design, where the encoder progressively reduces the spatial dimension with pooling layers, and the decoder then progressively recovers the object details and spatial dimension. The unique aspect of U-Net is the addition of skip connections, which forward the output of encoder layers to the corresponding decoder layers, combining coarse, high-level features with fine, low-level details. Figure 9.8 provides an initial overview of the U-Net architecture, a renowned convolutional neural network designed primarily for biomedical image segmentation. The U-shaped design consists of a contracting (downsampling) path on the left and an expansive (upsampling) path on the right, connected by a bottom neck. Each step in this structure typically comprises convolutional operations followed by either pooling or upsampling, making it adept at both capturing high-level features and retaining spatial information. The subsequent figures, Figures 9.9–9.12, delve deeper into the intricacies

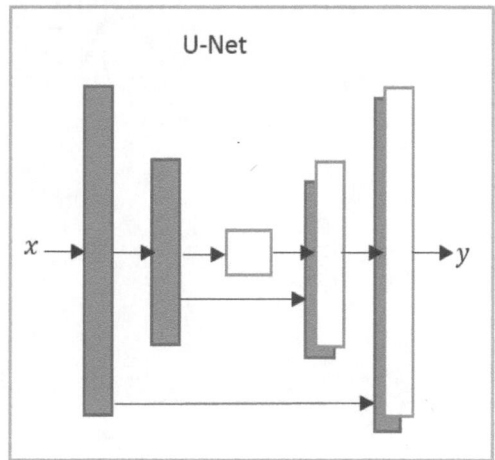

FIGURE 9.8
The U-Net general shape.

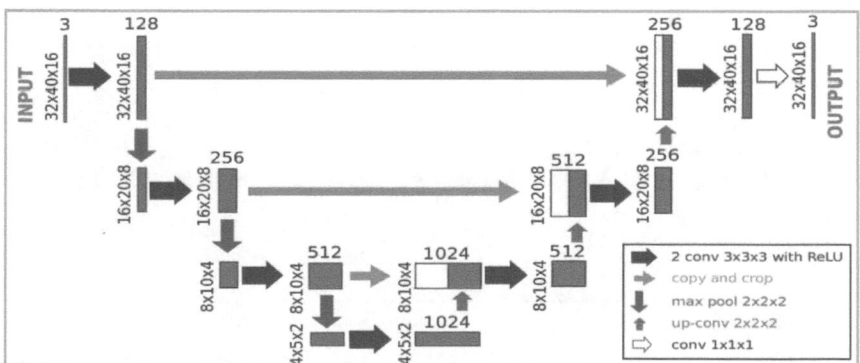

FIGURE 9.9
The U-Net in more detail.

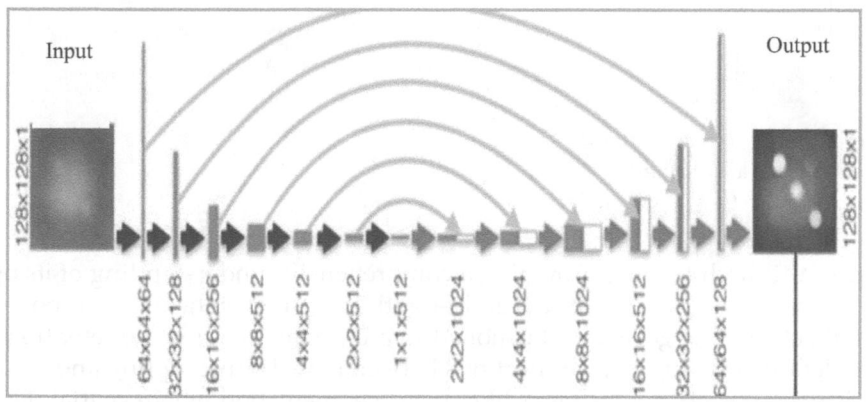

FIGURE 9.10
The generator in U-Net.

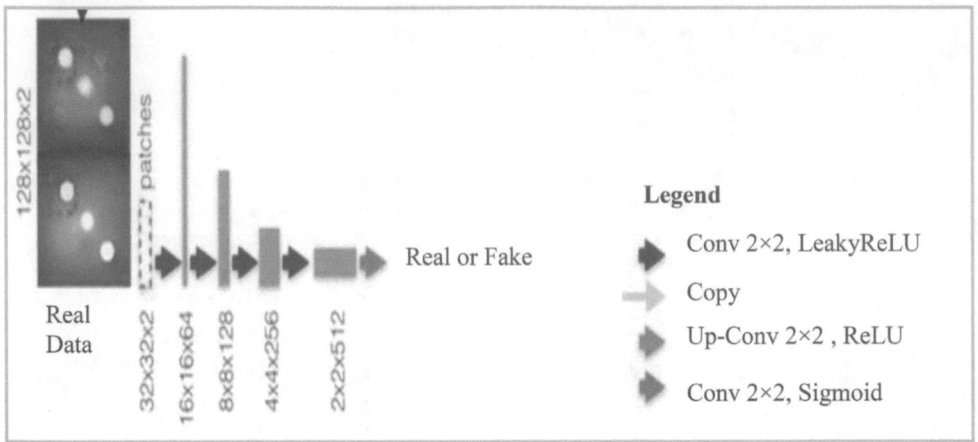

FIGURE 9.11
The discriminator in U-Net.

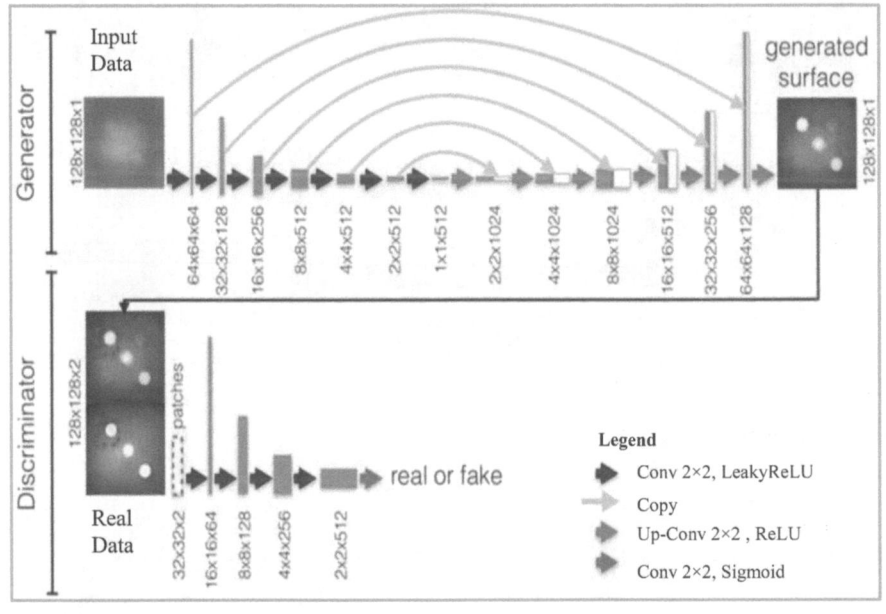

FIGURE 9.12
General Pix2Pix GAN architecture.

and layers of this architecture, providing a comprehensive understanding of its operation and design nuances. Figure 9.10 offers an in-depth look at the generator component of the U-Net architecture. The generator, fashioned in a U-shape, ensures the retention of high-resolution details by using skip connections between the downsampling and upsampling paths. This design is crucial for tasks like image segmentation where spatial details play a significant role in generating precise and coherent outputs. Figure 9.11 showcases the discriminator component within the U-Net framework. Unlike the generator's U-shape, the discriminator follows a more straightforward convolutional pathway, aiming to distinguish between real and generated samples. Its structure, while simpler, plays a critical role in guiding the generator toward producing more realistic outputs by assessing the authenticity of generated images. Figure 9.12 provides an overarching view of the Pix2Pix GAN architecture. This conditional GAN setup leverages the U-Net structure as its generator and includes a dedicated discriminator, similar to the one detailed in Figure 9.11. By integrating these components, the Pix2Pix model efficiently transforms input images into desired outputs, utilizing the power of both U-Net's detail retention and the GAN framework's adversarial training.

9.5.1 Generator

In the context of a GAN, U-Net is often used as the generator model. This model receives an image as input and generates a corresponding output image. Both the generator and discriminator models often use batch normalization and ReLU activation functions to stabilize the training process and promote the learning of a variety of features. It employs a dropout approach within each layer, with the provided image serving as its input. The image received from the source is processed as part of this procedure, and the output is placed in the target domain. The generator uses a U-Net model, which is similar to the Encoder-Decoder model but has a U-shaped structure in the decoder that merges feature maps of the same size. Apart from that, the Encoder-Decoder and U-Net models are exactly the same, and they can be interchanged.

9.5.2 Discriminator

The discriminator receives pairs of input images and generated images, or input images and target images, and must determine whether the images are real (from the dataset) or fake (generated by the generator). This process provides a strong incentive for the generator to produce realistic output images that closely resemble the target images. It accomplishes this by selecting one image from the source and one from the target and then assessing the similarity between the two images. It takes images from the source as input and generates output related to the target domain. The target domain determines the authenticity of each image and also provides a likelihood estimation of whether the images are real or fake. The images are categorized using a PatchGAN approach, resulting in a feature map that produces scores indicating the authenticity of the data. Figure 9.11 illustrates the discriminator component of cGAN, which includes a portion of the U-Net architecture in the general structure.

9.5.3 General Model

Figure 9.12 illustrates the generator and discriminator of the Pix2Pix GAN arranged side by side, showcasing their interconnectivity. The flow starts with the input to the generator and progresses toward the discriminator outputs that discern between real and fake images. The output of the generator comprises the generated image, which is then fed into both the discriminator and the real image. Blue arrows indicate Conv 2×2 and leaky ReLU operations, gray arrows represent the copy operation, green arrows denote Up-Conv 2×2 and ReLU operations, and red arrows signify Conv 2×2 and Sigmoid operations. The input and output data size for the generator is $128 \times 128 \times 1$, while the input data size for the discriminator is $128 \times 128 \times 2$.

9.5.4 Loss Function

The loss function employed combines L_1 loss and adversarial loss, with their relative weightage determined by a hyperparameter known as λ. This hyperparameter enables control over the relative significance of each loss function within the total loss computation.

$$\text{Generator Loss} = \text{Adversarial Loss} + \lambda \times L_1 \text{ Loss}$$

9.6 cGAN Applications

cGANs have a wide range of applications in various fields.

9.6.1 Image and Video Editing

cGANs can be used to edit or transform images and videos in various ways. For example, cGANs can be trained to colorize grayscale images or convert low-resolution images to high-resolution ones.

9.6.2 Data Augmentation

cGANs can be used to generate synthetic data to augment existing datasets, which can be useful in tasks, such as image classification, object detection, and segmentation.

9.6.3 Text-to-image Synthesis

cGANs can be used to generate images from textual descriptions, which can be useful in fields, such as advertising and e-commerce.

9.6.4 Face Recognition

cGANs can be trained to generate face images for different poses, lighting conditions, and expressions, which can be useful in face recognition applications.

9.6.5 Fashion and Interior Design

cGANs can be trained to generate new designs of clothes or furniture, which can be useful for the fashion and interior design industries.

9.6.6 Medical Imaging

cGANs can be used to generate synthetic medical images that can be useful in medical diagnosis and treatment planning.

9.6.7 Speech Synthesis

cGANs can be trained to generate realistic speech from textual input, which can be useful in text-to-speech applications.

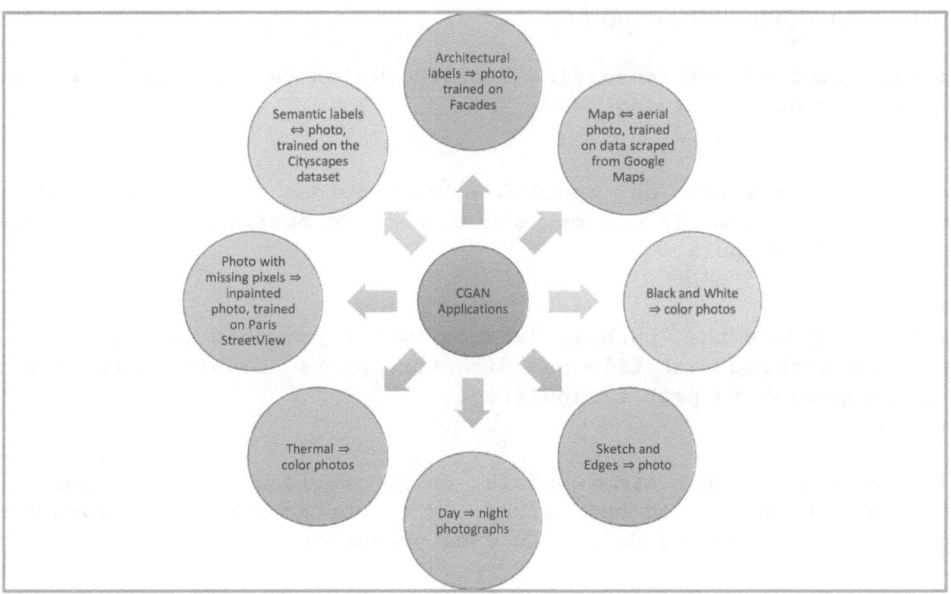

FIGURE 9.13
cGAN applications.

Overall, cGANs have a wide range of applications in various fields, and their potential for generating realistic and diverse images, videos, and other types of data makes them an attractive tool for many industries. The cGAN approach has several applications, as illustrated in Figure 9.13.

9.7 Implementation Pix2Pix

This approach as Pix2Pix (image-to-image translation with a conditional GAN) is implemented here to understand better how it works.

9.7.1 Import Libraries

Importing TensorFlow and other libraries. The code imports the required libraries for working with TensorFlow and other necessary modules. These imports provide the necessary tools and functionalities for working with TensorFlow, file operations, time-related tasks, plotting, and display control.

```
import tensorflow as tf
import os
import pathlib
import time
import datetime
from matplotlib import pyplot as plt
from IPython import display
```

Here's a breakdown of the imports:

```
#This line imports the TensorFlow library, which is a popular open-source
framework for deep learning.
import tensorflow as tf

#This line imports the `os` module, which provides a way to interact with
the operating system. It can be used to perform operations such as file
and directory manipulation.
import os

#This line imports the `pathlib` module, which provides classes and
methods for working with file and directory paths. It offers an object-
oriented approach to path manipulation.
import pathlib

#This line imports the `time` module, which provides functions for
working with time-related operations. It can be used for measuring time
durations or introducing delays in code execution.
import time

#This line imports the `datetime` module, which provides classes and
functions for working with dates and times. It can be used for tasks such
as date formatting and time calculations.
import datetime

#This line imports the `pyplot` module from the `matplotlib` library,
which is a plotting library for creating visualizations in Python. The
`plt` alias is used for convenience.
from matplotlib import pyplot as plt

#This line imports the `display` module from the `IPython` library. It
provides functions for controlling the display behavior in IPython
environments, such as Jupyter notebooks.
from IPython import display
```

9.7.2 Load the Dataset

Loading data from local or online paths. The code loads a dataset and displays a sample data image. Overall, this code loads a dataset using the provided URL, reads and decodes a sample image from the dataset, and displays the sample image using matplotlib.

```
dataset_name="maps"#@param ["cityscapes","edges2handbags","edges2shoes","
facades","maps", "night2day"]
_URL = f'http://efrosgans.eecs.berkeley.edu/pix2pix/datasets/{dataset_
name}.tar.gz'
path_to_zip = tf.keras.utils.get_file(fname=f"{dataset_name}.tar.
gz",origin=_URL,extract=True)
path_to_zip  = pathlib.Path(path_to_zip)
PATH = path_to_zip.parent/dataset_name
_URL = f'http://efrosgans.eecs.berkeley.edu/pix2pix/datasets/{dataset_
name}.tar.gz'
```

```
sample_image = tf.io.read_file(str(PATH /'train/1.jpg'))
sample_image = tf.io.decode_jpeg(sample_image)
print(sample_image.shape)
plt.figure()
plt.imshow(sample_image)
```

Here's a breakdown of the code:

```
#These lines define the dataset name (`dataset_name`) and the URL (`_URL`)
to download the dataset. The `get_file` function from `tf.keras.utils` is
used to download the dataset file and extract it. The `pathlib.Path`
module is used to handle file paths, and the `PATH` variable represents
the path to the extracted dataset.
dataset_name = "maps"
_URL = f'http://efrosgans.eecs.berkeley.edu/pix2pix/datasets/{dataset_
name}.tar.gz'
path_to_zip = tf.keras.utils.get_file(fname=f"{dataset_name}.tar.gz",
origin=_URL, extract=True)
path_to_zip = pathlib.Path(path_to_zip)
PATH = path_to_zip.parent / dataset_name
```

```
#This line redefines the `_URL` variable with the same URL for clarity.
It is not necessary since it was already defined earlier.
_URL = f'http://efrosgans.eecs.berkeley.edu/pix2pix/datasets/{dataset_
name}.tar.gz'
```

```
#These lines read the content of the file `1.jpg` from the `train` folder
in the dataset. The `tf.io.read_file` function reads the file content as
a binary string, and `tf.io.decode_jpeg` decodes the binary string into a
tensor representing the image.
sample_image = tf.io.read_file(str(PATH / 'train/1.jpg'))
sample_image = tf.io.decode_jpeg(sample_image)
```

```
#This line prints the shape of the sample image tensor, which represents
the dimensions of the image (e.g., height, width, channels).
print(sample_image.shape)
```

```
#These lines create a new figure using `plt.figure` and display the sample
image using `plt.imshow`. This shows the image in a matplotlib plot.
plt.figure()
plt.imshow(sample_image)
```

Figure 9.14 presents sample images from the dataset, specifically designed for the Pix2Pix mode. Overall, this code defines a function to load and preprocess an image file and sets constants for dataset loading and processing.

```
def load(image_file):
  image = tf.io.read_file(image_file)
  image = tf.io.decode_jpeg(image)
  w = tf.shape(image)[1]
  w = w // 2
  input_image = image[:, w:, :]
  real_image = image[:, :w, :]
```

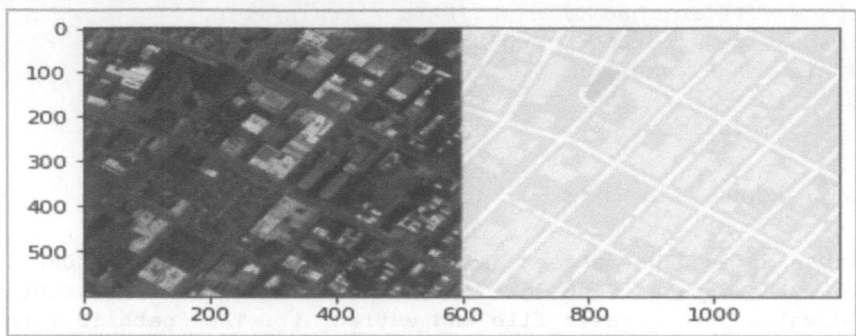

FIGURE 9.14
The data set sample.

```
  input_image = tf.cast(input_image, tf.float32)
  real_image = tf.cast(real_image, tf.float32)
  return input_image, real_image
BUFFER_SIZE = 400
BATCH_SIZE = 1
IMG_WIDTH = 256
IMG_HEIGHT = 256
```

Here's a breakdown of the code:

#This is a function definition for loading and preprocessing an image file. It takes one parameter, `image_file`, which represents the path to the image file.
```
def load(image_file):
```

#These lines read the content of the image file as a binary string using `tf.io.read_file`, and then decode the binary string into a tensor representing the image using `tf.io.decode_jpeg`.
```
image = tf.io.read_file(image_file)
image = tf.io.decode_jpeg(image)
```

#These lines split the image tensor into two tensors: `input_image` and `real_image`. The image is split at the halfway point horizontally (`w // 2`). The `input_image` represents the architecture label image, and the `real_image` represents the real building facade image.
```
w = tf.shape(image)[1]
w = w // 2
input_image = image[:, w:, :]
real_image = image[:, :w, :]
```

#These lines convert both `input_image` and `real_image` tensors to `tf.float32` data type.
```
input_image = tf.cast(input_image, tf.float32)
real_image = tf.cast(real_image, tf.float32)
```

#This line returns the `input_image` and `real_image` tensors as the output of the `load` function.
```
return input_image, real_image
```

```
#These lines set several constants for loading and processing the
dataset. `BUFFER_SIZE` represents the buffer size used for shuffling the
dataset, `BATCH_SIZE` represents the batch size for training, `IMG_WIDTH`
represents the desired width of the images, and `IMG_HEIGHT` represents
the desired height of the images.
BUFFER_SIZE = 400
BATCH_SIZE = 1
IMG_WIDTH = 256
IMG_HEIGHT = 256
```

9.7.3 Generator

It has three parts: an encoder, a decoder, and a generator.

9.7.3.1 Encoder

Overall, this code defines a downsample block with convolutional, batch normalization, and activation layers. It demonstrates the usage of the downsample block by applying it to an input tensor and printing the shape of the resulting tensor.

```
OUTPUT_CHANNELS = 3
def downsample(filters, size, apply_batchnorm=True):
  initializer = tf.random_normal_initializer(0., 0.02)
  result = tf.keras.Sequential()
result.add(tf.keras.layers.Conv2D(filters,size,strides=2,padding='same',
kernel_initializer=initializer,use_bias=False))
  if apply_batchnorm:
    result.add(tf.keras.layers.BatchNormalization())
  result.add(tf.keras.layers.LeakyReLU())
  return result
down_model = downsample(3, 4)
down_result = down_model(tf.expand_dims(inp, 0))
print (down_result.shape)
```

Here's a breakdown of the code:

```
#This line sets the number of output channels for the convolutional
layers in the `downsample` function.
OUTPUT_CHANNELS = 3
```

```
#This is a function definition for creating a downsample block. It
takes three parameters: `filters`, which represents the number of
filters in the convolutional layer, `size`, which represents the size
of the filters, and `apply_batchnorm`, which determines whether batch
normalization is applied after the convolutional layer.
def downsample(filters, size, apply_batchnorm=True):
```

```
#This line initializes the weights of the convolutional layer using a
random normal distribution with a mean of 0 and a standard deviation
of 0.02.
initializer = tf.random_normal_initializer(0., 0.02)
```

```
#These lines create a sequential model (`result`) and add a `Conv2D`
layer to it. The `Conv2D` layer performs a convolution operation with the
specified number of filters, filter size, stride of 2 for downsampling,
'same' padding, and the specified weight initializer. The `use_bias`
parameter is set to `False` to exclude the bias term.
result = tf.keras.Sequential()
result.add(tf.keras.layers.Conv2D(filters, size, strides=2,
padding='same', kernel_initializer=initializer, use_bias=False))

#These lines conditionally add a batch normalization layer
(`BatchNormalization`) and a LeakyReLU activation layer (`LeakyReLU`) to
the model, based on the value of `apply_batchnorm`.
if apply_batchnorm:
    result.add(tf.keras.layers.BatchNormalization())
result.add(tf.keras.layers.LeakyReLU())

#This line returns the created downsample block as the output of the
function.
return result

#This line creates a downsample block (`down_model`) by calling the
`downsample` function with `filters=3` and `size=4`.
down_model = downsample(3, 4)

#This line applies the downsample block to an input tensor (`inp`) by
expanding its dimensions and passing it through the `down_model`.
down_result = down_model(tf.expand_dims(inp, 0))

#This line prints the shape of the resulting tensor from the downsample
operation.
print(down_result.shape)
```

9.7.3.2 Decoder

Overall, this code defines an upsampling block with transposed convolutional, batch normalization, dropout (optional), and activation layers. The "upsample" function can be used to build the upsampling layers in a model architecture.

```
def upsample(filters, size, apply_dropout=False):
  initializer = tf.random_normal_initializer(0., 0.02)
  result = tf.keras.Sequential()
result.add(tf.keras.layers.Conv2DTranspose(filters,size,strides=2,padding
='same',kernel_initializer=initializer, use_bias=False))
  result.add(tf.keras.layers.BatchNormalization())
  if apply_dropout:
      result.add(tf.keras.layers.Dropout(0.5))
  result.add(tf.keras.layers.ReLU())
  return result
```

Here's a breakdown of the code:

```
#This is a function definition for creating an upsampling block. It takes
three parameters: `filters`, which represents the number of filters in
the transposed convolutional layer, `size`, which represents the size of
```

the filters, and `apply_dropout`, which determines whether dropout
regularization is applied after the transposed convolutional layer.

```
def upsample(filters, size, apply_dropout=False):
```

#This line initializes the weights of the transposed convolutional layer
using a random normal distribution with a mean of 0 and a standard
deviation of 0.02.

```
initializer = tf.random_normal_initializer(0., 0.02)
```

#These lines create a sequential model (`result`) and add a
`Conv2DTranspose` layer to it. The `Conv2DTranspose` layer performs an
upsampling operation with the specified number of filters, filter
size, stride of 2 for upsampling, 'same' padding, and the specified
weight initializer. The `use_bias` parameter is set to `False` to
exclude the bias term. Batch normalization is then applied to the
resulting tensor.

```
result = tf.keras.Sequential()
result.add(tf.keras.layers.Conv2DTranspose(filters, size, strides=2,
padding='same', kernel_initializer=initializer, use_bias=False))
result.add(tf.keras.layers.BatchNormalization())
```

#These lines conditionally add a dropout layer (`Dropout`) with a dropout
rate of 0.5 and a ReLU activation layer (`ReLU`) to the model, based on
the value of `apply_dropout`.

```
if apply_dropout:
    result.add(tf.keras.layers.Dropout(0.5))
result.add(tf.keras.layers.ReLU())
```

#This line returns the created upsampling block as the output of the
function.

```
return result
```

9.7.3.3 *Generator*

Overall, this code defines the generator architecture for the Pix2Pix model, which consists
of downsample and upsample layers with skip connections. The generator takes an input
image and produces a corresponding output image.

```
def Generator():
  inputs = tf.keras.layers.Input(shape=[256, 256, 3])
  down_stack = [
    downsample(64, 4, apply_batchnorm=False),
    downsample(128, 4),
    downsample(256, 4),
    downsample(512, 4),
    downsample(512, 4),
    downsample(512, 4),
    downsample(512, 4),
    downsample(512, 4),
  ]
  up_stack = [
    upsample(512, 4, apply_dropout=True),
    upsample(512, 4, apply_dropout=True),
    # (batch_size, 8, 8, 1024)
```

```
      upsample(512, 4, apply_dropout=True),
      upsample(512, 4),
      upsample(256, 4),
      upsample(128, 4),
      upsample(64, 4),
  ]
  initializer = tf.random_normal_initializer(0., 0.02)
last=tf.keras.layers.Conv2DTranspose(OUTPUT_CHANNELS,5,strides=3,padding=
'same',kernel_initializer=initializer,activation='tanh')
  x = inputs
  skips = []
  for down in down_stack:
    x = down(x)
    skips.append(x)
  skips = reversed(skips[:-1])
  for up, skip in zip(up_stack, skips):
    x = up(x)
    x = tf.keras.layers.Concatenate()([x, skip])
  x = last(x)
  return tf.keras.Model(inputs=inputs, outputs=x)
```

Here's a breakdown of the code:

```
#This function definition creates the generator model. It starts by
defining the input shape as `[256, 256, 3]`, representing the dimensions
of the input images.
def Generator():
  inputs = tf.keras.layers.Input(shape=[256, 256, 3])
```

```
#This block of code defines the downsample layers of the generator. It
creates a list called `down_stack` and adds downsample blocks with
different numbers of filters and filter sizes to the list. These
downsample blocks progressively reduce the spatial dimensions of the
input image.
down_stack = [
  downsample(64, 4, apply_batchnorm=False),
  downsample(128, 4),
  downsample(256, 4),
  downsample(512, 4),
  downsample(512, 4),
  downsample(512, 4),
  downsample(512, 4),
  downsample(512, 4),
]
```

```
#This block of code defines the upsample layers of the generator. It
creates a list called `up_stack` and adds upsample blocks with different
numbers of filters and filter sizes to the list. These upsample blocks
progressively increase the spatial dimensions of the input image.
up_stack = [
  upsample(512, 4, apply_dropout=True),
  upsample(512, 4, apply_dropout=True),
  upsample(512, 4, apply_dropout=True),
  upsample(512, 4),
```

```
    upsample(256, 4),
    upsample(128, 4),
    upsample(64, 4),
]
```

#This line defines the final convolutional layer (`last`) of the generator. It uses `Conv2DTranspose` with the specified number of output channels (`OUTPUT_CHANNELS`), filter size of 5, stride of 3 for upsampling, 'same' padding, and a tanh activation function.
```
initializer = tf.random_normal_initializer(0., 0.02)
last = tf.keras.layers.Conv2DTranspose(OUTPUT_CHANNELS, 5, strides=3,
padding='same', kernel_initializer=initializer, activation='tanh')
```

#These lines perform the downsampling operations through the generator model. The input tensor `x` is sequentially passed through the downsample blocks in `down_stack`. The intermediate outputs of each downsample block are stored in the `skips` list, excluding the last output.
```
x = inputs
skips = []
for down in down_stack:
  x = down(x)
  skips.append(x)
skips = reversed(skips[:-1])
```

#These lines perform the upsampling operations and establish skip connections in the generator. The tensor `x` is sequentially passed through the upsample blocks in `up_stack`. At each upsample block, the corresponding skip connection from `skips` is concatenated with `x`.
```
for up, skip in zip(up_stack, skips):
  x = up(x)
  x = tf.keras.layers.Concatenate()([x, skip])
```

#This line applies the final convolutional layer `last` to the output of the upsampling operations, producing the generator's output.
```
x = last(x)
```

#This line creates and returns the generator model using the defined inputs and outputs.
```
return tf.keras.Model(inputs=inputs, outputs=x)
```

9.7.4 Generator Loss

Overall, this code defines the generator loss function, which combines the adversarial loss and the L_1 loss. The generator loss is used to train the generator in the Pix2Pix model.

```
LAMBDA = 100
loss_object = tf.keras.losses.BinaryCrossentropy(from_logits=True)
def generator_loss(disc_generated_output, gen_output, target):
  gan_loss = loss_object(tf.ones_like(disc_generated_output),
disc_generated_output)
  l1_loss = tf.reduce_mean(tf.abs(target - gen_output))
  total_gen_loss = gan_loss + (LAMBDA * l1_loss)
  return total_gen_loss, gan_loss, l1_loss
```

Here's a breakdown of the code:

```
#This line sets the value of `LAMBDA` to 100, which is a hyperparameter
used to weight the importance of the L1 loss term in the generator
loss.
LAMBDA = 100
```

```
#This line creates a binary cross-entropy loss object to compute the
adversarial loss for the generator. The `from_logits=True` argument
indicates that the input to the loss function is logits (i.e., the output
of the discriminator without activation).
loss_object = tf.keras.losses.BinaryCrossentropy(from_logits=True)
```

```
#This function definition takes three parameters: `disc_generated_
output`, which represents the output of the discriminator for the
generated output, `gen_output`, which represents the generated output
from the generator, and `target`, which represents the target (ground
truth) output.
def generator_loss(disc_generated_output, gen_output, target):
```

```
#This line calculates the adversarial loss by comparing the
discriminator's output for the generated output (`disc_generated_output`)
to a tensor of ones (`tf.ones_like(disc_generated_output)`). The binary
cross-entropy loss is computed.
gan_loss = loss_object(tf.ones_like(disc_generated_output),
disc_generated_output)
```

```
#This line calculates the L1 loss by computing the mean absolute
difference between the target output (`target`) and the generated output
(`gen_output`).
l1_loss = tf.reduce_mean(tf.abs(target - gen_output))
```

```
#This line computes the total generator loss by adding the adversarial
loss (`gan_loss`) and the L1 loss (`l1_loss`) multiplied by the
hyperparameter `LAMBDA`.
total_gen_loss = gan_loss + (LAMBDA * l1_loss)
```

```
#This line returns the total generator loss, the adversarial loss, and
the L1 loss as the output of the `generator_loss` function.
return total_gen_loss, gan_loss, l1_loss
```

9.7.5 Discriminator

Overall, this code defines the discriminator architecture for the Pix2Pix model, which takes an input image and a target image and produces a binary classification output.

```
def Discriminator():
  initializer = tf.random_normal_initializer(0., 0.02)
  inp = tf.keras.layers.Input(shape=[256, 256, 3], name='input_image')
  tar = tf.keras.layers.Input(shape=[256, 256, 3], name='target_image')
  x = tf.keras.layers.concatenate([inp, tar])
  # (batch_size, 128, 128, 64)
```

```
  down1 = downsample(64, 4, False)(x)
  down2 = downsample(128, 4)(down1)
  down3 = downsample(256, 4)(down2)
  zero_pad1 = tf.keras.layers.ZeroPadding2D()(down3)
  conv = tf.keras.layers.Conv2D(512, 4, strides=1,kernel_
initializer=initializer,use_bias=False)(zero_pad1)
  batchnorm1 = tf.keras.layers.BatchNormalization()(conv)
  leaky_relu = tf.keras.layers.LeakyReLU()(batchnorm1)
  zero_pad2 = tf.keras.layers.ZeroPadding2D()(leaky_relu)
  last = tf.keras.layers.Conv2D(1, 4, strides=1, kernel_
initializer=initializer)(zero_pad2)
  return tf.keras.Model(inputs=[inp, tar], outputs=last)
```

Here's a breakdown of the code:

```
#This function definition creates the discriminator model. It starts by
defining two input tensors `inp` and `tar`, with the shape `[256, 256,
3]`, representing the input and target images, respectively.
def Discriminator():
  initializer = tf.random_normal_initializer(0., 0.02)
  inp = tf.keras.layers.Input(shape=[256, 256, 3], name='input_image')
  tar = tf.keras.layers.Input(shape=[256, 256, 3], name='target_image')
```

```
#This line concatenates the input and target images along the channel
axis, creating a tensor `x` with shape `(batch_size, 256, 256,
channels*2)`.
x = tf.keras.layers.concatenate([inp, tar])
```

```
#These lines apply the downsample blocks to the concatenated tensor `x`.
The output of each downsample block is stored in variables `down1`,
`down2`, and `down3`, respectively.
down1 = downsample(64, 4, False)(x)
down2 = downsample(128, 4)(down1)
down3 = downsample(256, 4)(down2)
```

```
#These lines continue the discriminator architecture by applying zero
padding, convolutional, batch normalization, LeakyReLU, and another
zero padding layer. Finally, a convolutional layer with 1 output
channel is applied to produce the discriminator's output tensor
`last`.
zero_pad1 = tf.keras.layers.ZeroPadding2D()(down3)
conv = tf.keras.layers.Conv2D(512, 4, strides=1, kernel_
initializer=initializer, use_bias=False)(zero_pad1)
batchnorm1 = tf.keras.layers.BatchNormalization()(conv)
leaky_relu = tf.keras.layers.LeakyReLU()(batchnorm1)
zero_pad2 = tf.keras.layers.ZeroPadding2D()(leaky_relu)
last = tf.keras.layers.Conv2D(1, 4, strides=1, kernel_
initializer=initializer)(zero_pad2)
```

```
#This line creates and returns the discriminator model using the defined
inputs and outputs.
return tf.keras.Model(inputs=[inp, tar], outputs=last)
```

9.7.6 Discriminator Loss

Overall, this code defines the discriminator loss function, which computes the binary cross-entropy loss for the discriminator's classification of real and generated images. The discriminator loss is used to train the discriminator in the Pix2Pix model.

```
def discriminator_loss(disc_real_output, disc_generated_output):
  real_loss = loss_object(tf.ones_like(disc_real_output),
disc_real_output)
  generated_loss = loss_object(tf.zeros_like(disc_generated_output),
disc_generated_output)
  total_disc_loss = real_loss + generated_loss
  return total_disc_loss
```

Here's a breakdown of the code:

```
#This function definition takes two parameters: `disc_real_output`, which
represents the discriminator's output for real images, and `disc_
generated_output`, which represents the discriminator's output for
generated (fake) images.
def discriminator_loss(disc_real_output, disc_generated_output):
```

```
#This line calculates the loss for the discriminator's classification of
real images. It uses the binary cross-entropy loss (`loss_object`) to
compare the discriminator's output for real images (`disc_real_output`)
to a tensor of ones (`tf.ones_like(disc_real_output)`), indicating the
real labels.
real_loss = loss_object(tf.ones_like(disc_real_output), disc_real_output)
```

```
#This line calculates the loss for the discriminator's classification of
generated images. It uses the binary cross-entropy loss (`loss_object`)
to compare the discriminator's output for generated images (`disc_
generated_output`) to a tensor of zeros (`tf.zeros_like(disc_generated_
output)`), indicating the fake labels.
generated_loss = loss_object(tf.zeros_like(disc_generated_output),
disc_generated_output)
```

```
#This line computes the total discriminator loss by summing the losses
for real and generated images.
total_disc_loss = real_loss + generated_loss
```

```
#This line returns the total discriminator loss as the output of the
`discriminator_loss` function.
return total_disc_loss
```

9.7.7 Optimizers

Overall, this code sets up the optimizer objects for the generator and discriminator models, as well as the checkpoint object for saving and restoring model weights. These components are crucial for training and checkpointing the models in the Pix2Pix training process.

```
generator_optimizer = tf.keras.optimizers.Adam(2e-4, beta_1=0.5)
discriminator_optimizer = tf.keras.optimizers.Adam(2e-4, beta_1=0.5)
checkpoint_dir = './training_checkpoints'
```

```
checkpoint_prefix = os.path.join(checkpoint_dir, "ckpt")
checkpoint = tf.train.Checkpoint(generator_optimizer=generator_
optimizer,discriminator_optimizer=discriminator_optimizer,generator=
generator,discriminator=discriminator)
```

Here's a breakdown of the code:

**#These lines create Adam optimizers for the generator and discriminator
models. The learning rate is set to 2e-4, and the beta_1 parameter of the
Adam optimizer is set to 0.5.**
```
generator_optimizer = tf.keras.optimizers.Adam(2e-4, beta_1=0.5)
discriminator_optimizer = tf.keras.optimizers.Adam(2e-4, beta_1=0.5)
```

**#These lines specify the directory path and the prefix for the checkpoint
files. The checkpoint files will be saved in the "training_checkpoints"
directory with the prefix "ckpt".**
```
checkpoint_dir = './training_checkpoints'
checkpoint_prefix = os.path.join(checkpoint_dir, "ckpt")
```

**#This line creates a checkpoint object using the `tf.train.Checkpoint`
class. It specifies the optimizer objects (`generator_optimizer` and
`discriminator_optimizer`) and the model objects (`generator` and
`discriminator`) to be saved and restored during training.**
```
checkpoint = tf.train.Checkpoint(generator_optimizer=generator_optimizer,
discriminator_optimizer=discriminator_optimizer,generator=generator,
discriminator=discriminator)
```

9.7.8 Image Generating

Overall, this function allows you to generate and visualize the input image, ground truth image, and predicted image using a generator model. It provides a convenient way to inspect the performance of the model during training or inference.

```
def generate_images(model, test_input, tar):
  prediction = model(test_input, training=True)
  plt.figure(figsize=(15, 15))
  display_list = [test_input[0], tar[0], prediction[0]]
  title = ['Input Image', 'Ground Truth', 'Predicted Image']
  for i in range(3):
    plt.subplot(1, 3, i+1)
    plt.title(title[i])
    plt.imshow(display_list[i] * 0.5 + 0.5)
    plt.axis('off')
  plt.show()
```

Here's a breakdown of the code:

**#This function definition takes three parameters: `model`, which
represents the generator model, `test_input`, which represents the input
image to the generator, and `tar`, which represents the ground truth
image.**
```
def generate_images(model, test_input, tar):
```

FIGURE 9.15
The first generated images.

```
#This line passes the `test_input` image through the generator model
(`model`) with the `training=True` flag. It generates a predicted image
(`prediction`).
prediction = model(test_input, training=True)

#These lines set up the figure and define the lists `display_list` and
`title` to store the images and titles for visualization.
plt.figure(figsize=(15, 15))
display_list = [test_input[0], tar[0], prediction[0]]
title = ['Input Image', 'Ground Truth', 'Predicted Image']

#These lines iterate over the images in `display_list` and plot them with
the corresponding title. The pixel values are rescaled to the range [0, 1]
before plotting. The resulting image visualization is displayed.
for i in range(3):
    plt.subplot(1, 3, i+1)
    plt.title(title[i])
    # To plot the pixel values in the [0, 1] range.
    plt.imshow(display_list[i] * 0.5 + 0.5)
    plt.axis('off')
plt.show()
```

Figure 9.15 depicts, from left to right, the input image, the ground truth image, and the initial generated image serving as the predicted image.

9.7.9 Training

Overall, this code defines and executes the training loop for the Pix2Pix model. It performs the forward pass, computes the losses, computes the gradients, applies the gradients to update the model weights, and saves the model checkpoints. It also displays the generated images and tracks the training progress using TensorBoard summaries.

```
@tf.function
def train_step(input_image, target, step):
  with tf.GradientTape() as gen_tape, tf.GradientTape() as disc_tape:
    gen_output = generator(input_image, training=True)
    disc_real_output = discriminator([input_image, target], training=True)
```

```
    disc_generated_output = discriminator([input_image, gen_output],
training=True)
    gen_total_loss, gen_gan_loss, gen_l1_loss = generator_loss(disc_
generated_output, gen_output, target)
    disc_loss = discriminator_loss(disc_real_output, disc_generated_output)
  generator_gradients = gen_tape.gradient(gen_total_loss,generator.
trainable_variables)
  discriminator_gradients = disc_tape.gradient(disc_loss,discriminator.
trainable_variables)
  generator_optimizer.apply_gradients(zip(generator_gradients,generator.
trainable_variables))
  discriminator_optimizer.apply_gradients(zip(discriminator_
gradients,discriminator.trainable_variables))
  with summary_writer.as_default():
    tf.summary.scalar('gen_total_loss', gen_total_loss, step=step//1000)
    tf.summary.scalar('gen_gan_loss', gen_gan_loss, step=step//1000)
    tf.summary.scalar('gen_l1_loss', gen_l1_loss, step=step//1000)
    tf.summary.scalar('disc_loss', disc_loss, step=step//1000)
def fit(train_ds, test_ds, steps):
  example_input, example_target = next(iter(test_ds.take(1)))
  start = time.time()
  for step, (input_image, target) in train_ds.repeat().take(steps).
enumerate():
    if (step) % 1000 == 0:
      display.clear_output(wait=True)
      if step != 0:
        print(f'Time taken for 1000 steps: {time.time()-start:.2f} sec\n')
      start = time.time()
      generate_images(generator, example_input, example_target)
      print(f"Step: {step//1000}k")
    train_step(input_image, target, step)
    if (step+1) % 10 == 0:
      print('.', end='', flush=True)
    if (step + 1) % 5000 == 0:
      checkpoint.save(file_prefix=checkpoint_prefix)
fit(train_dataset, test_dataset, steps=4000)
```

Here's a breakdown of the code:

```
#This function decorator (`@tf.function`) converts the `train_step`
function into a TensorFlow graph function, improving its performance.
@tf.function
def train_step(input_image, target, step):
```

```
#These lines define the training step within the gradient tape context.
The generator and discriminator models are called with the input image to
generate the output and calculate the discriminator outputs for both real
and generated images. The generator and discriminator losses are computed
using the generator_loss and discriminator_loss functions, respectively.
with tf.GradientTape() as gen_tape, tf.GradientTape() as disc_tape:
    gen_output = generator(input_image, training=True)
    disc_real_output = discriminator([input_image, target], training=True)
    disc_generated_output = discriminator([input_image, gen_output],
training=True)
```

```
    gen_total_loss, gen_gan_loss, gen_l1_loss = generator_loss(disc_
generated_output, gen_output, target)
    disc_loss = discriminator_loss(disc_real_output,
disc_generated_output)
```

#These lines compute the gradients of the generator and discriminator losses with respect to their trainable variables using the respective gradient tapes.
```
generator_gradients = gen_tape.gradient(gen_total_loss, generator.
trainable_variables)
discriminator_gradients = disc_tape.gradient(disc_loss, discriminator.
trainable_variables)
```

#These lines apply the computed gradients to update the trainable variables of the generator and discriminator using their respective optimizers.
```
generator_optimizer.apply_gradients(zip(generator_gradients, generator.
trainable_variables))
discriminator_optimizer.apply_gradients(zip(discriminator_gradients,
discriminator.trainable_variables))
```

#These lines write the generator and discriminator losses as scalar summaries for visualization using TensorBoard.
```
with summary_writer.as_default():
    tf.summary.scalar('gen_total_loss', gen_total_loss, step=step//1000)
    tf.summary.scalar('gen_gan_loss', gen_gan_loss, step=step//1000)
    tf.summary.scalar('gen_l1_loss', gen_l1_loss, step=step//1000)
    tf.summary.scalar('disc_loss', disc_loss, step=step//1000)
```

#This function `fit` takes three parameters: `train_ds`, `test_ds`, and `steps`. It represents the training loop for the Pix2Pix model. It iterates over the training dataset (`train_ds`) for the specified number of steps and performs the training step for each batch. It also displays the generated images and prints the progress during training.
```
fit(train_ds, test_ds, steps):
```

#This line generates and displays example images using the generator model (`generator`) and example input and target images (`example_input` and `example_target`).
```
generate_images(generator, example_input, example_target)
```

#This line saves the model weights using the `checkpoint` object and the specified checkpoint prefix.
```
checkpoint.save(file_prefix=checkpoint_prefix)
```

#The line `fit(train_dataset, test_dataset, steps=4000)` is a function call that starts the training process for the Pix2Pix model using the specified training and testing datasets. Here's what it does:
```
fit(train_dataset, test_dataset, steps=4000)
```

By calling "fit(train_dataset, test_dataset, steps=4000)", you initiate the training loop to train the Pix2Pix model. The training loop iterates over the "train_dataset" for the specified number of steps and performs the necessary operations for training, including computing gradients, updating weights, and saving checkpoints. The progress of training is displayed at regular intervals, including the generation of example images and

FIGURE 9.16
Generated images after 4000 epochs.

FIGURE 9.17
Generate some images using the test set.

printing of the step number. Make sure you have defined the necessary components, such as the generator, discriminator, optimizers, loss functions, and checkpoints, before calling the "fit()" function. Figure 9.16 displays the generated images after 4000 epochs, while Figure 9.17 presents the image generated using the test set.

9.8 cGAN Issues

cGANs have some issues that can affect their performance. Here are some common problems and possible solutions.

9.8.1 Mode Collapse

Mode collapse is a notorious problem in training GANs, and it affects cGANs as well. In the context of GANs, mode collapse refers to the situation where the generator produces limited diversity in its outputs, often generating very similar or even identical samples, regardless of the variation in the input noise vector. This happens when the generator finds a particular point in the space that can fool the discriminator and, therefore, keeps producing similar samples around that point. When mode collapse occurs in a cGAN, the generator starts ignoring the provided conditional input, and instead of generating different outputs for different conditions, it produces the same output irrespective of the condition.

Solutions:

1. **Mini-batch discrimination:** This technique introduces a mechanism that allows the discriminator to look at multiple data examples in combination, thus being able to tell if the generator is collapsing all samples to the same point.

2. **Unrolled GANs:** In this approach, the generator's objective is defined with respect to the parameters of an unrolled optimization of the discriminator. By including future steps of the discriminator in the generator's objective, the generator can avoid changes that would make the discriminator better in the future.

3. **Wasserstein GANs (WGANs):** The Wasserstein GAN uses a different approach to measure the distance between the real and generated distributions. This change in the loss function has been shown to mitigate the problem of mode collapse.

4. **Gradient penalty:** WGANs with a gradient penalty (WGAN-GP) further improve stability by enforcing a Lipschitz constraint via a penalty term in the discriminator's objective function.

5. **Feature matching:** In this approach, the generator is tasked to match the expected features on an intermediate layer of the discriminator. This way, instead of directly fooling the discriminator, the generator is forced to produce samples that have similar features as real ones.

These are just some of the many solutions researchers have proposed to alleviate the mode collapse problem. Please note that training GANs and specifically managing mode collapse remains an active area of research.

9.8.2 Lack of Diversity

Lack of diversity, or mode collapse, is a common issue when training cGANs. This happens when the generator produces the same or similar outputs regardless of changes in the input noise vector and the conditional input. This lack of diversity in the generated samples greatly reduces the utility of the model, as it is unable to cover the broad range of data that should be possible given the different conditional inputs.

Solutions:

1. **Conditional Variational Autoencoder-GAN (CVAE-GAN):** This model integrates a Variational Autoencoder (VAE) with a cGAN. The CVAE part of the model ensures high diversity by forcing the generated samples to follow a predefined distribution (usually a Gaussian), while the cGAN part ensures the quality of the generated samples.

2. **Mixup training technique:** In this approach, during training, two different latent vectors and the corresponding labels are mixed together before being fed into the generator. This encourages the generator to create diverse outputs, even for similar inputs.

3. **Mode seeking regularization:** This technique applies a regularization term to the generator's loss function to encourage it to generate diverse outputs. The regularization term encourages the generator to map different noise vectors to different outputs, increasing the diversity of the generated samples.

4. **Auxiliary Classifier GAN (ACGAN):** ACGAN is a variant of cGAN where the discriminator is also tasked with classifying the generated images. This provides an additional signal to the generator, helping it to generate more diverse samples.

5. **Ensemble learning:** This involves training multiple cGANs with different architectures and then using all of them to generate samples. This can lead to greater diversity in the generated samples.

6. **PACGAN (Packing two or more samples into a tensor):** PACGAN fights mode collapse by modifying the discriminator to take in two or more samples at once, allowing it to discern when the generator produces multiple similar outputs.

All these techniques aim to encourage the generator to explore more modes of data distribution and increase the diversity of its outputs. Still, achieving diversity while maintaining high sample quality remains a significant challenge in training cGANs.

9.8.3 Difficulty in Training

Training cGANs can indeed be challenging, due to reasons similar to those for standard GANs. These challenges include balancing the generator and discriminator during training, mode collapse, and vanishing gradients.

Solutions:

1. **Improved training techniques:** Techniques, such as WGAN and WGAN-GP, help improve the training stability of cGANs. They modify the objective function of the GAN to create a more stable and balanced training process.

2. **Better initialization and normalization:** Methods like Batch Normalization, Layer Normalization, and Spectral Normalization can be used to stabilize the learning dynamics and speed up convergence.

3. **Label smoothing:** Instead of using hard labels (0 and 1), we can use soft labels (values close to 0 and 1) to help with the discriminator's overconfidence, which can lead to more stable training.

4. **Feature matching:** Instead of directly comparing the generated samples and the real samples, compare their statistics (like means and variances) in the discriminator's feature space.

5. **Use of auxiliary classifiers:** The Auxiliary Classifier GAN (ACGAN) is an extension of the cGAN, which includes an auxiliary classifier to aid in the learning process. The auxiliary classifier helps the generator to produce samples that are not only visually realistic but also accurately meet the conditional requirements.

6. **Mini-batch discrimination:** This technique enables the discriminator to look at multiple examples in combination, rather than in isolation, which helps it to avoid being fooled by the generator and improves the overall stability of the training process.

7. **Progressive growing of GANs:** This involves starting training with lower-resolution images and then progressively adding layers to increase the resolution over time. This technique can lead to improved training stability and output quality.

8. **Two-Timescale Update Rule (TTUR):** This technique involves using different learning rates for the generator and the discriminator, which can help to balance their training.

9. **Using different loss functions:** Different types of loss functions, such as hinge loss or Least Squares loss, can be employed to improve the training of the GAN.

Despite these solutions, training cGANs remains a non-trivial task, and finding the right strategy often involves a fair amount of experimentation and tweaking.

9.8.4 Sensitivity to Input Noise

In cGANs, sensitivity to input noise is a commonly encountered issue. This issue arises because the generator of a cGAN receives both a random noise vector and some conditional input. The random noise is intended to enable the generator to produce diverse outputs given the same conditional input, but if the generator becomes too sensitive to this noise, it can lead to unpredictable and low-quality results.

Solutions:

1. **Noise regularization:** This technique involves adding a regularization term to the loss function that encourages the generator to be less sensitive to small changes in the input noise. This can help ensure that similar noise vectors produce similar outputs.

2. **Noise injection:** This involves adding noise not just at the input layer but also at various points within the generator network. This can help the generator learn to treat noise as a source of diversity rather than something to be overly sensitive to.

3. **Consistency regularization:** This technique encourages the generator to produce similar outputs for similar inputs. It involves computing the generator's loss for multiple noise vectors that are close to each other and encouraging the corresponding outputs to also be close to each other.

4. **Adversarial training of the generator:** This involves using a second discriminator to specifically target the generator's sensitivity to noise. The second discriminator is trained to distinguish between real and generated samples that are produced using similar but not identical noise vectors. The generator is then trained to fool this second discriminator.

5. **Controlled input noise:** Instead of using completely random noise vectors, you can use noise vectors that follow a certain structure or distribution. For example, you could use noise vectors that lie along a manifold in the noise space or noise vectors that are produced by a separate generative model. This can give you more control over the diversity of the generator's outputs and reduce its sensitivity to noise.

6. **Gradual noise reduction:** This involves starting the training process with a high level of noise and then gradually reducing the noise level as training progresses. This can help the generator learn to produce high-quality outputs even when the input noise is minimal.

As with all GAN training issues, it's important to keep in mind that the effectiveness of these solutions can depend heavily on the specific application and dataset.

9.8.5 Overfitting

Overfitting in cGANs is a common problem where the generator learns to produce outputs that are too similar to the training data and fails to generalize well to new inputs. This could result in a lack of diversity in generated samples and an inability to generate realistic samples for unseen conditional inputs.

Solutions:

1. **Regularization:** Techniques like dropout, weight decay (L_2 regularization), and batch normalization can be used to reduce overfitting. Regularization techniques apply constraints to the learning algorithm, which discourages learning overly complex models, thereby improving the model's ability to generalize.

2. **Data augmentation:** This involves creating new training samples by applying transformations (such as rotation, scaling, or cropping) to the existing data. This can effectively increase the size of the training data and help the model generalize better.

3. **Early stopping:** This technique involves monitoring the model's performance on a validation set during training and stopping training when the performance starts to degrade. This helps prevent the model from fitting too closely to the training data.

4. **Noise injection:** Adding noise to the inputs or the outputs of the generator can help to prevent overfitting. This forces the generator to learn to produce realistic outputs despite the presence of noise, which can improve its ability to generalize.

5. **Use of a validation set:** Just like in traditional machine learning tasks, using a validation set to tune hyperparameters and make decisions about the model architecture can help to prevent overfitting.

6. **Use of larger datasets:** The larger the dataset, the less likely the model is to overfit. If possible, using a larger and more diverse dataset can be beneficial.

7. **Training with more diverse conditions:** In the case of cGANs, providing a wider range of conditions during training can help the generator learn to generalize better. This can mean using a more diverse set of labels or data for the conditioning input.

Remember that overfitting is a common challenge in machine learning, and it's important to monitor for signs of overfitting during model training and evaluation.

By addressing these issues, you can improve the performance of cGANs and make them more effective in a range of applications.

9.9 cGAN Implementation Tips

Here are some implementation tips for cGAN.

9.9.1 Choose Appropriate Dataset

Choose the dataset that is suitable for your cGAN application. Make sure that the dataset has enough diversity to generate a wide range of images.

9.9.2 Use One-hot Encoding

Use one-hot encoding to encode the class labels of the conditional input. This will help in better representation of the conditional input and improve the quality of generated images.

9.9.3 Normalize Inputs

Normalize the input data before feeding it into the cGAN. This will help in better convergence and prevent the generator from generating unrealistic images.

9.9.4 Use Convolutional Layers

Use convolutional layers in both the generator and discriminator. This will help in capturing the spatial features of the images and improve the quality of generated images.

9.9.5 Use Batch Normalization

Use batch normalization in both the generator and discriminator. This will help in better convergence and prevent the generator from generating mode collapse.

9.9.6 Use Appropriate Loss Functions

Use appropriate loss functions, such as binary cross-entropy loss for the discriminator and adversarial loss for the generator.

9.9.7 Use Appropriate Hyperparameters

Use appropriate learning rate, batch size, and number of epochs. These hyperparameters can greatly affect the performance of the cGAN.

9.9.8 Monitor the Training Process

Monitor the training process and keep track of the generator and discriminator losses. This will help in determining when to stop the training and prevent overfitting.

9.9.9 Experiment with Different Architectures

Experiment with different architectures for both the generator and discriminator. This can greatly affect the performance of the cGAN and lead to better quality generated images.

9.9.10 Evaluate the Generated Images

Evaluate the quality of the generated images using appropriate metrics, such as inception score or FID score. This will help in determining the performance of the cGAN and can guide further improvements.

Remember, hands-on experience is key when working with cGANs or any other machine learning models. Therefore, consistently practicing implementation and troubleshooting is crucial for mastering these concepts.

9.10 Lessons Learned

- Learn cGAN architecture, its parts, and how it works.
- Learn cGAN implementation for Fashion dataset.
- Learn CDCGAN as a GAN variant with all the characteristics of the conditional DCGAN.
- Learn Pix2Pix as an image-to-image translation with a conditional GAN.
- Learn cGAN applications.
- Learn Implement an example for Pix2Pix.
- Learn cGAN issues.
- Learn cGAN implementation tips.

9.11 Problems

9.11.1 What is the difference between a conditional GAN and an unconditional GAN?

9.11.2 How do you define the conditional variable in a cGAN?

9.11.3 Can cGANs be used for image-to-image translation tasks? If so, how?

9.11.4 What is label smoothing, and how is it used in cGANs?

9.11.5 How can the mode collapse issue be addressed in cGANs?

9.11.6 Can cGANs be used for text generation tasks? If so, how?

9.11.7 How does the generator in a cGAN make use of the conditional information?

9.11.8 How can overfitting be prevented in cGANs?

9.11.9 What are some advantages of using cGANs over other types of GANs?

9.11.10 How can cGANs be used for data augmentation in a classification task?

9.11.11 What is the role of the discriminator in a cGAN?

9.11.12 What is the difference between a one-hot encoding and a soft encoding in the context of cGANs?

9.11.13 How can the quality of the generated samples be evaluated in a cGAN?

9.11.14 How can the performance of a cGAN be improved by using pre-trained models?

9.11.15 What is the role of batch normalization in cGANs?

9.11.16 Can cGANs be used for style transfer tasks? If so, how?

9.11.17 What is the impact of the choice of loss function on the performance of a cGAN?

9.11.18 How can the learning rate be adjusted to optimize the performance of a cGAN?

9.11.19 Can cGANs be used for speech generation tasks? If so, how?

9.11.20 How can the use of regularization techniques improve the performance of a cGAN?

9.12 Programming Questions

- **Easy**

    9.12.1 Implement a cGAN for generating images of handwritten digits conditioned on their corresponding labels.

    9.12.2 Train a cGAN to generate images of different types of clothes (e.g., shirts, pants, shoes) given their corresponding labels.

    9.12.3 Use a cGAN to generate realistic images of faces conditioned on attributes, such as age, gender, and hair color.

    9.12.4 Train a cGAN to generate realistic images of animals conditioned on their species labels.

    9.12.5 How do you define the conditioning variable in a cGAN?

    9.12.6 What is the role of the generator in a cGAN?

    9.12.7 What is the role of the discriminator in a cGAN?

    9.12.8 How do you combine the conditioning variable and the noise input in the generator?

- **Medium**

    9.12.9 Implement a cGAN for generating musical notes conditioned on their corresponding labels or genres.

    9.12.10 Train a cGAN to generate realistic images of different types of food conditioned on their recipe or cuisine labels.

    9.12.11 Use a cGAN to generate realistic images of furniture items conditioned on their type labels (e.g., chairs, tables, sofas).

    9.12.12 How do you choose the conditioning variable for a given task in a cGAN?

    9.12.13 How do you choose the size of the conditioning variable for a given task in a cGAN?

    9.12.14 How do you preprocess the conditioning variable before feeding it to the generator and discriminator?

9.12.15 How do you train a cGAN with a batch size larger than one?

9.12.16 How do you evaluate the performance of a cGAN on a given task?

- **Hard**

  9.12.17 Implement a cGAN for generating images of cars conditioned on their brand or model labels.

  9.12.18 Train a cGAN to generate realistic images of different types of plants conditioned on their species or habitat labels.

  9.12.19 Use a cGAN to generate realistic images of buildings conditioned on their architectural style or location labels.

  9.12.20 How do you use a pre-trained cGAN for generating new samples on a new dataset?

  9.12.21 How do you design the architecture of a cGAN for a complex multi-modal dataset?

  9.12.22 How do you apply transfer learning to a pre-trained cGAN for a related task?

  9.12.23 How do you handle class imbalance in the conditioning variable in a cGAN?

  9.12.24 How do you add regularization to a cGAN to prevent overfitting?

10

Cycle Generative Adversarial Network (CycleGAN)

The following topics are covered in this chapter about Cycle Generative Adversarial Network (CycleGAN):

- CycleGANs
- CycleGANs Applications
- CycleGAN Implementation Using TensorFlow
- CycleGAN Implementation Tips
- CycleGAN Issues

10.1 Preface

CycleGAN is a technique used for training models to translate from one domain to another without the need for paired examples. The models are trained using samples from both the source and target domains, which can be unrelated. To enhance the stability of the generator models and guide the process of sample generation, cycle consistency is incorporated into the CycleGAN architecture. This consistency ensures that a sample generated by the first generator is fed into the second generator and vice versa. CycleGAN is a type of GAN that allows unsupervised learning of image-to-image translation models, making it a powerful tool for various applications, such as style transfer, image colorization, and domain adaptation. CycleGAN doesn't require paired training data, and it learns to translate images from one domain to another through cycle consistency loss. This ensures that the translated images stay close to the original images in the source domain while also maintaining consistency in both directions. CycleGAN has been used in various applications, including artistic style transfer, image-to-image translation, voice conversion, and domain adaptation. It has also been utilized for text-to-image synthesis. The general architecture of CycleGAN consists of two parts, each with two generators and two discriminators. Its potential for creative expression and problem-solving is vast, and its applications are numerous. In this chapter, we will review the architecture and applications of CycleGAN and engage in practical programming exercises to learn how to use CycleGAN.

10.2 CycleGANs

Image-to-image translation challenges aim to find a mapping between input and output images using a training set of pre-aligned image pairs. Traditionally, creating an image-to-image translation model necessitated a training set of paired instances. That is, numerous

DOI: 10.1201/9781003281344-10

instances of an input image **X** (such as summer landscapes) and the corresponding image with the desired change that could serve as the expected output image **Y** (for instance, winter landscapes) would be used. However, for many tasks, paired training data are not available, and typically, a significant number of paired samples are needed when training a model for image-to-image translation. The need for a paired training dataset is one of the limitations, as compiling these databases is a challenging and time-consuming task. Some of these datasets are difficult, expensive, or even impossible to create. For instance, capturing photographs of artworks created by deceased artists or taking photos under different settings and lighting conditions can be challenging. Moreover, often, datasets simply do not exist, especially in the case of great paintings. As a result, people seek alternative training methods when they aim to train an image-to-image translation system without using paired samples. CycleGAN is a training model technique proven effective for unpaired image-to-image translation. One of the most intriguing aspects of CycleGAN is that it can be trained without paired data, and the training in the first version of the publication was done with unpaired data. CycleGAN is based on the GAN architecture, which has been extended, and the training is done on two generator models and two discriminator models simultaneously. One generator's output is used to generate images for another domain, while the other generator's output is used to generate images for the first domain. Both generators use images from their respective domains. Then, discriminator models are used to determine the likelihood that the images truly represent something that exists, and the generator models are accordingly adjusted. This extension may be sufficient on its own to generate realistic images in each domain; however, it is not enough to generate translations of the provided input images. CycleGAN promotes cycle consistency by introducing a new loss that computes the difference between the second generator's output and the original image and vice versa. This loss also computes the difference between the first generator's output and the original image. This enhances the stability of the generator models and directs the process of producing images in the new domain toward image translation. This also makes the image-creation process more efficient. For example, if we need to swap photos from summer to winter and vice versa, which present very different scenery, CycleGAN can be used.

- **Collection 1**: Photos of summer landscapes.
- **Collection 2**: Photos of winter landscapes.

The architecture will consist of two GANs, each with its own discriminator and generator models, resulting in a total of four models. The first GAN will be responsible for converting summer images into winter images, while the second GAN will perform the opposite task of converting winter images into summer images.

- **GAN 1**: Translates photos from collection 1 (summer images) to collection 2 (winter images).
- **GAN 2**: Translates photos from collection 2 (winter images) to collection 1 (summer images).

Figure 10.1 illustrates the distinction between paired and unpaired training data. In the paired setup, training examples $\{x_i, y_i\}$ exist where a direct correspondence between x_i and y_i is evident. On the other hand, unpaired images originate from different scenes, resulting in pairs X and Y that are distinct from each other. The general design of a Cycle GAN

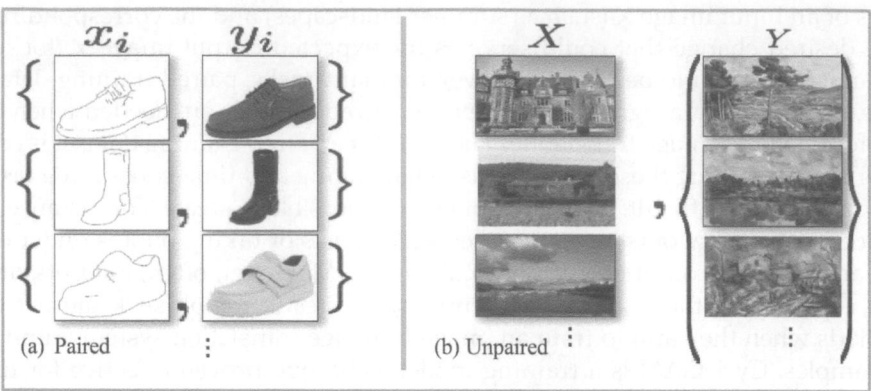

FIGURE 10.1
(a) Paired training data consists of training examples {x_i, y_i}, where the correspondence between x_i and y_i exists.
(b) Unpaired images are from different scenes. The pair X and Y are different.

can be divided into three main parts. The first part is the generator models, which are conditional models that generate a new image based on the input image. The second part is the discriminator models, which determine the likelihood that the generated image came from the target image collection. Both the generator and discriminator models are trained using adversarial loss, similar to traditional GAN models. However, these models alone are not enough to translate the input image to the target domain. To achieve this, cycle consistency loss is introduced, which compares the input image with the output image produced by the Cycle GAN using methods like the L_1 norm or the sum of absolute differences in pixel values. There are two GANs used in the Cycle GAN architecture to calculate cycle consistency loss and update the generator models with each new round of training. For instance, GAN 1 takes a photo of a summer scene and converts it into a winter landscape. The resulting image is passed through GAN 2, which transforms it back to a summer landscape image. The difference in appearance between the input image and the output image from GAN 2 is used to modify the generator models to minimize the appearance difference. The same procedure is repeated in reverse to achieve a backward cycle consistency loss from generator 2 to generator 1 and to compare the original winter image with the generated photo.

1. In the translation process, we need two generators (G_1 and G_2) and two discriminators (D_x and D_y). The generator G_1 will be translated from **X** to **Y**, and the G_2 will do it from **Y** to **X**. Also, discriminator D_y will check the output of the G_1, and D_x will check the output of the G_2. Figure 10.2 shows these processes. It elucidates the fundamental architecture of CycleGAN, focusing on its dual mapping functions: G_1: X → Y and G_2: Y → X. These generators are responsible for translating images from domain X to Y and vice versa. Complementing these generators are the adversarial discriminators D_Y and D_X. While D_Y attempts to discern between real images from domain Y and fake images generated by G_1, D_X differentiates between genuine images from domain X and those produced by G_2. The interplay between these components is crucial for the model to master the domain translation without the need for paired training sample.

2. CycleGAN reconstructs the estimation of **X** as **X**^ using G_2 from the **Y** as **Y**^ that is evaluated by **X** using G_1. Figure 10.3 offers a visual insight into the forward cycle-consistency mechanism within CycleGAN. Starting with an image x from

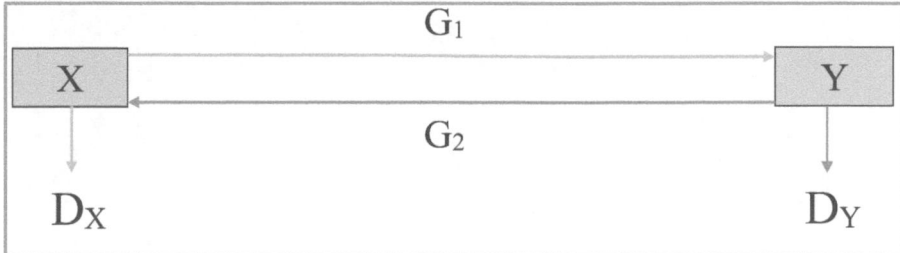

FIGURE 10.2
The mapping functions, G_1: $X \rightarrow Y$ and G_2: $Y \rightarrow X$, and their adversarial discriminators D_Y and D_X.

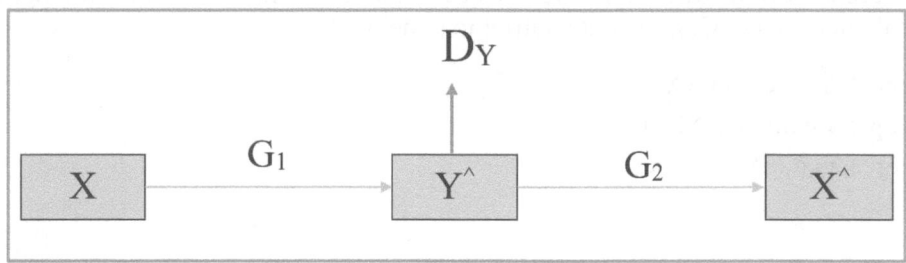

FIGURE 10.3
Forward cycle-consistency loss: $x \rightarrow G_1(x) \rightarrow G_2(G_1(x)) \approx x$.

domain X, the generator G_1 is applied, producing a translated image Y^. This translated image is then further processed by the second generator G_2, aiming to reconstruct the original image x. The underlying principle is to ensure the translated and then retranslated image $G_2(G_1(x))$ is consistent with the original, hence the term "cycle-consistency". Alongside this process, the discriminator D_Y evaluates the authenticity of the translated image Y^, determining how well it resembles genuine images from domain Y. This combination of transformations and evaluations facilitates the model's capability to maintain consistent and meaningful translations between domains. Now the G_2, the second generator, goes over the first output and gives the X^.

Step 1: $X \rightarrow G_1(X) = Y^$
Step 2: Evaluate Y^ by D_Y
Step 3: $G_2(G_1(X)) = G_2(Y^) = X^ \approx X$

3. It also reconstructs the estimation of **Y** as **Y^** using G_1 from the estimated **X** as **X^** using G_2, which **Y** evaluates. Figure 10.4 visually portrays the backward cycle-consistency process within CycleGAN. Beginning with an image **y** from domain **Y**, it undergoes transformation by the generator $\mathbf{G_2}$, yielding a translated image in domain X. To validate the consistency of this translation, the translated image is further passed through the generator $\mathbf{G_1}$, attempting to revert it back to the original image **y**. The overarching aim is to ensure that the image translated to domain X and subsequently retranslated back to domain **Y** (as $\mathbf{G_1(G_2(y))}$) remains congruent with the initial image. This backward cycle-consistency ensures that the translations between the domains are not just unidirectional but are meaningful and

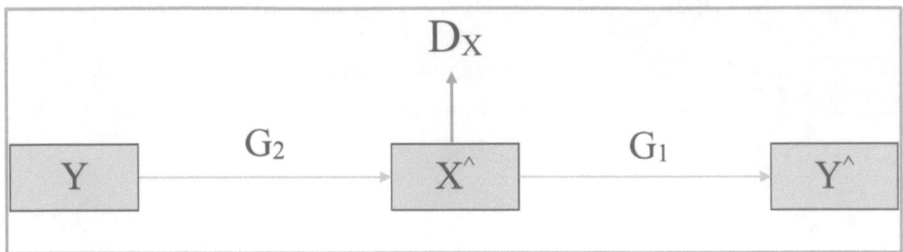

FIGURE 10.4
Backward cycle-consistency loss: $y \rightarrow G_2(y) \rightarrow G_1(G_2(y)) \approx y$.

coherent in both directions. G2 goes over the **Y**, giving **X^**, and then it will be evaluated by D_X. G_1 goes to its output to generate the **Y^**.

Step 1: $Y \rightarrow G_2(Y) = X^{\wedge}$
Step 2: Evaluate $X^{\wedge}$ by D_X
Step 3: $G_1(G_2(Y)) = G_1(X^{\wedge}) = Y^{\wedge} \approx Y$

10.3 CycleGANs Applications

CycleGAN has been deployed in various contexts, including style transfer, object transformation, season translation, photograph generation from paintings, and photo enhancement. During the style transfer process, the network converts data, which could be any photograph, into other artworks, such as a Van Gogh painting. The process by which a network changes the class of an object from one to another is referred to as object transfiguration. Here we review some of these applications.

10.3.1 Artistic Style Transfer

CycleGAN can be used to transfer the style of an artist from one image to another. This has applications in the fields of art and design.

10.3.2 Image-to-image Translation

CycleGAN can be used to translate images from one domain to another. For example, it can be used to translate images of horses to images of zebras.

10.3.3 Medical Image Analysis

CycleGAN can be used to translate images from one modality to another. This has applications in medical image analysis, where images from one modality can be translated to another to aid in diagnosis.

10.3.4 Video Stabilization

CycleGAN can be used to stabilize videos by translating frames from one domain to another.

10.3.5 Virtual Try-on

CycleGAN can be used to generate images of people wearing clothes that they haven't actually worn. This has applications in the fashion industry.

10.3.6 Colorization

CycleGAN can be used to colorize black and white images by translating them to color images.

10.3.7 3D Shape Synthesis

CycleGAN can be used to generate 3D shapes from 2D images.

10.3.8 Domain Adaptation

CycleGAN can be used to adapt models trained on one dataset to perform well on another dataset.

Overall, CycleGAN has the potential to revolutionize many fields by providing a simple yet effective way to translate images from one domain to another without the need for paired training data. Here are some other main applications presented in some reference research papers.

10.3.9 Style Transfer

The process by which an artist modifies the artistic qualities of one work of art, such as a painting, to another form, such as a photograph, is referred to as "style transfer". Many artists' styles, such as those of Monet, Van Gogh, Cezanne, and Ukiyo-e, have been applied to landscape photographs to demonstrate how CycleGAN works. Figure 10.5 shows how the style transfer transforms the input image (on the left) into a different artist's style (on the right).

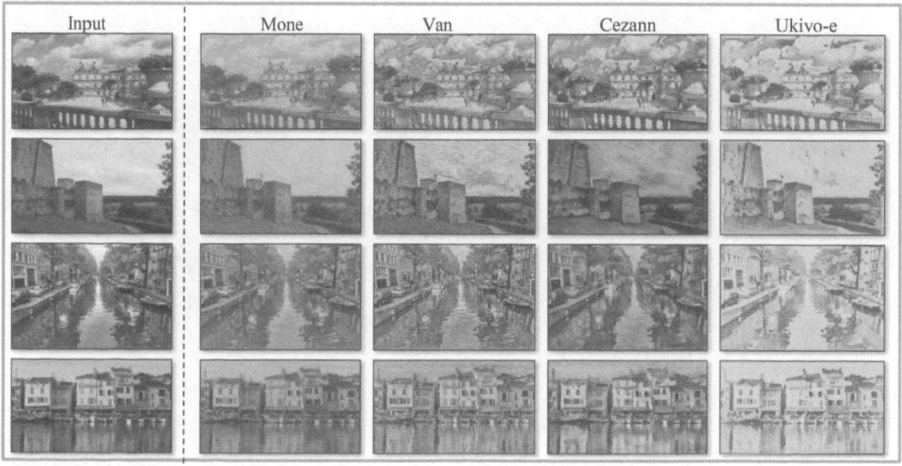

FIGURE 10.5
Collection style transfer I: we transfer input images into the artistic styles of Monet, Van Gogh, Cezanne, and Ukiyo-e.

FIGURE 10.6
These images show results on object transfiguration between horses and zebras, trained on 939 images from the wild horse class and 1177 images from the zebra class in ImageNet.

10.3.10 Object Transfiguration

When an object transforms from one class to another, such as a dog transforming into a cat, it is referred to as "object transfiguration". CycleGAN demonstrates this concept by transforming images of horses into zebras and then reversing the process to show how zebras can be transformed into images of horses. The only distinguishing feature between horses and zebras is their coat color; otherwise, they are physically identical. Figure 10.6 shows these transformations in different poses from horses to zebras (first row) and zebras to horses (second row).

It is also demonstrated how to use CycleGAN to transform apples into oranges (first row) and oranges into apples (second row). This makes perfect sense because apples and oranges are the same size and shape. Figure 10.7 showcases the results of training method on a dataset comprising 996 apple images and 1020 navel orange images sourced from ImageNet.

FIGURE 10.7
We train our method on 996 apple images and 1020 navel orange images from ImageNet.

FIGURE 10.8
Results on season transfer, training in winter and summer.

10.3.11 Season Transfer

The process of transforming a photograph taken during one season, such as summer, to make it appear as though it was taken during another season, such as winter, is known as "season transfer". CycleGAN is demonstrated by cycling through photographs of winter landscapes, summer landscapes, and back-to-winter landscapes. Figure 10.8 illustrates these processes.

10.3.12 Photograph Generation from Paintings

The technique of creating photorealistic photographs from a painting, which is often done by a well-known artist or illustrates a well-known setting, is known as "photograph generation from paintings". Several of Monet's paintings have been used to demonstrate how CycleGAN works by photographing them and converting them into digital images. Figure 10.9 displays – from left to right: the input image – results from Gatys et al. when utilizing two distinct representative artworks as style images; outcomes from Gatys et al. when applying the entire artist's collection; and finally, the result using CycleGAN.

FIGURE 10.9
Left to right: input image results from Gatys et al. using two different representative artworks as style images result from Gatys et al. using the entire collection of the artist and CycleGAN.

FIGURE 10.10
Photo enhancement: The system often learns to produce shallow focus by mapping from a set of smartphone snaps to professional DSLR photographs.

10.3.13 Photograph Enhancement

CycleGAN can also be used to enhance photographs by making changes to them that result in an improvement. For example, it can increase the depth of field in close-up shots of flowers to create a macro effect. Figure 10.10 showcases photo enhancement techniques. Notably, the system frequently learns to generate images with a shallow focus by transforming a collection of smartphone snapshots into images resembling those taken with a professional DSLR camera.

10.4 CycleGAN Implementation Using TensorFlow

In this section, let us implement CyclegGAN for horse and zebra examples.

10.4.1 Import Libraries and Setup

In this step, as in previous examples, we import libraries and set some parameters. We use the Pix2Pix library from TensorFlow examples. If you want to try this code, make sure to change the path of the data set for loading data. I encourage you to experiment with different parameters, such as buffer size and batch size, to see how they affect the network's performance, including its accuracy and speed.

```
import tensorflow as tf
import tensorflow_datasets as tfds
from tensorflow_examples.models.pix2pix import pix2pix
import os
import time
import matplotlib.pyplot as plt
from IPython.display import clear_output
AUTOTUNE = tf.data.AUTOTUNE
dataset, metadata = tfds.load('cycle_gan/horse2zebra',with_info=True,
as_supervised=True)
train_horses1, train_zebras1 = dataset['trainA'], dataset['trainB']
test_horses, test_zebras = dataset['testA'], dataset['testB']
BUFFER_SIZE = 2000
BATCH_SIZE = 1
IMG_WIDTH = 256
IMG_HEIGHT = 256
```

Here's an explanation of each line of code:

```
#The `import` statements import the necessary packages for building a
CycleGAN model using TensorFlow, accessing operating system
functionality, timing the model training, visualizing the generated
images, and clearing the output before displaying the new output.
import tensorflow as tf
import tensorflow_datasets as tfds
from tensorflow_examples.models.pix2pix import pix2pix
import os
import time
import matplotlib.pyplot as plt
from IPython.display import clear_output

#This line sets the `AUTOTUNE` constant to `tf.data.AUTOTUNE`, which
allows TensorFlow to automatically tune the data pipeline's parameters
for optimal performance.
AUTOTUNE = tf.data.AUTOTUNE

#This line loads the Horse-to-Zebra dataset from TensorFlow Datasets and
assigns it to `dataset`. The `metadata` variable retrieves information
about the dataset, including the number of training and testing examples.
dataset, metadata = tfds.load('cycle_gan/horse2zebra',with_info=True,
as_supervised=True)

#These lines unpack the `dataset` dictionary and retrieve the `trainA`,
`trainB`, `testA`, and `testB` splits of the Horse-to-Zebra dataset and
assigns them to their respective variables.
train_horses1, train_zebras1 = dataset['trainA'], dataset['trainB']
test_horses, test_zebras = dataset['testA'], dataset['testB']

#These lines set hyperparameters for the model. `BUFFER_SIZE` is the
number of elements from the dataset to buffer during shuffling. `BATCH_
SIZE` is the number of images to process in each batch. `IMG_WIDTH` and
`IMG_HEIGHT` are the size of the input and output images for the model.
BUFFER_SIZE = 2000
BATCH_SIZE = 1
IMG_WIDTH = 256
IMG_HEIGHT = 256
```

10.4.2 Import and Reuse the Pix2Pix Models

Using the Pix2Pix module, you can now locate the generator and discriminator and generate the first set of images. There are two discriminators (X and Y) and two generators (G_1 and G_2). Figure 10.11 represents the first set of samples generated. This code block is a continuation of the previous block of code, which defines two generators and two discriminators using the Pix2Pix model from TensorFlow examples. It generates Horse-to-Zebra and Zebra-to-Horse images using the generators and displays them using "matplotlib".

```
OUTPUT_CHANNELS = 4
generator_g1 = pix2pix.unet_generator(OUTPUT_CHANNELS,
norm_type='instancenorm')
generator_g2 = pix2pix.unet_generator(OUTPUT_CHANNELS,
norm_type='instancenorm')
d_x = pix2pix.discriminator(norm_type='instancenorm', target=False)
d_y = pix2pix.discriminator(norm_type='instancenorm', target=False)
```

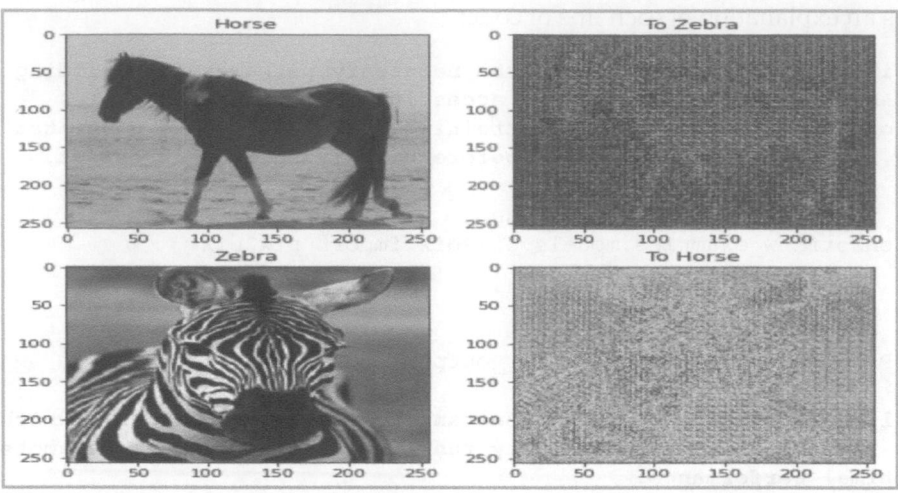

FIGURE 10.11
The first generated samples.

```
horse_to_zebra  = generator_g1(horse)
zebra_to_horse  = generator_g2(zebra)
plt.figure(figsize=(8, 8))
contrast = 8
imgs1 = [horse, horse_to_zebra,  zebra, zebra_to_horse ]
title = ['Horse', 'Horse_To Zebra', 'Zebra', 'Zebra_To Horse']
for i in range(len(imgs1)):
  plt.subplot(2, 2, i+1)
  plt.title(title[i])
  if i % 2 == 0:
    plt.imshow(imgs1[i][0] * 0.5 + 0.5)
  else:
    plt.imshow(imgs1[i][0] * 0.5 * contrast + 0.5)
plt.show()
```

Here are the details of the codes:

```
#These lines define two generators and two discriminators using the
Pix2Pix model from TensorFlow examples. `OUTPUT_CHANNELS` is set to 4,
which represents the number of channels in the output images. `generator_
g1` and `generator_g2` are two instances of the UNet generator, which is
a commonly used generator architecture for image-to-image translation.
`d_x` and `d_y` are the discriminators for the Horse-to-Zebra and Zebra-
to-Horse translation, respectively.
generator_g1 = pix2pix.unet_generator(OUTPUT_CHANNELS,
norm_type='instancenorm')
generator_g2 = pix2pix.unet_generator(OUTPUT_CHANNELS,
norm_type='instancenorm')
d_x = pix2pix.discriminator(norm_type='instancenorm', target=False)
d_y = pix2pix.discriminator(norm_type='instancenorm', target=False)
```

```
#These lines generate the Horse-to-Zebra and Zebra-to-Horse images using
the two generators. `horse_to_zebra` is generated by passing a `horse`
image through `generator_g1`. Similarly, `zebra_to_horse` is generated by
passing a `zebra` image through `generator_g2`.
horse_to_zebra  = generator_g1(horse)
zebra_to_horse  = generator_g2(zebra)

#This line creates a new figure with a size of 8x8 inches using
`matplotlib.pyplot.figure()`.
plt.figure(figsize=(8, 8))

#This line sets the `contrast` variable to 8, which is used to enhance
the contrast in the generated images.
contrast = 8

#This line creates a list `imgs1` containing the four images that will be
displayed in the figure: the original `horse` image, the Horse-to-Zebra
translation `horse_to_zebra`, the original `zebra` image, and the Zebra-
to-Horse translation `zebra_to_horse`.
imgs1 = [horse, horse_to_zebra,  zebra, zebra_to_horse ]

#This line creates a list `title` containing the titles for each of the
four images.
title = ['Horse', 'Horse_To Zebra', 'Zebra', 'Zebra_To Horse']

#This `for` loop plots each image in `imgs1`. Inside the loop, `plt.
subplot(2, 2, i+1)` creates a 2x2 grid of subplots and selects the
`i+1`th subplot to plot the current image. `plt.title(title[i])` sets the
title of the current subplot using the corresponding title from `title`.
The `if` statement applies contrast enhancement to the translated images
by multiplying the pixel values by `contrast` before adding 0.5 to each
pixel value and displaying the image using `plt.imshow()`. Finally, `plt.
show()`
for i in range(len(imgs1)):
  plt.subplot(2, 2, i+1)
  plt.title(title[i])
  if i % 2 == 0:
    plt.imshow(imgs1[i][0] * 0.5 + 0.5)
  else:
    plt.imshow(imgs1[i][0] * 0.5 * contrast + 0.5)
plt.show()
```

Check out Figure 10.12 for the discriminator's (Y and X) outputs. Can you see the zebra in these two images? It should be better in the next iterations. This code block plots the output of the two discriminators on the original "horse" and "zebra" images.

```
plt.figure(figsize=(8, 8))
plt.subplot(121)
plt.title('Is a real zebra?')
plt.imshow(d_y(zebra)[0, ..., -1], cmap='RdBu_r')
plt.subplot(122)
plt.title('Is a real horse?')
plt.imshow(d_x(horse)[0, ..., -1], cmap='RdBu_r')
plt.show()
```

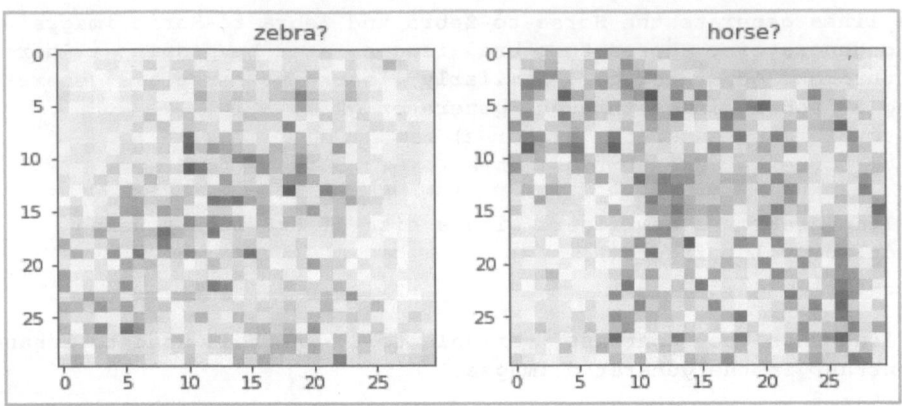

FIGURE 10.12
Discriminator data sample.

Here are the details of the codes:

```
#This line creates a new figure with a size of 8x8 inches using
`matplotlib.pyplot.figure()`.
plt.figure(figsize=(8, 8))
```

```
#This code block creates a subplot on the left side of the figure using
`plt.subplot(121)`. `plt.title('Is a real zebra?')` sets the title of the
subplot to "Is a real zebra?" using `plt.title()`. `plt.imshow(d_y(zebra)
[0, ..., -1], cmap='RdBu_r')` displays the output of the Zebra-to-Horse
discriminator on the original `zebra` image by passing it through `d_y`
and displaying the last channel of the output using the `RdBu_r`
colormap.
plt.subplot(121)
plt.title('Is a real zebra?')
plt.imshow(d_y(zebra)[0, ..., -1], cmap='RdBu_r')
```

```
#This code block creates a subplot on the right side of the figure using
`plt.subplot(122)`. `plt.title('Is a real horse?')` sets the title of the
subplot to "Is a real horse?" using `plt.title()`. `plt.imshow(d_x(horse)
[0, ..., -1], cmap='RdBu_r')` displays the output of the Horse-to-Zebra
discriminator on the original `horse` image by passing it through `d_x`
and displaying the last channel of the output using the `RdBu_r`
colormap.
plt.subplot(122)
plt.title('Is a real horse?')
plt.imshow(d_x(horse)[0, ..., -1], cmap='RdBu_r')
```

```
#This line displays the entire figure using `plt.show()`.
plt.show()
```

10.4.3 Loss Functions

This code block defines several loss functions and optimizers for training the CycleGAN model. First, the discriminator and generator loss functions are defined, and then the loss values are calculated and identified. The Adam optimizer is used to find the optimal parameters for generators G_1 and G_2, as well as for discriminators X and Y.

```
LAMBDA = 100
loss_object = tf.keras.losses.BinaryCrossentropy(from_logits=True)
def discriminator_loss(real_image, generated_image):
  real_loss = loss_object(tf.ones_like(real_image), real_image)
  generated_loss = loss_object(tf.zeros_like(generated_image),
generated_image)
  total_disc_loss = real_loss + generated_loss
  return total_disc_loss * 0.5
def generator_loss(generated_image):
  return loss_object(tf.ones_like(generated_image), generated_image)
def calc_cycle_loss(real_image-1, cycled_image-1):
  loss1 = tf.reduce_mean(tf.abs(real_image-1 - cycled_image-1))
  return LAMBDA * loss1
def identity_loss(real_image-1, same_image):
  loss = tf.reduce_mean(tf.abs(real_image-1 - same_image))
  return LAMBDA * 0.5 * loss
generator_g1_optimizer = tf.keras.optimizers.Adam(2e-4, beta_1=0.5)
generator_g2_optimizer = tf.keras.optimizers.Adam(2e-4, beta_1=0.5)
d_x_optimizer = tf.keras.optimizers.Adam(2e-4, beta_1=0.5)
d_y_optimizer_1 = tf.keras.optimizers.Adam(2e-4, beta_1=0.5)
```

Here are the details of the codes:

```
#This line sets the `LAMBDA` hyperparameter to 100, which is used to
weight the cycle consistency loss and identity loss during training.
LAMBDA = 100
```

```
#This line defines the binary cross-entropy loss function using `tf.
keras.losses.BinaryCrossentropy()`, which is used to calculate the
adversarial loss for the discriminators.
loss_object = tf.keras.losses.BinaryCrossentropy(from_logits=True)
```

```
#This function calculates the adversarial loss for the discriminators.
`real_loss` calculates the binary cross-entropy loss between the real
image and a tensor of ones using `loss_object`. `generated_loss`
calculates the binary cross-entropy loss between the generated image
and a tensor of zeros using `loss_object`. `total_disc_loss` calculates
the sum of the two losses, and the final output is half of the total
loss.
def discriminator_loss(real_image, generated_image):
  real_loss = loss_object(tf.ones_like(real_image), real_image)
  generated_loss = loss_object(tf.zeros_like(generated_image),
generated_image)
  total_disc_loss = real_loss + generated_loss
  return total_disc_loss * 0.5
```

```
#This function calculates the generator loss. It calculates the binary
cross-entropy loss between the generated image and a tensor of ones using
`loss_object`.
def generator_loss(generated_image):
  return loss_object(tf.ones_like(generated_image), generated_image)
```

```
#This function calculates the cycle consistency loss. It calculates the
mean absolute difference between the real image and the cycled image
using `tf.abs()`, and multiplies the result by the `LAMBDA`
hyperparameter.
def calc_cycle_loss(real_image-1, cycled_image-1):
  loss1 = tf.reduce_mean(tf.abs(real_image-1 - cycled_image-1))
  return LAMBDA * loss1
```

```
#This function calculates the identity loss. It calculates the mean
absolute difference between the real image and the same image (which
should be the real image passed through the identity generator) using
`tf.abs()`, and multiplies the result by half of the `LAMBDA`
hyperparameter.
def identity_loss(real_image-1, same_image):
  loss = tf.reduce_mean(tf.abs(real_image-1 - same_image))
  return LAMBDA * 0.5 * loss
```

```
#These lines define four different optimizers for training the
CycleGAN model. They use the Adam optimizer with a learning rate of
2e-4 and a beta1 value of 0.5. `generator_g1_optimizer` and
`generator_g2_optimizer` are the optimizers for the two generators,
`d_x_optimizer` is the optimizer for the Horse-to-Zebra discriminator,
and `d_y_optimizer_1` is the optimizer for the Zebra-to-Horse
discriminator.
generator_g1_optimizer = tf.keras.optimizers.Adam(2e-4, beta_1=0.5)
generator_g2_optimizer = tf.keras.optimizers.Adam(2e-4, beta_1=0.5)
d_x_optimizer = tf.keras.optimizers.Adam(2e-4, beta_1=0.5)
d_y_optimizer_1 = tf.keras.optimizers.Adam(2e-4, beta_1=0.5)
```

10.4.4 Checkpoints

The following code block is used to extract and save the model checkpoints during training, by calling the generators, discriminators, and their optimizers.

```
checkpoint_path = "./checkpoints/train"
ckpt_1 = tf.train.Checkpoint(generator_g1=generator_g1,
                             generator_g2=generator_g2,
                             d_x=d_x,
                             d_y=d_y,
                             generator_g1_optimizer=generator_g1_optimizer,
                             generator_g2_optimizer=generator_g2_optimizer,
                             d_x_optimizer=d_x_optimizer,
                             d_y_optimizer_1=d_y_optimizer_1)
ckpt_manager = tf.train.CheckpointManager(ckpt_1, checkpoint_path,
max_to_keep=5)
if ckpt_manager.latest_checkpoint:
  ckpt.restore(ckpt_manager.latest_checkpoint)
  print ('Latest checkpoint restored!!')
```

Here are the details of the codes:

```
#This line sets the path for saving the model checkpoints.
checkpoint_path = "./checkpoints/train"
```

```
#This line creates a new checkpoint object using `tf.train.Checkpoint()`.
It takes the generators, discriminators, and optimizers as arguments.
ckpt_1 = tf.train.Checkpoint(generator_g1=generator_g1,
                             generator_g2=generator_g2,
                             d_x=d_x,
                             d_y=d_y,
                             generator_g1_optimizer=generator_g1_optimizer,
                             generator_g2_optimizer=generator_g2_optimizer,
                             d_x_optimizer=d_x_optimizer,
                             d_y_optimizer_1=d_y_optimizer_1)

#This line creates a new checkpoint manager object using `tf.train.
CheckpointManager()`. It takes the checkpoint object, checkpoint path,
and `max_to_keep` argument (which specifies the maximum number of
checkpoints to keep) as arguments.
ckpt_manager = tf.train.CheckpointManager(ckpt_1, checkpoint_path,
max_to_keep=5)

#These lines check if there is a latest checkpoint in the checkpoint
manager, and if so, restores it using `ckpt.restore()`. It also prints a
message indicating that the latest checkpoint has been restored. This is
useful for resuming training from a previously saved checkpoint.
if ckpt_manager.latest_checkpoint:
  ckpt.restore(ckpt_manager.latest_checkpoint)
  print ('Latest checkpoint restored!!')
```

10.4.5 Training

In this section, we define the training function that will be used to train the CycleGAN model and generate new images. Figure 10.13 shows an example of a generated image after 40 iterations. The model can be trained for more iterations to produce different results.

```
EPOCHE_1 = 40
def generate_images(model, test_input1):
  prediction = model(test_input1)
        plt.figure(figsize=(12, 12))
    Display_list = [test_input1[0], prediction[0]]
  title = ['Input Image', 'Predicted Image']
```

FIGURE 10.13
Generated data after several iterations.

```
  for i in range(2):
    plt.subplot(1, 2, i+1)
    plt.title(title[i])
    plt.imshow(display_list[i] * 0.5 + 0.5)
    plt.axis('off')
  plt.show()
@tf.function
def train_step(real_x_1, real_y_1):
  with tf.GradientTape(persistent=True) as tape:
    fake_y = generator_g1(real_x_1, training=True)
    cycled_x_1 = generator_g2(fake_y, training=True)
    fake_x = generator_g2(real_y_1, training=True)
    cycled_y = generator_g1(fake_x, training=True)
    same_x = generator_g2(real_x_1, training=True)
    same_y_1 = generator_g1(real_y_1, training=True)
    disc_real_x_1 = d_x(real_x_1, training=True)
    disc_real_y_1 = d_y(real_y_1, training=True)
    disc_fake_x = d_x(fake_x, training=True)
    disc_fake_y = d_y(fake_y, training=True)
    gen_g_loss_1 = generator_loss_1(disc_fake_y)
    gen_f_loss = generator_loss_1(disc_fake_x_1)
    total_cycle_loss_1 = calc_cycle_loss(real_x_1, cycled_x_1) + calc_
cycle_loss(real_y_1, cycled_y)
    total_gen_g_loss_1 = gen_g_loss_1 + total_cycle_loss_1 + identity_
loss(real_y_1, same_y_1)
    total_gen_f_loss_1 = gen_f_loss + total_cycle_loss_1 + identity_
loss(real_x_1, same_x)
    disc_x_loss = discriminator_loss(disc_real_x_1, disc_fake_x)
    disc_y_loss = discriminator_loss(disc_real_y_1, disc_fake_y)
  generator_g1_gradients = tape.gradient(total_gen_g_loss_1,
generator_g1.trainable_variables)
  generator_g2_gradients = tape.gradient(total_gen_f_loss_1,
generator_g2.trainable_variables)
  d_x_gradients = tape.gradient(disc_x_loss, d_x.trainable_variables)
  d_y_gradients = tape.gradient(disc_y_loss, d_y.trainable_variables)
  generator_g1_optimizer.apply_gradients(zip(generator_g_gradients,
generator_g1.trainable_variables))
  generator_g2_optimizer.apply_gradients(zip(generator_g2_gradients,
generator_g2.trainable_variables))  d_x_optimizer.apply_gradients(zip(d_
x_gradients,d_x.trainable_variables))    d_y_optimizer_1.apply_
gradients(zip(d_y_gradients,d_y.trainable_variables))
for epoch in range(EPOCHE_1):
  start_1 = time.time()
  n = 0
  for image_x1, image_y1 in tf.data.Dataset.zip((train_horses1,
train_zebras1)):
    train_step(image_x1, image_y1)
    if n % 10 == 0:
      print ('.', end='')
    n += 1
  clear_output(wait=True)
  generate_images(generator_g1, horse)
```

```
  if (epoch + 1) % 6 == 0:
    ckpt_save_path1 = ckpt_manager.save()
    print ('Save the checkpoint for epoch {} at {}'.format(epoch+1,
ckpt_save_path1))
  print ('Time for epoch {} is {} sec\n'.format(epoch + 1,time.
time()-start_1))
```

Here's an explanation of each line of code:

```
#This line applies the gradients computed for the generator network G1 to
the corresponding trainable variables using the optimizer defined
earlier.
generator_g1_optimizer.apply_gradients(zip(generator_g_gradients,
generator_g1.trainable_variables))
```

```
#This line applies the gradients computed for the generator network G2 to
the corresponding trainable variables using the optimizer defined earlier.
generator_g2_optimizer.
apply_gradients(zip(generator_g2_gradients,generator_g2.trainable_
variables))
```

```
#This line applies the gradients computed for the discriminator network
Dx to the corresponding trainable variables using the optimizer defined
earlier.
d_x_optimizer.apply_gradients(zip(d_x_gradients,d_x.trainable_variables))
```

```
#This line applies the gradients computed for the discriminator network
Dy to the corresponding trainable variables using the optimizer defined
earlier.
d_y_optimizer_1.apply_gradients(zip(d_y_gradients,d_y.trainable_
variables))
```

```
#This line initiates a loop over the specified number of epochs for
training the model.
for epoch in range(EPOCHE_1):
```

```
#This line records the start time of the current epoch.
start_1 = time.time()
```

```
#This line initializes a counter variable `n` to keep track of the number
of batches processed in the current epoch.
n = 0
```

```
#This line iterates over the pairs of images in the training datasets for
horses and zebras, respectively.
for image_x1, image_y1 in tf.data.Dataset.zip((train_horses1,
train_zebras1)):
```

```
#This line calls the `train_step()` function defined earlier to compute
the gradients and update the weights of the generator and discriminator
networks.
train_step(image_x1, image_y1)
```

```
#These lines print a dot every 10 batches processed, to indicate the
progress of the training process.
if n % 10 == 0:
  print ('.', end='')
n += 1
```

```
#This line clears the output from the previous epoch to avoid cluttering
the display.
clear_output(wait=True)
```

```
#This line generates and displays a sample of images produced by the
generator network G1 using a fixed input image of a horse.
generate_images(generator_g1, horse)
```

```
#This line saves a checkpoint of the model weights after every sixth epoch.
if (epoch + 1) % 6 == 0:
  ckpt_save_path1 = ckpt_manager.save()
  print ('Save the checkpoint for epoch {} at {}'.format(epoch+1,
ckpt_save_path1))
```

```
#This line prints the time taken to complete the current epoch.
print ('Time for epoch {} is {} sec\n'.format(epoch + 1,time.time()-
start_1))
```

10.4.6 Generate Using the Test Dataset

Using the test data sample, we can generate new data by deploying a current generator. This code loops over the first five images in the test_horses dataset and calls the generate_images function for each of them using the generator_g_1 model. The generate_images function takes in the generator_g_1 model and an input image, generates a prediction using the model, and displays the input and generated images in a figure. Figure 10.14 displays the images generated using the test dataset.

```
#This is a loop that iterates over the first 5 elements of the test_
horses dataset.
for inp in test_horses.take(5):
```

```
#This function call generates images using the generator_g1 model by
passing in inp as the test input. The generate_images() function takes
care of plotting the input image and the predicted output image.
  generate_images(generator_g1, inp)
```

FIGURE 10.14
Generated images from the test dataset.

10.5 CycleGAN Issues

There are several issues that can arise when using CycleGAN.

10.5.1 Lack of Diversity in Generated Images

One of the most common issues with CycleGAN, and GANs in general, is the lack of diversity in the generated images, a problem also known as mode collapse. In this scenario, the generator produces very similar outputs for different inputs, which means that the model is not effectively learning to represent the full range of the target data distribution.

Solution:

A potential solution to the problem of mode collapse is to use techniques, such as mini-batch discrimination. This method allows the discriminator to examine multiple examples together, which makes it more difficult for the generator to always produce the same output. By doing this, it can help to ensure that the generator creates a more diverse set of images.

10.5.2 Poor Image Quality

Another common issue with CycleGAN is that the generated images may have poor quality. This can be due to a variety of reasons, such as the model not being able to fully capture the details of the input images, the presence of noise in the training data, or the model overfitting to the training data.

Solution:

One way to address the issue of poor image quality is to use a higher-capacity model. This can help the model to better capture the details of the input images. However, using a higher-capacity model also increases the risk of overfitting, so it is important to use techniques such as dropout and weight decay to prevent this. Another potential solution is to use a different loss function. The standard loss function used in CycleGAN is a combination of adversarial loss and cycle consistency loss. However, there are other types of loss functions that can be used, such as perceptual loss or feature matching loss, which can help to improve the quality of the generated images. Improving the quality of the training data can also help to improve the quality of the generated images. This can involve using higher-resolution images, removing noisy data, or using data augmentation techniques to increase the diversity of the training data. Finally, incorporating additional constraints into the model can also help to improve image quality. For example, adding an identity loss can help to ensure that the model preserves the identity of the input image when translating it to the target domain. Similarly, adding a structural similarity index measure (SSIM) loss can encourage the model to preserve the structure of the input image in the output image.

10.5.3 Unbalanced Image Domains

In some cases, the two image domains that are to be translated by CycleGAN might be unbalanced. That is, there may be significantly more images in one domain than the other, or the complexity of images in one domain may be much higher than that of the other domain. This can lead to the model overfitting to the larger or more complex domain, resulting in poor translation performance for the smaller or less complex domain.

Solution:

One potential solution for this problem is to use a balanced dataset. This might involve gathering more data for the smaller or less complex domain or downsampling the larger or more complex domain to match the size of the smaller domain. Alternatively, techniques like weighted loss functions can be used to balance the influence of each domain during training. This would involve giving a larger weight to the loss associated with the smaller domain, effectively increasing its influence on the model's learning process. Another strategy could be to use domain adaptation techniques. These methods aim to align the distributions of the two domains in some feature space, reducing the model's sensitivity to the difference in the number of samples in each domain. Finally, when dealing with differences in complexity between domains, a two-step training process could be used. In the first step, a simple model could be trained on the less complex domain. Then, in the second step, this model could be fine-tuned on the more complex domain, allowing it to gradually learn the more complex mapping while leveraging the simpler mapping learned in the first step.

10.5.4 Difficulty in Choosing Hyperparameters

Selecting hyperparameters in CycleGAN can be tricky because they significantly impact the model's performance and training stability. These include the learning rate, number of generator/discriminator layers, batch size, and the lambda value for cycle consistency loss.

Solutions:

1. **Grid search or random search:** They are traditional methods for hyperparameter tuning, where you train models with different hyperparameters and choose the one that performs best.

2. **Bayesian optimization:** This method builds a probability model of the objective function and uses it to select the most promising hyperparameters to evaluate in the true objective function.

3. **Automated machine learning (AutoML):** Tools like Google's AutoML, H2O, and others use sophisticated methods to automatically adjust hyperparameters.

4. **Learning rate schedulers:** They can adjust the learning rate during training. For example, the learning rate could decrease after a certain number of epochs, which often improves results.

5. **Hyperparameter tuning libraries:** Libraries, such as Optuna, Hyperopt, and Keras Tuner, provide sophisticated methods for hyperparameter tuning, which can help achieve optimal model performance.

10.5.5 Long Training Times

Training a CycleGAN can be computationally intensive and may require a large amount of data and processing power. This can make it difficult to iterate quickly on the model and experiment with different settings. CycleGAN involves training two generative adversarial networks simultaneously, which can be computationally expensive and result in long training times.

Solutions:

1. **Hardware improvements:** Using GPUs or TPUs can speed up the training process considerably compared to CPUs.
2. **Reduce model complexity:** You can reduce the number of layers or number of units per layer in your networks, at the cost of potential performance drop.
3. **Use pre-trained models:** You can use weights from a pre-trained model as a starting point. This technique, called transfer learning, can significantly reduce training time.
4. **Batch size adjustment:** Increasing the batch size can lead to faster training, provided the hardware can handle the increased memory demand.
5. **Distributed training:** By training the model on multiple GPUs or machines, the workload can be spread out, and training times can be reduced.

10.5.6 Mode Collapse

One common problem in GANs is mode collapse, where the generator starts producing the same outputs (or a small set of outputs) for different inputs. This is a significant issue because it means the network is not learning to represent the full complexity of the target data distribution.

Solution:

A potential solution to mode collapse is to apply techniques, such as mini-batch discrimination, which allows the discriminator to look at multiple examples in combination, making it harder for the generator to always produce the same output. Another approach could be using different types of GAN architectures, such as Wasserstein GANs, that have been shown to mitigate mode collapse.

10.5.7 Overfitting

The model performs well on the training data but poorly on the test data. CycleGAN, like other deep learning models, can overfit if not properly regularized. Overfitting means the model learns the training data too well, including its noise and outliers, resulting in poor performance on unseen data.

Solutions:

1. **Data augmentation:** This involves increasing the size of your training set by adding slight modifications to your existing data, helping the model generalize better.
2. **Regularization techniques:** Techniques like dropout or weight decay (L2 regularization) can be applied to prevent the model from fitting too closely to the training data.
3. **Early stopping:** This involves stopping the training process when performance on a validation set stops improving, even if performance on the training set continues to improve.
4. **Use a simpler model:** Reducing the complexity of the model (fewer layers or neurons per layer) can help to mitigate overfitting.
5. **Use of noise:** Injecting noise into the generator and/or discriminator during training can improve the robustness of the GAN and prevent overfitting.

10.5.8 Gradient Vanishing/Exploding

In CycleGANs, the vanishing/exploding gradient problem can occur during backpropagation, making the network hard to train. This is when gradient values become so large (exploding gradients) or so small (vanishing gradients) that they hinder the model's learning process.

Solutions:

1. **Normalized initialization:** Techniques like Xavier or He initialization can help manage this issue by maintaining the variance of activations and back-propagated gradients as one goes up or down the network.

2. **Gradient clipping:** This technique limits the value of gradients to a defined range to prevent them from getting too large or too small.

3. **Use of advanced optimization methods:** Optimizers like Adam, RMSProp, or Nadam are more capable of mitigating these problems than vanilla Stochastic Gradient Descent.

4. **Batch normalization:** This technique normalizes the input layer by adjusting and scaling the activations, which can help manage the vanishing/exploding gradient problem.

5. **Residual connections (skip connections):** They allow gradients to flow directly through several layers by having shortcuts from earlier layers to later ones, which can alleviate the vanishing gradient problem.

10.5.9 Unbalanced Data

CycleGAN is designed for unpaired image-to-image translation, which inherently tackles some unbalanced data issues. However, if there's a severe imbalance within each domain or between domains, the model may perform poorly.

Solutions:

1. **Data augmentation:** By synthesizing new data from existing samples, you can balance out the representation in each domain.

2. **Class weighting:** Modify your loss function to give more importance to under-represented classes.

3. **Oversampling and undersampling:** You can oversample the minority class or undersample the majority class to achieve a balance.

4. **Cost-sensitive training:** This method associates a higher cost with the misclassification of the minority class.

5. **Use of balanced datasets:** If possible, gather data in such a way to ensure a balance between different classes or domains.

10.5.10 Image Artifacts

CycleGANs can sometimes produce images with noticeable artifacts or irregularities, affecting the quality of the generated images.

Solutions:

1. **Increasing model capacity:** A model with more layers or neurons may be able to generate higher quality images.

2. **Refinement architectures:** After the initial generation, another network can be used to refine the generated images and reduce artifacts.

3. **Advanced loss functions:** Loss functions like Perceptual Loss or Style Loss can be used to encourage the generation of more visually pleasing images.

4. **Higher-quality training data:** Ensuring that your training data is of high quality and free from artifacts can help improve the quality of generated images.

5. **Post-processing techniques:** Techniques like blurring or smoothing can be applied to the generated images to reduce visible artifacts.

10.5.11 Lack of Diversity

Lack of diversity (or mode collapse) is a common issue in GANs, where the generator starts to produce limited or identical outputs regardless of varying inputs.

Solutions:

1. **Mini-batch discrimination:** This technique allows the discriminator to look at multiple examples in combination rather than in isolation, discouraging the generator from always generating the same image.

2. **Unrolled GANs:** It involves using a few steps of the discriminator's gradient to update the generator, adding diversity to the generated images.

3. **Adding noise:** Injecting noise into the generator's input or directly to its parameters can enhance the diversity of outputs.

4. **Regularization techniques:** Techniques like spectral normalization or instance noise can be used to improve the stability of GAN training and promote diversity in the output.

5. **Use of multiple generators:** Using more than one generator can improve diversity, as different generators may learn to produce different styles of images.

10.6 CycleGAN Implementation Tips

The majority of these suggestions can be found in more recent papers discussing CycleGAN in depth. Here, we'll review some tips to help you construct a more efficient architecture.

10.6.1 Preprocessing

Preprocessing of images is vital to ensure that the model can effectively learn the underlying features. This could include normalization of pixel values, resizing the images to a fixed size, and implementing data augmentation techniques, such as random flipping or rotation.

10.6.2 Model Architecture

It is important to design the generator and discriminator models carefully for the task at hand. For instance, for image-to-image translation tasks, the generator and discriminator models should be designed to manage the spatial information in the images.

10.6.3 Loss Functions

The loss functions used for training the CycleGAN should be chosen based on the task. For instance, for image-to-image translation tasks, commonly used loss functions include cycle consistency loss, adversarial loss, and identity loss.

10.6.4 Hyperparameters

Hyperparameters, such as learning rate, batch size, and the number of training epochs, should be carefully tuned to ensure the optimal performance of the model.

10.6.5 Data Preparation

Data preparation should be carried out carefully to ensure a good balance between the number of samples in each domain. This is crucial to prevent the model from learning a biased mapping between the two domains.

10.6.6 Training

It is important to monitor the training process closely to ensure that the model is learning the underlying patterns effectively. This could include visualizing the generated images during training and monitoring the loss values.

10.6.7 Evaluation

Once the model has been trained, it's important to evaluate its performance on a separate test dataset. This could involve qualitative evaluation of the generated images and quantitative evaluation using metrics, such as SSIM, PSNR, or FID.

10.6.8 Deployment

Lastly, it's important to choose the appropriate deployment strategy for the task at hand. This could include deploying the model as a standalone application, as part of a larger system, or as a web service.

Remember, hands-on experience is key when working with CycleGANs or any other machine learning models. Therefore, consistently practicing implementation and trouble-shooting is crucial for mastering these concepts.

10.7 Lessons Learned

- Learn CycleGAN architecture
- Learn CycleGAN application

- Learn CycleGAN implementation using TensorFlow
- Learn Tips for Implementing CycleGAN
- Learn Issues with CycleGAN

10.8 Problems

10.8.1 What is CycleGAN?

10.8.2 How does CycleGAN differ from other GANs?

10.8.3 What is the objective of CycleGAN?

10.8.4 How is CycleGAN trained?

10.8.5 What are some real-world applications of CycleGAN?

10.8.6 What types of data can be used with CycleGAN?

10.8.7 What is the architecture of CycleGAN?

10.8.8 How does CycleGAN use cycle consistency loss?

10.8.9 What is the importance of adversarial loss in CycleGAN?

10.8.10 How does CycleGAN handle image translation with unpaired data?

10.8.11 How does CycleGAN deal with mode collapse?

10.8.12 What is a generator in CycleGAN?

10.8.13 What is a discriminator in CycleGAN?

10.8.14 How does CycleGAN ensure that generated images are realistic and retain important features?

10.8.15 What is a cyclic mapping in CycleGAN?

10.8.16 How does CycleGAN handle multi-modal image-to-image translation?

10.8.17 Can CycleGAN be used for style transfer?

10.8.18 What are some challenges of using CycleGAN?

10.8.19 How can the performance of CycleGAN be evaluated?

10.8.20 What are some future directions for research on CycleGAN?

10.9 Programming Questions

- **Easy**

    10.9.1 Implement a CycleGAN model to convert images from a source domain to a target domain.

    10.9.2 Train a CycleGAN model on a custom dataset and evaluate its performance.

    10.9.3 Modify the CycleGAN architecture to include additional convolutional layers and experiment with different kernel sizes.

      10.9.4 Implement a CycleGAN model with spectral normalization to improve stability during training.

      10.9.5 Train a CycleGAN model with weight sharing to reduce the number of parameters and improve generalization.

- **Medium**

      10.9.6 Implement a CycleGAN model with conditional generators to control the style of the output images.

      10.9.7 Experiment with different loss functions for the CycleGAN, such as the Wasserstein loss or hinge loss.

      10.9.8 Modify the CycleGAN architecture to include skip connections between the generator and discriminator networks.

      10.9.9 Implement a CycleGAN model with attention mechanisms to focus on important image features during translation.

      10.9.10 Train a CycleGAN model on a large dataset with distributed training to speed up the training process.

      10.9.11 Modify the CycleGAN architecture to include a U-Net structure for the generator network.

      10.9.12 Implement a CycleGAN model with multiple discriminators to provide more fine-grained feedback during training.

      10.9.13 Experiment with different image preprocessing techniques, such as random cropping or data augmentation, to improve the model's performance.

      10.9.14 Train a CycleGAN model with cycle consistency loss only and compare its performance to the full CycleGAN model.

- **Hard**

      10.9.15 Implement a CycleGAN model with weight clipping or gradient penalty regularization to improve the model's stability during training.

      10.9.16 Experiment with different hyperparameters for the CycleGAN, such as the learning rate or batch size.

      10.9.17 Modify the CycleGAN architecture to include instance normalization instead of batch normalization.

      10.9.18 Implement a CycleGAN model with a self-attention module to improve the model's ability to capture global image features.

      10.9.19 Train a CycleGAN model with a multi-scale discriminator to capture both local and global image features.

      10.9.20 Modify the CycleGAN architecture to include a style loss term to enforce a desired style in the output images.

11

Semi-Supervised Generative Adversarial Network (SGAN)

This chapter covers the following topics about Generative Adversarial Network with Semi-Supervision (SGAN):

- What Is the Semi-Supervised GAN?
- Semi-Supervised GAN for MNIST
- Semi-Supervised Learning GAN Applications
- Semi-Supervised Learning GAN Issues
- Semi-Supervised Learning GAN Implementation Tips

11.1 Preface

The Semi-Supervised Generative Adversarial Network (SGAN) is an extension of GAN that uses both labeled and unlabeled data to improve the training of generative models. Semi-supervised learning plays a crucial role, given the cost and availability of labeled data. Its networks combine supervised learning loss with unsupervised loss and can work with any neural network architecture, including feedforward and recurrent networks. The goal of semi-supervised learning is to generalize from a small subset of labeled data. Discriminators are trained on both labeled and unlabeled data to distinguish between real and fake data and to categorize the labeled training images into the appropriate groups. The labeled data is used to train both the discriminator and the generator models, and then the unlabeled data is used to further train the generator model. By doing so, SGAN can generate high-quality data that is more diverse and better reflects the underlying distribution of the training data. It has been shown to outperform traditional supervised and unsupervised learning methods in many tasks.

However, SGAN also faces challenges, such as selecting the labeled data and balancing the supervised and unsupervised loss functions. The discriminator is trained to not only distinguish between real and fake data but also to classify the labeled data into their respective classes. The generator is trained to generate data that not only fools the discriminator but also produces realistic samples that belong to the labeled classes. SGAN has found applications in various fields, such as image and speech recognition, natural language processing, and even drug discovery. It has shown promising results in improving the quality and quantity of generated data, which can benefit various industries. Figure 11.1 provides a visual representation of the overarching architecture of the SGAN. Typically, an SGAN incorporates both unsupervised and supervised learning elements, allowing it to make use of both labeled and unlabeled data. The diagram

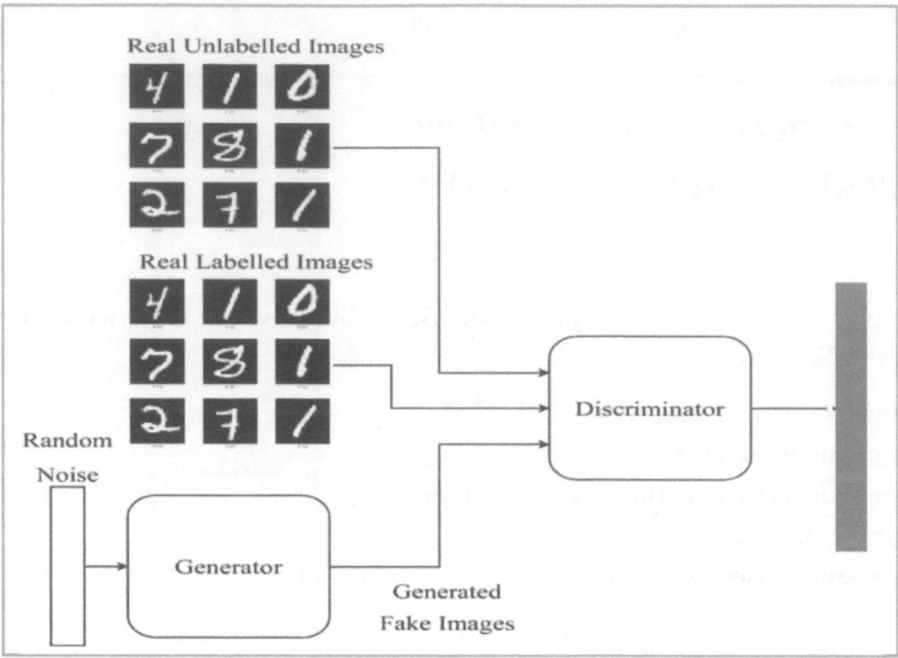

FIGURE 11.1
SGAN general architecture.

is likely to exhibit the interplay between the generator, which produces synthetic data samples, and the discriminator, which classifies these samples either as real or fake while also assigning class labels to real data. By learning from a combination of both types of data, SGANs aim to optimize generative capabilities and classification accuracy simultaneously. We explain more about these methods and provide a coding practice example in this chapter.

11.2 What Is the Semi-Supervised GAN?

Deep supervised learning methods have recently achieved significant success in both research and industry, but their success heavily depends on the availability of large amounts of labeled data. However, labeled data is more expensive to collect than unlabeled data in most applications. This problem motivates the use of semi-supervised learning, which can be trained to perform well with a small amount of labeled data. Semi-supervised learning is a well-known machine learning method where only a portion of the data in a set is labeled. In this approach, the discriminator uses three types of data: labeled training, unlabeled training, and generator-generated fake data. This is effective because discriminators are trained on both labeled and unlabeled data. What the discriminator learns about images without labels should help it describe the features of images with labels. In practice, this means that the discriminator has a SoftMax output that minimizes the cross-entropy. Semi-supervised learning attempts to generalize from a small subset of labeled

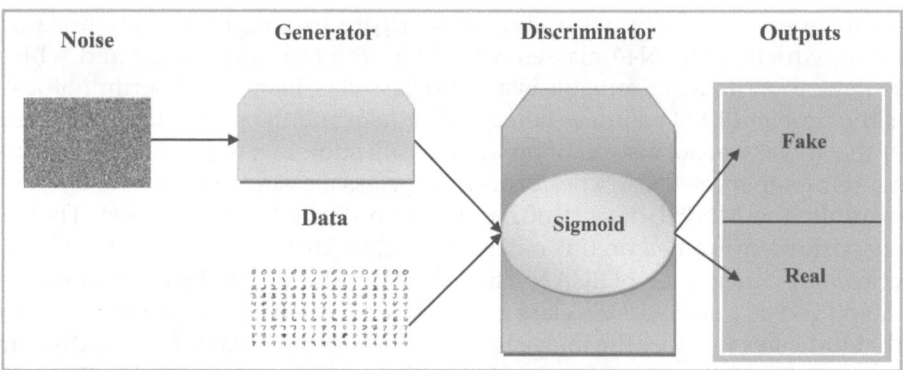

FIGURE 11.2
General GAN architecture.

data points to classify previously unseen examples effectively. It accomplishes this by internalizing hidden data structures and requiring that labeled and unlabeled data come from the same distribution. Figure 11.2 shows the entire regular GAN, including input data (both noise and real data), generator, discriminator, and outputs. Figure 11.3 presents the general architecture of the SGAN. Central to the visualization is the network's unique dual-input design: one for noise and the other two for labeled and unlabeled data. The generator module takes in random noise and crafts synthetic data samples. Simultaneously, the discriminator receives both labeled and unlabeled data samples, effectively discerning real from fake and, for labeled samples, classifying them into their respective categories. Please take a look at Figure 11.3 and compare it to Figure 11.2. It shows the general architecture of a semi-supervised GAN, with the main differences being in the input data (labeled and unlabeled data) and the activation function in the discriminator. These components are explained in more detail in the coding section of this chapter.

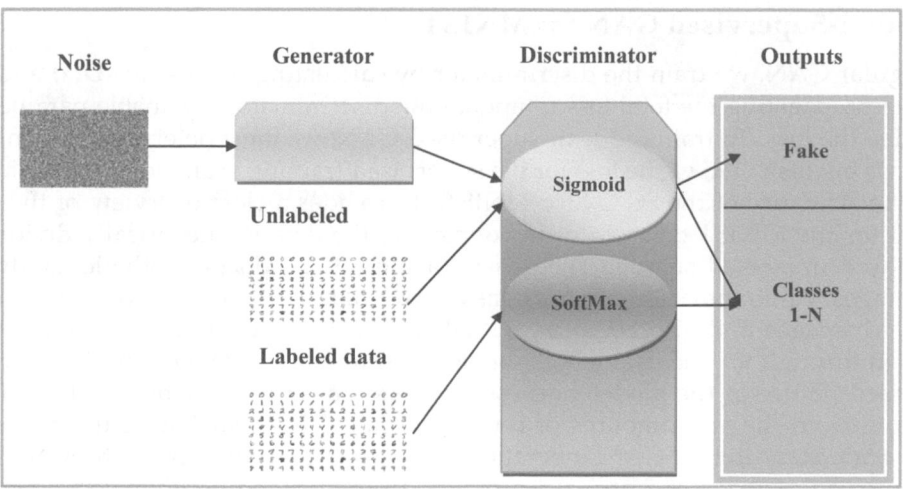

FIGURE 11.3
Semi-supervised GAN architecture.

The semi-supervised GAN has a similar structure to a regular GAN, but instead of determining which of the **N+1** classes come from the training dataset and which come from the generator, its discriminator is a multiclass classifier. The discriminator's output includes the probability of an image being real or fake and the probabilities of it belonging to one of the **N** classes. So, instead of binary classification in a regular GAN, the discriminator in a semi-supervised GAN performs multi-class classification.

For example, the MNIST dataset of handwritten digits has ten classes. Therefore, an SGAN discriminator trained on this dataset would predict between 10 + 1 = 11 classes. In the practical implementation of SGAN using the MNIST dataset, the discriminator output will be displayed as a vector of ten class probabilities that add up to one and another probability that indicates whether the image is real or fake. In a regular GAN, the discriminator calculates the loss of two inputs and uses that information to adjust the discriminator's parameters to keep the loss as low as possible. SGAN computation is based on three inputs and is trained differently than a regular GAN. The generator provides one input, which takes in a vector of random numbers and outputs fake data. The training dataset provides the other two inputs, one labeled and one not. The generator's input is a random number vector (**z**), and it generates fake examples (**x***), real examples from the training dataset without labels (**x**), and real examples from the training dataset with labels (**x, y**), where **y** is the label for the given example (**x**). A discriminator's output is a set of probabilities indicating whether the input data is real or fake. The output is a set of fake examples (**x***) that attempt to be as convincing as possible, as well as probabilities indicating the likelihood that the input example belongs to one of the **N** real classes or the fake class (**N+1** classes (labels) in total). The loss values show that the SGAN discriminator must learn two things at the same time: how to tell real examples from fake ones and how to classify real examples. In the original paper's terminology, these two goals are known as supervised and unsupervised losses. After training, the generator is removed, and the trained discriminator is used as a classifier.

11.3 Semi-Supervised GAN for MNIST

In a regular GAN, we train the discriminator by calculating the loss for **D(x)** and **D(x*)** and backpropagating the total loss to update the discriminator's trainable parameters to minimize the loss. To train the semi-supervised GAN, we must determine not only **D(x)** and **D(x*)** but also **D(x, y)**, the loss for the supervised training examples. Figure 11.4 illustrates the structure of the SGAN for MNIST. It provides a clear overview of the SGAN tailored for the MNIST dataset. In this depiction, the data is categorically divided into labeled and unlabeled subsets. The generator module produces synthetic handwritten digit images, while the discriminator's task is twofold. It discerns between genuine and fabricated images and also classifies the labeled real images into one of the ten digit classes (0 through 9). The use of both labeled and unlabeled data exemplifies the semi-supervised nature of the model, harnessing the strength of available labels while also benefiting from the vast amounts of unlabeled data. This visual structure facilitates a deeper understanding of SGAN's operation and learning mechanism on the MNIST dataset. Comparing Figures 11.3 and 11.4 provides an understanding of how the input data is divided into labeled and unlabeled data, and how the outputs are classified data that have been labeled.

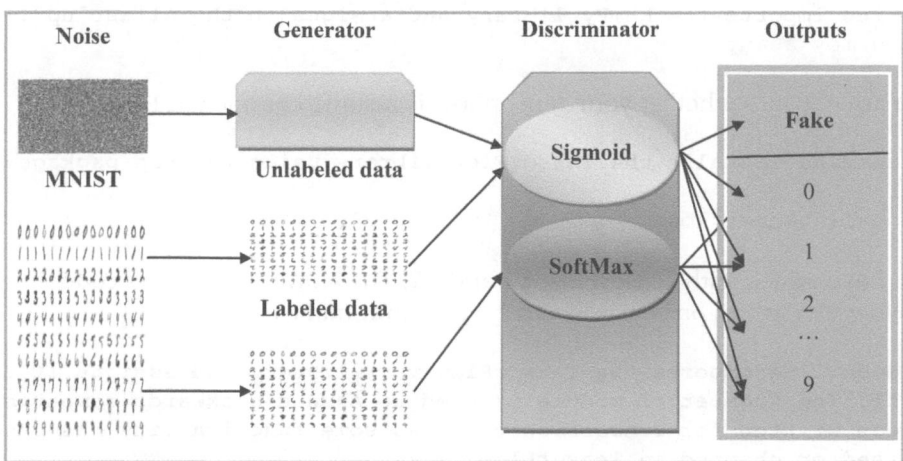

FIGURE 11.4
Semi-supervised GAN for MNIST.

11.3.1 Set Up and Import Libraries

To start, we need to import all the necessary packages, such as TensorFlow, Keras, Matplotlib, and NumPy. We also need to set certain parameters, such as the image rows and columns, and define the number of classes in the dataset, which is 10.

```
from keras.layers import Input, Dense, Reshape, BatchNormalization
from keras.models import Model
from tensorflow.keras.optimizers import Adam
from keras.datasets import mnist
from tensorflow.keras.utils import to_categorical
import numpy as np
```

Here's a breakdown of each line of code:

```
#This line imports the `Input`, `Dense`, `Reshape`, and
`BatchNormalization` layers from the `keras.layers` module.
from keras.layers import Input, Dense, Reshape, BatchNormalization

#This line imports the `Model` class from the `keras.models` module.
from keras.models import Model

#This line imports the `Adam` optimizer from the `tensorflow.keras.
optimizers` module.
from tensorflow.keras.optimizers import Adam

#This line imports the MNIST dataset from the `keras.datasets` module.
from keras.datasets import mnist

#This line imports the `to_categorical` function from the `tensorflow.
keras.utils` module.
from tensorflow.keras.utils import to_categorical
```

```
#This line imports the NumPy library and assigns it the alias `np`.
import numpy as np
```

If you are not sure whether your TensorFlow is installed or not, use this:

```
#This command installs the TensorFlow library using the pip package
manager.
pip install tensorflow
```

If you have issues with TensorFlow V1 and V2, The blowe code allows code written for TensorFlow v1.x to run on TensorFlow v2.x with minimal changes.

```
#this code line imports the TensorFlow v1.x library and assigns it the
alias tf. The. compat.v1 module is used to ensure backwards compatibility
with code written for TensorFlow v1.x, as some functionality has been
deprecated or changed in TensorFlow v2.x.
import tensorflow.compat.v1 as tf
```

11.3.2 Preprocess the Dataset

The dataset will be a subset of the entire training set and will be used to train the unsupervised discriminator. The batch labeled () function prepares the dataset for the supervised discriminator by selecting a subset of samples and their labels. Here, only 100 labeled examples, or 10 examples per class (10 classes in total), will be used to train the classifier. The batch unlabeled () function selects images at random from the dataset.

```
(x_train, y_train), (x_test, y_test) = mnist.load_data()
batch_size = 100
half_batch_size = 50
latent_dim = 100
iterations = 10000
optimizer = Adam(0.0002, 0.5)
```

These lines of code define and initialize several variables. Here's a breakdown of each line of code:

```
#This line loads the MNIST dataset into memory and splits it into
training and testing sets, which are assigned to the variables `x_train`,
`y_train`, `x_test`, and `y_test`.
(x_train, y_train), (x_test, y_test) = mnist.load_data()
#This line defines the batch size, which is the number of training
examples that are processed together in a single iteration of the
training loop. In this case, the batch size is set to 100.
batch_size = 100

#This line defines the half batch size, which is half of the batch size.
It will be used later in the code for the discriminator training.
half_batch_size = 50

#This line defines the size of the latent space, which is the
dimensionality of the noise vector that will be used as input to the
generator. In this case, the latent space size is set to 100.
latent_dim = 100
```

```
#This line defines the number of training iterations, which is the number
of times the generator and discriminator will be trained on the dataset.
In this case, the number of iterations is set to 10000.
iterations = 10000

#This line initializes the optimizer that will be used to update the
weights of the neural network during training. In this case, the
optimizer is Adam, with a learning rate of 0.0002 and a momentum of 0.5.
optimizer = Adam(0.0002, 0.5)
```

11.3.3 Generator

It has three hidden layers, including batch normalization, dense, and ReLU activation functions. The generator takes the random noise vector as input in the first hidden layer, uses hidden layer 1 output as input in hidden layer 2, and uses hidden layer 2 output as input in hidden layer 3. The final output layer uses hidden layer 3 output and the tanh activation function. The output of this module is the generator model. The code defines a function called "generator()" that returns a Keras model for the generator neural network. The model summary and the number of parameters are also displayed.

```
def generator():
    input_gen = Input(shape=(latent_dim,))
    hidden1 = BatchNormalization(momentum=0.8)(Dense(256,
activation='relu')(input_gen))
    hidden2 = BatchNormalization(momentum=0.8)(Dense(512,
activation='relu')(hidden1))
    hidden3 = BatchNormalization(momentum=0.8)(Dense(1024,
activation='relu')(hidden2))
    output = Dense(784, activation='tanh')(hidden3)
    reshaped_output = Reshape((28, 28, 1))(output)
    gen_model = Model(input_gen, reshaped_output)
    gen_model.compile(loss='binary_crossentropy', optimizer=optimizer)
    return gen_model
generator_model = generator()
generator_model.summary()
Model: "model"
```

Layer (type)	Output Shape	Param #
input_1 (InputLayer)	[(None, 100)]	0
dense (Dense)	(None, 256)	25856
batch_normalization (BatchNormalization)	(None, 256)	1024
dense_1 (Dense)	(None, 512)	131584
batch_normalization_1 (BatchNormalization)	(None, 512)	2048
dense_2 (Dense)	(None, 1024)	525312
batch_normalization_2 (BatchNormalization)	(None, 1024)	4096
dense_3 (Dense)	(None, 784)	803600
reshape (Reshape)	(None, 28, 28, 1)	0

```
Total params: 1,493,520
Trainable params: 1,489,936
Non-trainable params: 3,584
```

Here's a breakdown of each line of code in the function:

```
#This line defines an input layer for the generator network with the same
shape as the noise vector. The `shape` argument specifies the dimensions
of the input, which in this case is a one-dimensional vector of size
`latent_dim`.
input_gen = Input(shape=(latent_dim,))
```

```
#This line defines the first hidden layer of the generator network. The
`Dense` layer creates a fully connected layer with 256 neurons and a ReLU
activation function, and the `BatchNormalization` layer applies batch
normalization to the outputs of the `Dense` layer. The `momentum`
parameter sets the momentum for the moving average used to compute the
mean and standard deviation of the batch. The output of the layer is
assigned to the variable `hidden1`.
hidden1 = BatchNormalization(momentum=0.8)(Dense(256, activation=
'relu')(input_gen))
```

```
#This line defines the second hidden layer of the generator network. The
`Dense` layer creates a fully connected layer with 512 neurons and a ReLU
activation function, and the `BatchNormalization` layer applies batch
normalization to the outputs of the `Dense` layer. The output of the
layer is assigned to the variable `hidden2`.
hidden2 = BatchNormalization(momentum=0.8)(Dense(512, activation=
'relu')(hidden1))
```

```
#This line defines the third hidden layer of the generator network. The
`Dense` layer creates a fully connected layer with 1024 neurons and a
ReLU activation function, and the `BatchNormalization` layer applies
batch normalization to the outputs of the `Dense` layer. The output of
the layer is assigned to the variable `hidden3`.
hidden3 = BatchNormalization(momentum=0.8)(Dense(1024, activation=
'relu')(hidden2))
```

```
#This line defines the output layer of the generator network. The `Dense`
layer creates a fully connected layer with 784 neurons and a hyperbolic
tangent activation function. The output of the layer is assigned to the
variable `output`.
output = Dense(784, activation='tanh')(hidden3)
```

```
#This line reshapes the output of the generator network into a 28x28x1
image. The `Reshape` layer takes a single argument, which is the desired
shape of the output tensor.
reshaped_output = Reshape((28, 28, 1))(output)
```

```
#This line creates a Keras `Model` object that takes the noise vector as
input and produces an image as output.
gen_model = Model(input_gen, reshaped_output)
```

```
#This line compiles the generator model, specifying the binary cross-
entropy loss function and the optimizer object that was defined earlier.
gen_model.compile(loss='binary_crossentropy', optimizer=optimizer)
```

```
#This line returns the generator model.
return gen_model
```

```
#This line creates an instance of the generator model by calling the
`generator()` function.
generator_model = generator()

#This line prints a summary of the generator model, including the layer
types, output shapes, and number of trainable parameters.
generator_model.summary()
```

11.3.4 Discriminator

The discriminator() function takes an image (real or fake) as input and outputs a binary value of either "1" (for real) or "0" (for fake). The input is passed through three hidden layers, with each layer's output serving as the input for the next one. The activation function used for all hidden layers is ReLU, except for the last two layers: one uses sigmoid, and the other uses SoftMax. The discriminator_supervised() function uses SoftMax activation to classify an image into one of ten categories based on the discriminator model, specifically for the MNIST dataset. The output of this module is the discriminator model, which is returned by the discriminator() function. The summary of the model includes information about the number of parameters.

```
def discriminator():
    input_disc = Input(shape=(784,))
    hidden1 = Dense(512, activation='relu')(input_disc)
    hidden2 = Dense(256, activation='relu')(hidden1)
    hidden3 = Dense(128, activation='relu')(hidden2)
    output = Dense(1, activation='sigmoid')(hidden3)
    output2 = Dense(10, activation='softmax', name='classification_
layer')(hidden3)
    disc_model = Model(input_disc, output)
    disc_model_2 = Model(input_disc, output2)
    disc_model.compile(loss=['binary_crossentropy'], optimizer=optimizer,
metrics=['accuracy'])
    disc_model_2.compile(loss=['categorical_crossentropy'], optimizer=
optimizer, metrics=['accuracy'])
    return disc_model, disc_model_2
discriminator_model, classification_model = discriminator()
discriminator_model.summary()
Model: "model_1"
```

Layer (type)	Output Shape	Param #
input_2 (InputLayer)	[(None, 784)]	0
dense_4 (Dense)	(None, 512)	401920
dense_5 (Dense)	(None, 256)	131328
dense_6 (Dense)	(None, 128)	32896
dense_7 (Dense)	(None, 1)	129

```
Total params: 566,273
Trainable params: 566,273
Non-trainable params: 0
```

Here's a breakdown of each line of code in the function:

```
#This line defines an input layer for the discriminator network with the
same shape as the MNIST images. The `shape` argument specifies the
```

dimensions of the input, which in this case is a one-dimensional vector
of size 784 (28x28x1).

```
input_disc = Input(shape=(784,))
```

#This line defines the first hidden layer of the discriminator network.
The `Dense` layer creates a fully connected layer with 512 neurons and a
ReLU activation function. The output of the layer is assigned to the
variable `hidden1`.

```
hidden1 = Dense(512, activation='relu')(input_disc)
```

#This line defines the second hidden layer of the discriminator network.
The `Dense` layer creates a fully connected layer with 256 neurons and a
ReLU activation function. The output of the layer is assigned to the
variable `hidden2`.

```
hidden2 = Dense(256, activation='relu')(hidden1)
```

#This line defines the third hidden layer of the discriminator network.
The `Dense` layer creates a fully connected layer with 128 neurons and a
ReLU activation function. The output of the layer is assigned to the
variable `hidden3`.

```
hidden3 = Dense(128, activation='relu')(hidden2)
```

#This line defines the output layer of the discriminator network. The
`Dense` layer creates a fully connected layer with 1 neuron and a sigmoid
activation function. The output of the layer is assigned to the variable
`output`.

```
output = Dense(1, activation='sigmoid')(hidden3)
```

#This line defines the output layer of the classification network. The
`Dense` layer creates a fully connected layer with 10 neurons and a
softmax activation function. The output of the layer is assigned to the
variable `output2`.

```
output2 = Dense(10, activation='softmax', name='classification_layer')
(hidden3)
```

#This line creates a Keras `Model` object that takes an image as input
and produces a binary classification output as output. This is the
discriminator network.

```
disc_model = Model(input_disc, output)
```

#This line creates a Keras `Model` object that takes an image as input
and produces a 10-class classification output as output. This is the
classification network.

```
disc_model_2 = Model(input_disc, output2)
```

#This line compiles the discriminator model, specifying the binary cross-
entropy loss function and the optimizer object that was defined earlier.
The `metrics` argument specifies that accuracy should be tracked during
training.

```
disc_model.compile(loss=['binary_crossentropy'], optimizer=optimizer,
metrics=['accuracy'])
```

#This line compiles the classification model, specifying the categorical
cross-entropy loss function and the optimizer object that was defined

```
earlier. The `metrics` argument specifies that accuracy should be tracked
during training
disc_model_2.compile(loss=['categorical_crossentropy'],
optimizer=optimizer, metrics=['accuracy'])

#This line returns both the discriminator and classification models.
return disc_model, disc_model_2

#This line creates instances of the discriminator and classification
models by calling the `discriminator()` function and unpacking the
returned tuple.
discriminator_model, classification_model = discriminator()

#This line prints a summary of the discriminator model, including the
layer types, output shapes, and number of trainable parameters.
discriminator_model.summary()
```

11.3.5 Combined Model

In this model, both the generator and discriminator are called. The generator model takes in latent data, and the discriminator model takes in the generator output. The model summary displays the number of parameters and details about the model. This code defines a function called "combined()" that returns a Keras model for the combined generator/discriminator network.

```
def combined():
    inputs = Input(shape=(latent_dim,))
    gen_img = generator_model(inputs)
    gen_img = Reshape((784,))(gen_img)
    discriminator_model.trainable = False
    outs = discriminator_model(gen_img)
    comb_model = Model(inputs, outs)
    comb_model.compile(loss='binary_crossentropy', optimizer=optimizer,
metrics=['accuracy'])
    print(comb_model.summary())
    return comb_model
combined_model = combined()
combined_model.summary()
Model: "model_3"
```

Layer (type)	Output Shape	Param #
input_3 (InputLayer)	[(None, 100)]	0
model (Functional)	(None, 28, 28, 1)	1493520
reshape_1 (Reshape)	(None, 784)	0
model_1 (Functional)	(None, 1)	566273

```
Total params: 2,059,793
Trainable params: 1,489,936
Non-trainable params: 569,857
```

Here's a breakdown of each line of code in the function:

```
#This line defines an input layer for the combined network with the same
shape as the noise vector. The `shape` argument specifies the dimensions
of the input, which in this case is a one-dimensional vector of size
`latent_dim`.
inputs = Input(shape=(latent_dim,))
```

```
#This line passes the noise vector through the generator network to
produce a generated image.
gen_img = generator_model(inputs)
```

```
#This line reshapes the generated image into a one-dimensional vector of
size 784.
gen_img = Reshape((784,))(gen_img)
```

```
#This line sets the `trainable` attribute of the discriminator model to
`False`, which freezes the weights of the discriminator during training
of the combined network.
discriminator_model.trainable = False
```

```
#This line passes the generated image through the discriminator network
to produce a classification output.
outs = discriminator_model(gen_img)
```

```
#This line creates a Keras `Model` object that takes the noise vector as
input and produces a binary classification output as output. This is the
combined network.
comb_model = Model(inputs, outs)
```

```
#This line compiles the combined model, specifying the binary cross-
entropy loss function and the optimizer object that was defined earlier.
The `metrics` argument specifies that accuracy should be tracked during
training.
comb_model.compile(loss='binary_crossentropy', optimizer=optimizer,
metrics=['accuracy'])
#This line prints a summary of the combined model, including the layer
types, output shapes, and number of trainable parameters.
print(comb_model.summary())
```

```
#This line returns the combined model.
return comb_model
```

```
#This line creates an instance of the combined model by calling the
`combined()` function.
combined_model = combined()
```

```
#This line prints a summary of the combined model, including the layer
types, output shapes, and number of trainable parameters.
combined_model.summary()
```

11.3.6 Sample the Dataset

The MNIST digits dataset contains 60,000 training images, of which 1,000 are labeled, and the remaining are unlabeled. To create a training dataset, we randomly select 1,000 labeled images, with 100 images from each of the 10 classes. The "sample_1000()" function takes in two arguments, "x" and "y", which represent the features and labels of the dataset, respectively. The function returns two lists, each containing 100 randomly selected samples from each class, for a total of 1,000 samples.

```
def sample_1000(x, y):
    x_1000 = []
    y_1000 = []
    for i in range(10):
        x_i = x[y == i]
        ix = np.random.randint(0, len(x_i), 100)
        [x_1000.append(x_i[j]) for j in ix]
        [y_1000.append(i) for j in ix]
    return x_1000, y_1000
```

Here's a breakdown of each line of code in the function:

```
#These lines initialize two empty lists that will be used to store the
selected samples and corresponding labels.
x_1000 = []
y_1000 = []
```

```
#These lines loop through the 10 possible classes and extract the subset
of samples from the input features `x` that correspond to each class.
for i in range(10):
    x_i = x[y == i]
```

```
#This line generates a random array of 100 integers between 0 and the
number of samples in the current class.
ix = np.random.randint(0, len(x_i), 100)
```

```
#[These lines append 100 randomly selected samples and their
corresponding label to the `x_1000` and `y_1000` lists for the current
class.
x_1000.append(x_i[j]) for j in ix]
[y_1000.append(i) for j in ix]
```

```
#This line returns the two lists containing 1000 samples and labels in
total. The samples are randomly selected from the input features `x`,
with 100 samples for each of the 10 possible classes.
return x_1000, y_1000
```

11.3.7 Training

The GAN is trained in two steps: first, the discriminator is trained, and then the generator. The cost function for an unsupervised discriminator is binary cross-entropy (BCE), while the cost function for a supervised discriminator is categorical cross-entropy (CCE). This module trains the model and provides some outputs. The following steps are taken to train this model:

1. Sample labeled and unlabeled data from MNIST, normalize the data, and categorize the data labels.

2. Train the multiclass discriminator model with labeled real-world images.

3. Train the binary-class discriminator model with unlabeled real-world images.

4. Train the binary-class discriminator model with fake images generated by the generator network and sample noise of vector size 100.

5. Train the generator network by sampling noise with a vector size of 100 and training the combined model.

6. Repeat steps 2–5 for a certain number of iterations.

Training begins by using a set of labeled real-world images to train the supervised discriminator. Then, the unsupervised discriminator is trained to distinguish between real unlabeled images (labeled "1") and generator-generated images (labeled "0"). The generator is trained through the discriminator using the combined model that was created earlier. These fake images are fed into the discriminator to be sorted, with the discriminator given the target label "1", which means "true". This code defines a function called "train()" that trains the generator and discriminator networks using the MNIST dataset.

```
def train():
    train_data, train_data_y = sample_1000(x_train, y_train)
    train_data = ((np.array(train_data).astype(np.float32)) - 127.5) /
127.5
    train_data_y = to_categorical(train_data_y)
    all_train_data = ((np.array(x_train).astype(np.float32)) - 127.5) /
127.5
    all_train_data_y = to_categorical(y_train)
    for j in range(iterations):
        batch_indx = np.random.randint(0, train_data.shape[0],
size=(half_batch_size))
        batch_x = train_data[batch_indx]
        batch_x = batch_x.reshape((-1, 784))
        batch_y = train_data_y[batch_indx]
        batch_indx_total = np.random.randint(0, all_train_data.shape[0],
size=(half_batch_size))
        batch_x_total = all_train_data[batch_indx_total]
        batch_x_total = batch_x_total.reshape((-1, 784))
        batch_y_total = all_train_data_y[batch_indx_total]
        input_noise = np.random.normal(0, 1, size=(half_batch_size, 100))
        gen_outs = generator_model.predict(input_noise)
        gen_outs = gen_outs.reshape((-1, 784))
        classi_loss = classification_model.train_on_batch(batch_x,
batch_y)
        real_loss1 = discriminator_model.train_on_batch(batch_x_total,
np.ones((half_batch_size, 1)))
        fake_loss = discriminator_model.train_on_batch(gen_outs,
np.zeros((half_batch_size, 1)))
        full_batch_input_noise = np.random.normal(0, 1, size=(batch_size,
100))
        gan_loss = combined_model.train_on_batch(full_batch_input_noise,
np.array([1] * batch_size))
        if j % 1000 == 0:
            test_data = ((x_test.astype(np.float32) - 127.5) / 127.5).
reshape((-1, 784))
```

```
            test_results = classification_model.predict(test_data)
            test_results_argmax = np.argmax(test_results, axis=1)
            count = 0
            for i in range(len(test_results_argmax)):
                if test_results_argmax[i] == y_test[i]:
                    count += 1
            print("Accuracy After", j, "iterations: ", (count / len(test_
data)) * 100)
if __name__ == '__main__':
    train()


Accuracy After 0 iterations:  9.53
```

Here's a breakdown of each line of code in the function:

```
#This line calls the `sample_1000()` function to randomly select a subset
of 1000 samples from the training set.
train_data, train_data_y = sample_1000(x_train, y_train)


#These lines convert the training data to float32 and normalize the pixel
values to the range [-1, 1]. The labels are also one-hot encoded using
`to_categorical()`.
train_data = ((np.array(train_data).astype(np.float32)) - 127.5) / 127.5
train_data_y = to_categorical(train_data_y)


#These lines convert all of the training data to float32 and normalize
the pixel values to the range [-1, 1]. The labels are also one-hot
encoded using `to_categorical()`.
all_train_data = ((np.array(x_train).astype(np.float32)) - 127.5) / 127.5
all_train_data_y = to_categorical(y_train)


#This line starts a loop that will train the networks for the
`iterations` number of iterations.
for j in range(iterations):


#These lines randomly select a half-batch of training samples from the
1000 selected earlier, reshape the samples to a one-dimensional vector,
and obtain their corresponding labels.
batch_indx = np.random.randint(0, train_data.shape[0],
size=(half_batch_size))
batch_x = train_data[batch_indx]
batch_x = batch_x.reshape((-1, 784))
batch_y = train_data_y[batch_indx]


#These lines randomly select another half-batch of training samples from
the entire training set, reshape the samples to a one-dimensional vector,
and obtain their corresponding labels.
batch_indx_total = np.random.randint(0, all_train_data.shape[0],
size=(half_batch_size))
batch_x_total = all_train_data[batch_indx_total]
batch_x_total = batch_x_total.reshape((-1, 784))
batch_y_total = all_train_data_y[batch_indx_total]
```

```
#These lines generate a batch of noise vectors and use the generator
network to produce a batch of generated images. The generated images are
reshaped to a one-dimensional vector.
input_noise = np.random.normal(0, 1, size=(half_batch_size, 100))
gen_outs = generator_model.predict(input_noise)
gen_outs = gen_outs.reshape((-1, 784))

#These lines train the discriminator and generator networks on the
current batch of samples and noise vectors. The discriminator is trained
on real and fake images, while the generator is trained to produce images
that the discriminator cannot distinguish from real images.
classi_loss = classification_model.train_on_batch(batch_x, batch_y)
real_loss1 = discriminator_model.train_on_batch(batch_x_total,
np.ones((half_batch_size, 1)))
fake_loss = discriminator_model.train_on_batch(gen_outs, np.zeros((half_
batch_size, 1)))
full_batch_input_noise = np.random.normal(0, 1, size=(batch_size, 100))
gan_loss = combined_model.train_on_batch(full_batch_input_noise,
np.array([1] * batch_size))

#This line checks if the current iteration is a multiple of 1000.
if j % 1000 == 0:

#This line normalizes the pixel values of the test set to the range [-1,
1] and reshapes each test image to a one-dimensional vector.
test_data = ((x_test.astype(np.float32) - 127.5) / 127.5).reshape((-1,
784))

#This line uses the trained classification model to predict the class
labels for the test set.
test_results = classification_model.predict(test_data)

#This line converts the predicted class probabilities to class labels
using the `argmax()` function along the second axis.
test_results_argmax = np.argmax(test_results, axis=1)

#These lines count the number of correct predictions by comparing the
predicted labels to the true labels in the test set.
count = 0
for i in range(len(test_results_argmax)):
    if test_results_argmax[i] == y_test[i]:
        count += 1

#This line prints the accuracy of the classification model on the test
set at the current iteration.
print("Accuracy After", j, "iterations: ", (count / len(test_data)) *
100)

#This line calls the `train()` function if the script is being run as the
main program.
if __name__ == '__main__':
    train()
```

11.3.8 Evaluation and Plotting

It should be noted that the discriminator is not updated during this step. We only used the discriminator after training and discarded the generator because our main goal was to create a classifier for MNIST. In this case, we use the Matplotlib library to plot the predicted results, as shown in Figure 11.5. This code generates a grid of 25 images using the trained generator model and displays them using Matplotlib.

```
import matplotlib.pyplot as plt
r, c = 5, 5
noise = np.random.normal(0, 1, (r * c, 100))
gen_imgs = generator_model.predict(noise)
new_gen_img = gen_imgs.reshape(25, 784)
output_class = classification_model.predict(new_gen_img)
# Rescale images 0 - 1
gen_imgs = 0.5 * gen_imgs + 0.5
fig, axs = plt.subplots(r, c)
cnt = 0
print('predicted labels for generated images')
for i in range(r):
    for j in range(c):
        axs[i,j].imshow(gen_imgs[cnt, :,:,0], cmap='gray')
        print(np.argmax(output_class[cnt]), end=' ')
        axs[i,j].axis('off')
        cnt += 1
plt.show()
fig.savefig("mnist.png")
plt.close()
predicted labels for generated images
1 5 5 1 1 0 4 4 3 7 6 9 6 2 4 4 4 6 7 3 7 3 0 4 0
```

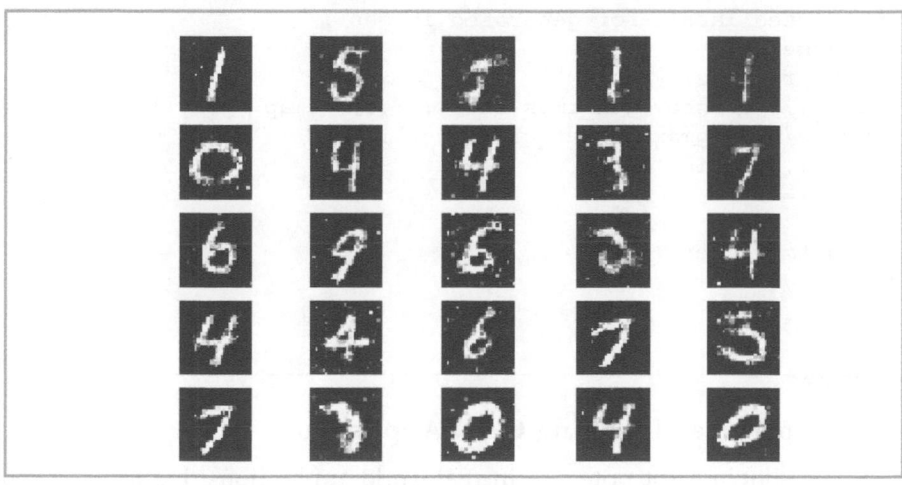

FIGURE 11.5
Predicted outputs.

Here's a breakdown of each line:

```
#This line imports the matplotlib library for data visualization.
import matplotlib.pyplot as plt

#These lines set the number of rows and columns for the generated image
grid.
r, c = 5, 5

#This line generates a batch of 25 noise vectors, each of size 100.
noise = np.random.normal(0, 1, (r * c, 100))

#These lines use the trained generator model to generate a batch of 25
images from the noise vectors. The images are reshaped to one-dimensional
vectors and then passed to the trained classification model to predict
their class labels.
gen_imgs = generator_model.predict(noise)
new_gen_img = gen_imgs.reshape(25, 784)
output_class = classification_model.predict(new_gen_img)

#This line rescales the generated images from the range [-1, 1] to the
range [0, 1].
gen_imgs = 0.5 * gen_imgs + 0.5

#This line creates a figure with `r` rows and `c` columns of subplots
using matplotlib.
fig, axs = plt.subplots(r, c)

#These lines loop through each of the 25 generated images, displaying
them in the corresponding subplot of the figure. The predicted class
label for each image is printed to the console. Finally, the figure is
displayed and saved as an image file.
cnt = 0
print('predicted labels for generated images')
for i in range(r):
    for j in range(c):
        axs[i,j].imshow(gen_imgs[cnt, :,:,0], cmap='gray')
        print(np.argmax(output_class[cnt]), end=' ')
        axs[i,j].axis('off')
        cnt += 1
plt.show()
fig.savefig("mnist.png")
plt.close()
```

11.4 Semi-Supervised Learning GAN Applications

The SGAN has shown great potential in real-world applications due to its benefits. For instance, GONet is a system that addresses the problem of traversability estimation for robots, and researchers have used SGANs to solve the issue of semantic image segmentation. Inspired by these findings, SGANs have been applied to the detection of road patches in images. Semi-supervised learning has also been used to address the problem of cross-modal information retrieval. Researchers have used SGANs to tackle novel problems that lack reasonable solutions as well as to conduct spoofing attacks on speaker recognition systems. In many cases, SGANs are useful when there is a shortage of labeled data available. Overall, semi-supervised learning GANs have numerous applications in various fields, and their potential for further use continues to be explored.

11.4.1 Image Classification

Semi-supervised GANs can be used to improve image classification by using both labeled and unlabeled data.

11.4.2 Object Detection

These GANs can be used to detect and identify objects in images with the help of labeled and unlabeled data.

11.4.3 Natural Language Processing

Semi-supervised GANs can be used for tasks, such as text classification, machine translation, and sentiment analysis.

11.4.4 Healthcare

These GANs can be used for medical image analysis, such as identifying tumors in MRI scans, with the help of labeled and unlabeled data.

11.4.5 Fraud Detection

Semi-supervised GANs can be used to detect fraud in financial transactions by using labeled and unlabeled data.

11.4.6 Autonomous Vehicles

These GANs can be used for object detection and recognition in autonomous vehicles with the help of labeled and unlabeled data.

11.4.7 Recommender Systems

Semi-supervised GANs can improve recommender systems by using labeled and unlabeled data to understand user preferences better.

11.4.8 Gaming

These GANs can generate new game levels, characters, and game assets in gaming.

11.4.9 Virtual Reality

Semi-supervised GANs can be used to generate realistic virtual environments by using both labeled and unlabeled data.

11.4.10 Advertising

These GANs can be used for targeted advertising by analyzing user behavior and preferences with the help of labeled and unlabeled data.

11.5 Semi-Supervised Learning GAN Issues

Semi-supervised learning with GANs is a relatively new area of research, and there are several issues that researchers are working to overcome.

11.5.1 Lack of Labeled Data

SGANs attempt to address the problem of scarce labeled data in machine learning. Collecting a large amount of labeled data is often time-consuming, costly, and, in some cases, practically impossible. However, unlabeled data is typically abundant and more easily accessible. Here are some problems associated with the lack of labeled data in SGANs.

1. **Model performance:** Models trained with less labeled data might not perform well due to high variance, which can lead to overfitting. The model may learn to perform very well on the training data but fail to generalize well to unseen data.

2. **Data representation:** With insufficient labeled data, the model might not learn an accurate representation of the true data distribution. This can lead to generating outputs that don't accurately represent the target domain.

Solutions:

1. **Data augmentation:** This technique creates new synthetic labeled data by applying transformations to the existing labeled examples. For example, an image can be flipped, rotated, or cropped to create a new labeled instance.

2. **Active learning:** This is an iterative process where the model is used to predict labels for the unlabeled data. The instances where the model is most uncertain are then labeled by human annotators and added to the training set.

3. **Transfer learning:** Use pre-trained models for similar tasks or domains and fine-tune them for the specific task. The idea is to leverage the knowledge gained from tasks with ample labeled data for tasks with less labeled data.

4. **Pseudo-labeling:** This involves generating labels for unlabeled data using a trained model, and then using this data to further train the model. The idea is that the model will learn more about the underlying data distribution, even from its mistakes.

5. **Self-training:** In this method, the model is initially trained with a small amount of labeled data, and then the model is used to predict labels for the unlabeled data. The model is retrained on its most confident predictions, along with the original labeled data.

6. **Co-training:** If there are two sets of features, two classifiers are trained, and each classifier labels the unlabeled instances for the other classifier. The process continues iteratively.

In conclusion, while the lack of labeled data presents a significant challenge in training SGANs, several strategies can be used to address this issue. The best approach will depend on the specific characteristics of the data and the problem at hand.

11.5.2 Difficulty in Finding the Right Balance between Labeled and Unlabeled Data

SGANs leverage both labeled and unlabeled data during the training process. However, finding the right balance between these two data types can pose a significant challenge for several reasons:

1. **Importance of unlabeled data:** Unlabeled data is typically used to improve the generator's performance in creating realistic examples. However, if too much emphasis is placed on the unlabeled data, the model might not learn enough about the structure of the labeled data to make accurate predictions.

2. **Influence of labeled data:** Conversely, if too much weight is given to the labeled data, the model could overfit to this data and fail to generalize well to unseen examples. It might also not generate diverse enough examples as it focuses too much on replicating the labeled examples.

Solutions:

1. **Dynamic loss balancing:** You could adjust the loss function contributions of labeled and unlabeled data dynamically throughout the training process. Initially, the model might place more emphasis on the labeled data to ensure it learns the correct structures. As training progresses, the emphasis could gradually shift more toward the unlabeled data to improve the diversity of the generated examples.

2. **Two-step training:** Another strategy could involve training in two steps. First, pre-train the discriminator using labeled data only, and then continue training with both labeled and unlabeled data.

3. **Confidence-based sampling:** In this approach, instances that the model predicts with high confidence are utilized more during training. This method usually involves a pseudo-labeling step where labels are predicted for the unlabeled data. Those predictions made with high confidence are added to the training set, effectively increasing the size of the labeled dataset.

4. **Ensemble methods:** You can also train multiple models with different balances of labeled and unlabeled data, and then combine their predictions. This can increase the robustness of your model to the balance of labeled and unlabeled data.

Striking the right balance between labeled and unlabeled data is a delicate task in semi-supervised learning and usually requires some experimentation and adjustment based on the specific data and task at hand.

11.5.3 Mode Collapse

Mode collapse is a common issue in GANs, including in the SGANs. When mode collapse occurs, the generator produces limited varieties of samples, often focusing on a few modes of the data distribution and ignoring others. As a result, the diversity of generated samples is significantly reduced.

Solutions:

1. **Mini-batch discrimination:** Mini-batch discrimination is a technique that allows the discriminator to assess a set of examples together and identify if they're too similar. If the generator is repeatedly producing the same output (a sign of mode collapse), the discriminator will be able to notice this during mini-batch discrimination and adjust accordingly.

2. **Unrolled GANs:** This technique involves updating the generator based on a "future" version of the discriminator. Essentially, the discriminator is "unrolled" several steps into the future, and the generator is updated based on this unrolled model. This encourages more stable learning and helps prevent mode collapse.

3. **Wasserstein GANs (WGANs):** WGANs use a different loss function (the Earth Mover's or Wasserstein distance) that has better theoretical properties and leads to more stable training. This can help prevent mode collapse.

4. **Spectral normalization:** This is a normalization method for the discriminator that can stabilize GAN training and help prevent mode collapse.

5. **Experience replay:** This technique involves storing past generator outputs and occasionally reusing them for training. This can encourage the generator to maintain diversity in its outputs and prevent it from collapsing to a single mode.

Remember that each technique might not work for all types of data or tasks, so it often requires some experimentation to find the best approach for a particular application.

11.5.4 Difficulty in Training

Semi-supervised learning with GANs can be challenging to train, as it involves optimizing two networks simultaneously. Training GANs, including SGANs, can be challenging due to the nature of their adversarial learning paradigm. This difficulty is often amplified in the semi-supervised setting due to the additional complexity of handling both labeled and unlabeled data. Specific issues might include the instability of the training process, the vanishing gradients problem, and the difficulty of achieving an equilibrium between the generator and the discriminator.

Solutions:

1. **Gradient clipping or spectral normalization:** These techniques control the magnitude of updates to the model weights, which can help to stabilize the training process.

2. **Alternative loss functions:** The traditional GAN loss function can lead to vanishing gradients when the discriminator is too strong. Alternative loss functions, such as the Wasserstein loss or the least-squares loss, can help to mitigate this issue.

3. **Modified training procedure:** Techniques, such as one-sided label smoothing, instance noise, and minibatch discrimination, can help to stabilize GAN training.

4. **Early stopping:** Monitor the model's performance on a validation set during training and stop training when performance starts to degrade.

5. **Learning rate schedules:** Adaptive learning rate schedules, such as learning rate decay or cyclical learning rates, can help to stabilize training and lead to better final model performance.

6. **Two time-scale update rule (TTUR):** Using different learning rates for the generator and the discriminator can also stabilize training. The TTUR suggests a larger learning rate for the discriminator than the generator.

7. **Use of pre-trained models:** Using pre-trained models as starting points can speed up the training process and also provide better results, as these models have already learned certain features from the data.

8. **Proportional control of labeled and unlabeled data:** Adjusting the ratio of labeled to unlabeled data used in each training batch can also help to stabilize training in the semi-supervised setting. Some approaches use more unlabeled data in the early stages of training and gradually increase the proportion of labeled data.

Keep in mind that these solutions are not mutually exclusive and can be combined to tackle the training difficulties more effectively. The choice of the solution also heavily depends on the specifics of your problem and data.

11.5.5 Stability Issues

GANs can be unstable, leading to poor training performance and results. Training GANs, including SGANs, often suffers from issues of instability. This instability often arises from the adversarial nature of GAN training, where the generator and the discriminator are in a constant push-pull dynamic. In many cases, one model may dominate the other, leading to poor performance. For instance, a too-strong discriminator can lead to vanishing gradients for the generator, causing it to stop learning.

Solutions:

1. **Gradient penalties:** Techniques, such as gradient clipping or gradient penalties, can be employed to control the magnitudes of the model updates, which can help stabilize training. One example is the Wasserstein GAN with Gradient Penalty (WGAN-GP), which adds a penalty term to the loss function to encourage 1-Lipschitz continuity and improve stability.

2. **Alternative loss functions:** The traditional GAN loss might lead to a vanishing gradients problem when the discriminator is too strong, causing the generator to stop learning. Alternative loss functions, such as Wasserstein loss or least-squares loss, can help alleviate this problem and improve stability.

3. **Modified training procedure:** Techniques, such as one-sided label smoothing, instance noise, or minibatch discrimination, can help stabilize the GAN training process.

4. **Spectral normalization:** This technique normalizes the weights of the model, which restricts the Lipschitz constant of the function approximated by the model and helps stabilize the training process.

5. **Two time-scale update rule (TTUR):** Using different learning rates for updating the generator and the discriminator can also improve stability. Generally, the discriminator is updated more frequently than the generator.

6. **Consistency regularization:** Encouraging the model to make consistent predictions on unlabeled data under small perturbations can also improve stability.

It's crucial to understand that these solutions aren't exclusive and can often be combined to tackle stability issues more effectively. The choice of solution often depends on the specifics of the data and the problem you're trying to solve.

11.5.6 Difficulty in Evaluating Performance

Evaluating the performance of semi-supervised learning with GANs can be challenging, as it involves evaluating the discriminator and generator networks. Evaluating the performance of SGANs can be quite challenging for a number of reasons.

1. **Lack of a ground truth:** For unsupervised tasks, such as generating images, there is no true label to compare the generated samples against. This makes it difficult to quantify how well the generator is doing.

2. **Quality vs. Diversity:** A good generator should generate samples that are both high in quality (i.e., each individual sample looks real) and diverse (i.e., the collection of samples covers the entire range of the data distribution). These two aspects are often in conflict. For example, a generator could achieve high quality by simply memorizing and regenerating training examples, but this would result in low diversity. Conversely, a generator could achieve high diversity by generating widely varying samples, but this might result in lower quality if the samples do not resemble real data.

3. **Instability of GAN training:** GANs are notoriously hard to train, and the generator's performance can fluctuate dramatically during training. This makes it hard to tell when to stop training (i.e., when has the generator's performance peaked?).

Solutions:

1. **Use supervised metrics where possible:** For tasks where some labeled data is available, we can apply traditional supervised metrics. For example, in semi-supervised classification, we can calculate accuracy, precision, recall, etc. on a held-out validation set.

2. **Inception Score (IS):** IS is a commonly used metric for evaluating the quality and diversity of generated images. It is calculated by applying a pre-trained classifier (e.g., Inception v3) to the generated samples, and then computing a score based on the classifier's output probabilities. However, it has its limitations and biases, so it should not be relied on as the sole evaluation metric.

3. **Frechet Inception Distance (FID):** FID is another popular metric for evaluating GANs. It compares the statistical distribution of the generated samples with that of the real samples in the feature space of a pre-trained classifier. Lower FID scores indicate better generated samples.

4. **Human evaluation:** Despite its scalability issues, human evaluation is often considered the gold standard for evaluating the performance of generative models. You can ask human evaluators to rank different models or to determine whether a given sample is real or generated.

5. **Track changes over time:** Due to the instability of GAN training, it's helpful to track the generator's performance over time, rather than just at the end of training. You can save generated samples at regular intervals during training to visually inspect the generator's progress. Additionally, you can compute quantitative metrics at regular intervals to plot a curve of the generator's performance over time.

Remember that no single evaluation method is perfect, and it's generally a good idea to use multiple methods in conjunction to get a fuller picture of the SGAN's performance.

11.6 Semi-Supervised Learning GAN Implementation Tips

Here are some implementation tips for semi-supervised learning GAN:

1. Use a small number of labeled examples and many unlabeled examples to train the model.
2. Use data augmentation techniques to increase the number of labeled examples.
3. Use a mix of labeled and unlabeled examples during training, and gradually decrease the weight of the supervised loss as the model gets better at classifying the data.
4. Use different learning rates for the generator and discriminator, and adjust them during training.
5. Use different loss functions for the generator and discriminator, and experiment with different weightings for each loss function.
6. Regularize the model to prevent overfitting using weight decay, dropout, and batch normalization techniques.
7. Use pre-trained models for the generator and discriminator to speed up training and improve performance.
8. Use techniques such as label smoothing and one-sided label smoothing to prevent the discriminator from overfitting to the labeled examples.
9. Experiment with different architectures for the generator and discriminator and adjust the number of layers and neurons in each.
10. Use different optimization algorithms, such as Adam, RMSProp, and Stochastic Gradient Descent, and experiment with different hyperparameters, such as learning rate and batch size.

Note that these tips are not exhaustive and may vary depending on the specific problem and dataset being used. Remember, hands-on experience is key when working with SGANs or any other machine learning models. Therefore, consistently practicing implementation and troubleshooting is crucial for mastering these concepts.

11.7 Lessons Learned

- Learn the Semi-Supervised GAN architecture and concepts
- Learn Semi-Supervised GAN implementation for MNIST
- Learn Semi-Supervised Learning GAN Applications
- Learn Semi-Supervised Learning GAN Issues
- Semi-Supervised Learning GAN Implementation Tips

11.8 Problems

11.8.1 What is an SGAN?

11.8.2 How does an SGAN differ from a traditional GAN?

11.8.3 What is the architecture of an SGAN?

11.8.4 How does an SGAN use labeled and unlabeled data in its training process?

11.8.5 How does the loss function differ in an SGAN compared to a traditional GAN?

11.8.6 What are the potential applications of SGANs?

11.8.7 How can an SGAN be used for image classification tasks?

11.8.8 What are the advantages and disadvantages of using an SGAN compared to other types of deep learning models?

11.8.9 How can the performance of an SGAN be evaluated?

11.8.10 What are some potential future directions for research on SGANs?

11.8.11 What is the difference between supervised and semi-supervised learning?

11.8.12 How does the discriminator in SGAN differ from the discriminator in regular GAN?

11.8.13 What is the role of labeled data in SGAN?

11.8.14 How does the generator in SGAN make use of both labeled and unlabeled data?

11.8.15 How is the loss function for SGAN different from regular GAN?

11.8.16 How does SGAN help with the problem of limited labeled data in machine learning?

11.8.17 What are some real-world applications of SGAN?

11.8.18 Can SGAN be used for unsupervised learning as well?

11.8.19 What are some limitations of SGAN?

11.8.20 How does SGAN compare to other semi-supervised learning techniques?

11.9 Programming Questions

- **Easy**

    11.9.1 Implement SGAN architecture for image classification using the MNIST dataset.

    11.9.2 Modify the SGAN architecture to perform semi-supervised text classification using a text dataset.

    11.9.3 Train an SGAN model on a subset of the CIFAR-10 dataset to generate realistic images.

11.9.4 Use SGAN to generate new data for a medical imaging dataset and evaluate the performance of the generated images using a pre-trained classification model.

11.9.5 Implement a variant of SGAN that includes a cycle-consistency loss for image-to-image translation tasks.

- **Medium**

11.9.6 Evaluate the performance of an SGAN model for anomaly detection in a dataset of industrial sensors.

11.9.7 Train an SGAN model on a dataset of audio recordings to generate new audio samples with specific characteristics.

11.9.8 Implement a conditional SGAN model that generates images based on specific input conditions.

11.9.9 Use SGAN to generate new data for a financial time-series dataset and evaluate the performance of the generated samples using a pre-trained predictive model.

11.9.10 Train an SGAN model on a subset of the ImageNet dataset to generate realistic images of specific objects or animals.

- **Hard**

11.9.11 Implement a semi-supervised GAN to generate handwritten digits (MNIST dataset) and classify them into their corresponding labels using TensorFlow.

11.9.12 Train a semi-supervised GAN on the CIFAR-10 dataset and evaluate its performance in generating realistic images and improving classification accuracy.

11.9.13 Build a semi-supervised GAN using TensorFLow and train it on the Fashion-MNIST dataset. Compare the results with a traditional supervised learning approach.

11.9.14 Use a semi-supervised GAN to generate realistic images of celebrities from the CelebA dataset and classify them based on their attributes (e.g., gender, age, hair color).

11.9.15 Implement a semi-supervised GAN to generate text data (e.g., product reviews and news articles) and classify them into their corresponding categories using natural language processing techniques.

12

Least Squares Generative Adversarial Network (LSGAN)

This chapter covers the following topics about Adversarial Network with Least Squares (LSGAN):

- LSGAN Architecture
- LSGAN Applications
- Develop an LSGAN for MNIST
- LSGAN for Caltech_birds2011 Dataset
- LSGAN Issues
- LSGAN Implementation Tips

12.1 Preface

LSGAN, or Least Squares GAN, is a type of generative adversarial network that uses the least squares loss function in its discriminator. This aims to improve the stability of GAN training and has demonstrated better results in some applications compared to standard GANs. The standard GAN loss function, which utilizes binary cross-entropy, can lead to issues like vanishing gradients and mode collapse, where the generator produces a limited range of samples failing to cover the complete distribution of the real data. LSGANs address this issue by training the generator and discriminator to minimize the least squares loss instead. This encourages the generator to produce more diverse samples and contributes to smoother and more stable training. LSGANs have been successfully applied to various tasks, such as image synthesis, text-to-image translation, and video prediction, and they have been shown to produce high-quality samples with better visual fidelity and diversity. However, LSGANs can be computationally expensive to train due to the quadratic optimization problem inherent in the least squares loss function. Techniques like mini-batch discrimination and spectral normalization have been proposed to mitigate this issue.

Overall, LSGANs hold promising potential to enhance the capabilities of generative models for various applications. This chapter provides an overview of LSGAN and coding examples for further practice. Figure 12.1 illustrates the general architecture of an LSGAN.

DOI: 10.1201/9781003281344-12

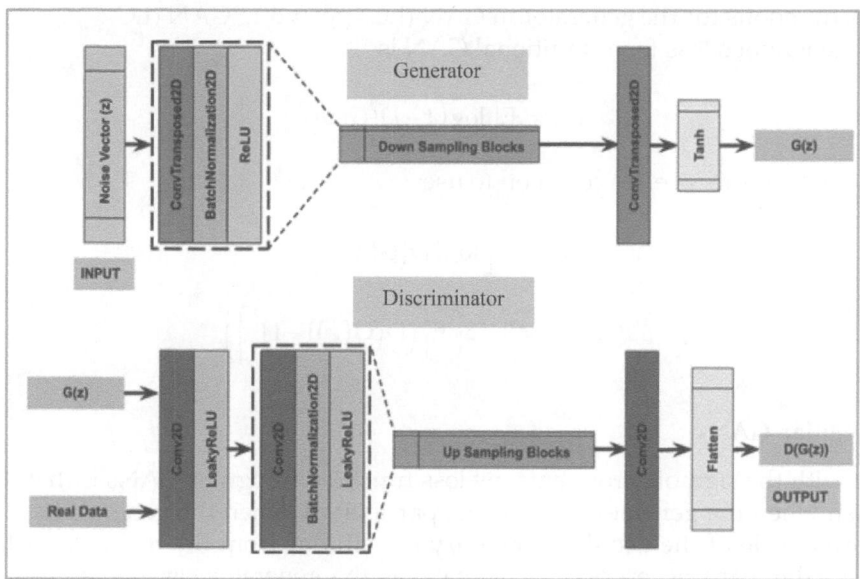

FIGURE 12.1
LSGAN architecture.

12.2 LSGAN Architecture

In a standard GAN, the generator and discriminator are trained using the binary cross-entropy loss function. The discriminator's goal is to classify the input images as real or fake, while the generator aims to create images that can fool the discriminator into believing they are real. Conversely, LSGANs employ a least squares loss function for both the generator and the discriminator. The discriminator is trained to assign high values to real images and low values to fake ones, while the generator strives to produce images that receive high values from the discriminator. This loss function encourages the generator to produce samples that are closer to the real data, and the discriminator can distinguish between real and fake samples using a more relaxed boundary, making the training process smoother and more stable. As a result, LSGANs have demonstrated the ability to produce high-quality samples with superior visual fidelity and diversity compared to standard GANs.

1. Loss functions for discriminator in GAN (LD_{GAN}) and LSGAN (LD_{LSGAN}):

$$L(G,D) = \mathrm{E}x \sim pdata(x)\left[\log D(x)\right] + \mathrm{E}z \sim pz(z)\left[\log\left(1 - D\left(G(z)\right)\right)\right]$$

where:
- E is the expectation.
- $D(x)$ is the discriminator's output for real data.
- $G(z)$ is the generator's output from noise z.
- $D(G(z))$ is the discriminator's output for fake data.

$$LD_{LSGAN} = \mathrm{E}\left[\left(D(x) - 1\right)^2\right] + \mathrm{E}\left[D\left(G(z)\right)^2\right]$$

2. Loss functions for the generator in GAN (LG_{GAN}) and LSGAN (LG_{LSGAN}):
The generator's loss for a traditional GAN is:

$$L_G = E\Big[\log\big(1 - D\big(G(z)\big)\big)\Big]$$

However, in practice, it's common to use:

$$L_G = E\Big[\log\big(D\big(G(z)\big)\big)\Big]$$

$$LG_{LSGAN} = 1/2\left(E\Big[\big(D\big(G(z)\big) - 1\big)^2\Big]\right)$$

12.2.1 Regular GANs

The issue with the sigmoid cross-entropy loss function in regular GANs is that the gradients vanish when the generator is updated, particularly when the generated samples are on the correct side of the decision boundary but still far from the real data distribution. This causes the learning process to stagnate, as the generator cannot produce samples that are closer to the real data. To address this issue, LSGANs introduce a new loss function based on the least squares method, which updates the data depending on how close it is to the decision boundary. The LSGAN's least squares loss function makes the training process more stable and produces samples that are closer to real data. The authors of the LSGAN paper presented Figures 12.2 and 12.3 to show the differences between the decision boundaries of the sigmoid cross-entropy loss function and the least squares loss function. In Figure 12.2, the two decision boundaries are shown, with the blue line indicating the sigmoid decision boundary and the red line indicating the least squares decision boundary. The blue plus symbols represent the fake data, while the red circles represent the real data. If a fake sample attempts to update the generator, and they are on the correct

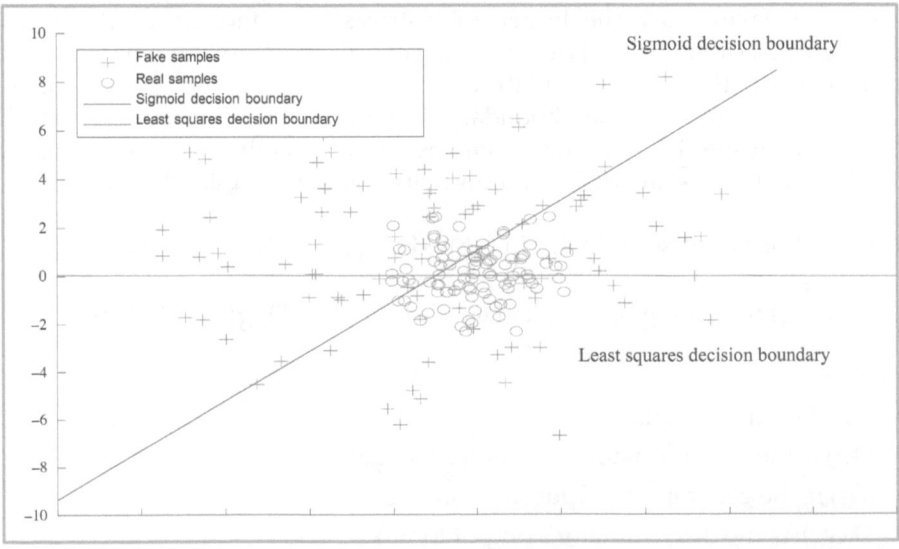

FIGURE 12.2
Two loss functions' decision boundaries for successful GANs learning.

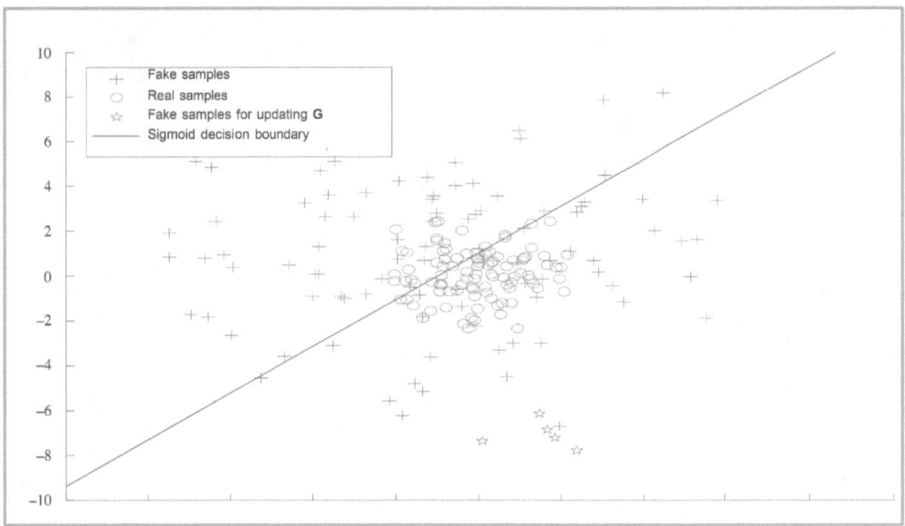

FIGURE 12.3
The sigmoid cross entropy loss function's decision boundary.

side of the decision boundary, the generator cannot be updated. It is crucial to note that the decision boundary must cross the real data distribution; otherwise, the learning process will come to a halt. In summary, the LSGAN's least squares loss function provides a more stable and consistent training process, leading to higher-quality generated samples that are closer to real data.

Figure 12.3 illustrates the decision boundary of the sigmoid cross-entropy loss function, where the fake samples have very small errors for updating the generator because they are on the correct side of the decision boundary. To address this issue, LSGAN was proposed.

12.2.2 LSGAN

Figure 12.4 displays the decision boundary of the least squares loss function and its ability to address the problem using the same data. The fake samples (in magenta) are penalized, compelling the generator to create models closer to the decision boundary. Suppose we select **a**, **b**, and **c** as coding for the discriminator, where **a** and **b** denote the labels of the fake and real data, respectively, and **c** represents the value that the generator wants the discriminator to associate with the fake data. As demonstrated earlier, this penalty forces the generator to generate samples closer to the decision boundary. Comparing Figure 12.3 with Figure 12.4, the discriminator's output must have a linear activation function, and the cost function is divided into separate parts for the discriminator and generator.

$$min_D V_{LSGAN}(D) = \frac{1}{2}E_{x \sim pdata}(x)\left[\left(D(x)-b\right)^2\right] + \frac{1}{2}E_{z \sim pz}(z)\left[\left(D\big(G(Z)\big)-a\right)^2\right]$$

$$min_G V_{LSGAN}(G) = \frac{1}{2}E_{z \sim pz}(z)\left[\left(D\big(G(Z)\big)-c\right)^2\right]$$

- E represents the expected value (or average).
- *pdata* is the distribution of the real data.

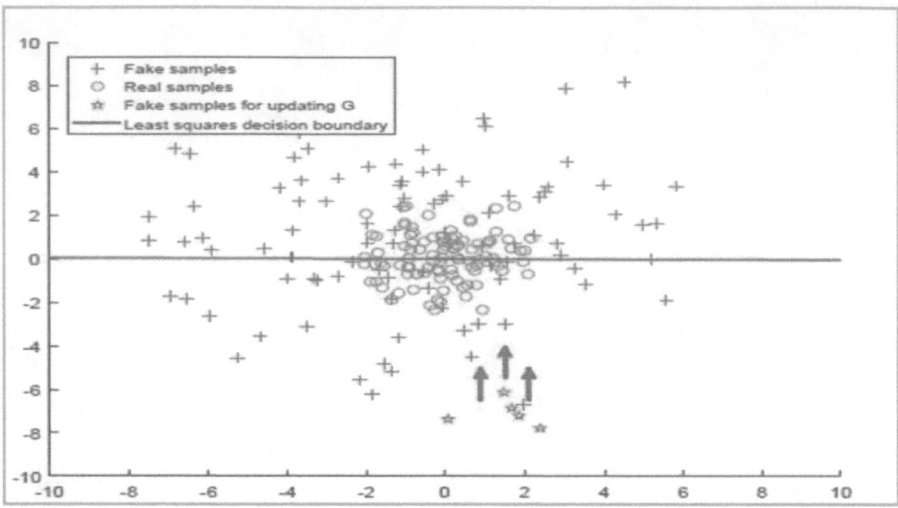

FIGURE 12.4
The least squares loss function's decision boundary.

- *pz* is the distribution of the input noise to the generator.
- *a* and *b* are labels for fake and real data, respectively. For LSGANs, typically $a = 0$ and $b = 1$, indicating that the discriminator should ideally label real data as 1 and fake data as 0.
- The objective for *D* is to minimize this value, making it as hard as possible for *G* to fool it.

Moving the generated samples closer to the decision boundary can make them appear more realistic. Figure 12.5 shows the loss functions for the LSGAN. Part (a) represents the LSGAN discriminator loss and Part (b) illustrates the LSGAN generator loss. On the other hand, the least squares loss function encourages the generator to produce samples closer to the real data distribution, resulting in a smoother and more stable training process.

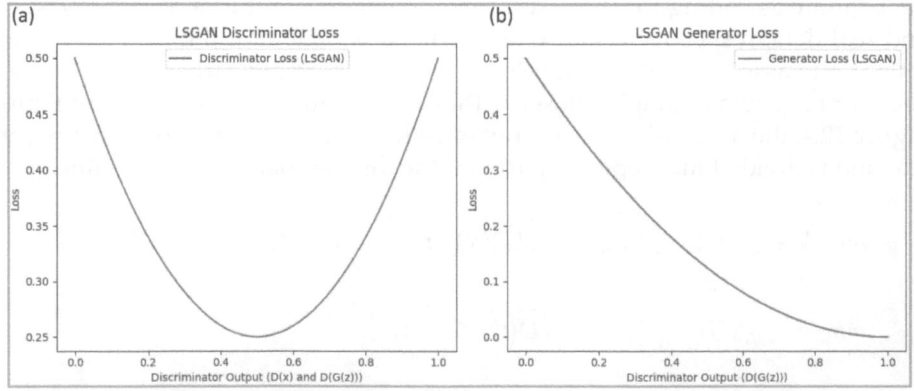

FIGURE 12.5
(a) LSGAN dicriminator loss. (b) LSGAN generator loss.

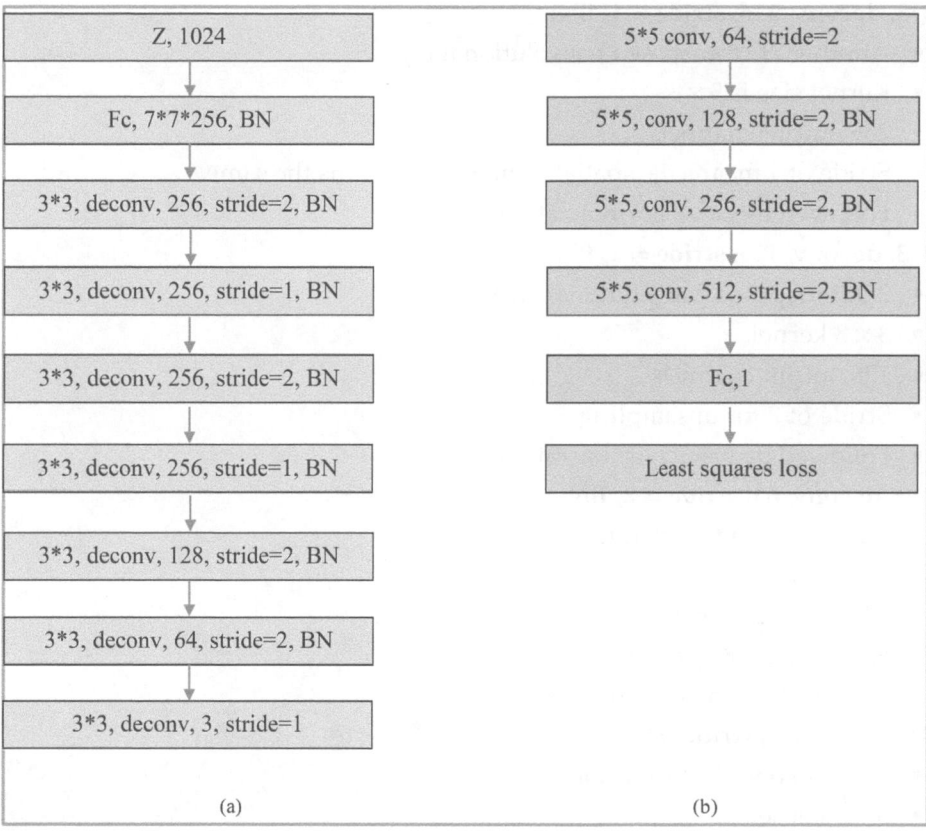

Z, 1024	5*5 conv, 64, stride=2
Fc, 7*7*256, BN	5*5, conv, 128, stride=2, BN
3*3, deconv, 256, stride=2, BN	5*5, conv, 256, stride=2, BN
3*3, deconv, 256, stride=1, BN	5*5, conv, 512, stride=2, BN
3*3, deconv, 256, stride=2, BN	Fc,1
3*3, deconv, 256, stride=1, BN	Least squares loss
3*3, deconv, 128, stride=2, BN	
3*3, deconv, 64, stride=2, BN	
3*3, deconv, 3, stride=1	
(a)	(b)

FIGURE 12.6
(a) The generator. (b) The discriminator.

The second approach to addressing the vanishing gradient problem involves penalizing samples that are far from the decision boundary. This encourages the generator to produce more diverse samples, thus maintaining a more consistent level of performance during training. This makes LSGANs more stable than regular GANs. The least squares loss function, used in LSGANs, has a single maximum value, unlike the sigmoid cross entropy loss function used in regular GANs that exhibits multiple maximum values when x is large. Figure 12.6 illustrates the architecture of the generator and the discriminator used in LSGANs. Figure 12.6 (a) describes the layers for a generator in an LSGAN. Here's a breakdown of each line to describe its meaning:

1. **3*3, deconv, 256, stride = 2, BN:**
   - This is a 2D transposed convolutional layer (often referred to as "deconvolution" or "up-sampling" layer).
   - The kernel size is 3×3.
   - It has 256 output channels (or filters).
   - It uses a stride of 2, which will generally upsample the spatial dimensions of the input by a factor of 2.
   - BN indicates that this layer is followed by a batch normalization layer.

2. **3*3, deconv, 256, stride = 1, BN:**
   - Another 2D transposed convolutional layer.
   - Kernel size is 3×3.
   - 256 output channels.
   - Stride of 1 means the spatial dimension remains the same.
   - Followed by batch normalization.

3. **3*3, deconv, 128, stride = 2, BN:**
   - 2D transposed convolutional layer.
   - 3×3 kernel.
   - 128 output channels.
   - Stride of 2 for upsampling.
   - Followed by batch normalization.

4. **3*3, deconv, 64, stride = 2, BN:**
   - 2D transposed convolutional layer.
   - 3×3 kernel.
   - 64 output channels.
   - Stride of 2 for upsampling.
   - Followed by batch normalization.

5. **3*3, deconv, 3, stride = 1:**
   - 2D transposed convolutional layer.
   - 3×3 kernel.
   - Three output channels (might indicate generating a three-channel image like RGB).
   - Stride of 1.

6. **Z, 1024:**
   - This is likely referring to the input layer. The generator takes a noise vector Z with 1024 dimensions.

7. **3*3, deconv, 256, stride = 2, BN:**
   - Another 2D transposed convolutional layer as described before.

8. **3*3, deconv, 256, stride = 1, BN:**
   - Again, a 2D transposed convolutional layer as described before.

9. **Fc, 7*7*256, BN:**
   - This is a fully connected (dense) layer, often used to reshape the flat input vector to a spatial format.
   - The output shape would be 7×7 spatially with 256 channels.
   - Followed by batch normalization.

It appears that some of these layers might be redundant or possibly presented out of order, especially when considering the sequence in which the layers should logically appear. Typically, in GAN generators, one would start with the noise vector, feed it into a dense layer to reshape it, and then progressively upsample using transposed convolution layers. Figure 12.5 (a) describes layers for the discriminator in an LSGAN:

1. **5 × 5 conv, 64, stride = 2:**
   - This layer uses a 5 × 5 convolutional kernel.
   - There are 64 output feature maps or channels.
   - The stride is set to 2, which means the spatial dimensions of the output will be half that of the input. This effectively downsamples the data.

2. **5 × 5 conv, 128, stride = 2, BN:**
   - This layer uses a 5 × 5 convolutional kernel.
   - The number of output channels is 128.
   - It uses a stride of 2 for downsampling.
   - Batch Normalization (BN) is applied after this layer, which helps in stabilizing the activations and potentially accelerates training.

3. **5 × 5 conv, 256, stride = 2, BN:**
   - This layer utilizes a 5 × 5 convolutional kernel.
   - There are 256 output channels.
   - The stride is set to 2, further downsampling the spatial dimensions.
   - Batch Normalization (BN) is again applied.

4. **5 × 5 conv, 512, stride = 2, BN:**
   - This layer uses a 5 × 5 convolutional kernel.
   - It has 512 output channels.
   - The stride of 2 continues the pattern of downsampling.
   - Batch Normalization (BN) is applied to this layer.

5. **Fc, 1:**
   - This is a Fully Connected (Fc) layer, which means every neuron in the previous layer is connected to every neuron in this layer.
   - The output has a single unit. Given that it's a discriminator, this single unit will likely produce a scalar value representing the probability that the input is real.

6. **Least squares loss:**
   - The LSGAN uses a least squares loss, which aims to minimize the squared error between the discriminator's predictions and the real labels (either 0 for fake or 1 for real). This can help mitigate some of the issues with the traditional GAN's loss, providing more stable and improved training.

This discriminator architecture sequentially downsamples its input through a series of convolutional layers, aiming to produce a single value at the end, which indicates whether the input is real or generated. The use of Batch Normalization after several layers can assist in stabilizing the training process and improving convergence.

The generator receives "**z**", which is a random noise value, and passes it through a fully-connected layer with batch normalization. Following this layer, the generator has seven deconvolution layers. The discriminator, conversely, contains one convolution layer and three deconvolution layers, followed by a fully-connected layer. The discriminator's output is a single value representing the probability of the input being real. Both the discriminator and the generator use the least squares loss function to calculate their respective losses during training.

12.2.3 Parameters Selection

Setting **b-c = 1** and **b-a = 2** is one of the things that must be done. When loss functions are minimized, the Pearson X_2 difference between **pd + pg** and **2pg** is kept as small as possible. For example, we got the following results when we set **a = 1, b = 1**, and **c = 0**.

$$\min_D V_{LSGAN}(D) = \frac{1}{2} E_{x \sim pdata}(x) \left[(D(x)-1)^2 \right] + \frac{1}{2} E_{z \sim pz}(z) \left[(D(G(Z))+1)^2 \right]$$

This equation represents the loss for the discriminator *D*.

- The first term penalizes the discriminator when it doesn't recognize real samples (*x*) as real (ideally outputting a value of 1).
- The second term penalizes the discriminator when it doesn't recognize fake samples *G(z)* as fake (ideally outputting a value of –1).

$$\min_G V_{LSGAN}(G) = \frac{1}{2} E_{z \sim pz}(z) \left[(D(G(Z)))^2 \right]$$

This equation represents the loss for the generator *G*.

- It penalizes the generator when the discriminator recognizes the generated samples *G(z)* as fake. Ideally, the generator wants the discriminator to think that its generated samples are real (thus the discriminator would output a value of 1).

    Setting **c = b** is another way to help **G** make samples as close to real as possible. To show this, let's use the **0-1** binary code as an example.

$$\min_D V_{LSGAN}(D) = \frac{1}{2} E_{x \sim pdata}(x) \left[(D(x)-1)^2 \right] + \frac{1}{2} E_{z \sim pz}(z) \left[(D(G(Z)))^2 \right]$$

$$\min_G V_{LSGAN}(G) = \frac{1}{2} E_{z \sim pz}(z) \left[(D(G(Z))-1)^2 \right]$$

12.3 LSGAN Applications

LSGAN is a type of GAN that employs a least squares loss function in lieu of the traditional cross-entropy loss function. This modification results in more stable training and enables the generation of sharper images. LSGAN has been utilized across various domains, including image synthesis, video synthesis, and style transfer. In image synthesis, LSGAN is used for generating high-quality images in numerous applications, such as face generation, object generation, and image inpainting. It has also demonstrated impressive results in generating high-quality 3D models, expanding its use to the creation of 3D objects. In the field of video synthesis, LSGAN has shown its effectiveness in generating high-quality videos. It has found various applications, such as video prediction, video super-resolution, and video style transfer. Moreover, LSGAN has been instrumental in generating realistic human motion and 3D pose estimation from 2D images. In the realm of style transfer, LSGAN has been deployed to generate images that capture the style of one image and the content of another. This technique has found applications in various domains like art, fashion, and design. In addition to visual applications, LSGAN has shown promise in natural language processing, where it has been used for tasks like text generation, translation, and summarization. It has also been applied in speech processing for tasks like speech recognition and synthesis. Furthermore, LSGAN has been beneficial in the field of drug discovery, where it has been used to generate new molecular structures with desirable properties. It has shown the potential to accelerate the drug discovery process by generating diverse and novel molecules that can be synthesized and tested in the lab. In summary, LSGAN has proven its effectiveness across a wide array of applications and shows great promise as a tool for generating high-quality images, videos, and data.

12.3.1 Some Experimental Results

DCGAN serves as a foundation upon which the least-square loss is implemented to form the LSGAN. The images produced by LSGANs surpass those generated by the baseline methods, namely DCGANs, and EBGANs. Figure 12.7 elucidates these differences and demonstrates how the image quality generated by LSGANs excels in comparison to DCGANs and EBGANs.

12.3.2 Stability Comparison on the LSUN Dataset

Both designs are built upon the DCGAN network topology and are evaluated for their stability. The first design involves disabling batch normalization in the generator (BN G), while the second design entails disabling batch normalization in both the generator and discriminator (BN GD). The tests were performed using both Adam and RMSProp optimizers. LSGANs consistently generate better quality images than standard GANs,

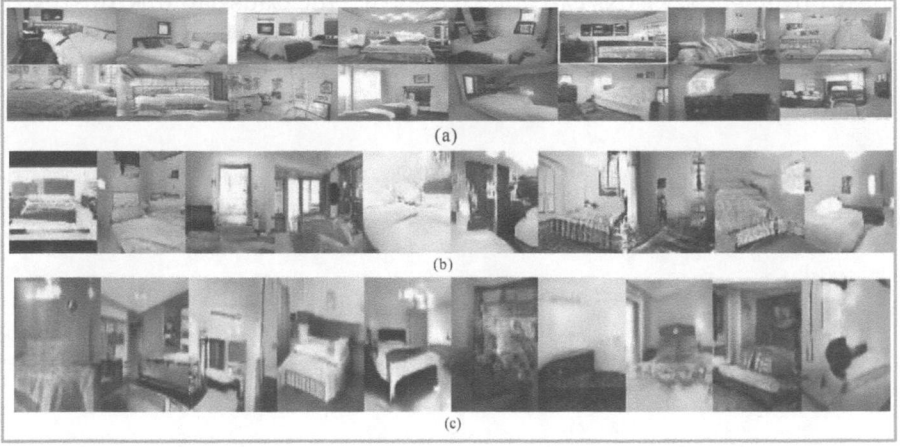

FIGURE 12.7
Generated images on LSUN-bedroom. (a) Generated by LSGANs. (b) Generated by DCGANs. (c) Generated by EBGANs.

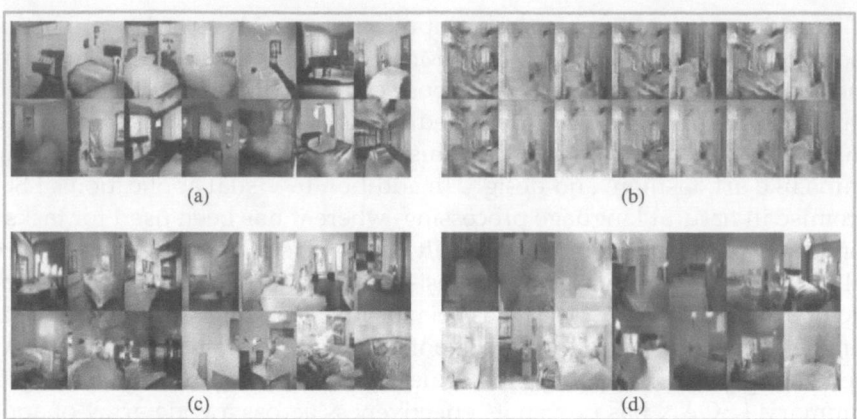

FIGURE 12.8
Comparison experiments by excluding batch normalization (BN).
(a) LSGANs without BN in G using RMSProp.
(b) LSGANs without BN in G and D using Adam.
(c) Regular GANs without BN in G using RMSProp.
(d) Regular GANs without BN in G and D using Adam.

exhibiting fewer instances of mode collapse. In the (BN G) with RMSProp and the (BN GD) with Adam benchmarks, LSGANs, and regular GANs show similar performance. Specifically, when BN G is trained with RMSProp, both LSGANs and regular GANs successfully learn the data distribution. Figure 12.8 demonstrates the results when batch normalization is disregarded, with the outputs of LSGANs in (a) and (b) surpassing those of standard GANs in (c) and (d).

12.3.3 Stability Comparison on Gaussian Mixture Distribution Dataset

In this dataset, a simple architecture consisting of three fully connected layers is used for both the generator and the discriminator. The mode collapse issue for standard GANs begins at step 15k, where they only generate samples following a single valid data distribution mode. Conversely, LSGANs can effectively learn the Gaussian mixture distribution, circumventing the mode collapse issue and generating samples with greater diversity. Figure 12.9 shows the dynamic results of Gaussian kernel estimation for LSGANs in comparison to regular GANs.

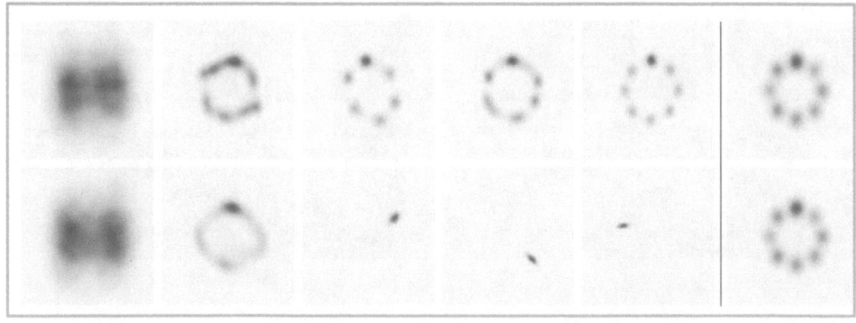

FIGURE 12.9
Dynamic results of Gaussian kernel estimation for LSGANs and regular GANs.

12.4 Develop an LSGAN for MNIST

LSGANs have been trained to generate Chinese characters of commendable visual quality, and some examples of these characters are provided for illustration. Human evaluators have affirmed that the generated characters are identifiable and visually analogous to actual Chinese characters. Furthermore, label vectors can be employed to assign suitable labels to the generated images. This positions LSGANs as a potentially useful instrument in generating Chinese characters for a variety of applications, such as font design, educational resources, and language learning tools. Figure 12.10 displays the generated images of handwritten Chinese characters produced by LSGANs.

Here, we use an approach tailored for MNIST data that has been rescaled from −1 to 1. The generator is a straightforward fully-connected neural network featuring leaky ReLU activation and batch normalization. It takes a "latent sample" composed of 100 randomly generated numbers and generates 784 (= 28 × 28) data points that constitute a digit image. In this case, we use a normal distribution, and the final activation is Tanh. The discriminator is also a simple fully-connected neural network with leaky ReLU activation, and the final activation is a sigmoid function. The loss function employed is the MSE, and the optimizer used is Adam.

12.4.1 Load Libraries

Import some libraries and modules here. Initialize some values as well, such as batch size and epoch. You can experiment with these parameters to see how they affect the results. The code imports the necessary libraries and modules from Keras and TensorFlow, defines an instance of the Adam optimizer with specific values for the learning rate and beta_1, and sets the batch size and number of epochs for training.

```
# Import the NumPy library and give it an alias np
import numpy as np
# Import the Matplotlib library and give it an alias plt
import matplotlib.pyplot as plt
# Import the MNIST dataset from Keras
from keras.datasets import mnist
# Import the Sequential and Model classes from Keras
from keras.models import Sequential, Model
```

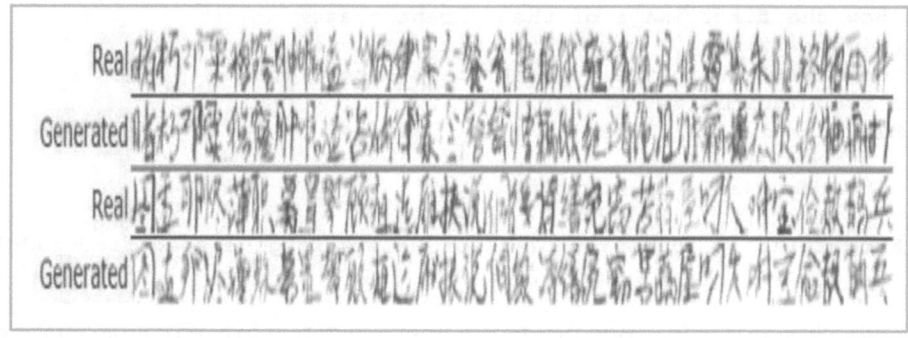

FIGURE 12.10
Generated images of handwritten Chinese characters by LSGANs.

```
# Import the Dense, LeakyReLU, and Batch Normalization layers from
Keras
from keras.layers import Dense, LeakyReLU, BatchNormalization
# Import the necessary layers from Keras
from keras.layers import Input, Flatten, Reshape, Conv2D,
Conv2DTranspose, UpSampling2D
# Import the Adam optimizer from TensorFlow
from tensorflow.keras.optimizers import Adam
# Import the initializers module from Keras
from keras import initializers
from keras import backend as K
# Define an instance of the Adam optimizer with a learning rate of 0.0002
and a beta_1 value of 0.5
Adam(lr=0.0002, beta_1=0.5)
# Define the batch size for training
batch_size = 64
# Define the number of epochs for training
epochs = 100
```

12.4.2 Loading and Exploring Data

The code demonstrates how to load the MNIST dataset using Keras, create a plot for visualization, and plot a sample of data from the first 10 classes of the training set. The subplot() function creates a grid of subplots with two rows and five columns. The loop selects a sample of data for each class, displays the first image in that sample using imshow(), adds a title with the class label, and hides the x and y axis ticks. The tight_layout() function is used to automatically adjust the subplot parameters to give specified padding.

```
# load mnist data
(X_train, y_train), (X_test, y_test) = mnist.load_data()
# Create a new figure for plotting
fig = plt.figure()
# plot some data sample
# Loop through the first 10 classes
for i in range(10):
    # Create a subplot for each class
    plt.subplot(2, 5, i+1)
    # Select a sample of data for the current class
    x_y = X_train[y_train == i]
    # Show the first image of the current class
    plt.imshow(x_y[0], cmap='gray', interpolation='none')
    # Add a title with the current class label
    plt.title("Class %d" % (i))
    # Hide the x-axis ticks
    plt.xticks([])
    # Hide the y-axis ticks
    plt.yticks([])
    # Automatically adjust subplot parameters to give specified padding
plt.tight_layout()
```

As previously stated, it is a good practice in implementation to explore the data and their distribution after importing and loading the libraries. The outputs ample of the dataset are shown in Figure 12.11.

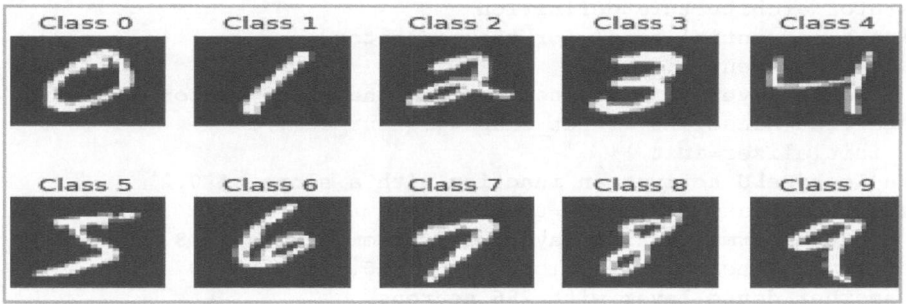

FIGURE 12.11
The initial data in the original dataset.

12.4.3 Preprocessing Data

Depending on the model and the problem being addressed, several preprocessing tasks can improve the performance of the model. Here, we use reshaping and normalization tasks to prepare the data for training. The following lines reshape the original X_train array, which is a 3D array of shape (60000, 28, 28), to a 2D array of shape (60000, 784). In the reshaped array, each row represents a single image that has been flattened into a vector of 784 values. After reshaping, the pixel values are normalized to be between −1 and 1, which is a common preprocessing step for training neural networks.

```
# Print the shape of the original X_train array
print('X_train.shape', X_train.shape)
# Reshape the X_train array to a 2D array of shape (60000, 784)
X_train = X_train.reshape(60000, 28*28)
# Normalize the pixel values to be between -1 and 1
X_train = (X_train.astype('float32') / 255 - 0.5) * 2
# Print the shape of the reshaped and normalized X_train array
print('X_train reshape:', X_train.shape)
```

12.4.4 Generator

Before defining the generator model, some parameters need to be initialized, as shown below. The generator model uses different parameters in its structure. It employs leaky ReLU and batch normalization in all layers and Tanh activation function in the final layer. The following lines define the architecture of the generator model in the cGAN. The generator model comprises a series of dense layers with leaky ReLU activation functions and batch normalization layers. The final layer has a Tanh activation function that produces a flattened image as output. The "latent_dim parameter defines the dimensionality of the noise vector used as input to the generator. The "init" parameter is a normal distribution initializer with a specific standard deviation used to initialize the weights of the layers.

```
# Define the dimensionality of the noise vector (latent space)
latent_dim = 100
# Define the dimensionality of the flattened image
img_dim = 784
# Define a normal distribution initializer with a specific standard
deviation
init = initializers.RandomNormal(stddev=0.02)
```

```
# Generator architecture definition
# Define a sequential model for the generator
generator = Sequential()
# Add a dense layer with 128 neurons and the noise vector as input
generator.add(Dense(128, input_shape=(latent_dim,),
kernel_initializer=init))
# Add a LeakyReLU activation function with a slope of 0.2
generator.add(LeakyReLU(alpha=0.2))
# Add a batch normalization layer with a momentum of 0.8
generator.add(BatchNormalization(momentum=0.8))
# Add another dense layer with 256 neurons
generator.add(Dense(256))
# Add another LeakyReLU activation function with a slope of 0.2
generator.add(LeakyReLU(alpha=0.2))
# Add another batch normalization layer with a momentum of 0.8
generator.add(BatchNormalization(momentum=0.8))
# Add another dense layer with 512 neurons
generator.add(Dense(512))
# Add another LeakyReLU activation function with a slope of 0.2
generator.add(LeakyReLU(alpha=0.2))
# Add another batch normalization layer with a momentum of 0.8
generator.add(BatchNormalization(momentum=0.8))
# Add a final dense layer with the flattened image as output and a tanh
activation function
generator.add(Dense(img_dim, activation='tanh'))
```

This generates a summary representation of your model. It is helpful to see the network structure and the values of the total, trainable, and non-trainable parameters.

```
generator.summary()
Model: "sequential"
```

Layer (type)	Output Shape	Param #
dense (Dense)	(None, 128)	12928
leaky_re_lu (LeakyReLU)	(None, 128)	0
batch_normalization (Batch Normalization)	(None, 128)	512
dense_1 (Dense)	(None, 256)	33024
leaky_re_lu_1 (LeakyReLU)	(None, 256)	0
batch_normalization_1(Batch normalization)	(None, 256)	1024
dense_2 (Dense)	(None, 512)	131584
leaky_re_lu_2 (LeakyReLU)	(None, 512)	0
batch_normalization_2 (Batch normalization)	(None, 512)	2048
dense_3 (Dense)	(None, 784)	402192

```
Total params: 583,312
Trainable params: 581,520
Non-trainable params: 1,792
```

12.4.5 Discriminator

As previously discussed, the discriminator is simpler than the generator. These lines define the architecture for the discriminator model in the cGAN. The discriminator model consists of a series of dense layers with leaky ReLU activation functions. The final layer has a single neuron that outputs a scalar value for the binary classification of whether the input is real or fake. The img_dim parameter is the dimensionality of the flattened image used as input to the discriminator, and init is the normal distribution initializer used to initialize the weights of the layers.

```
# Define a sequential model for the discriminator
discriminator = Sequential()
# Add a dense layer with 128 neurons and the flattened image as input
discriminator.add(Dense(128, input_shape=(img_dim,),
kernel_initializer=init))
# Add a LeakyReLU activation function with a slope of 0.2
discriminator.add(LeakyReLU(alpha=0.2))
# Add another dense layer with 256 neurons
discriminator.add(Dense(256))
# Add another LeakyReLU activation function with a slope of 0.2
discriminator.add(LeakyReLU(alpha=0.2))
# Add another dense layer with 512 neurons
discriminator.add(Dense(512))
# Add another LeakyReLU activation function with a slope of 0.2
discriminator.add(LeakyReLU(alpha=0.2))
# Add a final dense layer with a single neuron (outputting a scalar value
for the binary classification)
discriminator.add(Dense(1))
```

Make a summary of the model to see the discriminator model structure and the number of parameters.

```
discriminator.summary()
Model: "sequential_1"
```

Layer (type)	Output Shape	Param #
dense_4 (Dense)	(None, 128)	100480
leaky_re_lu_3 (LeakyReLU)	(None, 128)	0
dense_5 (Dense)	(None, 256)	33024
leaky_re_lu_4 (LeakyReLU)	(None, 256)	0
dense_6 (Dense)	(None, 512)	131584
leaky_re_lu_5 (LeakyReLU)	(None, 512)	0
dense_7 (Dense)	(None, 1)	513

```
Total params: 265,601
Trainable params: 265,601
Non-trainable params: 0
```

12.4.6 Compile Discriminator

These lines define and compile the discriminator model. The optimizer parameter is set to an instance of the Adam optimizer with a learning rate of 0.0002 and a beta_1 value of 0.5. The compile() function is used to specify the optimizer, loss function, and evaluation metric for the model. The loss function is mean squared error (MSE), and the evaluation metric is binary accuracy.

```
# Define the optimizer for the models with a learning rate of 0.0002 and
a beta_1 value of 0.5
optimizer = Adam(lr=0.0002, beta_1=0.5)
# Compile the discriminator model with the specified optimizer, mean
squared error loss, and binary accuracy metric
discriminator.compile(optimizer=optimizer, loss='mse',
metrics=['binary_accuracy'])
```

12.4.7 Combined Network and Model Summary

Here, we create and compile a combined model that includes both the generator and discriminator. The discriminator's trainable property is set to False, indicating that its weights should not be updated during training of the combined model. The noise vector z is defined as input to the generator, and an image is generated using the generator's img output. The discriminator then evaluates whether the generated image is real or fake, and the decision output is used as the output of the combined model. The compile() function is used to specify the optimizer, loss function, and evaluation metric for the combined model. The loss function is MSE, and the evaluation metric is binary accuracy. Finally, we print a summary of the combined model's architecture using the summary() function.

```
# Set the discriminator as non-trainable in the combined model
discriminator.trainable = False
# Define a noise vector with shape (latent_dim,) as input to the generator
z = Input(shape=(latent_dim,))
# Generate an image using the noise vector as input to the generator
img = generator(z)
# Use the discriminator to evaluate whether the generated image is real
or fake
decision = discriminator(img)
# Create a new model with the noise vector as input and the
discriminator's decision as output
d_g = Model(inputs=z, outputs=decision)
# Compile the combined model with the specified optimizer, mean squared
error loss, and binary accuracy metric
d_g.compile(optimizer=optimizer, loss='mse', metrics=['binary_accuracy'])
# Print a summary of the combined model's architecture
d_g.summary()

Model: "model_1"

Layer (type)                   Output Shape            Param #
=============================================================
input_2 (InputLayer)           [(None, 100)]           0
sequential (Sequential)        (None, 784)             583312
sequential_1 (Sequential)      (None, 1)               265601
=============================================================
Total params: 848,913
Trainable params: 581,520
Non-trainable params: 267,393
```

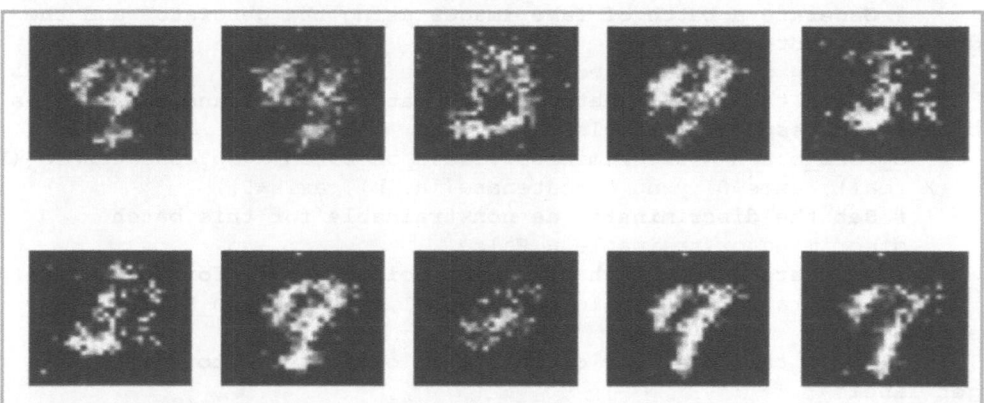

FIGURE 12.12
Epoch one.

12.4.8 Training Model

In each iteration, use the generator to see the generated sample. We showed you the first iteration output in Figure 12.12.

```python
# Set the number of epochs to train the cGAN for
epochs = 100
# Set the batch size for training the cGAN
batch_size = 32
# Create a numpy array of zeros with shape (batch_size//2, 1) to use as
fake labels
a = np.zeros(shape=(batch_size//2, 1))
# Create a numpy array of ones with shape (batch_size//2, 1) to use as
real labels
b = np.ones(shape=(batch_size//2, 1))
# Create a numpy array of ones with shape (batch_size, 1) to use as
labels for the generator
c = np.ones(shape=(batch_size, 1))
# Create an empty list to store the discriminator loss values for each
batch
d_loss = []
# Create an empty list to store the combined model loss values for each
batch
d_g_loss = []
# call the discriminator and generator in a loop
for e in range(epochs + 1):
    for i in range(len(X_train) // batch_size):
        # Set the discriminator as trainable for this batch
        discriminator.trainable = True
        # Select a batch of real images from the training set
        X_real = X_train[i*batch_size//2:(i+1)*batch_size//2]
        # Generate a batch of random noise vectors for the generator
        z = np.random.normal(loc=0, scale=1, size=(batch_size//2,
latent_dim))
```

```
        # Generate a batch of fake images using the generator and the
random noise vectors
        X_fake = generator.predict_on_batch(z)
        # Train the discriminator on the batch of real and fake images
with their corresponding labels
        d_loss_batch = discriminator.train_on_batch(x=np.concatenate((X_
fake, X_real), axis=0),y=np.concatenate((a, b), axis=0))
        # Set the discriminator as non-trainable for this batch
        discriminator.trainable = False
        # Generate a new batch of random noise vectors for the generator
        z = np.random.normal(loc=0, scale=1, size=(batch_size,
latent_dim))
        # Train the generator on the batch of noise vectors with the
target labels
        d_g_loss_batch = d_g.train_on_batch(x = z, y = c)
        # Print the loss values for the current batch in a formatted string
        print('epoch = %d/%d, batch = %d/%d, d_loss=%.3f, g_loss=%.3f' %
(e + 1, epochs, i, len(X_train) // batch_size, d_loss_batch[0], d_g_loss_
batch[0]),100*' ',end='\r')
    # Append the discriminator loss value for the current batch to the
list of discriminator loss values
    d_loss.append(d_loss_batch[0])
    # Append the combined model loss value for the current batch to the
list of combined model loss values
    d_g_loss.append(d_g_loss_batch[0])
    # plot the generated data
    # Print the discriminator and combined model loss values for the
current epoch
    print('epoch = %d/%d, d_loss=%.3f, g_loss=%.3f' % (e + 1, epochs,
d_loss[-1], d_g_loss[-1]), 100*' ')
    # If this is a multiple of 10 epochs, generate and plot a set of fake
images
    if e % 10 == 0:
        # Set the number of samples
        samples = 10
# Generate a set of fake images using the generator and a set of random
noise vectors
x_fake = generator.predict(np.random.normal(loc=0, scale=1,
size=(samples, latent_dim)))
        # Iterate over the set of fake images
        for k in range(samples):
            # Create a subplot for the current fake image
            plt.subplot(2, 5, k+1)
            # Plot the current fake image
            plt.imshow(x_fake[k].reshape(28, 28), cmap='gray')
            # Remove the x-axis ticks from the plot
            plt.xticks([])
            # Remove the y-axis ticks from the plot
            plt.yticks([])
        # Adjust the subplot layout to fit the figures within the figure
area
        plt.tight_layout()
        # Display the plot of fake images
        plt.show()
```

12.5 LSGAN for Caltech_birds2011 Dataset

Here, we will use LSGAN on different datasets with some network modifications as another example to help you learn how to implement LSGAN for your dataset.

12.5.1 Import Libraries

Here, we will use LSGAN on different datasets with some network modifications as another example to help you learn how to implement LSGAN for your dataset.

```
# Import the sys module for accessing system-specific parameters and
functions
import sys
# Import the TensorFlow library for building and training deep learning
models
import tensorflow as tf
# Import the Keras API from TensorFlow for building high-level neural
networks
from tensorflow import keras
# Add the '/content/gan-flavours-keras' directory to the system path
sys.path.insert(0,'/content/gan-flavours-keras')
# Import the prepare_dataset function from the 'dataset' module in the '/
content/gan-flavours-keras' directory
from dataset import prepare_dataset
# Import the get_generator and get_discriminator functions from the
'architecture' module in the '/content/gan-flavours-keras' directory
from architecture import get_generator, get_discriminator
# Import the AdaptiveAugmenter class from the 'augmentation' module in
the '/content/gan-flavours-keras' directory
from augmentation import AdaptiveAugmenter
# Import the various GAN loss functions from the 'losses' module in the
'/content/gan-flavours-keras' directory
from losses import (MiniMaxGAN, NonSaturatingGAN,LeastSquaresGAN,
HingeGAN, WassersteinGAN, RelativisticGAN, RelativisticAverageGAN,)
# Import the generate_images_with and plot_history functions from the
'utils' module in the '/content/gan-flavours-keras' directory
from utils import generate_images_with, plot_history
```

12.5.2 Set the Hyperparameters

After loading the necessary libraries, the next step in the model is to set and initialize the hyperparameters. These values can be changed to observe how they affect the results and performance of the model.

```
# Name of the dataset to use
dataset_name = "caltech_birds2011"
# Size of the images in pixels
image_size = 64
# Number of epochs to train the GAN model
num_epochs = 500
# Resolution of the KID measurement
kid_image_size = 75
```

```
# Interval of epochs to plot the generated images
plot_interval = 10
# Number of samples per batch for training the GAN model
batch_size = 128
# Smoothing factor for the labels of the real samples in the GAN model
one_sided_label_smoothing = 0.0
# Exponential moving average for the GAN model
ema = 0.99
# Learning rate for the generator in the GAN model
generator_lr = 2e-4
# Learning rate for the discriminator in the GAN model
discriminator_lr = 2e-4
# Exponential decay rate for the first moment estimates in Adam optimizer
in the GAN model
beta_1 = 0.5
# Exponential decay rate for the second moment estimates in Adam
optimizer in the GAN model
beta_2 = 0.999
# Dimensionality of the random noise vector used as input to the
generator in the GAN model
noise_size = 64
# Number of up- and downsampling layers in the generator and
discriminator of the GAN model
depth = 4
# Number of filters in the first layer of the generator and discriminator
of the GAN model
width = 128
# Weight initialization method for the generator and discriminator of the
GAN model
initializer = "glorot_uniform"
# Whether to use residual connections in the generator and discriminator
of the GAN model
residual = False
# Whether to use transposed convolutions or upsampling and convolutions
in the generator of the GAN model
transposed = True
# Slope of the negative part of the LeakyReLU activation function in the
generator and discriminator of the GAN model
leaky_relu_slope = 0.2
# Dropout rate in the generator of the GAN model
dropout_rate = 0.4
# Whether to use spectral normalization in the discriminator of the GAN
model
spectral_norm = False
# Target accuracy for the discriminator in the GAN model, set to None to
disable
target_accuracy = None
# Number of integration steps for the FID score calculation in the GAN
model
integration_steps = 1000
# Maximal probability for the adaptive augmentation in the GAN model
max_probability = 0.8
# ID of the current run of the GAN model
id = 0
```

12.5.3 Load Dataset

In this step, you should load the dataset from either a local path or an online address. Then, you can split the data into separate categories for training and validation.

```
# Load the training dataset
train_dataset = prepare_dataset(dataset_name, "train", image_size,
batch_size)
# Load the validation dataset
val_dataset = prepare_dataset(dataset_name, "validation", image_size,
batch_size)
```

12.5.4 Create the Model

To create the model, use the generator and discriminator models that were loaded in the previous step.

```
#Instantiate an instance of the NonSaturatingGAN class.
model = NonSaturatingGAN(
#Assign the value of the id variable to the id parameter of the
NonSaturatingGAN constructor.
    id=id,
#Call the get_generator function with the specified arguments to create
the generator model for the GAN and assign it to the generator parameter
of the NonSaturatingGAN constructor.
    generator=get_generator(noise_size, depth, width, initializer,
residual, transposed),
#Call the get_discriminator function with the specified arguments to
create the discriminator model for the GAN, and assign it to the
discriminator parameter of the NonSaturatingGAN constructor.
discriminator=get_discriminator(image_size,depth,width,initializer,residu
al,leaky_relu_slope,dropout_rate,       spectral_norm,),
#Instantiate an instance of the AdaptiveAugmenter class with the
specified arguments to be used for data augmentation during training,
and assign it to the augmenter parameter of the NonSaturatingGAN
constructor.
    augmenter=AdaptiveAugmenter(
        target_accuracy=target_accuracy,
        integration_steps=integration_steps,
        max_probability=max_probability,
        input_shape=(image_size, image_size, 3),
    ),
    #Assign the value of the one_sided_label_smoothing variable to the
one_sided_label_smoothing parameter of the NonSaturatingGAN constructor.
    one_sided_label_smoothing=one_sided_label_smoothing,
    #Assign the value of the ema variable to the ema parameter of the
NonSaturatingGAN constructor.
    ema=ema,
    #Assign the value of the kid_image_size variable to the kid_image_
size parameter of the NonSaturatingGAN constructor.
    kid_image_size=kid_image_size,
    #Assign the value of the plot_interval variable to the plot_interval
parameter of the NonSaturatingGAN constructor.
    plot_interval=plot_interval,
```

```
#Assign the value of True to the is_jupyter parameter of the
NonSaturatingGAN constructor.
    is_jupyter=True,
)
#Compile the GAN model.
model.compile(
#Specify the optimizer to be used for updating the generator weights
during training, using the Adam optimizer with the specified learning
rate, beta_1, and beta_2 values.
    generator_optimizer=keras.optimizers.Adam(learning_rate=generator_lr,
beta_1=beta_1, beta_2=beta_2),
#Specify the optimizer to be used for updating the discriminator weights
during training, using the Adam optimizer with the specified learning
rate, beta_1, and beta_2 values
    discriminator_optimizer=keras.optimizers.Adam(learning_
rate=discriminator_lr, beta_1=beta_1, beta_2=beta_2),)
```

12.5.5 Training and Testing

The final step is to train the model using the prepared data and evaluate its performance using the test set. The generated output results can be visualized and analyzed over a range of iterations, from 1 to 1000, as shown in Figures 12.13–12.16.

```
defines the path to save the model checkpoints where {} is replaced with
the id of the model.
checkpoint_path = "checkpoints/model_{}".format(id)
creates a callback to save the model weights during training.
checkpoint_callback = tf.keras.callbacks.ModelCheckpoint(
    specifies the path to save the checkpoint.
    filepath=checkpoint_path,
    specifies to save only the weights of the model, not the entire model.
    save_weights_only=True,
    specifies the validation KID (Kernel Inception Distance) as the
metric to monitor during training.
    monitor="val_kid",
```

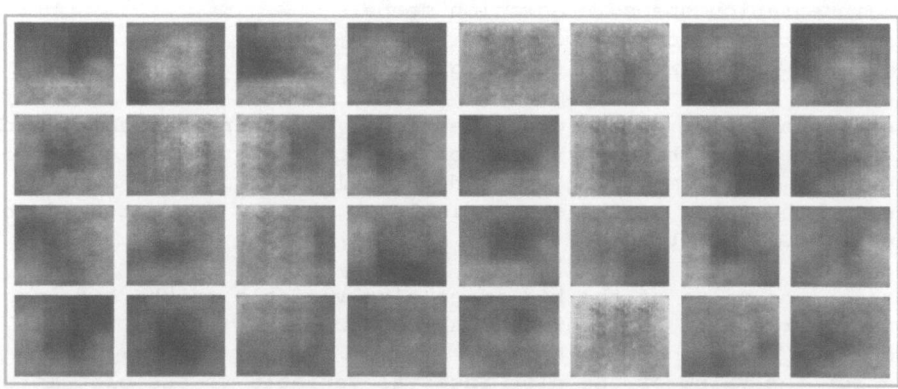

FIGURE 12.13
Output results after Epoch 1.

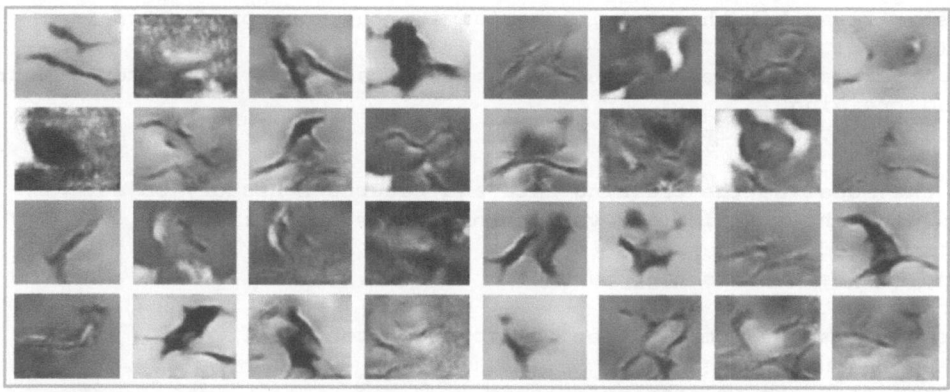

FIGURE 12.14
Output results after Epoch 100.

FIGURE 12.15
Output results after Epoch 500.

FIGURE 12.16
Output results after Epoch 1000.

```
    specifies that the goal is to minimize the monitored metric.
    mode="min",
    specifies to save only the best model (based on the monitored metric)
during training.
    save_best_only=True,
)
fits the model to the training data and returns a History object
containing the training and validation losses and metrics.
history = model.fit(
    specifies the training dataset.
    train_dataset,
    specifies the number of epochs to train the model.
    epochs=num_epochs,
    specifies the validation dataset.
    validation_data=val_dataset,
    specifies a list of callbacks to use during training.
    callbacks=[
        specifies a callback to plot the generated images after each epoch.
        keras.callbacks.LambdaCallback(on_epoch_end=model.plot_images),
        specifies the previously defined checkpoint callback to save the
model weights.
        checkpoint_callback,
    ],
)
loads the best model weights based on the monitored metric during training.
model.load_weights(checkpoint_path)
generates and plots sample images using the trained model and the History
object.
generate_images_with(model, history, id, is_jupyter=True)
plots the training and validation losses and metrics over the epochs
using the History object.
plot_history(history, id, is_jupyter=True)
```

12.6 LSGAN Issues

One of the main issues with LSGANs is the instability during training. While the objective function of LSGANs is less prone to mode collapse than traditional GANs, the optimization process can still be difficult to converge. This can result in the generator producing poor quality images or the discriminator failing to accurately distinguish real and fake samples. Additionally, LSGANs can suffer from gradient vanishing or exploding, which can hinder the learning process. Another challenge is the selection of hyperparameters, such as the learning rate, batch size, and number of layers, which can significantly impact the performance of the LSGAN. Some of the issues with LSGAN and their possible solutions are disused in the below subsections.

12.6.1 Mode Collapse

While LSGAN already improves stability over the standard GAN loss; it can still suffer from mode collapse and can benefit from some solutions. Mode collapse is a common issue in GANs, including LSGANs, where the generator starts producing a limited range of samples, failing to cover the full diversity of the real data. This often occurs when the generator discovers that certain outputs are more likely to fool the discriminator, leading it to produce these outputs repeatedly. Consequently, the GAN fails to generate a diverse set of samples, limiting its usefulness.

Solutions:

1. **Mini-batch discrimination:** This technique introduces a new feature to the discriminator that contains information about the variety of samples within a mini-batch. If the generator starts producing the same sample over and over (i.e., it starts to collapse), this feature will detect it.

2. **Experience replay:** This strategy stores the generated samples from the previous steps and mixes them with the current batch of generated samples for the discriminator's training. This technique helps to maintain diversity in the generator's outputs.

3. **Regularization techniques:** Techniques, such as gradient penalty or spectral normalization, enforce the discriminator to be a 1-Lipschitz function, which leads to a more stable training process and can prevent mode collapse.

4. **Use of multiple GANs or generators:** Implementing several generators could help in maintaining the diversity of the generated samples. The diversity is encouraged by promoting competition among the generators to cover different parts of the data distribution.

12.6.2 Gradient Vanishing/Exploding

Gradient vanishing or exploding is a common problem in deep learning models, including LSGANs. The issue arises during backpropagation, where the gradients of the loss function either become too small (vanish) or too large (explode) the further you go in the layers of the network. When gradients vanish, the weights of the earlier layers in the network aren't updated effectively during training, making it difficult for the network to learn. When gradients explode, the weights of the earlier layers can fluctuate wildly, leading to instability in the model's training process.

Solutions:

1. **Weight initialization:** Appropriate initialization of the weights can help mitigate this problem. Techniques, such as He or Xavier initialization, can be beneficial depending on the activation function used.

2. **Normalization:** Techniques like batch normalization or layer normalization can prevent the range of layer activations from becoming too large or too small, mitigating the vanishing/exploding gradient problem.

3. **Gradient clipping:** This technique sets a threshold value and rescales the gradients if they exceed this threshold. It's particularly useful for handling exploding gradients.

4. **Use of ReLU or leaky ReLU activations:** These activation functions are less prone to vanishing gradients because their derivatives do not saturate. ReLU has a

constant derivative of 1 for positive inputs, and leaky ReLU has a small, constant derivative for negative inputs.

5. **Skip/Residual connections:** Used extensively in deep networks, these allow gradients to propagate directly through several layers by having identity shortcuts from earlier layers to later ones. Residual networks (ResNets) use this technique extensively.

While these solutions can help mitigate the gradient vanishing/exploding problem, it's important to note that the choice of technique will depend on the specifics of the problem and the model architecture.

12.6.3 Unstable Training

GANs, including, can be notoriously difficult to train due to their adversarial nature, often leading to unstable training dynamics. Unstable training in LSGANs could manifest as:

1. **Mode collapse:** This is where the generator starts to collapse to producing the same or very similar outputs (one mode of the data distribution), instead of generating diverse samples from the data distribution.

2. **Oscillations:** This is where the generator's and discriminator's losses fail to converge and instead oscillate indefinitely.

3. **Vanishing/Exploding gradients:** As discussed earlier, these problems can also lead to unstable training.

Solutions:

1. **Alternate training:** Instead of updating the generator and discriminator at the same time, alternate between training the generator and discriminator. This approach can help maintain a better balance in the adversarial game.

2. **Gradient penalty or spectral normalization:** These methods constrain the discriminator's capacity, ensuring it doesn't overpower the generator. They are widely used techniques to promote stability in GANs.

3. **Learning rate scheduling:** Lowering the learning rate over time can help stabilize training.

4. **Adding noise:** Adding some noise to the inputs of the discriminator or the labels can help stabilize training.

5. **Modified objective functions:** Modifying the objective functions, like the use of the least squares loss function in LSGANs, can help improve the stability of the training process.

Remember that tuning a GAN (including an LSGAN) often requires much experimentation and patience, as finding the right balance between the generator and discriminator can be somewhat of an art.

12.6.4 Hyperparameter Tuning

Hyperparameter tuning in LSGANs, like in many machine learning models, is an important and challenging task. Choosing the right hyperparameters can drastically affect the performance and stability of the model. In LSGANs, there are numerous hyperparameters to consider, such as:

1. **Architecture parameters:** These include the number of layers, the number of units per layer, the type of layers (fully connected, convolutional, etc.), and the type of activation functions.

2. **Learning rate:** This is crucial to ensure the model is learning at an appropriate pace. Too high a learning rate can lead to instability and failure to converge, while too low a learning rate can result in slow training or getting stuck in local minima.

3. **Batch size:** This affects how well the model generalizes and its computational efficiency.

4. **Noise dimension:** This is the dimension of the noise vector input to the generator. It can affect the diversity of the generated samples.

5. **Optimizer:** The choice of optimizer (e.g., Adam, RMSProp, SGD) can have a significant impact on the training dynamics.

6. **Regularization parameters:** These include dropout rates or the weight for gradient penalty.

Solutions:

1. **Grid search or random search:** These are traditional hyperparameter optimization techniques, where different combinations of hyperparameters are systematically tested.

2. **Automated machine learning (AutoML) techniques:** More advanced methods, such as Bayesian Optimization, Evolutionary Algorithms, or Gradient-based optimization, can automate the process of hyperparameter tuning.

3. **Transfer learning:** Use the architecture and hyperparameters of a model that has been pre-trained on a similar task.

4. **Learning rate schedulers:** Dynamically adjust the learning rate during training.

5. **Early stopping:** Stop training when performance on a validation set stops improving to prevent overfitting.

It's also worth noting that hyperparameter tuning for LSGANs, like for many GANs, can be more art than science. Some trial and error, as well as experience and intuition, can often go a long way toward achieving good results.

12.6.5 Evaluation Metrics

In GANs and their variants like LSGANs, evaluating the quality and diversity of the generated samples can be quite challenging. Here are some issues and solutions related to evaluation metrics in LSGANs.

1. **Lack of ground truth:** Unlike in supervised learning, where we have a clear ground truth for comparison, in generative models like LSGANs, the objective is to generate samples that are similar to the real data distribution, and there's no clear-cut ground truth.

2. **Quality vs. Diversity:** A key challenge is evaluating both the quality (how realistic individual samples look) and diversity (how much the samples cover the whole data distribution) of the generated samples. It's possible for a model to generate very high-quality samples that lack diversity (e.g., by always generating the same realistic-looking image) or highly diverse but low-quality samples.

3. **Subjective evaluation:** Traditional metrics often involve human evaluation, which can be highly subjective and non-scalable.

Solutions:

1. **Inception Score (IS):** This is a commonly used metric for evaluating the quality and diversity of generated images. It's based on the classification scores of the generated samples using a pre-trained model (like Inception). It encourages high-confidence predictions for each generated sample (indicating high quality) and a diverse set of predictions across samples (indicating diversity). However, it's mostly applicable to natural image datasets and may not translate well to other types of data.

2. **Fréchet Inception Distance (FID):** FID calculates the Wasserstein-2 distance between real and generated samples in the feature space of a pre-trained model. It has been shown to correlate well with human judgment and is currently one of the most popular GAN evaluation metrics. But like IS, it's primarily for natural image datasets.

3. **Precision, Recall, and F_1 Score:** These are newer metrics for GANs that directly evaluate the trade-off between quality and diversity. Precision measures how many of the generated samples are close to the real data, recall measures how much of the real data distribution is covered by the generated samples, and the F_1 score provides a balanced measure of both.

4. **User Studies:** In some cases, human evaluators are still used to judge the quality and diversity of generated samples. This is often the case when other quantitative metrics are difficult to apply or interpret, such as in text generation.

It's important to note that no single metric is perfect, and it's generally a good practice to use a combination of different metrics and human evaluation to assess the performance of LSGANs or any other GAN models.

12.6.6 Memory Usage

In LSGANs and other generative models, memory usage can become a significant concern, particularly when working with large-scale datasets or high-resolution images. Here are some specific issues and potential solutions:

1. **High-Resolution images:** Training LSGANs on high-resolution images can be memory-intensive. The higher the resolution, the more memory is required to store the intermediate computations for both forward and backward passes.

2. **Large batch sizes:** LSGANs and other GANs often benefit from larger batch sizes, which provide a more accurate estimate of the gradient. However, larger batch sizes also require more memory.

3. **Model complexity:** The complexity of the generator and discriminator models in terms of the number of layers, filter sizes, etc. also significantly impacts memory usage.

Solutions:

1. **Gradient checkpointing:** This technique reduces memory usage by storing some intermediate outputs in the forward pass and recomputing them during the backward pass. This approach trades-off computation for memory, which can be beneficial when memory is the limiting factor.

2. **Model simplification:** Simplifying the model architecture, for instance, by reducing the number of layers or filters, can reduce memory usage but may also affect the quality of generated samples.

3. **Use of mixed precision training:** Training models with lower precision (e.g., float16 instead of float32) can save memory and potentially speed up computations, especially on GPUs that are optimized for lower precision.

4. **Distributed training:** Distributing the training across multiple GPUs allows you to effectively increase the available memory and thus handle larger batch sizes or more complex models.

5. **Progressive growing of GANs:** A technique introduced for training GANs where the model starts learning from low-resolution images, and, as training progresses, the resolution is increased. This method helps manage memory use efficiently.

Remember, it's often a trade-off between memory, computational resources, and model performance. The solutions would depend on the specific constraints of the system being used for training the LSGANs.

12.6.7 Limited Training Data

Training GANs, including LSGANs, requires substantial amounts of data. Limited data could lead to issues, such as overfitting, poor generalization, and lack of diversity in the generated samples. When the available training data is scarce, the model might not be able to learn the underlying distribution effectively, resulting in generated outputs that are not diverse or realistic.

Solutions:

1. **Data augmentation:** Techniques like rotation, scaling, flipping, or even more sophisticated methods like generative methods (VAEs, GANs themselves) can be used to increase the amount of training data.

2. **Transfer learning:** One could use a pre-trained model, perhaps trained on a larger dataset, and fine-tune it on the available limited data. This approach can help learn general features from the larger dataset and then adapt to the specific characteristics of the smaller dataset.

3. **Few-Shot learning:** Techniques, such as meta-learning, where the model is trained to learn from a small number of examples, can be employed.

4. **Regularization:** Regularization methods, like weight decay, dropout, or early stopping, can be used to prevent overfitting when training with a limited amount of data.

5. **Synthetic data:** If possible, synthetic data that mimics the characteristics of the real data can be generated and used to augment the training set.

Remember, all these solutions have their own trade-offs and should be considered depending on the specific use case and the nature of the data. It's also worth noting that research is ongoing in this area, and new methods for dealing with limited data are continually being developed.

12.7 LSGAN Implementation Tips

Here are some implementation tips for LSGAN:

1. Use the MSE loss function for the generator and discriminator, as it is well-suited for LSGANs.
2. Normalize the input data to have a zero mean and unit variance, which can help improve training stability and performance.
3. Use batch normalization to speed up training and improve the stability of the discriminator.
4. Use weight initialization techniques, such as Xavier or He initialization, to ensure that the weights are properly scaled and prevent the vanishing or exploding gradient problem.
5. Use a smaller learning rate for the discriminator than for the generator to prevent the discriminator from overpowering the generator during training.
6. Train the generator for more steps than the discriminator to ensure that the generator is able to catch up and produce high-quality images.
7. Use a larger batch size for training to improve the stability and speed of training.
8. Use data augmentation techniques, such as random cropping and flipping, to increase the diversity of the training data and improve the robustness of the model.
9. Use early stopping techniques, such as monitoring the validation loss, to prevent overfitting and improve generalization performance.
10. Visualize the generated samples and monitor the loss curves during training to ensure that the model is converging to a good solution.

Remember, hands-on experience is key when working with LSGANs or any other machine learning models. Therefore, consistently practicing implementation and troubleshooting is crucial for mastering these concepts.

12.8 Lessons Learned

- Learn about the LSGAN's architecture and all of its components.
- Learn about the LSGAN Applications.
- Learn how to implement LSGANs and the steps involved for MNIST.

- Learn how to implement LSGANs and the steps involved for Caltech_birds2011 Dataset.
- Learn about the most common LSGAN issues.
- Learn about LSGAN Implementation Tips.

12.9 Problems

12.9.1 What is LSGAN, and how does it differ from traditional GANs?

12.9.2 How does LSGAN use MSE loss in the discriminator and generator?

12.9.3 How does the use of MSE loss in LSGAN lead to more stable training than traditional GANs?

12.9.4 How is the architecture of an LSGAN generator similar to that of a traditional GAN generator, and how does it differ?

12.9.5 How does LSGAN compare to other GAN variants, such as WGAN and DCGAN, in terms of stability and quality of generated images?

12.9.6 How can LSGAN be used for tasks beyond image generation, such as text generation or anomaly detection?

12.9.7 What are some potential drawbacks of using LSGAN, and how can these be addressed?

12.9.8 What is the LSGAN architecture, and how many components does it have?

12.10 Programming Questions

- **Easy**

  12.10.1 What is the loss function used in LSGAN?

  12.10.2 How does LSGAN differ from traditional GAN?

  12.10.3 What are the advantages of using LSGAN over traditional GAN?

  12.10.4 How is the generator in LSGAN trained?

  12.10.5 How is the discriminator in LSGAN trained?

- **Medium**

  12.10.6 How does the hyperparameter "lambda" affect the performance of LSGAN?

  12.10.7 How can the training stability of LSGAN be improved?

  12.10.8 How can LSGAN be used for image synthesis?

  12.10.9 How can LSGAN be used for text-to-image synthesis?

  12.10.10 What are some techniques used to improve the quality of LSGAN-generated images?

- **Hard**

12.10.11 How can LSGAN be used for video generation?

12.10.12 How can LSGAN be used for cross-modal image synthesis?

12.10.13 How can LSGAN be used for anomaly detection?

12.10.14 What are some techniques for fine-tuning the LSGAN generator and discriminator?

12.10.15 What are some limitations of LSGAN, and how can they be addressed?

13

Wasserstein Generative Adversarial Network (WGAN)

This chapter covers the following topics about Wasserstein Generative Adversarial Network (WGAN):

- What is a Wasserstein GAN?
- Wasserstein GAN Implementation for MNIST
- WGAN-GP (WGAN with Gradient Penalty (GP)) on Fashion-MNIST
- Wasserstein GAN Applications
- WGAN's Issues
- Wasserstein GAN Implementation Tips

13.1 Preface

The Wasserstein Generative Adversarial Network (WGAN), proposed in 2017, aims to improve learning stability, solve issues such as mode collapse, and generate meaningful learning curves that can be used for debugging and hyperparameter searches. WGAN is a type of GAN that uses Wasserstein distance as a loss function instead of the traditional binary cross-entropy loss. The WGAN architecture was proposed in a paper titled "Wasserstein GAN" by Martin Arjovsky, Soumith Chintala, and Léon Bottou, which was published in 2017. The Wasserstein distance, also known as Earth-Mover (EM) distance, is a measure of the distance between two probability distributions. It provides a more stable and meaningful training signal for the generator in GANs compared to binary cross-entropy loss, which suffers from mode collapse and instability issues. In WGAN, the discriminator is not limited to outputting a probability between 0 and 1; instead, it outputs a scalar value representing the estimated Wasserstein distance between the generated and real distributions. The generator is trained to minimize this distance, while the discriminator is trained to maximize it. This creates a more informative feedback signal for the generator, which encourages it to generate samples that are closer to the real data distribution. WGAN has been successfully applied to various tasks, such as image generation, super-resolution, and style transfer. Its stability and ability to generate high-quality samples make it a popular choice for generative modeling tasks. However, WGAN also has its own set of challenges and limitations. One of the main issues is the difficulty in tuning the hyperparameters, such as the number of critic updates per generator update and the Lipschitz constant of the discriminator. Additionally, the weight clipping method used to enforce the Lipschitz constraint can lead to gradient vanishing or exploding problems, which can affect the training stability. Overall, WGAN is a powerful and promising

DOI: 10.1201/9781003281344-13

approach for generative modeling, but it requires careful tuning and implementation to overcome its challenges and achieve good results. This chapter reviews this approach's architecture and provides some coding examples for learning about the MNIST and Fashion MNIST datasets.

13.2 What Is a Wasserstein GAN?

WGAN is an extension of GAN that aims to make the training process more stable and less affected by the model's architecture and hyperparameter settings. Stable training involves finding and maintaining a balance between the capabilities of the generator and the discriminator. WGAN achieves this by modifying or replacing the discriminator with a critic that rates how real or fake an image is based on mathematical reasoning that minimizes the difference between the data's distribution in the training dataset and the generated examples. The EM distance is used to measure this difference. To convert GAN and DCGAN architectures to WGAN, several modifications are made, including using a linear activation function instead of a sigmoid in the critic's output layer, training the critic and generator models with Wasserstein loss, and setting a range of critic model weights after each mini-batch update. For example, consider the moving boxes problem shown in Figure 13.1, where two boxes must be moved to minimize transport costs. In P_1, moving box A from position 2 to position 3 costs 1, and moving box B from position 6 to position 5 costs 1, resulting in a total cost of 2. In P_2, moving box B from position 2 to position 5 costs 3, while moving box A from position 6 to position 3 costs 3, resulting in a total cost of 6. Although the outputs are the same in both P_1 and P_2 (box A in position 3 and box B in position 5), the total cost is different. The Wasserstein distance used in WGAN provides the minimum cost, like P_1, whereas normal GAN does not guarantee this.

The Wasserstein distance formula is:

$$W\left(p_r, p_g\right) = \inf_{\gamma \sim \Pi\left(p_r, p_g\right)} \mathbb{E}_{(x,y) \sim \gamma}\left[\|x - y\|\right]$$

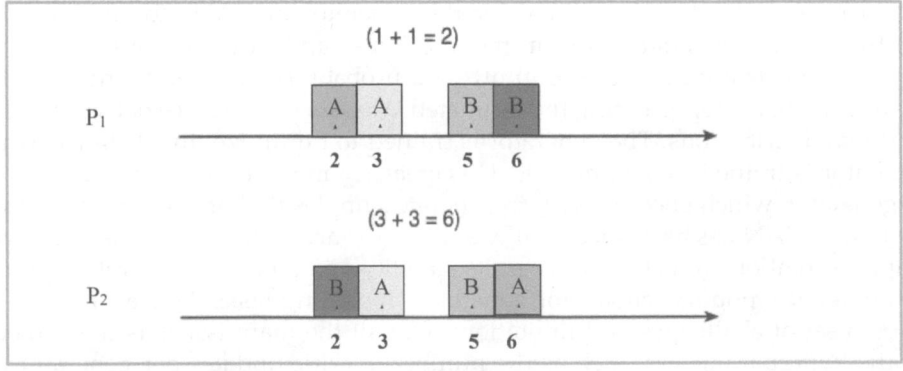

FIGURE 13.1
Example of using moving boxes.

In the above equation, $\prod(p_r, p_g)$ is the set of all possible combinations of two probability distributions p_r and p_g. The joint distribution $\gamma \in \prod(p_r, p_g)$ describes one plan for moving, just like in the example above, and the $\gamma(x, y)$ shows how much it should be moved from point x to point y (the point x has the same probability distribution as point y). When x is used as the starting point, and y is used as the destination, the traveling distance is $|x - y|$ and the cost (the total amount of movement) is $\gamma(x, y)$:

$$\sum_{x,y} \gamma(x,y) \|x - y\| = \mathbb{E}_{x,y\sim\gamma} \|x - y\|$$

In WGAN, the EM distance is used to find the cheapest way to move from one distribution to another. The "inf" in the definition of the Wasserstein distance stands for "infinity" or "greatest lower bound", indicating that only the lowest cost matters. Moreover, instead of using a discriminator to classify whether an image is real or fake, the WGAN replaces the discriminator with a critic that assigns a score to an image based on its realism. The amount of generator loss has a significant impact on the WGAN's convergence. The following are the average loss values for a small batch.

Critic Loss = [average critic score on real images]−[average critic score on fake images]

Generator Loss = −[average critic score on fake images]

We can calculate the Wasserstein loss by this formula:

Wasserstein Loss = label × average critic score

or

Wasserstein Loss (real images) = + 1 × average predicted score

Wasserstein Loss (fake images) = − 1 × average predicted score

In WGAN, a lower critic loss indicates a higher output quality. For instance, if there are 30 real images and 40 fake images, the loss is −10, but if there are 20 real images and 40 fake images, the loss is −20, which is lower, and the output quality is higher. These values depend on the ratio of real to fake images. Figures 13.2 and 13.3 illustrate the differences between the general architecture of GAN and WGAN. To identify the key differences between the two figures, explore numbers 1–3.

The network designs for GAN and WGAN are nearly identical, with the exception that WGAN uses a critic instead of a discriminator, and the critic's output function is not a sigmoid. The only other significant difference is the cost function used for the discriminator/critic and generator. Table 13.1 shows the cost functions for the discriminator and generator in GAN and WGAN.

WGAN has two main contributions:

1. No sign of collapse in experiments
2. The generator can still learn when the critic performs well

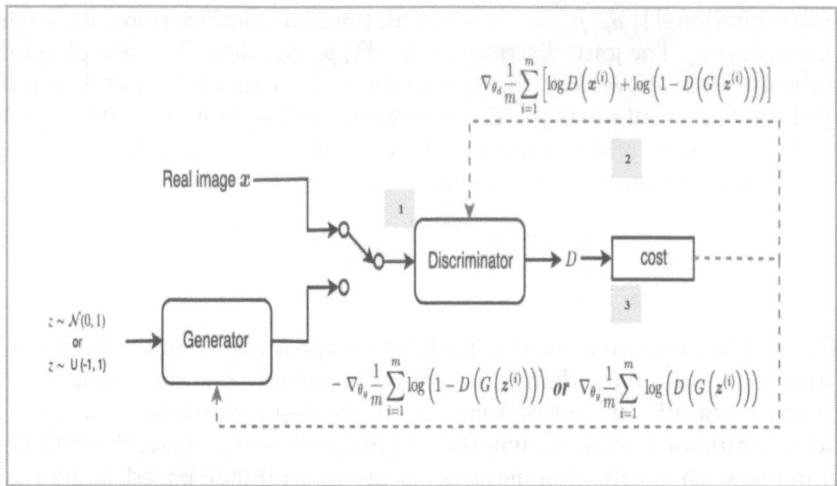

FIGURE 13.2
Normal GAN architecture.

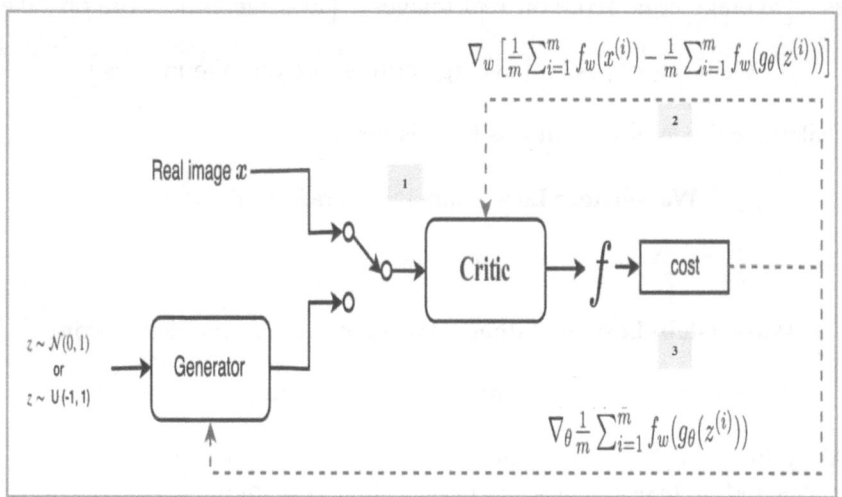

FIGURE 13.3
The WGAN architecture.

The implementation of WGAN differs in several ways, including:

- Using a linear activation function in the critic model's output layer instead of a sigmoid,
- Assigning –1 labels to real images and 1 to fake images instead of 0 and 1,
- Training the critic and generator models with Wasserstein loss,
- Limiting the weights of critic models to a certain range after each mini-batch update,
- Updating the critic model more frequently than the generator model, and
- Using a small learning rate.

TABLE 13.1

The Critic and Generator Cost Function in Normal GAN and WGAN

	Discriminator/Critic	Generator
GAN	$\nabla_{\theta_d} \dfrac{1}{m} \sum\limits_{i=1}^{m} \left[\log D\left(x^i\right) + \log\left(1 - D\left(G\left(z^i\right)\right)\right) \right]$	$\nabla_{\theta_g} \dfrac{1}{m} \sum\limits_{i=1}^{m} \left[\log\left(D\left(G\left(z^i\right)\right)\right) \right]$
WGAN	$\nabla_{w} \dfrac{1}{m} \sum\limits_{i=1}^{m} \left[f\left(x^i\right) - f\left(G\left(z^i\right)\right) \right]$	$\nabla_{\theta} \dfrac{1}{m} \sum\limits_{i=1}^{m} \left[f\left(G\left(z^i\right)\right) \right]$

Here we present two pseudo-code algorithms for WGAN and WGAN with gradient penalty.

13.2.1 WGAN Algorithm

All experiments used the default values $\alpha = 0.00005$, $c = 0.01$, $m = 64$, $n_{\text{critic}} = 5$.

Require: α the learning rate. c the clipping parameter. m the batch size. n_{critic} *the iterations of the critic per generator iteration.*

Require: w_0 initial critic parameters. θ_0 initial generator's parameters.
WGAN

1: **while** θ has not converged **do**
2:     **for** $t = 0, ..., n_{\text{critic}}$ **do**
3:         Sample $\{x^{(i)}\}_{i=1}^{m} \sim P_r$ a batch from the real data.
4:         Sample $\{z^{(i)}\}_{i=1}^{m} \sim p(z)$ a batch of prior samples.
5:         $g_w \leftarrow \nabla_w \left[1/m \sum_{i=1}^{m} f_w\left(x^{(i)}\right) - 1/m \sum_{i=1}^{m} f_w\left(g_\theta\left(z^{(i)}\right)\right) \right]$
6:         $w \leftarrow w + \alpha \cdot RMSProp(w, g_w)$
7:         $w \leftarrow clip(w, -c, c)$
8:     **end for**
9:     Sample $\{z^{(i)}\}_{i=1}^{m} \sim p(z)$ a batch of prior samples.
10:    $g_\theta \leftarrow -\nabla_\theta \sum_{i=1}^{m} f_w\left(g_\theta\left(z^{(i)}\right)\right)$
11:    $\theta \leftarrow \theta - \alpha \cdot RMSProp(\theta, g_\theta)$
12: **end while**

13.2.2 WGAN-GP Algorithm

WGAN with gradient penalty algorithm. default values of $\lambda = 10$, $n_{\text{critic}} = 5$, $\alpha = 0.0001$, $\beta_1 = 0$, $\beta_2 = 0.9$.

Require: The gradient penalty coefficient λ, the number of critic iterations per generator iteration n_{critic}, the batch size m, *Adam* hyperparameters α, β_1, β_2.

Require: initial critic parameters w_0, initial generator parameters θ_0.

1: **while** θ has not converged **do**
2:     **for** $t = 1, ..., n_{\text{critic}}$ **do**
3:         **for** $i = 1, ..., m$ **do**
4:             Sample real data $x \sim P_r$, latent variable $z \sim p(z)$, a random number $E \sim U[0, 1]$.

5:          $\tilde{x} \leftarrow G_\theta(z)$

6:          $\hat{x} \leftarrow Ex + (1-E)\tilde{x}$

7:          $L^{(i)} \leftarrow D_w(\tilde{x}) - D_w(x) + \lambda\left(\left\|\nabla_{\hat{x}} D_W(\hat{x})\right\|_2 - 1\right)^2$

8:      **end for**

9:          $w \leftarrow Adam(\nabla_{w\frac{1}{m}} \sum_{i=1}^{m} L^{(i)}, w, a, B_1, B_2)$

10:     **end for**

11:     Sample a batch of latent variables $\left\{z^{(i)}\right\}_{i=1}^{m} \sim p(z)$.

12:     $\theta \leftarrow Adam(\nabla_\theta 1/m \sum_{i=1}^{m} -D_w(G_\theta(z)), \theta, \alpha, \beta_1, \beta_2)$

13: **end while**

13.3 Wasserstein GAN for MNIST

Let's begin with the standard DCGAN model and explore each implementation detail individually, using the MNIST dataset.

13.3.1 Import Libraries

Setting up the program and system requirements for implementation is critical. As with previous steps, the first step in putting it all together is to import the necessary libraries, including TensorFlow and Keras for building the WGAN architecture, NumPy for array calculations, and Matplotlib for visualizations if needed.

```
#This line imports the `glob` module which is used to find all the
pathnames matching a specified pattern according to the rules used by the
Unix shell, although results are returned in arbitrary order.
import glob

#This line imports the `image` module which is used for processing image
data.
import image

#This line imports the `pyplot` module from the `matplotlib` library.
This module provides a way to create a variety of charts and plots,
including line plots, scatter plots, bar plots, and more.
import matplotlib.pyplot as plt

#This line imports the `numpy` library which is used for numerical
operations on arrays. It provides support for various numerical data
types and mathematical functions for manipulating arrays.
import numpy as np

#This line imports the `os` module, which provides a way of using
operating system dependent functionality like reading or writing to the
file system.
import os

#This line imports the `PIL` (Python Imaging Library) module, which
provides image processing capabilities.
import PIL
```

```
#This line imports the `layers` module from the `keras` package of
`TensorFlow`. It is used for building neural network models with the
Keras API.
from tensorflow.keras import layers
```

```
#This line imports the `time` module, which provides various time-related
functions. It is used for measuring the execution time of code.
import time
```

```
This line imports the `display` module from the `IPython` library which
is used for displaying output in the IPython environment.
from IPython import display
```

```
#This line imports the `datetime` module, which provides classes for
working with dates and times.
import datetime
```

13.3.2 Import Dataset

In this step, we load the MNIST dataset and define some parameters. The size of each image in the dataset is set to $28 \times 28 \times 1$, indicating that it is a grayscale image with a height and width of 28 and only one channel. Additionally, a base batch size and a noise dimension are defined to enable the generator to create the desired number of "digit" images. The MNIST dataset is loaded using Keras and normalized to the range of [–1, 1] for more accurate results. Batch normalization is performed, and the data is shuffled using a buffer size of 1024 to optimize performance. This code block loads the MNIST dataset from Keras, reshapes it to the desired shape of (28, 28, 1), normalizes the pixel values to the range of [–1, 1], and creates a "tf.data.Dataset" object for training.

```
#This line loads the MNIST dataset using Keras and unpacks the training
images and labels into `train_images1` and `train_labels1`, respectively.
The validation data is discarded by assigning it to `_`.
(train_images1, train_labels1), (_,_) = tf.keras.datasets.mnist.
load_data()
```

```
#This line reshapes the training images to the desired shape of `(28, 28,
1)` and converts them to `float32` data type.
train_images1 = train_images1.reshape(train_images1.shape[0], 28, 28,
1).astype('float32')
```

```
#This line normalizes the pixel values of the training images to the
range of [-1, 1].
train_images1 = (train_images1 - 127.5) / 127.5
```

```
#This line defines the shape of the images as a tuple of `(28, 28, 1)`.
IMG_SHAPE = (28, 28, 1)
```

```
#This line creates a `tf.data.Dataset` object from the tensor of training
images, shuffles it with a buffer size of 60000, and creates batches of
size 256 for training.
BUFFER_SIZE = 60000
BATCH_SIZE = 256
train_dataset = tf.data.Dataset.from_tensor_slices(train_images1).
shuffle(BUFFER_SIZE).batch(BATCH_SIZE)
```

13.3.3 Generator

In this section, we define the generator using Keras. We specify the data image format, upsample layers, an output layer, and return the model. After building the generator, we generate random numbers to serve as the initial inputs. This code block defines the generator architecture, creates an instance of the generator model, generates initial noise data, and initializes the generator module with the noise data to create a generated image. Here's an explanation of each line:

```
#This code defines the `make_generator1_model()` function that creates a
sequential model consisting of multiple layers such as Dense,
BatchNormalization, ReLU, Reshape, and Conv2DTranspose. It takes 100
random noise vectors as input and generates a 28 x 28 x 1 image as
output. The model's architecture has been designed to upsample the noise
vectors into an image-like format.
def make_generator1_model():
    model = tf.keras.Sequential()
    model.add(layers.Dense(128, use_bias1=False, input_shape=(100,)))
    model.add(layers.BatchNormalization())
    model.add(layers.ReLU())
    model.add(layers.Dense(7*7*256, use_bias1=False))
    model.add(layers.BatchNormalization())
    model.add(layers.ReLU())
    model.add(layers.Reshape((7, 7, 256)))
    assert model.output_shape == (None, 7, 7, 256)
    model.add(layers.Conv2DTranspose(128, (5, 5), strides1=(1, 1),
padding='same', use_bias1=False))
    assert model.output_shape == (None, 7, 7, 128)
    model.add(layers.BatchNormalization())
    model.add(layers.ReLU())
    model.add(layers.Conv2DTranspose(64, (5, 5), strides1=(2, 2),
padding='same', use_bias1=False))
    assert model.output_shape == (None, 14, 14, 64)
    model.add(layers.BatchNormalization())
    model.add(layers.ReLU())
    model.add(layers.Conv2DTranspose(1, (5, 5), strides1=(2, 2),
padding='same', use_bias1=False, activation='tanh'))
    assert model.output_shape == (None, 28, 28, 1)
    return model

#This line creates an instance of the generator model by calling the
`make_generator1_model()` function.
generator1 = make_generator1_model()

#This line creates an initial noise vector of shape (1, 100) using a
uniform distribution with a range of -1 to 1.
noise1 = tf.random.uniform([1, 100], -1, 1)

#This line initializes the generator module by passing the initial noise
data to the generator and creates a generated image with a shape of (1,
28, 28, 1).
generated_image = generator1(noise1, training=False)
```

13.3.4 Critic

In this module, we add the necessary layers, such as downsample and activation layers, and return the model. The code block defines the critic (discriminator) architecture using Keras. The layers include convolutional, activation, max pooling, flatten, and dense layers. After defining the architecture, we create an instance of the critic model and feed the generated data to it. Finally, we define the binary cross-entropy loss. Here's an explanation of each line:

```
#We define the critic architecture using a Keras sequential model. The
layers include two convolutional layers with LeakyReLU activation, a max
pooling layer, a flatten layer, a dense layer with ReLU activation and
dropout, and an output layer with sigmoid activation.
def make_discriminator1_model():
    model = tf.keras.Sequential()
    model.add(layers.Conv2D(64, (5, 5), strides=(2, 2), padding='same',
input_shape=[28, 28, 1]))
    model.add(layers.LeakyReLU(alpha=0.2))
    model.add(layers.Conv2D(128, (5, 5), strides=(2, 2), padding='same'))
    model.add(layers.LeakyReLU(alpha=0.2))
    model.add(layers.MaxPooling2D())
    model.add(layers.Flatten())
    model.add(layers.Dense(128, activation='relu'))
    model.add(layers.Dropout(0.2))
    model.add(layers.Dense(1, activation='sigmoid'))
    return model
```

```
#We create an instance of the critic model.
discriminator1 = make_discriminator1_model()
We feed the generated image to the critic model to obtain its decision.
decision = discriminator1(generated_image)
```

```
#We define the binary cross-entropy loss, which we'll use in the training
loop later.
cross_entropy = tf.keras.losses.BinaryCrossentropy(from_logits=False)
```

13.3.5 Loss Functions

Here, we define the loss functions for both the discriminator (critic) and the generator. We can experiment with different loss functions to observe how they affect the accuracy of the WGAN model.

```
def discriminator1_loss(real_output, fake_output):
    total_loss = -tf.reduce_mean(real_output) + tf.reduce_mean(fake_output)
    return total_loss
def generator1_loss(fake_output):
    return -tf.reduce_mean(fake_output)
```

```
#This line defines a function called `discriminator1_loss` that takes two
arguments, `real_output` and `fake_output`.
def discriminator1_loss(real_output, fake_output):
```

```
#This line calculates the total loss for the discriminator based on the
outputs of the real and fake inputs. It first calculates the mean of the
real output using `tf.reduce_mean`, negates it, and then adds the mean of
the fake output to get the total loss.
total_loss = -tf.reduce_mean(real_output) + tf.reduce_mean(fake_output)


#This line returns the total loss value.
return total_loss

#This line defines a function called `generator1_loss` that takes a
single argument, `fake_output`.
def generator1_loss(fake_output):

#This line returns the negative mean of the fake output, which is the
loss for the generator.
return -tf.reduce_mean(fake_output)
```

13.3.6 Optimizer

The previous model uses the RMSprop optimizer. It's possible to experiment with different optimizers to observe how the results vary in your implementation.

```
generator1_optimizer = tf.keras.optimizers.RMSprop(learning_rate=5e-5)
discriminator1_optimizer = tf.keras.optimizers.RMSprop(learning_rate=5e-5)


#This line initializes an instance of the RMSprop optimizer for the
generator network.
`tf.keras.optimizers` is the module used for defining the optimizer.
`RMSprop` is the name of the optimizer.
`learning_rate` is a parameter of the optimizer that sets the step size
at each iteration.
generator1_optimizer = tf.keras.optimizers.RMSprop(learning_rate=5e-5)

#This line initializes an instance of the RMSprop optimizer for the
discriminator network (or critic in this case).
`tf.keras.optimizers` is the module used for defining the optimizer.
`RMSprop` is the name of the optimizer.
`learning_rate` is a parameter of the optimizer that sets the step size
at each iteration.
discriminator1_optimizer = tf.keras.optimizers.RMSprop(learning_rate=5e-5)
```

13.3.7 Training

In this step, we define the necessary parameters and use the previously implemented functions for the generator, discriminator, loss, and optimizer to train the network and obtain the results. Finally, we generate and save the images.

```
# initialize some training hyperparameters
EPOCHS1 = 200
```

```
noise_dim = 100
num_examples_to_generate = 64

# define initial data (noise)
seed = tf.random.uniform([num_examples_to_generate, noise_dim], -1, 1)
current_time = datetime.datetime.now().strftime("%Y%m%d-%H%M%S")
gen_log_dir = 'logs/wgan_gradient_tape/' + current_time + '/gen'
disc_log_dir = 'logs/wgan_gradient_tape/' + current_time + '/disc'
gen_summary_writer = tf.summary.create_file_writer(gen_log_dir)
disc_summary_writer = tf.summary.create_file_writer(disc_log_dir)
@tf.function

# define the generator training module
def train_generator1():
    noise1 = tf.random.uniform([BATCH_SIZE, noise_dim], minval=-1,
maxval=1)
    with tf.GradientTape() as gen_tape:
        generated_images = generator1(noise1, training=True)
        fake_output = discriminator1(generated_images, training=True)
        gen_loss = generator1_loss(fake_output)
    gradients_of_generator1 = gen_tape.gradient(gen_loss, generator1.
trainable_variables)
    generator1_optimizer.apply_gradients(zip(gradients_of_generator1,
generator1.trainable_variables))
    return gen_loss
@tf.function

# define the discriminator training module
def train_discriminator1(images):
    noise1 = tf.random.uniform([BATCH_SIZE, noise_dim], minval=-1,
maxval=1)
    with tf.GradientTape() as disc_tape:
        generated_images = generator1(noise1, training=True)
        real_output = discriminator1(images, training=True)
        fake_output = discriminator1(generated_images, training=True)
        disc_loss = discriminator1_loss(real_output, fake_output)
    gradients_of_discriminator1 = disc_tape.gradient(disc_loss,
discriminator1.trainable_variables)
    discriminator1_optimizer.apply_gradients(zip(gradients_of_
discriminator1, discriminator1.trainable_variables))
    _ = [p.assign(tf.clip_by_value(p, -0.01, 0.01)) for p in
discriminator1.trainable_variables]
    return disc_loss

# define the general training module
def train(dataset, epochs1):
    for epoch in range(epochs1):
        start = time.time()
        for image_batch in dataset:
            for _ in range(5):
                disc_loss = train_discriminator1(image_batch)
            gen_loss = train_generator1()
        with gen_summary_writer.as_default():
            tf.summary.scalar('loss', gen_loss, step=epoch)
```

```
        with disc_summary_writer.as_default():
            tf.summary.scalar('loss', disc_loss, step=epoch)
        display.clear_output(wait=True)
        generate_and_save_images(generator1,epoch + 1,seed)
        print ('Time for epoch {} is {} sec'.format(epoch + 1, time.
time()-start))
    display.clear_output(wait=True)
    generate_and_save_images(generator1,epochs1, seed)
```

```
#Defines the number of epochs to train for, the size of the input noise
vector for the generator, and the number of examples to generate.
EPOCHS1 = 200
noise_dim = 100
num_examples_to_generate = 64
```

```
#Creates an initial random noise vector to use for generating images.
seed = tf.random.uniform([num_examples_to_generate, noise_dim], -1, 1)
```

```
#Defines directories for logging generator and discriminator training
progress.
current_time = datetime.datetime.now().strftime("%Y%m%d-%H%M%S")
gen_log_dir = 'logs/wgan_gradient_tape/' + current_time + '/gen'
disc_log_dir = 'logs/wgan_gradient_tape/' + current_time + '/disc'
gen_summary_writer = tf.summary.create_file_writer(gen_log_dir)
disc_summary_writer = tf.summary.create_file_writer(disc_log_dir)
```

```
#Defines the training step for the generator. Generates random noise
data, uses it to generate fake images, calculates the loss, computes the
gradients, and updates the generator parameters.
@tf.function
def train_generator1():
    noise1 = tf.random.uniform([BATCH_SIZE, noise_dim], minval=-1,
maxval=1)
    with tf.GradientTape() as gen_tape:
        generated_images = generator1(noise1, training=True)
        fake_output = discriminator1(generated_images, training=True)
        gen_loss = generator1_loss(fake_output)
    gradients_of_generator1 = gen_tape.gradient(gen_loss, generator1.
trainable_variables)
    generator1_optimizer.apply_gradients(zip(gradients_of_generator1,
generator1.trainable_variables))
    return gen_loss
```

```
#Defines the training step for the discriminator. Generates random noise
data, uses it to generate fake images, and real images from the training
dataset. Calculates the loss, computes the gradients, and updates the
discriminator parameters. Also, performs weight clipping to enforce the
Lipschitz constraint.
@tf.function
def train_discriminator1(images):
    noise1 = tf.random.uniform([BATCH_SIZE, noise_dim], minval=-1,
maxval=1)
    with tf.GradientTape() as disc_tape:
        generated_images = generator1(noise1, training=True)
```

```
            real_output = discriminator1(images, training=True)
            fake_output = discriminator1(generated_images, training=True)
            disc_loss = discriminator1_loss(real_output, fake_output)
        gradients_of_discriminator1 = disc_tape.gradient(disc_loss,
discriminator1.trainable_variables)
        discriminator1_optimizer.apply_gradients(zip(gradients_of_
discriminator1, discriminator1.trainable_variables))
        _ = [p.assign(tf.clip_by_value(p, -0.01, 0.01)) for p in
discriminator1.trainable_variables]
    return disc_loss
```

#This code block contains the main training module. It loops through the specified number of epochs, iterating through the dataset to train the generator and discriminator using the previously defined training modules. Within each epoch, the discriminator is trained five times for improved stability, while the generator is trained once. The losses for each module are written to tensorboard logs. The generated images are also saved and displayed after each epoch. The training function returns no value.

```
def train(dataset, epochs1):
    for epoch in range(epochs1):
        start = time.time()
        for image_batch in dataset:
            for _ in range(5):
                disc_loss = train_discriminator1(image_batch)
            gen_loss = train_generator1()
        with gen_summary_writer.as_default():
            tf.summary.scalar('loss', gen_loss, step=epoch)
        with disc_summary_writer.as_default():
            tf.summary.scalar('loss', disc_loss, step=epoch)
        display.clear_output(wait=True)
        generate_and_save_images(generator1,epoch + 1,seed)
        print ('Time for epoch {} is {} sec'.format(epoch + 1, time.
time()-start))
    display.clear_output(wait=True)
    generate_and_save_images(generator1,epochs1, seed)
```

13.3.8 Generate Image

The model can be run for a specified number of epochs and can be tested on image data. It is recommended to experiment with different numbers of epochs to observe the stability of the output and whether the error is small enough.

```
BATCH_SIZE = 64
def generate_and_save_images(model, epoch, test_input):
    predictions = model(test_input, training=False)
    fig = plt.figure(figsize=(8,8))
    for i in range(predictions.shape[0]):
        plt.subplot(8, 8, i+1)
        plt.imshow(predictions[i, :, :, 0] * 127.5 + 127.5, cmap='gray')
        plt.axis('off')
    plt.show()
train(train_dataset, EPOCHS1)
```

```
#This line sets the batch size for the training data.
BATCH_SIZE = 64
```

```
#This function generates and saves the images that are created by the
generator during training. The `model` argument refers to the generator
model, `epoch` is the current epoch number, and `test_input` is the input
noise data for the generator. The function generates the images by
calling the generator with the `test_input` data and setting
`training=False` to indicate that the model should not update its
weights. The generated images are then displayed in an 8x8 grid using
`plt.subplot()` and `plt.imshow()`. The `cmap` argument is set to 'gray'
to indicate that the images are grayscale. Finally, the images are
displayed using `plt.show()`.
def generate_and_save_images(model, epoch, test_input):
    predictions = model(test_input, training=False)
    fig = plt.figure(figsize=(8,8))
    for i in range(predictions.shape[0]):
        plt.subplot(8, 8, i+1)
        plt.imshow(predictions[i, :, :, 0] * 127.5 + 127.5, cmap='gray')
        plt.axis('off')
    plt.show()
```

```
#This line starts the training process by calling the `train()` function
with the training dataset and the number of epochs to train for. The
`train()` function is defined in an earlier code block and contains the
training loop for both the generator and discriminator models.
train(train_dataset, EPOCHS1)
```

Figure 13.4 displays the output after 100 epochs. Results after training a WGAN on the
MNIST dataset for 100 epochs. The displayed images demonstrate clear and recognizable

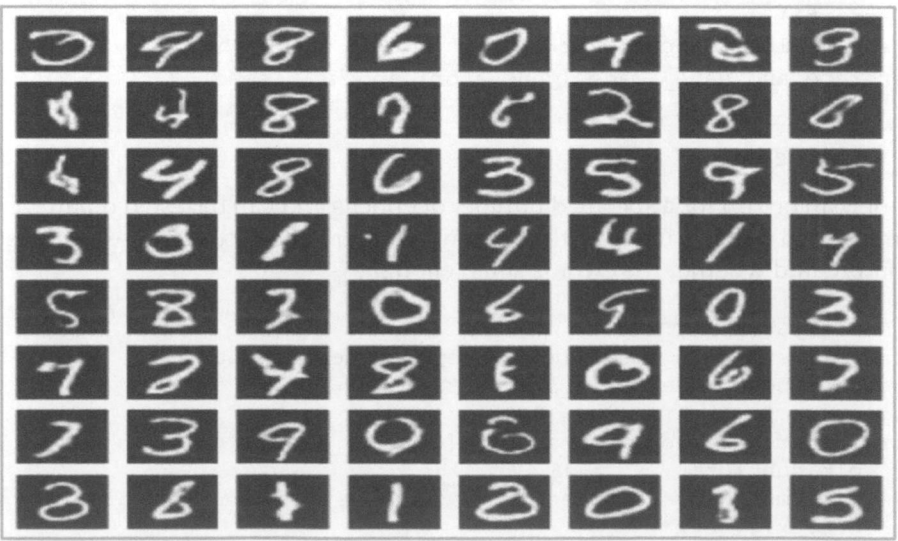

FIGURE 13.4
The output after 100 epochs.

handwritten digits, reflecting the effectiveness of the Wasserstein GAN in capturing the nuances of the dataset. The fidelity of the generated digits underscores the model's robustness and the advantages of using the Wasserstein loss.

13.4 WGAN-GP (WGAN with Gradient Penalty (GP)) on Fashion-MNIST

In the original Wasserstein GAN, a value function incorporating the Wasserstein distance is utilized, resulting in a value function with superior theoretical properties compared to the value function employed in the original GAN study. In WGAN, the discriminator, also known as the critic, must exist within the 1-Lipschitz functions, and the idea of "weight clipping" is used to address this limitation. However, weight clipping may be challenging to implement to impose a 1-Lipschitz constraint. When weight clipping is used, the WGAN discriminator (critic) often fails to converge, and the WGAN-GP method replaces weight clipping with a GP, resulting in more effective training. This is achieved by including a loss term that ensures the discriminator gradient L_2 norm remains very close to 1. In this section, we use this method to generate images from the Fashion-MNIST dataset.

13.4.1 Import Libraries

The code imports several commonly used libraries in deep learning and machine learning projects. TensorFlow is a popular deep learning framework developed by Google, NumPy is a library for numerical computing in Python, and Keras is a high-level neural networks API. By importing these libraries, we make their functionalities available to our code.

```
#This imports the NumPy library and aliases it as "np" for brevity in the
code.
import numpy as np

#This imports the TensorFlow library and aliases it as "tf" for brevity
in the code.
import tensorflow as tf

#This imports the Keras module from TensorFlow, which provides a high-
level API for building and training neural networks.
from tensorflow import keras

#This imports the layers module from Keras, which contains various types
of layers used to build neural networks.
from tensorflow.keras import layers
```

13.4.2 Prepare the Data

The dataset contains grayscale images of size 28×28 pixels, each associated with one of ten categories, such as trousers, pullovers, sneakers, etc. Once the hyperparameters are initialized, the loaded data is reshaped and normalized.

```
# initial the hyperparameters
IMG_SHAPE = (28, 28, 1)
BATCH_SIZE = 512
noise_dim = 128

# load the fashion mnist dataset from keras
fashion_mnist = keras.datasets.fashion_mnist
(train_images1, train_labels1), (test_images1, test_labels) = fashion_
mnist.load_data()
print(f"Number of examples: {len(train_images1)}")
print(f"Shape of the images in the dataset: {train_images1.shape[1:]}")

# reshape the training data
train_images1 = train_images1.reshape(train_images1.shape[0], *IMG_
SHAPE).astype("float32")

# normalize the training data
train_images1 = (train_images1 - 127.5) / 127.5
```

#In this block, we define the hyperparameters for the model. `IMG_SHAPE` represents the shape of the input images, `BATCH_SIZE` determines the number of images to use for each training batch, and `noise_dim` represents the size of the input noise for the generator model.
```
IMG_SHAPE = (28, 28, 1)
BATCH_SIZE = 512
noise_dim = 128
```

#In this block, we load the Fashion-MNIST dataset from Keras, which is a dataset of grayscale images of clothing items belonging to 10 categories. We then print out the number of examples in the training set and the shape of the images.
```
fashion_mnist = keras.datasets.fashion_mnist
(train_images1, train_labels1), (test_images1, test_labels) = fashion_
mnist.load_data()
print(f"Number of examples: {len(train_images1)}")
print(f"Shape of the images in the dataset: {train_images1.shape[1:]}")
```

#In this block, we reshape the training images to match the `IMG_SHAPE` hyperparameter we defined earlier. We then normalize the pixel values of the training images to be between -1 and 1 by subtracting 127.5 and dividing by 127.5.
```
train_images1 = train_images1.reshape(train_images1.shape[0], *IMG_
SHAPE).astype("float32")
train_images1 = (train_images1 - 127.5) / 127.5
```

13.4.3 Discriminator (Critic)

The samples in the dataset are in the format of (28, 28, 1). If the upsampling in the generator component is not handled carefully, the output shape might differ from the original photos. To address this issue, a simpler solution can be used. In the discriminator, the input for each sample can be "zero padded" to change the shape to (32, 32, 1). In the generator, the final output can be cropped to match the input format.

```
# define the convolutional layers
def conv_block(x,filters,activation,kernel_size1=(3, 3),strides1=(1,
1),padding="same",
    use_bias1=True,use_bn=False,use_dropout1=False,drop_value=0.5,):
    x = layers.Conv2D(filters, kernel_size1, strides1=strides1,
padding=padding, use_bias1=use_bias1)(x)

# deploying batch normalization and dropout
    if use_bn:
        x = layers.BatchNormalization()(x)
    x = activation(x)
    if use_dropout1:
        x = layers.Dropout(drop_value)(x)
    return x

#  define the discriminator model
def get_discriminator1_model():
    img_input = layers.Input(shape=IMG_SHAPE)
    x = layers.ZeroPadding2D((2, 2))(img_input)
    x = conv_block(x,64,kernel_size1=(5,5),strides1=(2, 2), use_bn=False,
use_bias1=True,activation=layers.LeakyReLU(0.2),use_dropout1=
False,drop_value=0.3,)
    x = conv_block(x,128,kernel_size1=(5,5),strides1=(2, 2),
use_bn=False,
        activation=layers.LeakyReLU(0.2),use_bias1=True,use_dropout1=
True,drop_value=0.3,)
    x = conv_block(x,256,kernel_size1=(5, 5),strides1=(2, 2),
use_bn=False,
        activation=layers.LeakyReLU(0.2),use_bias1=True,use_dropout1=True,
drop_value=0.3,)
    x = conv_block(x, 512, kernel_size1=(5, 5),strides1=(2, 2),
use_bn=False,
        activation=layers.LeakyReLU(0.2), use_bias1=True, use_dropout1=
False,drop_value=0.3,)

# define the flatten layer
    x = layers.Flatten()(x)

# define the dropout layer
    x = layers.Dropout(0.2)(x)

# define the dense layer
    x = layers.Dense(1)(x)

# define the model
    d_model1 = keras.models.Model(img_input, x, name="discriminator1")
    return d_model1

# define the discriminator model
d_model1 = get_discriminator1_model()

# Show the model summary
d_model1.summary()
Model: "discriminator1"
```

```
Layers (type)                        Outputs Shape              Params #
========================================================================
input_11   (InputLayer)              [(None, 28, 28, 1)]        0
zero_padding2d1(ZeroPadding 2D)      (None, 32, 32, 1)          0
conv2d (Conv2D)                      (None, 16, 16, 64)         1664
leaky_re_lu (LeakyReLU)              (None, 16, 16, 64)         0
conv2d_1 (Conv2D)                    (None, 8, 8, 128)          204928
leaky_re_lu_1 (LeakyReLU)            (None, 8, 8, 128)          0
dropout (Dropout)                    (None, 8, 8, 128)          0
conv2d_2 (Conv2D)                    (None, 4, 4, 256)          819456
leaky_re_lu_2 (LeakyReLU)            (None, 4, 4, 256)          0
dropout_1 (Dropout)                  (None, 4, 4, 256)          0
conv2d_3 (Conv2D)                    (None, 2, 2, 512)          3277312
leaky_re_lu_3 (LeakyReLU)            (None, 2, 2, 512)          0

flatten (Flatten)                    (None, 2048)               0
dropout_2 (Dropout)                  (None, 2048)               0
dense (Dense)                        (None, 1)                  2049
========================================================================
Total params: 4,305,409
Trainable params: 4,305,409
Non-trainable params: 0
```

```
#This function defines a convolutional block that will be used in the
discriminator model. The `x` argument is the input tensor, `filters` is
the number of filters in the convolutional layer, `activation` is the
activation function used, `kernel_size1` is the size of the convolutional
kernel, `strides1` is the stride of the convolutional kernel, `padding`
specifies the padding used in the convolutional layer, `use_bias1` is a
Boolean that determines whether bias is used in the convolutional layer,
`use_bn` is a Boolean that determines whether batch normalization is
used, `use_dropout1` is a Boolean that determines whether dropout is
used, and `drop_value` is the rate of dropout.
def conv_block(x,filters,activation,kernel_size1=(3, 3),strides1=(1, 1),
padding="same",
    use_bias1=True,use_bn=False,use_dropout1=False,drop_value=0.5,):
    x = layers.Conv2D(filters, kernel_size1, strides1=strides1,
padding=padding, use_bias1=use_bias1)(x)
    if use_bn:
        x = layers.BatchNormalization()(x)
    x = activation(x)
    if use_dropout1:
        x = layers.Dropout(drop_value)(x)
    return x

#This function defines the discriminator model using the `conv_block`
function defined earlier. The `img_input` is the input tensor, `x` is the
result of padding the input with zeros, and four convolutional blocks are
used to extract features from the input. The output is then flattened,
dropout is applied, and a fully connected layer is used to produce the
final output. The model is then returned as a `keras.models.Model`
object.
def get_discriminator1_model():
```

```
    img_input = layers.Input(shape=IMG_SHAPE)
    x = layers.ZeroPadding2D((2, 2))(img_input)
    x = conv_block(x,64,kernel_size1=(5,5),strides1=(2,2), use_bn=False,
use_bias1=True,activation=layers.LeakyReLU(0.2),use_dropout1=False,
drop_value=0.3,)
    x = conv_block(x,128,kernel_size1=(5,5),strides1=(2, 2),
use_bn=False,
        activation=layers.LeakyReLU(0.2),use_bias1=True,use_dropout1=True,
drop_value=0.3,)
    x = conv_block(x,256,kernel_size1=(5, 5),strides1=(2,
2),use_bn=False,
        activation=layers.LeakyReLU(0.2),use_bias1=True,use_dropout1=True,
drop_value=0.3,)
    x = conv_block(x, 512, kernel_size1=(5, 5),strides1=(2, 2),
use_bn=False,
        activation=layers.LeakyReLU(0.2), use_bias1=True,
use_dropout1=False,drop_value=0.3,)
    x = layers.Flatten()(x)
    x = layers.Dropout(0.2)(x)
    x = layers.Dense(1)(x)
    d_model1 = keras.models.Model(img_input, x, name="discriminator1")
    return d_model1

#These lines define the discriminator model using the `get_
discriminator1_model()` function and print a summary of the model. The
summary includes information such as the
d_model1 = get_discriminator1_model()
d_model1.summary()
```

13.4.4 Generator

We will define the architecture and network for the generator, including the layers and a model that incorporates an upsample block.

```
def upsample_block1(x,filters,activation, kernel_size1=(3, 3),
strides1=(1, 1),
    up_size=(2, 2),padding="same",use_bn=False,
use_bias1=True,use_dropout1=False,drop_value=0.3,):
    x = layers.UpSampling2D(up_size)(x)
    x = layers.Conv2D(filters, kernel_size1, strides1=strides1,
padding=padding, use_bias1=use_bias1)(x)
    if use_bn:
        x = layers.BatchNormalization()(x)
    if activation:
        x = activation(x)
    if use_dropout1:
        x = layers.Dropout(drop_value)(x)
    return x
def get_generator1_model():
    noise1 = layers.Input(shape=(noise_dim,))
    x = layers.Dense(4 * 4 * 256, use_bias1=False)(noise1)
    x = layers.BatchNormalization()(x)
    x = layers.LeakyReLU(0.2)(x)
```

```
    x = layers.Reshape((4, 4, 256))(x)
    x = upsample_block1(x,128,layers.LeakyReLU(0.2),strides1=(1, 1),
use_bias1=False,
        use_bn=True,padding="same",use_dropout1=False,)
    x = upsample_block1(x,64,layers.LeakyReLU(0.2),strides1=(1, 1),
use_bias1=False,
        use_bn=True, padding="same",use_dropout1=False,    )
    x = upsample_block1(x, 1, layers.Activation("tanh"), strides1=(1, 1),
use_bias1=False, use_bn=True)
    x = layers.Cropping2D((2, 2))(x)
    g_model1 = keras.models.Model(noise1, x, name="generator1")
    return g_model1
g_model1 = get_generator1_model()
g_model1.summary()

Model: "generator1"
```

Layer (type)	Output Shape	Param #
input_21 (InputLayer)	[(None, 128)]	0
dense_11 (Dense)	(None, 4096)	524288
batch_normalization (BatchN normalization)	(None, 4096)	16384
leaky_re_lu_41 (LeakyReLU)	(None, 4096)	0
reshape (Reshape)	(None, 4, 4, 256)	0
up_sampling2d (UpSampling2D)	(None, 8, 8, 256)	0
conv2d_41 (Conv2D)	(None, 8, 8, 128)	294912
batch_normalization_1(Batch Normalization)	(None, 8, 8, 128)	512
leaky_re_lu_51 (LeakyReLU)	(None, 8, 8, 128)	0
up_sampling2d_11 (UpSampling 2D)	(None, 16, 16, 128)	0
conv2d_51 (Conv2D)	(None, 16, 16, 64)	73728
batch_normalization_21(Batch Normalization)	(None, 16, 16, 64)	256
leaky_re_lu_61 (LeakyReLU)	(None, 16, 16, 64)	0
up_sampling2d_21 (UpSampling 2D)	(None, 32, 32, 64)	0
conv2d_61 (Conv2D)	(None, 32, 32, 1)	576
batch_normalization_31(Batch Normalization)	(None, 32, 32, 1)	4
activation (Activation)	(None, 32, 32, 1)	0
cropping2d (Cropping2D)	(None, 28, 28, 1)	0

```
Total params: 910,660
Trainable params: 902,082
Non-trainable params: 8,578
```

**#This function defines a block that upsamples an input tensor `x` using
`UpSampling2D` and applies convolution using `Conv2D` with the given
`filters`, `kernel_size1`, `strides1`, and `padding`. If `use_bn` is
`True`, then batch normalization is applied. If `activation` is given,
then it is applied to the output tensor. If `use_dropout1` is `True`,
then dropout is applied with `drop_value`. The upsampled and convolved
output tensor is returned.**

```
def upsample_block1(x,filters,activation, kernel_size1=(3,
3),strides1=(1, 1),
    up_size=(2, 2),padding="same",use_bn=False,
use_bias1=True,use_dropout1=False,drop_value=0.3,):
    x = layers.UpSampling2D(up_size)(x)
```

```
        x = layers.Conv2D(filters, kernel_size1, strides1=strides1,
padding=padding, use_bias1=use_bias1)(x)
    if use_bn:
        x = layers.BatchNormalization()(x)
    if activation:
        x = activation(x)
    if use_dropout1:
        x = layers.Dropout(drop_value)(x)
    return x
```

#This function defines the generator model. It first defines an input layer with the shape of the noise vector. Then, a dense layer with `4 * 4 * 256` units is applied to the input noise. Batch normalization and LeakyReLU activation are then applied to the output of the dense layer. The output is then reshaped to a tensor of shape `(4, 4, 256)`. Three upsample blocks are applied to the tensor, each with a different number of filters and an activation function. Finally, the output tensor is cropped using `Cropping2D` to match the input image size, and the generator model is returned.

```
def get_generator1_model():
    noise1 = layers.Input(shape=(noise_dim,))
    x = layers.Dense(4 * 4 * 256, use_bias1=False)(noise1)
    x = layers.BatchNormalization()(x)
    x = layers.LeakyReLU(0.2)(x)
    x = layers.Reshape((4, 4, 256))(x)
    x = upsample_block1(x,128,layers.LeakyReLU(0.2),strides1=(1,
1),use_bias1=False,
        use_bn=True,padding="same",use_dropout1=False,)
    x = upsample_block1(x,64,layers.LeakyReLU(0.2),strides1=(1, 1),
use_bias1=False,
        use_bn=True, padding="same",use_dropout1=False,    )
    x = upsample_block1(x, 1, layers.Activation("tanh"), strides1=(1, 1),
use_bias1=False, use_bn=True)
    x = layers.Cropping2D((2, 2))(x)
    g_model1 = keras.models.Model(noise1, x, name="generator1")
    return g_model1
```

#This code calls the `get_generator1_model()` function to get the generator model and displays the model summary.

```
g_model1 = get_generator1_model()
g_model1.summary()
```

13.4.5 WGAN-GP Model

The WGAN-GP model will be implemented using the generator and discriminator defined previously. The training procedure will also be modified accordingly.

```
class WGAN1(keras.Model):
    def __init__(self, discriminator1,generator1, latent_dim,
discriminator1_extra_steps=4, gp_weight=11.0,):
        super(WGAN1, self).__init__()
        self.discriminator1 = discriminator1
        self.generator1 = generator1
        self.latent_dim = latent_dim
```

```
            self.d_steps = discriminator1_extra_steps
            self.gp_weight = gp_weight
        def compile(self, d_optimizer1, g_optimizer1, d_loss_fn, g_loss_fn1):
            super(WGAN1, self).compile()
            self.d_optimizer1 = d_optimizer1
            self.g_optimizer1 = g_optimizer1
            self.d_loss_fn = d_loss_fn
            self.g_loss_fn1 = g_loss_fn1
        def gradient_penalty(self, batch_size, real_images1, fake_images1):
            alpha1 = tf.random.normal([batch_size, 1, 1, 1], 0.0, 1.0)
            diff = fake_images1 - real_images1
            interpolated = real_images1 + alpha1 * diff
            with tf.GradientTape() as gp_tape:
                gp_tape.watch(interpolated)
                pred = self.discriminator1(interpolated, training=True)
            grads1 = gp_tape.gradient(pred, [interpolated])[0]
            norm 1 = tf.sqrt(tf.reduce_sum(tf.square(grads1), axis=[1, 2, 3]))
            gp = tf.reduce_mean((norm 1 - 1.0) ** 2)
            return gp
        def train_step(self, real_images1):
            if isinstance(real_images1, tuple):
                real_images1 = real_images1[0]
            batch_size = tf.shape(real_images1)[0]
            for i in range(self.d_steps):
                random_latent_vectors = tf.random.normal(shape=(batch_size,
self.latent_dim))
                with tf.GradientTape() as tape:
                    fake_images1 = self.generator1(random_latent_vectors,
training=True)
                    fake_logits = self.discriminator1(fake_images1,
training=True)
                    real_logits = self.discriminator1(real_images1,
training=True)
                    d_cost1 = self.d_loss_fn(real_img1=real_logits,
fake_img1=fake_logits)
                    gp = self.gradient_penalty(batch_size, real_images1,
fake_images1)
                    d_loss = d_cost1 + gp * self.gp_weight
                d_gradient = tape.gradient(d_loss,self.discriminator1.
trainable_variables)
self.d_optimizer1.apply_gradients(zip(d_gradient,self.discriminator1.
trainable_variables))
            random_latent_vectors = tf.random.normal(shape=(batch_size, self.
latent_dim))
            with tf.GradientTape() as tape:
                generated_images = self.generator1(random_latent_vectors,
training=True)
                gen_img_logits = self.discriminator1(generated_images,
training=True)
                g_loss = self.g_loss_fn1(gen_img_logits)
            gen_gradient = tape.gradient(g_loss, self.generator1.
trainable_variables)
            self.g_optimizer1.apply_gradients(zip(gen_gradient, self.
generator1.trainable_variables)               )
            return {"d_loss": d_loss, "g_loss": g_loss}
```

```
#This line defines the class `WGAN1` which inherits from the `keras.
Model` class.
class WGAN1(keras.Model):

#This line defines the constructor method for the `WGAN1` class, which
initializes the discriminator, generator, latent dimension, number of
discriminator steps, and gradient penalty weight.
def __init__(self, discriminator1,generator1, latent_dim, discriminator1_
extra_steps=4, gp_weight=11.0,):

#This line calls the constructor of the parent class `keras.Model`.
super(WGAN1, self).__init__()

#These lines initialize the class variables for the `WGAN1` class.
self.discriminator1 = discriminator1
self.generator1 = generator1
self.latent_dim = latent_dim
self.d_steps = discriminator1_extra_steps
self.gp_weight = gp_weight

#This line defines the `compile` method for the `WGAN1` class, which
specifies the optimizer and loss function for both the generator and
discriminator.
def compile(self, d_optimizer1, g_optimizer1, d_loss_fn, g_loss_fn1):

#This line calls the `compile` method of the parent class `keras.Model`.
super(WGAN1, self).compile()

#These lines initialize the optimizer and loss function variables for the
`WGAN1` class.
self.d_optimizer1 = d_optimizer1
self.g_optimizer1 = g_optimizer1
self.d_loss_fn = d_loss_fn
self.g_loss_fn1 = g_loss_fn1

#This line defines the `gradient_penalty` method, which computes the
gradient penalty.
def gradient_penalty(self, batch_size, real_images1, fake_images1):

#This line generates a tensor of random values for alpha, used to compute
the interpolated values.
alpha1 = tf.random.normal([batch_size, 1, 1, 1], 0.0, 1.0)
#These lines compute the interpolated values between the real and fake
images.
diff = fake_images1 - real_images1
interpolated = real_images1 + alpha1 * diff

#These lines compute the gradient of the interpolated values with respect
to the discriminator's output.
with tf.GradientTape() as gp_tape:
    gp_tape.watch(interpolated)
    pred = self.discriminator1(interpolated, training=True)
grads1 = gp_tape.gradient(pred, [interpolated])[0]
```

```
#These lines compute the gradient penalty by calculating the L2 norm of
the gradients and taking the mean of the difference from 1.
norm 1 = tf.sqrt(tf.reduce_sum(tf.square(grads1), axis=[1, 2, 3]))
gp = tf.reduce_mean((norm 1 - 1.0) ** 2)

#This line returns the gradient penalty.
return gp

#This line defines the `train_step` method for the `WGAN1` class, which
performs a single training step.
def train_step(self, real_images1):

#This line checks whether the real images are in a tuple and extracts
them if they are.
if isinstance(real_images1, tuple):
    real_images1 = real_images1[0]

#This line gets the batch size of the real images.
batch_size = tf.shape(real_images1)[0]

#The `train_step` method is called during each training iteration and
receives the real images as input.
def train_step(self, real_images1):

#This line is checking whether the input `real_images1` is a tuple and,
if so, selects the first element of the tuple as the input.
if isinstance(real_images1, tuple):
            real_images1 = real_images1[0]

#This line gets the batch size of the input `real_images1`.
batch_size = tf.shape(real_images1)[0]

#This loop performs the training steps for the discriminator. It iterates
for `self.d_steps` steps, defined during initialization.
- For each step, it generates random latent vectors and feeds them to the
generator to generate fake images. It also gets the real image logits and
fake image logits from the discriminator.
- It calculates the loss for the discriminator (`d_cost1`) using the
`d_loss_fn` method and applies the gradient penalty using the `gradient_
penalty` method.
- It calculates the total loss (`d_loss`) and applies the gradients to
the discriminator.
 for i in range(self.d_steps):
            random_latent_vectors = tf.random.normal(shape=(batch_size,
self.latent_dim))
            with tf.GradientTape() as tape:
                fake_images1 = self.generator1(random_latent_vectors,
training=True)
                fake_logits = self.discriminator1(fake_images1,
training=True)
                real_logits = self.discriminator1(real_images1,
training=True)
                d_cost1 = self.d_loss_fn(real_img1=real_logits,
fake_img1=fake_logits)
```

```
                gp = self.gradient_penalty(batch_size, real_images1,
fake_images1)
                d_loss = d_cost1 + gp * self.gp_weight
            d_gradient = tape.gradient(d_loss,self.discriminator1.
trainable_variables)
            self.d_optimizer1.apply_gradients(zip(d_gradient,self.
discriminator1.trainable_variables))
```

  #This block trains the generator.
  - It generates random latent vectors and feeds them to the generator to
  generate fake images.
  - It calculates the loss for the generator (`g_loss`) using the `g_loss_
  fn1` method.
  - It calculates the gradients for the generator and applies them.
```
random_latent_vectors = tf.random.normal(shape=(batch_size, self.
latent_dim))
        with tf.GradientTape() as tape:
            generated_images = self.generator1(random_latent_vectors,
training=True)
            gen_img_logits = self.discriminator1(generated_images,
training=True)
            g_loss = self.g_loss_fn1(gen_img_logits)
        gen_gradient = tape.gradient(g_loss, self.generator1.
trainable_variables)
        self.g_optimizer1.apply_gradients(zip(gen_gradient, self.
generator1.trainable_variables))
```

#This line returns the dictionary with the discriminator and generator
losses.
```
return {"d_loss": d_loss, "g_loss": g_loss}
```

13.4.6 Saves Images

It is good practice to save the generated data for future use or to continue the training process from where it left off. This can save time and computational resources, as the model doesn't have to start from scratch every time. Additionally, the saved generated data can be used for various downstream tasks, such as testing, evaluation, or further analysis.

```
class GANMonitor(Keras.callbacks.Callback):
    def __init__(self, num_img=6, latent_dim=128):
        self.num_img = num_img
        self.latent_dim = latent_dim
    def on_epoch_end(self, epoch, logs=None):
        random_latent_vectors = tf.random.normal(shape=(self.num_img,
self.latent_dim))
        generated_images = self.model.generator1(random_latent_vectors)
        generated_images = (generated_images * 127.5) + 127.5
        for i in range(self.num_img):
            img = generated_images[i].numpy()
            img = keras.preprocessing.image.array_to_img(img)
            img.save("generated_img_{i}_{epoch}.png".format(i=i,
epoch=epoch))
```

```
#This line defines a class named `GANMonitor`, which is a subclass of the
`Keras.callbacks.Callback` class.
class GANMonitor(Keras.callbacks.Callback):

# This line defines a constructor method for the `GANMonitor` class that
takes two optional parameters `num_img` and `latent_dim`, which are set
to `6` and `128` respectively if not specified.
def __init__(self, num_img=6, latent_dim=128):

# These lines initialize instance variables `num_img` and `latent_dim`
with the values passed to the constructor.
self.num_img = num_img
self.latent_dim = latent_dim

# This line defines a method named `on_epoch_end` that is called at the
end of each epoch during training. It takes two parameters, `epoch` and
`logs`, where `epoch` is the current epoch number and `logs` is a
dictionary containing the training metrics.
def on_epoch_end(self, epoch, logs=None):

# This line generates a tensor of random noise vectors with shape `(num_
img, latent_dim)` using the `tf.random.normal` function from the
TensorFlow library.
random_latent_vectors = tf.random.normal(shape=(self.num_img, self.
latent_dim))

# This line uses the generator model (`generator1`) of the GAN to
generate fake images from the random noise vectors.
generated_images = self.model.generator1(random_latent_vectors)

# This line scales the pixel values of the generated images from the
range `[-1, 1]` to the range `[0, 255]` by multiplying them with `127.5`
and adding `127.5`.
generated_images = (generated_images * 127.5) + 127.5

# This loop iterates over the generated images, converts each image from
a tensor to a PIL image object, and saves it to a file with a filename
containing the image index (`i`) and the current epoch number (`epoch`).
The `array_to_img` method is used to convert the tensor to a PIL image
object. The images are saved in PNG format in the current working
directory.
for i in range(self.num_img):
    img = generated_images[i].numpy()
    img = keras.preprocessing.image.array_to_img(img)
    img.save("generated_img_{i}_{epoch}.png".format(i=i, epoch=epoch))
```

13.4.7 Train Model

Calling and utilizing the generated modules in the training model is a crucial step. This allows us to train the model using the defined architecture, loss function, optimizer, and other necessary parameters.

```
generator1_optimizer = keras.optimizers.Adam(learning_rate=0.0002,
beta_1=0.7, beta_2=0.8)
```

```
discriminator1_optimizer = keras.optimizers.Adam(learning_rate=0.0002,
beta_1=0.7, beta_2=0.8)
def discriminator1_loss(real_img1, fake_img1):
    real_loss = tf.reduce_mean(real_img1)
    fake_loss = tf.reduce_mean(fake_img1)
    return fake_loss - real_loss
def generator1_loss(fake_img1):
    return -tf.reduce_mean(fake_img1)
epochs1 = 20
cbk = GANMonitor(num_img=4, latent_dim=noise_dim)
wgan =
WGAN(discriminator1=d_model1,generator1=g_model1,latent_dim=noise_
dim,discriminator1_extra_steps=5,)
wgan.compile(d_optimizer1=discriminator1_optimizer,
g_optimizer1=generator1_optimizer,
    g_loss_fn1=generator1_loss, d_loss_fn=discriminator1_loss,)
wgan.fit(train_images1, batch_size=BATCH_SIZE, epochs1=epochs1,
callbacks=[cbk])
```

#Define the Adam optimizer with a learning rate of 0.0002, beta_1 of 0.7, and beta_2 of 0.8 for the generator.
```
generator1_optimizer = keras.optimizers.Adam(learning_rate=0.0002,
beta_1=0.7, beta_2=0.8)
```

#Define the Adam optimizer with a learning rate of 0.0002, beta_1 of 0.7, and beta_2 of 0.8 for the discriminator.
```
discriminator1_optimizer = keras.optimizers.Adam(learning_rate=0.0002,
beta_1=0.7, beta_2=0.8)
```

#Define the loss function for the discriminator. The function takes two inputs, real_img1 and fake_img1. The real_img1 and fake_img1 represent the real and fake images that the discriminator evaluates. The function returns the difference between the mean of the fake_img1 and the real_img1.
```
def discriminator1_loss(real_img1, fake_img1):
    real_loss = tf.reduce_mean(real_img1)
    fake_loss = tf.reduce_mean(fake_img1)
    return fake_loss - real_loss
```

#Define the loss function for the generator. The function takes the fake_img1 as an input and returns the negative mean of the fake_img1.
```
def generator1_loss(fake_img1):
    return -tf.reduce_mean(fake_img1)
```

#Define the number of epochs for training the WGAN model.
```
epochs1 = 20
```
#Define an instance of the GANMonitor class to generate and save four images after each epoch.
```
cbk = GANMonitor(num_img=4, latent_dim=noise_dim)
```

#Define an instance of the WGAN class with the discriminator and generator models, the latent dimension, and the number of extra discriminator steps.
```
wgan =
WGAN(discriminator1=d_model1,generator1=g_model1,latent_dim=noise_
dim,discriminator1_extra_steps=5,)
```

```
#Compile the WGAN model with the discriminator and generator optimizer,
generator loss function, and discriminator loss function.
wgan.compile(d_optimizer1=discriminator1_optimizer,
g_optimizer1=generator1_optimizer,
    g_loss_fn1=generator1_loss, d_loss_fn=discriminator1_loss,)
```

```
#Fit the WGAN model on the training images with the batch size, epochs,
and callbacks as inputs.
wgan.fit(train_images1, batch_size=BATCH_SIZE, epochs1=epochs1,
callbacks=[cbk])
```

13.4.8 Generated Image

It is a good practice to check the results and outputs of the algorithms in each step. You can check at the beginning of the coding, for example, by checking the initial data and after specific steps that they are generated and finally, the final output after the final epoch. Figure 13.5 shows the generated images.

```
from IPython.display import Image, display
display(Image("generated_img_0_19.png"))
display(Image("generated_img_1_19.png"))
display(Image("generated_img_2_19.png"))
```

```
#Importing the `Image` and `display` modules from the `IPython.display`
package, which is used to display image files in the Jupyter notebook.
from IPython.display import Image, display
```

```
#Using the `display()` function to show three images (`generated_
img_0_19.png`, `generated_img_1_19.png`, `generated_img_2_19.png`) that
were generated by the GAN model during the last epoch of training. The
images are displayed using the `Image()` function and their filenames are
passed as arguments.
display(Image("generated_img_0_19.png"))
display(Image("generated_img_1_19.png"))
display(Image("generated_img_2_19.png"))
```

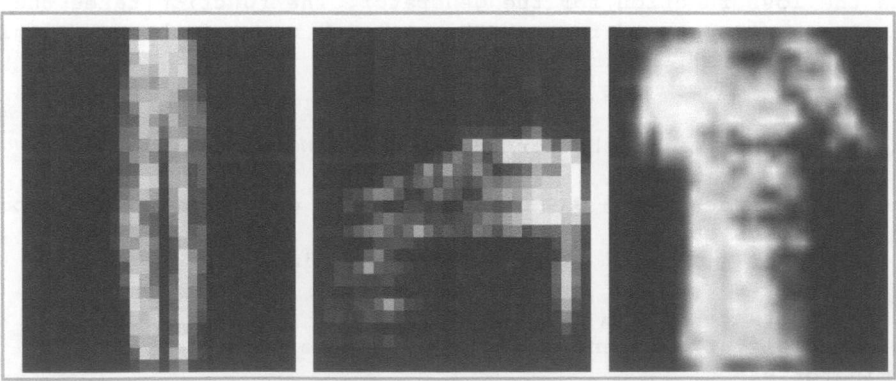

FIGURE 13.5
Generated images.

13.5 Wasserstein GAN Applications

WGAN has been successfully applied in a wide range of applications.

13.5.1 Image Synthesis

WGAN has shown promising results in generating high-quality images, especially in domains where GANs have struggled, such as medical imaging.

13.5.2 Style Transfer

WGAN has been used for style transfer tasks, where it can preserve the content of an image while transferring the style from another image.

13.5.3 Super-resolution

WGAN has been applied to super-resolution tasks, where it can generate high-resolution images from low-resolution inputs.

13.5.4 Data Augmentation

WGAN can be used for data augmentation in various applications, such as in the medical domain, where there may be limited data available.

13.5.5 Anomaly Detection

WGAN has been used for anomaly detection in various fields, such as in detecting fraud in financial transactions or identifying anomalies in medical images.

13.5.6 Speech Synthesis

WGAN has shown promising results in synthesizing human-like speech.

13.5.7 Music Generation

WGAN has also been applied to music generation tasks, where it can generate novel and diverse music compositions.

13.5.8 Video Generation

WGAN has been used for video generation tasks, such as generating realistic video sequences from still images or generating novel video sequences.

Overall, WGAN has shown promising results in a wide range of applications and has the potential to be used in various fields to generate high-quality and diverse data.

13.6 WGAN's Issues

Several WGAN issues make it challenging to use in any capacity. One of the main issues with traditional GANs is that the loss function used to train them is not very informative and can be difficult to optimize. The WGAN was introduced as a way to address this issue. However, it also has its own set of issues that need to be addressed.

13.6.1 Vanishing Gradients

WGANs were specifically designed to address the vanishing gradients problem found in traditional GANs. This issue arises when the discriminator becomes too powerful and the generator struggles to learn due to minimal gradient feedback. WGANs solve this issue by replacing the standard GAN loss function with the Wasserstein loss function. This function provides smooth and meaningful gradients almost everywhere, even when the discriminator is very confident about its decisions. Thus, the generator always has useful feedback to learn from, mitigating the vanishing gradient problem. The Wasserstein loss also reduces the risk of mode collapse, which is another common issue in GANs. Moreover, the WGAN model implements a Lipschitz constraint by weight clipping or GP, ensuring the function doesn't become too steep and keeping the gradients manageable, further contributing to solving the vanishing gradients problem.

13.6.2 Hyperparameter Tuning

In WGANs, hyperparameters play a crucial role in balancing the learning of the generator and the discriminator, and can influence the quality and diversity of the generated samples. However, choosing optimal hyperparameters can be tricky and time-consuming. One common issue in WGAN is the need to tune the weight clipping parameter or the GP lambda, which helps enforce the Lipschitz constraint. If these parameters are set incorrectly, they can lead to undesired behaviors, such as discriminator saturation or inadequate learning of the generator. A common solution to this issue is using a systematic approach like grid search or random search to find the best hyperparameters. Additionally, modern approaches like Bayesian Optimization or Automated Machine Learning (AutoML) tools can be used for hyperparameter optimization. It's also beneficial to leverage the research community's findings. For instance, in WGANs, it's often recommended to use RMSProp or Adam as the optimizer, and it's often suggested to use more discriminator updates per generator update than in traditional GANs. Also, monitoring the Wasserstein distance during training can provide a more reliable metric for tracking GAN training than traditional GAN loss. However, as the specifics can vary greatly based on the dataset and the problem at hand, the most effective strategy is often a combination of leveraging existing research and conducting careful experimentation.

13.6.3 Computational Resources

WGANs, like other GAN architectures, can be computationally intensive, requiring a significant amount of processing power and memory. The requirement to train two networks (the generator and the discriminator) simultaneously, the use of deep convolutional layers, and the need for large numbers of training iterations all contribute to the high computational cost. Moreover, WGANs employ a technique known as weight clipping or GP to ensure that the discriminator (or critic) follows the Lipschitz constraint. This technique involves additional computations, further adding to the computational burden. To mitigate this issue, several strategies can be adopted.

1. **Hardware acceleration:** Use of Graphics Processing Units (GPUs) or Tensor Processing Units (TPUs) can dramatically speed up the training process as these devices are designed for high-performance computation, which is required for training deep learning models.

2. **Efficient coding practices:** Techniques, such as batch processing, in-place operations, and reduced precision calculations, can help to optimize memory usage and computational efficiency.

3. **Model simplification:** If feasible, reducing the complexity of the generator and discriminator networks can save computational resources. This might involve using fewer layers or reducing the dimensionality of the latent space.

4. **Distributed training:** Leveraging distributed computing resources can help to scale the training process across multiple devices or machines, thus shortening the overall training time.

5. **Transfer learning:** Instead of training the model from scratch, one can use a pre-trained model and fine-tune it on the specific task, which can save a significant amount of computational resources.

13.6.4 Evaluation of Results

Evaluation of GANs, including WGANs, is challenging because they do not optimize a well-defined likelihood function. This makes it hard to compare the performance of different models or even different runs of the same model. One of the common issues is that traditional metrics, such as accuracy or loss value, may not directly translate into the quality or diversity of the generated samples. This is especially true for WGANs, where the discriminator (called the critic in WGAN terminology) is trained to estimate the Wasserstein distance between the real and generated distributions, rather than to classify samples as real or fake.

Solutions:

1. **Frequentist evaluation metrics:** This involves the use of metrics such as Inception Score (IS) and Frechet Inception Distance (FID) that provide a quantitative measure of the quality and diversity of generated samples.

2. **Qualitative evaluation:** This involves visually inspecting the generated samples. While this is subjective, it can provide a good sense of the model's performance.

3. **Wasserstein distance:** One of the unique advantages of WGANs is that the loss value of the critic (after it has been trained to optimality) provides an estimate of the Wasserstein distance between the real and generated distributions. This value can be used as a measure of the model's performance, with a smaller value indicating a better model.

4. **Application-specific metrics:** Depending on the specific task or application, other domain-specific metrics may be used. For instance, in the case of generating text, metrics, such as BLEU, ROUGE, or METEOR, might be employed.

Remember, no single evaluation metric is perfect, and it is often best to use a combination of different evaluation methods to assess a model's performance.

13.6.5 Gradient Clipping

In the original WGAN formulation, gradient clipping is used to enforce the Lipschitz constraint on the discriminator (critic) function, which is essential for the Wasserstein distance estimation to be valid. However, this method has some issues:

1. **Too much or too little:** If the range for the weight clipping is too big, the critic might become too complex and violate the Lipschitz constraint; if it's too small, the critic might be too simple to model the difference between the real and generated distributions effectively.

2. **Impact on capacity:** Gradient clipping can limit the capacity of the critic, leading to suboptimal performance.

3. **Impact on gradients:** The practice can lead to vanishing or exploding gradients, making training unstable.

To address these issues, an improved version of WGAN, known as WGAN-GP (Gradient Penalty), was proposed. WGAN-GP replaces the weight clipping with a gradient penalty term, which enforces the Lipschitz constraint more naturally and effectively. The penalty term is added to the critic's loss function, penalizing deviations from a gradient norm of 1, ensuring smoother critic functions, and stabilizing training. The gradient is computed on interpolated points between real and generated samples, allowing the model to consider the entire data space.

13.6.6 Mode Collapse

Mode collapse in a GAN occurs when the generator produces a limited variety of outputs, often just a single or a few types, instead of a diverse range that accurately represents the true data distribution. In essence, the generator finds and exploits certain patterns in the data that can fool the discriminator most easily, resulting in lack of diversity in the generated samples. While WGANs are generally more resistant to mode collapse than traditional GANs due to their use of the Wasserstein loss, which provides more meaningful gradients for the generator, mode collapse can still potentially occur. Several approaches can be taken to mitigate mode collapse in WGANs.

1. **Mini-batch discrimination:** This technique introduces a mechanism that allows the discriminator to look at multiple examples in combination, instead of in isolation. This makes it more difficult for the generator to collapse all samples to a single point, since the discriminator can identify and penalize lack of diversity across a batch.

2. **Unrolled GANs:** In this approach, the generator's gradient is calculated with respect to the future state of the discriminator. This allows the generator to account for how the discriminator will react to its new samples, making it more difficult for the generator to exploit short-term weaknesses in the discriminator that can lead to mode collapse.

3. **Adding noise:** Some noise can be added to the generator's output or the discriminator's input, making the generator's task harder and forcing it to learn to generate a wider range of samples to consistently fool the discriminator.

Remember that these solutions are general techniques for mitigating mode collapse in GANs and are not exclusive to WGANs. Their effectiveness may vary depending on the specific setup and data.

13.6.7 Hyperparameter Tuning

Hyperparameter tuning is a common challenge in machine learning, and WGANs are no exception. Hyperparameters, such as the learning rate, the batch size, the number of discriminator iterations per generator iteration, and the weight clipping threshold in WGANs, can significantly impact the training dynamics and the quality of the generated samples.

1. **Learning rate:** An inappropriate learning rate can cause the model to converge slowly or not at all, or can lead to unstable training dynamics. While it's typically a matter of trial and error, common practices include using a learning schedule (such as decreasing the learning rate over time), or using adaptive learning rate methods like Adam or RMSProp.

2. **Batch size:** The size of the mini-batch can impact the stability of the training and the quality of the model. A smaller batch size can lead to noisy gradient estimates, while a larger batch size can smooth the landscape but might not fit into memory. It's usually a trade-off.

3. **Number of discriminator iterations per generator iteration:** In WGAN, it's common to train the discriminator more times per generator update (e.g., 5 discriminator updates for each generator update). However, the exact ratio can significantly impact results. Tuning this parameter may lead to improved performance.

4. **Weight clipping in WGAN:** The choice of the weight clipping threshold can affect the Lipschitz constraint, influencing the effectiveness of the Wasserstein loss. If it's set too high or too low, the model may not train effectively. This parameter needs to be tuned carefully.

13.7 Wasserstein GAN Implementation Tips

Here are some implementation tips for Wasserstein GAN.

1. Use the Wasserstein loss function instead of the binary cross-entropy loss function used in traditional GANs.

2. Use weight clipping or GP regularization to enforce the Lipschitz constraint on the discriminator.

3. Increase the number of iterations for the critic (discriminator) compared to the generator.

4. Use a smaller learning rate for the discriminator than the generator.

5. Use the RMSProp or Adam optimizer instead of SGD for better convergence.

6. Monitor the Wasserstein distance during training instead of the generator and discriminator loss.

7. Use batch normalization in the generator to improve the stability of the training process.

8. Add Gaussian noise to the input of the discriminator to improve the robustness of the model.

9. Use a larger batch size to reduce the noise in the gradient estimates.

10. Use the same learning rate for both the generator and discriminator to prevent one from dominating the other.

11. These tips can help to improve the stability and performance of Wasserstein GAN models.

Remember, hands-on experience is key when working with WGANs or any other machine learning models. Therefore, consistently practicing implementation and trouble-shooting is crucial for mastering these concepts.

13.8 Lessons Learned

- Learn What is a Wasserstein GAN?
- Learn Wasserstein GAN for MNIST
- Learn WGAN-GP (WGAN with Gradient Penalty (GP)) on Fashion-MNIST
- Learn Wasserstein GAN Applications
- Learn WGAN's Issues
- Learn Wasserstein GAN Implementation Tips

13.9 Problems

13.9.1 What is the difference between a traditional GAN and a WGAN?

13.9.2 Explain the concept of a critic in WGAN.

13.9.3 How is the Wasserstein loss function different from the binary cross-entropy loss function used in GANs?

13.9.4 How do you set the weight clipping parameter in WGAN?

13.9.5 How can you evaluate the quality of the generated images in a WGAN?

13.9.6 What is the role of the gradient penalty term in WGAN-GP?

13.9.7 How can you modify a DCGAN to turn it into a WGAN?

13.9.8 How does the choice of optimizer affect the training of a WGAN?

13.9.9 Can you explain the intuition behind the EM distance and how it is used in WGANs?

13.9.10 How does using a WGAN instead of a GAN affect the visual quality of the generated images?

13.9.11 What exactly is the WGAN architecture? Give an example similar to the one given in Section 13.2.

13.9.12 What are the distinctions between regular WGAN and WGAN with gradient penalty?

13.9.13 What are the issues of the WGAN?

13.10 Programming Questions

- **Easy**

  13.10.1 What is the loss function used in LSGAN?

  13.10.2 How does LSGAN differ from traditional GAN?

  13.10.3 What are the advantages of using LSGAN over traditional GAN?

  13.10.4 How is the generator in LSGAN trained?

  13.10.5 How is the discriminator in LSGAN trained?

- **Medium**

  13.10.6 How does the hyperparameter "lambda" affect the performance of LSGAN?

  13.10.7 How can the training stability of LSGAN be improved?

  13.10.8 How can LSGAN be used for image synthesis?

  13.10.9 How can LSGAN be used for text-to-image synthesis?

  13.10.10 What are some techniques used to improve the quality of LSGAN-generated images?

- **Hard**

  13.10.11 How can LSGAN be used for video generation?

  13.10.12 How can LSGAN be used for cross-modal image synthesis?

  13.10.13 How can LSGAN be used for anomaly detection?

  13.10.14 What are some techniques for fine-tuning the LSGAN generator and discriminator?

  13.10.15 What are some limitations of LSGAN, and how can they be addressed?

14

Generative Adversarial Networks (GANs) for Images

This chapter covers the following topics about Image Generative Adversarial Networks (GANs):

- Architectures
- Image Synthesis
- Image Restoration Using SRGAN
- Image Synthesis Using GAN Issues
- Implementation Tips for Image Synthesis Using GANs

14.1 Preface

GANs have been used for a variety of applications, including generating photorealistic images of objects, animals, and even human faces. They have also been used to generate new images that combine characteristics from multiple existing images, such as a new car design that incorporates features from various existing car designs. One of the main challenges of GANs is finding the right balance between the generator and discriminator networks so that the generator creates realistic images without being too easily fooled by the discriminator. Despite this challenge, GANs have shown great promise in the field of image generation and are likely to be a key tool in future developments in this area. This chapter provides an overview of the methods used in image synthesis with GANs in practice and highlights their strengths and weaknesses. Figure 14.1 depicts the foundational structure of a Generative Adversarial Network (GAN) tailored for image synthesis. Within the architecture:

1. **Generator:** Beginning with a random noise vector, the generator produces synthetic images. Its objective is to produce images so authentic that the discriminator struggles to differentiate them from real images.

2. **Discriminator:** This component acts as a critic, aiming to distinguish between genuine images from the dataset and the synthesized ones from the generator. As training progresses, the discriminator becomes better at identifying and differentiating between real and fake images.

3. **Training loop:** The GAN operates in a cyclical manner: the generator produces images, the discriminator evaluates them, and based on this feedback, the generator refines its process. This push and pull dynamic ensures that both components improve over time.

DOI: 10.1201/9781003281344-14

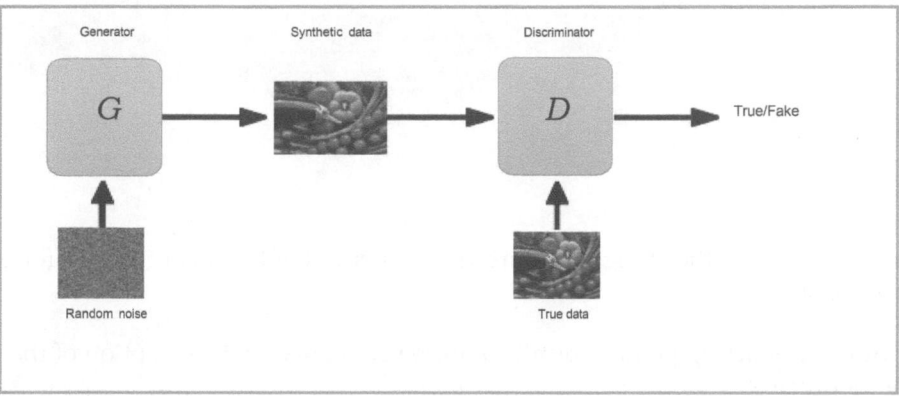

FIGURE 14.1
General GAN architecture for image synthetic.

4. **Loss function:** A crucial part of the architecture, the loss function guides the training process. For the generator, the goal is to minimize the difference between its output and real images, while the discriminator aims to maximize its ability to distinguish between the two.

5. **Synthesized images:** The figure likely showcases samples of images created by the generator at different stages of training. As epochs increase, the synthetic images become more detailed, clearer, and closer in resemblance to genuine images.

Overall, it elucidates the intricate dance between the generator and discriminator in a GAN, emphasizing their roles in the image synthesis process and how they collaboratively evolve to produce high-quality images.

14.2 Architectures

GANs can be used for image synthesis in three ways: (1) the direct method uses a single generator and discriminator to do everything; (2) the hierarchical approach uses two layers of GANs, with each GAN serving a fundamentally different purpose from the other GANs in the layer; and (3) the iterative method uses multiple GANs to perform the same function at varying levels of resolution. We go over these methods in more detail in this chapter.

14.2.1 Direct Methods

All the methods in this category follow the philosophy of using one generator and one discriminator. This category includes many of the earliest GAN models, such as GAN, DCGAN, and Improved GAN, among others, some of which will be discussed later. DCGAN is one of the most classic direct methods, and its structure has been used in many subsequent models.

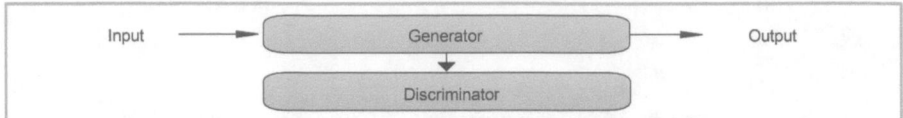

FIGURE 14.2
Direct method.

Figure 14.2 outlines the straightforward direct method of GANs optimized for efficient image synthesis:

- **Input:** The starting point, typically a noise vector, marks the inception of the synthesis process.
- **Generator:** A singular, robust unit that ingests the input noise and transforms it into a synthetic image. Drawing inspiration from models like DCGAN, the generator is engineered to craft images directly from noise without additional intermediate stages.
- **Discriminator:** This unit receives the generated image to assess its realism. By comparing it to genuine images, the discriminator guides the generator's improvements, ensuring it produces increasingly realistic outputs.
- **Output:** The final synthetic image produced after passing through the generator, representing the culmination of the model's image synthesis capabilities.

The essence of the direct method lies in its simplicity. By using only one generator and one discriminator, it builds upon foundational GAN models, such as the original GAN and DCGAN. Its inherent advantage is its uncomplicated design, making it both intuitive and efficient, often yielding satisfactory results without the complexity of its hierarchical and iterative counterparts.

This description offers a clear overview of the direct method, highlighting its foundational roots, basic components, and inherent simplicity.

14.2.2 Hierarchical Methods

Hierarchical method algorithms employ two generators and two discriminators. These algorithms' generators serve a variety of functions and aim to separate an image into two distinct parts known as "texture (style) and structure" and "foreground and background", respectively. The connection between the two generators could be either parallel or sequential, depending on the circumstances. For example, one proposed method suggests the use of two GANs:

1. a surface-GAN to generate a normal surface map from random noise **z**, and
2. a style-GAN to take both the generated normal surface map and noise **z** as input and output an image.

The normal surface map is created by the surface-GAN, and after passing through several convolutional and transposed convolutional layers, the generated normal surface map and noise vector are concatenated into a single tensor that continues to pass through the remaining style-generator layers. Each normal surface map and its associated image are concatenated at the channel dimension to produce a single input for the style discriminator.

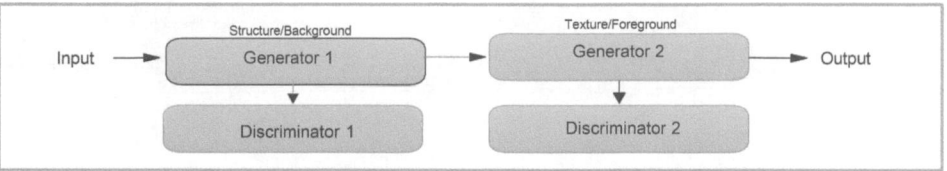

FIGURE 14.3
Hierarchical method.

Figure 14.3 delineates the hierarchical method of GANs designed for nuanced image synthesis:

- **Input-Output flow:** The diagram begins with an input and ends with the synthesized output, illustrating the journey of data through the system.
- **Generators:**
  1. **Generator 1 (Surface-GAN):** It takes random noise z as input and produces a "normal surface map". This layer focuses on the "structure/background" details of the image.
  2. **Generator 2 (Style-GAN):** Working sequentially after the first, it ingests the normal surface map from Generator 1, along with noise z, to emit a more refined image. This layer is responsible for imparting "texture/foreground" details.
- **Discriminators**:
  1. **Discriminator 1:** Evaluates the realism of the normal surface map produced by Generator 1.
  2. **Discriminator 2:** Assesses the final synthesized image, ensuring it harmoniously blends both structure and texture.

The hierarchical architecture allows for a sequential refinement of images, dividing the image synthesis process into distinct stages: first laying down the structure and then adding texture. The fusion of the normal surface map with noise helps create an image that's rich in both background context and intricate foreground details.

14.2.3 Iterative Methods

This method differs from hierarchical methods in a number of ways. First, rather than using two distinct generators to perform different functions, the models in this category employ multiple generators with comparable, if not identical, structures. Second, iterative methods can use weight-sharing among generators when the generators use the same structures, whereas hierarchical methods usually cannot. For example, StackGAN is an iterative method that employs only two generator layers. The first generator takes (z, c) as input and produces a blurry image with a rough shape and blurry details of the objects, whereas the second generator takes (z, c) as input and produces a larger image with more photorealistic details. Another example of iterative methods is SGAN, which stacks generators so that the top generator outputs an image, the bottom generator receives a noise vector as input, and the middle generator outputs higher-level

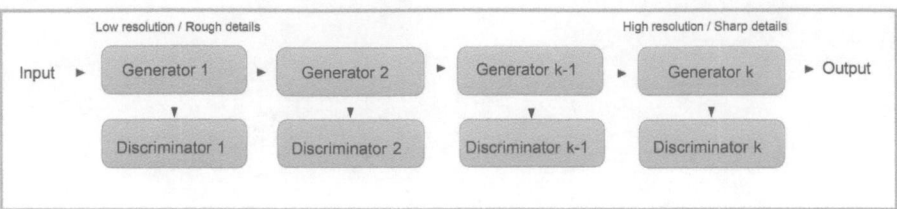

FIGURE 14.4
Iterative method.

features. Separate generators are required to constrain and improve the quality of those features because SGAN associates an encoder, a discriminator, and a Q-network with each generator.

Figure 14.4 provides a visual representation of the iterative GAN method:

- **Input-Output channel:** At the beginning, raw data flows through the system, with the final output capturing the synthesized high-resolution image with intricate details.
- **Generators:** A sequence of generators, from "Generator 1" to "Generator k", is displayed. Each subsequent generator refines the image further:
  - Generator 1 begins by producing a low-resolution image with rough details.
  - The intermediate generators (like Generator 2 and Generator k-1) refine the image's resolution and clarity iteratively.
  - Generator k finalizes the synthesis, producing a high-resolution image with sharp details.
- **Discriminators:** Parallel to the generators are discriminators, starting from "Discriminator 1" up to "Discriminator k". Each discriminator evaluates the output from its corresponding generator, ensuring that the synthesized images are realistic at every iterative step.

This figure showcases the progressive enhancement of images through iterative processes, where each generator refines the image further, and each discriminator ensures its realism.

14.2.4 Other Methods

Plug and Play Generative Network (PPGN) is a method that can produce stunning images in various tasks, including class-conditioned image synthesis, text-to-image synthesis, and image inpainting. Unlike the other methods mentioned previously, it uses activation maximization to generate images and is based on sampling with a prior learned using a denoising autoencoder (DAE). Instead of employing a feed-forward method, PPGN uses an optimization process to find an input **z** to the generator that causes the output image to highly activate a specific neuron in another pre-trained classifier. This method allows the model to first learn raw structure and then focus on refining details later, rather than dealing with all details at all scales at the same time.

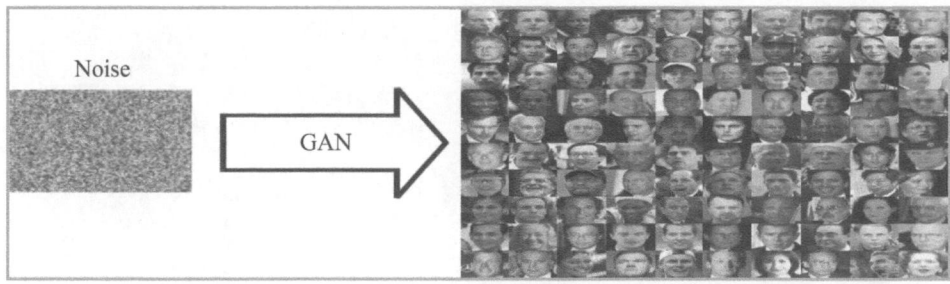

FIGURE 14.5
GAN models generate the photos (faces) from noise input data.

14.3 Image Synthesis

We can divide image synthesis using GANs into two types: (1) Text to Image, and (2) Image to Image. Figure 14.5 showcases the capability of GAN models to transform noise input data into realistic photo renderings, specifically generating detailed facial images.

14.3.1 Text to Image

When using GANs for image synthesis, the ability to control the content of the generated images is desired. Text-to-image synthesis is one of the most sought-after techniques in computer vision because if an algorithm can generate realistic images from text descriptions alone, it indicates that the algorithm understands the content of the images. Figure 14.6 presents the results from a text-to-image synthesis approach, where textual descriptions are transformed into corresponding visual representations, highlighting the model's ability to bridge semantic understandings between text and its associated imagery. Figure 14.7 offers a side-by-side comparison between authentic images and their synthesized counterparts generated using a GAN model. The juxtaposition underscores the GAN's prowess in replicating intricate details and nuances, revealing its potential in mimicking real-world imagery with remarkable accuracy.

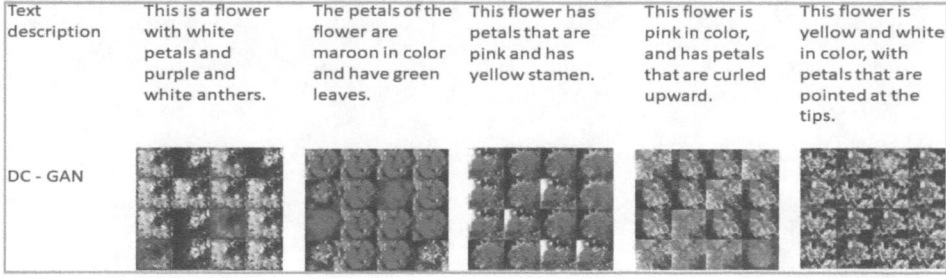

FIGURE 14.6
The output of the text-to-image approach.

FIGURE 14.7
Compare the real images and the synthesized images using GAN.

14.3.2 Image to Image

Image-to-image translation involves using images as the conditional input for this type of image synthesis. It is the challenge of translating a representation of one scene into another. For example, mapping black-and-white images into RGB images, or vice versa, is a type of image-to-image translation. This method is more generalized than style transfer because, in addition to transferring image styles, it can also change the properties of objects. Evaluating the quality of synthetic images is extremely difficult, and metrics such as RMSE are ineffective because there is no exact one-to-one relationship between actual and synthetic images. Figure 14.8 demonstrates the diverse potential of GANs by showcasing various renditions of an input image. By slightly altering internal parameters or leveraging conditional inputs, the GAN produces an array of images, each bearing unique alterations or features. This highlights not just the versatility of GANs but also their capability to introduce variations based on a single reference, emphasizing their prowess in creative and adaptive synthesis.

In this section, we will explore some examples of image synthesis using GANs on different datasets, such as MNIST, Colab, and CIFAR-10.

FIGURE 14.8
GAN can generate a variety of an input image.

14.3.3 MNIST Dataset

The MNIST dataset will be used to demonstrate image synthesis.

14.3.3.1 Import Libraries

TensorFlow, Python, and plotting and displaying tools are required to get started with the implementation.

```
#Imports the TensorFlow library and its functions.
import tensorflow as tf
#Imports the glob module, which is used to search for files or
directories that match a specified pattern.
import glob
#Imports the imageio module, which is used to read and write image data.
import imageio
#Imports the pyplot module from the matplotlib library, which is used for
plotting graphs and figures.
import matplotlib.pyplot as plt
#Imports the numpy library, which provides support for large,
multi-dimensional arrays and matrices, as well as a large collection of
high-level mathematical functions to operate on these arrays.
import numpy as np
#Imports the os module, which provides a way of using operating system
dependent functionality, like reading or writing to the file system.
import os
#Imports the Python Imaging Library (PIL), which adds support for
opening, manipulating, and saving many different image file formats.
import PIL
#Imports the layers module from the TensorFlow library, which provides a
set of commonly used neural network layers, such as Conv2D, Dense,
Dropout, etc.
from tensorflow.keras import layers
#Imports the time module, which provides various time-related functions.
import time
#Imports the display module from the IPython library, which is used to
display output in a Jupyter notebook environment.
from IPython import display
```

14.3.3.2 Load Dataset

There are multiple links available to download the MNIST dataset. Once the dataset is imported, it needs to be normalized to be in the range of [−1, +1]. Next, the dataset can be batched and shuffled to preserve its unpredictability. The type of normalization, batch size, and buffer size can be adjusted to affect performance and accuracy.

```
#Loads the MNIST dataset from the Keras library, which consists of 60,000
training images and 10,000 test images of handwritten digits. The
training images and labels are assigned to `train_images1` and `train_
labels1`, respectively, while the test data is discarded using the `_`
symbol.
(train_images1, train_labels1), (_, _) = tf.keras.datasets.mnist.
load_data()
```

```
#Reshapes the `train_images1` array to have four dimensions - the first
dimension corresponds to the number of training examples, the next two
dimensions correspond to the height and width of each image, and the last
dimension corresponds to the number of color channels (1 for grayscale).
The resulting array is then cast to `float32` data type.
train_images1 = train_images1.reshape(train_images1.shape[0], 28, 28,
1).astype('float32')
```

```
#Normalizes the pixel values in the `train_images1` array to be between
-1 and 1. This is done by subtracting 127.5 from each pixel value and
then dividing by 127.5.
train_images1 = (train_images1 - 127.5) / 127.5
```

```
#Defines the size of the buffer used for shuffling the training data
and the batch size used during training. `BUFFER_SIZE` is set to
60,000, which is the number of training examples, and `BATCH_SIZE` is
set to 256.
BUFFER_SIZE = 60000
BATCH_SIZE = 256
```

```
#Creates a TensorFlow dataset object from the `train_images1` array,
shuffles the dataset using a buffer of size `BUFFER_SIZE`, and creates
batches of size `BATCH_SIZE`. The resulting `train_dataset` object can be
used for training a machine learning model.
train_dataset = tf.data.Dataset.from_tensor_slices(train_images1).
shuffle(BUFFER_SIZE).batch(BATCH_SIZE)
```

14.3.3.3 Generator

The generator consists of three convolution layers, three leaky ReLU layers, and three batch normalization layers. Additionally, there is a single dense layer in the generator. To improve generator performance, one can adjust the number of layers, activation functions, and normalization techniques.

```
#Defines a function named `make_generator_model1()` that returns a
generator model for GAN.
def make_generator_model1():
```

```
#Creates a sequential model using the Keras API.
model1 = tf.keras.Sequential()
```

```
#Adds a fully connected (Dense) layer with 7x7x256 units to the model,
with no bias and an input shape of 100.
model1.add(layers.Dense(7*7*256, use_bias=False, input_shape=(100,)))
```

```
#Adds a batch normalization layer and a LeakyReLU activation layer to the
model.
model1.add(layers.BatchNormalization())
model1.add(layers.LeakyReLU())
```

```
#Reshapes the output of the previous layer to have a shape of (7, 7,
256).
model1.add(layers.Reshape((7, 7, 256)))
```

```
#Checks that the output shape of the current layer matches the
expected shape of (None, 7, 7, 256), where `None` corresponds to the
batch size.
assert model1.output_shape == (None, 7, 7, 256)
```

```
#Adds a transposed convolutional layer to the model with 128 filters, a
kernel size of 5x5, stride of 1x1, same padding, and no bias.
model1.add(layers.Conv2DTranspose(128, (5, 5), strides=(1, 1),
padding='same', use_bias=False))
```

```
#Checks that the output shape of the current layer matches the expected
shape of (None, 7, 7, 128).
assert model1.output_shape == (None, 7, 7, 128)
```

```
#Adds a batch normalization layer and a LeakyReLU activation layer to the
model.
model1.add(layers.BatchNormalization())
model1.add(layers.LeakyReLU())
```

```
#Adds another transposed convolutional layer to the model with
64 filters, a kernel size of 5x5, stride of 2x2, same padding, and no
bias.
model1.add(layers.Conv2DTranspose(64, (5, 5), strides=(2, 2),
padding='same', use_bias=False))
```

```
#Checks that the output shape of the current layer matches the expected
shape of (None, 14, 14, 64).
assert model1.output_shape == (None, 14, 14, 64)
```

```
#Adds a batch normalization layer and a LeakyReLU activation layer to the
model.
model1.add(layers.BatchNormalization())
model1.add(layers.LeakyReLU())
```

```
#Adds a final transposed convolutional layer to the model with 1 filter,
a kernel size of 5x5, stride of 2x2, no padding, no bias, and a
hyperbolic tangent (tanh) activation function.
model1.add(layers.Conv2DTranspose(1, (5, 5), strides=(2, 2), padding='',
use_bias=False, activation='tanh'))
Checks that the output shape of the current layer matches the expected
shape of (None, 28, 28, 1).
assert model1.output_shape == (None, 28, 28, 1)
```

```
#Returns the final generator model.
return model1
```

Use the generator model function to create the generator, and generate noise data from a normal distribution to use as the initial input for the generator. This code generates a single image using the generator model created by the make_generator_model1() function and displays it using Matplotlib.

```
#Creates a generator model using the `make_generator_model1()` function
and assigns it to the variable `Generator1`.
Generator1 = make_generator_model1()
```

```
#Generates a random noise tensor of shape (1, 100) using TensorFlow's
`tf.random.normal()` function and assigns it to the variable `noise1`.
noise1 = tf.random.normal([1, 100])

#Generates an image using the `Generator1` model and the `noise1` tensor.
The `training1` argument is set to `False` to ensure that the batch
normalization layers in the generator are not updated during this step.
generated_image1 = generator(noise1, training1=False)

#Displays the generated image using Matplotlib. The `[0, :, :, 0]`
indexing is used to select the first (and only) image in the batch, and
the grayscale colormap (`cmap='gray'`) is used to display the image in
black and white.
plt.imshow(generated_image1[0, :, :, 0], cmap='gray')
```

14.3.3.4 Discriminator

Two convolutional layers, two leaky ReLU layers, two dropout layers, one flatten layer, and one dense layer are used in the discriminator function. Additional layers can be added to observe their impact on performance. Other factors, such as the dropout rate, can also affect performance. This code defines a discriminator model using the Keras API.

```
#Defines a function named `make_discriminator_model1()` that returns a
discriminator model for GAN.
def make_discriminator_model1():

#Creates a sequential model using the Keras API.
model1 = tf.keras.Sequential()

#Adds a 2D convolutional layer with 64 filters, a kernel size of 5x5,
stride of 2x2, no padding, and an input shape of (28, 28, 1).
model1.add(layers.Conv2D(64, (5, 5), strides=(2, 2), padding='',input_
shape=[28, 28, 1]))

#Adds a LeakyReLU activation layer to the model.
model1.add(layers.LeakyReLU())

#Adds a dropout layer to the model with a rate of 0.3 to prevent
overfitting.
model1.add(layers.Dropout(0.3))

#Adds another 2D convolutional layer to the model with 128 filters, a
kernel size of 5x5, stride of 2x2, same padding, and no bias.
model1.add(layers.Conv2D(128, (5, 5), strides=(2, 2), padding='same'))

#Adds a LeakyReLU activation layer to the model.
model1.add(layers.LeakyReLU())

#Adds another dropout layer to the model with a rate of 0.3.
model1.add(layers.Dropout(0.3))

#Flattens the output of the previous layer into a 1D tensor.
model1.add(layers.Flatten())
```

```
#Adds a fully connected (Dense) layer with 1 unit to the model. This
layer outputs a scalar value that represents the probability of the input
image being real or fake.
model1.add(layers.Dense(1))

#Returns the final discriminator model.
return model1
```

The next step in implementing the discriminator is to create an instance of the discriminator model and apply it to a generated image. Then, a binary cross-entropy loss function is initialized to compute the cross-entropy loss.

```
#Creates an instance of the discriminator model using the `make_
discriminator_model1()` function and assigns it to the variable
`discriminator`.
discriminator = make_discriminator_model1()

#Applies the discriminator model to the generated image `generated_
image1` to get a prediction score (`decision`) for whether the image is
real or fake.
decision = discriminator(generated_image1)

#Initializes a binary cross-entropy loss function using TensorFlow's `tf.
keras.losses.BinaryCrossentropy()` method with the `from_logits` argument
set to `True`. The `from_logits` argument indicates that the input to the
loss function will be unnormalized logits instead of normalized
probabilities.
cross_entropy = tf.keras.losses.BinaryCrossentropy(from_logits=True)
```

14.3.3.5 Discriminator and Generator Loss

The discriminator loss is calculated using cross-entropy, and there are two types of loss: real loss and fake loss. These two loss values are used to determine the total loss. This code defines the discriminator loss function for GAN training.

```
#Defines a function named `discriminator_loss()` that takes two
arguments: `real_output1` (output from the discriminator for real images)
and `fake_output1` (output from the discriminator for fake images).
def discriminator_loss(real_output1, fake_output1):

#Calculates the loss for real images by computing the binary cross-
entropy between the discriminator output for real images (`real_output1`)
and a tensor of ones with the same shape as `real_output1`. The `tf.
ones_like()` method creates a tensor of ones with the same shape as
`real_output1`.
real_loss1 = cross_entropy(tf.ones_like(real_output1), real_output1)

#Calculates the loss for fake images by computing the binary cross-
entropy between the discriminator output for fake images (`fake_output1`)
and a tensor of zeros with the same shape as `fake_output1`. The `tf.
zeros_like()` method creates a tensor of zeros with the same shape as
`fake_output1`.
fake_loss1 = cross_entropy(tf.zeros_like(fake_output1), fake_output1)
```

```
#Computes the total loss by adding the losses for real and fake images.
total_loss = real_loss1 + fake_loss1

#Returns the total loss.
return total_loss
```

The generator loss is computed using cross-entropy on the fake output. This code defines the generator loss function for GAN training.

```
#Defines a function named `generator_loss()` that takes one argument:
`fake_output1` (output from the discriminator for fake images generated
by the generator).
def generator_loss(fake_output1):

#Calculates the binary cross-entropy between the discriminator output for
fake images (`fake_output1`) and a tensor of ones with the same shape as
`fake_output1`. The `tf.ones_like()` method creates a tensor of ones with
the same shape as `fake_output1`. The resulting loss represents how well
the generator is able to generate images that can fool the discriminator
into thinking they are real.
return cross_entropy(tf.ones_like(fake_output1), fake_output1)
```

14.3.3.6 Optimizers

The optimization function is an important aspect of the network, and its performance can be tested by adjusting various parameters. The generator and discriminator models each have their own optimizer, which can be customized. This code sets up the optimizer for the generator and discriminator models and creates a checkpoint to save the model weights during training.

```
#Creates an instance of the Adam optimizer for the generator model
with a learning rate of 1e-4, and assigns it to the variable
`generator_optimizer`.
generator_optimizer = tf.keras.optimizers.Adam(1e-4)

#Creates an instance of the Adam optimizer for the discriminator model
with a learning rate of 1e-4, and assigns it to the variable
`discriminator_optimizer`.
discriminator_optimizer = tf.keras.optimizers.Adam(1e-4)

#Sets up a checkpoint directory (`./training_checkpoints`) and a prefix
for the checkpoint files (`ckpt`). The prefix will be used to name the
saved checkpoint files.
checkpoint_dir = './training_checkpoints'
checkpoint_prefix = os.path.join(checkpoint_dir, "ckpt")

#Creates a checkpoint instance that saves the generator optimizer,
discriminator optimizer, generator model, and discriminator model. The
saved checkpoint files will include these variables' values, allowing the
model to be restored later for continued training or inference.
checkpoint=tf.train.Checkpoint(generator_optimizer=generator_optimizer,
discriminator_optimizer=discriminator_optimizer,generator=generator,
discriminator=discriminator)
```

14.3.3.7 Training

At this point, we assign values to the parameters of the random normal distribution to generate the seed as the first data. This code sets up some training parameters for the GAN model.

```
#Sets the number of epochs (iterations over the training data) to 50.
EPOCHS = 50

#Sets the size of the random noise vector that will be input to the
generator model to 100.
noise_dim = 100

#Sets the number of images that will be generated by the generator model
after each epoch to 16.
num_examples_to_generate = 16

#Creates a random noise tensor of shape (`num_examples_to_generate`,
`noise_dim`) using TensorFlow's `tf.random.normal()` function. This
tensor will be used to generate images during training and can be thought
of as a set of random seeds for the generator model.
seed = tf.random.normal([num_examples_to_generate, noise_dim])
```

The train() function is used to generate new images by invoking the developed modules. It receives real-world images as input. The first step is to feed the generator the seed, which is the generated noise data. Next, provide the discriminator with the real images as well as the images generated by the generator in the previous phase. This enables determining which outputs are real and which are fake. The final step in this process is to compute the loss and gradient values. This code defines the train_step() function using TensorFlow's tf.function() decorator to improve the training performance of the function.

```
#The `@tf.function` decorator compiles the `train_step()` function into a
graph computation, allowing TensorFlow to optimize the execution of the
function.
@tf.function
def train_step(images):

#Creates a batch of random noise vectors with shape (`BATCH_SIZE`,
`noise_dim`), where `BATCH_SIZE` is the number of images in the batch and
`noise_dim` is the size of the noise vector.
noise1 = tf.random.normal([BATCH_SIZE, noise_dim])

#Opens two gradient tapes, one for the generator and one for the
discriminator, to record the gradients of the loss functions with respect
to the trainable variables.
with tf.GradientTape() as gen_tape, tf.GradientTape() as disc_tape:

#Computes the generated images using the generator model, and computes
the real and fake outputs using the discriminator model.
generated_images = generator(noise1, training=True)
real_output1 = discriminator(images, training=True)
fake_output1 = discriminator(generated_images, training=True)
```

```
#Computes the generator loss and discriminator loss using the output of
the discriminator.
gen_loss = generator_loss(fake_output1)
disc_loss = discriminator_loss(real_output1, fake_output1)
```

```
#Computes the gradients of the generator loss and discriminator loss with
respect to the trainable variables of the generator and discriminator,
respectively.
gradients_of_generator = gen_tape.gradient(gen_loss, generator.
trainable_variables)
gradients_of_discriminator = disc_tape.gradient(disc_loss, discriminator.
trainable_variables)
```

```
#Updates the trainable variables of the generator and discriminator
models using the computed gradients and the optimizer instances.
generator_optimizer.apply_gradients(zip(gradients_of_generator,
generator.trainable_variables))
discriminator_optimizer.apply_gradients(zip(gradients_of_discriminator,
discriminator.trainable_variables))
```

Here, there is a train() function that takes in dataset values and epochs as input parameters. You can also select the maximum number of saved images, and here we chose to keep the images after every m (where m = 15) epochs. This code defines a train() function that trains the generator and discriminator models using the train_step() function for a specified number of epochs.

```
def train(dataset, epochs):
#Iterates through the specified number of epochs.
  for epoch in range(epochs):
      #Starts the timer for the epoch.
      start = time.time()
      #Iterates through each batch of images in the dataset and trains the
generator and discriminator models using the `train_step()` function.
      for image_batch in dataset:
          train_step(image_batch)
      #Generates and saves a set of sample images using the generator
model at the current epoch.
      generate_and_save_images(generator1,epoch + 1,seed)
      if (epoch + 1) % 15 == 0:
      #Saves the current state of the generator and discriminator models
every 15 epochs using a TensorFlow checkpoint.
          checkpoint.save(file_prefix = checkpoint_prefix)
```

This function is used to save the images generated by the model and display them as output. Changing the values passed to the function will result in a corresponding change in the displayed images. The function generate_and_save_images() defined in this code generates and saves a set of sample images using the generator model. It takes in three arguments: the generator model, the current epoch, and a set of input noise vectors.

```
def generate_and_save_images(model1, epoch, test_input1):
#Generates a set of image predictions using the generator model and the
input noise vectors.
predictions = model1(test_input1, training=False)
```

```
#Creates a new figure for displaying the sample images.
fig = plt.figure(figsize=(4,4))
#Iterates through each image in the predictions set and displays it as a
subplot in the figure.
for i in range(predictions.shape[0]):
    plt.subplot(4, 4, i+1)
    plt.imshow(predictions[i, :, :, 0] * 127.5 + 127.5, cmap='gray')
    plt.axis('off')
#Saves the figure as a PNG file with a filename indicating the current
epoch.
plt.savefig('image_at_epoch_{:04d}.png'.format(epoch))
#Displays the figure with the sample images.
plt.show()
```

The function "train()" trains the generator and discriminator models using the "train_step()" function for a specified number of epochs with the MNIST dataset. The function is called with two arguments: the training dataset ("train_dataset") and the number of epochs to train for ("EPOCHS"). A loop in the "train()" function iterates over the dataset for the specified number of epochs, calling "train_step()" function to perform a single training step on each batch of images. After each epoch, the "generate_and_save_images()" function is called to generate a set of sample images using the generator model and save them to a file. If the current epoch is a multiple of 15, the current state of the generator and discriminator models is saved to a checkpoint file. When executed, this code generates and saves a set of sample images after the specified number of epochs. Figure 14.9 showcases synthesized images from the MNIST dataset generated by a GAN after 1000 training iterations. The displayed images reflect the model's evolving capability to replicate handwritten digits, ranging from "0" to "9". As the iterations progressed, the generator has been fine-tuned to capture the nuances and unique styles of handwritten numerals. The variability and detail in these synthesized outputs highlight the GAN's proficiency in understanding and emulating the essence of the MNIST dataset, offering a glimpse into the model's journey from its inception to its refined stages.

```
train(train_dataset, EPOCHS)
```

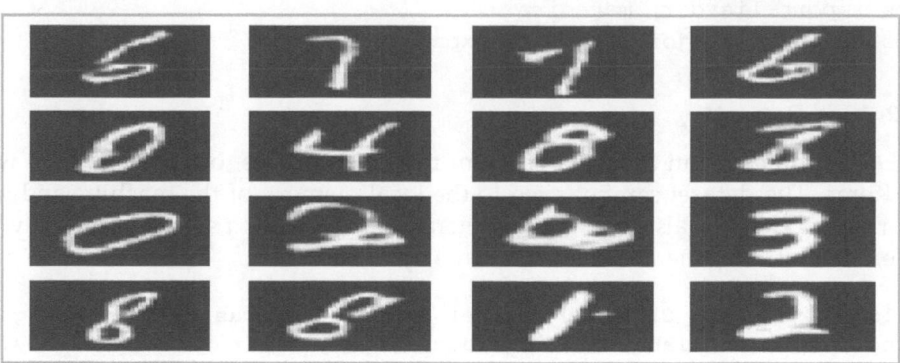

FIGURE 14.9
Generated data from initial noise data after 1000 epochs.

14.3.4 CIFAR-10 Dataset

In this demonstration, the images are generated using the CIFAR-10 dataset and GAN models.

14.3.4.1 Import Libraries

The first step is to import any relevant libraries. We use these libraries to take advantage of the modules provided by Keras, NumPy, Python, and OS libraries. This code imports various libraries and modules needed for building and training a GAN model for image synthesis using Keras. Here's a brief description of each library/module:

- **Input, Dense, Reshape, Flatten, Dropout:** layers for building the generator and discriminator models
- **BatchNormalization, Activation, ZeroPadding2D, leaky ReLU:** activation and normalization layers for building the generator and discriminator models
- **UpSampling2D, Conv2D:** convolutional layers for building the generator and discriminator models
- **Sequential, Model:** classes for creating the generator and discriminator models
- **Adam, SGD:** optimizers for training the GAN
- **matplotlib.pyplot:** library for plotting images
- **NumPy:** library for numerical computations
- **os:** library for interacting with the operating system

```
from keras.layers import Input, Dense, Reshape, Flatten, Dropout
from keras.layers import BatchNormalization, Activation, ZeroPadding2D
from keras.layers.advanced_activations import LeakyReLU
from keras.layers.convolutional import UpSampling2D, Conv2D
from keras.models import Sequential, Model
from tensorflow.keras.optimizers import Adam,SGD
import keras
import matplotlib.pyplot as plt
import sys
import numpy as np
import os
from os import listdir, makedirs
from os.path import join, exists, expanduser
```

14.3.4.2 Load Dataset

The CIFAR-10 dataset can be accessed from multiple sources, but in this code, we load it from Keras. The dataset can be saved to the local memory of the machine and used as input for the model. It is also possible to generate images from a specific class only. In this example, we chose to generate images of birds by default.

```
#This line loads the CIFAR-10 dataset using the Keras API and assigns the
training images and labels to `X_train` and `y_train`, respectively. The
second set of parentheses assigns empty variables to the test images and
labels, as we don't need them for this example.
(X_train, y_train), (_, _) = keras.datasets.cifar10.load_data()
```

```
#This line filters the training images to only include images with the
label "2", which corresponds to the class "bird" in the CIFAR-10 dataset.
This is done to reduce the complexity of the problem and speed up
training time.
X_train = X_train[y_train.flatten() == 2]
```

14.3.4.3 Network Shape

Before defining the generator and discriminator, you can establish the network's structure by inputting some initial parameters, such as the number of picture rows and columns and the number of channels. These lines of code initialize the network parameters' values for the DCGAN model.

- img_rows and img_cols are set to 32 since CIFAR-10 images are 32 × 32 pixels.
- channels are set to 3 since CIFAR-10 images are color images with RGB channels.
- img_shape is a tuple that specifies the dimensions and number of channels for the input images.
- latent_dim is the dimensionality of the latent space, which is the input to the generator. It is set to 100.

```
img_rows = 32
img_cols = 32
channels = 3
img_shape = (img_rows, img_cols, channels)
latent_dim = 100
```

14.3.4.4 Generator

In this example, you can see that the structure of the generator differs from that of the previous example. It uses three convolutional layers as well as two different activation layers (ReLU and Tanh). Additionally, a batch normalization layer, as well as reshaping and upsampling, are used to change the size. For example, the first upsample2D module will change the size to 16 × 16 × 128, while the second will change it to 32 × 32 × 128. The code defines a function called build_generator that returns a generator model for a GAN. The generator model is defined using the Keras Sequential API.

```
def build_generator():
#creates a new Sequential model object.
model1 = Sequential()`:

#adds a fully connected layer with 8x8x128 neurons and a ReLU activation
function. The input shape is (latent_dim,), which is the size of the
noise vector that will be used as input to the generator.
model1.add(Dense(128 * 8 * 8, activation="relu", input_dim=latent_dim))
#reshapes the output of the previous layer into a 3D tensor of shape (8,
8, 128).
model1.add(Reshape((8, 8, 128)))

#performs upsampling of the feature maps by a factor of 2 using nearest
neighbor interpolation. This doubles the spatial resolution of the tensor.
model1.add(UpSampling2D())
```

```
#adds a 2D convolutional layer with 128 filters, a kernel size of 3x3,
and "same" padding (i.e., the output tensor has the same spatial
dimensions as the input tensor). No activation function is specified.
model1.add(Conv2D(128, kernel_size=3, padding="same"))

#applies batch normalization to the output of the convolutional layer,
using a momentum value of 0.8 to smooth the mean and variance estimates.
model1.add(BatchNormalization(momentum=0.8))

applies a ReLU activation function to the output of the batch
normalization layer.
model1.add(Activation("relu"))

#performs another upsampling operation using nearest neighbor
interpolation, again doubling the spatial resolution of the tensor.
model1.add(UpSampling2D())

#adds another convolutional layer with 64 filters, a kernel size of 3x3,
and "same" padding.
model1.add(Conv2D(64, kernel_size=3, padding="same"))

#applies batch normalization again.
model1.add(BatchNormalization(momentum=0.8))

applies a ReLU activation function.
model1.add(Activation("relu"))

#adds a final convolutional layer with `channels` filters (i.e., the same
number of channels as the output images), a kernel size of 3x3, and
"same" padding. No activation function is specified.
model1.add(Conv2D(channels, kernel_size=3, padding="same"))

#applies a hyperbolic tangent (tanh) activation function to the output of
the convolutional layer, which maps the output values to the range [-1, 1].
model1.add(Activation("tanh"))

#creates a Keras Input object representing the noise vector input to the
generator, with shape (latent_dim,).
noise1 = Input(shape=(latent_dim,))

#applies the generator model to the noise input, producing a generated
image.
img = model1(noise1)

#constructs and returns a Keras Model object that takes the noise input
and produces the generated image output.
return Model1(noise1, img)
```

14.3.4.5 Discriminator

The discriminator architecture in this example involves four convolution layers with a leaky ReLU activation function as well as four dropout layers. Furthermore, three batch normalization layers, one flatten layer, and one dense layer were employed. By altering the number and values of each layer's parameters, you can observe how it impacts the performance of the discriminator.

```
def build_discriminator():
    # define a sequential model
    model1 = Sequential()
    # add a convolutional layer with 32 filters, 3x3 kernel size, stride
of 2 and same padding
    model1.add(Conv2D(32, kernel_size=3, strides=2, input_shape=img_
shape, padding="same"))
    # add a LeakyReLU activation function with alpha value of 0.2
    model1.add(LeakyReLU(alpha=0.2))
    # add a dropout layer with a rate of 0.25
    model1.add(Dropout(0.25))
    # add a convolutional layer with 64 filters, 3x3 kernel size, stride
of 2 and same padding
    model1.add(Conv2D(64, kernel_size=3, strides=2, padding="same"))
    # add zero padding of 1 to the bottom and right of the feature map
    model1.add(ZeroPadding2D(padding=((0,1),(0,1))))
    # add a batch normalization layer with a momentum value of 0.8
    model1.add(BatchNormalization(momentum=0.8))
    # add a LeakyReLU activation function with alpha value of 0.2
    model1.add(LeakyReLU(alpha=0.2))
    # add a dropout layer with a rate of 0.25
    model1.add(Dropout(0.25))
    # add a convolutional layer with 128 filters, 3x3 kernel size, stride
of 2 and same padding
    model1.add(Conv2D(128, kernel_size=3, strides=2, padding="same"))
    # add a batch normalization layer with a momentum value of 0.8
    model1.add(BatchNormalization(momentum=0.8))
    # add a LeakyReLU activation function with alpha value of 0.2
    model1.add(LeakyReLU(alpha=0.2))
    # add a dropout layer with a rate of 0.25
    model1.add(Dropout(0.25))
    # add a convolutional layer with 256 filters, 3x3 kernel size, stride
of 1 and same padding
    model1.add(Conv2D(256, kernel_size=3, strides=1, padding="same"))
    # add a batch normalization layer with a momentum value of 0.8
    model1.add(BatchNormalization(momentum=0.8))
    # add a LeakyReLU activation function with alpha value of 0.2
    model1.add(LeakyReLU(alpha=0.2))
    # add a dropout layer with a rate of 0.25
    model1.add(Dropout(0.25))
    # flatten the feature map
    model1.add(Flatten())
    # add a dense layer with 1 neuron and sigmoid activation function
    model1.add(Dense(1, activation='sigmoid'))
    # create an input tensor of the shape specified by img_shape
    img = Input(shape=img_shape)
    # get the discriminator's prediction on the input tensor
    validity = model1(img)
    # return a Keras model with the input tensor and the discriminator's
prediction as outputs
    return Model1(img, validity)
```

14.3.4.6 *Build and Compile the Generator and Discriminator*

At this stage of the procedure, we begin by constructing and compiling the discriminator and generator models. The generator model is then fed with noise input to generate images, while only the generator is trained for the GAN model we are working on. The discriminator, on the other hand, receives both the real images and the generated images as input and determines whether they are real or fake. Finally, we create a combined model, consisting of a stacked generator and a discriminator, to train the generator to deceive the discriminator.

```
#Define the discriminator using the build_discriminator function.
discriminator = build_discriminator()
#Compile the discriminator using binary cross-entropy loss, Adam
optimizer with learning rate 0.0002, momentum 0.5, and accuracy as a
metric.
discriminator.compile(loss='binary_crossentropy',optimizer=Adam(0.0002,0.
5),metrics=['accuracy'])
#Define the generator using the build_generator function.
generator1 = build_generator()
#Define an input tensor for the generator.
z = Input(shape=(latent_dim,))
#Generate an image using the generator by passing the input tensor.
img = generator1(z)
#Set the discriminator to non-trainable.
discriminator.trainable = False
#Pass the generated image through the discriminator to get the validity
score.
valid = discriminator(img)
#Combine the generator and discriminator using the input tensor and
validity score as output.
combined = Model1(z, valid)
#Compile the combined model using binary cross-entropy loss and Adam
optimizer with learning rate 0.0002 and momentum 0.5.
combined.compile(loss='binary_crossentropy', optimizer=Adam(0.0002,0.5))
```

14.3.4.7 *Train the Model*

We start by defining the values of various parameters, such as epochs and batch size. Normalizing the data makes calculations faster. Then, we introduce some noise and generate initial fake data that is fed into the generator. The generator and discriminator are then trained using real images, generated images, and fake images, and the final generated images are displayed. Figure 14.10 presents a collection of synthesized images representing the bird class, generated by the model after undergoing 1000 training epochs. These images emphasize the model's progression in capturing the intricate features, colors, and postures unique to various bird species. As the epochs advanced, the generator refined its understanding and depiction of avian attributes. The assortment of birds showcased demonstrates the GAN's adeptness at creating diverse and lifelike representations, mirroring the rich variability found in nature.

```
# Start training the model
sets the number of epochs to train the GAN.
epochs=15000
```

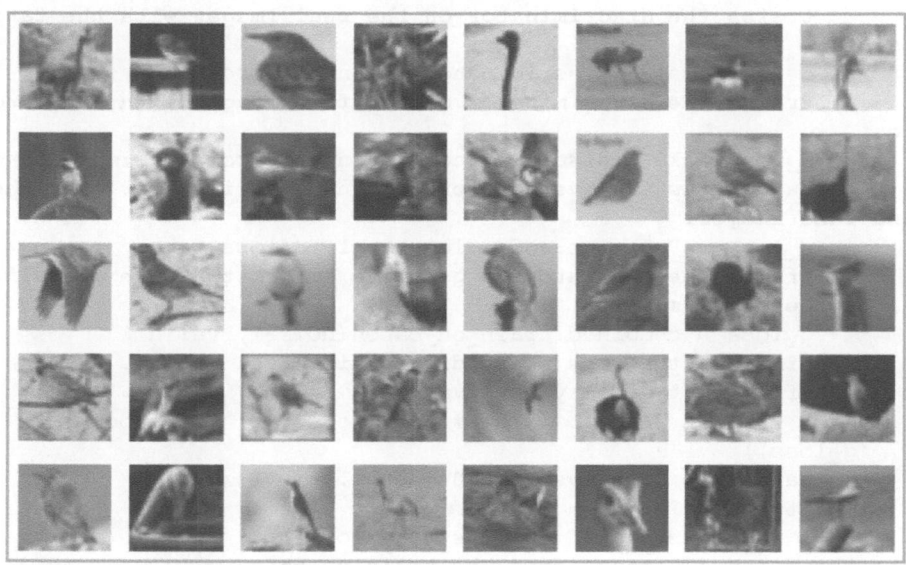

FIGURE 14.10
Generated data from initial data (bird class) after 1000 epochs.

```
#determines the number of samples to use for each training iteration.
batch_size=32
#determines the interval at which the loss is displayed during training.
display_interval=1000
#initializes an empty list to store the losses.
losses=[]
#normalizes the pixel values of the training data to the range of
[-1,1].
X_train = X_train / 127.5 - 1
#creates a numpy array of ones with the shape of (batch_size, 1) to be
used as the target for the real images.
valid = np.ones((batch_size, 1))
#adds a small random noise to the target values of the real images.
valid += 0.05 * np.random.random(valid.shape)
#creates a numpy array of zeros with the shape of (batch_size, 1) to be
used as the target for the fake images.
fake = np.zeros((batch_size, 1))
#adds a small random noise to the target values of the fake images.
fake += 0.05 * np.random.random(fake.shape)
#loops over the number of epochs.
for epoch in range(epochs):
          selects a random set of indices from the training data.
          idx = np.random.randint(0, X_train.shape[0], batch_size)
          selects the images corresponding to the random indices.
          imgs = X_train[idx]
          generates random noise for the generator.
          noise1 = np.random.normal(0, 1, (batch_size, latent_dim))
          generates fake images from the random noise using the
generator.
          gen_imgs = generator.predict(noise1)
```

```
            trains the discriminator on the real images with the target
of ones.
            d_loss_real = discriminator.train_on_batch(imgs, valid)
            trains the discriminator on the fake images with the target
of zeros.
            d_loss_fake = discriminator.train_on_batch(gen_imgs, fake)
            calculates the average loss of the discriminator over the
real and fake images.
            d_loss = 0.5 * np.add(d_loss_real, d_loss_fake)
            trains the generator to generate images that are classified
as real by the discriminator.
            g_loss = combined.train_on_batch(noise1, valid)
            displays the loss every display_interval epochs.
            if epoch % display_interval==0:
                print ("%d [D loss: %f] [G loss: %f]" % (epoch, d_
loss[0], g_loss))
            saves the loss every 1000 epochs.
            if epoch % 1000==0:
                losses.append((d_loss[0],g_loss))
#selects the first 40 images from the training data.
s=X_train[:40]
#denormalizes the pixel values of the images.
s = 0.5 * s + 0.5
#creates a 5x8 grid of subplots to display the images.
f, ax = plt.subplots(5,8, figsize=(12,8))
#loops over the selected images.
for i, img in enumerate(s):
        displays the image on the corresponding subplot.
        ax[i//8, i%8].imshow(img)
        removes the axis labels from the subplot.
        ax[i//8, i%8].axis('off')
#displays the image grid.
plt.show()
```

14.3.5 Generating Faces with DCGANs

DCGAN is another GAN technique widely used for creating and synthesizing visual media. DCGANs differ from other types of GANs in their use of convolution layers in the discriminator and transposing convolution layers in the generator. This technique was discussed in detail in Chapter 8, and this section will demonstrate how to use it to generate faces.

14.3.5.1 Import Libraries

This code block imports the necessary libraries for the project, including TensorFlow, Keras, NumPy, Matplotlib, OS, gdown, and ZipFile.

```
#imports the TensorFlow library.
import tensorflow as tf

#imports the Keras API, a high-level API to build and train deep learning
models using TensorFlow as the backend.
from tensorflow import keras
```

```
#imports the layers module from Keras, which provides a set of building
blocks for creating deep learning models.
from tensorflow.keras import layers
```

```
#imports the NumPy library, which is used for numerical operations in
Python.
import numpy as np
```

```
#imports the Pyplot module from the Matplotlib library, which provides a
convenient interface for creating plots and visualizations.
import matplotlib.pyplot as plt
```

```
#imports the os module, which provides a way of interacting with the file
system in Python.
import os
```

```
#imports the gdown library, which is a Python module for downloading
files from Google Drive.
import gdown
```

```
#imports the ZipFile class from the zipfile module, which provides tools
for working with ZIP archives.
from zipfile import ZipFile
```

14.3.5.2 Prepare CelebA Data

In this case, we will use the CelebA dataset, which is already pre-processed. You are still free to perform any data preparation procedure you see fit. You can also download it and import the data from your computer or provide the proper online link to access it. The database here contains a total of 202599 images.

```
#This creates a new directory named "celeba_gan" in the current working
directory. If the directory already exists, nothing happens.
os.makedirs("celeba_gan")
```

```
#This line sets the variable url to a Google Drive link that contains the
CelebA dataset for use in a GAN.
url = https://drive.google.com/uc?id=1O7m1O1OEJjLE5QxLZiM9Fpjs7Oj6e684
```

```
#This line sets the variable output to the path where the downloaded data
will be stored.
output = "celeba_gan/data.zip"
```

```
#This downloads the file from the Google Drive link in url and saves it
to the file path in output. The quiet=True argument prevents console
output during the download.
gdown.download(url, output, quiet=True)
```

```
#This line opens the downloaded zip file in read mode and extracts all
the contents to the "celeba_gan" directory. This unpacks the CelebA
dataset into the "celeba_gan" directory for use in the GAN.
with ZipFile("celeba_gan/data.zip," "r") as zipobj:
    zipobj.extractall("celeba_gan")
```

We can now create a dataset and then normalize it. Normalization, in this case, places the image data value in the range [0, 1].

```
#This line creates a dataset using images from the directory celeba_gan.
It specifies that the images do not have labels and sets their size to
64x64 pixels. The batch size is set to 32.
dataset = keras.preprocessing.image_dataset_from_directory("celeba_gan",
label_mode=None, image_size=(64, 64), batch_size=32)

#This line maps the dataset using a lambda function that divides each
image by 255 to scale the pixel values between 0 and 1. This is a common
pre-processing step for image data.
dataset = dataset.map(lambda x: x / 255.0)
```

It is good practice to show the data before passing it on to the next step for processing.

```
#This starts a loop that will iterate through each batch of images in the
dataset.
for x in dataset:
    This turns off the axis labels in the plot.
    plt.axis("off")

#This displays the first image in the current batch as a plot. The x
variable is a batch of images in tensor format, so  we first convert it
to a NumPy array using numpy() and then multiply it by 255 to scale the
pixel values to the 0-255 range. Finally, we convert the result to an
integer data type using astype("int32"). The [0] at the end selects the
first image in the batch for display.
    plt.imshow((x.numpy() * 255).astype("int32")[0])

    This exits the loop after displaying the first image.
    break
```

14.3.5.3 Discriminator

The discriminator function converts image data into a score vector. In this case, the function comprises of three convolution layers and three leaky ReLU layers. The final section of the network includes a flattening layer, a dropout layer, and a dense layer. Experimenting with different parameter and hyperparameter values can help observe how they affect the results and network performance.

```
#Create a new instance of a sequential model in Keras for the
discriminator network.
discriminator = keras.Sequential(
    [ Define an input layer with the shape of (64, 64, 3) which
corresponds to the shape of the input image.
        keras.Input(shape=(64, 64, 3)),

        Add a convolutional layer with 64 filters of size 4x4, a stride of
2, and "same" padding to the model.
        layers.Conv2D(64, kernel_size=4, strides=2, padding="same"),
```

Add a LeakyReLU activation layer with a negative slope coefficient of 0.2 to the model.

```
layers.LeakyReLU(alpha=0.2),
```

Add another convolutional layer with 128 filters of size 4x4, a stride of 2, and "same" padding to the model.

```
layers.Conv2D(128, kernel_size=4, strides=2, padding="same"),
```

Add another LeakyReLU activation layer with a negative slope coefficient of 0.2 to the model.

```
layers.LeakyReLU(alpha=0.2),
```

Add another convolutional layer with 128 filters of size 4x4, a stride of 2, and "same" padding to the model.

```
layers.Conv2D(128, kernel_size=4, strides=2, padding="same"),
```

Add another LeakyReLU activation layer with a negative slope coefficient of 0.2 to the model.

```
layers.LeakyReLU(alpha=0.2),
```

Flatten the output of the last convolutional layer into a 1D vector.

```
layers.Flatten(),
```

Add a dropout layer with a rate of 0.2 to the model to prevent overfitting.

```
layers.Dropout(0.2),
```

Add a fully connected layer with a single output unit and sigmoid activation function to the model. #This output unit is used to determine whether the input image is real or fake.

```
layers.Dense(1, activation="sigmoid"),],name="discriminator",)
```

14.3.5.4 Generator

The structure is nearly identical to that of the discriminator, except for the addition of Conv2DTranspose.

```
#Sets the dimensionality of the noise vector used as input for the
generator.
latent_dim = 128


#Creates a sequential model for the generator.
generator = keras.Sequential(
        Defines the input shape of the generator as a noise vector of
dimension latent_dim.
    [   keras.Input(shape=(latent_dim,)),
        Applies a dense layer with 8 8 128 output units to the input
noise vector.
        layers.Dense(8 * 8 * 128),
        Reshapes the output of the dense layer to a 3D tensor with shape
(8, 8, 128).
        layers.Reshape((8, 8, 128)),
```

Applies a transpose convolution with 128 filters, a kernel size of 4x4, a stride of 2x2, and same padding to increase the spatial dimensions of the input tensor.

```
        layers.Conv2DTranspose(128, kernel_size=4, strides=2,
padding="same"),
```

Applies a LeakyReLU activation function to the output of the convolutional layer.

```
        layers.LeakyReLU(alpha=0.2),
```

Applies another transpose convolution with 256 filters, a kernel size of 4x4, a stride of 2x2, and same padding to further increase the spatial dimensions of the input tensor.

```
        layers.Conv2DTranspose(256, kernel_size=4, strides=2,
padding="same"),
```

Applies another LeakyReLU activation function to the output of the convolutional layer.

```
        layers.LeakyReLU(alpha=0.2),
```

Applies another transpose convolution with 512 filters, a kernel size of 4x4, a stride of 2x2, and same padding to further increase the spatial dimensions of the input tensor.

```
        layers.Conv2DTranspose(512, kernel_size=4, strides=2,
padding="same"),
```

Applies another LeakyReLU activation function to the output of the convolutional layer.

```
        layers.LeakyReLU(alpha=0.2),
```

```
#Applies a convolutional layer with 3 filters, a kernel size of 5x5, and
same padding to produce the final image output of the generator. The
activation function used is sigmoid, which scales the output values
between 0 and 1.
        layers.Conv2D(3, kernel_size=5, padding="same",
activation="sigmoid"),],
    name="generator",)
```

14.3.5.5 Training

The following is a training step that includes several functions.

```
#Defines a new class named GAN which is derived from the keras.Model1
class, which will serve as the base class for our GAN model.
class GAN(keras.Model1):
```

```
#This method is the constructor of the class GAN. It is called when an
object of this class is created. The method takes three parameters -
discriminator, generator1, and latent_dim - which are the discriminator
network, generator network, and the dimension of the latent space,
respectively.
    def __init__(self, discriminator, generator1, latent_dim):
        This line calls the constructor of the base class
        super(GAN, self).__init__()
        It initializes the inherited properties of the GAN class from the.
        keras.Model1
        This line assigns the discriminator network to the self.
discriminator attribute of the GAN class.
        self.discriminator = discriminator
```

```
        This line assigns the generator network to the self.generator1
attribute of the GAN class.
        self.generator1 = generator1
        This line assigns the dimension of the latent space to the self.
latent_dim attribute of the GAN class.
        self.latent_dim = latent_dim
```

The optimizers and loss functions are defined in the compiled module.

```
#This is a method definition for the `compile` method of the `GAN` class,
with `d_optimizer`, `g_optimizer`, and `loss_fn` as its parameters.
def compile(self, d_optimizer, g_optimizer, loss_fn):

#This line calls the `compile` method of the parent class `keras.Modell`.
super(GAN, self).compile()

#These lines set instance variables `d_optimizer`, `g_optimizer`, and
`loss_fn` to the values passed in as arguments.
self.d_optimizer = d_optimizer
self.g_optimizer = g_optimizer
self.loss_fn = loss_fn

#These lines create two instance variables, `d_loss_metric` and `g_loss_
metric` using `keras.metrics.Mean` to track the loss values for the
discriminator and generator models, respectively.
self.d_loss_metric = keras.metrics.Mean(name="d_loss")
self.g_loss_metric = keras.metrics.Mean(name="g_loss")

#This is a property method that returns a list of the two instance
variables created earlier, `d_loss_metric` and `g_loss_metric`. This
allows the loss values to be accessed externally from the class.
@property
def metrics(self):
    return [self.d_loss_metric, self.g_loss_metric]
```

The train_step module is used to randomly sample points in the latent space and decode them into fake images. The fake images are then combined with real images to create labels that can distinguish between real and fake images. The discriminator can now be trained using these labels, and the generator can be trained using latent space samples without updating the discriminator's weights. Figures 14.11 and 14.12 offer a visual comparison of the generated images from the CelebA dataset after distinct stages of training: 10 and 30 iterations, respectively. In Figure 14.11, after just ten iterations, the model begins to form basic facial features and structures. By Figure 14.12, at 30 iterations, there's a noticeable improvement in image clarity, facial detail precision, and overall resemblance to authentic celebrity portraits. These figures underscore the model's capability to progressively refine and improve image quality with increased training iterations..

```
#Defines the training step method for the GAN model.
def train_step(self, real_images):

#Randomly generates latent vectors for the generator and combines them
with the real images to create a batch of combined images. Creates
labels for the combined images where the labels for the generated
```

FIGURE 14.11
Generated data from initial data after 10 epochs.

FIGURE 14.12
Generated data from initial data after 30 epochs.

```
images are zeros with a small random offset and the labels for the real
images are ones.
batch_size = tf.shape(real_images)[0]
random_latent_vectors = tf.random.normal(shape=(batch_size, self.
latent_dim))
generated_images = self.generator(random_latent_vectors)
combined_images = tf.concat([generated_images, real_images], axis=0)
labels = tf.concat([tf.ones((batch_size, 1)), tf.zeros((batch_size, 1))],
axis=0)
labels += 0.05 * tf.random.uniform(tf.shape(labels))

#Calculates the discriminator loss by making predictions on the combined
images and comparing the labels to the predictions using the binary
cross-entropy loss. Calculates the gradients of the discriminator loss
with respect to the discriminator trainable weights using backpropagation.
```

Updates the discriminator trainable weights using the optimizer and the gradients.

```
with tf.GradientTape() as tape:
    predictions = self.discriminator(combined_images)
    d_loss = self.loss_fn(labels, predictions)
grads = tape.gradient(d_loss, self.discriminator.trainable_weights)
self.d_optimizer.apply_gradients(zip(grads, self.discriminator.
trainable_weights))
```

#Generates new random latent vectors and creates misleading labels (all zeros) for them. Calculates the generator loss by making predictions on the generated images using the discriminator and comparing the predictions to the misleading labels using the binary cross-entropy loss. Calculates the gradients of the generator loss with respect to the generator trainable weights using backpropagation. Updates the generator trainable weights using the optimizer and the gradients.

```
random_latent_vectors = tf.random.normal(shape=(batch_size, self.
latent_dim))
misleading_labels = tf.zeros((batch_size, 1))
with tf.GradientTape() as tape:
    predictions = self.discriminator(self.generator(random_latent_vectors))
    g_loss = self.loss_fn(misleading_labels, predictions)
grads = tape.gradient(g_loss, self.generator.trainable_weights)
self.g_optimizer.apply_gradients(zip(grads, self.generator.
trainable_weights))
```

#Updates the discriminator and generator loss metrics with the latest loss values.
Returns a dictionary with the discriminator and generator loss metrics.

```
self.d_loss_metric.update_state(d_loss)
self.g_loss_metric.update_state(g_loss)
return {"d_loss": self.d_loss_metric.result(),"g_loss": self.g_loss_
metric.result(),
```

#Defines a callback for monitoring the GAN during training.
Generates random latent vectors and uses them to generate a batch of new images.
Saves the generated images to files.

```
class GANMonitor(keras.callbacks.Callback):
    def __init__(self, num_img=3, latent_dim=128):
        self.num_img = num_img
        self.latent_dim = latent_dim
    def on_epoch_end(self, epoch, logs=None):
        random_latent_vectors = tf.random.normal(shape=(self.num_img,
self.latent_dim))
        generated_images = self.model1.generator(random_latent_vectors)
        generated_images *= 255
        generated_images.numpy()
        for i in range(self.num_img):
            img = keras.preprocessing.image.array_to_img(generated_
images[i])
            img.save("generated_img_%03d_%d.png" % (epoch, i))
```

```
#Sets the number of epochs (iterations) for which the GAN will be
trained.
epochs = 30

#Initializes a new GAN object with the specified discriminator,
generator, and latent dimension.
gan = GAN(discriminator=discriminator, generator1=generator1,
latent_dim=latent_dim)

#Configures the GAN for training by specifying the optimizers and loss
function to use.
gan.compile(
    d_optimizer=keras.optimizers.Adam(learning_rate=0.0001),
    g_optimizer=keras.optimizers.Adam(learning_rate=0.0001),
    loss_fn=keras.losses.BinaryCrossentropy(),)

#Trains the GAN on the dataset for the specified number of epochs, using
the specified callbacks to monitor the training process.
gan.fit(dataset, epochs=epochs, callbacks=[GANMonitor(num_img=10,
latent_dim=latent_dim)])
```

14.4 Image Restoration Using SRGAN

Image restoration is an intriguing topic in computer vision, and a lot of research has been done on it. Technical issues encountered during the image or video capture process may result in suboptimal output. Deep learning, particularly GANs, provides some methods for improving image resolution. Super-Resolution GANs, or SRGANs, can be used to over-come technical limitations or other issues. These amazing GAN structures can convert many low-resolution photos and videos into high-resolution versions. In this project, we will build the SRGAN model and train it using the TensorFlow and Keras deep learning frameworks.

14.4.1 Import Libraries and Install Prerequisites

Before starting the SRGAN project, you need to ensure that all the required libraries are installed. Additionally, you need to ensure that the datasets and utils directories are present in your working directory as they will help in preparing the dataset for training the models.

```
#This line is a compatibility feature to allow code to be compatible with
both Python 2 and Python 3.
from __future__ import print_function, division

#This imports the `scipy` library, which provides functions for
scientific computing and optimization.
import scipy

#This imports the `InstanceNormalization` layer from the `tensorflow_
addons` package, which provides additional functionality to TensorFlow.
from tensorflow_addons.layers import InstanceNormalization
```

```
#This imports the `uuid4` function from the `uuid` module, which
generates a random UUID (Universal Unique Identifier).
from uuid import uuid4

#This imports the MNIST dataset from the `tensorflow.keras.datasets`
module. The MNIST dataset is a set of 70,000 handwritten digits, commonly
used for image classification.
from tensorflow.keras.datasets import mnist

#This imports several types of layers from the `tensorflow.keras.layers`
module. These layers are used to build neural networks for deep learning.
from tensorflow.keras.layers import Add, BatchNormalization, Conv2D,
Dense, Flatten, Input, LeakyReLU, PReLU, Lambda

#This imports the `Model` class from the `tensorflow.keras.models` module.
The `Model` class is used to define and train deep learning models.
from tensorflow.keras.models import Model

#This imports the pre-trained VGG19 model from the `tensorflow.keras.
applications` module. The VGG19 model is a convolutional neural network
that was trained on the ImageNet dataset and is often used as a feature
extractor for image classification tasks.
from tensorflow.keras.applications.vgg19 import VGG19
#This imports the `datetime` module, which provides classes for working
with dates and times.
import datetime

#This imports the `pyplot` module from the `matplotlib` library, which is
used for creating data visualizations in Python.
import matplotlib.pyplot as plt

#This imports the `sys` module, which provides access to system-specific
parameters and functions.
import sys

#This imports the `Image` class from the `PIL` (Python Imaging Library)
module, which is used for image processing tasks in Python.
from PIL import Image

#This imports the `os` module, which provides a way to interact with the
file system in Python.
import os

#This imports the `glob` function from the `glob` module, which is used
to find all the pathnames matching a specified pattern.
from glob import glob

#This imports the `numpy` library, which provides support for large,
multi-dimensional arrays and matrices, along with a large collection of
high-level mathematical functions to operate on these arrays.
import numpy as np

#This imports the `timeit` module, which provides a simple way to time
small bits of Python code.
import timeit
```

```
#This imports the OpenCV library, which is a popular computer vision
library used for image and video processing.
import cv2

#This imports the `backend` module from the `tensorflow.keras` package,
which provides a set of functions for building and manipulating deep
learning models.
import tensorflow.keras.backend as K

#This imports the `tensorflow` library, which is a popular deep learning
framework for building and training machine learning models.
import tensorflow as tf

#This imports the `requests` library, which is used to send HTTP requests
in Python.
import requests

#This block of code downloads
with open("weights-srgan.tar.gz", "wb") as wf:
    wf.write(requests.get("https://martin-krasser.de/sisr/weights-srgan.
tar.gz").content)
```

14.4.2 Data Preprocessing

To train our SRGAN model, we will use the DIVerse 2K dataset, which contains high-quality images of varying resolutions. You should download the four separate zip files mentioned in the code below. The four folders contain training and validation files in both low and high resolution. We will use both the low-resolution and high-resolution versions of the photos to train our model.

```
#DIV2K_RGB_MEAN` is a numpy array representing the mean RGB values of
the DIV2K dataset, which is a benchmark dataset for single-image
super-resolution. The values are multiplied by 255 to bring them in the
range of 0-255.
DIV2K_RGB_MEAN = np.array([0.4488, 0.4371, 0.4040]) * 255

#resolve_single` is a function that takes a model and a low-resolution
image and returns the corresponding super-resolved image. The function
first expands the dimensions of the low-resolution image using `tf.
expand_dims`, so that it can be passed as a batch of size 1 to the
`resolve` function. The `resolve` function is called with the model and
the expanded low-resolution image, and the resulting super-resolved image
is returned.
def resolve_single(model1, lr):
    return resolve(model1, tf.expand_dims(lr, axis=0))[0]

#resolve` is a function that takes a model and a batch of low-resolution
images and returns the corresponding super-resolved images.
The function first casts the low-resolution images to float32 using `tf.
cast`.
The low-resolution images are passed to the model to get the super-resolved
images.
The super-resolved images are clipped to the range of 0-255 using
`tf.clip_by_value`.
```

The values of the super-resolved images are rounded to the nearest integer using `tf.round`.
The super-resolved images are cast to uint8 using `tf.cast` and returned.

```
def resolve(model1, lr_batch):
    lr_batch = tf.cast(lr_batch, tf.float32)
    sr_batch = model1(lr_batch)
    sr_batch = tf.clip_by_value(sr_batch, 0, 255)
    sr_batch = tf.round(sr_batch)
    sr_batch = tf.cast(sr_batch, tf.uint8)
    return sr_batch
```

#evaluate` is a function that takes a model and a dataset of low-resolution and high-resolution image pairs and returns the mean PSNR value of the super-resolved images produced by the model. The function iterates over the images in the dataset and calls the `resolve` function to get the corresponding super-resolved images. The `psnr` function is called to compute the PSNR value between the super-resolved and high-resolution images. The PSNR values are appended to a list of PSNR values. The mean PSNR value is computed using `tf.reduce_mean` and returned.

```
def evaluate(model1, dataset):
    psnr_values = []
    for lr, hr in dataset:
        sr = resolve(model1, lr)
        psnr_value = psnr(hr, sr)[0]
        psnr_values.append(psnr_value)
    return tf.reduce_mean(psnr_values)
```

You can normalize the data to get better performance.

#This function takes an image tensor `x` and subtracts the DIV2K_RGB_MEAN value from it and then divides by 127.5.

```
def normalize(x, rgb_mean=DIV2K_RGB_MEAN):
    return (x - rgb_mean) / 127.5
```

#This function takes a normalized image tensor `x` and undoes the normalization by multiplying by 127.5 and then adding the DIV2K_RGB_MEAN value.

```
def denormalize(x, rgb_mean=DIV2K_RGB_MEAN):
    return x * 127.5 + rgb_mean
```

#This function takes an image tensor `x` and normalizes it to be between 0 and 1 by dividing by 255.

```
def normalize_01(x):
    return x / 255.0
```

#This function takes an image tensor `x` and normalizes it to be between -1 and 1 by dividing by 127.5 and then subtracting 1.

```
def normalize_m11(x):
    return x / 127.5 - 1
```

#This function takes a normalized image tensor `x` that is between -1 and 1 and undoes the normalization by adding 1 and then multiplying by 127.5.

```
def denormalize_m11(x):
    return (x + 1) * 127.5
```

The peak signal-to-noise ratio (PSNR) is a measure of the quality of a signal or image, expressed as the ratio of the maximum possible power of the signal to the power of the noise that affects the fidelity of its representation.

```
#This is a function that calculates the peak signal-to-noise ratio (PSNR)
between two images `x1` and `x2`. It uses the `tf.image.psnr` function
from TensorFlow, which takes the two images and the maximum pixel value
(`max_val`) as inputs.
def psnr(x1, x2):
    return tf.image.psnr(x1, x2, max_val=255)
```

```
#This is a function that returns a lambda function for performing pixel
shuffling with a given `scale`. Pixel shuffling is a technique used in
some super-resolution models to increase the spatial resolution of an
image by rearranging the pixels in a low-resolution image. The `depth_to_
space` function from TensorFlow is used to perform the pixel shuffling
operation. The lambda function returned by this function can be applied
to a tensor using the `tf.keras.layers.Lambda` layer.
def pixel_shuffle(scale):
    return lambda x: tf.nn.depth_to_space(x, scale)
```

14.4.3 Generator and Discriminator

We create a new function for the residual blocks by repeatedly stacking a feed-forward and skip connection layer, a batch normalization layer, a parametric ReLU activation function, and a final 3 × 3 convolutional layer with batch normalization. The leaky ReLU activation function with an alpha of 0.2 is used immediately after a convolutional layer.

```
#`LR_SIZE` is a constant variable representing the low-resolution size of
the image.
#`HR_SIZE` is a constant variable representing the high-resolution size
of the image.
LR_SIZE = 24
HR_SIZE = 96
```

```
#upsample` is a function that takes two arguments:
x_in`: an input tensor
num_filters`: the number of filters to use in the convolution operation
Conv2D` applies a 2D convolution to the input tensor.
Lambda` is a layer that applies a custom function to the input tensor.
pixel_shuffle` is a function that reorganizes the input tensor by
rearranging its dimensions in a certain way.
PReLU` is a layer that applies the parametric rectified linear unit
activation function element-wise to the input tensor.
def upsample(x_in, num_filters):
    x = Conv2D(num_filters, kernel_size=3, padding='same')(x_in)
    x = Lambda(pixel_shuffle(scale=2))(x)
    return PReLU(shared_axes=[1, 2])(x)
```

```
#res_block` is a function that takes three arguments:
x_in`: an input tensor
num_filters`: the number of filters to use in the convolution operations
momentum`: the momentum value for the batch normalization layers
```

Add` **is a layer that adds two input tensors element-wise.**

```
def res_block(x_in, num_filters, momentum=0.8):
    x = Conv2D(num_filters, kernel_size=3, padding='same')(x_in)
    x = BatchNormalization(momentum=momentum)(x)
    x = PReLU(shared_axes=[1, 2])(x)
    x = Conv2D(num_filters, kernel_size=3, padding='same')(x)
    x = BatchNormalization(momentum=momentum)(x)
    x = Add()([x_in, x])
    return x
```

#sr_resnet` **is a function that takes two optional arguments:**
num_filters`: the number of filters to use in the convolution operations
num_res_blocks`: the number of residual blocks to use in the model
Input` **is a layer that defines the input shape for the model.**
Conv2D` **applies a 2D convolution to the input tensor.**
normalize_01` **is a function that normalizes the input tensor to the range**
[0, 1].
BatchNormalization`

```
def sr_resnet(num_filters=64, num_res_blocks=16):
    x_in = Input(shape=(None, None, 3))
    x = Lambda(normalize_01)(x_in)
    x = Conv2D(num_filters, kernel_size=9, padding='same')(x)
    x = x_1 = PReLU(shared_axes=[1, 2])(x)
    for _ in range(num_res_blocks):
        x = res_block(x, num_filters)
    x = Conv2D(num_filters, kernel_size=3, padding='same')(x)
    x = BatchNormalization()(x)
    x = Add()([x_1, x])
    x = upsample(x, num_filters * 4)
    x = upsample(x, num_filters * 4)
    x = Conv2D(3, kernel_size=9, padding='same', activation='tanh')(x)
    x = Lambda(denormalize_m11)(x)
    return Modell(x_in, x)
```

14.4.4 Training

After completing the SRGAN infrastructure, we can proceed to model training. Both the generative and discriminative models can be safely archived.

14.4.5 Load and Display

You can now use the trained model to create a higher-resolution image.

#This function takes in a path to an image as input and returns the
loaded image as a numpy array using the `Image.open()` method from the
PIL library.

```
def load_image(path):
    return np.array(Image.open(path))
```

 # Define a function to plot low-resolution (LR) and super-resolution (SR)
images
This function takes in two images, low-resolution (LR) and super-
resolution (SR), as input and plots them side by side using `plt.
imshow()` method from the `matplotlib` library.

The dimensions of the SR image are automatically calculated based on the scale factor between the LR and SR images.

```
def plot_sample(lr, sr):
    plt.figure(figsize=(20, 10))
    images = [lr, sr]
    titles = ['LR', f'SR (x{sr.shape[0] // lr.shape[0]})']
    for i, (img, title) in enumerate(zip(images, titles)):
        plt.subplot(1, 2, i+1)
        plt.imshow(img)
        plt.title(title)
        plt.xticks([])
        plt.yticks([])
```

```
# Define a function to load an LR image, generate its SR equivalent using
the GAN model, and plot both images
- This function takes in the path to an LR image as input, loads the image
using `load_image()` function, and generates its SR equivalent using the GAN
model by calling `resolve_single()` function with the LR image as input.
- The LR and SR images are plotted side by side using `plot_sample()`
function.
- The dimensions of the SR image are automatically calculated based on
the scale factor between the LR and SR images.
def resolve_and_plot(lr_image_path):
    lr = load_image(lr_image_path)
    gan_sr = resolve_single(model1, lr)
    print(lr.shape, gan_sr.shape)
    plt.figure(figsize=(20, 20))
    images = [lr, gan_sr]
    titles = ['LR', 'SR (GAN)']
    positions = [1, 2]
    for i, (img, title, pos) in enumerate(zip(images, titles, positions)):
        plt.subplot(2, 2, pos)
        plt.imshow(img)
        plt.title(title)
        plt.xticks([])
        plt.yticks([])
```

Figure 14.13 displays the prowess of advanced generative techniques in producing image data of superior resolution. The visual examples underscore the stark clarity, detail,

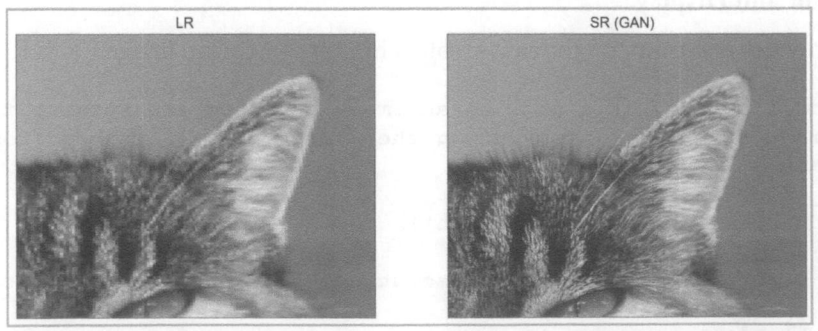

FIGURE 14.13
Generated image data with better resolution.

and precision with which the images have been generated, highlighting the capability of GANs or similar models to not just replicate reality but to do so with remarkable fidelity and sharpness.

14.5 Image Synthesis Using GAN Issues

Image synthesis with GANs has gotten much interest, but there are still a few issues to work out. Here are some of the main issues.

14.5.1 Mode Collapse

In some cases, the generator in a GAN may produce a limited range of output images, resulting in a phenomenon known as mode collapse. This issue can occur when the generator learns to produce a few modes of the target distribution and ignores the rest.

14.5.2 Lack of Diversity

Even when mode collapse is not an issue, GANs can produce images that lack diversity, resulting in repeated patterns or artifacts in the output images.

14.5.3 Training Instability

GANs can be challenging to train, and the training process can be unstable. In some cases, the discriminator can overpower the generator, leading to poor-quality images or a failure to converge.

14.5.4 Limited Applicability to Specific Domains

While GANs have been successful in generating high-quality images for many applications, they may not be suitable for all image synthesis tasks. For example, GANs may not be effective for generating images with fine details or textures.

14.5.5 Lack of Interpretability

GANs are typically considered black-box models, and it can be difficult to interpret how the generator produces the output images. This lack of interpretability can be a challenge in applications where understanding the underlying process is essential.

14.5.6 Dataset Bias

GANs are only as good as the training data they are provided with. If the training dataset is biased or lacks diversity, the generated images may also exhibit similar biases and limitations.

14.5.7 Computational Complexity

GANs can be computationally expensive to train, especially when generating high-resolution images. This computational complexity can limit the scalability of GAN-based image synthesis systems.

14.5.8 Ethical Concerns

GANs can be used to create fake images or deepfakes that can be used for malicious purposes, such as disinformation spread or the creation of false identities. This raises ethical concerns about the use of GAN-based image synthesis technology.

Addressing these issues is an active area of research, and many new techniques have been proposed to mitigate them, including improved training algorithms, better regularization methods, and more effective architectures for the generator and discriminator.

14.6 Implementation Tips for Image Synthesis Using GANs

Here are some implementation tips for image synthesis using GANs.

14.6.1 Choose an Appropriate GAN Architecture for Your Task

There are many different types of GAN architectures, and choosing the right one can have a significant impact on the quality of the generated images. Consider the specific requirements of your task, such as image resolution, input/output format, and the complexity of the target distribution.

14.6.2 Preprocess and Normalize Your Data

Preprocessing and normalizing your data can improve the stability and convergence of your GAN. This can include techniques such as resizing, cropping, and centering your input images and scaling pixel values to a standardized range.

14.6.3 Use Data Augmentation Techniques

Data augmentation techniques can help to increase the diversity of your training data and improve the performance of your GAN. This can include techniques, such as random cropping, flipping, and rotating your input images.

14.6.4 Regularize Your GAN to Prevent Mode Collapse

Regularization techniques, such as weight decay, dropout, and batch normalization, can help to prevent mode collapse in your GAN by encouraging the generator to produce diverse output images.

14.6.5 Monitor Your GAN Training

Monitoring your GAN training is essential to ensure that it is progressing correctly. This can include monitoring loss functions, visualizing generated images at various stages of training, and evaluating the performance of your GAN on a validation dataset.

14.6.6 Use Transfer Learning to Improve Your GAN

Transfer learning techniques can be used to improve the performance of your GAN by leveraging pre-trained models on similar tasks. For example, you can start with a pre-trained GAN model and train a new model on a similar but different dataset.

14.6.7 Experiment with Hyperparameters

Experimenting with different hyperparameters, such as learning rates, batch sizes, and regularization strengths, can help you to find the optimal configuration for your GAN.

14.6.8 Consider Using a Pre-trained GAN Model

Using a pre-trained GAN model can save you time and computational resources, especially if your task is similar to the pre-trained model's original task. You can fine-tune the pre-trained model on your dataset to generate high-quality images.

14.6.9 Evaluate the Quality of Your Generated Images

Evaluating the quality of your generated images is essential to ensure that your GAN is producing high-quality outputs. You can use metrics, such as Inception Score, Frechet Inception Distance, or Perceptual Path Length, to evaluate the quality of your generated images.

Remember, hands-on experience is key when working with GANs or any other machine learning models. Therefore, consistently practicing implementation and troubleshooting is crucial for mastering these concepts.

14.6.10 Use GANs Responsibly

GANs can be used to create false images or deepfakes for malicious purposes. It is critical to use GANs responsibly and to think about the ethical implications of your work.

14.7 Lessons Learned

- Learn SRGAN Architectures
- Learn Image Synthesis using SRGAN
- Learn Image Restoration using SRGAN
- Learn Image Synthesis using GAN Issues
- Learn Implementation Tips for Image Synthesis using GANs

14.8 Problems

14.8.1 What are the main image synthesis architectures in GAN?

14.8.2 Explain each of the two main types of image synthesis.

14.8.3   Change some parameters and layers in the code example in section 14.3.3 to see how they change the results through iteration and discuss it.

14.8.4   Change some parameters and layers in the code example in section 14.3.4 to see how iteration affects the results and discuss it.

14.8.5   Change some parameters and layers in the code example in section 14.3.5 to see how iteration affects the results and discuss it.

14.8.6   Change some parameters and layers in the code example in section 14.4 to see how iteration affects the results and discuss it.

14.8.7   What are some common loss functions used in GAN-based image synthesis?

14.8.8   What is mode collapse in GAN-based image synthesis, and how can it be addressed?

14.8.9   How can conditional GANs be used for image synthesis?

14.8.10   What is a Pix2Pix GAN, and how is it used for image-to-image translation?

14.8.11   How can cycle-consistent GANs be used for image synthesis, and what are some applications of this approach?

14.8.12   How can adversarial loss be combined with other loss functions in GAN-based image synthesis?

14.8.13   What are some techniques for improving the stability of GAN-based image synthesis, such as the use of spectral normalization?

14.8.14   What is progressive growing in GAN-based image synthesis, and how can it improve the quality of generated images?

14.8.15   What are some applications of GAN-based image synthesis in the field of fashion and design, such as generating new clothing designs or textures?

14.8.16   What are some challenges in GAN-based image synthesis, such as overfitting or vanishing gradients, and how can they be addressed?

14.8.17   How can GAN-based image synthesis be used for data augmentation in training deep learning models?

14.8.18   How can GAN-based image synthesis be used in the creation of new art, such as generating new paintings or sculptures?

14.8.19   What are some techniques for improving the diversity of generated images in GAN-based image synthesis, such as the use of style-based generators?

14.8.20   How can GAN-based image synthesis be used in the generation of synthetic data for use in robotics or other applications?

14.8.21   What are some promising directions for future research in GAN-based image synthesis and its applications?

14.9 Programming Questions

- **Easy**

   14.9.1   How do you load and preprocess image data in TensorFlow or Keras before training a GAN?

   14.9.2   How can you define and compile the generator and discriminator models in Keras for a simple GAN?

14.9.3 How can you use the Adam optimizer to train a GAN in TensorFlow or Keras?

14.9.4 How can you use the MNIST dataset for training a GAN in TensorFlow or Keras?

14.9.5 How can you visualize the generated images during training in TensorFlow or Keras?

- **Medium**

14.9.6 How can you implement a Wasserstein GAN with gradient penalty in TensorFlow or Keras?

14.9.7 How can you use a pre-trained VGG network for perceptual loss in a GAN in Keras or TensorFlow?

14.9.8 How can you implement a CycleGAN for image-to-image translation in TensorFlow or Keras?

14.9.9 How can you use the FID metric to evaluate the quality of generated images in a GAN in TensorFlow or Keras?

14.9.10 How can you use a pre-trained GPT-2 model for text-to-image generation in a GAN in TensorFlow or Keras?

- **Hard**

14.9.11 How can you implement a StyleGAN in TensorFlow or Keras for high-quality image synthesis?

14.9.12 How can you use a variational autoencoder (VAE) for unsupervised image synthesis in TensorFlow or Keras?

14.9.13 How can you use a generative query network (GQN) for 3D scene generation from 2D images in TensorFlow or Keras?

14.9.14 How can you implement a GAN with progressive growing in TensorFlow or Keras for high-resolution image synthesis?

14.9.15 How can you use a pre-trained StyleGAN2 model for fine-tuning on a new dataset in TensorFlow or Keras?

14.9.16 How can you implement a BigGAN in TensorFlow or Keras for large-scale image synthesis with hundreds of millions of parameters?

14.9.17 How can you use a spatio-temporal GAN (STGAN) for video synthesis in TensorFlow or Keras?

14.9.18 How can you implement a conditional GAN with an attention mechanism for image synthesis in TensorFlow or Keras?

14.9.19 How can you use a pre-trained T5 model for text-to-image generation in a GAN in TensorFlow or Keras?

14.9.20 How can you optimize a GAN for deployment on a mobile device using TensorFlow Lite or Keras?

15

Generative Adversarial Networks (GANs) for Voice, Music, and Song

The following topics are covered in this chapter about Generative Adversarial Networks (GANs) for Voice, Music, and Song:

- What is Sound?
- Audio Synthesis
- Human Voice Conversion
- Song Conversion
- Song Conversion using TensorFlow
- Issues in Generative Adversarial Networks (GANs) for Voice, Music, and Song
- Implementation Tips in Generative Adversarial Networks (GANs) for Voice, Music, and Song

15.1 Preface

GANs can analyze sound wave data across crucial wave domains, including voice, music, and song. In physics, sound is defined as the vibration of acoustic waves as they pass through a solid, liquid, or gas, and in human physiology, it is perceived as waves by the brain. While GANs have been extensively used in the field of image synthesis to generate realistic images, they can also be applied to other types of data, such as voice, music, and songs. Some of the main areas of application include GANs for Voice Synthesis, Music Synthesis, and Song Synthesis. Voice synthesis with GANs involves generating speech signals that mimic natural human voices. The process involves training a GAN model on a dataset of speech signals to learn the underlying patterns and structures of human speech. Once trained, the GAN model can generate new speech signals that resemble natural human speech. It has several applications, including in voice assistants, language translation, and speech therapy. GANs for music synthesis entail creating new musical compositions that sound as though they were composed by a human musician. The process involves training a GAN model on a dataset of musical compositions to learn the underlying patterns and structures of music. Once trained, the GAN model can generate new musical compositions that mimic those composed by a human musician. It has several applications, including in music production, composition, and education. Song synthesis with GANs involves generating new songs that sound like they were composed and sung by a human singer. The process involves training a GAN model on a dataset of songs to learn the underlying patterns and structures of music and vocals. Once trained, the GAN model can generate new songs that sound like they were

DOI: 10.1201/9781003281344-15

composed and sung by a human singer. It has several applications, including in music production, composition, and education. However, several challenges exist in synthesizing voice, music, and songs using GANs. One of the most significant challenges is the scarcity of high-quality datasets for training GAN models. Another challenge is the complex and diverse nature of sound, which makes it difficult for GAN models to capture all of the nuances and subtleties of human speech and music. Additionally, GAN models for sound synthesis tend to be more computationally intensive than those for image synthesis, which makes them more difficult to train and use in real-time applications. Despite these obstacles, GANs have demonstrated great promise in the field of sound synthesis and are expected to play a major role in the development of new technologies for voice, music, and song generation. This chapter provides an overview of sound and its characteristics, which can be useful when deploying GAN for voice, music, and song generation.

15.2 What Is Sound?

Sound is a type of energy transmitted via vibrations in a channel, such as air, water, or solids. When an object vibrates, it creates pressure waves that travel through the medium, causing the molecules to vibrate and transfer energy to adjacent molecules. Our ears detect these pressure waves, and our brain interprets them as sound. Sound can be characterized by its frequency, which determines the pitch or tone of the sound, and its amplitude, which determines the loudness or volume of the sound. Different types of sounds, such as speech, music, and environmental noise, have distinct frequency and amplitude patterns that can be analyzed and synthesized using signal processing techniques.

In various branches of science, there are several definitions of sound. For example, in physics, sound is defined as the vibration of acoustic waves as they pass through a solid, liquid, or gas. On the other hand, in human physiology, sound is defined as the waves that the brain perceives (audible for humans between 20 Hz and 20 kHz). Sound waves have properties, such as frequencies (measured in Hertz), amplitudes (which are the density and are measured in decibels), and directions (e.g., the brain determines it by comparing the times when sound reaches the left and right ears). It also has pitch (how low or high is it?), duration (how long or short is it?), loudness (how loud or soft is it?), timbre (the quality of the sound), and texture. Figure 15.1 illustrates the various perception ranges of entities, such as animals, humans, and planets. The wave is represented differently in each domain, and we can analyze sound wave data for the two most important wave domains using time and frequency. Figure 15.2 shows examine and compare two distinct sound waves: one with a low pitch and another with a high pitch.

1. **3D Visualization:** This plot offers a holistic perspective by combining the three crucial parameters: time, amplitude, and frequency. One curve signifies the low-pitch wave, oscillating at a frequency of 5 Hz, while the other, represented with a dashed line, corresponds to the high-pitch wave at a frequency of 50 Hz. By observing the depth of this plot (the z-axis representing frequency), one can clearly discern the difference in pitches of the two waves.

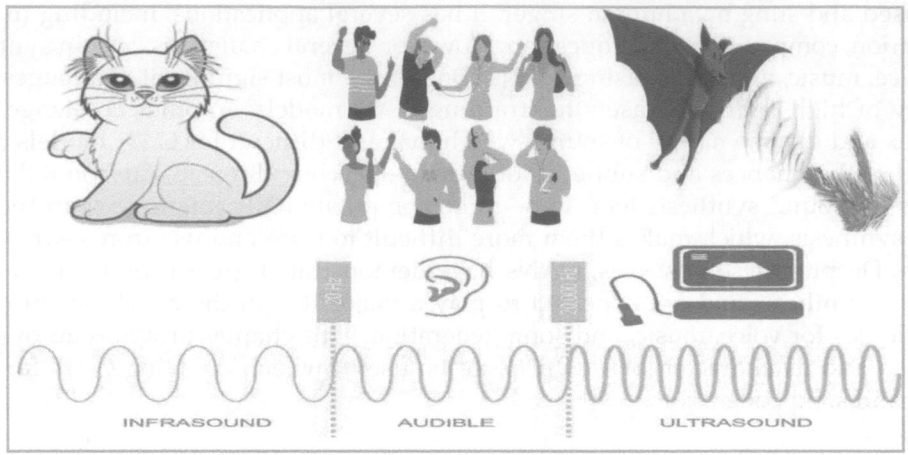

FIGURE 15.1
Different entities perceive different frequencies.

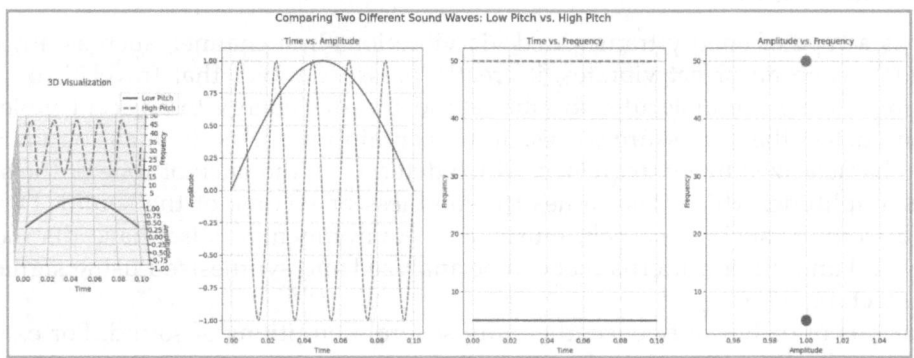

FIGURE 15.2
Time and frequency domain of the wave sound.

2. **Time vs. Amplitude:** In this 2D plot, the time domain representation of both sound waves is showcased. The waveform of the low-pitch sound has broader oscillations compared to the more tightly packed oscillations of the high-pitch sound, represented with a dashed line. This difference in oscillation density over time gives an auditory distinction between low and high pitches.

3. **Time vs. Frequency:** Here, the frequency values of the two sounds are visualized over time. The low-pitch sound is represented by a constant line at 5 Hz, while the high-pitch sound is denoted by a dashed line consistently at 50 Hz. This plot emphasizes that frequency, which is instrumental in distinguishing pitch, remains constant for pure sinusoidal tones.

4. **Amplitude vs. Frequency:** The peak amplitudes of the two waves are plotted against their respective frequencies. It provides insight into the relationship between the amplitude and frequency of the two sounds. In this case, both waves have comparable amplitudes but significantly different frequencies, further emphasizing their distinction in pitch.

Sound waves are characterized by several essential properties, including: Frequency, Amplitude, Wavelength, Speed, and Phase. Let us review some of these features, which are needed for training the GAN model.

15.2.1 Pitch

Pitch is one of the essential properties of sound waves, referring to the perceived highness or lowness of a sound. It is determined by the frequency of the sound wave, which is measured in Hertz (Hz) or cycles per second. The higher the frequency of a sound wave, the higher its pitch, and vice versa. For example, a 440-Hz sound wave is perceived as the musical note A above middle C, whereas a 220-Hz sound wave is perceived as the musical note A below middle C. Pitch perception varies from person to person and is influenced by factors, such as age, gender, and hearing ability. Additionally, some sounds, like noise or harmonics-rich sounds like music, can have complex or ambiguous pitch structures, making the perception of the pitch more challenging.

15.2.2 Sound Duration

Sound duration refers to the length of time a sound persists before it fades away. It is determined by the characteristics of the sound wave, such as its amplitude and frequency, as well as the properties of the medium through which it travels. The duration of a sound can vary widely, depending on the source of the sound and the environment in which it is produced. For example, a short sound like a hand clap may last only a few milliseconds, while a sustained musical note can last several seconds or more. Additionally, the duration of a sound can be influenced by various signal processing techniques, such as filtering, compression, and reverberation, which can modify the characteristics of the sound wave and affect its perceived duration.

15.2.3 Sound Intensity

Sound intensity, also known as sound level or loudness, is another crucial property of sound waves. It refers to the amount of energy carried by the sound wave and is determined by its amplitude, which is the maximum displacement of the wave from its equilibrium position. Sound intensity is measured in decibels (dB), a logarithmic scale that relates the intensity of the sound wave to a reference level. The reference level for sound intensity is usually set at the threshold of human hearing, which corresponds to a sound intensity of 0 dB. As the intensity of a sound wave increases, so does its perceived loudness or volume. For example, a sound wave with an intensity of 10 dB is perceived to be twice as loud as one with an intensity of 0 dB. The perception of sound intensity can vary among individuals and can be influenced by several factors, such as age, gender, and hearing ability. In addition, prolonged exposure to high-intensity sounds can lead to hearing damage or loss.

15.2.4 Timbre

Timbre is a characteristic of sound that distinguishes one sound source from another, even when they are producing sounds of the same pitch and loudness. It is often described as the "color" or "quality" of a sound. Timbre is determined by the complex interaction of different frequency components in a sound wave, which are known as

Qualities	Distinction	Shape	Produced by
Pitch	LOW		Wave frequency (Hz)
	High		
Duration	Long		Wave persistence
	Short		
Intensity	Loud		Wave amplitude (dB)
	Soft		
Timbre	Voices		Harmonic sound
	Instrument		

FIGURE 15.3
Overview of the Four Primary Characteristics of Sound Waves, Accompanied by Outputs Illustrating Their Distinct Properties.

harmonics or overtones. The specific combination of harmonics in a sound wave gives it its unique timbre. For example, a guitar and a piano playing the same note at the same volume will produce different timbres because the sound waves they produce have different harmonic structures. The guitar produces more harmonics and overtones, which give it a richer and more complex timbre, while the piano produces fewer harmonics and overtones, resulting in a simpler and more straightforward timbre. Timbre is an important characteristic in music and sound design because it can convey emotions, moods, and even identities. It is also a key factor in speech recognition and language understanding, as it allows us to distinguish different speakers and identify the emotions they are expressing. Signal processing techniques can be used to extract information about the source and characteristics of the sound by measuring and analyzing these properties. Figure 15.3 offers a concise overview of the principal properties defining sound waves. Within the table, four critical characteristics of sound waves are delineated. Accompanying each of these characteristics are visual representations or outputs that elucidate their meanings and implications. This layout facilitates a clear understanding of the nuances and significance of each sound wave property, making it an essential reference for anyone exploring the realm of acoustics.

Figure 15.3 summarizes the essential properties of sound waves. The table displays the four most important characteristics of sound waves, with a presentation of the output that helps to clarify these characteristics.

15.2.5 Preparing audio Data and Feature Extraction

The human voice, music, and song are all examples of audio, which are the data types used by all the formats we've looked at. If your data is analog at the start of the process, you must convert it to digital or binary format. Audio files can be saved in various formats, such as MP3, WMA, and WAV.

15.2.5.1 *Librosa*

Librosa is a Python library for analyzing and processing audio signals. It provides a wide range of functionality for working with audio data, including tools for loading and saving audio files, feature extraction, pitch and tempo estimation, time and frequency-domain processing, and more. Some of the key features of Librosa include:

- Loading and saving audio files in various formats, including WAV, MP3, and FLAC.
- Calculating a wide range of audio features, including spectral features, rhythm features, and timbral features.
- Estimating pitch and tempo of an audio signal.
- Converting between time and frequency domains using a variety of transforms, including the discrete Fourier transform (DFT), the short-time Fourier transform (STFT), and the constant-Q transform (CQT).
- Visualizing audio data using various types of plots, including waveform, spectrogram, and chromagram.

Librosa is widely used in research and industry applications, including music information retrieval, speech processing, and audio analysis for machine learning. Its flexible and intuitive API makes it easy to use for both beginners and experienced users. It has a wide range of modules for audio data processing, and the first step is to install it, which can be done in two ways on jupyter notebook or Conda.

15.2.5.1.1 *Installing on Jupyter Notebook*

This command is used to install the Python package "librosa". Librosa is a library for analyzing and processing audio data, such as music and speech. It provides tools for tasks, such as loading audio files, computing spectrograms, and extracting features like Mel-frequency cepstral coefficients (MFCCs) and chroma features. The package is commonly used in applications, such as music information retrieval, speech processing, and sound classification.

```
pip install librosa
```

15.2.5.1.2 *Installing on Conda*

This command is used to install the "librosa" package through the conda package manager. The "-c conda-forge" flag specifies the channel from which to install the package. "librosa" is a Python library for analyzing and processing audio signals, and is often used in tasks, such as music information retrieval and audio feature extraction.

```
conda install -c conda-forge librosa
```

Please note that Librosa, Conda, and Jupyter versions may support different features. It is recommended to use virtual environments to configure different coding environments for different versions.

15.2.5.2 Loading and Playing the Audio Data

Before using audio modules, it is important to load the data and perform some initial checks to ensure its quality and characteristics. This can include checking the data's value, distribution, and features. Here are some examples of how this can be done.

```
# loading the audio data, you can provide the path for loading data on
your local computer or website URL. This line of code loads an audio file
named "JCV.wav" located in the "sample_data" directory using the librosa
library, and assigns the audio data to the variable "x" and the sampling
rate to the variable "sr".
x, sr = librosa.load('/content/sample_data/JCV.wav')

# playing the audio data, This code plays the audio signal 'x' at the
sampling rate 'sr' using IPython.display Audio module.
ipd.Audio(x, rate=sr)
```

15.2.5.3 Plot the Audio Data

The data plotting provides some insight into the nature of the data as well as its distribution. Plotting audio data allows you to observe the shape of the data and how it evolves at each step. Here's an example of plotting audio data.

```
#This code imports the required libraries for plotting and displaying
audio data. Specifically, it imports the matplotlib.pyplot library and
the librosa.display library.
import matplotlib.pyplot as plt
import librosa.display

#This code uses the Matplotlib library to create a new figure with a
specific size of 14x5. Then it uses the librosa.display module to plot
the waveform of the loaded audio data 'x' with a sampling rate 'sr' on
the figure. The waveplot shows the amplitude of the audio signal as a
function of time, allowing us to visualize the overall shape of the audio
waveform.
plt.figure(figsize=(14, 5))
librosa.display.waveplot(x, sr=sr)
```

Figure 15.4 presents is a waveform display of an audio signal, generated using the Librosa library. The visualization serves as an intuitive representation of the audio signal's amplitude variations over its duration, providing an initial glimpse into its loudness dynamics and potential structure.

15.2.5.4 Spectrum

In signal processing and physics, a spectrum is a representation of the frequency content of a signal. In other words, it shows how much of the signal's energy is contained at each frequency. The spectrum of a signal is typically calculated using a Fourier transform, which converts the time-domain signal into the frequency domain. The result is a complex-valued function that represents the amplitude and phase of each frequency component of the signal. The most common type of spectrum is the power spectrum,

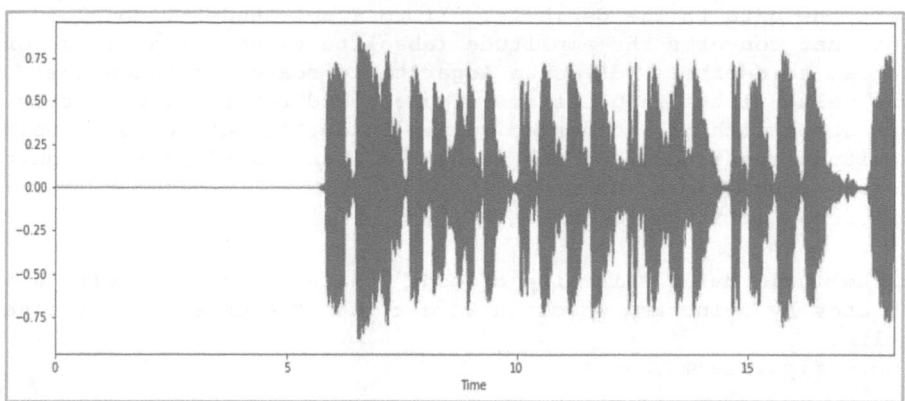

FIGURE 15.4
The audio data representation.

which shows the squared magnitude of each frequency component of the signal. The power spectrum is often plotted as a function of frequency, and it can be used to identify the frequency content of a signal and detect the presence of specific frequencies or frequency bands. Another type of spectrum is the amplitude spectrum, which shows the magnitude (without squaring) of each frequency component of the signal. This type of spectrum is often used for visualizing harmonic structures in signals, such as musical notes. Spectra are widely used in many areas of science and engineering, including acoustics, telecommunications, and signal processing. They provide valuable information about the frequency content of a signal and can be used for various applications, such as noise reduction, signal filtering, and feature extraction for machine learning. It is a graphical representation of a signal's frequency spectrum as it evolves over time, and it is known as a spectral plot. It has a librosa module as specshow for displaying the spectrum.

```
# librosa.display.specshow is a function in the Librosa library for
displaying a spectrogram or a mel spectrogram of an audio signal. It
takes as input a matrix of spectrogram or mel spectrogram values, as well
as optional arguments for customizing the plot, such as the sampling rate
and frequency limits. The function uses the matplotlib library to
generate the plot.
librosa.display.specshow
```

Here's an example of computing the STFT of an audio signal with the stft module, converting the extracted values to decibels with the amplitude_to_db module, and plotting the resulting spectrum.

```
# Extract the short-time Fourier transform values. This code applies the
short-time Fourier transform (STFT) on the audio signal 'x' using the
default parameters of Librosa. The STFT converts the time-domain signal
into the frequency domain and returns a 2-dimensional complex-valued
matrix 'X', where each element represents the magnitude and phase of a
frequency component at a specific time frame.
X = librosa.stft(x)
```

```
# Convert the data to the decibels. `librosa.amplitude_to_db()` is a
function that converts the amplitude (absolute value) of a signal or
spectrogram to decibels (dB) on a logarithmic scale. It takes the
absolute value of the input as its argument and returns a new array of
the same shape with the converted values in dB. In this case, `abs(X)` is
the magnitude spectrogram of the signal `x`, and `Xdb` is the magnitude
spectrogram converted to dB scale.
Xdb = librosa.amplitude_to_db(abs(X))

# plot the audio data. This line of code creates a new plot with a size
of 14 inches by 5 inches, which is larger than the default plot size in
Matplotlib.
plt.figure(figsize=(14, 5))

# This code generates a spectrogram of the audio signal x using the
Short-time Fourier Transform (STFT) computed using librosa.stft(). The
amplitude values of the STFT are converted to decibels using librosa.
amplitude_to_db(). The resulting spectrogram is displayed using librosa.
display.specshow(), with the x-axis representing time and the y-axis
representing frequency in Hz. plt.colorbar() adds a colorbar to the plot
to show the mapping of amplitude values to colors.
librosa.display.specshow(Xdb, sr=sr, x_axis='times', y_axis='hz')
plt.colorbar()
```

Figure 15.5 represents a spectrogram, which is a set of values commonly used in deep learning approaches, such as GANs. Unlike a spectrum, which provides a snapshot of the sound at a specific point in time, a spectrogram gives a display of a sound signal as it occurs in real-time. It is a method of describing the loudness or signal intensity of audio data over time, making it an ideal data format for deep learning techniques that work with image data. The visual format of a spectrogram can be 2D or 3D, and Figure 15.5 shows a 2D example, while Figure 15.6 shows a 3D example of the output of audio data. Figure 15.7 depicts a 2D spectrogram of a man's voice, and it is a good practice to compare these outputs and change some of their parameters to learn how the spectrum shape changes.

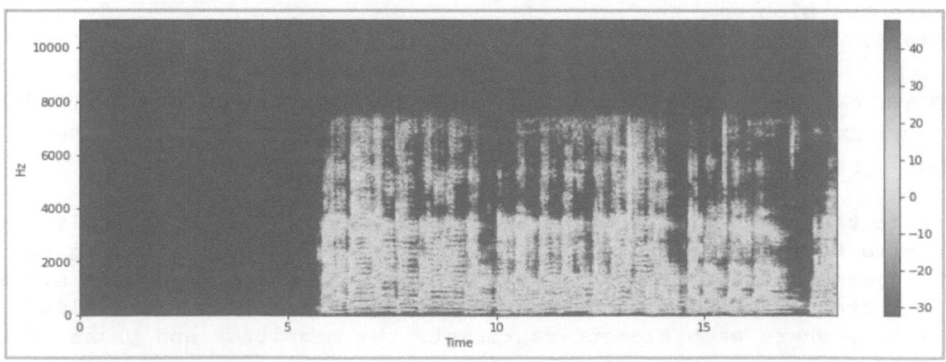

FIGURE 15.5
The 2D spectrogram of audio data based on the Hz on the *y*-axis and time on the *x*-axis.

FIGURE 15.6
A 3D spectrogram of a piece from a musical work.

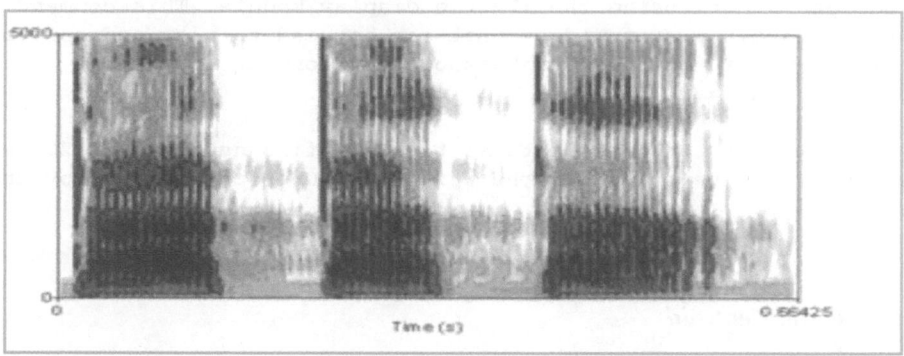

FIGURE 15.7
A 2D spectrogram that illustrates the sound of a man.

15.2.5.5 Create an Audio Signal

To work effectively with audio signals, it is important to understand how to generate them and describe their parameters using libraries, such as NumPy.

```
# This line imports the NumPy library and makes it available in the
current code. NumPy is a powerful library for numerical computing in
Python, providing support for multi-dimensional arrays and a large
collection of mathematical functions.
import numpy as np


# This line sets the value of the variable `Sr1` to 22050, which
represents the sample rate of an audio signal in Hertz (Hz). Sample rate
refers to the number of samples of audio that are taken per second to
represent the continuous audio signal digitally.
Sr1 = 22050


# This line of code defines a variable named `T1` and assigns it the
value of 5.0. The variable `T1` represents the duration of an audio
signal or a segment of an audio signal in seconds. In this case, it
represents a duration of 5 seconds.
T1 = 5.0
```

```
# This line creates a 1D NumPy array `T1` that contains a sequence of
evenly spaced numbers from 0 to `T1` with a step size of `1/sr1` (the
time duration of one sample at the given sampling rate `sr1`). The number
of elements in the array is calculated using `int(T1*sr1)`, which rounds
down the total number of samples needed to represent a time period of
`T1` seconds at the given sampling rate `sr1`. `endpoint=False` is used
to exclude the end point `T1` from the sequence.
T1 = np.linspace(0, T, int(T1*sr1), endpoint=False)

# The line generates a sine wave with a frequency of 220 Hz and an
amplitude of 0.5, sampled at the time points defined in T1. The formula
used to generate the sine wave is A*sin(2*pi*f*t), where A is the
amplitude, f is the frequency, and t is time.
X1 = 0.5*np.sin(2*np.pi*220*T1)

# The ipd.Audio(x1, rate=sr1) command plays the audio signal x1 at the
sampling rate of sr1 using the IPython display module. This command
generates an audio player widget that can be used to play and control the
audio signal within the Jupyter Notebook environment.
ipd.Audio(x1, rate=sr1)

# This code writes the audio data x1 to a WAV file named 'tone_220.wav'
at the sampling rate sr1 using the write_wav function provided by the
librosa library.
librosa.output.write_wav('tone_220.wav', x1, sr1)
```

15.2.5.6 Spectral Centroid

It works similarly to a weighted mean in determining the gravitational center of the spectrum and the value of f_c is:

$$f_c = \sum_k S(k)f(k) / \sum_k S(k)$$

The $S(k)$ and $f(k)$ are spectral and frequency at k, respectively, and the module in librosa for extracting its value is:

```
librosa.feature.spectral_centroid
```

Consider the following example, which demonstrates how to calculate, plot, and display the spectral centroid value of a signal.

```
# This line of code loads the audio data from a WAV file named 'JCV.wav'
located in the '/content/sample_data' directory, using the librosa
library. The audio waveform is stored in the variable 'x', and the
sampling rate in Hz is stored in the variable 'sr'.
x, sr = librosa.load('/content/sample_data/JCV.wav')

# This line of code generates an audio player in the Jupyter Notebook
environment that allows the user to listen to the audio data stored in
the `x` variable at the specified `sr` (sampling rate). The audio data
may have been loaded from a file using `librosa.load()` function.
ipd.Audio(x, rate=sr)
```

```
# This code calculates the spectral centroid of the audio signal 'x'
using librosa library. The spectral centroid is a measure of the
"center of gravity" of the spectrum and represents the average
frequency of the signal weighted by its magnitude. The function
returns a numpy array of size (1, n) where n is the number of frames
in the signal, and the [0] index is used to extract the spectral
centroid vector.
spectral_centroids = librosa.feature.spectral_centroid(x, sr=sr)[0]

# The first line calculates the spectral centroids of the audio signal x
using librosa.feature.spectral_centroid() function and storing the result
in the spectral_centroids variable.
spectral_centroids.shape

# The second line retrieves the number of frames in the spectral_
centroids array and assigns them to the variable frames.
frames = range(len(spectral_centroids))

# The third line converts the frame indices to time values using librosa.
frames_to_time() function and assigns the result to the variable t. The
frames variable is passed as argument to frames_to_time() function to get
the time value for each frame.
t = librosa.frames_to_time(frames)

# This is a user-defined function that applies min-max normalization on
an input array along a specified axis. The normalization scales the
values of the input array to be within the range [0,1]. The `axis`
parameter specifies the axis along which the normalization is performed,
with the default value of `axis=0` indicating normalization along
columns. The function returns the normalized array.
def normalize(x, axis=0):
    return sklearn.preprocessing.minmax_scale(x, axis=axis)

# This code displays the waveform of the audio signal `x` with a
sampling rate of `sr` in the background, and then plots the spectral
centroid as a red line on top of it. The `librosa.display.waveplot()`
function generates the waveform plot, while the `normalize()` function
scales the spectral centroid values to a range of [0, 1] for better
visualization. The `t` variable is an array of time values corresponding
to each frame of the spectral centroid feature. The `alpha` parameter in
the `librosa.display.waveplot()` function specifies the opacity of the
waveform plot.
librosa.display.waveplot(x, sr=sr, alpha=0.3)
plt.plot(t, normalize(spectral_centroids), color='r')
```

Figure 15.8 presents the waveform of an audio signal, with the spectral centroid distinctly marked. This waveform progresses over time (horizontal axis) with amplitude variations (vertical axis). The spectral centroid, indicating the "center of mass" of the spectrum, provides insights into the sound's texture. A position towards the upper part of the graph denotes a brighter sound with more high-frequency content, while a position closer to the bottom suggests a deeper or muddier sound. This visual representation offers a glimpse into the audio's tonal qualities and how they evolve throughout its duration.

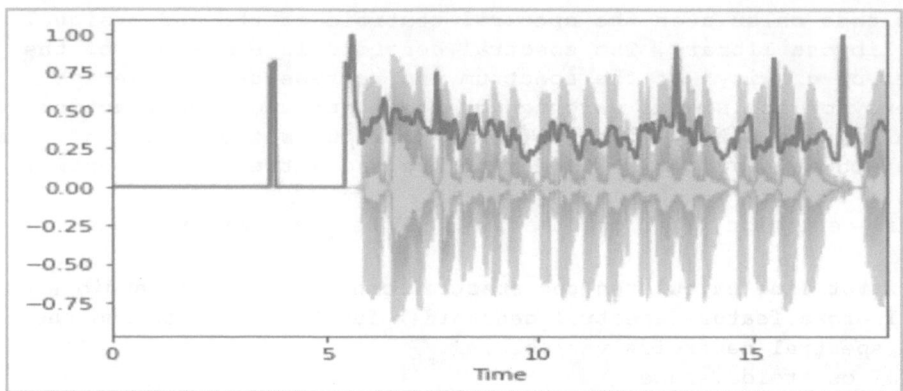

FIGURE 15.8
Spectral Centroid Visualization of the audio signal: Comparison of Two Signal Profiles.

15.2.5.7 Spectral Rolloff

The spectral rolloff is a measure of the frequency below which a specified percentage of the total spectral energy is contained. The spectral_rolloff module in Librosa can be used to calculate this value. Here's an example of how to use the spectral_rolloff module.

```
# `librosa.feature.spectral_rolloff` is a function in the librosa library
that computes the spectral rolloff frequency for each frame in an audio
signal. Spectral rolloff frequency is defined as the frequency below
which a given percentage of the total spectral energy lies. It is a
useful metric for analyzing the spectral shape of a signal, and can be
used to extract features for tasks such as music genre classification,
instrument recognition, and speech recognition.
librosa.feature.spectral_rolloff
```

Here's an example of how to use the spectral_rolloff module with audio data, and Figure 15.9 shows the resulting spectral rolloff plot. Figure 15.9 showcases a spectral rolloff plot, illustrating the threshold below which a specified percentage (typically around 85%) of the total spectral energy is contained. Positioned over time on the horizontal axis,

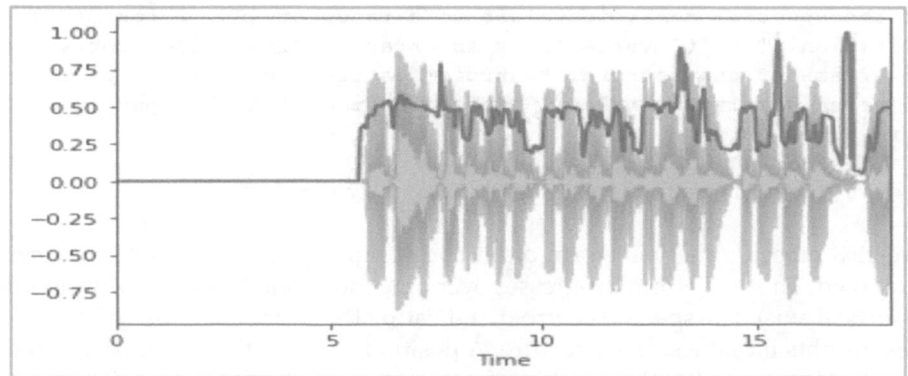

FIGURE 15.9
Spectral Rolloff Representation of an Audio Signal.

the curve (often represented as a line) on the plot provides a clear view of the frequency cutoff point for each time segment. Peaks in the rolloff can indicate the presence of harmonic content, while valleys may suggest more noise-like elements. By analyzing the spectral rolloff, one can gather essential insights into the sound's content and its changes throughout the audio's duration.

```
# `librosa.feature.spectral_rolloff` is a function that computes the
spectral rolloff frequency for each frame of an audio signal. The
spectral rolloff frequency is defined as the frequency below which a
specified percentage of the total spectral energy lies. The function
takes an audio signal as input and returns an array of size `(n_frames,)`
containing the spectral rolloff frequency for each frame. In the given
code, the spectral rolloff frequency is computed for the audio signal `x`
with a sampling rate of `sr`, and the results are stored in the variable
`spectral_rolloff`.
spectral_rolloff = librosa.feature.spectral_rolloff(x+0.01, sr=sr)[0]

# The code visualizes the spectral rolloff of an audio signal `x` using
`librosa`. The function `librosa.feature.spectral_rolloff` is used to
extract the spectral rolloff feature from the audio signal `x`. The
resulting feature is then normalized using the `normalize` function
defined earlier. Finally, the wave plot of the audio signal is displayed
along with the spectral rolloff feature plotted against time.
librosa.display.waveplot(x, sr=sr, alpha=0.5)
plt.plot(t, normalize(spectral_rolloff), color='r')
```

15.2.5.8 Spectral Bandwidth

It is spectral width at one-half the spectral maximum.

$$\left(\frac{\sum_k |S(k)|^p (f(k) - f_c)^p}{\sum_k |S(k)|^p} \right)^{1/p}$$

$S(k)$ is the magnitude, $f(k)$ is the frequency at k, and f_c is the center of spectral. Figure 15.10 shows the spectral bandwidth of an audio signal. Figure 15.10 presents the spectral

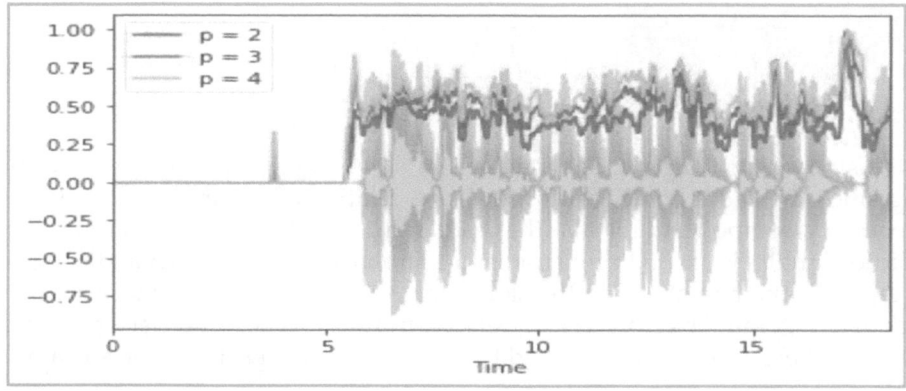

FIGURE 15.10
Spectral bandwidth (for three bandwidths) of an audio signal.

bandwidth for p = 2 is represented by the first curve, offering a general sense of the spectrum's spread. The second curve, representing p = 3, delves deeper into the signal's texture and frequency nuances. Meanwhile, the third curve for p = 4 offers an even finer granularity of the spectrum's details. Observing these curves in tandem provides insights into the complexity and distribution of the audio signal's frequency components.

```
# These lines of code compute three different values for spectral
bandwidth, using the `librosa.feature.spectral_bandwidth()` function. The
first line computes spectral bandwidth using the default `p=2` value,
where `p` is the exponent used in the formula. The second line computes
it with `p=3`, and the third line computes it with `p=4`. The `+0.02`
value added to `x` is a small offset used to avoid numerical errors when
computing the logarithm of small values. The resulting values are stored
in three different variables: `spectral_bandwidth_1`, `spectral_
bandwidth_2`, and `spectral_bandwidth_3`.
spectral_bandwidth_1 = librosa.feature.spectral_bandwidth(x+0.02, sr=sr)[0]
spectral_bandwidth_2 = librosa.feature.spectral_bandwidth(x+0.02, sr=sr,
p=3)[0]
spectral_bandwidth_3 = librosa.feature.spectral_bandwidth(x+0.02, sr=sr,
p=4)[0]
```

```
# This code computes the spectral bandwidth of an audio signal `x` using
different values of the exponent `p` and stores them in `spectral_
bandwidth_1`, `spectral_bandwidth_2`, and `spectral_bandwidth_3`. It then
plots the waveform of the audio signal and the three spectral bandwidths
over time, with the legend indicating the value of `p` for each
bandwidth. The `librosa.feature.spectral_bandwidth` function is used to
compute the spectral bandwidth, and the `normalize` function is used to
scale the values of the bandwidths to the range [0, 1].
librosa.display.waveplot(x, sr=sr, alpha=0.4)
plt.plot(t, normalize(spectral_bandwidth_1), color='r')
plt.plot(t, normalize(spectral_bandwidth_2), color='g')
plt.plot(t, normalize(spectral_bandwidth_3), color='y')
plt.legend(('p = 2', 'p = 3', 'p = 4'))
```

15.2.5.9 Zero-crossing Rate

It is the number of zero-crossing within the part of the signal.

$$z_{cr} = \frac{1}{T-1}\sum_{t=1}^{T-1}I\{s_t s_{t-1} < 0\}$$

S_t is the signal with length **t**. For instance, in this case, we take advantage of the zero crossing since the first period of stillness has a relatively low amplitude, which allows high-frequency components to take the lead. Figure 15.11 shows the zero-crossing rate of an audio signal. Figure 15.11 illustrates the zero-crossing rate of an audio signal. This metric captures the rate at which the signal transitions from positive to negative values and vice versa. A higher zero-crossing rate typically suggests a noisier or more percussive sound, whereas a lower rate might indicate a more harmonic or sustained tone.

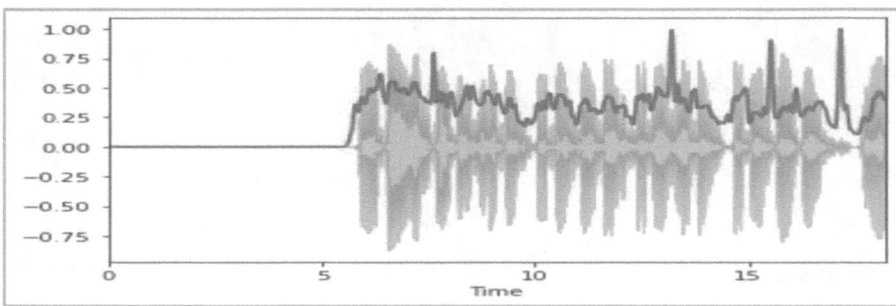

FIGURE 15.11
Zero-crossing rate of the audio signal.

The displayed plot provides insights into the signal's temporal characteristics and its potential timbral textures.

```
# This line of code computes the spectral centroid of an audio signal `x`
using the `librosa` library. Spectral centroid is a measure of the
distribution of spectral energy in the audio signal, and it represents
the center of mass of the spectrum. It is calculated as the weighted mean
of the frequencies present in the signal, where the weighting is the
magnitude of the spectrum at each frequency. The function `librosa.
feature.spectral_centroid` takes the audio signal `x` and the sampling
rate `sr` as input, and returns a matrix of shape `(n_features, n_frames)`
containing the spectral centroid values for each frame of the audio
signal. The `[0]` index is used to extract only the first row of the
matrix, which contains the spectral centroid values.
spectral_centroids = librosa.feature.spectral_centroid(x+0.01, sr=sr)[0]
```

```
# This code segment computes the spectral centroid of the audio signal
x with sampling rate sr and plots it on top of the waveform plot of x.
The spectral centroid is a measure of the "center of mass" of the
spectral content of an audio signal, and can provide information about
the perceived "brightness" or "darkness" of the sound. The librosa.
feature.spectral_centroid function is used to compute the spectral
centroid, and the resulting values are normalized and plotted as a red
line on top of the waveform plot using the normalize and plot
functions.
librosa.display.waveplot(x, sr=sr, alpha=0.4)
plt.plot(t, normalize(spectral_centroids), color='r')
```

15.2.5.10 Mel-frequency Cepstral Coefficients (MFCCs)

Extracting the MFCCs from audio data is a popular feature extraction technique. MFCCs are a set of characteristics that represent the general contour of the spectral envelope of the human voice. Figure 15.12 shows an example of the MFCCs of an audio signal. Figure 15.12 presents the Mel-Frequency Cepstral Coefficients (MFCCs) of an audio signal. The MFCCs are a representation of the short-term power spectrum of sound, emphasizing the characteristics of the human auditory system. In the plot, each coefficient captures distinct features of the audio's timbre and texture. Commonly used in audio analysis and speech

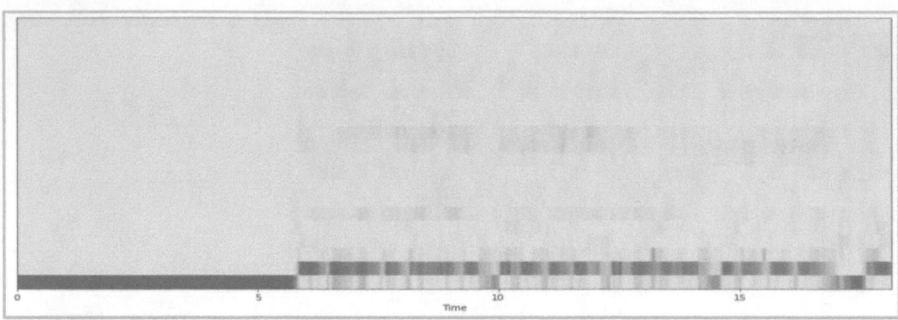

FIGURE 15.12
MFCCs of an audio signal.

recognition, the visualization in Figure 15.12 offers a deeper understanding of the signal's spectral nature across different mel-frequency bands.

```
# This will compute 20 Mel Frequency Cepstral Coefficients (MFCCs) for
the audio signal x sampled at sr Hz. The MFCCs are a widely used feature
representation for audio signals in tasks such as speech recognition
and music genre classification. They are obtained by first applying a
mel-scale filterbank to the audio signal to extract frequency bands, and
then computing the Discrete Cosine Transform (DCT) of the log-magnitude
spectrum of each band. The resulting coefficients capture the spectral
shape of the audio signal at different frequencies, similar to how the
human ear perceives sound.
mfccs = librosa.feature.mfcc(x, sr=sr, n_mfcc=20)
```

```
# The code generates a visualization of the Mel-Frequency Cepstral
Coefficients (MFCCs) of an audio signal using the librosa library. The
MFCCs are computed from the audio signal `x` with sampling rate `sr`
using the `librosa.feature.mfcc()` function. The resulting MFCCs are then
displayed as a spectrogram-like plot with time on the x-axis and
frequency on the y-axis using `librosa.display.specshow()`. The `figsize`
parameter of `plt.figure()` sets the size of the plot.
plt.figure(figsize=(15, 7))
librosa.display.specshow(mfccs, sr=sr, x_axis='time')
```

15.2.5.11 Chroma Feature

Figure 15.13 shows an example of a feature vector that represents the amount of energy contributed by each pitch to the overall signal. Figure 15.13 showcases the chroma feature of an audio signal. Chroma features are typically a representation of the energy distribution across the 12 different pitch classes and are derived from the 12 different semitone pitches of Western music. Within the visualization, one can observe the strength or activity of each pitch class over time. This feature is instrumental in recognizing harmonies, chords, and capturing the essence of musical content in the signal.

```
# The code calculates the chroma feature from the audio signal `x` using
the short-time Fourier transform (STFT) with a window length of 2048
samples, hop length of 12 samples, and the number of chroma bins equal
```

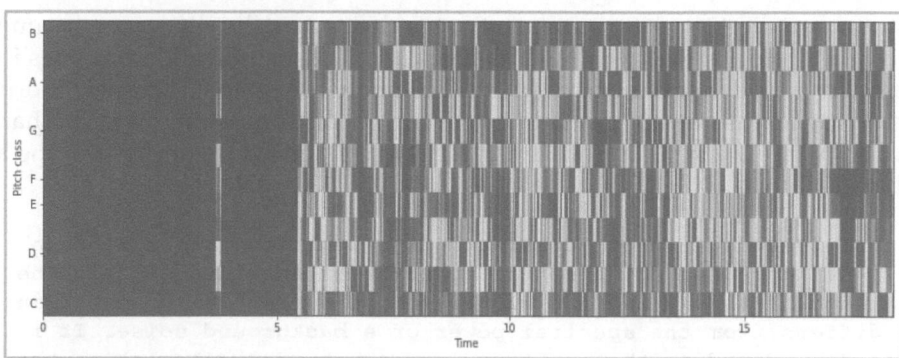

FIGURE 15.13
Chroma feature of an audio signal.

to 12. The resulting chroma feature represents the distribution of energy in each chromatic pitch class over time.

```
chromagram = librosa.feature.chroma_stft(x, sr=sr, hop_length=12)
```

```
# The code generates a chromagram of the audio signal `x` using the
`librosa.feature.chroma_stft` function. The resulting chromagram is
displayed using `librosa.display.specshow`, where the x-axis represents
time and the y-axis represents the chroma scale. The `hop_length`
parameter specifies the number of samples between successive frames in the
STFT calculation. The `cmap` parameter sets the color map to be used in
the display. The figure size is set using `plt.figure(figsize=(15, 4))`.
plt.figure(figsize=(15, 4))
librosa.display.specshow(chromagram, x_axis='time', y_axis='chroma',
hop_length=10, cmap='coolwarm')
```

15.2.5.12 Spectral Contrast

The spectral contrast is a feature that describes the spectral peaks and valleys, as well as the differences between them, in each frequency sub-band of an audio signal. The Librosa module for computing spectral contrast is called spectral_contrast, and Figure 15.14 shows an example of its audio data value format. Figure 15.14 displays the spectral

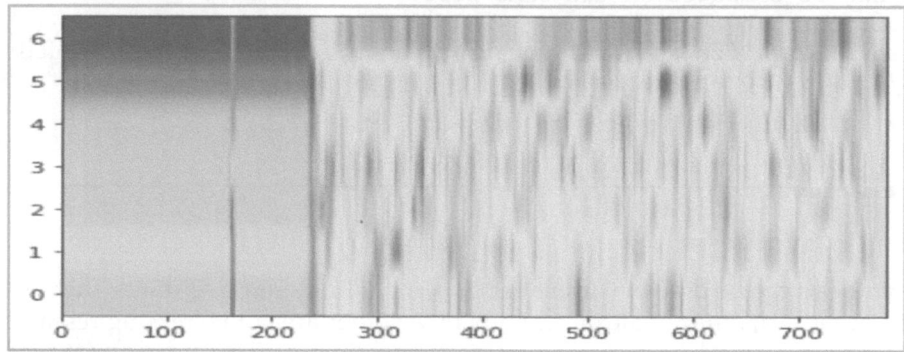

FIGURE 15.14
Spectral contrast of an audio signal.

contrast of an audio signal. Spectral contrast is defined as the difference in amplitude between peaks and valleys in the sound spectrum. The visualization provides insights into the relative loudness of distinct spectral components against their neighboring frequencies. This feature can be particularly useful in distinguishing between harmonic content and noise-like parts in the signal, offering a nuanced perspective of the audio's tonal characteristics.

```
# `librosa.feature.spectral_contrast` is a function in the librosa
library that computes the spectral contrast of an audio signal. The
spectral contrast is a measure of how much the spectral power of an audio
signal differs from the spectral power of a background noise. It is
calculated by dividing the spectrum into sub-bands, calculating the mean
of the power spectrum in each sub-band, and then calculating the
difference between the highest and lowest mean values.
librosa.feature.spectral_contrast

# This line of code calculates the spectral contrast of an audio signal
`x` using Librosa's `spectral_contrast()` function, and stores the
resulting feature matrix in the variable `spectral_contrast_value`. The
function computes the spectral contrast of the audio signal across
frequency bands, which represents how much the energy in one frequency
subband differs from the energy in other subbands. The resulting matrix
is a 2D array, where each column corresponds to a short-time window of
the audio signal and each row corresponds to a different spectral
contrast feature value.
spectral_contrast_value = librosa.feature.spectral_contrast(x, sr=sr)

# It seems like you are missing the variable name for `spectral_contrast_
value` in the code you provided. Assuming it is `spectral_contrast_
value`, this line of code displays a heatmap of the spectral contrast
values over time and frequency, with lower frequencies at the bottom and
higher frequencies at the top. The `aspect='auto'` argument sets the
aspect ratio of the plot to fit the data, and `origin='lower'` sets the
origin of the plot to the lower left corner. The `cmap='coolwarm'`
argument sets the color map of the plot to a blue-red gradient, with blue
representing lower values and red representing higher values. The
`normalize()` function scales the values of `spectral_contrast_value`
between 0 and 1 along the frequency axis, so that different frequency
ranges can be compared on the same plot.
spectral_contrast.shape
plt.imshow(normalize(spectral_contrast_value, axis=1), aspect='auto',
origin='lower', cmap='coolwarm')
```

15.3 Audio Synthesis

Audio synthesis can be used in various settings, including smart assistants, such as Google assistant, apple siri, amazon alexa, and others. Another area of increasing research interest is the use of such technologies in music production. In fact, the use of AI for music production is becoming more popular, and a variety of competing solutions and research are being conducted in this area. Researchers on Google's mgenta3 project are pushing the

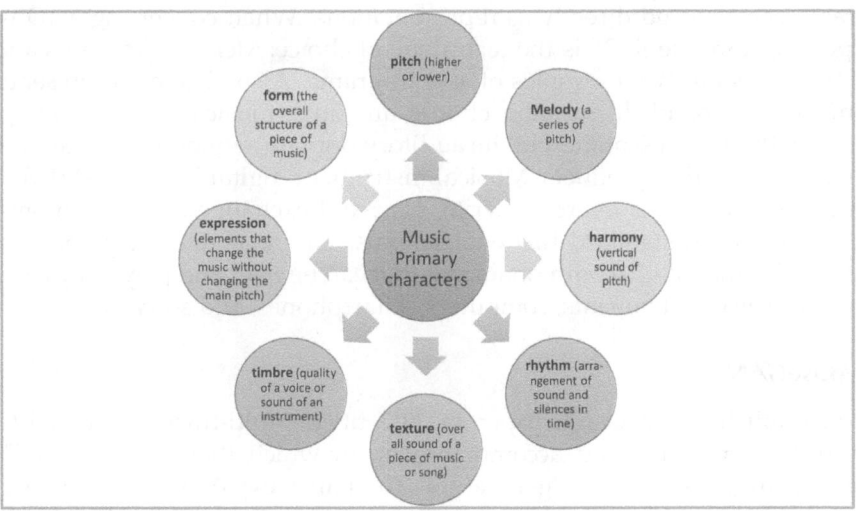

FIGURE 15.15
Several musical aspects as some of the primary characteristics.

boundaries of music production to unprecedented heights. They are accomplishing this by experimenting with various technologies, tools, and research initiatives that will allow anyone with little to no prior knowledge of such complex issues to independently compose stunning pieces of music. This section will explore music, voice, and song synthesis using GAN and some of today's most popular methodologies.

15.3.1 Music Synthesis

Music is the process of organizing sound to create different combinations, such as harmony and rhythm. Various machines are used to generate different types of music, depending on their shape and function. Figure 15.15 visualizes the spectral contrast of an audio signal, highlighting several types of musical characteristics. Within the displayed spectrum, one can identify elements such as forms, pitch, and other listed attributes. By observing this representation, viewers can understand the diverse components and nuances inherent in the musical piece.

Furthermore, different cultures have different music, and we can see the evolution of music in human existence over time. Despite this, music generation remains a fascinating research field with many unanswered questions and exciting works to investigate. There are numerous methods for creating music. Several approaches construct their methodology using machine learning and artificial neural network techniques, and GAN is one of the most recent methods used in this industry. The next section will explore the use of GAN and MuseGAN for music synthesis, which are among the most recent methods used in this industry.

15.3.1.1 Music Representation

The notation and conventions used to write music scores are distinctive. The two primary categories that can be used to classify various types of musical representation are continuous and discrete. Continuous musical representation works with waveforms to represent musical data. In the audio domain, one-dimensional waveforms or two-dimensional spectrograms can be used directly as representations. When converting a 1D waveform to a 2D spectrogram, the STFT is the technique of choice. Mel-spectrograms and magnitude spectrograms are two examples of spectrograms. Also, discrete representation can capture information on pitch, duration, chords, and other musical elements. Despite being less expressive than representation in the auditory domain, symbolic expression is widely used in music-generating products. Musical instrument digital interface (MIDI) is a standard that allows musicians to create, write, play, and exchange music with one another. MIDI is a widely used standard that enables musicians to create, write, play, and share music with each other. It is a common format that can be read and played by a wide range of electronic musical instruments, computers, smartphones, and software.

15.3.1.2 MuseGAN

Dong et al. published a research paper in 2017 titled Multi-track sequential GANs for symbolic music generation and accompaniment, in which they proposed a GAN-type framework for multi-track music generation. The paper explores various musical topics in-depth and provides an outline of Dong and his team's approach to addressing them. The MuseGAN approach seeks to address three primary aspects of music, which are as follows:

1. the multi-track interdependency, which refers to how all of the instruments work together to create an acceptable sound for the listener;
2. the melodic; and
3. the harmonic content of the music.

MuseGAN works within a framework that utilizes three distinct methods to address these three ideas:

- jamming,
- hybrid, and
- composer.

MuseGAN's authors believe a bar is the basic compositional unit, not notes. Figure 15.16 shows their presented structure. Bar 1–4 that create phrase 2 is an example that presented in Figure 15.6. Let's go over these techniques in more details.

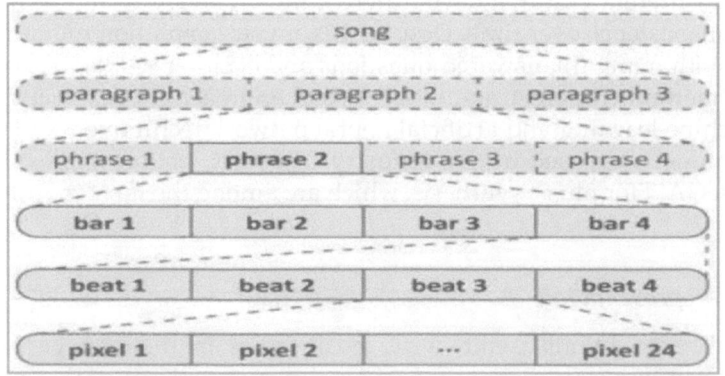

FIGURE 15.16
A bar as the basic compositional unit.

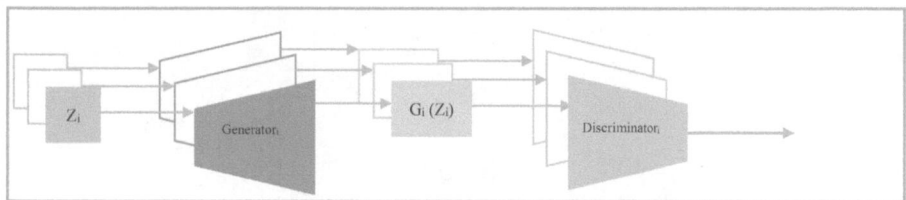

FIGURE 15.17

The jamming model generates multi-track outputs and is made up of **i** generator and discriminator pairs.

15.3.1.3 Jamming

There are **i** generators for the first approach; each has its own discriminator to train the overall GAN and generate the combination of all instruments. The jamming setup, as shown in Figure 15.17, simulates a group of musicians improvising together to create music without any predetermined arrangement or structure. Figure 15.17 presents the structure of the jamming model, a subsequent evolution in music generation following MusGAN. The model is uniquely designed to produce multi-track outputs, underlining its complexity and advancement. It employs multiple generator-discriminator pairs, with each pair working cohesively. The generators are responsible for creating distinct musical elements, while the discriminators evaluate the authenticity of these outputs. This schematic suggests an enhanced capability for producing diverse and layered musical compositions, pushing the boundaries of automated music generation.

15.3.1.4 Composer

In this case, the generator is a human composer who is in charge of creating a large number of instrument tracks. As shown in Figure 15.18, the configuration includes a single discriminator for identifying genuine or fabricated samples. Unlike the jamming model that required **M** random vectors, this model only requires one random vector (indicated by the letter **Z**) and a single discriminator for identifying genuine or fabricated samples, as shown in Figure 15.18. Figure 15.18 showcases the model of a composer, a progressive development post the jamming model. This model streamlines its design, leveraging a single yet powerful generator capable of producing up to M tracks simultaneously. Accompanying this generator is a singular discriminator whose task is to discern between genuine and fabricated music samples. The compact architecture of this model emphasizes efficiency and specialization, offering a simplified yet effective approach to music composition in the realm of automated music generation.

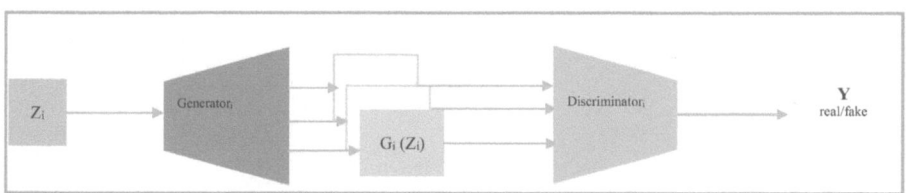

FIGURE 15.18

Model of a composer made of a single generator that can produce **M** tracks and a single discriminator that can tell the difference between fake and real samples.

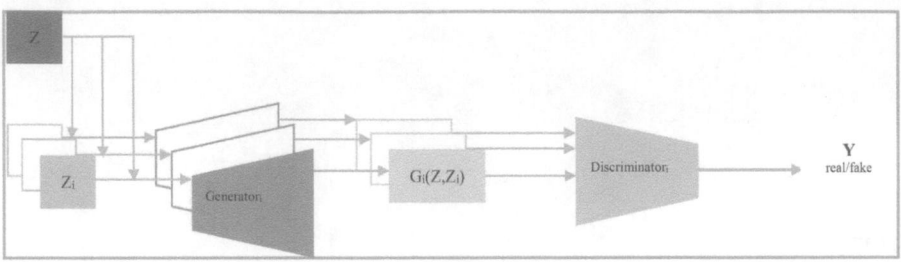

FIGURE 15.19
A hybrid model consists of **i** generators and just one discriminator. Each generator requires two inputs in the form of random vectors: one for the inter-track and one for the intra-track.

15.3.1.5 *Hybrid*

The hybrid model, which is a combination of the jamming and composer models, uses intra-track and inter-track random vectors to simulate composer inputs. It takes two types of random vectors as inputs and has **M** generators and a single discriminator that can determine whether the output is fake or not. The image demonstrates that the hybrid model, with **i** generators, requires only one discriminator to accurately determine whether a sample is authentic. Since there are **i** different generators, the configuration allows for the use of different architectures for the various tracks. Figure 15.19 presents a hybrid music generation model that integrates **i** generators and a singular discriminator. Unique to this design, each generator necessitates two distinct random vector inputs. The first is for the inter-track, governing the relationships between different tracks, while the second concerns the intra-track, shaping the internal structure and nuances of individual tracks. This dual-input mechanism accentuates the model's capacity to simultaneously fine-tune both global and local musical dynamics, ensuring a more holistic and intricate audio output.

15.3.1.6 *Temporal*

Another model that MuseGAN can generate is the temporal model, which preserves the coherence between two bars generated successively by other models. It treats the progression of the bars as an additional dimension and generates a fixed-length phrase. Figure 15.20 illustrates the temporal model used in music generation, which is

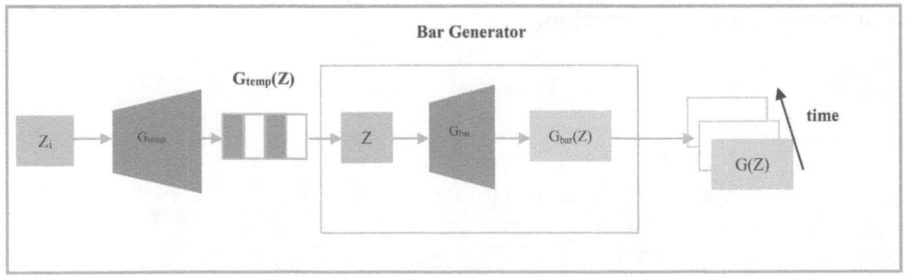

FIGURE 15.20
The temporal model and its two subcomponents are the generator of the temporal structure (G_{temp}) and the bar generator (G_{bar}).

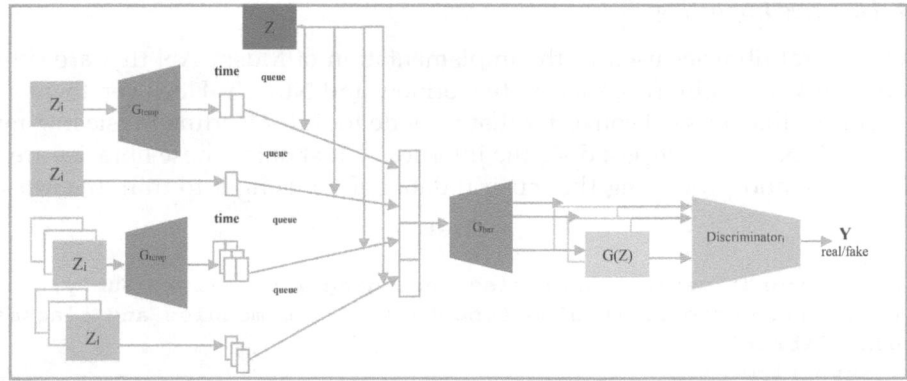

FIGURE 15.21
Simplified MuseGAN design with **i** generators, one discriminator, and two temporal stages for phrase coherent output.

compartmentalized into two main subcomponents. The first, G_{temp}, is responsible for crafting the temporal structure, ensuring the flow and progression of the musical piece align with desired temporal dynamics. The second, G_{bar}, zeroes in on generating individual bars, meticulously shaping the shorter segments that collectively form the broader rhythmic structure. Together, these components collaborate to produce music with both coherent long-term structure and detailed bar-by-bar intricacy.

15.3.1.7 MuseGAN

MuseGAN's setup employs a two-step temporal model technique, as discussed in the previous section, to ensure proper organization within the timeline. Some tracks in the configuration use a temporal model, while others use direct random vectors. Concatenation, or summing, is performed on the temporal model outputs and direct inputs before passing them on to the bar generator model. Figure 15.21 showcases the streamlined architecture of MuseGAN, a pivotal model in music generation. Within this structure, there are **i** distinct generators, each tasked with crafting specific musical components or features. In tandem with these, a singular discriminator evaluates the authenticity of the generated music, discerning between genuine and fabricated outputs. Integral to this design are two temporal stages, meticulously devised to ensure phrase coherence. These stages ensure that the output not only has individual musical merit but also maintains consistency and fluidity throughout, resulting in a harmonious and cohesive musical composition.

This step comes immediately before the bar generator model. The bar generator then composes music one bar at a time, which is then evaluated by either a critic or a discriminator model. In the following section, we will discuss the implementation details for both the generator model and the critic model.

15.3.2 MuseGAN Implementation

In this section, we will discuss the implementation of the architecture and prepare a reduced set of generators for a 4-track MuseGAN. Then, we will train MuseGAN using the Boulanger-JSB Lewandowsk's Chorales dataset.

15.3.2.1 Libraries Importing

There are several libraries used in the implementation of MuseGAN that are similar to other commonly used libraries, such as TensorFlow and NumPy. However, there are also unique libraries like music21.converter that provide tools for loading music into music21 from different sources, such as a disk, the internet, or text data. These libraries are essential in handling and processing the musical data before using it to train the MuseGAN model.

```
# The code imports several libraries including TensorFlow, NumPy,
Matplotlib, and music21. It also imports specific modules and classes
from these libraries.
import tensorflow as tf
from tensorflow.keras.initializers import RandomNormal
tf.compat.v1.disable_eager_execution()
import os
import matplotlib.pyplot as plt
import numpy as np
from music21 import converter
import matplotlib.pyplot as plt
from tensorflow.keras.layers import Input, Flatten, Dense
from tensorflow.keras.layers import Conv2Dtranspose, Reshape, Lambda
from tensorflow.keras.layers import BatchNormalization, LeakyReLU
from tensorflow.keras.layers import Concatenate, Conv3D
from tensorflow.keras.layers import Layer, Activation
from tensorflow.keras.models import Model
from tensorflow.keras import backend as K
from tensorflow.keras.optimizers import Adam
from functools import partial
from music21 import note, stream, duration, tempo
```

15.3.2.2 Hyperparameters Setup

The next step is to assign initial values to the hyperparameters, such as batch size and epochs, to begin with.

```
# Weight_init is an instance of the RandomNormal class from tensorflow.
keras.initializers, which will be used as the weight initializer for the
network weights.
Weight_init = RandomNormal(mean=0., stddev=0.02)

# batch_size is an integer specifying the number of samples in each
training batch.
batch_size = 128

#n_bars is an integer specifying the number of bars in each generated
music sequence.
n_bars = 2

#n_steps_per_bar is an integer specifying the number of time steps per
bar in each generated music sequence.
n_steps_per_bar = 32
```

```
#n_pitches is an integer specifying the number of different pitches that
can be used in the music sequence.
n_pitches = 84

#n_tracks is an integer specifying the number of tracks in the generated
music sequence.
n_tracks = 4

#grad_weight is a float specifying the weight applied to the gradient
penalty term in the WGAN-GP loss function.
grad_weight = 10

#z_dim is an integer specifying the dimensionality of the random noise
input vector.
z_dim = 32

#epochs is an integer specifying the number of training epochs.
epochs = 1000

#sampling_frequency is an integer specifying how often to generate a
sample from the generator network during training.
sampling_frequency = 10

#n_critic is an integer specifying the number of times to update the critic
network per generator network update in the WGAN-GP training procedure.
n_critic = 5

#use_gen is a boolean indicating whether to use the generator network
during training (as opposed to only training the critic network).
use_gen = False
```

15.3.2.3 Data Processing

You can perform some data processing to prepare the data for the next step. The data can be imported in any format and then normalized or altered, which can help to improve performance.

```
# This code initializes a variable data_path with a string value
representing the file path to the JSB-Chorales dataset in npz format.
The load_music function is then called with data_path, n_bars, and
n_steps_per_bar as arguments to load and encode the music data into a
multi-dimensional numpy array called encoded_scores. np.squeeze is then
used to remove any dimensions with size 1 from encoded_scores. Finally,
the shape of encoded_scores is assigned to input_dim, which represents
the dimensions of each input sample in the dataset.
data_path = "JSB-Chorales-dataset/Jsb16thSeparated.npz"
encoded_scores = load_music(data_path, n_bars, n_steps_per_bar)
encoded_scores = np.squeeze(encoded_scores)
input_dim = encoded_scores.shape[1:]
```

15.3.2.4 Build and Train Critic Model

The critic model is much easier to understand than the generator model. It is a convolutional WGAN-GP model that takes both the output of the bar generator and real samples to determine whether the generator output is fake or not. This is a function that builds a critic model for the WGAN architecture used for music generation. It takes the input dimensions (input_dim), weight initialization method (weight_init), and number of bars (n_bars) as input. It first defines an input layer (critic_input) with the input dimensions. Then it applies a series of convolutional layers with different parameters and number of filters. After flattening the output of the last convolutional layer, it applies a dense layer with 512 units and a leaky ReLU activation function. Finally, it outputs the critic score with a dense layer with a single output and no activation function. The function returns the critic model.

```
def build_critic(input_dim, weight_init, n_bars):
    critic_input = Input(shape=input_dim, name='critic_input')
    x = critic_input
    x = conv_3d(x,num_filters=128,kernel_size=(2, 1, 1),stride=(1, 1,
1),padding='valid',weight_init=weight_init)
    x = conv_3d(x,num_filters=64,kernel_size=(n_bars - 1, 1,
1),stride=(1, 1, 1),padding='valid',weight_init=weight_init)
    x = conv_3d(x,num_filters=64,kernel_size=(1, 1, 12),stride=(1, 1,
12),padding='same',weight_init=weight_init)
    x = conv_3d(x,num_filters=64,kernel_size=(1, 1, 7),stride=(1, 1,
7),padding='same',weight_init=weight_init)
    x = conv_3d(x,num_filters=64,kernel_size=(1, 2, 1),stride=(1, 2,
1),padding='same',weight_init=weight_init)
    x = conv_3d(x,num_filters=64,kernel_size=(1, 2, 1),stride=(1, 2,
1),padding='same',weight_init=weight_init)
    x = conv_3d(x,num_filters=128,kernel_size=(1, 4, 1),stride=(1, 2,
1),padding='same',weight_init=weight_init)
    x = conv_3d(x,num_filters=256,kernel_size=(1, 3, 1),stride=(1, 2,
1),padding='same',weight_init=weight_init)
    x = Flatten()(x)
    x = Dense(512, kernel_initializer=weight_init)(x)
    x = LeakyReLU()(x)
    critic_output = Dense(1,activation=None,kernel_initializer=weight_
init)(x)
    critic = Model(critic_input, critic_output)
    return critic
```

This model also needs to be trained, and you can define the training module for critic training. This is a function to train a critic model in a Wasserstein GAN. The function takes as input the training data (x_train), the critic model (critic_model), the latent space dimension (z_dim), batch size (batch_size), the number of tracks (n_tracks), and a boolean indicating whether or not to use a generator (use_gen). Inside the function, the valid and fake labels for the loss function are defined as arrays of ones and negative ones, respectively. The function then generates random noise for each track in the batch using numpy's random.normal function. The true images are randomly selected from the training data if not using a generator; otherwise, they are taken from the generator's output. Finally, the function trains the critic model on the batch of true and fake images along with the generated noise for each track, and returns the critic's loss on this batch.

```
def train_critic(x_train,critic_model,z_dim,batch_size,n_tracks,use_gen):
    valid = np.ones((batch_size, 1), dtype=np.float32)
    fake = -np.ones((batch_size, 1), dtype=np.float32)
```

```
        dummy = np.zeros((batch_size, 1), dtype=np.float32)
        if use_gen:
            true_imgs = next(x_train)[0]
            if true_imgs.shape[0] != batch_size:
                true_imgs = next(x_train)[0]
        else:
            idx = np.random.randint(0, x_train.shape[0], batch_size)
            true_imgs = x_train[idx]
        track1_noise = np.random.normal(0, 1, (batch_size, z_dim))
        track2_noise = np.random.normal(0, 1, (batch_size, z_dim))
        track3_noise = np.random.normal(0, 1, (batch_size, n_tracks, z_dim))
        track4_noise = np.random.normal(0, 1, (batch_size, n_tracks, z_dim))
        d_loss = critic_model.train_on_batch([true_imgs,track1_noise,track2_
noise,track3_noise,track4_noise], [valid, fake, dummy])
        return d_loss
```

15.3.2.5 Temporal Model

As discussed earlier in this chapter, the generator configuration depends on whether we use the jamming, composer, or hybrid technique. To simplify things, we will focus on the hybrid configuration, which has multiple generators, one for each track. One set of generators is dedicated to creating tracks that require temporal coherence, such as a melody that is a long sequence and requires coherence between bars. For these types of tracks, we use a temporal architecture similar to the one described below.

```
# Define a function called build_temporal_network with input parameters
z_dim, n_bars, and weight_init.
def build_temporal_network(z_dim, n_bars, weight_init):

#Create an input layer with shape (z_dim,) and name 'temporal_input'.
    input_layer = Input(shape=(z_dim,), name='temporal_input')

#Reshape the input layer to have shape [1, 1, z_dim] and store the result
in x.
    x = Reshape([1, 1, z_dim])(input_layer)

#Add a 2D transposed convolutional layer with 512 filters, kernel size
(2, 1), valid padding, stride (1, 1), and weight initializer weight_init
to x.
    x = Conv2DTranspose(filters=512, kernel_size=(2, 1), padding='valid',
strides=(1, 1), kernel_initializer=weight_init)(x)

#Add batch normalization with momentum 0.9 to x.
    x = BatchNormalization(momentum=0.9)(x)
#Add a ReLU activation layer to x.
    x = Activation('relu')(x)

#Add another 2D transposed convolutional layer with z_dim filters, kernel
size (n_bars - 1, 1), valid padding, stride (1, 1), and weight
initializer weight_init to x.
    x = Conv2DTranspose(filters=z_dim, kernel_size=(n_bars - 1, 1),
padding='valid', strides=(1, 1), kernel_initializer=weight_init)(x)
```

```
#Add batch normalization with momentum 0.9 to x.
    x = BatchNormalization(momentum=0.9)(x)

#Add another ReLU activation layer to x.
    x = Activation('relu')(x)

#Reshape x to have shape [n_bars, z_dim] and store the result in
output_layer.
    output_layer = Reshape([n_bars, z_dim])(x)

# Create a Keras model with input_layer as input and output_layer as
output, and return it.
    return Model(input_layer, output_layer)
```

15.3.2.6 Bar Generator Model

As shown, the temporal model reformats the random vector to the desired dimensions before passing it through transposed convolutional layers to expand the output vector to the length of the bars set. For tracks where inter-bar coherence is not necessary, we use the random vector **z** directly in its current form. The first step in generating a larger coordinated vector is to concatenate the outputs of the temporal generator and the direct random vectors. This vector is then used as input to the bar generator, known as G_{bar}. This function defines a generator model that takes a four-dimensional latent vector as input and outputs a bar of music.

- **"z_dim"**: the dimensionality of the input latent vector
- **"n_steps_per_bar"**: the number of time steps (or subdivisions) per bar of music
- **"n_pitches"**: the number of distinct pitch values in the musical vocabulary
- **"weight_init"**: an initializer for the model weights

The function begins by defining an input layer that expects an input tensor of shape (z_dim * 4,), which corresponds to a concatenated latent vector for each of the four tracks in the musical composition. The input tensor is then fed through a dense layer with 1024 units, followed by batch normalization and a ReLU activation. The resulting tensor is then reshaped to (2, 1, 512) and passed through a 2D transposed convolutional layer with 512 filters, a kernel size of (2, 1), and a stride of (2, 1). This is followed by batch normalization and a ReLU activation. The tensor is then passed through two more 2D transposed convolutional layers with 256 filters, kernel size (2, 1), and stride (2, 1), each followed by batch normalization and a ReLU activation. The tensor is then passed through another 2D transposed convolutional layer with 256 filters, kernel size (1, 7), and stride (1, 7), followed by batch normalization and a ReLU activation. Finally, the tensor is passed through a 2D transposed convolutional layer with 1 filter, kernel size (1, 12), and stride (1, 12). The output of this layer is then passed through a hyperbolic tangent activation function, which produces a tensor of shape (1, n_steps_per_bar, n_pitches, 1). The model is then instantiated and returned.

```
Def build_bar_generator(z_dim, n_steps_per_bar, n_pitches, weight_init):
    input_layer = Input(shape=(z_dim * 4,), name='bar_generator_input')
    x = Dense(1024)(input_layer)
    x = BatchNormalization(momentum=0.9)(x)
```

```
    x = Activation('relu')(x)
    x = Reshape([2, 1, 512])(x)
    x = Conv2Dtranspose(filters=512,kernel_size=(2,
1),padding='same',strides=(2, 1),kernel_initializer=weight_init)(x)
    x = BatchNormalization(momentum=0.9)(x)
    x = Activation('relu')(x)
    x = Conv2Dtranspose(filters=256,kernel_size=(2, 1),padding='same',
strides=(2, 1),kernel_initializer=weight_init)(x)
    x = BatchNormalization(momentum=0.9)(x)
    x = Activation('relu')(x)
    x = Conv2Dtranspose(filters=256,kernel_size=(2, 1),padding='same',
strides=(2, 1),kernel_initializer=weight_init)(x)
    x = BatchNormalization(momentum=0.9)(x)
    x = Activation('relu')(x)
    x = Conv2Dtranspose(filters=256,kernel_size=(1, 7),padding='same',
strides=(1, 7),kernel_initializer=weight_init)(x)
    x = BatchNormalization(momentum=0.9)(x)
    x = Activation('relu')(x)
    x = Conv2Dtranspose(filters=1,kernel_size=(1, 12),padding='same',
strides=(1, 12),kernel_initializer=weight_init)(x)
    x = Activation('tanh')(x)
    output_layer = Reshape([1, n_steps_per_bar, n_pitches, 1])(x)
    return Model(input_layer, output_layer)
```

15.3.2.7 Generator

This function builds a generator model for the MCTGAN architecture. The generator takes as input four tensors of different shapes, which represent the latent noise vectors for each of the four tracks in the generated music. The function takes in several parameters, including the latent noise vector dimension (z_dim), the number of tracks in the generated music (n_tracks), the number of bars in each track (n_bars), the number of steps per bar (n_steps_per_bar), the number of pitches (n_pitches), and the weight initialization function (weight_init). The function first defines four input layers for each of the four tracks. It then builds a temporal network for track 1 using the build_temporal_network() function. The track 1 over time tensor is generated by passing the track 1 input tensor through the track 1 temporal network. For tracks 2, 3, and 4, a temporal network is also built, and the corresponding over time tensors are generated by passing their respective input tensors through the appropriate temporal networks. Next, a bar generator is built for each of the tracks using the build_bar_generator() function. For each bar in the music, the function concatenates the track over time tensors with the noise vectors for each of the tracks, and passes the resulting tensor through the appropriate bar generator. The output tensors from each bar generator are concatenated along the pitch axis to form the output tensor for the entire music sequence. Finally, the function constructs and returns a Model object that takes in the four input tensors and outputs the generated music sequence tensor.

```
def build_generator(z_dim,n_tracks,n_bars,n_steps_per_bar,n_pitches,
weight_init):
    track1_input = Input(shape=(z_dim,), name='track1_input')
    track2_input = Input(shape=(z_dim,), name='track2_input')
    track3_input = Input(shape=(n_tracks, z_dim), name='track3_input')
    track4_input = Input(shape=(n_tracks, z_dim), name='track4_input')
```

```
    # track1 temporal network
    track1_temp_network = build_temporal_network(z_dim, n_bars,
weight_init)
    track1_over_time = track1_temp_network(track1_input)
    # track3 temporal network
    track3_over_time = [None] * n_tracks
    track3_temp_network = [None] * n_tracks
    for track in range(n_tracks):
        track3_temp_network[track] = build_temporal_network(z_dim,
n_bars,weight_init)
        melody_track = Lambda(lambda x: x[:, track, :])(track3_input)
        track3_over_time[track] = track3_temp_network[track]
(melody_track)
    # bar generator for each track
    bar_gen = [None] * n_tracks
    for track in range(n_tracks):
        bar_gen[track] = build_bar_generator(z_dim,n_steps_per_bar,
n_pitches,weight_init)
    # output for each track-bar
    bars_output = [None] * n_bars
    for bar in range(n_bars):
        track_output = [None] * n_tracks
        t1 = Lambda(lambda x: x[:, bar, ],name='track1_input_bar_' +
str(bar))(track1_over_time)
        t2 = track2_input
        for track in range(n_tracks):
            t3 = Lambda(lambda x: x[:, bar, :])(track3_over_time[track])
            t4 = Lambda(lambda x: x[:, track, :])(track4_input)
            z_input = Concatenate(axis=1,name='total_input_bar_{}_track_
{}'.format(bar, track))([t1, t2, t3, t4])
            track_output[track] = bar_gen[track](z_input)
        bars_output[bar] = Concatenate(axis=-1)(track_output)
    generator_output = Concatenate(axis=1, name='concat_bars')(bars_output)
    generator = Model([track1_input, track2_input, track3_input,
track4_input],generator_output)
    return generator
```

15.3.2.8 Build GAN

This function builds a GAN model by taking in the following arguments:

- **"generator"**: a Keras model that generates a musical piece from a set of random noise vectors and control parameters
- **"critic"**: a Keras model that evaluates the quality of a musical piece generated by the generator
- **"input_dim"**: a tuple that represents the shape of the input to the critic
- **"z_dim"**: an integer representing the dimension of the noise vectors
- **"n_tracks"**: an integer representing the number of tracks in the musical piece
- **"batch_size"**: an integer representing the batch size
- **"grad_weight"**: a float representing the weight of the gradient penalty in the critic loss function

The function starts by setting the generator layers to be non-trainable, and then it defines the input for the real and fake images. It creates a weighted average between the real and fake images and computes the validity of the real and fake images and the validity of the interpolated images. It defines the critic model that takes in the real and fake images and the interpolated images, and outputs the validity of each. The critic model is compiled with three loss functions: the Wasserstein loss for the validity of the real images, the Wasserstein loss for the validity of the fake images, and the gradient penalty loss for the validity of the interpolated images. The critic and generator layers are then swapped, and the GAN model is defined by taking in the input noise vectors and outputting the validity of the generated musical piece. The GAN model is compiled with the Wasserstein loss function. Finally, the critic layers are set to be trainable again, and the critic model and GAN model are returned.

```
def build_gan(generator,critic,input_dim,z_dim,n_tracks,batch_size,
grad_weight):
    # Generator layers for critic training
    set_trainable(generator, False)
    # Image input (real sample)
    real_img = Input(shape=input_dim)
    # Fake image
    track1_input = Input(shape=(z_dim,), name='track1_input')
    track2_input = Input(shape=(z_dim,), name='track2_input')
    track3_input = Input(shape=(n_tracks, z_dim), name='track3_input')
    track4_input = Input(shape=(n_tracks, z_dim), name='track4_input')
    fake_img = generator([track1_input,track2_input,track3_input,
track4_input])
    # Critic determines the validity of the real and fake images
    fake = critic(fake_img)
    valid = critic(real_img)
    # Construct a weighted average between the real and fake images
    interpolated_img = RandomWeightedAverage(batch_size)([real_img,
fake_img])
    validity_interpolated = critic(interpolated_img)
    partial_gp_loss = partial(gradient_penalty_loss,interpolated_samples=
interpolated_img)
    partial_gp_loss.__name__ = 'gradient_penalty'
    critic_model = Model(inputs=[real_img,track1_input,track2_input,track3_
input,track4_input],outputs=[valid,fake,validity_interpolated])
    critic_model.compile(loss=[wasserstein,wasserstein,partial_gp_
loss],optimizer=Adam(lr=0.001, beta_1=0.5, beta_2=0.9), loss_weights=[1, 1,
grad_weight)
    # Critic layers for generator training
    set_trainable(critic, False)
    set_trainable(generator, True)
    # Sampled noise for the input to generator
    track1_input = Input(shape=(z_dim,), name='track1_input')
    track2_input = Input(shape=(z_dim,), name='track2_input')
    track3_input = Input(shape=(n_tracks, z_dim), name='track3_input')
    track4_input = Input(shape=(n_tracks, z_dim), name='track4_input')
    # Generate the images based of noise
    img = generator([track1_input, track2_input, track3_input,
track4_input])
    model_output = critic(img)
```

```
    # Define the gan
    gan = Model([track1_input,track2_input,track3_input,track4_input],
model_output)
    gan.compile(optimizer=Adam(lr=0.001, beta_1=0.5,
beta_2=0.9),loss=wasserstein)
    # Reset the critic layers
    set_trainable(critic, True)
    return critic_model, gan
```

15.3.2.9 Train Generator

The "train_generator" function takes the GAN model, noise dimension, number of tracks, and batch size as input. It generates noise vectors for each track and trains the generator part of the GAN to produce valid outputs for this noise. It returns the loss of the GAN on this batch. The "argmax_output" function takes the output of the generator and finds the index of the maximum value in the last dimension (which represents the pitch). It returns a numpy array of the same shape but with the pitch values replaced with their respective indices. The "notes_to_midi" function takes the number of bars, steps per bar, number of tracks, epoch number, output folder, and output tensor from the generator. For each score in the output, it finds the pitch indices using "argmax_output" and converts them to a midi file. It uses the "music21" library to create a score for each track, where each note has a duration of 0.25 and a pitch determined by the pitch index. It then writes the score as a midi file to the output folder with a filename based on the epoch number and score number.

```
def train_generator(gan_model, z_dim, n_tracks, batch_size):
    valid = np.ones((batch_size, 1), dtype=np.float32)
    track1_noise = np.random.normal(0, 1, (batch_size, z_dim))
    track2_noise = np.random.normal(0, 1, (batch_size, z_dim))
    track3_noise = np.random.normal(0, 1, (batch_size, n_tracks, z_dim))
    track4_noise = np.random.normal(0, 1, (batch_size, n_tracks, z_dim))
    return gan_model.train_on_batch([track1_noise,track2_noise,track3_
noise,track4_noise], valid)
def argmax_output(output):
    max_pitches = np.argmax(output, axis=3)
    return max_pitches
def notes_to_midi(n_bars,n_steps_per_bar,n_tracks,epoch,output_folder,
output):
    for score_num in range(len(output)):
        max_pitches = argmax_output(output)
        midi_note_score = max_pitches[score_num].reshape([n_bars
*n_steps_per_bar,n_tracks])
        parts = stream.Score()
        parts.append(tempo.MetronomeMark(number=66))
        for I in range(n_tracks):
            last_x = int(midi_note_score[:, i][0])
            s = stream.Part()
            dur = 0
            for idx, x in enumerate(midi_note_score[:, i]):
                x = int(x)
                if (x != last_x or idx % 4 == 0) and idx > 0:
                    n = note.Note(last_x)
                    n.duration = duration.Duration(dur)
```

```
                s.append(n)
                dur = 0
            last_x = x
            dur = dur + 0.25
        n = note.Note(last_x)
        n.duration = duration.Duration(dur)
        s.append(n)
        parts.append(s)
    parts.write('midi', fp=os.path.join(output_folder,"sample_{}_
{}.midi".format(epoch, score_num)))
```

15.3.2.10 Predictions

The "sample_predictions" function generates new scores using the trained generator model and saves them as MIDI files. The function takes as input the "output_folder" to save the generated scores, "z_dim", "n_tracks", "n_bars", "n_steps_per_bar", and "epoch" to name the generated files, and the "generator" model to generate new scores. The function first generates random noise for each track using numpy's "np.random.normal" function. It then uses the generator model to generate scores by calling "generator.predict" with the generated noise as input. The resulting scores are then passed to the "notes_to_midi" function, which converts the scores to MIDI files and saves them to the specified "output_folder". The "save_models" function saves the weights of the trained models as HDF5 files in the specified "output_folder". The function takes as input the "gan_model", "critic_model", "generator_model", and "output_folder". It calls the "save_weights" method of each model and saves the weights with the corresponding names "model.h5", "critic.h5", and "generator.h5" in the specified "output_folder".

```
def sample_predictions(output_folder,z_dim,n_tracks,n_bars,n_steps_per_bar,
epoch,generator):
    r = 5
    track1_noise = np.random.normal(0, 1, (r, z_dim))
    track2_noise = np.random.normal(0, 1, (r, z_dim))
    track3_noise = np.random.normal(0, 1, (r, n_tracks, z_dim))
    track4_noise = np.random.normal(0, 1, (r, n_tracks, z_dim))
    gen_scores = generator.predict([track1_noise,track2_noise,
track3_noise,track4_noise])
    notes_to_midi(n_bars,n_steps_per_bar,n_tracks,epoch,output_folder,
gen_scores)
def save_models(gan_model, critic_model, generator_model, output_folder):
    gan_model.save_weights(os.path.join(output_folder, 'model.h5'))
    critic_model.save_weights(os.path.join(output_folder, 'critic.h5'))
    generator_model.save_weights(os.path.join(output_folder, 'generator.
h5'))
```

15.3.2.11 Train MuseGAN

This code defines several functions that are used to train a MuseGAN model for music generation. The "train_musegan" function is the main training function that takes as input the training data ("x_train"), the critic, generator, and GAN models ("critic_model", "gen_model", "gan_model"), the size of the latent space ("z_dim"), the number of tracks, bars, and steps per bar, the batch size, the number of epochs to train for, the output folder for saving generated music, and some optional parameters ("print_every_n_batches" and "n_critic"). This function trains the critic and generator models, prints the loss values, and saves the generated music to the specified output folder. The "load_music" function loads the training data from a specified file path ("data_path") and returns it in the format required by the model. The "train_critic" function trains the critic model on a batch of real and generated data. The "build_temporal_network" function builds a convolutional neural network for processing temporal data. The "build_bar_generator" function builds a generator model for generating individual bars of music. The "build_generator" function builds the full generator model for generating multi-track music. The "build_gan" function builds the GAN model for training the generator and critic models. The "train_generator" function trains the generator model on a batch of noise data. The "argmax_output" function returns the index of the maximum value in a tensor. The "notes_to_midi" function converts generated music from tensor format to MIDI format and saves it to a file. The "sample_predictions" function generates music samples using the generator model and saves them to MIDI files. The "save_models" function saves the weights of the critic, generator, and GAN models to files.

```python
def train_musegan (x_train,critic_model,gen_model,gan_model,z_dim,n_
tracks,n_bars,n_steps_per_bar,batch_size, epochs,output_folder,  print_
every_n_batches=10,n_critic=5, use_gen=False):
    d_losses = []
    g_losses = []
    for epoch in range(epochs):
        for _ in range(n_critic):
            d_loss = train_critic(x_train,critic_model,z_dim,batch_size,
n_tracks,use_gen)
        g_loss = train_generator(gan_model, z_dim, n_tracks, batch_size)
        print("Epoch=%d [D loss: (%.1f)(Real=%.1f,Fake=%.1f, Grad.
Penalty=%.1f)] [Gen loss: %.1f]" % (epoch,d_loss[0],d_loss[1],
d_loss[2],d_loss[3],g_loss))
        d_losses.append(d_loss)
        g_losses.append(g_loss)
        if epoch % print_every_n_batches == 0:
            sample_predictions(output_folder,z_dim,n_tracks,n_bars,
n_steps_per_bar,epoch,gen_model)
    return d_losses, g_losses
def load_music(data_path, n_bars, n_steps_per_bar):
    filename = data_path
    with np.load(filename, encoding='bytes', allow_pickle=True) as nf:
        data = nf['train']
    data_ints = []
    for x in data:
        counter = 0
        cont = True
        while cont:
            if not np.any(np.isnan(x[counter+counter+4)])):
                cont = False
            else:
                counter += 4
        if n_bars * n_steps_per_bar < x.shape[0]:
            data_ints.append(x[counter +(counter + (n_bars *n_steps_per_
bar)), :])
```

```
    data_ints = np.array(data_ints)
    n_songs = data_ints.shape[0]
    n_tracks = data_ints.shape[2]
    data_ints = data_ints.reshape([n_songs, n_bars, n_steps_per_bar,
n_tracks])
    max_note = 83
    where_are_NaNs = np.isnan(data_ints)
    data_ints[where_are_NaNs] = max_note + 1
    max_note = max_note + 1
    data_ints = data_ints.astype(int)
    num_classes = max_note + 1
    encoded_scores = np.eye(num_classes)[data_ints]
    encoded_scores[encoded_scores == 0] = -1
    encoded_scores = np.delete(encoded_scores, max_note, -1)
    encoded_scores = encoded_scores.transpose([0, 1, 2, 4, 3])
    return encoded_scores
```

15.3.2.12 Model Object

These lines of code build and initialize the critic and generator models, and then create the GAN by combining the critic and generator. Here is a breakdown of each line.

Calls the function `build_critic` to create the critic model with the specified input dimension, weight initialization method, and number of bars.
```
Critic = build_critic(input_dim, weight_init, n_bars)
```

Calls the function `build_generator` to create the generator model with the specified latent dimension, number of tracks, number of bars, steps per bar, number of pitches, and weight initialization method.
```
gen_model = build_generator(z_dim,n_tracks,n_bars,n_steps_per_bar,
n_pitches,weight_init)
```

Calls the function `build_gan` to create the GAN by combining the generator and critic models. It returns two models: the critic model and the GAN model. The GAN is created by setting the critic's trainable weights to false, and then training the generator to maximize the critic's output on fake samples. The `grad_weight` parameter controls the weight given to the gradient penalty term in the loss function.
```
critic_model, gan_model = build_gan(gen_model,critic,input_dim,z_dim,
n_tracks,batch_size,grad_weight)
```

15.3.2.13 MuseGAN Training Variables Setup

The variables "encoded_scores", "output_folder", "sampling_frequency", "n_critic", "use_gen", and "epochs" were not defined in the conversation so far, so it cannot execute as is. "encoded_scores" should be a numpy array containing the encoded music data, "output_folder" should be a string specifying the folder path where the generated MIDI files will be saved, "sampling_frequency" and "n_critic" are hyperparameters that determine the training behavior, and "epochs" is the number of epochs for which the MuseGAN model should be trained.

You will need to define these variables before executing this line of code.

```
d_losses, g_losses = train_musegan(encoded_scores,critic_model,gen_model,
gan_model,z_dim,n_tracks,n_bars, n_steps_per_bar,batch_size,epochs,
output_folder,sampling_frequency,n_critic,use_gen=use_gen)
```

15.3.2.14 Generate Music

Generate some music as final outputs. It generates random noise arrays using the NumPy library. It creates noise arrays for individual tracks as well as overall tracks. The generated noise is then fed into a MuseGAN model to produce generated scores. An inference ID is set, and the generated scores are saved as a MIDI file for further processing.

```
track1_noise = np.random.normal(0, 1, (1, z_dim))
track2_noise = np.random.normal(0, 1, (1, z_dim))
track3_noise = np.random.normal(0, 1, (1, n_tracks, z_dim))
track4_noise = np.random.normal(0, 1, (1, n_tracks, z_dim))
gen_scores = gen_model.predict([track1_noise, track2_noise, track3_noise,
track4_noise])
inference_id = "musegan"
sample_musegan_0.midi =
notes_to_midi(n_bars,n_steps_per_bar,n_tracks,inference_id,output_
folder,gen_scores)
gen_score = converter.parse(os.path.join(output_folder, 'sample_
musegan_0.midi'))
```

15.4 Human Voice Conversion

The process of human voice conversion involves altering the characteristics of a recorded human voice to achieve a desired target voice, which may involve changes to pitch, duration, timbre, or other voice attributes. This can be useful in various applications, such as creating voiceovers for animations, video games, or dubbing foreign movies or TV shows, as well as aiding speech therapy or language translation. Voice conversion can be achieved through different methods, such as rule-based or statistical techniques, as well as deep learning methods like GANs. GANs have shown promise in producing more accurate and natural-sounding voice conversions by training a generator network to produce target voices from source voices, while a discriminator network distinguishes between generated and real target voices. Despite recent advancements in voice conversion techniques, the complexity and variability of human voices present challenges in achieving high-quality results, requiring careful consideration of conversion techniques and evaluation metrics.

15.4.1 What Is the Human Voice?

The human voice is created through vocal derivatives, which include speech or talking, singing, sobbing, and any other sounds that come from the human mouth and have

FIGURE 15.22
The human voice generates structures and parts.

meaning. The vocal components include the lungs (which amplify the flow to the vocal), the box (which changes the length through laryngeal muscles), and the articulators (which filter the sound through the tongue, palate, cheek, and lips). Figure 15.22 provides a detailed visualization of the physiological structures involved in human voice production, including the trachea, mouth, and tongue. The diagram intricately displays how these elements work in tandem to generate voice. From the initial airflow in the trachea to the modulation and articulation carried out by the mouth and tongue, the image offers a clear insight into the complex orchestration of components that give rise to the distinctive sounds of human speech and singing.

Generally, three variables can be used to identify a speaker:

1. linguistic elements, such as sentence structure and vocabulary selection;
2. supra-segmental factors, such as prosodic properties of a speech signal; and
3. segmental factors, such as spectrum and formants.

There are several approaches to voice conversion, and a good approach should be capable of converting both supra-segmental and segmental characteristics.

15.4.2 Voice Conversion Approaches

Voice conversion is the process of transferring the speech of one person to another while preserving the original content, and it can be categorized into two basic types: parallel and non-parallel. Parallel conversion occurs when both speakers say the same sentence, while non-parallel conversion occurs when the phrases are not the same. Deep learning has made significant contributions to speech conversion, which can be divided into three categories. Firstly, it allows the mapping module to learn from a large amount of speech data, significantly improving the quality and similarity of the imitated voice. Secondly, deep learning has had a significant impact on the evolution of vocoding technology. Finally, it is an alternative to more traditional analysis methods and illustrates the pipeline reconstruction process. GAN is one of the DL methods that has recently demonstrated extremely promising results in voice conversion. There are various approaches to voice conversion, and some popular ones will be discussed in detail in the following section, providing additional information.

1. **YourTTS:** Toward Zero-Shot Multi-Speaker TTS and Zero-Shot Voice Conversion for everyone.
2. **S3PRL-VC:** Open-Source Voice Conversion Framework with Self-Supervised Speech Representations.
3. **Assem-VC:** Realistic Voice Conversion by Assembling Modern Speech Synthesis Techniques.
4. **NVC-Net:** End-to-End Adversarial Voice Conversion.
5. **DGC-vector:** A new speaker embedding for zero-shot voice conversion.
6. **Glow-WaveGAN 2:** High-quality Zero-shot Text-to-speech Synthesis and Any-to-any Voice Conversion.
7. **AGAIN-VC:** A One-shot Voice Conversion using Activation Guidance and Adaptive Instance Normalization.
8. **StarGANv2-VC:** A Diverse, Unsupervised, Non-parallel Framework for Natural-Sounding Voice Conversion.
9. **S2VC:** A Framework for Any-to-Any Voice Conversion with Self-Supervised Pre-trained Representations.
10. **MediumVC:** Any-to-any voice conversion using synthetic specific-speaker speeches as intermedium features.

And some research papers on this topic:

1. "Voice Conversion Using Deep Recurrent Neural Networks" by Sercan Ö. Arık, Aydın A. Bulut, İlker Kılıç, and Tuğba Yılmaz.
2. "Voice Conversion with Non-Parallel Data Using Adversarial Networks" by Kanichi Fukui, Takuhiro Kaneko, Daichi Mochihashi, and Hiroshi Saruwatari.
3. "CycleGAN-VC: Non-parallel Voice Conversion Using Cycle-Consistent Adversarial Networks" by Yi-Chiao Wu, Yen-Cheng Liu, Chieh-Chi Kao, and Hsin-Min Wang.
4. "StarGAN-VC: Non-parallel many-to-many voice conversion with star generative adversarial networks" by Hong-Wei Ng, Lazaros Nalpantidis, and Eng-Jon Ong.
5. "Phonetic Posteriorgrams for Many-to-One Voice Conversion Without Parallel Data Training" by Shinnosuke Takamichi, Hirokazu Kameoka, and Tatsuya Kawahara.

In this section, we will discuss YourTTS as one of the most recent approaches.

15.4.3 YourTTS Approach

VITS is an end-to-end, text-to-speech conditional variational autoencoder (VAE) that utilizes adversarial learning. YourTTS is an extension of VITS that includes several novel features enabling zero-shot multi-speaker and multilingual training. Unlike some other systems, YourTTS takes unprocessed text as input rather than phonemes, which results in more realistic results in languages where strong open-source grapheme-to-phoneme converters are not available. YourTTS also employs a transformer-based text encoder. For training in multiple languages, it concatenates four-dimensional trainable language embeddings into the embeddings of each input letter. It uses the HiFi-GAN version 1 vocoder but with discriminator modifications from a previous study. Additionally, it uses a VAE to facilitate effective end-to-end training to establish a link between the text-to-speech (TTS) model and the vocoder. This is achieved by utilizing the posterior encoder introduced in another study, which enables the model to learn an intermediate representation. As a result, it outperforms a two-stage approach system in which the vocoder and the TTS model are trained independently.

The model also employs the stochastic duration predictor presented in yet another study to incorporate synthesis speech with various rhythms based on the text provided as input. All affine coupling layers of the flow-based decoder, posterior encoder, and vocoder are trained on external speaker embeddings to provide the model with zero-shot multi-speaker generation capabilities. Global conditioning is used in both the coupling layers' residual blocks and the posterior encoder. The external speaker embeddings are also added to the outputs of the text encoder and decoder before passing them to the duration predictor and vocoder. Linear projection layers are used to match the dimensions before element-wise summing (Figure 15.23). Figure 15.23 presents a schematic

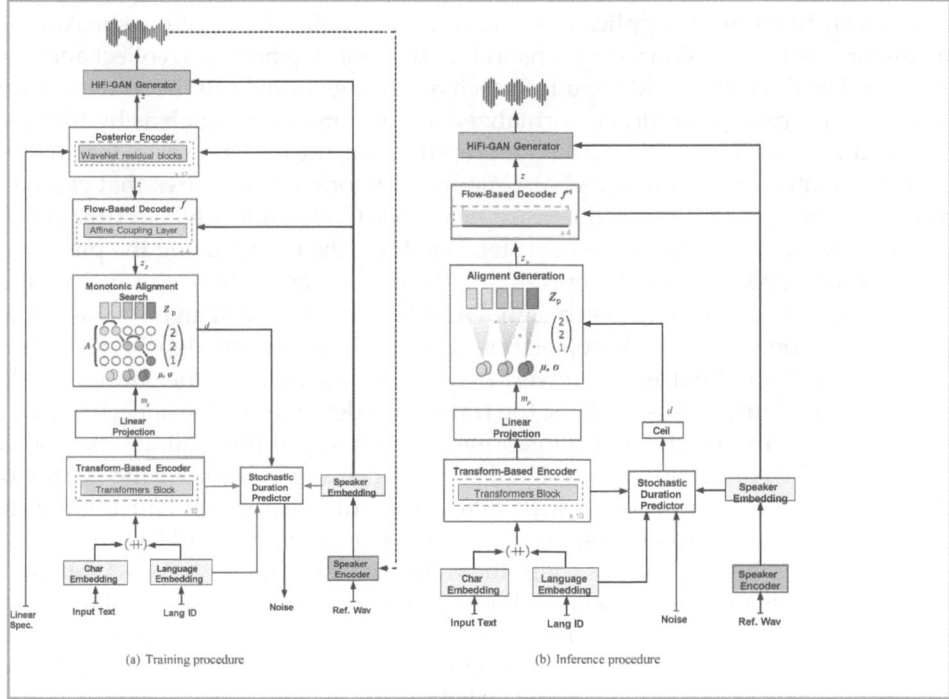

FIGURE 15.23

The processes of YourTTS: (a) Training procedure and (b) Inference procedure. The symbol (++) denotes concatenation, solid lines represent connections with no gradient transmission, and dashed lines signify optional connections.

representation of the "YourTTS" system during its training and inference stages. Key elements to note include:

- **Concatenation points:** These are marked with "(++)" symbols, showing where different input or intermediate tensors are combined.
- **Red connections:** These signify pathways where no gradient information is transmitted during backpropagation. Such connections are non-trainable or deliberately isolated from gradient updates.
- **Dashed connections:** Represent optional pathways, suggesting that depending on the configuration or certain conditions, these connections might be utilized or ignored.

The diagram provides a comprehensive view of how data flows within "YourTTS", helping users understand both its operational phases and architectural nuances.

For more information on their approach, testing the findings, and interacting with their code, refers to their article.

15.4.4 Voice Conversion Using TensorFlow

Voice conversion using TensorFlow involves training a neural network to learn a mapping between two different speakers' voices. The basic idea is to train a model to take in a speech signal from a source speaker and transform it into a speech signal that sounds like the target speaker. This process can be used for various applications, such as dubbing in movies, adding voice effects in games or applications, and improving the clarity of the speaker's voice. To implement voice conversion using TensorFlow, the first step here is to collect and preprocess the data. The dataset should include speech recordings from both the source and target speakers. The recordings should be normalized and preprocessed, such as by filtering out noise and reducing silence. Once the data is preprocessed, the next step is to design the neural network architecture. There are several neural network architectures that can be used for voice conversion, including feedforward networks, CNNs, and RNNs. After designing the neural network architecture, the next step is to train the model using the preprocessed data. The training process involves optimizing the model parameters to minimize the difference between the predicted speech signal and the target speech signal. The optimization is typically done using backpropagation and gradient descent algorithms. When the model is trained, it can be used to convert the speech signals from the source speaker to the target speaker. During this process, the trained model takes in the speech signal from the source speaker and produces a transformed speech signal that sounds like the target speaker. Finally, the converted speech signal is postprocessed to improve the quality of the speech. This can involve techniques, such as filtering out noise and enhancing the signal-to-noise ratio. Overall, voice conversion using TensorFlow is a powerful technique that can be used for a variety of applications. With the right data, neural network architecture, and training process, it is possible to achieve high-quality voice conversion results that sound natural and realistic. The voice conversion is the task of converting a source speaker's voice into a target speaker's voice without changing the linguistic content. For this task, we can use a pre-trained CycleGAN-based model called CycleGAN-VC2.

1. Clone the CycleGAN-VC2 repository

```
git clone https://github.com/leimao/Voice-Conversion-CycleGAN-VC2.git
cd Voice-Conversion-CycleGAN-VC2
```

2. Install the required libraries

```
pip install -r requirements.txt
```

3. Download the pre-trained CycleGAN-VC2 model

```
wget https://github.com/leimao/Voice-Conversion-CycleGAN-VC2/raw/master/
pre_trained_model/ckpt.zip
unzip ckpt.zip
```

4. Create a Python script and import the necessary libraries

```python
import os
import sys
import tensorflow as tf
import numpy as np
import librosa
import soundfile as sf
sys.path.append('Voice-Conversion-CycleGAN-VC2')
from model.cyclegan_vc2 import CycleGANVC2
from preprocess import *
os.environ['TF_CPP_MIN_LOG_LEVEL'] = '3'  # Suppress TensorFlow logging
```

5. Load the pre-trained CycleGAN-VC2 model

```python
def load_model(checkpoint_dir):
    model = CycleGANVC2(num_features=24, mode='test')
    model.load(filepath=os.path.join(checkpoint_dir, 'model.ckpt'))
    return model
checkpoint_dir = 'ckpt'
model = load_model(checkpoint_dir)
```

6. Create a function to convert a source voice into a target voice

```python
def voice_conversion(input_audio, output_audio, model,
sample_rate=16000):
    wav, _ = librosa.load(input_audio, sr=sample_rate, mono=True)
    wav = wav_padding(wav=wav, sr=sample_rate, frame_period=5,
multiple=4)
    f0, timeaxis, sp, ap = world_decompose(wav=wav, fs=sample_rate,
frame_period=5)
    coded_sp = world_encode_spectral_envelop(sp=sp, fs=sample_rate,
dim=24)
    coded_sp_converted = model.test(inputs=np.array([[coded_sp]]),
direction='A2B')[0]
    coded_sp_converted = np.asarray(coded_sp_converted)
    sp_converted = world_decode_spectral_envelop(coded_sp=coded_sp_
converted, fs=sample_rate)
    wav_transformed = world_speech_synthesis(f0=f0, coded_sp=sp_
converted, ap=ap, fs=sample_rate, frame_period=5)
    sf.write(output_audio, wav_transformed, sample_rate,
subtype='PCM_16')
```

7. Convert a source voice to a target voice

```python
input_audio = 'path/to/source_voice.wav'
output_audio = 'path/to/target_voice.wav'
voice_conversion(input_audio, output_audio, model)
```

This example demonstrates how to use the pre-trained CycleGAN-VC2 model for voice conversion. You can adapt this code to perform voice conversion on your own dataset by training a new model or fine-tuning the existing model on your data. Note that the quality of the conversion will depend on the quality of the pre-trained model, and it may not work well for voices that are very different from those in the training dataset.

15.5 Song Conversion

Song conversion, also known as music style transfer, involves modifying the characteristics of a recorded song to produce a desired target song style. This process may involve changing the tempo, rhythm, melody, harmony, or other aspects of the song to make it sound like a different genre or artist. Song conversion has several applications in areas, such as music production, entertainment, and education. For example, it can be used to create new versions of existing songs, to help students learn to play different styles, or to generate background music for video games and films. There are several approaches to song conversion, including rule-based methods, statistical methods, and deep learning techniques, such as GANs. GANs have shown promising results in recent years, allowing for more accurate and natural-sounding song conversion by training a generator network to produce a target song style from a source song and a discriminator network to distinguish between the generated and real target songs. However, song conversion is still a challenging task due to the complexity of music and the large variability in individual song styles. It requires careful consideration of the desired target style and the source song characteristics, as well as the selection of appropriate conversion techniques and evaluation metrics to ensure the quality and musicality of the converted song.

15.5.1 What Is a Song?

It is a piece of music in which the human voice serves as the primary instrument. So, there you have it:

$$Song = Human's\ voice + Music$$

As a result, the song is divided into genres, such as art, folk, sporting, lute, part, and patter. A song is created when music and spoken words are combined, as we discussed in the previous section. While converting songs, a few different approaches may be used.

1. **Learn2Sing 2.0:** Diffusion and Mutual Information-Based Target Speaker SVS by Learning from Singing Teacher, INTERSPEECH 2022.
2. **DiffSVC:** A Diffusion Probabilistic Model for Singing Voice Conversion, ASRU 2022.
3. **FastSVC:** Fast Cross-Domain Singing Voice Conversion with Feature-wise Linear Modulation, ICME 2021.
4. **PitchNet:** Unsupervised Singing Voice Conversion with Pitch Adversarial Network, ICASSP 2020.
5. **DurIAN-SC:** Duration Informed Attention Network based Singing Voice Conversion System, INTERSPEECH 2020.

Also some of which are discussed in these publications:

1. Unsupervised Cross-Domain Singing Voice Conversion, INTERSPEECH 2020.
2. VAW-GAN for Singing Voice Conversion with Non-parallel Training Data, APSIPA 2020.
3. Phonetic Posteriorgrams based Many-to-Many Singing Voice Conversion via Adversarial Training, 2020.
4. Improving Adversarial Waveform Generation based Singing Voice Conversion with Harmonic Signals, ICASSP 2022.
5. Unsupervised Singing Voice Conversion by Kou Tanaka, Hirokazu Kameoka, Kaoru Tashiro, and Nobukatsu Hojo.
6. Cross-Synthesis of Singing Voice with Single-Mode Synthesizer by Yuki Saito, Hirokazu Kameoka, Kou Tanaka, and Nobukatsu Hojo.
7. A Hierarchical Speaker Representation Framework for One-shot Singing Voice Conversion, INTERSPEECH 2022.

15.5.2 Song Generation Using TensorFlow

Song generation is a challenging problem in the field of music information retrieval and deep learning. With the progress of deep learning techniques, it is now possible to generate songs that sound like they were created by humans. TensorFlow, a popular deep learning framework, can be used to create deep neural networks that can learn the patterns of music and generate new songs. One approach to song generation is to use DCGAN. To use TensorFlow for song generation, one needs a large dataset of songs. The dataset can be in the form of MIDI files, audio files, or spectrograms. MIDI files are preferred because they contain information about the notes, timing, and other musical elements that can be easily used for training the neural network. Once the dataset is prepared, it is preprocessed by converting the MIDI files into a format that can be used by the neural network. This can be done by representing each note as a one-hot vector or by using a piano roll representation. The next step is to build the DCGAN model in TensorFlow. The generator and discriminator networks are typically designed as CNNs with several layers. The generator network takes in a random noise vector and outputs a song, while the discriminator network takes in a song and outputs a probability of whether it is real or generated. The model is trained by alternating between training the generator network and the discriminator network. During training, the generator tries to generate songs that trick the discriminator, while the discriminator tries to distinguish between real and generated songs. And then, when the model is trained, it can be used to generate new songs by feeding in a random noise vector to the generator network. The output is a generated song that can be played back as an audio file or converted to a MIDI file for further editing. Overall, song generation using TensorFlow is a complex and challenging task, but with the right dataset and training techniques, it is possible to create deep neural networks that can generate high-quality songs. To generate a song using TensorFlow, you can utilize the Magenta library, which is a TensorFlow-powered framework for generating music and art. In this example, we'll use the pre-trained performance RNN model to generate a song in MIDI format.

1. Install the necessary libraries
```
pip install magenta
pip install tensorflow
```

2. Import the necessary libraries

```
import os
import magenta
import tensorflow as tf
from magenta.models.performance_rnn import performance_sequence_generator
from magenta.models.shared import sequence_generator_bundle
from magenta.music import DEFAULT_QUARTERS_PER_MINUTE
from magenta.protobuf import generator_pb2
from magenta.protobuf import music_pb2
from note_seq import midi_io
```

3. Download a pre-trained model bundle, which is used for generating the song. For this example, we'll use the "performance_with_dynamics" model

```
Wget https://storage.googleapis.com/magentadata/models/performance_rnn/
colab2/checkpoints/performance_with_dynamics.mag
```

4. Load the pre-trained model

```
bundle_path = 'performance_with_dynamics.mag'
bundle = sequence_generator_bundle.read_bundle_file(bundle_path)
generator_map = performance_sequence_generator.get_generator_map()
generator = generator_map['performance_with_dynamics'](checkpoint=None,
bundle=bundle)
generator.initialize()
```

5. Create a function to generate a MIDI file

```
def generate_midi_file(output_file, primer_midi=None, total_seconds=30,
temperature=1.0):
    generator_options = generator_pb2.GeneratorOptions()
    if primer_midi:
        primer_sequence = midi_io.midi_file_to_note_sequence(primer_midi)
        generator_options.input_sections.add(
            start_time=0.0,
            end_time=primer_sequence.total_time,
            sequence=primer_sequence,
        )
    generator_options.generate_sections.add(
        start_time=generator_options.input_sections[0].end_time if
primer_midi else 0.0,
        end_time=total_seconds,
    )
    generator_options.args['temperature'].float_value = temperature
    generator_options.args['beam_size'].int_value = 1
    generator_options.args['branch_factor'].int_value = 1
    generator_options.args['steps_per_iteration'].int_value = 1
    # Generate the song
    generated_sequence = generator.generate(generator_options)
    # Save the generated song as a MIDI file
    midi_io.note_sequence_to_midi_file(generated_sequence, output_file)
```

6. Generate a MIDI file

```
output_midi_file = 'generated_song.mid'
primer_midi_file = None
generate_midi_file(output_midi_file, primer_midi=primer_midi_file, total_
seconds=30, temperature=1.0)
```

This example demonstrates how to use the pre-trained Performance RNN model from the Magenta library to generate a song in MIDI format. You can experiment with different pre-trained models and adjust the parameters (e.g., temperature, total_seconds) to influence the generated song's style, complexity, and duration.

15.6 Song Conversion Using TensorFlow

Song conversion refers to the process of converting a song from one style or genre to another while preserving its essence and structure. TensorFlow, an open-source machine learning framework, can be used for song conversion by training neural networks, such as GANs or VAEs, to learn the mapping between songs in different styles. The process of song conversion using TensorFlow typically involves the following steps:

15.6.1 Data Collection

Collecting a large dataset of songs in the original style and the desired style for conversion.

15.6.2 Data Preprocessing

Preprocessing the collected dataset to extract useful features such as notes, chords, and rhythms and encoding them into a suitable format for input to the neural network.

15.6.3 Neural Network Architecture

Designing and implementing a suitable neural network architecture, such as GAN or VAE, that can learn the mapping between songs in the original and desired styles.

15.6.4 Training the Model

Training the neural network using the preprocessed dataset to learn the mapping between the songs in the original and desired styles.

15.6.5 Testing and Evaluation

Testing the trained model on a separate dataset of songs and evaluating its performance by comparing the original and converted songs using metrics, such as MSE or SSIM. There are several challenges involved in song conversion using TensorFlow, such as the need for a large and diverse dataset, the complexity of the neural network architecture, and the difficulty in evaluating the quality of the converted songs. However, with proper implementation and tuning, song conversion using TensorFlow can lead to impressive results and enable the creation of new and exciting music styles.

15.6.6 Code Example

To create a song converter using TensorFlow, you can utilize the Magenta library, which is a TensorFlow-powered framework for generating music and art. Here's a simple example that demonstrates how to use the Magenta library to convert a MIDI file into a different style. This example shows a simple way to convert a drum track in a MIDI file into a new style using a pre-trained MusicVAE model from the Magenta library. Note that this model only works with drum tracks. You can experiment with different pre-trained models to convert other types of tracks or even entire songs.

15.6.6.1 Install the Necessary Libraries

```
pip install magenta
pip install tensorflow
```

15.6.6.2 Import the Necessary Libraries

```
import os
import magenta
import tensorflow as tf
from magenta.models.music_vae import configs
from magenta.models.music_vae.trained_model import TrainedModel
from note_seq import midi_io
from note_seq import sequences_lib
```

15.6.6.3 Download a Pre-trained Model

Retrieve a pre-trained model checkpoint for song conversion. In this demonstration, we'll employ the "cat-drums_2bar_small" model.

```
wget https://storage.googleapis.com/magentadata/models/music_vae/
checkpoints/cat-drums_2bar_small.tar
tar xf cat-drums_2bar_small.tar
```

15.6.6.4 Load the Pre-trained Model

```
model_config = configs.CONFIG_MAP['cat-drums_2bar_small']
model = TrainedModel(model_config, batch_size=4, checkpoint_dir_or_
path='./cat-drums_2bar_small/checkpoint')
```

15.6.6.5 Create a Function to Convert a MIDI File to a New Style

```
def convert_midi_file(input_file, output_file, temperature=1.0):
    # Load the input MIDI file
    input_sequence = midi_io.midi_file_to_note_sequence(input_file)

    # Extract the drum track from the input sequence
    drums = sequences_lib.extract_drum_tracks(input_sequence)[0]

    # Encode the drum track
    encoded_drums, _ = model.encode([drums])

    # Decode the encoded drum track to a new style
    decoded_drums = model.decode(encoded_drums, length=32,
temperature=temperature)[0]
```

```
    # Replace the drum track in the input sequence with the new style
    output_sequence = sequences_lib.replace_sequence_track(input_
sequence, decoded_drums)

    # Save the output sequence as a MIDI file
    midi_io.note_sequence_to_midi_file(output_sequence, output_file)
```

15.6.6.6 Convert a MIDI File to a New Style

```
# input_midi_file = 'input_song.mid' # Replace with your input MIDI file
output_midi_file = 'converted_song.mid'
convert_midi_file(input_midi_file, output_midi_file, temperature=1.0)
```

15.7 Issues in GANs for Voice, Music, and Song

GANs have been used for generating synthetic voice, music, and song. However, they come with a set of challenges that may affect the quality and usability of the generated content. Here are some of the issues with GANs in these domains, along with possible solutions:

15.7.1 Mode Collapse

GANs may suffer from mode collapse, where the generator produces limited varieties of output, causing a lack of diversity in generated samples.

Solution: Techniques, such as mini-batch discrimination, unrolled GANs, or spectral normalization, can help mitigate mode collapse and ensure diversity in the generated content.

15.7.2 Training Instability

GAN training can be unstable, leading to poor convergence or oscillations in the learning process.

Solution: Improved training techniques, such as Wasserstein GAN (WGAN), WGAN with gradient penalty (WGAN-GP), or spectral normalization, can help stabilize training and produce better results.

15.7.3 High-quality Audio Generation

Generating high-quality audio samples, especially for music and voice, is challenging due to the complex temporal structure and high dimensionality of audio data.

Solution: Utilize advanced GAN architectures, such as WaveGAN or MelGAN, which are specifically designed for generating high-quality audio. Alternatively, consider using other generative models, such as VAEs or autoregressive models (e.g., WaveNet, SampleRNN).

15.7.4 Real-time Generation

Real-time generation of audio can be difficult due to the computational complexity of GANs and the need for fast synthesis.

Solution: Use parallel processing, efficient algorithms, or optimized hardware to speed up the synthesis process. Also, consider using lightweight GAN models that can generate audio samples with lower computational requirements.

15.7.5 Evaluation Metrics

Quantitatively evaluating the quality and diversity of generated voice, music, and song is challenging, as traditional metrics (e.g., Inception Score, Frechet Inception Distance) may not be suitable for audio data.

Solution: Develop custom evaluation metrics tailored for audio data, such as the Mel Cepstral Distortion (MCD) for voice, or use subjective evaluation methods involving human listeners.

15.7.6 Controllability

Controlling specific attributes (e.g., pitch, timbre, emotion) in the generated audio samples is challenging with vanilla GANs.

Solution: Use cGANs or other conditional generative models, which allow control over specific attributes by conditioning the generation process on additional input information.

By addressing these challenges, researchers and practitioners can improve GAN-based voice, music, and song generation and create more diverse, high-quality, and usable content.

15.8 Implementation Tips in GANs for Voice, Music, and Song

When implementing GANs for voice, music, and song generation, consider the following tips to help improve the quality of the generated content and ensure a smooth training process.

15.8.1 Choose the Right Architecture

Select a GAN architecture suitable for audio generation, such as WaveGAN or MelGAN. These models are specifically designed to handle the complexities of audio data, leading to better results.

15.8.2 Use Appropriate Input Representations

Pick suitable input representations, such as spectrograms or waveforms, that capture relevant information for the target application. Mel spectrograms, for instance, are a popular choice for voice synthesis due to their perceptual relevance.

15.8.3 Preprocess the Data

Normalize and preprocess the audio data to ensure consistency and facilitate learning. Techniques, such as silence trimming, data augmentation, and scaling, can help improve the quality of the generated samples.

15.8.4 Handle Long-range Dependencies

Voice, music, and song data have long-range temporal dependencies. Consider using recurrent or attention-based layers in the generator and discriminator to capture these dependencies effectively.

15.8.5 Use Conditional GANs

If you need control over specific attributes in the generated audio (e.g., pitch, timbre, emotion), use cGANs or other conditional generative models.

15.8.6 Monitor Training Progress

Track the training progress by regularly generating samples and inspecting them. This helps identify issues such as mode collapse, training instability, or other artifacts in the generated content.

15.8.7 Stabilize GAN Training

Employ techniques that stabilize GAN training, such as gradient clipping, learning rate schedules, or advanced training methods like WGAN and WGAN-GP.

15.8.8 Experiment with Different Loss Functions

Use different loss functions, such as L_1 or L_2 losses, in addition to the adversarial loss, to guide the generator toward producing realistic samples with fewer artifacts.

15.8.9 Gradually Increase Model Complexity

Start with a smaller, less complex model and gradually increase the complexity as needed. This approach can help avoid overfitting and promote better generalization.

15.8.10 Use Domain-specific Knowledge

Incorporate domain-specific knowledge into the GAN architecture or training process. For example, use a pre-trained model for feature extraction or enforce constraints that ensure the generated content follows certain musical rules.

15.8.11 Evaluate the Results

Develop custom evaluation metrics tailored for audio data or use subjective evaluation methods involving human listeners to assess the quality and diversity of the generated content.

Remember, hands-on experience is key when working with GANs or any other machine learning models. Therefore, consistently practicing implementation and troubleshooting is crucial for mastering these concepts.

15.9 Lessons Learned

- Learn What is Sound?
- Learn Audio Synthesis
- Learn Human Voice Conversion
- Learn Song Conversion
- Learn Song Conversion using TensorFlow
- Learn Issues in GANs for Voice, Music, and Song
- Learn Implementation Tips in GANs for Voice, Music, and Song

15.10 Problems

15.10.1 What is the basic architecture of a GAN and how does it work for generating audio samples?

15.10.2 What are some common input representations (e.g., spectrograms, waveforms) used for training GANs on audio data?

15.10.3 What are some challenges in generating high-quality audio samples using GANs?

15.10.4 How do conditional GANs (cGANs) differ from regular GANs, and how can they be used to control specific attributes (e.g., pitch, instrument) in generated audio samples?

15.10.5 What are some techniques to stabilize GAN training, such as Wasserstein GAN (WGAN) and WGAN with gradient penalty (WGAN-GP)?

15.10.6 How do GANs with recurrent layers (e.g., LSTM or GRU) handle long-range dependencies in audio data, and how do they improve the quality of generated audio samples?

15.10.7 What are some evaluation metrics for assessing the quality and diversity of generated audio samples, and what are the challenges in developing such metrics?

15.10.8 How can attention mechanisms (e.g., self-attention) be used in GANs for audio generation, and what are their benefits?

15.10.9 How can domain-specific knowledge (e.g., musical rules, pre-trained feature extraction) be incorporated into GAN architectures to generate more realistic and coherent audio samples?

15.11 Programming Questions

- **Easy**

  15.11.1 How to load audio data for GAN training?

  15.11.2 How to preprocess audio data before feeding it into the GAN?

  15.11.3 How to implement a simple GAN for audio generation?

  15.11.4 How to visualize the generated audio waveforms?

  15.11.5 How to calculate the audio quality metrics for generated audio samples?

  15.11.6 How to train a GAN model for audio classification?

  15.11.7 How to evaluate the classification performance of a trained audio GAN model?

  15.11.8 Implement a simple GAN to generate short audio samples (e.g., single notes or drum beats) using TensorFlow or PyTorch.

  15.11.9 Preprocess audio data to create input representations (e.g., spectrograms) suitable for GAN training.

  15.11.10 Implement a function to convert the output of a GAN (e.g., generated spectrogram) back to an audio waveform.

- **Medium**

  15.11.11 How to implement a Wasserstein GAN for audio generation?

  15.11.12 How to implement a conditional GAN for audio generation with a given genre label?

  15.11.13 How to implement a multi-scale GAN for audio generation?

  15.11.14 How to use transfer learning with a pre-trained audio GAN model?

  15.11.15 How to use feature matching in the GAN loss function for improved audio generation?

  15.11.16 How to implement a CycleGAN for audio style transfer?

  15.11.17 How to generate audio samples with controllable attributes using a GAN model?

  15.11.18 Implement a conditional GAN (cGAN) for generating audio samples with specific attributes (e.g., pitch, instrument) using TensorFlow or PyTorch.

  15.11.19 Use a pre-trained GAN model (e.g., WaveGAN or MelGAN) to generate audio samples and fine-tune the model on a custom dataset.

  15.11.20 Implement a GAN with recurrent layers (e.g., LSTM or GRU) in the generator and discriminator to handle long-range dependencies in audio data.

- **Hard**

  15.11.21 How to implement a progressive GAN for high-resolution audio generation?

  15.11.22 How to implement a VAE-GAN for audio generation with a disentangled latent representation?

15.11.23   How to generate a large dataset of realistic audio samples using a GAN?

15.11.24   How to train a GAN model for music transcription from audio signals?

15.11.25   How to perform real-time audio generation with a GAN model on a mobile device?

15.11.26   How to incorporate lyrics or textual information into the GAN model for song generation?

15.11.27   How to optimize the GAN training process for faster convergence and better results?

15.11.28   Develop a custom evaluation metric for assessing the quality and diversity of generated audio samples and use it to compare different GAN models.

15.11.29   Implement a GAN with attention mechanisms (e.g., self-attention) in the generator and discriminator to improve the quality of generated audio samples.

15.11.30   Design and implement a GAN architecture that incorporates domain-specific knowledge (e.g., musical rules, pre-trained feature extraction) to generate more realistic and coherent audio samples.

Appendix

Chapter 1 Questions Responses

Problems

1.15.1 Machine learning is a subset of artificial intelligence that involves the development of algorithms that allow computers to learn from and make decisions or predictions based on data. There are three main types: supervised learning, unsupervised learning, and reinforcement learning. The benefits include automation, scalability, and adaptability. Drawbacks include the requirement for large amounts of data, the potential for overfitting, and challenges with interpretability.

1.15.2 Deep learning is a subset of machine learning that's based on artificial neural networks with multiple layers, or "deep" networks. It has found applications in numerous areas, including image and speech recognition, natural language processing, and even art creation.

1.15.3 Generative Adversarial Networks (GANs) are a type of deep learning model that consists of two neural networks contesting with each other in a game. As part of AI, machine learning uses algorithms to parse data, learn from it, and then make determinations or predictions. Deep learning is a subset of machine learning where neural networks learn from vast amounts of data, while GANs are a particular type of deep learning model.

1.15.4 Supervised learning is a type of machine learning where a model is trained on labeled data, that is, it knows the output for each example during training. Unsupervised learning, on the other hand, involves training a model on data where the outcome is unknown, and the goal is to find structure in the data, such as clustering or association.

1.15.5 Overfitting occurs when a machine learning model learns the noise in the training data to the point where it negatively impacts the performance of the model on new data. This is typically a result of a model that is too complex, such as having too many parameters. Methods to avoid overfitting include using more data, reducing model complexity, and applying techniques like cross-validation, regularization, and early stopping.

1.15.6 Regularization is a technique used to prevent overfitting by adding a penalty term to the loss function. The penalty term discourages the coefficients from taking extreme values, leading to a simpler and more generalized model.

1.15.7 Cross-validation is a technique used to assess the performance of a machine learning model on an independent data set and to tune model parameters. The most common method of cross-validation is K-fold cross-validation, where the data set is randomly partitioned into k equal-sized subsamples.

1.15.8 Clustering is an unsupervised learning technique used to group similar instances on the basis of features into clusters. Popular clustering algorithms include K-Means, Hierarchical Clustering, and DBSCAN.

1.15.9 Logistic vs. Linear Regression: Linear regression predicts a continuous value, while logistic regression predicts a binary outcome.

1.15.10 Generative vs. Discriminative Models: Generative models learn the joint probability distribution P(X,Y), and then derive P(Y|X) for prediction, while discriminative models learn P(Y|X) directly.

1.15.11 Reinforcement Learning: Reinforcement learning is learning how to act to maximize a reward signal. Applications include game playing, robotics, and resource allocation.

1.15.12 Parametric vs. Non-parametric Models: Parametric models assume the data follows a certain distribution and describe it with a set of parameters. Non-parametric models don't make strong assumptions about the data distribution.

1.15.13 Classification vs. Regression: Classification predicts discrete labels, while regression predicts continuous values.

1.15.14 L1 vs. L2 Regularization: L1 regularization (also known as Lasso) can lead to sparse models, while L2 regularization (also known as Ridge) does not.

1.15.15 Batch vs. Stochastic Gradient Descent: Batch GD uses all data points for each update, while stochastic GD uses one random data point.

1.15.16 K-Nearest Neighbors vs. K-Means Clustering: K-NN is a supervised learning algorithm that predicts a label for a new data point based on its closest neighbors, while K-means is an unsupervised learning algorithm that groups similar data points together.

1.15.17 Evaluation Metrics: Common metrics include accuracy, precision, recall, F1 score, ROC AUC for classification, and MSE, RMSE, MAE, R-squared for regression.

1.15.18 Precision vs. Recall: Precision is the fraction of true positives among all positive predictions, while recall is the fraction of true positives among all actual positives.

1.15.19 Bias-Variance Tradeoff: High bias can cause underfitting (model is too simple), while high variance can cause overfitting (model is too complex).

1.15.20 Deep Learning vs. Traditional Machine Learning: Deep learning can automatically learn feature representations from raw data, often leading to superior performance, especially for complex tasks like image or speech recognition.

1.15.21 Neural Network: A neural network is a machine learning model inspired by the human brain. It consists of interconnected layers of nodes or "neurons".

1.15.22 Backpropagation: Backpropagation is a method used to calculate the gradient of the loss function with respect to the weights in the neural network.

1.15.23 Neural Network Architectures: Popular architectures include feedforward networks (like MLPs), convolutional neural networks (CNNs), and recurrent neural networks (RNNs).

1.15.24 Transfer Learning: Transfer learning is a technique where a pre-trained model is used as the starting point for a related task.

1.15.25 Challenges in Training Deep Neural Networks: Challenges include overfitting, vanishing/exploding gradients, and the need for large amounts of data and computing power.

1.15.26 Deep Learning Frameworks: Popular frameworks include TensorFlow, PyTorch, and Keras.

1.15.27 CNN vs. RNN: CNNs are typically used for spatial data (like images), while RNNs are used for sequential data (like time series or sentences).

1.15.28 Applications of NLP: Applications include machine translation, sentiment analysis, and chatbots.

1.15.29 Single-Layer vs. Multi-Layer Perceptron: A single-layer perceptron can only learn linearly separable patterns, while a multi-layer perceptron can learn non-linear patterns.

1.15.30 Bias Term: The bias term allows the model to fit the data when all input features are zero.

1.15.31 Data Preprocessing Techniques: These include handling missing values, standardization, normalization, encoding categorical variables, and feature selection/extraction.

1.15.32 Ensemble Learning Methods: These include bagging (like random forest), boosting (like gradient boosting), and stacking.

1.15.33 Dealing with Imbalanced Datasets: Techniques include oversampling the minority class, undersampling the majority class, and using appropriate metrics.

1.15.34 Hyperparameter vs. Parameter: A parameter is learned from the data, while a hyperparameter is set before training (like learning rate).

1.15.35 Data Cleaning Techniques: Techniques include removing duplicates, handling missing values, and removing outliers.

1.15.36 Perceptron vs. Neural Network: A perceptron is a single-layer neural network, while a neural network can have multiple layers.

1.15.37 "Deep" in Deep Learning: "Deep" refers to the number of layers in a neural network. Deep learning models typically have many layers.

1.15.38 Supervised vs. Unsupervised vs. Reinforcement Learning: Supervised learning learns from labeled data, unsupervised learning learns from unlabeled data, and reinforcement learning learns from reward-based feedback.

1.15.39 Activation Function: The activation function introduces non-linearity into the model, allowing it to learn complex patterns.

1.15.40 Loss Function: The loss function measures how well the model's predictions match the true values. It's what the model tries to minimize during training.

1.15.41 Batch Size: Batch size is the number of training examples used in one iteration.

1.15.42 Regularization: Regularization is a technique used to prevent overfitting by adding a penalty term to the loss function.

1.15.43 Overfitting vs. Underfitting: Overfitting occurs when the model learns the training data too well, including its noise. Underfitting occurs when the model is too simple to learn the underlying pattern.

1.15.44 Dropout Layer: A dropout layer randomly sets a fraction of input units to 0 at each update, which helps prevent overfitting.

1.15.45 Generative Model: A generative model is a model for randomly generating observable data, often used in unsupervised learning.

1.15.46   Transfer Learning: Transfer learning is a method where a pre-trained model is used as the starting point for a related task.

1.15.47   Model vs. Algorithm: A model is a specific representation learned from data by an algorithm. An algorithm is a method or set of rules for learning from data.

1.15.48   Validation Set: A validation set is used to tune hyperparameters and prevent overfitting during training.

1.15.49   Backpropagation: Backpropagation is a method used to calculate the gradient of the loss function with respect to the weights in the neural network.

1.15.50   Gradient Descent vs. Stochastic Gradient Descent: Gradient descent uses all training samples for each update, while stochastic gradient descent uses one random sample.

1.15.51   Hyperparameter vs. Model Parameter: A hyperparameter is set before training and guides the learning process, while a model parameter is learned during training.

1.15.52   Convolutional Layer: A convolutional layer applies a series of filters to the input, capturing local patterns.

1.15.53   Pooling Layer: A pooling layer reduces the spatial size of the representation, reducing computation and helping to make the representation invariant to small translations.

1.15.54   RNN: A recurrent neural network (RNN) is a type of neural network that has internal loops and can process sequential data.

1.15.55   LSTM: A long short-term memory (LSTM) network is a type of RNN that can learn and remember over long sequences, avoiding the vanishing gradient problem.

1.15.56   One-Hot vs. Label Encoding: One-hot encoding represents each category as a binary vector, while label encoding assigns each category a unique integer.

1.15.57   Regression vs. Classification Problem: In regression, the model predicts a continuous value, while in classification, the model predicts a discrete class label.

1.15.58   Confusion Matrix: A confusion matrix is used to measure the performance of a classification model, showing the true and false positives and negatives.

1.15.59   PCA: Principal Component Analysis (PCA) is used for dimensionality reduction; it transforms features into a set of orthogonal (uncorrelated) components.

Chapter 2 Questions Responses

Problems

2.14.1   The three major types of data cleaning approaches are: data auditing, workflow specification, and workflow execution. General steps involved are identifying, correcting or removing errors, and inconsistencies in the data.

2.14.2   Data transformation is the process of converting data from one format or structure into another. Three primary approaches are normalization, aggregation, and generalization.

2.14.3 Data balancing refers to techniques that adjust the class distribution of a dataset. Oversampling and undersampling are common data balancing techniques, where oversampling increases the minority class instances and undersampling decreases the majority class instances.

2.14.4 Data augmentation is the process of creating new data instances by applying various transformations to existing data. It is crucial because it can help improve the performance of machine learning models by providing more diverse examples during training.

2.14.5 Data reduction is the process of reducing the amount of data by obtaining a reduced dataset that is much smaller in volume but still produces the same analytical results. Principal Component Analysis (PCA) and Linear Discriminant Analysis (LDA) are dimensionality reduction techniques used in data reduction.

2.14.6 In data splitting, there are usually three partitions: training set, validation set, and test set.

2.14.7 The main steps involved in data preparation include data cleaning, data transformation, data integration, data reduction, and data discretization.

2.14.8 Sample Data:

First Name	Last Name	IDid	Grade
John	Doe	1001	85
Jane	Smith	1002	90
Alice	Brown	1003	88
Bob	White	1004	NA

Cleaning and Transformation:

- Remove non-numeric characters from IDid.
- Replace "NA" in Grade with the median grade.

2.14.9 Steps:

1. Load Excel file into a data processing tool (like Python's `pandas`).
2. Clean missing or inconsistent data.
3. Transform columns to desired formats (e.g., date to datetime format).
4. Reduce data size or dimensions if necessary using techniques like PCA.

2.14.10 Steps:

- For PCA: Normalize data, compute covariance matrix, and select top "k" eigenvectors based on eigenvalues to transform data.
- For LDA: Compute within-class and between-class scatter matrices, find eigenvalues and eigenvectors, and transform data using top "k" eigenvectors.
- Using either method can reduce computation cost by reducing data dimensions while retaining key information.

2.14.11 Data preprocessing is the process of cleaning and transforming raw data before feeding it into a machine learning model. It is significant because it helps to improve the accuracy and efficiency of machine learning models.

2.14.12 Common techniques used for the imputation of missing data include mean/ mode/median imputation, prediction models, and multiple imputation.

2.14.13 Noisy data can be handled using techniques like binning, regression, and clustering.

2.14.14 Feature scaling is a method used to normalize the range of independent variables or features of data. It is necessary in algorithms that use gradient descent and in algorithms that use distance-based metrics.

2.14.15 Imbalanced datasets can be managed using techniques like resampling, generating synthetic samples, and using cost-sensitive learning methods.

2.14.16 Data augmentation is a strategy that enables practitioners to significantly increase the diversity of data available for training models, without actually collecting new data. Data generation, on the other hand, involves creating new data based on the existing dataset or from scratch.

2.14.17 Dimensionality reduction is the process of reducing the number of random variables under consideration by obtaining a set of principal variables. It is employed in machine learning to reduce computational costs and to avoid overfitting.

2.14.18 Common techniques used for the detection and removal of outliers include Z-Score, IQR (Interquartile Range), and DBScan clustering.

Programming

Easy

2.15.1 Remove missing values using pandas

```
import pandas as pd
data = pd.read_csv("data.csv")
data_clean = data.dropna()
data_clean.to_csv("data_clean.csv", index=False)
```

2.15.2 Normalize values using Min-Max scaling

```
import pandas as pd
from sklearn.preprocessing import MinMaxScaler
data = pd.read_csv("data.csv")
scaler = MinMaxScaler()
data_normalized = scaler.fit_transform(data)
data_normalized = pd.DataFrame(data_normalized, columns=data.columns)
data_normalized.to_csv("data_normalized.csv", index=False)
```

2.15.3 One-hot encoding for categorical variables

```
import pandas as pd
data = pd.read_csv("data.csv")
data_encoded = pd.get_dummies(data, columns=["categorical_column"])
data_encoded.to_csv("data_encoded.csv", index=False)
```

2.15.4 Split dataset into training and testing sets

```
import pandas as pd
from sklearn.model_selection import train_test_split
data = pd.read_csv("data.csv")
X_train, X_test, y_train, y_test = train_test_split(data.
drop("target_column", axis=1), data["target_column"], test_
size=0.2, random_state=42)
```

2.15.5 Remove outliers using z-score

```
import numpy as np
import pandas as pd
from scipy import stats
data = pd.read_csv("data.csv")
data_no_outliers = data[(np.abs(stats.zscore(data)) < 3).all(axis=1)]
data_no_outliers.to_csv("data_no_outliers.csv", index=False)
```

2.15.6 Apply PCA

```
import pandas as pd
from sklearn.decomposition import PCA
data = pd.read_csv("data.csv")
pca = PCA(n_components=2)
data_pca = pca.fit_transform(data)
data_pca = pd.DataFrame(data_pca, columns=["PC1", "PC2"])
data_pca.to_csv("data_pca.csv", index=False)
```

2.15.7 Feature scaling using standardization

```
import pandas as pd
from sklearn.preprocessing import StandardScaler
data = pd.read_csv("data.csv")
scaler = StandardScaler()
data_standardized = scaler.fit_transform(data)
data_standardized = pd.DataFrame(data_standardized, columns=data.
columns)
data_standardized.to_csv("data_standardized.csv", index=False)
```

2.15.8 Data discretization using k-means

```
import pandas as pd
from sklearn.cluster import KMeans
data = pd.read_csv("data.csv")
kmeans = KMeans(n_clusters=4)
data["cluster"] = kmeans.fit_predict(data)
data.to_csv("data_discretized.csv", index=False)
```

2.15.9 Text preprocessing

```
import re
from nltk.corpus import stopwords
from nltk.stem import PorterStemmer
```

```python
def text_preprocessing(text):
    text = text.lower()
    text = re.sub(r"[^a-z0-9]+", " ", text)
    words = text.split()
    stemmer = PorterStemmer()
    stop_words = set(stopwords.words("english"))
    words = [stemmer.stem(w) for w in words if w not in stop_words]
    return " ".join(words)
```

2.15.10 Data augmentation with Keras

```python
from keras.preprocessing.image import ImageDataGenerator
from keras.preprocessing import image
datagen = ImageDataGenerator(
        rotation_range=40,
        width_shift_range=0.2,
        height_shift_range=0.2,
        shear_range=0.2,
        zoom_range=0.2,
        horizontal_flip=True,
        fill_mode='nearest')
img = image.load_img('path_to_your_image', target_size=(150, 150))
# replace with your image path
x = image.img_to_array(img)
x = x.reshape((1,) + x.shape)
i = 0
for batch in datagen.flow(x, batch_size=1, save_to_dir='preview',
save_prefix='img', save_format='jpeg'):
    i += 1
    if i > 20:  # decide how many augmented images you want
        break
```

2.15.11 Remove duplicates from a list of strings

```python
def remove_duplicates(lst):
    return list(set(lst))
```

2.15.12 Convert a CSV file to a JSON file

```python
import pandas as pd
data = pd.read_csv("data.csv")
data.to_json("data.json", orient="records")
```

2.15.13 Count the number of occurrences of each word in a text file

```python
from collections import Counter
with open('text.txt', 'r') as f:
    words = f.read().split()
    word_count = Counter(words)
```

2.15.14 Tokenize a sentence into words

```python
def tokenize_sentence(sentence):
    return sentence.split()
```

2.15.15 Remove stop words from a text file

```python
from nltk.corpus import stopwords
stop_words = set(stopwords.words('english'))
with open('text.txt', 'r') as f:
    words = f.read().split()
    words = [word for word in words if word not in stop_words]
```

2.15.16 Merge multiple CSV files into a single CSV file

```python
import pandas as pd
from glob import glob
csv_files = glob("*.csv")
df = pd.concat((pd.read_csv(f) for f in csv_files))
df.to_csv("merged.csv", index=False)
```

2.15.17 Perform stemming on a list of words

```python
from nltk.stem import PorterStemmer
def stem_words(words):
    stemmer = PorterStemmer()
    return [stemmer.stem(word) for word in words]
```

2.15.18 Convert text to lowercase and remove punctuation marks

```python
import string
def preprocess_text(text):
    text = text.lower()
    return text.translate(str.maketrans('', '', string.
punctuation))
```

2.15.19 Split a large text file into smaller files based on the number of lines

```python
def split_file(filename, lines_per_file):
    with open(filename, 'r') as f:
        lines = f.readlines()
    for i in range(0, len(lines), lines_per_file):
        with open(f'file_{i//lines_per_file}.txt', 'w') as f:
            f.writelines(lines[i:i+lines_per_file])
```

2.15.20 Replace missing values in a dataset with the mean or median of the feature

```python
import pandas as pd
data = pd.read_csv('data.csv')
data.fillna(data.mean(), inplace=True)
# or data.fillna(data.median(), inplace=True) for median
data.to_csv('data_clean.csv', index=False)
```

2.15.21 Remove duplicate rows from a CSV file

```python
import pandas as pd
data = pd.read_csv('data.csv')
data.drop_duplicates(inplace=True)
data.to_csv('data_no_duplicates.csv', index=False)
```

2.15.22 Replace all occurrences of a specific value in a CSV file with a new value

```
import pandas as pd
data = pd.read_csv('data.csv')
data.replace('old_value', 'new_value', inplace=True) # replace
'old_value' and 'new_value' with your values
data.to_csv('data_replaced.csv', index=False)
```

2.15.23 Merge two CSV files based on a common column

```
import pandas as pd
data1 = pd.read_csv('data1.csv')
data2 = pd.read_csv('data2.csv')
merged = pd.merge(data1, data2, on='common_column') # replace
'common_column' with your column
merged.to_csv('merged.csv', index=False)
```

Medium

2.15.24 Convert all categorical variables in a dataset to one-hot encoded variables

```
import pandas as pd
def one_hot_encode(data):
    categorical_cols = data.select_dtypes(include=['object']).
columns
    data = pd.get_dummies(data, columns = categorical_cols)
    return data
data = pd.read_csv('data.csv')
data = one_hot_encode(data)
```

2.15.25 Perform feature scaling on a dataset

```
from sklearn.preprocessing import StandardScaler
import pandas as pd
data = pd.read_csv('data.csv')
scaler = StandardScaler()
scaled_data = scaler.fit_transform(data)
scaled_data = pd.DataFrame(scaled_data, columns=data.columns)
```

2.15.26 Impute missing values in a dataset using mean imputation

```
import pandas as pd
def mean_imputation(data):
    return data.fillna(data.mean())
data = pd.read_csv('data.csv')
data = mean_imputation(data)
```

2.15.27 Perform PCA on a dataset

```
from sklearn.decomposition import PCA
import pandas as pd
data = pd.read_csv('data.csv')
```

```
    pca = PCA(n_components=2) # replace 2 with the number of
    components you want
    principalComponents = pca.fit_transform(data)
```

2.15.28 Detect and remove outliers from a dataset

```
import pandas as pd
from scipy import stats
def remove_outliers(data):
    z_scores = stats.zscore(data)
    abs_z_scores = np.abs(z_scores)
    filtered_entries = (abs_z_scores < 3).all(axis=1)
    new_data = data[filtered_entries]
    return new_data
data = pd.read_csv('data.csv')
data = remove_outliers(data)
```

Hard

2.15.29 Preprocess text data for natural language processing (NLP)

```
import nltk
from nltk.corpus import stopwords
from nltk.tokenize import word_tokenize
from nltk.stem import PorterStemmer
def preprocess_text(text):
    stop_words = set(stopwords.words('english'))
    word_tokens = word_tokenize(text)
    filtered_text = [w for w in word_tokens if not w in
stop_words]
    ps = PorterStemmer()
    stemmed_text = [ps.stem(word) for word in filtered_text]
    return stemmed_text
```

Chapter 3 Questions Responses

Problems

3.10.1 Hyperparameters guide the learning process of a model. They can be optimized through techniques like grid search, random search, or Bayesian optimization.

3.10.2 The correct model is the one that best generalizes from training data to unseen data. Model error is the difference between the model's predictions and the actual values. It can be calculated using metrics like Mean Squared Error (MSE) for regression tasks and accuracy for classification tasks.

3.10.3 Noise refers to irrelevant or random data points that don't represent the underlying pattern. Noise is generally hard to quantify, but overfitting (i.e., a model learning the noise) can indicate its presence.

3.10.4   Bias is the difference between the average prediction of the model and the correct value. It's an indication of the model's assumptions about the data. It can be calculated as the difference between the expected prediction and the true value.

3.10.5   Variance indicates how much the model's predictions would change if it were trained on a different dataset. It can be calculated by measuring the variability of model predictions for a given data point.

3.10.6   The bias-variance tradeoff is a balance between a model's ability to fit data well (low bias) and also adapt to different data (low variance). The best results typically come from a balance between the two.

3.10.7   A model's flaws can include overfitting, underfitting, lack of generalization, etc. These can be identified through techniques like cross-validation and examining learning curves.

3.10.8   The three main approaches to model evaluation are holdout method (splitting data into train and test sets), cross-validation (dividing data into "k" subsets and rotating the test set), and bootstrap methods (sampling with replacement).

3.10.9   The purpose of model evaluation is to assess how well a model will generalize to new data.

3.10.10   Common evaluation metrics for classification models include accuracy, precision, recall, F1 score, and AUC-ROC.

3.10.11   A confusion matrix summarizes the counts of true positive, true negative, false positive, and false negative predictions. It's used to calculate several classification metrics.

3.10.12   Precision, recall, and F1 score are calculated from the confusion matrix. Precision is TP/(TP+FP), recall is TP/(TP+FN), and F1 score is 2*(precision*recall)/(precision+recall).

3.10.13   Overfitting is when a model learns the training data too well, including noise. It can be prevented by techniques like regularization, early stopping, or gathering more data.

3.10.14   Cross-validation is a technique to assess model performance using different subsets of the data. It's important because it provides a more robust estimate of the model's performance.

3.10.15   A ROC curve plots the true positive rate against the false positive rate for different threshold values, and it's used to assess the performance of a binary classifier.

3.10.16   Precision is the ratio of correctly predicted positive observations to the total predicted positives, while recall is the ratio of correctly predicted positive observations to all observations in actual class.

3.10.17   The choice of evaluation metric depends on the problem at hand, the business objective, and the cost of different types of errors.

3.10.18   Validation set is used for tuning the model parameters during training, while the test set is used for evaluating the final model performance.

3.10.19   Overfitting can be detected by comparing model performance on training data and validation/test data. If a model performs significantly better on training data, it's likely overfitting.

3.10.20 Common evaluation metrics for binary classification problems include accuracy, precision, recall, F1 score, and AUC-ROC.

3.10.21 Precision and recall are used to evaluate the performance of classification models, especially in cases of imbalanced classes.

3.10.22 The F1 score is derived from the harmonic average of precision and recall.

3.10.23 Cross-validation is a resampling technique used to evaluate machine learning models on a limited data sample. It partitions the data into subsets, holds out one as a validation set, and trains the model on the remaining subsets. This process repeats, holding out a different subset each time. The final model performance is the average of the performances on each subset. It helps to prevent overfitting and provides a better understanding of the model's generalization performance.

3.10.24 Regression model performance is evaluated using metrics, such as Mean Absolute Error (MAE), MSE, Root Mean Squared Error (RMSE), or R-squared (R^2). These metrics compare the model's predictions with the actual values, providing a quantifiable measure of the model's prediction accuracy.

3.10.25 For multi-class classification problems, some common evaluation metrics include multi-class versions of precision, recall, and F1-score, as well as the confusion matrix, macro averaged metrics, and micro averaged metrics.

3.10.26 A confusion matrix is a table that is often used to describe the performance of a classification model on a set of data for which the true values are known. It summarizes the counts of true positive, true negative, false positive, and false negative predictions. This helps to identify the types of errors made by the model.

3.10.27 The Receiver Operating Characteristic (ROC) curve is a graphical representation of the sensitivity (true positive rate) versus 1-specificity (false positive rate) for a binary classifier as its discrimination threshold is varied. It is used to assess the performance of a binary classifier and to choose the best probability threshold for classification. The area under the ROC curve (AUC-ROC) is often used as a single-number summary of the model's performance.

Programming

Easy

3.11.1 You can use the "accuracy_score" function from scikit-learn's metrics module to evaluate the accuracy of a classification model. You would pass the true labels and the predicted labels to this function.

3.11.2 Accuracy measures the overall correctness of the classifier (i.e., how many predictions it got right), while precision measures the classifier's ability to correctly identify only relevant instances (i.e., how many of the identified positive instances were actually positive).

3.11.3 You can use TensorFlow's "metrics.ConfusionMatrix" class to compute the confusion matrix of a classification model. You can use TensorFlow's "tf.math.confusion_matrix" function to compute the confusion matrix of a classification model. You would pass the true labels and the predicted labels to this function.

Appendix

3.11.4 Here's an example of a Python function to calculate and print the accuracy of a binary classification model:

```
from sklearn.metrics import accuracy_score
def print_accuracy(y_true, y_pred):
    accuracy = accuracy_score(y_true, y_pred)
    print(f'Accuracy: {accuracy}')
```

3.11.5 Here's an example of a Python function to calculate and print the precision and recall of a multiclass classification model:

```
from sklearn.metrics import precision_score, recall_score
def calculate_precision_recall(y_true, y_pred):
    precision = precision_score(y_true, y_pred, average='macro')
    recall = recall_score(y_true, y_pred, average='macro')
    return precision, recall
```

3.11.6 The F1 score is not typically calculated for regression models. It is a metric used for classification tasks.

3.11.7 Here's an example of a Python function to calculate the MSE of a regression model:

```
from sklearn.metrics import mean_squared_error
def calculate_mse(y_true, y_pred):
    mse = mean_squared_error(y_true, y_pred)
    return mse
```

3.11.8 Here's an example of a Python function to calculate and print the confusion matrix of a classification model:

```
from sklearn.metrics import confusion_matrix
def print_confusion_matrix(y_true, y_pred):
    cm = confusion_matrix(y_true, y_pred)
    print('Confusion Matrix:')
    print(cm)
```

Medium

3.11.9 In TensorFlow, you can perform K-fold cross-validation using the "KFold" class from the "sklearn.model_selection" module. In scikit-learn, you can perform K-fold cross-validation using the "KFold" class from the "sklearn.model_selection" module. You would need to split your data into k subsets, and then train and evaluate your model k times, each time using a different subset as your validation set.

3.11.10 AUC-ROC (Area Under the Receiver Operating Characteristic Curve) is a performance measurement for binary classification problems. It can be interpreted as the probability that the model ranks a random positive instance more highly than a random negative instance. In Keras, you can use the "AUC" class from "tensorflow.keras.metrics" to compute the AUC-ROC of a binary classification model.

3.11.11 Here's an example of a Python function to calculate and print the ROC curve of a binary classification model:

```
from sklearn.metrics import roc_curve
def print_roc_curve(y_true, y_scores):
    fpr, tpr, thresholds = roc_curve(y_true, y_scores)
    print('ROC Curve:')
    print(f'FPR: {fpr}')
    print(f'TPR: {tpr}')
```

3.11.12 Here's an example of a Python function to calculate and print the precision-recall curve of a binary classification model:

```
from sklearn.metrics import precision_recall_curve
def print_precision_recall_curve(y_true, y_scores):
    precision, recall, thresholds = precision_recall_curve(y_true,
y_scores)
    print('Precision-Recall Curve:')
    print(f'Precision: {precision}')
    print(f'Recall: {recall}')
```

3.11.13 Here's an example of a Python function to calculate the AUC of an ROC curve:

```
from sklearn.metrics import roc_auc_score
def calculate_auc(y_true, y_scores):
    auc = roc_auc_score(y_true, y_scores)
    return auc
```

3.11.14 Here's an example of a Python function to perform cross-validation on a classification model using K-fold cross-validation:

```
from sklearn.model_selection import cross_val_score
def perform_cross_validation(model, X, y, cv):
    scores = cross_val_score(model, X, y, cv=cv)
    return scores
```

3.11.15 Here's an example of a Python function to calculate the R-squared score of a regression model:

```
from sklearn.metrics import r2_score
def calculate_r2_score(y_true, y_pred):
    r2 = r2_score(y_true, y_pred)
    return r2
```

Hard

3.11.16 You can use Bayesian optimization libraries like "Scikit-Optimize" or "Hyperopt" with scikit-learn to tune hyperparameters. These libraries provide a function that you can call to evaluate the model with different hyperparameters and use Bayesian optimization to select the next set of hyperparameters to evaluate.

3.11.17 In TensorFlow, you can evaluate the performance of a deep learning model using the "Precision" and "Recall" classes from "tensorflow.keras.metrics". To plot precision-recall curves for such models, you can use the "precision_recall_curve" function from sklearn.metrics and matplotlib for visualization.

3.11.18 Keras does not directly support leave-one-out cross-validation. However, you can use "sklearn.model_selection.LeaveOneOut" to generate train/test indices and use them to train and evaluate your Keras model.

3.11.19 Here's an example of a Python function to perform nested cross-validation on a classification model:

```
from sklearn.model_selection import cross_val_score, KFold
def perform_nested_cross_validation(model, X, y, outer_cv,
inner_cv):
    outer_scores = []
    for train_index, test_index in outer_cv.split(X):
        X_train, X_test = X[train_index], X[test_index]
        y_train, y_test = y[train_index], y[test_index]
        model.fit(X_train, y_train)
        inner_scores = cross_val_score(model, X_train, y_train,
cv=inner_cv)
        outer_scores.append(model.score(X_test, y_test))
    return outer_scores, inner_scores
```

3.11.20 Here's an example of a Python function to calculate the Brier score of a binary classification model:

```
from sklearn.metrics import brier_score_loss
def calculate_brier_score(y_true, y_prob):
    brier_score = brier_score_loss(y_true, y_prob)
    return brier_score
```

3.11.21 Here's an example of a Python function to calculate and plot the learning curve of a classification or regression model:

```
from sklearn.model_selection import learning_curve
import matplotlib.pyplot as plt
def plot_learning_curve(model, X, y):
    train_sizes, train_scores, test_scores = learning_
curve(model, X, y)
    plt.plot(train_sizes, train_scores.mean(axis=1), label='train
score')
    plt.plot(train_sizes, test_scores.mean(axis=1), label='test
score')
    plt.legend(loc='best')
    plt.show()
```

3.11.22 Here's an example of a Python function to calculate the average precision (AP) of a binary classification model:

```
from sklearn.metrics import average_precision_score
def calculate_average_precision(y_true, y_scores):
    average_precision = average_precision_score(y_true, y_scores)
    return average_precision
```

3.11.23 Here's an example of a Python function to perform hyperparameter tuning on a classification or regression model using grid search:

```
from sklearn.model_selection import GridSearchCV
def perform_grid_search(model, X, y, param_grid):
    grid_search = GridSearchCV(model, param_grid)
    grid_search.fit(X, y)
    return grid_search.best_params_
```

Chapter 4 Questions Responses

Problems

4.14.1 TensorFlow is an open-source library developed by the Google Brain Team for numerical computation and machine learning. It uses data flow graphs and offers APIs for beginners and experts, supports various platforms (CPU, GPU, TPU), and includes tools for visualization (TensorBoard), deployment (TF Serving), mobile and IoT (TF Lite), and more.

4.14.2 TensorFlow can be installed using pip: "pip install tensorflow", or conda: "conda install tensorflow".

4.14.3 Tensors in TensorFlow are n-dimensional arrays. They can be rank-0 (scalars), rank-1 (vectors), rank-2 (matrices), or higher-rank tensors.

4.14.4 A TensorFlow session is a context for running a computation graph. It's created using "with tf.Session() as sess:".

4.14.5 A computation graph is defined by creating TensorFlow operations and tensors, which are automatically added to the graph.

4.14.6 Variables are stateful nodes that hold parameters. Placeholders are nodes whose values are fed at runtime. Variables are used for trainable parameters, placeholders for input data and labels.

4.14.7 Training a model involves defining a loss function, an optimizer, and calling "optimizer.minimize(loss)" inside a session.

4.14.8 A tensor is a general term for n-dimensional arrays. A variable is a special tensor that maintains state across executions of the graph.

4.14.9 A placeholder is a tensor that expects to receive a value, while a variable is a tensor that can change its value during execution.

4.14.10 Common activation functions include "tf.nn.relu", "tf.nn.sigmoid", "tf.nn.tanh", "tf.nn.softmax".

4.14.11 Backpropagation is a method for training neural networks by adjusting weights based on the calculated gradient of the loss function.

4.14.12 Models can be saved with the "tf.train.Saver" API and restored with "saver.restore(session, save_path)".

4.14.13 TensorFlow offers various optimizers like Gradient Descent, Adagrad, Adam, RMSProp.

4.14.14 TensorFlow Serving is a flexible, high-performance serving system for machine learning models, designed for production environments.

4.14.15 TensorFlow Lite is a lightweight version for mobile and embedded devices.

4.14.16 Keras is a high-level neural networks API capable of running on top of TensorFlow, Theano, and CNTK. It offers more user-friendly interfaces.

4.14.17 Keras offers Sequential model for linear stack of layers, and Functional API for complex architectures.

4.14.18 Callbacks in Keras are functions applied during the training process, like model checkpointing, early stopping, learning rate scheduling.

4.14.19 Overfitting can be addressed with techniques like regularization, dropout, or early stopping.

4.14.20 Keras models can be saved with "model.save(filepath)" and loaded with "keras. models.load_model(filepath)".

4.14.21 Keras offers various layers like Dense, Conv2D, MaxPooling2D, Dropout, LSTM, etc.

4.14.22 Sequential API is for simple models with single input/output, while Functional API is for complex models with multiple inputs/outputs or shared layers.

4.14.23 Transfer learning in Keras can be done by loading a pre-trained model, freezing some layers, and training the remaining layers on the new task.

4.14.24 Data augmentation in Keras can be done with "keras.preprocessing.image. ImageDataGenerator".

4.14.25 Image classification tasks in Keras typically involve Convolutional Neural Networks (CNNs), which can be built using the Sequential or Functional API.

Programming

Easy

4.15.1 Linear regression model:
- Define placeholders for input features (X) and labels (Y).
- Create variables for weights (W) and bias (b).
- Define the linear model: Y_pred = X * W + b.
- Define the loss function (e.g., mean squared error).
- Create an optimizer and minimize the loss function.
- Run the training loop within a TensorFlow session.

4.15.2 2D convolutional layer:
- Use "tf.nn.conv2d" function with input tensor, filter/kernel tensor, strides, and padding.

4.15.3 Simple feedforward neural network:
- Create input placeholders.
- Define fully connected (dense) layers using "tf.layers.dense" or "tf.matmul" and activation functions.
- Define the loss function, optimizer, and training operation.
- Run the training loop within a TensorFlow session.

4.15.4 Calculate model accuracy:
- Define an accuracy metric (e.g., correct predictions percentage).
- Calculate the accuracy using the true labels and model predictions.
- Run the evaluation within a TensorFlow session.

4.15.5 Visualize training progress:
- Use TensorBoard by creating summary operations and writing summaries to a log directory.
- Launch TensorBoard to visualize the training progress.

4.15.6 Basic neural network with Keras for MNIST:
- Load the MNIST dataset.
- Create a Sequential model.
- Add Dense layers with activation functions.
- Compile the model with a loss function, optimizer, and accuracy metric.
- Train the model using "model.fit".
- Evaluate the model with "model.evaluate".

4.15.7 Logical OR gate:
- Create a dataset for OR gate inputs and outputs.
- Build a simple Sequential model with one Dense layer.
- Compile and train the model.
- Test the model with OR gate input combinations.

4.15.8 CIFAR-10 classification:
- Load the CIFAR-10 dataset.
- Preprocess the data (e.g., normalization).
- Build a CNN using the Sequential model with Conv2D, MaxPooling2D, and Dense layers.
- Compile and train the model.
- Evaluate the model on the test set.

4.15.9 House price prediction:
- Load and preprocess the house price dataset.
- Create a Sequential model with Dense layers.
- Compile the model with a loss function (e.g., mean squared error) and optimizer.
- Train the model.
- Evaluate the model on the test set.

4.15.10 Gender prediction based on height and weight:
- Load and preprocess the dataset.
- Create a Sequential model with Dense layers and appropriate activation functions.
- Compile the model with a loss function (e.g., binary_crossentropy), optimizer, and accuracy metric.
- Train the model.
- Evaluate the model on the test set.

Medium

4.15.11 Implementing a Recurrent Neural Network (RNN) with TensorFlow:
- Initialize your RNN with the required number of layers and neurons.
- Define your cost/loss function and optimizer (like Adam Optimizer).
- Run your computational graph within a TensorFlow session.

4.15.12 Image Classification with Pre-trained Model in TensorFlow:
- Import a pre-trained model from TensorFlow Hub or use "tf.keras.applications" module.
- Extract features from your images using this pre-trained model.
- Train a new model on top of these features to classify your images.

4.15.13 Implementing a Generative Adversarial Network (GAN) with TensorFlow:
- Define your generator and discriminator networks.
- Define your loss functions and optimizers for both networks.
- Train both networks in a loop, with the generator trying to fool the discriminator and the discriminator getting better at telling real from fake.

4.15.14 Training a CNN for Image Recognition with TensorFlow:
- Define your CNN with the desired architecture.
- Compile your model, specifying the optimizer and loss function.
- Fit your model to the training data.

4.15.15 Implementing a Long Short-Term Memory (LSTM) Network in TensorFlow:
- Define your LSTM with the desired number of units.
- Compile your model, specifying the optimizer and loss function.
- Fit your model to the training data.

4.15.16 Building a Keras Model for Sentiment Analysis on Movie Reviews:
- Preprocess your text data (tokenization, padding, etc.)
- Define your model architecture (could be an LSTM or a simple Dense network).
- Compile and train your model.

4.15.17 Training a Keras Model to Generate New Text:
- Preprocess your text data and create sequences.
- Define a model with LSTM layer(s) followed by a Dense layer with a softmax activation function.
- Train your model and then use it to generate new text.

4.15.18 Designing a Keras Model to Recognize Emotions in Speech:
- Extract features from your audio data.
- Define your model architecture (could be a Conv1D, LSTM, or simple Dense network).
- Compile and train your model.

4.15.19 Training a Keras Model for Image Segmentation on Medical Images:
- Define your model architecture (U-Net is a commonly used architecture for image segmentation tasks).
- Compile and train your model.

4.15.20 Developing a Keras Model to Predict Company Stock Prices:
- Preprocess your time series data.
- Define your model architecture (an LSTM network is often used for time series prediction).
- Compile and train your model.

Please note that these are high-level steps. Each task involves more detailed steps like data preprocessing, model evaluation, and fine-tuning.

Hard

Here are brief outlines of how you might approach these tasks:

4.15.21 Implementing a Deep Neural Network with Multiple Hidden Layers in TensorFlow:
- Define your deep neural network with the desired number of hidden layers and units in each layer.
- Compile your model, specifying the optimizer and loss function.
- Fit your model to the training data.

4.15.22 Transfer Learning Using a Pre-trained Model in TensorFlow:
- Import a pre-trained model from TensorFlow Hub or tf.keras.applications.
- Freeze the weights of the pre-trained model and add your custom layers on top.
- Compile and train your model on your new data.

4.15.23 Implementing a Variational Autoencoder (VAE) for Image Generation in TensorFlow:
- Define the encoder and decoder parts of your VAE.
- Define the VAE loss function, which includes both the reconstruction loss and the KL divergence loss.
- Train your VAE on your image data.

4.15.24 Developing a Multi-GPU Training Program for a Deep Learning Model Using TensorFlow:
- Use the "tf.distribute.MirroredStrategy" for synchronous training on multiple GPUs.
- Define and compile your model within the strategy's scope.
- Train your model.

4.15.25 Building a Program for Object Detection Using a Deep Learning Model Trained with TensorFlow:
- Use a pre-trained model like SSD or Faster R-CNN available in the TensorFlow Model Zoo.
- Depending on the task, fine-tune the model on your specific data if needed.
- Use the model to make predictions and visualize the bounding boxes.

4.15.26 Building a Keras Model for Object Detection in Real-Time Video Streams:
- This is a complex task and usually requires using a pre-trained model.
- The model can be fine-tuned on a specific object detection task if necessary.
- The trained model can then be used on video frames for object detection.

4.15.27 Training a Keras Model to Generate Realistic 3D Models from 2D Images:

- This is an advanced task that might involve GANs or VAEs.
- The training process involves the generation of a latent representation of the 2D images that can then be decoded into 3D models.

4.15.28 Developing a Keras Model to Generate New Music Based on a Given Style or Genre:

- This task might involve sequence generation models like RNNs or LSTMs.
- The network can be trained on a large dataset of music in the desired style or genre.
- The trained model can then be used to generate new music.

4.15.29 Designing a Keras Model for Automatic Machine Translation:

- This task typically involves sequence-to-sequence (Seq2Seq) models.
- The model is trained to translate from the source language to the target language.

4.15.30 Training a Keras Model for Real-Time Facial Recognition and Identification:

- This is typically a multi-step process involving face detection (e.g., using a pre-trained model like MTCNN), face alignment, and then face recognition/identification.
- The face recognition/identification model can be trained on a large dataset of faces.

Please note that these are high-level steps. Each task involves more detailed steps like data preprocessing, model evaluation, and fine-tuning.

Chapter 5 Questions Responses

Problems

5.8.1 Artificial Neural Networks (ANNs) are computational models inspired by the biological neural networks in the human brain. They consist of interconnected artificial neurons that process and transmit information.

5.8.2 ANNs are similar to the biological neuron system as they are composed of artificial neurons that receive inputs, apply weights and activation functions, and produce outputs, mimicking the transmission and processing of information in the human brain.

5.8.3 The main difference between a feedforward neural network and a recurrent neural network (RNN) is that feedforward networks have a unidirectional flow of information, while recurrent networks have feedback connections, allowing them to process sequential and time-dependent data.

5.8.4 Backpropagation is a training algorithm for neural networks that calculates and adjusts the weights and biases based on the gradient of the loss function. It works by propagating the error backward from the output layer to the hidden layers, enabling the network to learn and improve its predictions.

5.8.5 Overfitting can be avoided in neural network training by using techniques, such as regularization (L1, L2), dropout, early stopping, and having a sufficient amount of diverse training data.

5.8.6 Activation functions determine the output of a neuron and introduce non-linearity in the neural network. Commonly used activation functions include sigmoid, tanh, ReLU, and softmax.

5.8.7 Dropout is a regularization technique that randomly sets a fraction of the neurons to zero during training, preventing them from being too dependent on each other and reducing overfitting.

5.8.8 A convolutional neural network (CNN) is a specialized type of neural network designed for processing grid-like data, such as images. Unlike traditional feedforward networks, CNNs utilize convolutional layers and pooling layers to effectively extract spatial and local patterns from input data.

5.8.9 An RNN is a type of neural network with feedback connections that allow it to process sequential and time-dependent data. It is useful in applications such as natural language processing, where the context and order of words matter.

5.8.10 Hyperparameters like the learning rate, number of hidden layers, and batch size can be optimized through techniques such as grid search, random search, or using optimization algorithms like Adam or RMSprop.

5.8.11 Transfer learning involves using pre-trained models on one task and applying them to a different but related task. It can save training time and improve performance, especially when the new task has limited training data.

5.8.12 Supervised learning involves training a neural network with labeled input-output pairs, unsupervised learning focuses on finding patterns and structure in the input data without labeled examples, and semi-supervised learning combines both labeled and unlabeled data for training.

5.8.13 In neural networks, regression tasks involve predicting continuous numerical values, while classification tasks involve predicting discrete categories or classes.

5.8.14 Regularization is a technique used to prevent overfitting in neural networks by adding additional terms to the loss function, penalizing large weights or complex model structures.

5.8.15 The vanishing gradient problem occurs when gradients become extremely small during backpropagation, making it difficult for deep neural networks to learn. Techniques like using different activation functions, weight initialization methods, or normalization techniques can help alleviate this problem.

5.8.16 Early stopping involves monitoring the validation loss during training and stopping the training process when the loss stops improving. It helps prevent overfitting by finding an optimal balance between training and generalization.

5.8.17 Normalization techniques like batch normalization adjust the mean and standard deviation of the input data within each batch, making the neural network more robust to variations in input values and improving training stability.

5.8.18 The performance of a trained neural network can be evaluated by metrics such as accuracy, precision, recall, F1 score, or using techniques like cross-validation and comparing against other models using appropriate evaluation measures.

5.8.19   Imbalanced data in classification tasks can be handled by techniques such as oversampling the minority class, undersampling the majority class, or using class weighting during training to give more importance to the minority class.

5.8.20   Common pitfalls to avoid when training neural networks include insufficient training data, inadequate preprocessing, improper choice of hyperparameters, overfitting, and not monitoring the training process effectively.

5.8.21   Neural networks can be used for unsupervised learning tasks such as clustering by using techniques like self-organizing maps (SOMs) or for dimensionality reduction by using methods like autoencoders or t-SNE.

5.8.22   Transfer learning involves utilizing knowledge from pre-trained models for specific tasks. In image recognition, for example, a pre-trained model can be fine-tuned on a new dataset, while in natural language processing, pre-trained language models like GPT or BERT can be used to improve performance on various tasks.

Programming

Easy

5.9.1   Implementing a single-layer perceptron in Python can be done using libraries like NumPy. Here's a basic example:

```python
import numpy as np
# Define input data
X = np.array([[0, 0], [0, 1], [1, 0], [1, 1]])
y = np.array([0, 0, 0, 1])
# Define activation function (step function)
def step_function(x):
    return 1 if x >= 0 else 0
# Initialize weights and bias
weights = np.array([0.0, 0.0])
bias = 0.0
learning_rate = 0.1
# Perceptron algorithm
for epoch in range(100):
    for i in range(len(X)):
        input_data = X[i]
        target = y[i]
        # Calculate weighted sum
        weighted_sum = np.dot(input_data, weights) + bias
        # Apply activation function (step function)
        prediction = step_function(weighted_sum)
        # Update weights and bias
        error = target - prediction
        weights += learning_rate * error * input_data
        bias += learning_rate * error
# Test the perceptron
test_input = np.array([1, 1])
weighted_sum = np.dot(test_input, weights) + bias
prediction = step_function(weighted_sum)
print("Prediction:", prediction)
```

5.9.2   Building a feedforward neural network with one hidden layer using Keras is straightforward. Here's an example:

```
from tensorflow import keras
# Define the model architecture
model = keras.Sequential([
    keras.layers.Dense(units=64, activation='relu',
input_shape=(input_dim,)),
    keras.layers.Dense(units=num_classes, activation='softmax')
])
# Compile the model
model.compile(optimizer='adam', loss='categorical_crossentropy',
metrics=['accuracy'])
# Train the model
model.fit(X_train, y_train, epochs=10, batch_size=32)
# Evaluate the model
loss, accuracy = model.evaluate(X_test, y_test)
print("Loss:", loss)
print("Accuracy:", accuracy)
```

In this example, the model is built with one hidden layer containing 64 units and a ReLU activation function. The output layer has the number of units equal to the number of classes in your classification problem, with a softmax activation function for multi-class classification. The model is compiled with an optimizer, a loss function, and optional metrics. Then, it is trained on the training data (X_train and y_train) for a specified number of epochs and batch size. Finally, the model is evaluated on the test data (X_test and y_test).

5.9.3   Training a neural network to classify the MNIST dataset in Python can be done using libraries like TensorFlow or Keras. Here's a brief example using Keras:

```
from tensorflow import keras
# Load and preprocess the MNIST dataset
(X_train, y_train), (X_test, y_test) = keras.datasets.mnist.
load_data()
X_train = X_train / 255.0
X_test = X_test / 255.0
# Convert labels to one-hot encoding
y_train = keras.utils.to_categorical(y_train)
y_test = keras.utils.to_categorical(y_test)
# Define the model architecture
model = keras.Sequential([
    keras.layers.Flatten(input_shape=(28, 28)),
    keras.layers.Dense(units=128, activation='relu'),
    keras.layers.Dense(units=10, activation='softmax')
])
# Compile the model
model.compile(optimizer='adam', loss='categorical_crossentropy',
metrics=['accuracy'])
# Train the model
model.fit(X_train, y_train, epochs=10, batch_size=32)
# Evaluate the model
loss, accuracy = model.evaluate(X_test, y_test)
print("Loss:", loss)
print("Accuracy:", accuracy)
```

In this example, the model is built with a flatten layer to convert the input data from 2D images to a 1D array, followed by a dense hidden layer with 128 units and a ReLU activation function. The output layer has 10 units with a softmax activation function for multi-class classification. The model is compiled with an optimizer, a loss function, and optional metrics. Then, it is trained on the training data (X_train and y_train) for a specified number of epochs and batch size. Finally, the model is evaluated on the test data (X_test and y_test).

Medium

5.9.4 To implement a multi-layer perceptron (MLP) in Python, you can use libraries like NumPy. An MLP consists of multiple layers of neurons, including an input layer, one or more hidden layers, and an output layer. Each neuron applies an activation function to its weighted inputs. Here's a basic example:

```python
import numpy as np
# Define input data
X = np.array([[0, 0], [0, 1], [1, 0], [1, 1]])
y = np.array([0, 1, 1, 0])
# Define activation function (sigmoid)
def sigmoid(x):
    return 1 / (1 + np.exp(-x))
# Initialize weights and biases
input_dim = X.shape[1]
hidden_dim = 2
output_dim = 1
W1 = np.random.randn(input_dim, hidden_dim)
b1 = np.zeros(hidden_dim)
W2 = np.random.randn(hidden_dim, output_dim)
b2 = np.zeros(output_dim)
# Forward pass
z1 = np.dot(X, W1) + b1
a1 = sigmoid(z1)
z2 = np.dot(a1, W2) + b2
output = sigmoid(z2)
# Backpropagation
error = y - output
delta_output = error * output * (1 - output)
delta_hidden = np.dot(delta_output, W2.T) * a1 * (1 - a1)
# Update weights and biases
learning_rate = 0.1
W2 += np.dot(a1.T, delta_output) * learning_rate
b2 += np.sum(delta_output, axis=0) * learning_rate
W1 += np.dot(X.T, delta_hidden) * learning_rate
b1 += np.sum(delta_hidden, axis=0) * learning_rate
# Test the MLP
test_input = np.array([[0, 0]])
z1 = np.dot(test_input, W1) + b1
a1 = sigmoid(z1)
z2 = np.dot(a1, W2) + b2
output = sigmoid(z2)
print("Output:", output)
```

5.9.5 To build a CNN using TensorFlow, you can use the TensorFlow library, which provides a comprehensive framework for building and training neural networks. Here's a brief example:

```
import tensorflow as tf
# Define the model architecture
model = tf.keras.Sequential([
    tf.keras.layers.Conv2D(filters=32, kernel_size=(3, 3),
activation='relu', input_shape=(28, 28, 1)),
    tf.keras.layers.MaxPooling2D(pool_size=(2, 2)),
    tf.keras.layers.Flatten(),
    tf.keras.layers.Dense(units=64, activation='relu'),
    tf.keras.layers.Dense(units=10, activation='softmax')
])
# Compile the model
model.compile(optimizer='adam', loss='sparse_categorical_
crossentropy', metrics=['accuracy'])
# Train the model
model.fit(X_train, y_train, epochs=10, batch_size=32)
# Evaluate the model
loss, accuracy = model.evaluate(X_test, y_test)
print("Loss:", loss)
print("Accuracy:", accuracy)
```

In this example, the model is built with convolutional layers, pooling layers, and fully connected layers. The model is then compiled with an optimizer, a loss function, and optional metrics. It is trained on the training data (X_train and y_train) for a specified number of epochs and batch size. Finally, the model is evaluated on the test data (X_test and y_test).

5.9.6 To train an RNN for sequence prediction in TensorFlow, you can utilize the TensorFlow library. RNNs are designed to process sequential data, making them suitable for tasks like sequence prediction or natural language processing. Here's a basic example:

```
import tensorflow as tf
# Define the model architecture
model = tf.keras.Sequential([
    tf.keras.layers.SimpleRNN(units=64, activation='relu', input_
shape=(T, input_dim)),
    tf.keras.layers.Dense(units=output_dim, activation='softmax')
])
# Compile the model
model.compile(optimizer='adam', loss='categorical_crossentropy',
metrics=['accuracy'])
# Train the model
model.fit(X_train, y_train, epochs=10, batch_size=32)
# Evaluate the model
loss, accuracy = model.evaluate(X_test, y_test)
print("Loss:", loss)
print("Accuracy:", accuracy)
```

In this example, the model is built with a SimpleRNN layer followed by a fully connected layer. The model is then compiled with an optimizer, a loss function, and optional metrics. It is trained on the training data (X_train and y_train) for a specified number of epochs and batch size. Finally, the model is evaluated on the test data (X_test and y_test).

Hard

5.9.7 Implementing a neural network from scratch using only NumPy involves building the basic components like layers, activation functions, and training algorithms. Here's a simplified example of a neural network implementation using NumPy:

```python
import numpy as np
# Define the activation function (sigmoid)
def sigmoid(x):
    return 1 / (1 + np.exp(-x))
# Define the neural network class
class NeuralNetwork:
    def __init__(self, input_dim, hidden_dim, output_dim):
        self.weights1 = np.random.randn(input_dim, hidden_dim)
        self.bias1 = np.zeros((1, hidden_dim))
        self.weights2 = np.random.randn(hidden_dim, output_dim)
        self.bias2 = np.zeros((1, output_dim))
    def forward(self, X):
        self.hidden_layer = sigmoid(np.dot(X, self.weights1) +
self.bias1)
        self.output_layer = sigmoid(np.dot(self.hidden_layer,
self.weights2) + self.bias2)
        return self.output_layer
    def backward(self, X, y, learning_rate):
        error = y - self.output_layer
        delta_output = error * self.output_layer * (1 - self.
output_layer)
        delta_hidden = np.dot(delta_output, self.weights2.T) *
self.hidden_layer * (1 - self.hidden_layer)
        self.weights2 += learning_rate * np.dot(self.hidden_
layer.T, delta_output)
        self.bias2 += learning_rate * np.sum(delta_output, axis=0)
        self.weights1 += learning_rate * np.dot(X.T, delta_hidden)
        self.bias1 += learning_rate * np.sum(delta_hidden, axis=0)
# Example usage
X = np.array([[0, 0], [0, 1], [1, 0], [1, 1]])
y = np.array([[0], [1], [1], [0]])
input_dim = X.shape[1]
hidden_dim = 4
output_dim = y.shape[1]
nn = NeuralNetwork(input_dim, hidden_dim, output_dim)
for epoch in range(10000):
    output = nn.forward(X)
    nn.backward(X, y, learning_rate=0.1)
# Test the trained neural network
test_input = np.array([[1, 0]])
output = nn.forward(test_input)
print("Output:", output)
```

5.9.8 Building a generative adversarial network (GAN) for image generation using TensorFlow involves creating a generator and a discriminator network and training them together. Here's a simplified example:

```python
import tensorflow as tf
# Define the generator network
class Generator(tf.keras.Model):
    def __init__(self, input_dim, output_dim):
        super(Generator, self).__init__()
        self.fc = tf.keras.layers.Dense(output_dim)
        self.relu = tf.keras.layers.ReLU()
    def call(self, x):
        x = self.fc(x)
        x = self.relu(x)
        return x
# Define the discriminator network
class Discriminator(tf.keras.Model):
    def __init__(self, input_dim):
        super(Discriminator, self).__init__()
        self.fc = tf.keras.layers.Dense(1)
        self.sigmoid = tf.keras.layers.Activation('sigmoid')
    def call(self, x):
        x = self.fc(x)
        x = self.sigmoid(x)
        return x
# Example usage
input_dim = 100
output_dim = 784
# Initialize generator and discriminator
generator = Generator(input_dim, output_dim)
discriminator = Discriminator(output_dim)
# Define the loss function and optimizers
loss_fn = tf.keras.losses.BinaryCrossentropy()
gen_optimizer = tf.keras.optimizers.Adam(learning_rate=0.001)
disc_optimizer = tf.keras.optimizers.Adam(learning_rate=0.001)
@tf.function
def train_step(real_samples):
    # Generate fake samples
    noise = tf.random.normal([batch_size, input_dim])
    with tf.GradientTape() as gen_tape, tf.GradientTape() as disc_tape:
        fake_samples = generator(noise, training=True)
        real_output = discriminator(real_samples, training=True)
        fake_output = discriminator(fake_samples, training=True)
        disc_loss_real = loss_fn(tf.ones_like(real_output),
real_output)
        disc_loss_fake = loss_fn(tf.zeros_like(fake_output),
fake_output)
        disc_loss = disc_loss_real + disc_loss_fake
        gen_loss = loss_fn(tf.ones_like(fake_output),
fake_output)
    gradients_of_discriminator = disc_tape.gradient(disc_loss,
discriminator.trainable_variables)
```

```
        gradients_of_generator = gen_tape.gradient(gen_loss,
generator.trainable_variables)
        disc_optimizer.apply_gradients(zip(gradients_of_discriminator,
discriminator.trainable_variables))
        gen_optimizer.apply_gradients(zip(gradients_of_generator,
generator.trainable_variables))
        return gen_loss, disc_loss
# Train the GAN
for epoch in range(num_epochs):
        real_samples = get_real_samples()  # Get real samples (This
function should be defined)
        gen_loss, disc_loss = train_step(real_samples)
# Generate new samples with the trained generator
noise = tf.random.normal([num_samples, input_dim])
generated_samples = generator(noise, training=False)
# Example usage of the generated samples
for sample in generated_samples:
        process_sample(sample.numpy())  # Assuming process_sample() is
already defined
```

5.9.9 Training a deep reinforcement learning agent to play a game using TensorFlow involves implementing an agent with a neural network model and using a reinforcement learning algorithm like Q-learning or policy gradients. Here's a simplified example:

```
import gym
import tensorflow as tf
from tensorflow.keras import layers
# Define the neural network model
model = tf.keras.Sequential([
    layers.Dense(128, activation='relu'),
    layers.Dense(64, activation='relu'),
    layers.Dense(num_actions)
])
# Define the agent
class DQNAgent:
    def __init__(self, num_actions):
        self.num_actions = num_actions
        self.model = model
    def get_action(self, state):
        return tf.argmax(self.model(state)[0]).numpy()
    def train(self, env, num_episodes, epsilon=1.0, epsilon_
decay=0.99, epsilon_min=0.01):
        optimizer = tf.keras.optimizers.Adam(learning_rate=0.001)
        loss_fn = tf.keras.losses.MeanSquaredError()
        for episode in range(num_episodes):
            state = env.reset()
            state = tf.expand_dims(tf.convert_to_tensor(state), 0)
            total_reward = 0
            while True:
                if tf.random.uniform(shape=()) < epsilon:
                    action = env.action_space.sample()
                else:
                    action = self.get_action(state)
```

```
                    next_state, reward, done, _ = env.step(action)
                    next_state = tf.expand_dims(tf.convert_to_
tensor(next_state), 0)
                    total_reward += reward
                    with tf.GradientTape() as tape:
                        q_values = self.model(state, training=True)
                        q_value = tf.reduce_sum(tf.multiply(q_values,
tf.one_hot(action, self.num_actions)))
                        target_q = reward + discount_factor *
tf.reduce_max(self.model(next_state, training=True))
                        loss = loss_fn(target_q, q_value)
                    grads = tape.gradient(loss, self.model.
trainable_variables)
                    optimizer.apply_gradients(zip(grads, self.model.
trainable_variables))
                    if done:
                        break
                    state = next_state
                epsilon *= epsilon_decay
                epsilon = max(epsilon, epsilon_min)
```

In this example, we define the neural network model using TensorFlow's Keras API, and then create a DQNAgent class that uses the model for action selection and training. The agent interacts with the OpenAI Gym environment to play a game over a specified number of episodes. During training, the agent performs Q-learning updates to update the Q-values based on the observed rewards and chooses actions based on an epsilon-greedy policy.

Chapter 6 Questions Responses

Problems

6.8.1 Deep learning is a subset of machine learning that focuses on training artificial neural networks with multiple layers to learn and extract representations from data. It differs from traditional machine learning in its ability to automatically learn hierarchical representations from raw data, eliminating the need for manual feature engineering. Deep learning models can handle complex patterns and large amounts of data, making them suitable for tasks such as image and speech recognition.

6.8.2 A neural network is a computational model inspired by the structure and functioning of biological neural networks. In deep learning, neural networks are composed of multiple interconnected layers of artificial neurons called nodes or units. Each node takes inputs, performs a weighted sum of the inputs, applies an activation function, and produces an output. The connections between nodes have associated weights that are adjusted during training to optimize the network's performance. Through a process called forward propagation, data flows through the network, and the network produces predictions or representations based on the learned weights.

6.8.3   There are different types of neural networks used in deep learning. Some common types include:

- Feedforward neural networks: These are the basic types of neural networks where information flows only in one direction, from the input layer to the output layer. They are used for tasks like classification and regression.

- Convolutional neural networks (CNNs): CNNs are particularly effective for image and video processing tasks. They use convolutional layers to capture spatial patterns and hierarchies of features in the data.

- Recurrent neural networks (RNNs): RNNs are designed to handle sequential data by introducing connections that allow feedback loops. They can capture temporal dependencies and are commonly used for tasks like natural language processing and speech recognition.

- Generative adversarial networks (GANs): GANs consist of a generator network and a discriminator network that compete against each other. GANs are used for tasks such as generating realistic images and data synthesis.

6.8.4   Choosing the right activation function for a neural network depends on the task and the network architecture. Some commonly used activation functions include:

- Sigmoid function: It maps inputs to a range between 0 and 1, making it suitable for binary classification problems or as an output activation in certain cases.

- Rectified Linear Unit (ReLU): ReLU sets negative inputs to zero and keeps positive inputs as they are. It helps in dealing with the vanishing gradient problem and is widely used in deep learning.

- Hyperbolic tangent (tanh): Tanh is similar to the sigmoid function but maps inputs to a range between -1 and 1. It is commonly used in RNNs.

- Softmax: Softmax is often used in the output layer for multi-class classification problems. It converts the outputs into a probability distribution over the classes.

6.8.5   Backpropagation is a key algorithm used in deep learning to train neural networks. It is a method for efficiently computing the gradients of the network's weights with respect to the loss function. Backpropagation involves two main steps: forward propagation and backward propagation. During forward propagation, input data is fed into the network, and activations are calculated layer by layer until the output is obtained. In backward propagation, the gradients of the loss function with respect to the network's output are computed. These gradients are then propagated backward through the layers, applying the chain rule to compute the gradients of the weights. By iteratively adjusting the weights based on these gradients using optimization algorithms, the network learns to minimize the loss function and improve its predictions.

6.8.6   Overfitting occurs when a deep learning model becomes too specialized to the training data and performs poorly on new, unseen data. Several techniques can help prevent overfitting in deep learning:

- Regularization: Regularization techniques such as L1 or L2 regularization can be used to add a penalty term to the loss function, discouraging the model from relying too heavily on any particular feature or combination of features.

- Dropout: Dropout randomly sets a fraction of the units in a layer to zero during training, which helps to prevent units from co-adapting and encourages the model to learn more robust representations.

- Early stopping: Early stopping involves monitoring the model's performance on a validation set during training and stopping the training when the performance on the validation set starts to degrade. This helps prevent the model from overfitting by finding the point of best generalization.

- Data augmentation: Data augmentation involves artificially expanding the training dataset by applying random transformations to the input data, such as rotations, translations, or flips. This increases the diversity of the data and reduces overfitting.

- Increasing the size of the training dataset: Having more training data can help reduce overfitting by providing the model with a more representative sample of the underlying distribution.

6.8.7 Transfer learning is a technique in deep learning where knowledge gained from training a model on one task or domain is transferred and applied to a different but related task or domain. Instead of training a model from scratch, transfer learning allows us to leverage the knowledge and representations learned from pre-trained models, often trained on large-scale datasets. By using a pre-trained model as a starting point, transfer learning offers several benefits, including improved performance with limited data, faster convergence, and reduced computational requirements. The pre-trained model's weights are usually frozen, and only the last few layers or specific parts of the model are fine-tuned for the target task using a smaller task-specific dataset. Transfer learning is commonly used in computer vision tasks, where pre-trained models trained on large image datasets like ImageNet are fine-tuned for specific image recognition or object detection tasks.

6.8.8 Optimization algorithms are used in deep learning to iteratively update the model's weights and minimize the loss function. Some common optimization algorithms used in deep learning include:

- Stochastic Gradient Descent (SGD): SGD updates the weights based on the gradients computed on a subset (batch) of the training data at each iteration.

- Adaptive Moment Estimation (Adam): Adam combines the advantages of AdaGrad and RMSprop algorithms by adapting the learning rate for each parameter based on past gradients.

- RMSprop: RMSprop is an adaptive learning rate optimization algorithm that scales the learning rate based on the moving average of squared gradients.

- AdaGrad: AdaGrad adapts the learning rate of each parameter based on the historical gradients, giving larger updates to parameters with smaller gradients.

- Adamax: Adamax is a variant of Adam that uses the infinity norm to scale the learning rate instead of the L2 norm.

6.8.9 The vanishing gradient problem occurs during training when the gradients calculated during backpropagation become extremely small, making it difficult for the model to learn and update the weights of early layers effectively.

This problem is especially common in deep neural networks with many layers. To mitigate the vanishing gradient problem, some techniques can be applied:

- Activation functions: Using activation functions like ReLU instead of sigmoid or tanh can help alleviate the vanishing gradient problem, as ReLU doesn't suffer from saturation issues and allows gradients to flow more easily.

- Weight initialization: Careful weight initialization techniques such as Xavier or He initialization can help ensure that the initial weights are within an appropriate range to prevent gradients from vanishing or exploding.

- Skip connections: Introducing skip connections or shortcuts in the network architecture, such as in residual networks (ResNet), allows gradients to bypass certain layers and flow more easily, addressing the vanishing gradient problem.

- Layer normalization or batch normalization: Applying normalization techniques within or across layers, such as layer normalization or batch normalization, can help stabilize the gradients and mitigate the vanishing gradient problem.

6.8.10 Choosing the right hyperparameters for a deep learning model is crucial for achieving optimal performance. Hyperparameters are parameters that are set before training the model and cannot be learned from the data. Some common hyperparameters in deep learning include the learning rate, batch size, number of layers, number of units per layer, activation functions, regularization parameters, and optimization algorithms. To choose the right hyperparameters:

- Start with reasonable default values based on prior knowledge or best practices.

- Perform a systematic search, such as grid search or random search, over a range of values for each hyperparameter while monitoring the model's performance on a validation set.

- Use techniques like cross-validation to evaluate the model's performance across different hyperparameter settings.

- Consider the trade-off between model complexity and generalization performance, avoiding overfitting or underfitting.

- Use visualization tools, such as learning curves or hyperparameter importance plots, to analyze the impact of different hyperparameters on the model's performance.

6.8.11 In deep learning, supervised learning refers to a learning paradigm where the training data includes both input samples and their corresponding target labels. The model learns to map inputs to outputs based on the labeled examples. Unsupervised learning, on the other hand, involves learning patterns and representations in the input data without explicit target labels. The model discovers hidden structures and dependencies within the data. Semi-supervised learning is a combination of both, where a small portion of the training data has labels, and the model leverages both labeled and unlabeled data to learn representations and make predictions. Deep learning models can be used for all three types of learning, depending on the availability of labeled data and the nature of the problem.

6.8.12 Reinforcement learning is a type of learning where an agent interacts with an environment and learns to take actions that maximize a reward signal. In deep reinforcement learning, deep neural networks are used to approximate the value function or policy of the agent. The agent receives feedback in the form of rewards or penalties based on its actions, and the neural network learns to optimize its policy to maximize the cumulative reward over time. Deep reinforcement learning has been successfully applied to various tasks, including game playing, robotics, and autonomous driving.

6.8.13 Adversarial training is a technique used in deep learning, specifically in the context of generative models, such as GANs. Adversarial training involves training two competing models simultaneously: a generator model that aims to generate realistic data samples and a discriminator model that tries to distinguish between real data and data generated by the generator. The generator and discriminator are trained iteratively, where the generator tries to fool the discriminator and the discriminator learns to better distinguish between real and generated data. This adversarial process leads to the generator improving its ability to generate more realistic samples over time.

6.8.14 The performance of a deep learning model can be measured using various evaluation metrics depending on the task. For classification tasks, metrics, such as accuracy, precision, recall, and F1-score, can be used to assess the model's performance. In regression tasks, metrics, such as mean squared error (MSE), mean absolute error (MAE), or R-squared, can be used. Additionally, depending on the specific problem, domain-specific metrics or evaluation methods may be used. It's important to carefully select the appropriate metrics that align with the goals and requirements of the task.

6.8.15 Regularization in deep learning refers to techniques used to prevent overfitting and improve the model's generalization performance. Regularization adds additional constraints or penalties to the model's objective function or loss function. Common regularization techniques in deep learning include L1 regularization, L2 regularization, and dropout. L1 regularization adds a penalty term proportional to the absolute value of the model's weights, encouraging sparsity and feature selection. L2 regularization adds a penalty term proportional to the squared value of the weights, promoting weight decay and smoothing the weight values. Dropout randomly sets a fraction of the units in a layer to zero during training, preventing units from co-adapting and improving the model's robustness. Regularization helps control the complexity of the model, avoids overfitting, and improves the model's ability to generalize to new, unseen data.

6.8.16 A CNN is a type of neural network commonly used in deep learning for tasks involving images and spatial data. CNNs are specifically designed to efficiently process data with a grid-like structure, leveraging the concept of convolution to extract local patterns and hierarchies of features. CNNs consist of multiple convolutional layers that apply convolution operations to the input data, followed by non-linear activation functions, such as ReLU. Pooling layers are often used to downsample the spatial dimensions and reduce the computational complexity. The outputs from the convolutional layers are typically passed through one or more fully connected layers for classification or regression. CNNs have achieved great success in tasks, such as image classification, object detection, and image segmentation.

6.8.17   A recurrent neural network (RNN) is a type of neural network commonly used in deep learning for tasks involving sequential data. Unlike feedforward neural networks, RNNs have feedback connections that allow information to persist and be processed across different time steps. This enables RNNs to capture temporal dependencies and learn from sequences of data. The key component of an RNN is the recurrent layer, which maintains a hidden state that serves as memory. At each time step, the RNN takes an input and combines it with the hidden state to produce an output and update the hidden state. The hidden state is then passed to the next time step, allowing the RNN to process sequences of arbitrary length. RNNs have been successfully applied to tasks, such as natural language processing, speech recognition, and time series analysis.

6.8.18   A GAN is a type of neural network architecture in deep learning that involves two components: a generator network and a discriminator network. The generator network takes random noise as input and generates synthetic data samples. The discriminator network takes both real data samples and generated samples as input and aims to distinguish between them. The generator and discriminator are trained iteratively in an adversarial process. The generator tries to generate samples that the discriminator cannot distinguish from real samples, while the discriminator aims to correctly classify real and generated samples. This adversarial training process leads to the generator improving its ability to generate realistic samples, while the discriminator becomes more effective at distinguishing real and generated data. GANs have been used for tasks, such as image synthesis, data augmentation, and anomaly detection.

6.8.19   Deep reinforcement learning is a combination of deep learning and reinforcement learning. It involves using deep neural networks to approximate the value function or policy of an agent in a reinforcement learning setting. Deep reinforcement learning differs from traditional reinforcement learning by leveraging the representational power of deep neural networks to learn complex mappings from observations to actions. Deep reinforcement learning has achieved impressive results in domains such as game playing and robotics, where high-dimensional inputs and complex decision-making are involved.

6.8.20   Scaling a deep learning model to handle large datasets can be achieved through various techniques:

- Mini-batch training: Instead of processing the entire dataset at once, mini-batch training involves dividing the data into smaller batches and updating the model's weights incrementally based on each batch. This allows efficient processing of large datasets while still updating the model's parameters.

- Data parallelism: Data parallelism involves distributing the training process across multiple devices or machines, where each device processes a subset of the data and updates the model's parameters. This enables parallelization and faster training on large datasets.

- Model parallelism: Model parallelism involves splitting a deep learning model across multiple devices or machines, where each device processes a different portion of the model's architecture. This allows training and inference on large models that may not fit into the memory of a single device.

- Distributed training: Distributed training involves training a deep learning model on multiple devices or machines that communicate and synchronize their updates. This allows for even larger-scale training on massive datasets by leveraging distributed computing resources.
- Data preprocessing and augmentation: Preprocessing techniques, such as data normalization, dimensionality reduction, and feature scaling, can help reduce the complexity of the data and improve the efficiency of training on large datasets. Data augmentation techniques, such as random cropping, rotation, and flipping, can artificially expand the training data and introduce diversity, improving the model's ability to generalize.

Programming

Easy

6.9.1 Here's an example of implementing a simple neural network to classify images of digits from the MNIST dataset using the TensorFlow library in Python:

```
import tensorflow as tf
from tensorflow.keras.datasets import mnist
from tensorflow.keras.models import Sequential
from tensorflow.keras.layers import Dense, Flatten
# Load the MNIST dataset
(x_train, y_train), (x_test, y_test) = mnist.load_data()
# Preprocess the data
x_train = x_train / 255.0
x_test = x_test / 255.0
# Define the model architecture
model = Sequential()
model.add(Flatten(input_shape=(28, 28)))
model.add(Dense(128, activation='relu'))
model.add(Dense(10, activation='softmax'))
# Compile the model
model.compile(optimizer='adam',
              loss='sparse_categorical_crossentropy',
              metrics=['accuracy'])
# Train the model
model.fit(x_train, y_train, epochs=5, batch_size=32,
validation_split=0.2)
# Evaluate the model
test_loss, test_acc = model.evaluate(x_test, y_test)
print('Test accuracy:', test_acc)
```

This code loads the MNIST dataset, preprocesses the image data by normalizing it, defines a simple neural network architecture with two dense layers, compiles the model with an optimizer and loss function, trains the model on the training data, and evaluates its performance on the test data.

6.9.2 Here's an example of a Python script to load and preprocess image data for use in a deep learning model using the TensorFlow library:

```
import tensorflow as tf
from tensorflow.keras.preprocessing.image import
ImageDataGenerator
# Define the data directories
train_dir = 'path/to/train/data'
validation_dir = 'path/to/validation/data'
# Define the image data generators
train_datagen = ImageDataGenerator(rescale=1.0/255.0)
validation_datagen = ImageDataGenerator(rescale=1.0/255.0)
# Load and preprocess the training data
train_generator = train_datagen.flow_from_directory(
    train_dir,
    target_size=(224, 224),
    batch_size=32,
    class_mode='binary'
)
# Load and preprocess the validation data
validation_generator = validation_datagen.flow_from_directory(
    validation_dir,
    target_size=(224, 224),
    batch_size=32,
    class_mode='binary'
)
# Define and train the deep learning model using the image data
model = tf.keras.models.Sequential(...)
model.compile(...)
model.fit(train_generator, validation_data=validation_generator,
epochs=10)
```

This code uses the "ImageDataGenerator" class from TensorFlow's Keras API to load and preprocess image data from directories. It rescales the pixel values to a range of 0–1, defines separate generators for training and validation data, and sets the target image size and batch size. The data is then loaded and preprocessed using the generators.

6.9.3 Here's an example of training a simple CNN to classify images of cats and dogs using the TensorFlow library in Python:

```
import tensorflow as tf
from tensorflow.keras.preprocessing.image import
ImageDataGenerator
# Define the data directories
train_dir = 'path/to/train/data'
validation_dir = 'path/to/validation/data'
# Define the image data generators
train_datagen = ImageDataGenerator(rescale=1.0/255.0)
validation_datagen = ImageDataGenerator(rescale=1.0/255.0)
# Load and preprocess the training data
train_generator = train_datagen.flow_from_directory(
    train_dir,
    target_size=(150,
```

```
150),
    batch_size=32,
    class_mode='binary'
)
# Load and preprocess the validation data
validation_generator = validation_datagen.flow_from_directory(
    validation_dir,
    target_size=(150, 150),
    batch_size=32,
    class_mode='binary'
)
# Define the CNN model
model = tf.keras.models.Sequential([
    tf.keras.layers.Conv2D(32, (3, 3), activation='relu', input_
shape=(150, 150, 3)),
    tf.keras.layers.MaxPooling2D((2, 2)),
    tf.keras.layers.Conv2D(64, (3, 3), activation='relu'),
    tf.keras.layers.MaxPooling2D((2, 2)),
    tf.keras.layers.Conv2D(128, (3, 3), activation='relu'),
    tf.keras.layers.MaxPooling2D((2, 2)),
    tf.keras.layers.Flatten(),
    tf.keras.layers.Dense(128, activation='relu'),
    tf.keras.layers.Dense(1, activation='sigmoid')
])
# Compile the model
model.compile(optimizer='adam', loss='binary_crossentropy',
metrics=['accuracy'])
# Train the model
model.fit(train_generator, validation_data=validation_generator,
epochs=10)
```

This code uses the "ImageDataGenerator" class to load and preprocess image data from directories, and then defines a CNN model using the Sequential API in TensorFlow. The model consists of convolutional and pooling layers followed by fully connected layers. It is compiled with an optimizer, loss function, and metrics, and then trained on the training data using the "fit" method.

6.9.4 Here's an example of implementing a feedforward neural network to predict housing prices based on input features, such as location, number of rooms, and square footage, using the TensorFlow library in Python:

```
import tensorflow as tf
from tensorflow.keras.models import Sequential
from tensorflow.keras.layers import Dense
# Define the input features and target variable
X = [[0.3, 0.5, 0.2], [0.1, 0.2, 0.3], [0.7, 0.8, 0.5]]
y = [100000, 200000, 300000]
# Define the model architecture
model = Sequential()
model.add(Dense(16, input_dim=3, activation='relu'))
model.add(Dense(8, activation='relu'))
model.add(Dense(1))
# Compile the model
model.compile(optimizer='adam', loss='mean_squared_error')
```

```
# Train the model
model.fit(X, y, epochs=100)
# Predict on new data
new_data = [[0.4, 0.3, 0.6]]
prediction = model.predict(new_data)
print('Predicted price:', prediction)
```

Medium

6.9.5 Here's an example of training a CNN on the CIFAR-10 dataset and evaluating its performance on the test set using the TensorFlow library in Python:

```
import tensorflow as tf
from tensorflow.keras.datasets import cifar10
from tensorflow.keras.models import Sequential
from tensorflow.keras.layers import Conv2D, MaxPooling2D, Flatten,
Dense
# Load the CIFAR-10 dataset
(x_train, y_train), (x_test, y_test) = cifar10.load_data()
# Preprocess the data
x_train = x_train / 255.0
x_test = x_test / 255.0
# Define the model architecture
model = Sequential()
model.add(Conv2D(32, (3, 3), activation='relu', input_shape=(32,
32, 3)))
model.add(MaxPooling2D((2, 2)))
model.add(Conv2D(64, (3, 3), activation='relu'))
model.add(MaxPooling2D((2, 2)))
model.add(Conv2D(64, (3, 3), activation='relu'))
model.add(Flatten())
model.add(Dense(64, activation='relu'))
model.add(Dense(10, activation='softmax'))
# Compile the model
model.compile(optimizer='adam',
              loss='sparse_categorical_crossentropy',
              metrics=['accuracy'])
# Train the model
model.fit(x_train, y_train, epochs=10, batch_size=32,
validation_split=0.2)
# Evaluate the model on the test set
test_loss, test_acc = model.evaluate(x_test, y_test)
print('Test accuracy:', test_acc)
```

6.9.6 Here's an example of implementing an RNN for sentiment analysis on movie reviews using the TensorFlow library in Python:

```
import tensorflow as tf
from tensorflow.keras.datasets import imdb
from tensorflow.keras.models import Sequential
from tensorflow.keras.layers import Embedding, LSTM, Dense
# Load the IMDB movie review dataset
(x_train, y_train), (x_test, y_test) = imdb.
load_data(num_words=10000)
```

```
# Preprocess the data
x_train = tf.keras.preprocessing.sequence.pad_sequences(x_train,
maxlen=500)
x_test = tf.keras.preprocessing.sequence.pad_sequences(x_test,
maxlen=500)
# Define the model architecture
model = Sequential()
model.add(Embedding(10000, 32))
model.add(LSTM(32))
model.add(Dense(1, activation='sigmoid'))
# Compile the model
model.compile(optimizer='adam',
              loss='binary_crossentropy',
              metrics=['accuracy'])
# Train the model
model.fit(x_train, y_train, epochs=5, batch_size=64,
validation_split=0.2)
# Evaluate the model on the test set
test_loss, test_acc = model.evaluate(x_test, y_test)
print('Test accuracy:', test_acc)
```

6.9.7 Here's an example of building a deep learning model to generate captions for images using the COCO dataset using the TensorFlow library in Python:

```
import tensorflow as tf
from tensorflow.keras.models import Sequential
from tensorflow.keras.layers import Dense, LSTM, Embedding,
RepeatVector, TimeDistributed
# Note: Assume you've already loaded and preprocessed the COCO
dataset
# The variables X_train, y_train, vocab_size, embedding_size, and
max_caption_length should be defined from this preprocessing.
# Define the model architecture
model = Sequential()
model.add(Embedding(vocab_size, embedding_size,
input_length=max_caption_length))
model.add(LSTM(256, return_sequences=False))
model.add(RepeatVector(max_caption_length))
model.add(LSTM(256, return_sequences=True))
model.add(TimeDistributed(Dense(vocab_size, activation='softmax')))
# Compile the model
model.compile(optimizer='adam', loss='categorical_crossentropy')
# Train the model
model.fit(X_train, y_train, epochs=10, batch_size=64)
# Generate captions for new images (assuming X_test is defined)
predicted_captions = model.predict(X_test)
```

6.9.8 Here's an example of implementing a variational autoencoder (VAE) to generate new images of faces from the CelebA dataset using the TensorFlow library in Python:

```
import tensorflow as tf
from tensorflow.keras.models import Model
from tensorflow.keras.layers import Input, Dense, Lambda, Flatten,
Reshape
```

```
from tensorflow.keras.losses import mse
from tensorflow.keras import backend as K
import numpy as np

# Note: Assume you've already loaded and preprocessed the CelebA
dataset into a variable called X_train
latent_dim = 100
input_shape = (64, 64, 3)
# Encoder
inputs = Input(shape=input_shape)
x = Flatten()(inputs)
x = Dense(256, activation='relu')(x)
z_mean = Dense(latent_dim)(x)
z_log_var = Dense(latent_dim)(x)
# Sampling function
def sampling(args):
    z_mean, z_log_var = args
    epsilon = K.random_normal(shape=(K.shape(z_mean)[0], latent_
dim), mean=0., stddev=1.)
    return z_mean + K.exp(0.5 * z_log_var) * epsilon
z = Lambda(sampling, output_shape=(latent_dim,))([z_mean,
z_log_var])
# Decoder
x = Dense(256, activation='relu')(z)
x = Dense(64 * 64 * 3, activation='sigmoid')(x)
outputs = Reshape(input_shape)(x)
# VAE model
model = Model(inputs, outputs)
# VAE loss
def vae_loss(inputs, outputs):
    reconstruction_loss = mse(K.flatten(inputs),
K.flatten(outputs))
    kl_loss = -0.5 * K.sum(1 + z_log_var - K.square(z_mean) -
K.exp(z_log_var), axis=-1)
    return K.mean(reconstruction_loss + kl_loss)
# Compile the model
model.compile(optimizer='adam', loss=vae_loss)
# Train the model
model.fit(X_train, X_train, epochs=10, batch_size=64)
# Generate new images
num_images = 10  # example number
latent_vectors = np.random.normal(size=(num_images, latent_dim))
generated_images = model.predict(latent_vectors)
```

Hard

6.9.9 Implementing a deep reinforcement learning algorithm for playing a game like Atari Breakout or Pac-Man requires combining deep learning with reinforcement learning techniques. Here's a high-level overview of the steps involved:

1. Set up the environment: Install the necessary libraries and frameworks for working with deep reinforcement learning. Popular choices include OpenAI Gym and TensorFlow.

2. Preprocess the game inputs: Convert the raw game frames into a suitable format for deep learning models. This may involve resizing, grayscale conversion, or other preprocessing steps.

3. Design the deep neural network: Create a deep neural network architecture that takes the game frames as input and outputs the Q-values for each possible action. CNNs are commonly used to process the game frames.

4. Define the agent: Implement an agent that interacts with the game environment, selects actions based on the current state, and updates the neural network based on the observed rewards. Techniques like epsilon-greedy exploration and experience replay can be used to improve learning.

5. Train the agent: Initialize the agent and repeatedly play the game, collecting experience and updating the neural network weights using techniques like Q-learning or policy gradients. The agent learns to make better decisions by optimizing the neural network based on the observed rewards.

6. Evaluate the performance: After training, evaluate the performance of the agent by playing the game and measuring metrics, such as the average score or success rate. You can also visualize the agent's gameplay to analyze its behavior.

Keep in mind that implementing a deep reinforcement learning algorithm for playing complex games like Atari Breakout or Pac-Man can be challenging and time-consuming. It often requires fine-tuning the hyperparameters, training for a significant number of episodes, and potentially using advanced techniques like double Q-learning or dueling architectures. However, with patience and experimentation, you can develop a capable agent that performs well in these games.

6.9.10 Training a deep learning model to predict the 3D structure of a protein from its amino acid sequence is a challenging task. Here's a high-level overview of the steps involved:

1. Prepare the data: Collect a dataset of protein sequences and their corresponding experimental 3D structures, such as those available in the Protein Data Bank (PDB). Preprocess the data by converting the amino acid sequences into numerical representations, such as one-hot encoding.

2. Design the deep learning architecture: Choose an appropriate deep learning architecture for the task, such as an RNN, CNN, or a combination of both. Consider using specialized architectures like residual networks (ResNets) or transformer networks designed for sequence modeling tasks.

3. Train the model: Split the dataset into training and validation sets. Use the training set to train the deep learning model to predict the 3D structure from the input amino acid sequences. You can use techniques like mini-batch gradient descent and backpropagation to update the model's weights.

4. Evaluate the model: Use the validation set to evaluate the performance of the trained model. Metrics like root mean square deviation (RMSD) or Global Distance Test (GDT) can be used to measure the similarity between the predicted 3D structure and the experimental structure.

5. Fine-tune and optimize: Experiment with different model architectures, hyperparameters, and regularization techniques to improve the model's

performance. Consider techniques like transfer learning, ensembling, or incorporating additional information, such as evolutionary conservation scores or protein contact maps.

6. Test the model: Once you have a trained and optimized model, you can apply it to predict the 3D structure of unseen protein sequences. Compare the predicted structures with experimental structures to assess the accuracy and reliability of the predictions.

It's worth noting that predicting protein structures from amino acid sequences is a highly complex problem, and current state-of-the-art methods often combine deep learning with other computational techniques and expert knowledge. Developing an accurate and reliable protein structure prediction model requires a deep understanding of both protein bioinformatics and deep learning methodologies.

6.9.11 Building a neural network to generate music using MIDI files and evaluating its performance using human evaluation metrics involves combining deep learning with music generation techniques. Here's a high-level overview of the steps involved:

1. Prepare the data: Collect a dataset of MIDI files containing musical compositions. MIDI files represent music as a sequence of musical events and can be converted into numerical representations suitable for deep learning models.

2. Design the deep learning architecture: Choose an appropriate deep learning architecture for music generation, such as RNNs or GANs. RNNs, particularly variants like long short-term memory (LSTM) or transformer-based architectures, are commonly used for sequence generation tasks.

3. Preprocess the data: Convert the MIDI files into a suitable format for deep learning models. This may involve encoding musical events, quantizing time steps, or applying other preprocessing steps specific to music data.

4. Train the model: Split the dataset into training and validation sets. Use the training set to train the deep learning model to generate music. You can use techniques like teacher forcing or reinforcement learning with reward models to guide the model's training.

5. Evaluate the generated music: Use human evaluation metrics, such as subjective ratings or user studies, to assess the quality and musicality of the generated compositions. Objective metrics like note diversity, harmony, or melodic structure can also be used to measure specific aspects of the generated music.

6. Fine-tune and optimize: Experiment with different model architectures, hyperparameters, and training strategies to improve the quality of the generated music. Techniques like temperature sampling, beam search, or conditional generation can be applied to control the output and generate music with desired characteristics.

7. Generate new music: Once you have a trained and optimized model, you can use it to generate new music compositions by sampling from the learned latent space. Explore the generated music and refine the model based on feedback and subjective evaluation.

Keep in mind that music generation is a subjective task, and evaluating the quality of generated music is inherently challenging. Human evaluation metrics, while valuable, may still involve some degree of subjectivity. Therefore, it's important to involve musicians or experts in the evaluation process to provide informed feedback and ensure the generated music meets the desired criteria.

6.9.12 Developing a deep learning model to detect and classify objects in satellite imagery for use in disaster response or urban planning involves combining deep learning with computer vision techniques. Here's a high-level overview of the steps involved:

1. Collect and preprocess the data: Gather a dataset of satellite images labeled with the objects or features of interest, such as buildings, roads, or vegetation. Preprocess the images by resizing, normalizing, and augmenting them to increase the diversity of the training data.

2. Design the deep learning architecture: Choose a suitable deep learning architecture for object detection and classification, such as a CNN or a combination of CNNs and RNNs. Popular architectures include Faster R-CNN, SSD, or YOLO.

3. Annotate the data: Annotate the satellite images with bounding boxes or segmentation masks to indicate the location and extent of the objects or features of interest. This annotated data will be used to train and evaluate the model.

4. Split the data: Divide the dataset into training, validation, and test sets. The training set is used to train the deep learning model, the validation set is used for hyperparameter tuning and model selection, and the test set is used to evaluate the final model's performance.

5. Train the model: Use the training set to train the deep learning model to detect and classify objects in the satellite images. This involves feeding the images into the model, computing the loss based on the predicted and ground truth labels, and updating the model's weights using optimization algorithms, such as SGD or Adam.

6. Evaluate the model: Use the validation set to assess the model's performance in terms of object detection accuracy, precision, recall, and other relevant metrics. Adjust the model's hyperparameters or architecture if necessary to improve performance.

7. Test the model: Use the test set to evaluate the final model's performance on unseen data. Measure the model's ability to accurately detect and classify objects in the satellite images.

8. Fine-tune and optimize: Experiment with different model architectures, hyperparameters, and data augmentation techniques to improve the model's performance. Techniques, such as transfer learning or ensembling multiple models, can also be employed to enhance the model's accuracy.

9. Deploy the model: Once the model achieves satisfactory performance, it can be deployed to analyze new satellite images and automatically detect and classify objects of interest. This can support disaster response efforts, urban planning, or other applications that require object recognition in satellite imagery.

Keep in mind that developing a robust and accurate object detection and classification model for satellite imagery may require a large and diverse dataset, careful selection of hyperparameters, and extensive experimentation. Domain knowledge and expert guidance in satellite imagery analysis can also significantly contribute to the success of the model.

Chapter 7 Questions Responses

Problems

7.12.1 The generator and discriminator in GANs have different roles. The generator creates fake data to mimic the real data distribution, while the discriminator tries to distinguish between real and fake data.

7.12.2 The training process of GANs involves two steps: the discriminator is trained to distinguish real from fake data, and the generator is trained to fool the discriminator.

7.12.3 The objective function of GANs is a minimax game where the generator tries to maximize the probability of the discriminator making a mistake while the discriminator tries to minimize this probability.

7.12.4 Some common loss functions used in GANs are Binary Cross-Entropy, Wasserstein Loss, and Hinge Loss.

7.12.5 The noise vector in GANs is a random input to the generator, which it uses to generate fake data.

7.12.6 The performance of GANs can be evaluated using measures like Inception Score (IS), Frechet Inception Distance (FID), and Precision and Recall (PR).

7.12.7 Mode collapse in GANs refers to the situation where the generator produces a limited variety of outputs.

7.12.8 Techniques, such as adding noise to the discriminator's inputs or labels, mini-batch discrimination, and training with gradient penalties, can prevent mode collapse in GANs.

7.12.9 Vanilla GANs are the simplest form of GANs, while DCGANs (Deep Convolutional GANs) introduce specific architectural constraints to improve the quality and stability of outputs.

7.12.10 Practical applications of GANs include image synthesis, style transfer, image super-resolution, and data augmentation.

7.12.11 High-resolution images can be generated using GANs through progressive growing, where the model starts from a low resolution and progressively adds layers to increase the resolution.

7.12.12 Unconditional GANs generate outputs from random noise, while conditional GANs generate outputs based on a given condition or input.

7.12.13 GAN for data augmentation: GANs can generate additional training data that closely resembles the distribution of the original data, thereby potentially improving the performance of machine learning models.

7.12.14 Batch normalization in GANs helps to stabilize training, reduce mode collapse, and helps the model converge faster.

7.12.15 New examples can be generated from a trained GAN model by feeding a noise vector into the generator.

7.12.16 Challenges in training GANs include mode collapse, unstable training dynamics, and difficulty in balancing the training of the generator and the discriminator.

7.12.17 The generator in GANs produces data from a noise vector, while an encoder, used in Variational Autoencoders (VAEs), maps input data to a lower-dimensional latent space.

7.12.18 GANs can be used for image-to-image translation by using conditional GANs where the condition is the input image and the output is the translated image.

7.12.19 Adversarial training involves a competition between two models (generator and discriminator), while traditional supervised training involves a model learning from labeled data.

7.12.20 GANs can be used for unsupervised learning as they can learn to mimic any data distribution without requiring labeled data. This is particularly useful for tasks, such as clustering, dimensionality reduction, and generative tasks.

Programming

Easy

7.13.1 Implementing a Normal GAN to Generate Images of a Specific Category To implement a Normal GAN to generate images of a specific category, such as cats or dogs, you will need a dataset of images containing the desired category. Here's an example of how you can implement a Normal GAN using the TensorFlow library in Python:

Step 1: Import the necessary libraries

```
import tensorflow as tf
from tensorflow.keras import layers
import numpy as np
```

Step 2: Define the generator and discriminator models

```
# Generator
def build_generator():
    model = tf.keras.Sequential()
    model.add(layers.Dense(256, input_dim=100, activation='relu'))
    model.add(layers.Dense(512, activation='relu'))
    model.add(layers.Dense(1024, activation='relu'))
    model.add(layers.Dense(784, activation='tanh'))
    model.add(layers.Reshape((28, 28, 1)))
    return model
# Discriminator
def build_discriminator():
    model = tf.keras.Sequential()
    model.add(layers.Reshape((784,), input_shape=(28, 28, 1)))
```

```
    model.add(layers.Dense(1024, activation='relu'))
    model.add(layers.Dense(512, activation='relu'))
    model.add(layers.Dense(256, activation='relu'))
    model.add(layers.Dense(1, activation='sigmoid'))
    return model
```

Step 3: Define the loss functions and optimizers

```
cross_entropy = tf.keras.losses.BinaryCrossentropy()
def discriminator_loss(real_output, fake_output):
    real_loss = cross_entropy(tf.ones_like(real_output),
real_output)
    fake_loss = cross_entropy(tf.zeros_like(fake_output),
fake_output)
    total_loss = real_loss + fake_loss
    return total_loss
def generator_loss(fake_output):
    return cross_entropy(tf.ones_like(fake_output), fake_output)
generator_optimizer = tf.keras.optimizers.Adam(1e-4)
discriminator_optimizer = tf.keras.optimizers.Adam(1e-4)
```

Step 4: Define the training loop

```
@tf.function
def train_step(images):
    noise = tf.random.normal([BATCH_SIZE, 100])
    with tf.GradientTape() as gen_tape, tf.GradientTape() as
disc_tape:
        generated_images = generator(noise, training=True)
        real_output = discriminator(images, training=True)
        fake_output = discriminator(generated_images,
training=True)
        gen_loss = generator_loss(fake_output)
        disc_loss = discriminator_loss(real_output, fake_output)
    gradients_of_generator = gen_tape.gradient(gen_loss,
generator.trainable_variables)
    gradients_of_discriminator = disc_tape.gradient(disc_loss,
discriminator.trainable_variables)
    generator_optimizer.apply_gradients(zip(gradients_of_
generator, generator.trainable_variables))
    discriminator_optimizer.apply_gradients(zip(gradients_of_
discriminator, discriminator.trainable_variables))
```

Step 5: Train the GAN

```
# Load your dataset containing images of the desired category
# images = load_dataset()
# Normalize and reshape images
images = (images - 127.5) / 127.5
images = np.expand_dims(images, axis=3)
# Set batch size and number of epochs
BATCH_SIZE = 32
EPOCHS = 100
# Build the generator and discriminator models
```

```
generator = build_generator()
discriminator = build_discriminator()
# Iterate over epochs
for epoch in range(EPOCHS):
    for i in range(len(images) // BATCH_SIZE):
        batch = images[i * BATCH_SIZE : (i + 1) * BATCH_SIZE]
        train_step(batch)
```

Step 6: Generate new images

```
# Generate new images using the trained generator
noise = tf.random.normal([NUM_SAMPLES, 100])
generated_images = generator(noise, training=False)
# Convert generated images to the desired format
generated_images = (generated_images * 127.5) + 127.5
generated_images = np.squeeze(generated_images, axis=3)
# Display or save the generated images
```

This implementation provides a basic structure for training a Normal GAN to generate images of a specific category. You may need to customize it further based on your specific requirements, such as adjusting the network architecture or hyperparameters.

7.13.2 Training a Normal GAN on Handwritten Digits and Generating New Samples
To train a Normal GAN on a small dataset of handwritten digits and generate new samples, you can follow a similar approach as described in the previous section. Here's an example using the MNIST dataset:

Step 1: Import the necessary libraries and load the MNIST dataset

```
import tensorflow as tf
from tensorflow.keras import layers
(train_images, _), (_, _) = tf.keras.datasets.mnist.load_data()
# Normalize and reshape the images
train_images = (train_images - 127.5) / 127.5
train_images = train_images.reshape(train_images.shape[0], 28, 28, 1)
```

Step 2: Define the generator and discriminator models

```
def build_generator():
    model = tf.keras.Sequential()
    model.add(layers.Dense(7 * 7 * 256, use_bias=False,
input_shape=(100,)))
    model.add(layers.BatchNormalization())
    model.add(layers.LeakyReLU())
    model.add(layers.Reshape((7, 7, 256)))
    model.add(layers.Conv2DTranspose(128, (5, 5), strides=(1, 1),
padding='same', use_bias=False))
    model.add(layers.BatchNormalization())
    model.add(layers.LeakyReLU())
    model.add(layers.Conv2DTranspose(64, (5, 5), strides=(2, 2),
padding='same', use_bias=False))
    model.add(layers.BatchNormalization())
    model.add(layers.LeakyReLU())
```

```
    model.add(layers.Conv2DTranspose(1, (5, 5), strides=(2, 2),
padding='same', use_bias=False, activation='tanh'))
    return model
def build_discriminator():
    model = tf.keras.Sequential()
    model.add(layers.Conv2D(64, (5, 5), strides=(2, 2),
padding='same', input_shape=[28, 28, 1]))
    model.add(layers.LeakyReLU())
    model.add(layers.Dropout(0.3))
    model.add(layers.Conv2D(128, (5, 5), strides=(2, 2),
padding='same'))
    model.add(layers.LeakyReLU())
    model.add(layers.Dropout(0.3))
    model.add(layers.Flatten())
    model.add(layers.Dense(1))
    return model
```

Step 3: Define the loss functions and optimizers

```
cross_entropy = tf.keras.losses.
BinaryCrossentropy(from_logits=True)
def discriminator_loss(real_output, fake_output):
    real_loss = cross_entropy(tf.ones_like(real_output),
real_output)
    fake_loss = cross_entropy(tf.zeros_like(fake_output),
fake_output)
    total_loss = real_loss + fake_loss
    return total_loss
def generator_loss(fake_output):
    return cross_entropy(tf.ones_like(fake_output), fake_output)
generator_optimizer = tf.keras.optimizers.Adam(1e-4)
discriminator_optimizer = tf.keras.optimizers.Adam(1e-4)
```

Step 4: Define the training loop

```
@tf.function
def train_step(images):
    noise = tf.random.normal([BATCH_SIZE, 100])
    with tf.GradientTape() as gen_tape, tf.GradientTape() as
disc_tape:
        generated_images = generator(noise, training=True)
        real_output = discriminator(images, training=True)
        fake_output = discriminator(generated_images,
training=True)
        gen_loss = generator_loss(fake_output)
        disc_loss = discriminator_loss(real_output, fake_output)
    gradients_of_generator = gen_tape.gradient(gen_loss,
generator.trainable_variables)
    gradients_of_discriminator = disc_tape.gradient(disc_loss,
discriminator.trainable_variables)
    generator_optimizer.apply_gradients(zip(gradients_of_
generator, generator.trainable_variables))
    discriminator_optimizer.apply_gradients(zip(gradients_of_
discriminator, discriminator.trainable_variables))
```

Step 5: Train the GAN

```
BATCH_SIZE = 128
EPOCHS = 50
generator = build_generator()
discriminator = build_discriminator()
for epoch in range(EPOCHS):
    for i in range(train_images.shape[0] // BATCH_SIZE):
        batch = train_images[i * BATCH_SIZE : (i + 1) *
BATCH_SIZE]
        train_step(batch)
```

Step 6: Generate new digit samples

```
NUM_SAMPLES = 10
# Generate new digit samples using the trained generator
noise = tf.random.normal([NUM_SAMPLES, 100])
generated_images = generator(noise, training=False)
# Convert generated images to the desired format
generated_images = (generated_images * 127.5) + 127.5
generated_images = tf.cast(generated_images, tf.uint8)
# Display or save the generated digit samples
```

You can modify this code to suit your specific requirements, such as adjusting the network architecture, hyperparameters, or number of training epochs.

7.13.3 Modifying the Normal GAN Code to Use Different Activation Functions to modify the Normal GAN code to use different activation functions in the generator and discriminator, you can simply replace the existing activation functions with the desired ones. Here's an example:

```
# Generator
def build_generator():
    model = tf.keras.Sequential()
    model.add(layers.Dense(256, input_dim=100,
activation='relu'))
    model.add(layers.Dense(512, activation='relu'))
    model.add(layers.Dense(1024, activation='sigmoid'))  # Modified
activation function
    model.add(layers.Dense(784, activation='tanh'))
    model.add(layers.Reshape((28, 28, 1)))
    return model
# Discriminator
def build_discriminator():
    model = tf.keras.Sequential()
    model.add(layers.Reshape((784,), input_shape=(28, 28, 1)))
    model.add(layers.Dense(1024, activation='sigmoid'))  # Modified
activation function
    model.add(layers.Dense(512, activation='relu'))
    model.add(layers.Dense(256, activation='relu'))
    model.add(layers.Dense(1, activation='sigmoid'))
    return model
```

In this example, the generator now uses the "sigmoid" activation function in the second-last layer instead of "relu", and the discriminator uses the "sigmoid" activation function in the first layer instead of "relu". You can choose different activation functions based on your requirements. Remember to adjust the rest of the code, such as loss functions, optimizers, training loop, and generating new samples, as per your modified GAN architecture.

Medium

7.13.4 Implementing a Normal GAN to Generate 3D Objects Generating 3D objects using a Normal GAN involves modifying the network architecture and the input data structure. Here's an example of how you can implement a Normal GAN to generate 3D objects:

Step 1: Import the necessary libraries

```
import tensorflow as tf
from tensorflow.keras import layers
import numpy as np
```

Step 2: Define the generator and discriminator models

```
# Generator
def build_generator():
    model = tf.keras.Sequential()
    model.add(layers.Dense(256, input_dim=100,
activation='relu'))
    model.add(layers.Dense(512, activation='relu'))
    model.add(layers.Dense(1024, activation='relu'))
    model.add(layers.Dense(4096, activation='relu'))
    model.add(layers.Reshape((4, 4, 256)))
    model.add(layers.Conv2DTranspose(128, (5, 5), strides=(2, 2),
padding='same', activation='relu'))
    model.add(layers.Conv2DTranspose(64, (5, 5), strides=(2, 2),
padding='same', activation='relu'))
    model.add(layers.Conv2DTranspose(3, (5, 5), strides=(2, 2),
padding='same', activation='tanh'))
    return model
# Discriminator
def build_discriminator():
    model = tf.keras.Sequential()
    model.add(layers.Conv2D(64, (5, 5), strides=(2, 2),
padding='same', input_shape=[32, 32, 3]))
    model.add(layers.LeakyReLU())
    model.add(layers.Dropout(0.3))
    model.add(layers.Conv2D(128, (5, 5), strides=(2, 2),
padding='same'))
    model.add(layers.LeakyReLU())
    model.add(layers.Dropout(0.3))
    model.add(layers.Flatten())
    model.add(layers.Dense(1))
    return model
```

Step 3: Define the loss functions and optimizers

```
cross_entropy = tf.keras.losses.BinaryCrossentropy(from_
logits=True)
def discriminator_loss(real_output, fake_output):
    real_loss = cross_entropy(tf.ones_like(real_output),
real_output)
    fake_loss = cross_entropy(tf.zeros_like(fake_output),
fake_output)
    total_loss = real_loss + fake_loss
    return total_loss
def generator_loss(fake_output):
    return cross_entropy(tf.ones_like(fake_output), fake_output)
generator_optimizer = tf.keras.optimizers.Adam(1e-4)
discriminator_optimizer = tf.keras.optimizers.Adam(1e-4)
```

Step 4: Define the training loop

```
@tf.function
def train_step(images):
    noise = tf.random.normal([BATCH_SIZE, 100])
    with tf.GradientTape() as gen_tape, tf.GradientTape() as
disc_tape:
        generated_images = generator(noise, training=True)
        real_output = discriminator(images, training=True)
        fake_output = discriminator(generated_images, training=True)
        gen_loss = generator_loss(fake_output)
        disc_loss = discriminator_loss(real_output, fake_output)
    gradients_of_generator = gen_tape.gradient(gen_loss,
generator.trainable_variables)
    gradients_of_discriminator = disc_tape.gradient(disc_loss,
discriminator.trainable_variables)
    generator_optimizer.apply_gradients(zip(gradients_of_
generator, generator.trainable_variables))
    discriminator_optimizer.apply_gradients(zip(gradients_of_
discriminator, discriminator.trainable_variables))
```

Step 5: Train the GAN

```
BATCH_SIZE = 128
EPOCHS = 100
# Load your dataset containing 3D objects
# images = load_dataset()
# Normalize and reshape images
images = (images - 127.5) / 127.5
images = images.reshape(images.shape[0], 32, 32, 3)
# Build the generator and discriminator models
generator = build_generator()
discriminator = build_discriminator()
# Iterate over epochs
for epoch in range(EPOCHS):
    for i in range(len(images) // BATCH_SIZE):
        batch = images[i * BATCH_SIZE : (i + 1) * BATCH_SIZE]
        train_step(batch)
```

Step 6: Generate new 3D object samples

```
NUM_SAMPLES = 10
# Generate new 3D object samples using the trained generator
noise = tf.random.normal([NUM_SAMPLES, 100])
generated_images = generator(noise, training=False)
# Convert generated images to the desired format
generated_images = (generated_images * 127.5) + 127.5
generated_images = generated_images.numpy()
# Display or save the generated 3D object samples
```

Please note that generating high-quality 3D objects requires more complex architectures and specialized techniques, such as using 3D convolutional layers or employing advanced generative models like VAEs or Generative Adversarial Networks (GANs) with 3D data. The provided implementation serves as a basic example and can be further enhanced and customized based on specific requirements.

7.13.5 Training a Normal GAN on a Large Dataset and Evaluating Image Quality
Training a Normal GAN on a large dataset and evaluating the quality of the generated images can be done using various metrics. Two commonly used metrics are IS and FID. Here's an example of how you can train a Normal GAN on a large dataset and evaluate the generated images using FID:

Step 1: Import the necessary libraries and load the large dataset

```
import tensorflow as tf
from tensorflow.keras import layers
import numpy as np
import os
from tensorflow.keras.applications.inception_v3 import
InceptionV3
from tensorflow.keras.applications.inception_v3 import
preprocess_input
from scipy.linalg import sqrtm
# Load your large dataset
# images = load_dataset()
# Normalize the images to the range [-1, 1]
images = (images - 127.5) / 127.5
```

Step 2: Define the generator and discriminator models, loss functions, and optimizers (similar to previous sections)
Step 3: Define a function to calculate the FID score

```
def calculate_fid_score(real_images, generated_images,
batch_size=50):
    real_images = preprocess_input(real_images)
    generated_images = preprocess_input(generated_images)
    # Load pre-trained InceptionV3 model without the final
classification layers
    inception_model = InceptionV3(include_top=False,
pooling='avg')
    # Extract feature vectors from real and generated images
```

```
    real_features = inception_model.predict(real_images,
batch_size=batch_size)
    generated_features = inception_model.predict(generated_images,
batch_size=batch_size)
    # Calculate mean and covariance for real and generated feature
vectors
    real_mean = np.mean(real_features, axis=0)
    generated_mean = np.mean(generated_features, axis=0)
    real_cov = np.cov(real_features, rowvar=False)
    generated_cov = np.cov(generated_features, rowvar=False)
    # Calculate the squared Frobenius norm between the means
    mean_diff = real_mean - generated_mean
    mean_squared_norm = np.dot(mean_diff, mean_diff)
    # Calculate the trace of the product of the covariances
    cov_product = np.dot(real_cov, generated_cov)
    cov_sqrt = sqrtm(cov_product)
    if np.iscomplexobj(cov_sqrt):
        cov_sqrt = cov_sqrt.real
    # Calculate the FID score
    fid_score = mean_squared_norm + np.trace(real_cov + generated_
cov - 2 * cov_sqrt)
    return fid_score
```

Step 4: Define the training loop

```
@tf.function
def train_step(images):
    noise = tf.random.normal([BATCH_SIZE, 100])
    with tf.GradientTape() as gen_tape, tf.GradientTape() as
disc_tape:
        generated_images = generator(noise, training=True)
        real_output = discriminator(images, training=True)
        fake_output = discriminator(generated_images,
training=True)
        gen_loss = generator_loss(fake_output)
        disc_loss = discriminator_loss(real_output, fake_output)
    gradients_of_generator = gen_tape.gradient(gen_loss,
generator.trainable_variables)
    gradients_of_discriminator = disc_tape.gradient(disc_loss,
discriminator.trainable_variables)
    generator_optimizer.apply_gradients(zip(gradients_of_
generator, generator.trainable_variables))
    discriminator_optimizer.apply_gradients(zip(gradients_of_
discriminator, discriminator.trainable_variables))
```

Step 5: Train the GAN

```
BATCH_SIZE = 128
EPOCHS = 100
generator = build_generator()
discriminator = build_discriminator()for epoch in range(EPOCHS):
    for i in range(len(images) // BATCH_SIZE):
        batch = images[i * BATCH_SIZE : (i + 1) * BATCH_SIZE]
        train_step(batch)
```

Step 6: Generate new samples and calculate the FID score

```
NUM_SAMPLES = 1000
# Generate new samples using the trained generator
noise = tf.random.normal([NUM_SAMPLES, 100])
generated_images = generator(noise, training=False)
# Convert generated images to the desired format
generated_images = (generated_images * 127.5) + 127.5
# Calculate the FID score
fid_score = calculate_fid_score(images[:NUM_SAMPLES],
generated_images)
print("FID Score:", fid_score)
```

This example demonstrates training a Normal GAN on a large dataset and evaluating the quality of the generated images using the FID score. You can modify the code to use other evaluation metrics like IS or customize it further based on your specific requirements.

7.13.6 Implementing a Normal GAN that Generates Conditioned Images
Implementing a Normal GAN that generates images conditioned on a specific input, such as a sentence describing the image, involves modifying the network architecture and the training process. Here's an example of how you can implement a conditional Normal GAN:

Step 1: Import the necessary libraries

```
import tensorflow as tf
from tensorflow.keras import layers
import numpy as np
```

Step 2: Define the generator and discriminator models

```
# Generator
def build_generator():
    # Define the input layers for both the noise and condition
    input_noise = layers.Input(shape=(100,))
    input_condition = layers.Input(shape=(10,))  # Example:
10-dimensional condition vector
    # Merge the noise and condition inputs
    combined_input = layers.concatenate([input_noise,
input_condition])
    # Generate the image based on the combined input
    model = layers.Dense(256)(combined_input)
    model = layers.LeakyReLU()(model)
    model = layers.BatchNormalization()(model)
    model = layers.Dense(512)(model)
    model = layers.LeakyReLU()(model)
    model = layers.BatchNormalization()(model)
    model = layers.Dense(1024)(model)
    model = layers.LeakyReLU()(model)
    model = layers.BatchNormalization()(model)
    model = layers.Dense(784, activation='tanh')(model)
    generated_image = layers.Reshape((28, 28, 1))(model)
    # Define the generator model with the input noise and condition
```

```python
    generator = tf.keras.Model(inputs=[input_noise, input_
condition], outputs=generated_image)
    return generator
# Discriminator
def build_discriminator():
    # Define the input layers for both the image and condition
    input_image = layers.Input(shape=(28, 28, 1))
    input_condition = layers.Input(shape=(10,))  # Example:
10-dimensional condition vector
    # Flatten the image and merge it with the condition input
    image_flatten = layers.Flatten()(input_image)
    combined_input = layers.concatenate([image_flatten,
input_condition])
    # Classify the image based on the combined input
    model = layers.Dense(1024)(combined_input)
    model = layers.LeakyReLU()(model)
    model = layers.Dropout(0.3)(model)
    model = layers.Dense(512)(model)
    model = layers.LeakyReLU()(model)
    model = layers.Dropout(0.3)(model)
    model = layers.Dense(256)(model)
    model = layers.LeakyReLU()(model)
    model = layers.Dropout(0.3)(model)
    output = layers.Dense(1, activation='sigmoid')(model)
    # Define the discriminator model with the input image and
condition
    discriminator = tf.keras.Model(inputs=[input_image, input_
condition], outputs=output)
    return discriminator
```

Step 3: Define the loss functions and optimizers (similar to previous sections)
Step 4: Define the training loop

```python
@tf.function
def train_step(images, conditions):
    noise = tf.random.normal([BATCH_SIZE, 100])
    with tf.GradientTape() as gen_tape, tf.GradientTape() as
disc_tape:
        generated_images = generator([noise, conditions],
training=True)
        real_output = discriminator([images, conditions],
training=True)
        fake_output = discriminator([generated_images,
conditions], training=True)
        gen_loss = generator_loss(fake_output)
        disc_loss = discriminator_loss(real_output, fake_output)
    gradients_of_generator = gen_tape.gradient(gen_loss,
generator.trainable_variables)
    gradients_of_discriminator = disc_tape.gradient(disc_loss,
discriminator.trainable_variables)
    generator_optimizer.apply_gradients(zip(gradients_of_
generator, generator.trainable_variables))
    discriminator_optimizer.apply_gradients(zip(gradients_of_
discriminator, discriminator.trainable_variables))
```

Step 5: Train the GAN

```
BATCH_SIZE = 128
EPOCHS = 100
# Load your dataset and conditions
# images = load_dataset()
# conditions = load_conditions()
# Normalize and reshape images
images = (images - 127.5) / 127.5
images = images.reshape(images.shape[0], 28, 28, 1)
# Iterate over epochs
for epoch in range(EPOCHS):
    for i in range(len(images) // BATCH_SIZE):
        batch_images = images[i * BATCH_SIZE : (i + 1) *
BATCH_SIZE]
        batch_conditions = conditions[i * BATCH_SIZE : (i + 1) *
BATCH_SIZE]
        train_step(batch_images, batch_conditions)
```

Step 6: Generate new conditioned images

```
NUM_SAMPLES = 10
# Generate new conditioned images using the trained generator
noise = tf.random.normal
([NUM_SAMPLES, 100])
sample_conditions = conditions[:NUM_SAMPLES]
generated_images = generator([noise, sample_conditions],
training=False)
# Convert generated images to the desired format
generated_images = (generated_images * 127.5) + 127.5
# Display or save the generated conditioned images
```

This example demonstrates how to implement a Normal GAN that generates images conditioned on a specific input, such as a sentence describing the image. You can modify the code based on your specific requirements, including the architecture of the generator and discriminator, the dimensionality of the condition vector, and the input data structure for conditions.

Hard

7.13.7 Implementing a Normal GAN that Generates High-Resolution Images Generating high-resolution images, such as 4K or 8K resolution, with a Normal GAN requires certain modifications to the architecture and training process. Here's an example of how you can implement a Normal GAN that generates high-resolution images:

Step 1: Import the necessary libraries

```
import tensorflow as tf
from tensorflow.keras import layers
import numpy as np
```

Step 2: Define the generator and discriminator models

```python
# Generator
def build_generator():
    model = tf.keras.Sequential()
    model.add(layers.Dense(64 * 64 * 256, input_dim=100))
    model.add(layers.Reshape((64, 64, 256)))
    model.add(layers.BatchNormalization())
    model.add(layers.LeakyReLU())
    model.add(layers.Conv2DTranspose(128, (5, 5), strides=(2, 2),
padding='same'))
    model.add(layers.BatchNormalization())
    model.add(layers.LeakyReLU())
    model.add(layers.Conv2DTranspose(64, (5, 5), strides=(2, 2),
padding='same'))
    model.add(layers.BatchNormalization())
    model.add(layers.LeakyReLU())
    model.add(layers.Conv2DTranspose(3, (5, 5), strides=(2, 2),
padding='same', activation='tanh'))
    return model
# Discriminator
def build_discriminator():
    model - tf.keras.Sequential()
    model.add(layers.Conv2D(64, (5, 5), strides=(2, 2),
padding='same', input_shape=[64, 64, 3]))
    model.add(layers.LeakyReLU())
    model.add(layers.Dropout(0.3))
    model.add(layers.Conv2D(128, (5, 5), strides=(2, 2),
padding='same'))
    model.add(layers.LeakyReLU())
    model.add(layers.Dropout(0.3))
    model.add(layers.Flatten())
    model.add(layers.Dense(1))
    return model
```

Step 3: Define the loss functions and optimizers (similar to previous sections)
Step 4: Define the training loop

```python
@tf.function
def train_step(images):
    noise = tf.random.normal([BATCH_SIZE, 100])
    with tf.GradientTape() as gen_tape, tf.GradientTape() as
disc_tape:
        generated_images = generator(noise, training=True)
        real_output = discriminator(images, training=True)
        fake_output = discriminator(generated_images,
training=True)
        gen_loss = generator_loss(fake_output)
        disc_loss = discriminator_loss(real_output, fake_output)
    gradients_of_generator = gen_tape.gradient(gen_loss,
generator.trainable_variables)
```

```
    gradients_of_discriminator = disc_tape.gradient(disc_loss,
discriminator.trainable_variables)
    generator_optimizer.apply_gradients(zip(gradients_of_
generator, generator.trainable_variables))
    discriminator_optimizer.apply_gradients(zip(gradients_of_
discriminator, discriminator.trainable_variables))
```

Step 5: Train the GAN

```
BATCH_SIZE = 128
EPOCHS = 100
# Load your dataset of high-resolution images
# images = load_dataset()
# Normalize and reshape images
images = (images - 127.5) / 127.5
# Build the generator and discriminator models
generator = build_generator()
discriminator = build_discriminator()
# Iterate over epochs
for epoch in range(EPOCHS):
    for i in range(len(images) // BATCH_SIZE):
        batch = images[i * BATCH_SIZE : (i + 1) * BATCH_SIZE]
        train_step(batch
)
```

Step 6: Generate new high-resolution images

```
NUM_SAMPLES = 10
# Generate new high-resolution images using the trained
generator
noise = tf.random.normal([NUM_SAMPLES, 100])
generated_images = generator(noise, training=False)
# Convert generated images to the desired format
generated_images = (generated_images * 127.5) + 127.5
# Display or save the generated high-resolution images
```

Generating high-resolution images requires more computational resources and training time compared to lower-resolution images. It may also require additional architectural adjustments, such as using larger convolutional filters or deeper models, to capture the complexity and details of high-resolution images.

7.13.8 Training a Normal GAN that Generates Video Sequences Training a Normal GAN to generate video sequences instead of static images involves modifying the network architecture and data structure to handle temporal information. Here's an example of how you can train a Normal GAN to generate video sequences:

Step 1: Import the necessary libraries

```
import tensorflow as tf
from tensorflow.keras import layers
import numpy as np
```

Step 2: Define the generator and discriminator models

```
# Generator
def build_generator():
    model = tf.keras.Sequential()
    model.add(layers.Dense(7 * 7 * 256, use_bias=False,
input_shape=(100,)))
    model.add(layers.BatchNormalization())
    model.add(layers.LeakyReLU())
    model.add(layers.Reshape((7, 7, 256)))
    model.add(layers.Conv2DTranspose(128, (5, 5), strides=(1, 1),
padding='same', use_bias=False))
    model.add(layers.BatchNormalization())
    model.add(layers.LeakyReLU())
    model.add(layers.Conv2DTranspose(64, (5, 5), strides=(2, 2),
padding='same', use_bias=False))
    model.add(layers.BatchNormalization())
    model.add(layers.LeakyReLU())
    model.add(layers.Conv2DTranspose(3, (5, 5), strides=(2, 2),
padding='same', use_bias=False, activation='tanh'))
    return model
# Discriminator
def build_discriminator():
    model = tf.keras.Sequential()
    model.add(layers.Conv2D(64, (5, 5), strides=(2, 2),
padding='same', input_shape=[64, 64, 3]))
    model.add(layers.LeakyReLU())
    model.add(layers.Dropout(0.3))
    model.add(layers.Conv2D(128, (5, 5), strides=(2, 2),
padding='same'))
    model.add(layers.LeakyReLU())
    model.add(layers.Dropout(0.3))
    model.add(layers.Flatten())
    model.add(layers.Dense(1))
    return model
```

Step 3: Define the loss functions and optimizers (similar to previous sections)

Step 4: Define the training loop

```
@tf.function
def train_step(videos):
    noise = tf.random.normal([BATCH_SIZE, 100])
    with tf.GradientTape() as gen_tape, tf.GradientTape() as
disc_tape:
        generated_videos = generator(noise, training=True)
        real_output = discriminator(videos, training=True)
        fake_output = discriminator(generated_videos,
training=True)
        gen_loss = generator_loss(fake_output)
        disc_loss = discriminator_loss(real_output,
fake_output)
    gradients_of_generator = gen_tape.gradient(gen_loss,
generator.trainable_variables)
```

```
    gradients_of_discriminator = disc_tape.gradient(disc_loss,
discriminator.trainable_variables)
    generator_optimizer.apply_gradients(zip(gradients_of_
generator, generator.trainable_variables))
    discriminator_optimizer.apply_gradients(zip(gradients_of_
discriminator, scriminator.trainable_variables))
```

Step 5: Train the GAN

```
BATCH_SIZE = 128
EPOCHS = 100
# Load your dataset of video sequences
# videos = load_dataset()
# Normalize and reshape videos
videos = (videos - 127.5) / 127.5
# Build the generator and discriminator models
generator = build_generator()
discriminator = build_discriminator()
# Iterate over epochs
for epoch in range(EPOCHS):
    for i in range(len(videos) // BATCH_SIZE):
        batch = videos[i * BATCH_SIZE : (i + 1) * BATCH_SIZE]
        train_step(batch)
```

Step 6: Generate new video sequences

```
NUM_SAMPLES = 10
# Generate new video sequences using the trained generator
noise = tf.random.normal([NUM_SAMPLES, 100])
generated_videos = generator(noise, training=False)
# Convert generated videos to the desired format
generated_videos = (generated_videos * 127.5) + 127.5
# Display or save the generated video sequences
```

Generating video sequences requires capturing temporal dependencies and structure. One approach is to use recurrent or convolutional architectures that can model sequential data effectively. You may also need to preprocess and format the video data appropriately, such as converting frames to a consistent size or applying video-specific transformations.

7.13.9 Implementing a Normal GAN that Generates Images with Multiple Objects and Complex Backgrounds Implementing a Normal GAN that can generate images with multiple objects and complex backgrounds involves designing a suitable architecture and training setup. Here's a high-level overview of the steps you can follow:

Step 1: Import the necessary libraries

```
import tensorflow as tf
from tensorflow.keras import layers
import numpy as np
```

Step 2: Define the generator and discriminator models

```
# Generator
def build_generator():
    model = tf.keras.Sequential()
    model.add(layers.Dense(256, input_dim=100))
    model.add(layers.LeakyReLU())
    model.add(layers.Dense(512))
    model.add(layers.LeakyReLU())
    model.add(layers.Dense(1024))
    model.add(layers.LeakyReLU())
    model.add(layers.Dense(784, activation='tanh'))
    model.add(layers.Reshape((28, 28, 1)))
    return model
# Discriminator
def build_discriminator():
    model = tf.keras.Sequential()
    model.add(layers.Reshape((784,), input_shape=(28, 28, 1)))
    model.add(layers.Dense(1024))
    model.add(layers.LeakyReLU())
    model.add(layers.Dense(512))
    model.add(layers.LeakyReLU())
    model.add(layers.Dense(256))
    model.add(layers.LeakyReLU())
    model.add(layers.Dense(1, activation='sigmoid'))
    return model
```

Step 3: Define the loss functions and optimizers (similar to previous sections)

Step 4: Define the training loop

```
@tf.function
def train_step(images):
    noise = tf.random.normal([BATCH_SIZE, 100])
    with tf.GradientTape() as gen_tape, tf.GradientTape() as
disc_tape:
        generated_images = generator(noise, training=True)
        real_output = discriminator(images, training=True)
        fake_output = discriminator(generated_images,
training=True)
        gen_loss = generator_loss(fake_output)
        disc_loss = discriminator_loss(real_output,
fake_output)
    gradients_of_generator = gen_tape.gradient(gen_loss,
generator.trainable_variables)
    gradients_of_discriminator = disc_tape.gradient(disc_loss,
discriminator.trainable_variables)
    generator_optimizer.apply_gradients(zip(gradients_of_
generator, generator.trainable_variables))
    discriminator_optimizer.apply_gradients(zip(gradients_of_
discriminator, discriminator.trainable_variables))
```

Step 5: Train the GAN

```
BATCH_SIZE = 128
EPOCHS = 100
# Load your dataset of images with multiple objects and complex
backgrounds
# images = load_dataset()
# Normalize and reshape images
images = (images - 127.5) / 127.5
images = images.reshape(images.shape[0], 28, 28, 1)
# Build the generator and discriminator models
generator = build_generator()
discriminator = build_discriminator()
# Iterate over epochs
for epoch in range(EPOCHS):
    for i in range(len(images) // BATCH_SIZE):
        batch = images[i * BATCH_SIZE : (i + 1) * BATCH_SIZE]
        train_step(batch)
```

Step 6: Evaluate the performance against other state-of-the-art GAN models to evaluate the performance of your Normal GAN against other state-of-the-art GAN models; you can use various evaluation metrics, such as IS, FID, or perceptual similarity metrics like LPIPS. Additionally, you can conduct a visual inspection and compare the generated images with those produced by other models. It's important to note that comparing GAN models can be subjective and dependent on the specific dataset and task at hand. To calculate the IS or FID, you can use external libraries or custom implementations that leverage pre-trained classifiers and feature extractors. These metrics provide insights into the quality and diversity of the generated images compared to the real data distribution. However, implementing these metrics is beyond the scope of this response.

Chapter 8 Questions Responses

Problems

8.9.1   A DCGAN, or Deep Convolutional Generative Adversarial Network, is a type of Generative Adversarial Network (GAN) that uses convolutional layers in its generator and discriminator networks. It's particularly suited for image generation tasks.

8.9.2   In a DCGAN, the generator and discriminator are convolutional neural networks (CNNs), which are known for their effectiveness in image processing. Traditional GANs do not necessarily utilize CNNs. Also, DCGANs implement certain modifications to the architecture of the networks, such as the use of batch normalization, strided convolutions, and the absence of fully connected layers.

8.9.3   DCGANs have a variety of applications including but not limited to: image generation, super-resolution, style transfer, data augmentation, and anomaly detection.

8.9.4 Mode collapse can be mitigated through several methods, including the use of minibatch discrimination, unrolled GANs, the Wasserstein loss function, or by introducing noise into the input data.

8.9.5 The role of the generator in a DCGAN is to create fake data, typically images that resemble the real data from the training set. The generator network takes in a random noise vector and transforms it into an image through a series of upscaling layers.

8.9.6 The discriminator in a DCGAN is a binary classifier that tries to distinguish between real and fake images. It takes an image as input and outputs a probability that the image came from the real dataset rather than being created by the generator.

8.9.7 The quality of images produced by a DCGAN can be assessed visually or by using quantitative metrics like the Inception Score (IS) or Fréchet Inception Distance (FID). These metrics compare the statistics of generated images to those of real ones.

8.9.8 The loss function typically used in a DCGAN is the binary cross-entropy loss function. The generator tries to minimize this function, while the discriminator tries to maximize it.

8.9.9 The quality of images produced by a DCGAN can be improved through various methods such as using a more complex network architecture, adjusting hyperparameters, increasing the size of the training dataset, implementing different regularization techniques, or using techniques such as progressive training, data augmentation, and style mixing.

8.9.10 Yes, while DCGANs are mostly used for image generation tasks, they can also be used for other types of data like speech or music. The principles of DCGANs can be applied to any kind of data that can be represented in a grid-like structure, such as time-series data or even text, if represented appropriately.

Programming

Easy

8.10.1 Implementing a DCGAN to generate images of a specific class involves training the DCGAN on a dataset that contains images of that class. For example, you could use a dataset of cat or dog images, such as the Cats vs. Dogs dataset available on Kaggle. The generator network will learn to generate new images that resemble the images in the training set.

8.10.2 Modifying a pre-trained DCGAN involves fine-tuning the generator network on a dataset that contains images with the desired attributes. For example, if you want to generate images of red objects, you could create a dataset of images of red objects and then fine-tune the generator on this dataset.

8.10.3 Implementing a conditional DCGAN involves modifying the generator network to take a label as input in addition to the random noise vector. The label can be represented as a one-hot vector and concatenated with the noise vector before being passed through the network.

8.10.4 Training a DCGAN on a large dataset involves setting up a training loop where the generator and discriminator networks are trained alternately on mini-batches of images from the dataset. The generator network learns to generate high-resolution images by trying to fool the discriminator into classifying its generated images as real.

8.10.5 Implementing a DCGAN that generates sequences of images is more complex and may involve using recurrent layers in the generator network to capture the temporal dependencies between frames. The input to the generator could be a sequence of noise vectors instead of a single noise vector.

8.10.6 Modifying a DCGAN to generate diverse images can involve using techniques, such as minibatch discrimination or unrolled GANs, to prevent mode collapse. Additionally, using a variety of regularization techniques and careful hyperparameter tuning can also help improve the diversity of the generated images.

8.10.7 Implementing a DCGAN to generate styled images might involve incorporating style transfer techniques into the DCGAN framework. This could be done by having a style loss term in the generator's loss function, which measures the difference between the style of the generated image and the style of a target image.

8.10.8 Datasets for DCGANs can be loaded using libraries like TensorFlow's tf.data or PyTorch's DataLoader. These libraries allow for efficient loading, shuffling, and batching of data.

8.10.9 The generator takes a random noise vector as input, typically of shape (batch_size, latent_dim), and outputs an image of shape (batch_size, height, width, channels). The discriminator takes an image as input of shape (batch_size, height, width, channels) and outputs a probability that the image is real, of shape (batch_size, 1).

8.10.10 The generator network can be created using Keras' Sequential API. It typically starts with a Dense layer that reshapes the input into a 3D tensor, followed by several Conv2DTranspose (also known as deconvolution) layers with batch normalization and ReLU activations.

8.10.11 The discriminator network can also be created using Keras' Sequential API. It typically consists of several Conv2D layers with leaky ReLU activations and Dropout layers, followed by a final Dense layer with a sigmoid activation.

8.10.12 The discriminator can be compiled using Keras' compile method, with "binary_crossentropy" as the loss and a suitable optimizer like Adam. For example: "discriminator.compile(loss='binary_crossentropy', optimizer=Adam())".

Medium

8.10.13 Training a DCGAN with limited resources would involve strategies such as:
- Reducing the complexity of the network, for example, by decreasing the number of layers or the number of neurons in each layer.
- Using a smaller batch size during training.
- Employing model compression techniques like quantization or pruning.
- Using lighter models like MobileNet as a base for the discriminator.

8.10.14 A loss function that encourages the generator to create informative images could involve a term that measures the usefulness of the generated images for a downstream task. This could be implemented by training a separate model on the downstream task and using this model's predictions on the generated images to compute the additional loss term.

8.10.15 Handling missing or incomplete data could involve training the generator to generate complete images from partial inputs. This could be done by modifying the generator to take both a noise vector and a partial image as input.

8.10.16 Generating images with multiple controllable attributes could be done with a conditional DCGAN. Each attribute could be represented as a one-hot vector and concatenated with the noise vector before being passed to the generator.

8.10.17 To improve interpretability in medical images, one could incorporate domain-specific knowledge into the DCGAN. This could be done, for example, by using a loss function that encourages the generator to produce images that align with medical diagnostic criteria.

8.10.18 Generating images of 3D objects or scenes could involve training the generator on a dataset of 3D images. The generator would need to be modified to output 3D tensors instead of 2D images.

8.10.19 Generating images in a constrained domain could be done by training the generator on a dataset of images from that domain. This would cause the generator to learn the specific features of that domain.

8.10.20 Creating a DCGAN model involves connecting the generator and the discriminator such that the output of the generator feeds into the input of the discriminator. This can be done using Keras' Functional API.

8.10.21 Training the DCGAN model involves alternately training the discriminator and the generator. The discriminator is trained to distinguish real images from fake ones, and the generator is trained to fool the discriminator.

8.10.22 Generating new images using the trained generator involves feeding a noise vector to the generator and taking its output. The output is a tensor that can be reshaped into an image.

8.10.23 Visualizing the generated images can be done using matplotlib's imshow function. Before showing the image, it may be necessary to post-process the image by rescaling the pixel values to the range 0–1 or 0–255 and converting the image to the correct data type.

8.10.24 Implementing gradient penalty regularization involves adding a term to the discriminator's loss that penalizes large gradients. This term is computed by taking the gradient of the discriminator's output with respect to its input, computing the norm of this gradient, and then computing the square difference between this norm and the target norm (usually 1).

Hard

8.10.25 To implement a DCGAN that generates images in real-time, you can optimize the generator network for faster inference, use lightweight architectures, and employ hardware acceleration techniques, such as running the model on a GPU or using model quantization.

8.10.26 Train a DCGAN to generate adversarial attack-resistant images by incorporating adversarial training techniques. This involves generating adversarial examples and including them in the training process, forcing the DCGAN to learn more robust image representations.

8.10.27 To implement a DCGAN with controllable attributes, use a conditional DCGAN. This involves providing additional input information to the generator, such as one-hot encoded labels representing the desired attributes (e.g., facial expressions or poses).

8.10.28 To increase the diversity of generated images, you can add noise or randomness to the generator input, use dropout layers in the generator, or implement techniques like minibatch discrimination to encourage the generator to produce a more diverse set of images.

8.10.29 Generating images with novel compositions or arrangements can be achieved by training the DCGAN on a dataset containing such images or by incorporating domain-specific knowledge into the model, such as using a loss function that encourages creativity.

8.10.30 Train a DCGAN to generate images for data augmentation by training it on a dataset similar to the one used for the supervised learning task. The generated images can be mixed with the original dataset to create a larger, augmented dataset for training the supervised model.

8.10.31 To implement a conditional GAN using the DCGAN architecture, modify the generator and discriminator to accept conditional input. For the generator, concatenate the conditional information (e.g., one-hot encoded labels) with the noise vector before feeding it into the network. For the discriminator, concatenate the conditional information with the input image before feeding it into the network.

8.10.32 To use spectral normalization in DCGAN, apply it to the weights of the layers in the discriminator network. In Keras, you can use the "SpectralNormalization" wrapper on the layers or implement a custom layer that incorporates spectral normalization.

8.10.33 To use progressive growing strategy for higher resolution images, start with a low-resolution version of the dataset and train the DCGAN. Then, gradually increase the resolution by adding layers to both the generator and discriminator networks while continuing the training process.

8.10.34 Implement WGAN-GP using DCGAN architecture by replacing the standard GAN loss functions with the Wasserstein loss and adding a gradient penalty term to the discriminator loss. The gradient penalty ensures that the discriminator's gradients have a consistent norm, which stabilizes the training process.

8.10.35 To implement a self-attention mechanism in DCGAN, you can use self-attention layers in both the generator and discriminator networks. This involves computing attention maps from the input feature maps and using them to weight the feature maps, allowing the network to focus on specific regions of the input. In Keras, you can implement this using custom layers or make use of existing libraries that provide self-attention layers.

Chapter 9 Questions Responses

Problems

9.11.1   The key difference between a conditional GAN (cGAN) and an unconditional GAN lies in the control of output. While an unconditional GAN generates data from noise, a cGAN allows us to condition the generation process on additional information, such as a class label or another image.

9.11.2   The conditional variable in a cGAN is typically defined as additional information that we want to condition the data generation process on. It is provided as input to both the generator and the discriminator.

9.11.3   Yes, cGANs can be used for image-to-image translation tasks. This involves conditioning the generation process on an input image and then generating a corresponding output image.

9.11.4   Label smoothing is a regularization technique where target labels are smoothed from hard 0s and 1s to softer values, like 0.9 and 0.1. This can help the discriminator generalize better.

9.11.5   Mode collapse can be addressed in cGANs using various techniques like adding noise to the inputs, using different types of regularization, and implementing different architectural choices.

9.11.6   Yes, cGANs can be used for text generation tasks by conditioning the generation process on some information, such as a preceding sequence of words.

9.11.7   The generator in a cGAN uses conditional information by receiving it as input along with noise. This conditional information guides the generation process.

9.11.8   Overfitting can be prevented in cGANs using strategies like regularization, dropout, and early stopping.

9.11.9   Advantages of using cGANs over other types of GANs include their ability to generate data conditioned on specific information and their potential for better control over the data generation process.

9.11.10   cGANs can be used for data augmentation in classification tasks by generating additional training examples based on the existing classes.

9.11.11   The discriminator in a cGAN determines whether a given sample is real or fake and also checks if the condition aligns with the sample.

9.11.12   One-hot encoding and soft encoding are ways to represent categorical variables. In the context of cGANs, one-hot encoding uses binary vectors while soft encoding allows for more gradual transitions.

9.11.13   The quality of the generated samples in a cGAN can be evaluated using various metrics like Inception Score (IS) and Fréchet Inception Distance (FID).

9.11.14   The performance of a cGAN can be improved by using pre-trained models to initialize the weights of the generator and/or discriminator, reducing the time and data required for training.

9.11.15   Batch normalization is a technique used in cGANs to stabilize training by normalizing the input layer by adjusting and scaling the activations.

9.11.16   Yes, cGANs can be used for style transfer tasks by conditioning the generation on a style image and a content image.

9.11.17   The choice of loss function impacts the performance of a cGAN as it determines how the network learns to generate realistic samples. Common choices include the binary cross-entropy and hinge loss.

9.11.18   The learning rate can be adjusted dynamically during the training of a cGAN to optimize performance, often starting with a larger rate and reducing it over time.

9.11.19   Yes, cGANs can be used for speech generation tasks by conditioning the generation process on a sequence of phonemes or other linguistic features.

9.11.20   Regularization techniques can improve the performance of a cGAN by preventing overfitting and improving the generalization of the discriminator and generator.

Programming

Easy

9.12.1   Implementing a cGAN for generating images of handwritten digits conditioned on their labels would involve conditioning the generator to produce images based on the digit labels (0–9) and training the discriminator to distinguish between real and generated images while considering the labels.

9.12.2   To train a cGAN to generate images of different types of clothes given their labels, you would use a similar process, this time conditioning the generator on clothing labels like "shirt", "pants", "shoes", and so on. A dataset like Fashion-MNIST could be used for this task.

9.12.3   A cGAN could be used to generate realistic images of faces conditioned on attributes, such as age, gender, and hair color, by incorporating these attributes as conditioning variables in the generator and discriminator. A dataset like CelebA, which includes such attributes, could be used for this task.

9.12.4   To train a cGAN to generate images of animals conditioned on species labels, the generator would be conditioned on labels representing different animal species, and a suitable dataset containing images of various animal species and their corresponding labels would be needed.

9.12.5   The conditioning variable in a cGAN is the additional information used to condition the data generation process. It is typically incorporated as input to both the generator and the discriminator.

9.12.6   The role of the generator in a cGAN is to generate fake samples conditioned on the conditioning variable. It aims to produce samples so realistic that the discriminator cannot distinguish them from real ones.

9.12.7   The role of the discriminator in a cGAN is to distinguish between real and fake samples while also considering the conditioning variable. It is trained to classify real samples as real and fake samples as fake.

9.12.8   The conditioning variable and the noise input in the generator are usually combined via concatenation or element-wise product. This combined input is then fed into the generator's neural network.

Medium

9.12.9   Implementing a cGAN for generating musical notes conditioned on labels or genres involves using these labels or genres as conditioning variables. Your generator will produce musical notes based on these conditions, while the discriminator will differentiate between real and generated music, considering the conditions.

9.12.10   To train a cGAN to generate realistic images of different types of food based on recipe or cuisine labels, you'd condition the generator on these labels. A suitable dataset with images of various foods and corresponding labels would be necessary.

9.12.11   A cGAN can generate realistic images of furniture items conditioned on their type labels by incorporating these labels into the generator and discriminator. You'd need a dataset with images of various furniture types and their corresponding labels.

9.12.12   The choice of the conditioning variable for a given task in a cGAN depends on the specific requirements of the task. It could be a class label, a set of attributes, or even another image, depending on what specific output you want from the generator.

9.12.13   The size of the conditioning variable typically depends on the number of possible conditions. For instance, if your conditions are categorical and have ten possible values, you might use a one-hot encoded vector of length ten as your conditioning variable.

9.12.14   Preprocessing the conditioning variable before feeding it to the generator and discriminator might involve normalizing it to a certain range or encoding categorical variables into a format that can be understood by the model, such as one-hot encoding.

9.12.15   Training a cGAN with a batch size larger than one involves feeding multiple data instances into the model simultaneously. Both the generator and discriminator are updated based on the average loss across the entire batch.

9.12.16   The performance of a cGAN can be evaluated using various metrics, depending on the specific task. For image generation tasks, you might use metrics like IS or FID. Human evaluation is also commonly used, as the ultimate goal of a cGAN is often to produce results that are convincing to humans.

Hard

9.12.17   To implement a cGAN for generating images of cars conditioned on their brand or model labels, you would use these labels as conditions, training your generator to create car images based on them. Your discriminator would differentiate between real and fake car images, considering the conditions.

9.12.18   Training a cGAN to generate images of different plant types conditioned on species or habitat labels would involve conditioning the generator on these labels. A dataset with images of various plants and corresponding labels would be necessary.

9.12.19 A cGAN could generate realistic images of buildings conditioned on architectural style or location labels by incorporating these labels into the generator and discriminator. You would need a dataset with images of various buildings and their corresponding labels.

9.12.20 Using a pre-trained cGAN for generating new samples on a new dataset could involve fine-tuning. You can load the pre-trained model and continue training on the new data, possibly with a lower learning rate to avoid destroying the pre-existing model weights.

9.12.21 Designing the architecture of a cGAN for a complex multi-modal dataset often involves using deeper or more complex architectures for both the generator and discriminator. You might use convolutional layers for image data, recurrent layers for sequential data, or even transformer models for more complex data structures.

9.12.22 Applying transfer learning to a pre-trained cGAN for a related task could involve fine-tuning the model on the new task. Depending on the similarity of the tasks, you might choose to only fine-tune certain layers while keeping others fixed.

9.12.23 Handling class imbalance in the conditioning variable in a cGAN might involve techniques such as oversampling the minority class, undersampling the majority class, or using a weighted loss function to give more importance to under-represented classes.

9.12.24 Regularization in a cGAN to prevent overfitting can be added in several ways. Dropout layers, weight decay, and early stopping are common techniques. Also, using a validation set to monitor the model's performance during training can help detect and prevent overfitting.

Chapter 10 Questions Responses

Problems

10.8.1 CycleGAN is a method for training Generative Adversarial Networks (GANs) to perform image-to-image translation tasks. It's unique in its ability to learn this translation without the need for paired data.

10.8.2 CycleGANs use a cycle-consistency loss to ensure that the transformation from one domain to another and back is consistent. This is a major difference from traditional GANs that typically require paired data for such tasks.

10.8.3 The objective of CycleGAN is to learn mapping functions between two domains without having paired training examples, allowing image-to-image translation tasks even when explicit pairing isn't feasible.

10.8.4 CycleGAN is trained using a combination of adversarial loss and cycle consistency loss. Adversarial loss ensures that the generated images look real, while cycle consistency loss maintains the content between an original image and an image that's been converted to another domain and back.

10.8.5 CycleGAN has applications in tasks such as photo enhancement, image colorization, style transfer, domain adaptation, and more. For example, it can transform images of horses into zebras, or convert real-life images into the style of famous painters.

10.8.6 CycleGAN can be used with any type of image data, from photographs to paintings, and even maps. The two datasets should correspond to the two domains you wish to translate between.

10.8.7 CycleGAN architecture consists of two generator networks and two discriminator networks. Each generator is associated with a direction of translation (from domain A to domain B, and vice versa). Each discriminator tries to distinguish between real and fake images from one domain.

10.8.8 Cycle consistency loss ensures that an original image, when translated to the other domain and then translated back, will be the same as the original. This makes CycleGAN learn meaningful translations even in the absence of paired data.

10.8.9 Adversarial loss is used to make the generated images indistinguishable from real images in their respective domain, thus making the image translation believable.

10.8.10 CycleGAN uses the cycle-consistency loss to learn to translate between unpaired data. It ensures that an image translated from one domain to another and then back will retain its original characteristics.

10.8.11 CycleGAN's use of cycle consistency loss helps prevent mode collapse by ensuring that the generators learn a broad distribution of the data, rather than just a few modes.

10.8.12 A generator in CycleGAN is a network that transforms an image from one domain to another.

10.8.13 A discriminator in CycleGAN is a network that tries to distinguish between real and fake images in a particular domain.

10.8.14 CycleGAN uses adversarial loss to make generated images realistic, and cycle consistency loss to ensure that the translated images retain the essential features of the original images.

10.8.15 Cyclic mapping in CycleGAN refers to the process of translating an image from one domain to another and then back to the original domain.

10.8.16 CycleGAN is primarily designed for unimodal translations. For multi-modal translations, modifications or alternative models like StarGAN or MUNIT might be better suited.

10.8.17 Yes, CycleGAN can be used for style transfer tasks, like changing the style of a photograph to match a particular artist's painting style.

10.8.18 Challenges of using CycleGAN include the need for large amounts of data, long training times, and potential for generating unrealistic or low-quality images.

10.8.19 Performance of CycleGAN can be evaluated using qualitative metrics (visual inspection, human judgment) and quantitative metrics like Fréchet Inception Distance (FID).

10.8.20 Future directions could include improving the quality and diversity of generated images, reducing training times, handling multimodal translations better, or applying CycleGAN to other types of data or tasks.

Programming

Easy

10.9.1 This involves using CycleGAN's architecture and training strategy to create a model that can convert images from one domain to another (like transforming photographs into paintings). This task requires a good understanding of CycleGAN's architecture, training process, and the TensorFlow or PyTorch libraries.

10.9.2 In this task, you have to prepare a custom dataset with two distinct image domains. You'll need to load and preprocess the dataset, then use it to train your CycleGAN model. Evaluating performance involves using both qualitative (visual) assessments and quantitative metrics, such as FID scores or Inception Scores (ISs).

10.9.3 The goal here is to understand the impact of depth (more convolutional layers) and the receptive field (determined by kernel sizes) on the model's performance. You can add additional convolutional layers to both the generator and discriminator models and experiment with different kernel sizes to see how they impact the model's results.

10.9.4 Spectral normalization is a technique to stabilize the training of GANs by normalizing the spectral norm of the weights of the neural network. This can help avoid the problem of mode collapse and improve the stability of the GAN during training.

10.9.5 Weight sharing is a method to reduce the number of trainable parameters in the model, which can help to improve the generalization of the model. In the context of CycleGAN, this could involve having the two generator models or the two discriminator models share weights, effectively halving the number of parameters for that part of the model.

Medium

10.9.6 A conditional generator in CycleGAN would mean modifying the generator to accept additional information that specifies the desired output style. This usually involves concatenating the style vector to the input noise vector.

10.9.7 This involves modifying the loss function used for training. Wasserstein loss and hinge loss are other common loss functions for training GANs that might provide more stable training or better results.

10.9.8 Adding skip connections between the generator and discriminator networks could involve concatenating the generator's output with its input, and feeding that into the discriminator.

10.9.9 Adding attention to a CycleGAN could be done with self-attention layers in the generator and discriminator networks. This can help the model focus on important image features.

10.9.10 Training on a large dataset would require more computational resources. Distributed training involves splitting the training data across multiple GPUs or machines to speed up the training process.

10.9.11 For the CycleGAN architecture, replace the standard generator with a U-Net structure. This integration will ensure better local and global information capture within the generator, potentially leading to more detailed synthesized images.

10.9.12 Incorporate multiple discriminators within the CycleGAN framework. By doing this, the model can gain more nuanced feedback during its training phase, addressing details at different scales and potentially leading to higher fidelity results.

10.9.13 Enhance the model's preprocessing steps by introducing techniques such as random cropping or advanced data augmentation. These methods can potentially make the model more robust and versatile, allowing it to generalize better across varied input images.

10.9.14 Experiment by training a version of CycleGAN that exclusively relies on cycle consistency loss. Afterward, compare its performance metrics and visual results with the traditional CycleGAN model to understand the impact of individual loss components on the overall output.

Hard

10.9.15 Weight clipping and gradient penalty are techniques to constrain the weights of the discriminator and can help improve the stability of GAN training.

10.9.16 This involves adjusting the parameters used for training, such as the learning rate and batch size, and observing how they affect the training process and results.

10.9.17 Replacing batch normalization with instance normalization in the CycleGAN architecture could potentially help with style transfer tasks.

10.9.18 A self-attention module can help the model focus on important features in an image, and capture long-range dependencies that a convolutional layer might miss.

10.9.19 A multi-scale discriminator implies having multiple discriminators each operating at different scales or resolutions. In the context of image translation, this allows the model to capture both local details and global structures effectively. Implementing this requires adjusting the discriminator architecture to include multiple discriminators, each processing the image at a different scale. During training, the real and fake loss terms for each discriminator are typically summed to compute the overall discriminator loss.

10.9.20 Style loss is often used in style transfer tasks to ensure that the generated image maintains the style of the target domain. It measures the difference in feature correlations (Gram matrices) between the style target and the generated image. To integrate a style loss term into CycleGAN, one could extract feature maps from a pre-trained model (like VGG-19) for both the generated and target images, compute their Gram matrices, and add the resulting style loss term to the overall loss function that is being optimized during training. This modification would guide the generator to produce images that not only lie in the target domain but also match a specific style.

Chapter 11 Questions Responses

Problems

11.8.1   An SGAN is an extension of the Generative Adversarial Network (GAN) that can use both labeled and unlabeled data for training. This makes it useful in scenarios where labeled data is scarce.

11.8.2   In a traditional GAN, the discriminator's task is to classify whether an image is real or generated. In an SGAN, the discriminator is also trained to classify real images into their correct classes, essentially becoming a multi-class classifier.

11.8.3   An SGAN has the same basic structure as a GAN, with a generator and discriminator. The main difference is that the discriminator also performs multi-class classification on the real images, besides distinguishing between real and generated images.

11.8.4   In the SGAN training process, both labeled and unlabeled data is used to train the discriminator to distinguish between real and generated images, but only the labeled data is used for multi-class classification.

11.8.5   The loss function in an SGAN consists of two parts: the traditional GAN loss, which measures the discriminator's ability to distinguish between real and generated images, and a supervised loss, which measures the discriminator's performance in multi-class classification.

11.8.6   SGANs have potential applications in fields such as image classification, object detection, natural language processing, healthcare, and fraud detection.

11.8.7   SGANs can be used to perform image classification in a semi-supervised manner. The discriminator is trained to classify the real images into their respective classes, and this learned representation can be used to classify new images.

11.8.8   The main advantage of SGANs is their ability to leverage both labeled and unlabeled data, which can be especially useful when labeled data is scarce. However, SGANs, like other GANs, can be difficult to train due to challenges like mode collapse, instability during training, and difficulties in balancing the generator and discriminator.

11.8.9   The classification performance of an SGAN's discriminator can be evaluated using traditional supervised metrics on the labeled data. For the quality of generated samples, metrics such as the Inception Score (IS) and Fréchet Inception Distance (FID) can be used.

11.8.10   Future research on SGANs could focus on improving the stability of training, developing better loss functions, investigating how to effectively use SGANs for different types of data, and exploring applications in new domains.

11.8.11   Supervised learning requires all data to be labeled for training, while semi-supervised learning can use both labeled and unlabeled data, making it more applicable when labeled data is limited.

11.8.12   In an SGAN, the discriminator performs both binary classification (distinguishing real from generated images) and multi-class classification (classifying real images into their respective classes).

11.8.13 The labeled data in SGAN is used for training the discriminator to perform multi-class classification.

11.8.14 The generator in an SGAN primarily learns from the feedback of the discriminator, which itself is trained on both labeled and unlabeled data. However, it doesn't directly use labeled or unlabeled data.

11.8.15 The SGAN loss function includes an additional term for supervised learning, which measures the discriminator's performance in multi-class classification.

11.8.16 SGANs leverage both labeled and unlabeled data for training, which can improve the model's performance when labeled data is limited.

11.8.17 Real-world applications of SGANs include image and text classification, object detection, and fraud detection among others.

11.8.18 While SGANs are primarily used for semi-supervised learning, the generator in an SGAN can be used for unsupervised tasks, such as generating new data samples.

11.8.19 Limitations of SGANs include difficulty in training, potential for mode collapse, and evaluation challenges.

11.8.20 SGANs provide a unique approach to semi-supervised learning by using a generative model. They can potentially leverage unlabeled data more effectively than some traditional semi-supervised learning methods. However, like other GANs, they can be challenging to train and evaluate.

Programming

Easy

11.9.1 The general steps to implement an SGAN on the MNIST dataset:
1. Prepare the MNIST dataset, splitting it into labeled and unlabeled data.
2. Define the generator model. This could be a simple convolutional neural network (CNN) that upsamples noise to the size of an MNIST image.
3. Define the discriminator model. This should be a CNN that classifies images into K+1 classes, where K is the number of classes in MNIST and the extra class represents fake images from the generator.
4. Define the combined model for updating the generator. This model takes noise as input and output the classification of generated images.
5. Train the model in alternating steps: first update the discriminator on real and fake samples, and then update the generator through the combined model.
6. Evaluate the model on the test set.

11.9.2 SGANs can be adapted for text data by using appropriate models for the generator and discriminator:
1. Instead of CNNs, use Recurrent Neural Networks (RNNs) or Transformers for the generator and discriminator models.
2. Train the generator to produce realistic sequences of text, and train the discriminator to classify these sequences into their appropriate classes, along with an additional class for fake/generated sequences.

11.9.3   The steps for training an SGAN on a subset of the CIFAR-10 dataset are similar to those for MNIST. The main difference would be the complexity of the models used for the generator and discriminator, as CIFAR-10 images are more complex and have more classes.

11.9.4   Training an SGAN on a medical imaging dataset is similar to training it on other image datasets. Once the SGAN is trained, the generator can be used to create new medical images. The quality of these generated images can be evaluated using a pre-trained classification model by seeing how well the generated images are classified.

11.9.5   Cycle-consistency loss is used in models like CycleGAN for image-to-image translation tasks. To integrate it into an SGAN, you would:

   1. Define two SGANs: one for translating from domain A to domain B and one for translating from domain B to domain A.

   2. When training the model, include an additional loss term for each generator that measures how well the generator can translate an image to the other domain and then back to the original domain. This is the cycle-consistency loss.

   3. Train the model with both the GAN loss and the cycle-consistency loss.

Medium

11.9.6   Train an SGAN on the "normal" sensor readings. After training, the generator should be able to generate new "normal" readings and the discriminator should be good at distinguishing between "normal" and "anomalous" readings. To detect anomalies, feed the sensor data into the discriminator: if it identifies the reading as "fake", it is likely to be an anomaly. To evaluate performance, use a labeled anomaly dataset and calculate metrics, such as precision, recall, F1 score, and Area Under the ROC Curve (AUC-ROC).

11.9.7   Convert the audio data into spectrograms or other suitable format. Train an SGAN on the converted data so that the generator learns to create new audio samples in the form of spectrograms. Convert these back into the time domain to listen to the generated audio. To make the model generate audio with specific characteristics, you could condition the generator's input on certain features.

11.9.8   The conditional GAN (cGAN) extension can also be applied to SGANs. For this, condition both the generator and discriminator on an additional input (like a class label). During training, feed the label into the generator along with the noise to guide the generation process, and into the discriminator to tell it what kind of image it should be expecting.

11.9.9   Prepare the financial time-series data and train an SGAN on it. Once the SGAN is trained, the generator can create new time-series data. Evaluate the quality of the generated data by using it as input to a pre-trained predictive model. The performance of the predictive model on the generated data compared to real data can give a measure of the quality of the generated data.

11.9.10   Choose the subset of the ImageNet dataset corresponding to the desired objects or animals. Train an SGAN on this subset so that the generator learns to create images of these specific classes. Since ImageNet images are more complex than

MNIST or CIFAR-10, you may need more complex generator and discriminator architectures. Also, use techniques like data augmentation and batch normalization to improve training.

Hard

11.9.11 TensorFlow provides a great platform to implement Semi-supervised GANs due to its flexible computational graph and high-level APIs. To implement an SGAN on the MNIST dataset, you will have to construct two primary components: the generator and the discriminator, which will also serve as the classifier. Once the model is trained, the generator can produce realistic-looking digits, and the discriminator can classify the digits into their corresponding labels.

11.9.12 CIFAR-10, a dataset of 60,000 small color images, is ideal for this task. Train an SGAN model on this dataset, evaluating both the quality of the generated images and the accuracy of the discriminator's classification of images into their correct classes. This involves both visual evaluation and measuring the classification accuracy of the model on a hold-out test set.

11.9.13 Fashion-MNIST serves as a contemporary alternative to the traditional MNIST dataset, often employed to benchmark machine learning techniques. Using TensorFlow, design a semi-supervised GAN and train it on the Fashion-MNIST dataset. After completing the training process, evaluate and compare the quality of the generated images and the classification accuracy of the discriminator against the outcomes from a conventional supervised learning model.

11.9.14 The CelebA dataset includes 202,599 celebrity images with 40 attribute annotations. Train an SGAN model on this dataset to generate realistic celebrity faces. Additionally, train the discriminator to classify these images based on various attributes like gender, age, and hair color. This task involves generating high-quality, high-resolution images, which may require more complex architectures and advanced techniques.

11.9.15 Creating GANs for text data is challenging due to the discrete nature of text. An approach like the GAN-based SeqGAN can be extended to a semi-supervised scenario, where the generator produces realistic text (like product reviews or news articles), and the discriminator classifies the text into categories. Use natural language processing techniques like word embeddings, RNNs, or transformers for the generator and discriminator models. Measure the quality of the generated text and the classification accuracy of the model.

Chapter 12 Questions Responses

Problems

12.9.1 Least Squares Generative Adversarial Networks (LSGANs) are a type of GAN that uses a least squares loss function, instead of the more common binary cross-entropy loss function used in traditional GANs. The primary difference is the type of loss function used, which influences the training dynamics and quality of generated samples.

12.9.2 The MSE loss function, also known as the least squares loss function, is used in both the discriminator and generator networks in LSGAN. This loss function assigns high values to real images and low values to fake images in the discriminator. Meanwhile, the generator tries to generate images that the discriminator will assign high values to. It is a measure of the average squared differences between the estimated and actual values.

12.9.3 MSE loss provides a more stable training process, producing samples that are closer to real data. In traditional GANs, the use of the sigmoid cross entropy loss function leads to a vanishing gradients problem, especially when the generated samples are far from the real data distribution. However, LSGAN's least squares loss function helps to alleviate this issue by producing more consistent gradients, leading to more stable training.

12.9.4 The architecture of an LSGAN generator can be quite similar to that of a traditional GAN generator. Both use a series of fully connected and deconvolution layers (or transposed convolutional layers) with non-linear activation functions. They also both take in a random noise vector and output a generated sample. However, the exact architecture can vary depending on the specific implementation, and there may be differences in the details such as the number of layers or the use of specific techniques like batch normalization.

12.9.5 LSGAN tends to generate higher quality samples with better visual fidelity than standard GANs and often has a more stable training process. Compared to WGAN, which improves stability by using a Wasserstein loss function, LSGAN often produces images with finer details. Compared to DCGAN, which is known for its deep convolutional architecture, LSGAN tends to provide more stability during training.

12.9.6 While LSGAN is often used for image generation, it can also be applied to other types of data. For text generation, LSGAN could be adapted to take in and produce sequences of word embeddings instead of image data. For anomaly detection, an LSGAN could be trained on normal data, and then used to identify anomalous data points as those that the LSGAN struggles to generate accurately.

12.9.7 Some potential drawbacks of LSGAN, similar to other GANs, include the possibility of mode collapse (where the generator only produces a limited variety of outputs) and difficulty in choosing appropriate hyperparameters. While the need for large amounts of training data is a common challenge in deep learning, it's not specific to LSGANs. These issues can often be addressed through techniques such as adjusting the model architecture, using different types of normalization, or employing methods for handling imbalanced or limited data.

12.9.8 Like all GANs, LSGAN consists of two main components: a generator and a discriminator. The generator is a neural network that takes a random noise vector as input and outputs a generated sample. The discriminator is another neural network that takes a sample (either a real one from the training data or a generated one from the generator) as input, and outputs a value indicating whether it believes the sample is real or fake. The architecture of these components can vary depending on the specific implementation, but often involves fully connected and deconvolution layers in the generator, and convolution and fully connected layers in the discriminator.

Programming

Easy

12.10.1 LSGAN uses a least squares (or mean squared error) loss function. This loss function assigns high scores to real images and low scores to fake images in the discriminator, while the generator tries to generate images that the discriminator will assign high scores to.

12.10.2 The primary difference between LSGAN and traditional GANs lies in the type of loss function used. While traditional GANs use a binary cross entropy loss function, LSGANs utilize a least squares (mean squared error) loss function. The use of the least squares loss function helps to address some of the issues encountered in training traditional GANs, such as the vanishing gradient problem.

12.10.3 LSGANs offer a few advantages over traditional GANs. The use of a least squares loss function can result in more stable training dynamics and improved quality of the generated samples. Furthermore, LSGANs tend to be less susceptible to the mode collapse problem, where the generator starts producing only a limited variety of outputs. LSGANs also tend to generate samples that are closer to the real data distribution, leading to improved realism in generated samples.

12.10.4 The generator in LSGAN is trained by minimizing the least squares loss function. It takes a random noise vector as input and tries to generate images that the discriminator will believe are real. During training, the generator's parameters are adjusted to minimize the difference between the discriminator's predictions for generated images and the value representing "real" in the loss function.

12.10.5 The discriminator in LSGAN is trained by minimizing the least squares loss function. It tries to assign high scores to real images and low scores to fake images. During training, the discriminator's parameters are adjusted to minimize the difference between its predictions for real images and the value representing "real" in the loss function, and to minimize the difference between its predictions for generated images and the value representing "fake".

Medium

12.10.6 In the context of LSGANs, "lambda" could represent the weight for a regularization term in the loss function. Its value can influence the balance between the generator and discriminator during training. If lambda is set too high, the discriminator might dominate the learning process, resulting in poor quality generations. If set too low, the generator might overpower, potentially leading to mode collapse. Fine-tuning "lambda" based on validation performance is usually required to achieve a good balance.

12.10.7 Training stability can be improved in LSGANs through several approaches. Implementing gradient clipping or normalization can help prevent exploding or vanishing gradients. Using advanced optimization algorithms, such as Adam or RMSProp, can also enhance stability. Lastly, techniques like batch normalization and layer normalization can improve the model's robustness to the initial weights and the regularity of the input distribution, improving the overall stability of the training process.

12.10.8 LSGAN, like other types of GANs, can be used for image synthesis by training the model on a large dataset of images. Once trained, the generator part of the LSGAN can take a random noise vector as input and generate new images that are similar to the training data. This is useful for tasks, such as generating new designs, creating artwork, or augmenting existing datasets.

12.10.9 For text-to-image synthesis, LSGAN can be adapted to take a text description as input (along with the random noise vector), and generate an image that matches the description. This requires a joint embedding space where both the text descriptions and the images can be represented. In the training phase, the discriminator is trained to distinguish between real image-text pairs and generated image-text pairs. This way, the generator learns to generate images that align with the given text descriptions.

12.10.10 Several techniques can be employed to improve the quality of LSGAN-generated images. Techniques like upsampling and convolution can help to preserve the details in the generated images. Using deeper architectures and adding more layers can also help in capturing complex patterns. Training the model for more epochs with a more extensive and diverse dataset can also improve the quality of the generated images. Additionally, using techniques like spectral normalization and adding noise to the inputs of the discriminator can also help to improve the quality of the generated images.

Hard

12.10.11 LSGANs can be used for video generation by extending the architecture to deal with sequences of frames rather than single images. For example, the generator and discriminator can be designed to process 3D tensors (width, height, time) instead of 2D images (width, height). The generator's goal would be to produce sequences of frames that the discriminator cannot distinguish from real video clips.

12.10.12 Cross-modal image synthesis involves generating an image from an input in a different modality (like text or sound). This requires a model that understands the correlations between different data modalities. For LSGANs, the generator can be conditioned on the input modality (such as text descriptions or audio signals) to generate corresponding images. During training, the discriminator learns to distinguish between real pairs (input, image) and fake pairs generated by the generator.

12.10.13 Anomaly detection using LSGAN involves training the model on "normal" data only. During inference, the discriminator assigns a score to incoming data. If the generated image significantly deviates from the real image (based on a predetermined threshold), the input is classified as an anomaly. This works because the generator learns the distribution of normal data and fails to generate sensible outputs for inputs that do not match this distribution.

12.10.14 Fine-tuning the generator and discriminator in LSGANs involves several techniques. For the generator, one could use different types of noise distributions or adjust the complexity of the model. For the discriminator, adjustments to its sensitivity can be made, ensuring that it's not too strong or too weak compared to the generator. Other strategies include experimenting with different archi-tectures, using advanced optimization algorithms, adjusting learning rates, and applying regularization techniques like dropout or weight decay.

12.10.15 While LSGANs have several advantages, they do have limitations. These include issues like mode collapse, wherein the generator produces limited varieties of samples, and instability during training, where the generator and discriminator may not converge. Hyperparameter tuning can be challenging due to the highly sensitive nature of GANs to these parameters. Overcoming these challenges often involves employing various strategies, including using different loss functions, incorporating regularization techniques, employ-ing different optimization algorithms, and implementing architectures designed to maintain balance between the generator and discriminator, such as Wasserstein GANs. Moreover, continual research in the field is leading to the development of novel techniques and architectures that mitigate these issues.

Chapter 13 Questions Responses

Problems

13.9.1 Traditional GANs and WGANs (Wasserstein GANs) differ mainly in their loss functions and training methods. Traditional GANs use a binary cross-entropy loss function, while WGANs employ a Wasserstein loss function, which helps alleviate the problem of mode collapse and results in more stable training.

13.9.2 The critic in WGAN replaces the discriminator in a traditional GAN. Unlike a discriminator which classifies, the critic in WGAN is trained to estimate the Wasserstein distance between the real and generated distributions.

13.9.3 The Wasserstein loss function measures the Earth Mover's distance between the real and generated distributions. It provides smoother gradients than the binary cross-entropy loss function, which can help during backpropagation and thus result in more stable training.

13.9.4 Weight clipping in WGAN is a parameter used to enforce the Lipschitz con-straint on the critic, which is necessary for the theoretical guarantees of the Wasserstein loss. The value of the weight clipping parameter is typically cho-sen via experimentation, though a common starting point is [-0.01, 0.01].

13.9.5 To evaluate the quality of the generated images in a WGAN, various metrics can be used, including the Inception Score (IS), the Fréchet Inception Distance (FID), and human evaluation. Additionally, the Wasserstein distance itself can be used as an evaluation metric.

13.9.6 The gradient penalty term in WGAN-GP is a regularization term added to the loss function of the critic. It penalizes deviations from a gradient norm of one, which enforces the Lipschitz constraint in a different, often better-behaved way than weight clipping.

13.9.7 To modify a DCGAN into a WGAN, replace the binary cross-entropy loss function with the Wasserstein loss function and use a critic instead of a discriminator. The critic does not employ sigmoid activation in the output layer. Also, you need to implement weight clipping or a gradient penalty to maintain the Lipschitz constraint.

13.9.8 The choice of optimizer can greatly affect the training of a WGAN. For example, RMSprop or Adam optimizers are usually favored over stochastic gradient descent (SGD) because they provide adaptive learning rates, which can help with the convergence of the model.

13.9.9 The Earth-Mover (EM) distance, also known as the Wasserstein-1 distance, measures the minimum cost of transporting mass to transform one distribution into another. In WGANs, the EM distance is used as a more meaningful and smooth metric of distance between the real data distribution and the model's generated data distribution.

13.9.10 Using a WGAN instead of a GAN generally results in better visual quality of the generated images. This is because the WGAN training process is more stable, and it often better avoids mode collapse, which results in a more diverse set of realistic-looking images.

13.9.11 The WGAN architecture is similar to a traditional GAN but replaces the discriminator with a critic and uses a different loss function (Wasserstein loss). For example, in a DCGAN-like WGAN, you would have a convolutional generator and a convolutional critic, with the critic's final layer being a linear output rather than a sigmoid output.

13.9.12 Regular WGAN uses weight clipping to enforce the Lipschitz constraint, while WGAN with gradient penalty (WGAN-GP) adds a gradient penalty term to the loss function of the critic to enforce the Lipschitz constraint. WGAN-GP often results in more stable training than regular WGAN.

13.9.13 Some issues with WGAN include the need for mechanisms like weight clipping or gradient penalty to enforce the Lipschitz constraint. Weight clipping can sometimes lead to undesirable training dynamics, and gradient penalty can increase the computational cost. Additionally, while WGANs can offer benefits in terms of training stability and output quality, they may require more nuanced hyperparameter tuning compared to traditional GANs.

Programming

Easy

13.10.1 The loss function used in LSGAN (Least Squares GAN) is the least squares loss function, or quadratic loss function. It is a variation of GANs that aims to minimize the square of the difference between the predictions and the targets.

13.10.2 LSGAN differs from traditional GAN in the type of loss function used. While traditional GANs use a binary cross-entropy loss function, LSGANs use a least squares loss function. This change helps alleviate problems, such as vanishing gradients and mode collapse, commonly observed in traditional GANs.

13.10.3 The advantages of using LSGAN over traditional GAN include more stable training and reduced likelihood of mode collapse, due to the nature of the least squares loss function. Moreover, the generated images often have better quality as the least squares loss function pushes the generated samples to lie near the decision boundary, leading to generated samples with characteristics more similar to real data.

13.10.4   The generator in LSGAN is trained to minimize the least squares distance between its generated samples (passed through the discriminator) and the target value of real samples. It is trained by backpropagating through both the generator and the discriminator, but updating only the weights of the generator.

13.10.5   The discriminator in LSGAN is trained to minimize the least squares distance between the real samples and the target value for real samples, and between the generated samples (passed through the discriminator) and the target value for fake samples. The weights of the discriminator are updated during this process.

Medium

13.10.6   In the context of LSGAN, the hyperparameter "lambda" isn't inherently a part of the LSGAN architecture. However, in general, lambda is often used as a regularization parameter in machine learning models. If it's being used in LSGAN, it might be part of a regularization term to prevent overfitting or to balance different components of the loss function. The value of lambda can significantly affect the performance of the LSGAN; a high value might lead to underfitting, while a low value might result in overfitting.

13.10.7   The training stability of LSGAN can be improved by careful tuning of hyperparameters and normalization techniques, such as batch normalization or layer normalization. Also, the choice of optimizer can greatly affect stability. Adam is often used as it automatically adjusts the learning rate during training. Additionally, techniques like gradient clipping or spectral normalization can be used to prevent the gradients from exploding or vanishing.

13.10.8   LSGAN can be used for image synthesis by training the model with a dataset of real images. Once trained, the generator part of the LSGAN can generate new images that resemble those in the training dataset. This can be useful in a variety of applications, including art generation, photo editing, and creating training data for other machine learning models.

13.10.9   For text-to-image synthesis, an LSGAN could be combined with a recurrent neural network (RNN) or transformer network that can process the text input. The text input would be embedded into a continuous space, and then fed into the LSGAN's generator to produce a corresponding image.

13.10.10 To improve the quality of LSGAN-generated images, various techniques can be employed, such as:

- Training for more epochs or using a larger dataset, assuming overfitting is not occurring.
- Careful tuning of the model's hyperparameters.
- Using architectures proven to work well with GANs, like DCGANs (Deep Convolutional GANs).

- Using techniques like label smoothing or adding noise to the inputs or the labels.
- Applying various regularization techniques like dropout, weight decay, or spectral normalization.
- Incorporating class labels in the generation process (if available), as in conditional GANs.

Hard

13.10.11 LSGAN can be used for video generation by considering each video as a sequence of frames (images). By extending the input dimensionality, LSGAN can generate sequences of frames to produce a video. This requires a 3D convolutional architecture, with the third dimension being time.

13.10.12 For cross-modal image synthesis, LSGAN can be combined with a model that can process the input from the other modality. For instance, in text-to-image synthesis, the text is first processed by a text-embedding model, and the output of that model is fed into the LSGAN to generate an image that corresponds to the text.

13.10.13 Anomaly detection with LSGAN involves training the model with normal data. Then, during inference, we measure the difference between the output of the discriminator for a given instance and the output for normal data. If the difference is significant, the instance is flagged as an anomaly.

13.10.14 Fine-tuning the LSGAN generator and discriminator often involves a delicate balancing act. Here are a few techniques:

- Adjusting the training ratio between the generator and the discriminator. It's often beneficial to train the discriminator more frequently than the generator.
- Modifying the learning rate. Using a learning rate that decreases over time (learning rate decay) might help.
- Incorporating regularization techniques, such as dropout or weight decay, can help prevent overfitting.
- Using different optimizers. For example, Adam is often used with GANs because of its adaptive learning rate.
- Introducing noise to the inputs can sometimes help with training dynamics, adding an element of stochasticity that can prevent the model from overfitting or getting stuck in particular states. However, adding noise directly to the labels isn't a standard practice and might not lead to the desired outcomes.

13.10.15 Some limitations of LSGANs include:

- Like other GANs, LSGANs can be challenging to train, with issues like mode collapse, vanishing gradients, and a delicate balance between the generator and discriminator.
- LSGANs can generate images that look realistic at a glance, but they can sometimes lack diversity (a symptom of mode collapse) or contain unrealistic features upon closer inspection.

- The quality of the output is heavily dependent on the quantity and quality of the training data.
- To address these limitations, researchers have proposed numerous techniques and variations on the GAN architecture, including the use of different loss functions, regularization techniques, architectural tweaks, and improved training procedures.

Chapter 14 Questions Responses

Problems

14.8.1 Main architectures of Generative Adversarial Networks include Deep Convolutional GANs (DCGANs), Conditional GANs (cGANs), and specialized GANs such as Pix2Pix, CycleGAN, and StyleGAN.

14.8.2 The two main types of image synthesis are text-to-image and image-to-image synthesis. The former uses text descriptions to generate corresponding images, while the latter transforms one type of image into another.

14.8.3 to 14.8.6 Generally, changing parameters and layers could affect model complexity, convergence speed, and the ability to generalize.

14.8.7 Common loss functions include the standard GAN loss, L1 and L2 losses, Wasserstein loss, and hinge loss.

14.8.8 Mode collapse occurs when the generator produces limited varieties of samples. This can be addressed with techniques, such as minibatch discrimination, unrolled GANs, or Wasserstein loss.

14.8.9 Conditional GANs can be used for image synthesis by providing additional input information to guide the image generation process.

14.8.10 Pix2Pix GAN is used for image-to-image translation tasks such as turning a sketch into a color image.

14.8.11 Cycle-consistent GANs ensure the learned image transformations are reversible, which is useful in tasks like photo style transfer.

14.8.12 Adversarial loss can be combined with other loss functions to enforce different properties on the generated images, such as L1 loss for enforcing image content consistency.

14.8.13 Techniques for improving GAN stability include using different normalization methods like spectral normalization, gradient penalty, or modifying the loss function.

14.8.14 Progressive growing, as introduced in StyleGAN, trains the model gradually by starting with low-resolution images and progressively increasing the resolution by adding layers, thereby improving image quality.

14.8.15 GANs can be used to generate new clothing designs, create realistic fabric textures, or simulate how clothes might look on different body types.

14.8.16 Challenges include overfitting, vanishing gradients, and mode collapse. Solutions involve varied techniques, such as regularization, alternative training methods, and different architectural designs.

14.8.17 GANs can generate additional training data, augmenting the original dataset, which can help improve model performance.

14.8.18 GANs can be used to generate new artistic designs, create novel paintings or sculptures, and experiment with different artistic styles.

14.8.19 Techniques to improve diversity include introducing randomness in the input or using methods like StyleGAN that explicitly model the variation in generated images.

14.8.20 GANs can be used to generate synthetic data for robotics applications, such as creating realistic sensor data or simulating different environments.

14.8.21 Future research directions include improving the stability and reliability of GAN training, increasing the diversity of the generated samples, and exploring novel applications of GANs in various fields.

Programming

Easy

14.9.1 In TensorFlow or Keras, you can load and preprocess image data using utilities like "mageDataGenerator" or "tf.data.Dataset". Preprocessing may include normalizing pixel values to be between -1 and 1, resizing images, and augmenting the dataset with transformations.

14.9.2 Both generator and discriminator can be defined as instances of the "Sequential" model in Keras. The generator often includes dense layers and upsampling layers, while the discriminator is a simple binary classifier. You compile the models separately, often using the Adam optimizer and binary cross-entropy loss.

14.9.3 To use the Adam optimizer in TensorFlow or Keras, you would specify it when compiling the model, like so: "model.compile(optimizer='adam', loss='binary_crossentropy')".

14.9.4 The MNIST dataset can be loaded directly in Keras using "keras.datasets.mnist.load_data()". The images need to be reshaped and normalized to be used in a GAN.

14.9.5 To visualize the generated images during training in TensorFlow or Keras, you could have the generator create images at the end of each epoch, then use a library like matplotlib to display these images. You can use the "imshow" function to display the images and save them for future reference.

Medium

14.9.6 Implementing a Wasserstein GAN with gradient penalty (WGAN-GP) in TensorFlow or Keras involves modifying the standard GAN architecture. In WGAN-GP, you use a different loss function, known as the Wasserstein loss. The gradient penalty is implemented by calculating the gradients of the discriminator's predictions with respect to the input images, and adding a penalty term to the discriminator's loss based on these gradients.

14.9.7 To use a pre-trained VGG network for perceptual loss in a GAN, you would first load a pre-trained VGG model without the top layers. You then feed both the generated images and real images into this network, and calculate the perceptual loss as the difference between the VGG representations of the real and generated images.

14.9.8 Implementing a CycleGAN for image-to-image translation involves defining two generators and two discriminators. Each generator translates images from one domain to the other, and each discriminator classifies images from one domain. The CycleGAN loss function includes terms for the GAN loss, forward cycle consistency loss, and backward cycle consistency loss.

14.9.9 The Fréchet Inception Distance (FID) metric requires the use of a pre-trained Inception model. You calculate the Inception activations for both the real and generated images, and then calculate the Fréchet distance between these two distributions. In TensorFlow or Keras, this involves loading the pre-trained Inception model, calculating the activations, and using a library like NumPy or SciPy to calculate the Fréchet distance.

14.9.10 Text-to-image generation typically involves models like AttnGAN or StackGAN. While GPT-2 can be used to generate text, feeding this text to a GAN to produce corresponding images requires an architecture specifically designed for this purpose.

Hard

14.9.11 To implement a StyleGAN in TensorFlow or Keras, you need to modify the architecture of the generator and discriminator in a standard GAN. Key elements of StyleGAN include: style modulation, noise injection, and the use of a mapping network.

14.9.12 Implementing a Variational Autoencoder (VAE) for unsupervised image synthesis involves defining an encoder that compresses input data into a lower-dimensional representation, and a decoder that reconstructs the input data from this representation. The loss function consists of a reconstruction term and a KL divergence term.

14.9.13 Implementing a Generative Query Network (GQN) in TensorFlow or Keras involves defining a representation network and a generation network. The representation network encodes the input images and camera viewpoints into a latent representation, and the generation network decodes this latent representation into a predicted image.

14.9.14 A GAN with progressive growing starts with a small resolution and gradually adds layers to increase the resolution during training. This can be implemented in TensorFlow or Keras by creating a list of models with increasing resolution and training each model sequentially.

14.9.15 Fine-tuning a pre-trained StyleGAN2 model on a new dataset involves loading the pre-trained model and continuing training on the new dataset without necessarily freezing any layers.

14.9.16 BigGAN is a GAN architecture designed for large-scale image synthesis, and it can be implemented in TensorFlow or Keras. It requires substantial computational resources due to the size of the model and the complexity of the training process.

14.9.17 A Spatio-Temporal GAN (STGAN) is used for video synthesis. This is a complex task that involves generating sequences of frames that are both spatially and temporally coherent.

14.9.18 A conditional GAN with an attention mechanism, like AttnGAN, requires integrating attention mechanisms into the architecture, allowing the model to focus on relevant parts of a text description when generating specific parts of an image. This involves both conditional information and attention layers.

14.9.19 Text-to-image generation with a GAN would typically involve taking a given text description and generating a corresponding image. While T5 can generate or transform text, it doesn't directly pair with a GAN for text-to-image generation. Instead, specific architectures like AttnGAN or StackGAN are used for this purpose.

14.9.20 Optimizing a GAN for deployment on a mobile device using TensorFlow Lite involves converting the trained GAN model to the TensorFlow Lite format using the TensorFlow Lite Converter. The model should be optimized for size and speed, and tested to ensure it performs well on the target device.

Chapter 15 Questions Responses

Problems

15.10.1 Basic Architecture of a GAN for Generating Audio Samples

A GAN for audio generation typically consists of a generator that creates audio samples, and a discriminator that distinguishes real samples from generated ones. They are trained together: the generator improves its ability to create realistic audio, and the discriminator improves its ability to distinguish fake audio from real ones.

15.10.2 Input Representations for Training GANs on Audio Data

Input representations can include time-domain waveforms, frequency-domain representations like spectrograms, or even more abstract representations, such as MFCCs (Mel-frequency cepstral coefficients).

15.10.3 Challenges in Generating High-Quality Audio Samples using GANs

Challenges include high dimensionality of audio data, managing temporal dependencies across various timescales, and ensuring phase consistency for frequency-based representations. Mode collapse, where the generator produces limited variety of samples, is also a challenge.

15.10.4 Conditional GANs for Audio

Conditional GANs (cGANs) can generate audio samples with specific characteristics by conditioning the model on additional information like pitch or instrument type. This differs from standard GANs, which generate outputs based on random noise.

15.10.5 Techniques to Stabilize GAN Training

Techniques include using Wasserstein GAN (WGAN) with its Earth Mover's distance, or WGAN-GP (gradient penalty) which stabilizes training by penalizing gradients of the discriminator that stray from 1.

15.10.6 GANs with Recurrent Layers for Audio

GANs with recurrent layers (like LSTM or GRU) can handle long-range temporal dependencies in audio data, producing more coherent and high-quality audio samples.

15.10.7 Evaluation Metrics for Generated Audio

Metrics could include Inception Score (IS) or Fréchet Inception Distance (FID), though these may not fully capture audio quality. Subjective human evaluation often remains the gold standard.

15.10.8 Attention Mechanisms in GANs for Audio Generation

Attention mechanisms allow the model to focus on different parts of the input sequence at different times, which can help handle long-term dependencies and improve audio quality.

15.10.9 Incorporating Domain-Specific Knowledge in GANs for Audio

Including musical rules or using pre-trained feature extractors can guide the learning process and produce more realistic and musically coherent audio samples.

Programming

Easy

15.11.1 You can use libraries such as Librosa or Soundfile in Python to load audio files. For example, using Librosa:

```
import librosa
audio, sr = librosa.load('filename.wav', sr=None)
```

15.11.2 The preprocessing steps may include normalization, framing, windowing and transformation to frequency domain (using Fourier Transform) or other suitable representations like Mel-spectrogram or MFCC.

15.11.3 A simple GAN for audio generation consists of a generator and discriminator network. The generator can take a random noise vector and generate an output that resembles the real audio data. The discriminator then tries to distinguish between real and fake (generated) audio data.

15.11.4 You can use Python libraries such as matplotlib to plot the audio waveforms. You can also use Librosa's display module to plot spectrograms.

15.11.5 Commonly used audio quality metrics include PESQ, STOI, and MOS. However, for GANs, it is challenging to define suitable metrics, and often subjective human evaluation is used.

15.11.6 GANs are typically not used for classification. Rather, they're used for generating new data. For classification, you may want to use a CNN or LSTM network instead.

15.11.7 While GANs are primarily for generation, there are adaptations like the auxiliary classifier GAN (AC-GAN) that can be used for classification. For evaluating classification performance, metrics like accuracy, precision, recall, or F1-score are appropriate.

15.11.8 To implement a GAN for audio generation using a framework like TensorFlow or PyTorch, you would define a generator that produces audio samples from a noise vector and a discriminator that determines if a given audio sample is real or generated. Training involves updating the generator to produce better samples and refining the discriminator to better distinguish between real and generated samples.

15.11.9 This could involve transforming the raw audio data into spectrograms or other frequency-domain representations, which could be achieved with libraries like Librosa.

15.11.10 If the output of your GAN is a spectrogram or other frequency-domain representation, you will need to perform an inverse transform to convert it back into a time-domain audio waveform. This could be done using functions provided by libraries like Librosa.

Medium

15.11.11 Wasserstein GAN (WGAN) uses a different loss function than traditional GANs, which helps in stabilizing training. You would implement the generator and discriminator similar to a standard GAN, but the loss function for the discriminator would be the mean output for real samples subtracted from the mean output for fake samples. You would then train the generator to minimize the mean output of the discriminator for fake samples.

15.11.12 In conditional GANs (cGANs), both the generator and discriminator are conditioned on some extra information (like genre). This can be done by feeding the genre label (after encoding it) as an input to both generator and discriminator along with the noise vector and real data, respectively.

15.11.13 Multi-scale GANs train multiple GANs on different scales (resolutions) of the data. Lower-resolution GANs are trained first, and their outputs are used as inputs to train higher-resolution GANs. In audio, this could be implemented by training different GANs on different time scales or frequency bands of the audio data.

15.11.14 You can initialize your GAN with weights from a pre-trained model and continue training on your specific data. This can help to improve performance and reduce training time.

15.11.15 Feature matching involves modifying the GAN loss function to encourage the generator to match the expected value of the features on an intermediate layer of the discriminator, rather than directly matching the data distribution.

15.11.16 CycleGAN is an architecture that can be used for tasks like style transfer without needing paired data. It uses two GANs and loss functions that encourage the original data to be reconstructed after going through both GANs (cycle consistency loss).

15.11.17 This would typically involve using a cGAN, where the condition vector includes the desired attributes. You can then set the attributes in the condition vector to generate audio with the desired properties.

15.11.18 As mentioned, in cGANs both the generator and discriminator are conditioned on some extra information. This condition could be specific attributes like pitch or instrument, which would be concatenated with the input to the generator and discriminator.

15.11.19 You can load a pre-trained model like WaveGAN or MelGAN and then continue training on your dataset. You should adjust the learning rate to be lower than it was during the initial training to avoid catastrophic forgetting.

15.11.20 This would involve replacing some or all of the layers in the generator and discriminator with LSTM or GRU layers. You would then need to format your data as sequences rather than as individual samples. This can help to model temporal dependencies in the audio data.

Hard

15.11.21 A progressive GAN grows both the generator and discriminator progressively during training. You start with low-resolution models, and then add layers that model finer details as training progresses. This approach helps with training stability and speeds up training.

15.11.22 VAE-GANs combine Variational Autoencoders (VAEs) and GANs to create a generative model with a disentangled latent space. First, a VAE is trained to map the input data to a structured latent space. Then, a GAN is trained to generate data from samples in this latent space.

15.11.23 After training a GAN on an existing audio dataset, you can generate a large number of audio samples by feeding random noise vectors into the generator and recording its output.

15.11.24 This would involve training a GAN to transform spectrograms of audio signals into piano-roll like representations (or another suitable format). The generator's input would be spectrograms, and the discriminator would try to distinguish between real and generated transcriptions.

15.11.25 This is a challenging task due to the computational constraints of mobile devices. You would need to use a lightweight GAN architecture, optimize the model for mobile (e.g., using TensorFlow Lite or PyTorch Mobile), and potentially use lower-resolution audio.

15.11.26 This could be achieved with a cGAN where the conditioning vector includes data derived from the lyrics or other textual information. Textual data would need to be encoded into a suitable format (e.g., word embeddings).

15.11.27 This could involve using advanced training techniques such as gradient penalty, different normalization methods (like spectral normalization), alternative loss functions (like Wasserstein loss or hinge loss), or techniques for balancing the generator and discriminator training (like the one-sided label smoothing).

15.11.28 There's no standard way to evaluate generated audio. You could combine existing metrics like IS or FID with audio-specific metrics like perceptual audio quality or even create your own based on musical theory.

15.11.29 This could involve adding self-attention layers to both the generator and discriminator, which can help them to model dependencies across different parts of the input.

15.11.30 This would depend on the domain knowledge you wish to incorporate. You might encode musical rules into the generator's architecture, use pre-trained feature extraction models as part of the discriminator, or incorporate music theory-based constraints into the loss function.

References

Arjovsky, M., Chintala, S., and Bottou, L. (2017). Wasserstein Generative Adversarial Networks. *Proceedings of the 34th International Conference on Machine Learning*, pp. 214–223.

Goodfellow, I., Pouget-Abadie, J., Mirza, M., Xu, B., Warde-Farley, D., Ozair, S., Courville, A., and Bengio, Y. (2014). Generative Adversarial Nets, NIPS.

Radford, A., Metz, L., and Chintala, S. (2015). Unsupervised Representation Learning with Deep Convolutional Generative Adversarial Networks. arXiv preprint arXiv:1511.06434.

References

Bibliography

Allen, J. (1995). Natural Language Understanding. Benjamin: Cummings.

Alon, U. (2019). An Introduction to Systems Biology: Design Principles of Biological Circuits. Boca Raton, FL: CRC Press.

Ash, R. B. (1970). Basic Probability Theory. New York, NY: Wiley.

Bengio, Y. (1991). Artificial Neural Networks and Their Application to Sequence Recognition. Ph.D. thesis, McGill University, (Computer Science), Montreal, Canada.

Berthelot, D., Schumm, T., and Metz, L. (2017). Began: Boundary Equilibrium Generative Adversarial Networks. arXiv preprint arXiv:1703.10717. BEGAN introduced a new way of balancing the generator and discriminator during training, leading to higher quality images.

Bishop, C. M. (2006). Pattern Recognition and Machine Learning. UK: Springer.

Bottou, L. (1991). Stochastic Gradient Learning in Neural Networks. Proceedings of Neuro-Nîmes 91, Nimes, France: EC2.

Brock, A., Donahue, J., and Simonyan, K. (2018). Large Scale GAN Training for High Fidelity Natural Image Synthesis. arXiv preprint arXiv:1809.11096.

Chollet, F. (2018). Deep Learning with Python. Shelter Island, NY: Manning Publications.

Christian, S., Sergey, I., Vincent, V., and Alexander, A. (2017). An Inception-v4, Inception-ResNet and the Impact of Residual Connections on Learning, ACM Digital Library. arXiv:1602.07261.

Coleman, C. (2020). Selection via Proxy: Efficient Data Selection for Deep Learning. Proceedings of the International Conference on Learning Representations (ICLR) [Virtual Conference].

Creswell, A., et al. (2018). Generative Adversarial Networks: An Overview. IEEE Signal Processing Magazine, 35(1), 53–65.

Delalleau, O., and Bengio, Y. (2011). Shallow vs. Deep Sum-Product Networks. Proceedings of the Neural Information Processing Systems Conference (NIPS), Granada, Spain.

Deng, J., Dong, W., Socher, R., Li, L.-J., Li, K., and Fei-Fei, L. (2009). ImageNet: A Large-Scale Hierarchical Image Database. Proceedings of the Conference on Computer Vision and Pattern Recognition (CVPR), Miami Beach, FL.

Donahue, J., and Krähenbühl, P. (2018). BigGAN: Large Scale Generative Adversarial Networks. arXiv preprint arXiv:1809.11096.

Dong, S., McKenna, S., and Psarrou, A. (2000). Dynamic Vision: From Images to Face Recognition. London, UK: Imperial College Press.

Edresson Casanova, E., et al. (2022). YourTTS: Towards Zero-Shot Multi-Speaker TTS and Zero-Shot Voice Conversion for Everyone. Ithaca, NY: Cornell University. arXiv preprint.

Erhan, D., Bengio, Y., Courville, A., and Vincent, P. (2009). Visualizing Higher-Layer Features of a Deep Network. University of Montreal, Vol. 1341, pp. 594–611.

Fei-Fei, L., Fergus, R., and Perona, P. (2006). One-Shot Learning of Object Categories. IEEE Transactions on Pattern Analysis and Machine Intelligence, 28(4), 594–611.

Ghayoumi, M. (2017). A Quick Review of Deep Learning in Facial Expression. Journal of Communication and Computer, 14, 34–38.

Ghayoumi, M. (2021). Deep Learning in Practice. Boca Raton, FL: Chapman and Hall/CRC.

Ghayoumi, M., and Bansal, A. K. (2017). Improved Human Emotion Analysis Using Facial Key Points and Dihedral Group. International Journal of Advanced Studies in Computer Science and Engineering, 6(1), 25–33.

Ghayoumi, M., et al. (2006). Color Images Segmentation Using a Self-Organizing Network with Adaptive Learning Rate. International Journal of Information Technology, Poland, 1, 629–638.

Ghayoumi, M., et al. (2016). A Formal Approach for Multimodal Integration to Drive Emotions. Journal of Visual Languages and Sentient Systems, 2, 48–54.

Ghayoumi, M., et al. (2019). A Time-Series Analysis with Machine Learning. 5th Annual International Conference on Computational Mathematics, Computational Geometry & Statistics.

Gulrajani, I., et al. (2017). Improved Training of Wasserstein GANs. Advances in Neural Information Processing Systems, pp. 5767–5777.

He, K., Zhang, X., Ren, S., and Sun, J. (2015). Deep Residual Learning for Image Recognition. 2016 IEEE Conference on Computer Vision and Pattern Recognition (CVPR).

Hochreiter, S., and Schmidhuber, J. (1997). Long Short-Term Memory. Neural Computation, 9(8), 1735–1780.

Honarmand, A. (2019). Semi-Supervised Learning in Generative Adversarial Networks. arXiv preprint arXiv:1606.01583.

Huang, G., Liu, Z., Laurens, V. D. M., and Weinberger, K. Q. (2017). Densely Connected Convolutional Networks, CVPR.

Isola, P., Zhu, J., Zhou, T., and Efros, A. A. (2017). Image-to-Image Translation with Conditional Adversarial Networks. Proceedings of the IEEE Conference on Computer Vision and Pattern Recognition, pp. 5967–5976.

Karras, T., et al. (2017). Progressive Growing of GANs for Improved Quality, Stability, and Variation. arXiv preprint arXiv:1710.10196.

Karras, T., Laine, S., and Aila, T. (2018). A Style-Based Generator Architecture for Generative Adversarial Networks. Proceedings of the IEEE/CVF Conference on Computer Vision and Pattern Recognition (CVPR), 4401–4410. This paper introduced StyleGAN, which is known for generating extremely high-quality images.

Kingma, D. P., and Ba, J. (2014). Adam: A Method for Stochastic Optimization. arXiv preprint arXiv:1412.6980.

Kingma, D. P., and Dhariwal, P. (2018). Glow: Generative Flow with Invertible 1×1 Convolutions. Advances in Neural Information Processing Systems, 10215–10224. While not a GAN, this work introduced an important class of generative models known as flow models.

Kolda, T. G., and Bader, B. W. (2009). Tensor Decompositions and Applications. SIAM Review, 51(3), 455–500.

Koonce, B., and Jefferson, M. O. (2021). Convolutional Neural Networks with Swift for Tensorflow: Image Recognition and Dataset Categorization. USA: Apress.

Krizhevsky, A., Sutskever, I., and Hinton, G. E. (2012). ImageNet Classification with Deep Convolutional Neural Networks, NIPS.

LeCun, Y., Bottou, L., Bengio, Y., and Haffner, P. (1998). Gradient-Based Learning Applied to Document Recognition. Proceedings of the IEEE.

Ledig, C., et al. (2017). Photo-Realistic Single Image Super-Resolution Using a Generative Adversarial Network. Proceedings of the IEEE Conference on Computer Vision and Pattern Recognition, pp. 4681–4690.

Manning, C., Surdeanu, M., Bauer, J., Finkel, J., Bethard, S., and McClosky, D. (2014). The Stanford CoreNLP Natural Language Processing Toolkit. Proceedings of 52nd Annual Meeting of the Association for Computational Linguistics: System Demonstrations.

Mao, X., et al. (2017). Least Squares Generative Adversarial Networks. Proceedings of the IEEE International Conference on Computer Vision, pp. 2794–2802.

Mescheder, L., Geiger, A., and Nowozin, S. (2018). Which Training Methods for GANs Do Actually Converge? Proceedings of the 35th International Conference on Machine Learning. PMLR 80:3481–3490. This paper provides a theoretical analysis of GAN training methods and their convergence properties.

Metz, L., Poole, B., Pfau, D., and Sohl-Dickstein, J. (2016). Unrolled Generative Adversarial Networks. arXiv preprint arXiv:1611.02163.

Mikolov, T., Chen, K., Corrado, G., and Dean, J. (2013). Efficient Estimation of Word Representations in Vector Space. arXiv preprint arXiv:1301.3781.

Mikolov, T., Sutskever, I., Chen, K., Corrado, G. S., and Dean, J. (2013). Distributed Representations of Words and Phrases and Their Compositionality, NIPS.

Mirza, M., and Osindero, S. (2014). Conditional Generative Adversarial Nets. arXiv preprint arXiv:1411.1784.

Miyato, T., Kataoka, T., Koyama, M., and Yoshida, Y. (2018). Spectral Normalization for Generative Adversarial Networks. arXiv preprint arXiv:1802.05957.

Moews, B. (2016). Computer Vision for Music Identification Cham: Springer International Publishing.

Odena, A., Olah, C., and Shlens, J. (2017). Conditional Image Synthesis with Auxiliary Classifier GANs. Proceedings of the 34th International Conference on Machine Learning, pp. 2642–2651.

Pedersen, T., Patwardhan, S., and Michelizzi, J. (2004). WordNet::Similarity: Measuring the Relatedness of Concepts. Demonstration Papers at HLT-NAACL.

Radford, A., Metz, L., and Chintala, S. (2016). Unsupervised Representation Learning with Deep Convolutional Generative Adversarial Networks. arXiv preprint arXiv:1511.06434.

Rumelhart, D. E., Hinton, G. E., and Williams, R. J. (1986). Learning Representations by Back-Propagating Errors. Nature, 323, 533–536.

Russakovsky, O., Deng, J., Su, H., Krause, J., Satheesh, S., Ma, S., Huang, Z., Karpathy, A., Khosla, A., Bernstein, M., Berg, A. C., and Fei-Fei, L. (2015). ImageNet Large Scale Visual Recognition Challenge. International Journal of Computer Vision (IJCV), 115, 211–252.

Szegedy, C., Liu, W., Jia, Y., Sermanet, P., Reed, S., Anguelov, D., Erhan, D., Vanhoucke, V., and Rabinovich, A. (2015). Going Deeper with Convolutions. Proceedings of the IEEE Conference on Computer Vision and Pattern Recognition.

Taigman, Y., Yang, M., Ranzato, M., and Wolf, L. (2014). DeepFace: Closing the Gap to Human-Level Performance in Face Verification, 2014 IEEE Conference on Computer Vision and Pattern Recognition.

Taylor, G., and Hinton, G. (2009). Factored Conditional Restricted Boltzmann Machines for Modeling Motion Style. Proceedings of the 26th Annual International Conference on Machine Learning.

Vaswani, A., Shazeer, N., Parmar, N., Uszkoreit, J., Jones, L., Gomez, A. N., Kaiser, Ł., and Polosukhin, I. (2017). Attention Is All You Need, NIPS.

Wah, C., Branson, S., Welinder, P., Perona, P., and Belongie, S. (2011). The Caltech-UCSD Birds-200-2011 Dataset.

Wang, J., Liu, Z., and Wu, Y. (2019). Deep Learning for Sensor-Based Activity Recognition: A Survey. Pattern Recognition Letters. Amsterdam: Elsevier.

Wang, Z., et al. (2019). Generative Adversarial Networks in Computer Vision: A Survey and Taxonomy. arXiv preprint arXiv:1906.01529.

Zhang, H., Goodfellow, I., Metaxas, D., and Odena, A. (2019). Self-Attention Generative Adversarial Networks. Proceedings of the 36th International Conference on Machine Learning, PMLR 97: 7354–7363. This work introduced the use of self-attention mechanisms in GANs, a technique that has proved very useful in many other areas of deep learning.

Zhu, J., Park, T., Isola, P., and Efros, A. A. (2017). Unpaired Image-to-Image Translation using Cycle-Consistent Adversarial Networks. Proceedings of the IEEE International Conference on Computer Vision, pp. 2223–2232.

Web Resources

http://colah.github.io/

http://www.bdhammel.com/

https://cs231n.github.io/

https://github.com/

https://keras.io/

https://paperswithcode.com/

https://probml.github.io/
https://salu133445.github.io/
https://towardsdatascience.com/
https://web.stanford.edu/
https://www.cs.cornell.edu/
https://www.javatpoint.com/
https://www.python.org/
https://www.tensorflow.org/
https://www.w3schools.com/

Index

Note: Locators in *italics* represent figures and **bold** indicate tables in the text.